# Reconstruction

# Reconstruction

*A Historical Encyclopedia of the American Mosaic*

Richard Zuczek, Editor

 GREENWOOD™

An Imprint of ABC-CLIO, LLC

Santa Barbara, California • Denver, Colorado

**Library of Congress Cataloging-in-Publication Data**

Reconstruction : a historical encyclopedia of the American mosaic /
   Richard Zuczek, editor.
      pages cm
   Includes bibliographical references and index.
   ISBN 978-1-61069-917-4 (alk. paper) — ISBN 978-1-61069-918-1
(eISBN)   1. Reconstruction (U.S. history, 1865–1877)—Encyclopedias.   I. Zuczek,
Richard, 1966–
   E668.R35 2016
   973.803—dc23       2015019206

ISBN: 978-1-61069-917-4
EISBN: 978-1-61069-918-1

20   19   18   17   16      1   2   3   4   5

This book is also available on the World Wide Web as an eBook.
Visit www.abc-clio.com for details.

Greenwood
An Imprint of ABC-CLIO, LLC

ABC-CLIO, LLC
130 Cremona Drive, P.O. Box 1911
Santa Barbara, California 93116-1911

This book is printed on acid-free paper ∞

Manufactured in the United States of America

# Contents

# List of Entries

# List of Primary Documents

President Abraham Lincoln's Emancipation Proclamation (January 1, 1863)
Thirteenth Amendment to the U.S. Constitution (Ratified December 18, 1865)
Mississippi Black Codes (1865)
Civil Rights Act (April 1866)
Military Reconstruction Acts (1867–1868)
Fourteenth Amendment to the U.S. Constitution (Ratified July 28, 1868)
Articles of Impeachment against President Andrew Johnson (February 21, 1868)
Sample Constitution under Congressional Reconstruction, Texas (1869)
Fifteenth Amendment to the U.S. Constitution (Ratified March 30, 1870)
Enforcement Act of April 1871 (Ku Klux Klan Act)

# Guide to Related Topics

**Economics and Labor**

Black Codes
Bourbons
Bureau of Refugees, Freedmen, and
  Abandoned Lands
Carpetbaggers
Confiscation Acts
Contraband, Slaves as
Edisto Island, South Carolina
Field Order No. 15
Freedman's Savings and Trust Company
Freedmen's Relief Societies
Howard, Oliver Otis (1830–1909)
Julian, George Washington (1817–1899)
Labor Systems
New South
Port Royal Experiment
Sherman, John (1823–1900)
Southern Claims Commission (SCC)
Southern Homestead Act (1866)
U.S. Army and Reconstruction

**Federal Activism/Rights (Civil,
Political, and Economic)**

Abolition of Slavery
Akerman, Amos Tappan (1821–1880)
Amnesty Proclamations
Black Suffrage
Chase, Salmon Portland (1808–1873)
Civil Rights
Civil Rights Act of 1866
Civil Rights Act of 1875
Confiscation Acts

Congressional Reconstruction
Enforcement Acts (1870, 1871, 1875)
Fifteenth Amendment (1870)
Fourteenth Amendment (1868)
Freedman's Savings and Trust Company
House Judiciary Committee
Joint Committee on Reconstruction
Military Reconstruction Acts (1867–1868)
Republicans, Moderate
Republicans, Radical
Southern Claims Commission (SCC)
Southern Homestead Act (1866)
Stevens, Thaddeus (1792–1868)
Suffrage
Sumner, Charles (1811–1874)
Supreme Court
Thirteenth Amendment (1865)
U.S. Army and Reconstruction

**Legal and Constitutional Issues**

Abolition of Slavery
Amnesty Proclamations
Black Codes
Black Suffrage
Chase, Salmon Portland (1808–1873)
Civil Rights
Civil Rights Act of 1866
Civil Rights Act of 1875
Command of the Army Act (1867)
Confiscation Acts
Congressional Reconstruction
Constitutional Conventions
Enforcement Acts (1870, 1871, 1875)

**Race Relations**

# Preface

This new, one-volume edition of *The Encyclopedia of the Reconstruction Era* represents part of ABC-CLIO/Greenwood Press's continuing effort to make complex periods of history accessible to a wider audience. American Reconstruction marked a complicated and chaotic phase of American history, as the nation faced unprecedented social, economic, and constitutional crises: a third of the country lay in ruin; some 4 million former slaves became free, and then became citizens; a new political party dominated the landscape; the Constitution added three amendments in four years; the U.S. military assumed a never-before-seen role in civilian governance; and America saw its first impeachment of a president.

This volume seeks to provide an introduction to Reconstruction by focusing on the most significant individuals, events, and issues. Like its larger predecessor, the two-volume *Encyclopedia of the Reconstruction Era*, this volume incorporates the latest scholarship from the most prominent historians in the field. Condensed and edited specifically for the high school student and lower-level college student, this new volume presents both the basics of Reconstruction and the most useful resources for further study. Students looking for subjects that occurred during Reconstruction, but are not related to Reconstruction directly, may need to look elsewhere. For instance, readers will not find information on Native Americans, foreign policy, or Northern labor strikes; while of importance to the larger period, these are peripheral to Reconstruction. For those seeking more details, or perhaps specifics on local individuals or events not captured here, the Further Reading sections and the Selected Bibliography offer substantial information.

This volume's Introduction summarizes the Reconstruction period and provides some historical background for the entries. The entries comprise the bulk of the book, with each including references to other entries (when applicable) and suggestions for further reading. The entries are arranged alphabetically, with biographical entries alphabetized by surname (Ames, Adelbert) and events by description, not by year (Elections of 1866, not 1866, elections of). Ten key primary documents follow the entries and an extensive bibliography delivers even more resources for the student researcher.

Readers may be confused by inconsistencies in some terms. For example, readers will see blacks, freedmen, freedpeople, and African Americans used interchangeably. The switching is often deliberate, to either avoid constant repetition, avert an awkward phrasing ("white and black males" is simpler than "white and African American males"), or make a clear distinction: "freedpeople" specifically refers to former slaves, not all African Americans. Usage of "confederate" and "Confederate" may also seem odd. In most cases, lower-case confederate refers to an individual, whereas Confederate refers to the political entity ("former confederates" but the "former Confederate states"). The term "conservative" will also appear frequently, sometimes as a noun and sometimes as an adjective. Both refer to those who seek stability and the status quo, and reject sudden or significant changes. As an adjective, Conservative can be applied at any time, such as Conservative Republicans who opposed support for black civil rights. As a noun, Conservative usually refers to white Democrats in the South; in fact, in Reconstruction writing, Southern Democrats, former confederates, and Conservatives are used almost interchangeably.

# Acknowledgments

I am grateful for the support of the team at ABC-CLIO/Greenwood Press—in particular Marian Perales—for their gentle style of patient supervision. Of course I remain in debt to the original contributors to the two-volume edition, as their initial efforts made my present undertaking easier. Finally, although it is certainly not final, my deepest thanks and respect go to my wife Etsuko, for her endless forbearance with my academic endeavors.

*The views expressed herein are those of the editor and the contributors and are not to be construed as official or reflecting the views of the Commandant or of the U.S. Coast Guard.*

# Introduction

In American history, "Reconstruction" is the term generally applied to the period between 1862 and 1877, during which the United States sought to bring order from the tremendous social, political, economic, physical, and constitutional changes caused by secession and the Civil War. The decision by 11 Southern states to attempt secession and reject the national government—and more important, the decision by the federal government under President Abraham Lincoln to deny that attempt and enforce federal law—unleashed forces that forever changed America. Some of these forces, and some of the changes that resulted, were confined to the war years. Others, once released, could not be contained. These included the abolition of slavery, the expansion of governmental power and constitutional jurisdiction, the rise of the Republican Party, the explosion of Northern industry and the national market, and the appearance of a social dynamism that supported struggles by new social groups for political and civil equality.

Unfortunately, history classes often sum up Reconstruction in nearly useless ways, or ignore it altogether. When compared to the glorious and rather straightforward years of the Civil War, Reconstruction seems wandering and confusing, a rambling collection of amendments and acts, generals and politicians, former slaves and former confederates. Even the historical viewpoints on Reconstruction are in flux, with debates on who was right, who was wrong, what could have been done differently, who gained, and who lost.

## Reconstruction: An Overview

### Wartime and Early Presidential Reconstruction

The changes—and the controversies—that came to characterize Reconstruction began early in the Civil War. Some of the great questions of Reconstruction—the status of freedpeople, the readmission of former Confederate states, the argument over who would control any reconciliation process—found expression well before any formal process began. At first, Congress led the way, taking aggressive steps geared toward weakening the Confederacy by attacking its core, slavery. In April 1862, Congress abolished slavery in the nation's capital, and by July endorsed informal emancipation in the Second Confiscation Act of July 1862, which allowed federal troops to seize the personal property of those in rebellion—including slaves. Whether interpreted as humanitarian efforts or simply necessary war measures, these acts carried huge ramifications; but these wartime actions carried no consideration for peacetime consequences. By spring 1862, President Abraham Lincoln had also taken the first steps toward political reconstruction by setting up military governors in conquered areas and seeking out Unionist support to construct new Southern state governments under what historians call "wartime reconstruction" (covered in this volume by Presidential Reconstruction). By summer 1862, Lincoln privately professed to his Cabinet his desire for emancipation. Issued on September 22, the preliminary Emancipation Proclamation declared that all slaves in areas still in rebellion, as of January 1, 1863, "shall be henceforth and forever free." Slavery was now directly linked to the fate of the rebellion, and the president had begun flexing his authority as commander in chief. Yet as with other measures, no one fully considered the consequences of the proclamation—including the fate of African Americans who might become free. In 1863, with the dual victories of Gettysburg and Vicksburg and more Confederate territory falling under federal control daily, Lincoln announced his program for "restoration," issuing his Proclamation of Amnesty and Pardon in December. Lincoln's generous granting of pardons, his rejection of punitive or vengeful actions, and liberal view of allegiance (only 10% of 1860 voters needed to declare allegiance for a Confederate state to begin constituting a new government) represented another carrot-and-stick approach to ending the war and restoring the Union. This so-called Ten Percent Plan made no mention of former slaves or their future status, except that former confederates has to acknowledge federal supremacy, including any federal measures relating to slavery (such as its possible abolition).

## President Lincoln and Congress Lock Horns

Lincoln's plan angered many in the North. Abolitionists and a growing pocket of aggressive Republicans in the army and Congress—Radical Republicans they would be called—wanted more change, more guarantees, and more punishment. In July 1864, Congress responded to the presidential program by passing the Wade-Davis Bill. This proposal required a majority of eligible Southern voters to take a loyalty oath, significantly restricted the political participation by former confederates, and guaranteed some civil rights to freedpeople (former slaves). Lincoln refused to sign the bill into law, so the initiative never went into effect. Congress retaliated by refusing to seat in Congress representatives from four states that had begun reconstructing new governments under Lincoln's program—Tennessee, Louisiana, Arkansas, and Virginia.

## President Johnson Seizes the Initiative

In early spring 1865, discussions over the future of Reconstruction took a back seat to celebrations of Union victory. But while Union soldiers went home to tremendous welcomes, and Congress adjourned in March to visit their thankful constituents, Abraham Lincoln—victorious war president—never saw home again. Shot by John Wilkes Booth on April 14, Lincoln died early the next morning, and the task of rebuilding the country fell to Vice President Andrew Johnson, a Unionist Democrat from Tennessee. With Lincoln dead, anxiety over the war evaporating, and Congress not in session, President Johnson seized the opportunity and embarked on a program to quickly bring former Confederate states back into the Union. Like his predecessor, Johnson stressed speed, leniency, and executive control; the freedpeople were nowhere in his plan.

Johnson's program was simple. Former confederates either needed to take a loyalty oath or petition the president directly for a presidential pardon. Then, these "loyal" white Southerners would create new state governments, nullify and repudiate secession and Confederate debts (in other words, affirm that neither ever existed nor could exist), and draft new state constitutions that abolished slavery. Once complete, these states would be readmitted to Congress with all their rights and privileges intact. Johnson saw the war and the readmission process as vehicles for preserving the Union and humbling an oppressive planter elite, not for inciting economic, racial, or constitutional revolution. He believed that a new South would be ruled by white Unionists, merchants, and artisans; in other words, people like Johnson. Through summer 1865, the former Confederate states elected new state governments, which, like Johnson himself, drastically misread the political and social atmosphere of the North. Several states ignored some of Johnson's meager requirements, such as repudiating the Confederate debt, declaring secession null and void, and even ratifying the Thirteenth Amendment. Their most obnoxious blunder was passage of "Black Codes," laws that regulated all aspects of black life in their respective states. To many white Southerners, Black Codes created order out of chaos, stabilizing everything from labor needs to social relationships.

Many African Americans and Northern Republicans believed differently, and saw the codes as an attempt to salvage a slave society. More "radical" Northerners responded with demands for land confiscation, a total redistribution of Southern land to secure economic power for blacks and punish former confederates. However, all agreed that the treatment of former slaves dredged up memories of the Old South, in total rejection of the spirit of emancipation and Confederate defeat. The losers were calling the shots, and the winners—or at least their African American Southern allies—were subjected to their whims.

The final requirement facing Johnson's state governments, and their last collective misstep, was the election of new federal representatives. When the 1865 fall elections were over, half of the senators and representatives elected had served in either the Confederate army or the Confederate government. This fact, added to the intransigence of the states toward Johnson's generous terms and the blatant arrogance apparent in the black codes, convinced Northerners and their federal representatives gathering in Washington that the white South seemed little, if at all, repentant.

## Congressional Republicans Seek a Compromise

Reminiscent of the earlier clash between Lincoln and Congress, Republicans blocked part of the president's program, and then sought an alternative to it. When it convened in December 1865, Congress refused to seat the new Southern members. Then Republicans created the Joint Committee of Fifteen on Reconstruction, and set to work on a series of bills that would allow the federal government to intervene on behalf of the former slaves and protect them from the outlandish public and private treatment rampant in the South. In spring 1866, Moderate Republicans presented the Freedmen's Bureau Bill and the Civil Rights Bill, two measures attempting to bridge gaps between factions in the party, the Congress and the Executive, and the North and South. While both bills authorized a more active and powerful federal presence, largely supporting and protecting the recently freed slaves, neither altered the political makeup of the Southern governments or mentioned black suffrage.

But President Johnson was in no mood to compromise. He vetoed both measures, which had a unifying effect on Republicans who believed that the South needed to accept defeat, federal supremacy, and some black rights. In April 1866, the Republicans introduced the Fourteenth Amendment, passed the Civil Rights Act over Johnson's veto, and then proposed and passed a new Freedmen's Bureau Act in July. Johnson retaliated by urging the Southern states not to ratify the Fourteenth Amendment. He formally abandoned his wartime alliance with Republicans and created a new party, one opposed to African American rights, extensions of federal power, and modifications to the Constitution. Johnson believed his National Union Movement would attract antiblack Northerners and win in the fall 1866 elections, ushering in a Conservative, pro-Johnson Congress. Again, the president was mistaken. Johnson and his alliance with white Southerners cost him dearly in the North, and bloody race riots in the South between whites and African Americans hardened Northern hearts toward this new party. Most Northerners rejected racial equality and African American voting, but this was different: Northern voters saw the choice between innocent, helpless pro-Union former slaves, and vicious, belligerent former rebels. Johnson's party did not have a chance. In many ways, the congressional elections of 1866 served as a referendum on Reconstruction. Republicans trounced President Johnson's National Union Party, in a clear message about Northern expectations for Reconstruction. Republican domination of Congress made the legislature "veto-proof," easily able to pass a measure with the requisite two-thirds majority to override a presidential veto. Rather than yielding, President Johnson stepped up his opposition to the Fourteenth Amendment, pushing Southern governments to reject its ratification. In the end, every former Confederate state except one—his own Tennessee—rejected the amendment (Tennessee was readmitted to Congress in the summer of 1866). Moderate Republicans watched in dismay as the last component of their compromise strategy collapsed.

### The Alternative: Congressional ("Radical") Reconstruction

Even more than the president's vetoes the previous spring, Johnson's actions in the summer and fall of 1866 brought a sense of unity to the Republican Party. With both Johnson's new party and his Southern governments discredited, a golden opportunity appeared for real change in the South. In March 1867, Republicans in control of Congress turned their considerable power toward instituting their version of Reconstruction. That program was embodied in a series of measures called the Military Reconstruction Acts. Congress passed the first in March 1867, and followed with three supplemental acts. Johnson vetoed them all, and saw each one become law over his opposition. On the surface, the measures did seem radical and unprecedented, and certain aspects were. Congress divided the South into five military districts, placed supervisory powers in the hands of army generals, and dictated the registration of all able-bodied, eligible males, as defined by the still-pending Fourteenth Amendment. Thus, in 10 former Confederate states, African American men could now register to vote and hold political office, but many former confederates could not. This new electorate then voted for a constitutional convention, which drafted a new state constitution that provided for a new state government, which, finally, needed to ratify the Fourteenth Amendment. When all this had occurred, the state could present itself to Congress for readmission to the Union.

As shown in various entries, this "Radical" Reconstruction was not as extreme as some made it sound. Republicans agreed that giving freedmen the vote was more important, more democratic, more American, and less controversial than giving them land. The acts only applied to the Southern states still awaiting readmission, so African American males in the

North, the Border States, and even Tennessee were not affected. Nonetheless, the Military Reconstruction Acts set in motion a political revolution in the South. Southern African Americans fully understood the power of the ballot. Educated or illiterate, free black or former slave, urban or rural, Upper South or delta, African American males eagerly registered under the provisions of the Reconstruction Acts—and the protective gaze of federal troops. Still, a fully developed Republican presence in the South required an alliance with whites. Although the Military Reconstruction Acts disfranchised many former confederates, Unionists could participate, and many did. Earning the pejorative label "scalawags," these Southern whites brought an important local experience to Southern politics, forging an at-times uneasy alliance with the black community. These two groups were joined by a third, which has traditionally borne the brunt of historical criticism: the "carpetbaggers," a derogative term applied to Northerners who settled in the South after the war.

In late 1867 eligible Southerners, black and white, voted for delegates to state constitutional conventions. These conventions established—at least on paper—state governments and policies that represented incredible reforms; one could argue they collectively embodied a revolution. As a whole, the new state constitutions were as progressive as any in existence and what followed, for a few brief years, was an incredible experiment in democratic process. Once the new state constitutions were complete, the new voters elected new governments, which were resoundingly Republican in makeup; these governments replaced the Johnson governments established during the Presidential Reconstruction phase.

In the South, the reaction from Conservative white Southerners came in many forms, some legal, some illegal, some economic, and some even literary. The response is best seen in two developments during this phase—the evolution of the agricultural labor system called sharecropping, and the rise of white violence. Both marked attempts by whites to regain control of elements within their society that had been traditionally theirs; the details of these developments are captured in the entries of this volume, but suffice it to say that in both cases the Conservatives' drive to defend old ideas was greater than Republican willpower to protect new ones.

## The Grant Administration: Climax and Denouement

Of course, the state of affairs in the South was partly dependent upon support from the North, be it public opinion or action by Republicans in Washington. For a time, that support was steady and strong, and embraced several far-reaching actions. Through 1867 and 1868, Congress passed the Command of the Army Act (as part of the 1867 Army Appropriations Act), the Tenure of Office Act, and supplements to the Military Reconstruction Act, all intended to strengthen the Reconstruction process and Republican positions in government. Ultimately, Johnson's obstinacy pushed Congress into entirely uncharted waters and, in 1868, resulted in the first impeachment of a president in American history. Again, divisions within the Republican Party brought about a moderate solution: the president was impeached and disgraced, but not convicted by the Senate or removed from office. The impeachment crushed the hopes of the Democratic Party, and allowed an easy victory for Ulysses S. Grant and the Republicans in the 1868 presidential contest. The Republican Party now firmly controlled the workings of the federal government.

The first few years of the Grant administration saw what many believe to be the climax of Reconstruction activism. In February 1869, Congress passed the Fifteenth Amendment and sent it to the states for ratification. A compromise, the amendment did not positively confer the right to vote; it merely prohibited voting restrictions that were based upon "race, color, or previous condition of servitude." Immediately in the North, and eventually in the South, this amendment led to a wide array of imaginative voting regulations and provisions designed to eliminate black voting without violating the letter of the law. However, more immediate problems held the Grant administration's interest, as antiblack and anti-Republican violence expanded in scope and intensity with the coming of the Republican state governments. Such organizations as the Ku Klux Klan and the Knights of the White Camellia had appeared soon after the war to enforce classic values of white supremacy and black obedience. With the formation of new state governments, these took on a more political aim and became terrorist agents of the Democratic Party in an attempt to demoralize Republican electoral majorities. Republicans in Washington fired back with three Enforcement Acts, passed in May 1870, and February and April 1871. Collectively, these acts extended federal jurisdiction over voting and voting practices, ensured that political rights were not being violated, outlawed organizations seeking to infringe on federally guaranteed rights, and allowed the president to suspend the writ of habeas corpus to enforce the laws. These measures would be the basis for the much-heralded federal crackdown on white supremacist groups in the early 1870s, when federal troops and Justice Department officials arrested thousands of whites accused of violating Republicans' civil rights.

## *Reconstruction Collapses*

The flurry of Republican activity in Congress and across the South did not last. On the one hand, Republican measures had been crafted to allow for local control—federalism, one might argue—as seen in granting African American suffrage. Its framers had intended that this burst of federal activity could then recede and Southern Republicans could take care of themselves. That clearly was not the case because federal officials from the War and Justice Departments were constantly required to intervene in some Southern dispute, riot, or electoral crisis. More than five years after the war, the former Confederate states seemed to be an endless sinkhole that demanded resources but produced no conclusive, stable results. That fact, added to the tales of political corruption in the Reconstruction governments and the prevailing antiblack sentiment in the United States, began to erode support in the North. On the other hand, some Northerners argued that stable, tangible results had been achieved, and so it was time to move on. After all, slavery was abolished, African Americans were now citizens with civil and political rights (according to the Fourteenth and Fifteenth Amendments), states were being readmitted to Congress under new constitutions, and the Southern economy—never a very progressive engine—seemed to be slowly making way. For many, it appeared as though the Union had been "reconstructed," and there was no more to do.

The presidential contest in 1872 captured this spirit, as many Moderate Republicans and Democrats merged into the Liberal Republican Party to challenge Grant for reelection. Although unsuccessful, the Liberal Republican movement foreshadowed significant changes in Northern priorities—the Panic of 1873 (a recession), monetary policy, political corruption and civil service reform, westward expansion, and immigrant issues were becoming hot topics. The fate of African Americans in the South seemed like something from far away and long ago, perhaps best left to the states to deal with. The congressional elections of 1874 drove this home, as Democrats gained control of Congress for the first time since before the Civil War.

Then in the mid-1870s, the Supreme Court entered the Reconstruction discussion and delivered several crippling blows to the Republican program. In the Slaughterhouse cases (1873), *United States v. Reese* (1876), and *United States v. Cruikshank* (1876), the court followed a conservative view of the Reconstruction amendments, limiting their scope and applicability. Added to this, the hostility, shrewdness, and perseverance of Southern Democrats became so organized by the mid-1870s that, without overt federal intervention, the "black and tan" governments in the South collapsed one by one. Southern Conservatives appealed to racism; applied economic and social coercion; developed mass intimidation techniques; and, when necessary, resorted to outright violence, kidnapping, and assassination. By the presidential election of 1876, all but three Southern Reconstruction governments had toppled, and those three—Florida, Louisiana, and South Carolina—were under siege.

These two trends, apathy in the North and focused ruthlessness in the South, intersected in the 1876 election. The so-called Compromise of 1877 allowed Republican Rutherford B. Hayes to become president, but signaled the overthrow of the last Republican governments in the South. Abandoned by Washington, black and white Republicans in the South could only look to their local governments for help. Since these relied on federal assistance, the last state regimes collapsed like a house of cards. The South had been "redeemed."

The effects were immediate, lasting, and predictable, since other states had returned to "home rule" earlier. Across the South, as had occurred under Andrew Johnson's restoration policy, many white Southerners were ready to implement their own version of "reconstruction." Certainly, Reconstruction meant much more than just who governed, for it took into account the vast range of social, familial, legal, geographic, economic, even spiritual changes that were under way. Unfortunately, those who governed often dictated the scope and focus of those changes, opportunities, and initiatives. Soon the backlash began, with prosecutions of former Republican politicians; amendments to state constitutions regarding fiscal policies, education, and welfare; and, of course, legal maneuvers to restrict black male suffrage.

However, the slow and steady erosion of the promise of Reconstruction cannot erase its accomplishments. Some historians place among these abolition, the destruction of the planter aristocracy and recognition of the Union as perpetual. Others disagree, noting these were products of the war, not its aftermath. Instead, they point to the social, religious, and economic achievements of the freedpeople; the genesis of Southern economic reforms built upon diversification and Northern capital; the progressive new state constitutions, parts of which outlived Redemption; the precedents set by the conscientious and subservient roles of the military during turbulent times; and, finally and perhaps most important, the three Reconstruction Amendments. While these represented expedient solutions at the time, they nonetheless placed before Americans a constant reminder that the nation still fell short of the ideals espoused in the Declaration of Independence. At least the pledge was now formal and official. It remains to be seen when and how that pledge will be fulfilled.

# Chronology

**1860**

**November 6**  Abraham Lincoln becomes the first Republican elected president.

**December 20**  South Carolina secedes from the federal Union.

**1861**

**January–June**  Ten other slave states secede from the Union.

**February**  Confederate States of America established with its capital in Montgomery, Alabama.

**May 25**  Gen. Benjamin Butler in Virginia declares runaway slaves "contraband of war."

**June 22**  House of Representatives passes John Crittenden's War Aims Resolution, declaring it the federal government's purpose to preserve the Union, not to interfere with the "internal affairs" of Southern states.

**July 25**  Senate passes Andrew Johnson's War Aims Resolution, stating same as House version.

**August 6**  Congress passes the First Confiscation Act.

**November 7**  Union forces seize territory along the South Carolina coast, allowing first experiments with contrabands (escaped slaves) to begin.

**December**  Congress creates the Joint Committee on the Conduct of the War to push a more aggressive Radical agenda for prosecuting the war.

**1862**

**March 2**  Abraham Lincoln appoints Andrew Johnson military governor of Union-occupied Tennessee.

**April 16**  Congress abolishes slavery in the District of Columbia and the federal territories.

**May 1**  In New Orleans, Gen. Benjamin Butler begins informal reconstruction by coordinating Unionist elements in Louisiana.

| | |
|---|---|
| **May 19** | President Lincoln appoints Edward Stanley as provisional governor of North Carolina. |
| **May 20** | Congress passes the Homestead Act. |
| **July 17** | Congress passes the Second Confiscation Act, specifically allowing the seizure of slaves from those in rebellion. Act also authorizes president to "employ" freed slaves "as necessary and proper for the suppression of the rebellion," the first federal pronouncement mentioning the use of blacks in the service. |
| **July 22** | President Lincoln, at a cabinet meeting, declares his support for emancipation. |
| **September 22** | Following the battle of Antietam, Lincoln announces the Preliminary Emancipation Proclamation, giving Confederate states three months to end the rebellion or lose their slaves. |

**1863**

| | |
|---|---|
| **January 1** | Promulgation of the Emancipation Proclamation, declaring free slaves in areas still under rebellion against the United States. Proclamation also allows for the enlistment of African Americans in the armed forces. |
| **April 20** | West Virginia is admitted to the Union. |
| **June 20** | Gradual emancipation begins under West Virginia's state constitution. |
| | President Lincoln appoints Francis H. Pierpont provisional governor of Virginia. |
| **December 8** | President Lincoln delivers his Proclamation of Amnesty and Reconstruction, also called the "Ten Percent Plan." |

**1864**

| | |
|---|---|
| **January 4** | Arkansas state constitutional convention opens under Lincoln's guidelines. |
| **January 20** | Isaac Murphy selected as provisional governor of Arkansas under Ten Percent Plan. |
| **May 21** | Congressmen from Arkansas denied admittance to federal legislature; breach between executive and Congress evident. |
| **July 2** | Congress passes Wade-Davis Bill as a more stringent alternative to Lincoln's Reconstruction plan. |
| **July 8** | Lincoln pocket-vetoes the Wade-Davis Bill. |
| | Republican National Convention in Baltimore nominates Abraham Lincoln on a "National Union Party" platform of Union, victory, and reconciliation. Andrew Johnson, War Democrat from Tennessee, selected as his running mate. |

| | |
|---|---|
| **August 29** | Democratic National Convention meets in Chicago and nominates ticket of Gen. George B. McClellan and George Pendleton. |
| **October 5** | Louisiana convenes its constitutional convention as per Lincoln's Ten Percent Plan. |
| **October 29** | Maryland adopts new constitution, abolishing slavery. |
| **November 8** | Abraham Lincoln is reelected president, receiving nearly 75 percent of the Union soldier vote; Democrat/Union Party Andrew Johnson elected vice president. |
| **December 6** | Salmon P. Chase, Lincoln's secretary of the treasury, becomes chief justice of the United States. |

**1865**

| | |
|---|---|
| **January 11** | Missouri, a "border state," emancipates its slaves. |
| **January 16** | In Savannah, Union general William T. Sherman issues Special Field Order No. 15, setting aside abandoned coastal lands for use by freed slaves; this begins the mythical federal grant of "forty acres and a mule." |
| **January 31** | Congress passes the Thirteenth Amendment, which will formally abolish slavery in the United States. It is sent to the states for ratification. |
| **February 13** | Virginia convenes its constitutional convention as per Lincoln's Ten Percent Plan. |
| **February 22** | Tennessee emancipates its slaves. |
| **March 3** | Congress creates, within the War Department, the Bureau of Refugees, Freedmen, and Abandoned Lands to help blacks in their transition from slavery to freedom. |
| **March 4** | Abraham Lincoln is inaugurated a second time as president. His address reflects his Reconstruction policy with the immortal "with malice toward none; with charity for all." |
| **April 5** | William G. Brownlow elected governor of Tennessee. |
| **April 9** | Confederate general Robert E. Lee surrenders the Army of Northern Virginia to Ulysses S. Grant at Appomattox Court House, Virginia. |
| **April 14** | John Wilkes Booth assassinates President Lincoln at Ford's Theater in Washington, D.C. |
| **April 15** | Lincoln dies; Andrew Johnson is sworn in as president. |
| **May 1** | President Johnson authorizes military trials for the Lincoln assassins. |
| **May 29** | Johnson issues his First Amnesty Proclamation, which includes a liberal amnesty but requires many to appeal for a special presidential pardon. |

|  | Johnson initiates his Reconstruction program with his Proclamation for North Carolina, appointing William W. Holden provisional governor. |
|---|---|
| **June 13** | Johnson appoints Benjamin F. Perry and William H. Sharkey provisional governors of South Carolina and Mississippi, respectively. |
| **June 17** | Johnson appoints James Johnson and Andrew J. Hamilton provisional governors of Georgia and Texas, respectively. |
| **June 21** | Johnson appoints Lewis Parsons provisional governor of Alabama. |
| **July 13** | Johnson appoints William Marvin provisional governor of Florida. |
| **August 14** | First constitutional convention to be held under Johnson's program opens in Mississippi; others follow through fall. |
| **October 2** | In Mississippi, Benjamin Humphries becomes the first governor elected under Johnson's Reconstruction plan. |
| **December 2** | New Mississippi legislature passes "black codes" to regulate freedpeople; other former Confederate states follow. |
| **December 3** | Thirty-Ninth Congress reconvenes and refuses to seat representatives and senators elected under Johnson's program. |
| **December 13** | Congress creates the Joint Committee of Fifteen on Reconstruction. |
| **December 18** | Thirteenth Amendment ratified and becomes part of the U.S. Constitution. |
| **1866** **February 19** | Johnson vetoes the Freedmen's Bureau Bill. |
| **March 27** | Johnson vetoes the Civil Rights Bill. |
| **April** | Ku Klux (from Greek *kuklos* or circle) founded in Pulaski, Tennessee (the "Klan" was added much later). |
| **April 2** | Johnson issues proclamation formally declaring the "insurrection" at an end. |
| **April 9** | Congress passes the Civil Rights Act over Johnson's veto, the first significant piece of legislation passed over an executive veto. |
| **April 30/May 1** | Race riot in Memphis, Tennessee. |
| **June 13** | Congress passes the Fourteenth Amendment and sends it to the states for ratification. |
| **June 21** | Congress passes the Southern Homestead Act. |
| **July 16** | Johnson vetoes second Freedmen's Bureau Bill. |
|  | Congress overrides Johnson's veto and passes the Freedmen's Bureau Renewal Act. |

| | |
|---|---|
| **July 24** | Tennessee, after ratifying the Fourteenth Amendment, becomes the first former Confederate state readmitted to the Union. |
| **July 30** | Race riot in New Orleans, Louisiana. |
| **August 14–15** | National Union Movement holds its convention in Philadelphia. |
| **October–November** | Republicans trounce Johnson's Conservative National Union Movement in fall congressional elections. |

**1867**

| | |
|---|---|
| **January 5** | Johnson vetoes bill to enfranchise blacks in the District of Columbia. |
| **January 8** | Congress overrides Johnson's veto; black male suffrage begins in District of Columbia. |
| **March 2** | Congress passes First Military Reconstruction Act, Tenure of Office Act, Army Appropriations Act, and Fortieth Congress Act. |
| | Johnson vetoes Military Reconstruction Act, Tenure of Office Act, and Fortieth Congress Act; approves but submits formal protest to Army Appropriations Act. |
| | Congress overrides presidential vetoes and passes into law Military Reconstruction, Tenure, and Fortieth Congress Acts. |
| **August 12** | Johnson suspends Secretary of War Edwin M. Stanton and appoints Gen. Ulysses S. Grant secretary *ad interim*. |
| **September 7** | Johnson issues Second Amnesty Proclamation. |
| **September 23** | In Louisiana, the first state constitutional convention under Congressional Reconstruction begins. |
| **October–November** | Democrats score sweeping surprise victories in state contests across the North. |
| **December 7** | First vote on impeachment fails in House of Representatives. |

**1868**

| | |
|---|---|
| **January 13** | Senate reconvenes and refuses to consent Johnson's suspension of Secretary Stanton and appointment of Ulysses S. Grant. |
| **February 4** | William H. Smith of Alabama becomes the first governor elected under Congressional Reconstruction and the Military Reconstruction Acts. |
| **February 21** | Johnson formally removes Stanton as secretary of war; appoints General Lorenzo Thomas. |
| **February 24** | House of Representatives votes to impeach President Johnson. |
| **March 2–3** | House adopts 11 Articles of Impeachment and names impeachment managers for the Senate trial. |

| | |
|---|---|
| **March 27** | Supreme Court rules in *Ex parte McCardle* that Congress can restrict the court's jurisdiction relating to "political issues." |
| **March 30** | Senate convenes as High Court of Impeachment as the president's trial opens. |
| **May 16** | Senate votes on Article Eleven, finding Johnson "not guilty" by a vote of 35 to 19, one shy of conviction. |
| **May 20** | Republican National Convention nominates Ulysses S. Grant for president and Speaker of the House Schuyler Colfax as vice president. |
| **May 26** | Senate votes on Article Two, finding Johnson "not guilty" by a vote of 35 to 19, one shy of conviction; Senate adjourns as High Court. |
| **May 30** | First official Memorial Day, established by the Grand Army of the Republic across the North to remember Union dead. |
| **June 22** | Congress readmits Arkansas to the Union as the first state readmitted under the Republican's plan of Reconstruction. |
| **July 25** | Congress passes bill dismantling the Freedmen's Bureau; all operations other than education will cease as of January 1, 1869. |
| **July 28** | Fourteenth Amendment ratified and added to the U.S. Constitution. |
| **November 3** | Ulysses S. Grant elected president. |
| **1869**<br>**February 25** | Congress passes the Fifteenth Amendment and sends it to the states for ratification. |
| **March 4** | Ulysses S. Grant inaugurated as president. |
| **April 12** | Supreme Court upholds constitutionality of the Military Reconstruction Acts in *Texas v. White*. |
| **October 4** | Tennessee, the first state readmitted, becomes the first state "redeemed" by Conservatives as DeWitt Senter wins governorship. |
| **October 5** | Virginia "redeemed" as elections result in a Conservative victory; Virginia is the only state redeemed before readmission. |
| **December 22** | Georgia directed to reconvene the 1868 legislature, which includes blacks, before Congress will consider readmission. |
| **1870**<br>**January 26** | Despite its Conservative government, Virginia is readmitted to the Union. |
| **February 23** | Congress readmits Mississippi to the Union. |
| **February 25** | Hiram R. Revels, Senate-elect from Mississippi, becomes the first black U.S. senator. |

| | |
|---|---|
| **March 30** | Upon ratification, the Fifteenth Amendment becomes part of the U.S. Constitution. |
| | Congress readmits Texas to the Union. |
| **May 31** | Congress passes the First Enforcement Act, placing certain forms of voting harassment under federal jurisdiction. |
| **June–August** | In North Carolina, the "Kirk-Holden War" begins, pitting state forces against the Ku Klux Klan. |
| **July 15** | Congress readmits Georgia to the federal Union for the second time. |
| **November 4** | Conservative legislature convenes, "redeeming" North Carolina. |
| **December 12** | Joseph H. Rainey, the first African American to serve in the House of Representatives, takes his seat in Washington; he will serve until 1879. |
| **December 19** | Lower house of North Carolina legislature passes formal Articles of Impeachment against Republican governor William W. Holden. |
| **1871** | |
| **March 3** | Congress creates the Southern Claims Commission, which will operate until 1880. |
| **March 22** | William W. Holden is convicted and removed by the North Carolina Senate—the first governor in American history thus removed. |
| **April 20** | Faced with growing evidence of well-organized terrorist challenges to the Southern Republican governments, Congress passes the Third Enforcement Act (also called the Ku Klux Act; later generations added the "Klan" portion of the title). |
| **October 17** | Citing the Ku Klux Act, President Grant suspends the writ of habeas corpus in portions of up-country South Carolina and orders military/Justice Department intervention. |
| **November 1** | After second readmission, Georgia is again "redeemed" with ascension of James M. Smith as governor. |
| **1872** | |
| **May 3** | "Liberal Republicans" bolt Grant's Republican Party and hold convention in Cincinnati; *New York Tribune* owner Horace Greeley nominated for president. |
| **May 22** | Congress passes the Amnesty Act, clearing nearly all former confederates from political liabilities imposed under the Military Reconstruction Acts and Fourteenth Amendment. |
| **June 5–6** | Republican National Convention nominates Ulysses S. Grant for reelection. |
| **July 9–10** | Democratic National Convention backs the Liberal Republicans and their candidate, Horace Greeley. |

| | |
|---|---|
| **November 5** | Ulysses S. Grant reelected president. |
| **December 9** | Division among Republicans in Louisiana leads the Republican legislature to impeach Republican governor Henry Clay Warmoth; although he is not removed, the governorship falls to P.B.S. Pinchback, making him the first black governor in U.S. history. |

**1873**

| | |
|---|---|
| **January 9** | Republican divisions in Louisiana result in disputed election and dual governments: Republicans assemble under William P. Kellogg, and Conservatives assemble under John McEnery. |
| **April 13** | White vigilantes murder black and white Republicans in the Colfax Massacre in Louisiana. |
| **April 14** | Supreme Court, in the Slaughterhouse Cases, renders very narrow interpretation of the scope of the Fourteenth Amendment. |
| **September 18** | Panic of 1873 begins with the failure of Jay Cooke's investment house. |

**1874**

| | |
|---|---|
| **March–May** | In the Brooks-Baxter War, Republican infighting in Arkansas moves from political disputes into court fights, and finally erupts in bloodshed. |
| **May 16** | Grant recognizes Elisha Baxter as governor of Arkansas, ending Brooks-Baxter War. |
| **June** | Appearance of White League in Louisiana, terrorist organization aimed at overthrowing Republican Kellogg. |
| **August 30** | White League murders Republicans in the Coushatta Massacre. |
| **September 16** | White League battles police in New Orleans; Kellogg temporarily overthrown; Grant sends federal troops to reinstate Kellogg. |
| **October–November** | Democrats score sweeping victories in congressional elections; the next House of Representatives, set to convene in fall 1875, will be under Democratic control. |
| **November 10** | Arkansas is "redeemed" with the election of Conservative Augustus H. Garland as governor. |
| **December** | Race riots and violence across Mississippi, as white Conservatives embark on a violent, terror-based campaign to seize control at the next election. Across the South, whites adopt the term "Mississippi Plan" when referring to brutal, overt tactics. |

**1875**

| | |
|---|---|
| **March 1** | Congress passes the Civil Rights Act of 1875. |

| | |
|---|---|
| **November 3** | Violence and fraud result in the redemption of Mississippi; Conservative whites regain control of the state legislature. |
| **1876** | |
| **January 4** | Conservative legislature convenes in Mississippi. |
| **March 27** | Supreme Court, in *United States v. Cruikshank* and *United States v. Reese*, restricts scope and use of Enforcement Acts. |
| **June 15–17** | In Cincinnati, Republican National Convention nominates Rutherford B. Hayes of Ohio for president. |
| **June 27–29** | In St Louis, Democratic National Convention nominates New Yorker Samuel Tilden for president. |
| **July 7** | Hamburg Massacre occurs in South Carolina, as election campaigning pits Republican black militiamen against white Conservative gun clubs. |
| **September 16–19** | In South Carolina a three-day, countywide killing spree conducted by white gun clubs earns the name the Ellenton Riot; ends with direct intervention by U.S. infantry units. |
| **October 16–17** | White attack on a Republican meeting, called the Cainhoy Riot, leads Grant to send more federal troops to South Carolina for the election. |
| **November 8** | Presidential and state elections disputed; state gubernatorial elections in South Carolina and Louisiana result in dual governments for both, while improprieties in state electoral returns deadlock the presidential decision. |
| **November 28–30** | Democrats and Republicans establish rival legislatures in South Carolina. |
| **December** | Republican legislature elects Daniel H. Chamberlain governor of South Carolina, with Democratic legislature selecting former confederate Wade Hampton III. |
| **1877** | |
| **January 1** | Democrat Zebulon Vance, governor of North Carolina during the Confederacy, is sworn in as governor once again. |
| **January 2** | Florida Democrats "redeem" the state; Democrat Charles F. Drew becomes governor. |
| **January 8** | In Louisiana, rival governors are sworn in: Stephen B. Packard has Republican (and federal) support, while Francis T. Nicholls is backed by Democrats. |
| **January 20** | The Federal Electoral Commission created to decide the presidential contest. |

| | |
|---|---|
| **February** | Discussion, rumors, and trips North and South occur as commission debates presidential decision. |
| **February 26** | Wormley House "deal" negotiates a complex series of trade-offs to settle the presidential controversy. |
| **March 2** | Disputed electoral votes go to Rutherford B. Hayes. |
| **March 4** | Hayes is inaugurated as president. |
| **April 3** | Hayes orders federal troops to leave state capitals and cease interfering in state political disputes. |
| **April 10** | Federal troops leave Columbia; Hampton becomes governor and South Carolina is formally "redeemed." |
| **April 24** | Federal troops withdraw from Baton Rouge; Francis T. Nicholls becomes governor of a "redeemed" Louisiana. |

**1878**

| | |
|---|---|
| **June 18** | Congress passes the Posse Comitatus Act, severely restricting the use of federal military forces as agents of law and order in civilian society. |

**1883**

| | |
|---|---|
| **October 15** | Supreme Court, in the Civil Rights Cases, overturns the Civil Rights Act of 1875 and declares that the Fourteenth Amendment only covers government action. Segregation by private individuals in privately owned establishments is legal, as Court creates difference between "civil rights" and "social rights": federal acceptance of Jim Crow laws fully under way. |

**1890**

| | |
|---|---|
| **November 1** | Mississippi becomes first Southern state to alter its state constitution to legally disfranchise blacks, using loopholes in the Fifteenth Amendment. Other Southern states follow over the next decade. |

**1892**

| | |
|---|---|
| **April** | In response to antiblack violence and the rise of lynchings across the South, African American journalist Ida B. Wells begins an anti-lynching crusade that grows to international dimensions. |

**1896**

| | |
|---|---|
| **May 18** | Supreme Court rules in *Plessy v. Ferguson* that accommodations that are separate but equal do not violate the Fourteenth Amendment. |

# ABOLITIONISTS

Abolitionists advocated ending slavery and emancipating slaves. African American and white American abolitionists were part of an antislavery movement that spanned the Atlantic world during the 18th and 19th centuries. Prior to 1830, most of them favored gradual elimination of slavery, but by the early 1830s, abolitionists began supporting immediate general emancipation. During the Civil War, they pressed the Lincoln administration to make emancipation a Union war aim. During Reconstruction, they advocated national protection of black rights. When people used the term "abolitionist" during the era of the Civil War and Reconstruction, they usually meant the immediatists—small radical groups of agitators, political activists, Underground Railroad leaders, and freedom fighters. Historians distinguish between these abolitionists and a larger, less radical, group of journalists and politicians who, to varying degrees, opposed the territorial expansion of slavery and the influence slaveholders exercised on the U.S. government. During the Civil War and Reconstruction, Radical Republicans constituted the majority of this larger group, which became less distinguishable from abolitionists as time passed.

## Early American Abolitionists

As soon as slavery came into existence in Great Britain's North American colonies during the 17th century, enslaved people sought freedom. They purchased freedom, sued for it, escaped, and—on rarer occasions—took up arms. During the 1690s, a few Quakers began to contend that slavery was sinful and dangerous. During the 1780s, white rationalists and evangelicals began to exercise considerable influence. These early abolitionists contributed to the decisions between 1783 and 1804 on the part of all the states north of Delaware to end slavery or provide for its gradual abolition. In 1787, Congress adopted the Northwest Ordinance banning slavery in the Northwest Territory. By the1790s, small gradual abolition societies had spread to Delaware, Maryland, and Virginia. Early abolitionism peaked during the 1780s.

During the following decades, the spread of cotton cultivation into the Old Southwest created a market for slaves that ended the southward spread of antislavery sentiment. Meanwhile white Northerners increasingly interpreted social status in racial terms and restricted black access to schools, churches, and jobs. In 1800, the Virginia slave Gabriel organized a revolt conspiracy that—when revealed to white authorities and crushed—intensified an anti-abolitionist reaction. As whites became convinced that free blacks encouraged slave revolt and constituted a dependent and criminal class, antislavery societies in Delaware, Maryland, and Virginia disbanded, became inactive, or declined.

The American Colonization Society (ACS), organized in Washington, D.C., in 1816, epitomized the linkage of gradual emancipation and expatriation. In 1821, the ACS established a colony for free African Americans at Liberia in West Africa. During the society's early years, it enjoyed the support of black and white abolitionists who later became immediatists. Yet, from its beginning, many African Americans were suspicious of the ACS. They feared that its real goal was to strengthen slavery by removing all free black people from the United States.

## Immediatism during the Late 1820s and 1830s

Black opposition to the ACS contributed to the rise of immediatism. In 1829, black abolitionist David Walker published in Boston his *Appeal to the Colored Citizens of the World.* He denounced the ACS, asserted the right of African Americans to U.S. citizenship, and suggested that black men must fight for freedom.

Several developments led a few young white men and women to become immediate abolitionists. The emergence in the North of factory production and wage labor made slave labor seem outmoded and barbaric. As middle-class family life developed in the North, the disruption slavery imposed on black families appeared increasingly reprehensible. The religious revival known as the Second Great Awakening encouraged evangelical Northerners to establish benevolent organizations designed to fight a variety of sins.

More than any other individual, white abolitionist William Lloyd Garrison spread immediatism during the 1830s. Influenced by black abolitionists, Garrison began publishing his weekly newspaper, *The Liberator*, in January 1831. Like Walker, Garrison rejected gradualism and colonization. He demanded immediate general emancipation and equal rights for African Americans. In late 1833, Garrison brought together a diverse group, including a few black men and a few white women, to form the American Anti-Slavery Society (AASS). Rejecting the violent abolitionist tactics endorsed by Walker and put into practice by slave rebel Nat Turner in his failed Virginia slave revolt of August 1831, the AASS pledged to use peaceful moral means to promote immediatism and convince masters to free their slaves. In 1835 and 1836, the organization sent thousands of antislavery petitions to Congress and stacks of abolitionist propaganda into the South. These efforts produced another anti-abolitionist and antiblack reaction, which strengthened proslavery sentiment in the South and encouraged mob violence against abolitionists and black communities in the North.

## Rise of a More Aggressive Abolitionism

The anti-abolitionist reaction and the failure of peaceful agitation to weaken slavery led immediatists in new directions. Garrison and his associates centered in New England became social perfectionists, feminists, and anarchists. They embraced dissolution of the Union as the only way to save the North from the sin of slavery and force the South to abolish it. The great majority of immediate abolitionists (both black and white), however, believed that church and government action could be effective against slavery. They became more willing to consider violent means and rejected radical assertions of women's rights.

At its 1840 annual meeting, the AASS split apart on these issues. The Garrisonian minority retained control of what became known as the "Old Organization," while the great majority of immediatists launched new organizations. The breakup of the AASS also encouraged autonomous organization among black abolitionists, who led in forming local vigilance associations designed to protect fugitive slaves. In 1846, black abolitionists joined church-oriented white abolitionists in the American Missionary Association (AMA), an outgrowth of the AASS that sent antislavery missionaries into the South.

In 1848, the conservative wing of the abolitionist Liberty Party merged into the Free Soil Party and its members, for all intents and purposes, ceased to be immediatists. They, nevertheless, had an enormous impact on those who by the Civil War were called Radical Republicans.

## Abolitionists during the Civil War and Reconstruction

White Southerners anticipated that the victory of Republican candidate Abraham Lincoln in the presidential election of 1860 would encourage Underground Railroad activity, abolitionist politics in the Upper South, and slave revolt. Such fears had an important role in the secession movement that led to the Civil War in April 1861. Lincoln, who was not an immediate abolitionist, hoped for the "ultimate extinction" of slavery and the colonization of African Americans outside of the United States, but as the war began, he promised not to interfere with slavery in the South. He believed that abolitionism of any sort would alienate Southern Unionists and weaken support of the war in the North.

Immediate abolitionists, nevertheless, almost universally supported the war as a means of ending slavery. By the late 1850s, Garrison and his associates had become less committed to nonviolence. When the Civil War began, they dropped their opposition to forceful means. Church-oriented and radical political abolitionists rejoined the AASS, and the organization's membership and influence grew. AASS leader Wendell Phillips emerged as the North's most popular public speaker. Well aware of their new standing, immediatists in alliance with Radical Republicans lobbied Lincoln to make emancipation and racial justice Union war aims. Immediatists—especially black immediatists—led in urging the president to enlist black troops.

Younger white immediatists became officers in the otherwise segregated black Union regiments. Immediatists led in wartime reconstruction efforts in the South. During the summer of 1861, the AMA and many smaller abolitionist organizations began sending missionaries and teachers into war zones to minister to the physical, spiritual, and educational needs of the former slaves. Women predominated, in part because younger immediatist men had enrolled in Union armies. The most ambitious abolitionist effort occurred in the South Carolina Sea Islands centered on Port Royal, which Union forces captured in 1861. With organizational and financial backing from Lewis Tappan and support from former immediatist Secretary of the Treasury Salmon P. Chase, younger abolitionists, who called themselves "Gideonites," launched the Port Royal Experiment in 1862. They provided medical care, taught school, and helped former slaves purchase land. At Port Royal and in a similar undertaking in southern Louisiana, immediatists attempted to transform an oppressed people into independent proprietors and wage laborers. In addition to providing clothing, food,

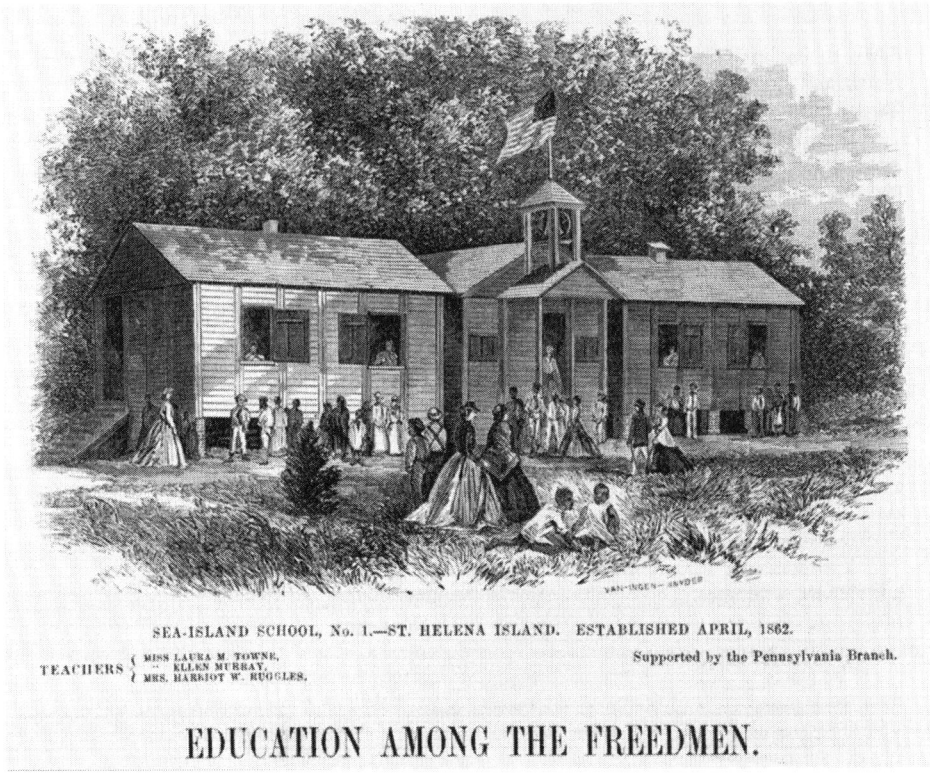

SEA-ISLAND SCHOOL, No. 1.—ST. HELENA ISLAND. ESTABLISHED APRIL, 1862.

TEACHERS { MISS LAURA M. TOWNE,
          " ELLEN MURRAY,
          MRS. HARRIOT W. RUGGLES.          Supported by the Pennsylvania Branch.

## EDUCATION AMONG THE FREEDMEN.

Following the Union's capture of South Carolina's Sea Islands in November 1861, Gideonites and the American Missionary Association established schools to aid former slaves in their transition to freedom and free labor. (Library of Congress)

medical care, and educational services, they lobbied for rent control, and helped former slaves find jobs locally and in the North.

In 1863, antislavery organizations began petitioning Congress in support of a constitutional amendment to prohibit forever slavery in the United States. When the ratification of the Thirteenth Amendment achieved this goal in December 1865, Garrison and his closest associates declared that their efforts had succeeded. Garrison ceased publication of *The Liberator* and urged the AASS to disband. He and those who agreed with him believed the Republican Party could best protect black rights and interests.

Early in the Civil War, immediate abolitionists advocated the right of black men to vote as a means of protecting their freedom. Immediatists favored land redistribution and advocated creating a federal agency to provide food and medical care to freedpeople, find jobs for them, and defend their civil and political rights. In December 1863, when Lincoln announced a mild Reconstruction plan that would leave former masters in control of the status of their former slaves, many immediatists criticized it as insufficient. They supported voting rights, education, and land for African Americans as recompense for generations of unrequited labor and as essential for black economic and political independence.

As the war ended, most immediatists believed that Lincoln's policy of reconciliation with former rebels threatened the rights of former slaves. After Lincoln's assassination, immediatists mistakenly anticipated that his presidential successor, Andrew Johnson, would be more active in establishing black rights in the South, but by the fall of 1865, they had become very critical of Johnson. Black abolitionists in particular lobbied in Washington on behalf of the freedpeople. Following Johnson's veto of the Civil Rights Act in February 1866, immediatists began calling for his impeachment. They were disappointed when Congress failed to remove Johnson from office in 1868.

Immediatist influence increased after the congressional election of 1866 in which their Radical Republican allies made impressive gains. Unlike the Radicals, however, most immediatists opposed the ratification of the Fourteenth Amendment, contending that its threat to reduce the representation in Congress of states that denied black men the right to vote was by no means a guarantee of black suffrage. Instead, immediatists advocated a revolutionary reordering of Southern society that would provide justice and full citizenship for African Americans. Immediatists supported the Fifteenth Amendment guaranteeing that the right to vote would not be denied to black men. With the ratification of this amendment in 1870, immediatists declared they had achieved their ultimate objective. Other abolitionists were not so sure, but the rump of the AASS voted to disband. Abolitionists, and in particular immediatists, had played a crucial role in ending slavery, in creating black institutions in the postwar South, and in placing protections for minority rights in the U.S. Constitution.

*Stanley Harrold*

*See also:* Abolition of Slavery; Garrison, William Lloyd (1805–1879).

## Further Reading

Curry, Richard O. "The Abolitionists and Reconstruction: A Critical Appraisal." *Journal of Southern History* 54 (1968): 529–32.

Fredrickson, George. *The Inner Civil War: Northern Intellectuals and the Crisis of the Union.* New York: Harper and Row, 1968.

Friedman, Lawrence J. *Gregarious Saints: Self and Community in American Abolitionism, 1830–1870.* New York: Cambridge University Press, 1982.

Gara, Larry. "A Glorious Time: The 1874 Abolitionist Reunion in Chicago." *Journal of the Illinois State Historical Society* 65 (1972): 280–92.

Harrold, Stanley. *American Abolitionists.* Harlow, UK: Longman, 2001.

McPherson, James M. *The Struggle for Equality: Abolitionists and the Negro in the Civil War and Reconstruction.* 1964. Reprint, Princeton, NJ: Princeton University Press, 1992.

Rose, Willie Lee. *Rehearsal for Reconstruction: The Port Royal Experiment.* Indianapolis: Bobbs-Merrill, 1964.

Stewart, James Brewer. *Holy Warriors: The Abolitionists and American Slavery.* 2nd ed. New York: Hill and Wang, 1997.

## ABOLITION OF SLAVERY

The abolition of slavery is usually associated with the Civil War. However, slavery's end arguably is the most important event associated with wartime Reconstruction.

## From Slave to Contraband

Freedom for the slaves did not appear likely in the early months of the Civil War. Both Unionists and confederates denied slavery was a cause for the war. White Southerners claimed they were fighting for independence, for states' rights, and to defend their homes against Northern aggression. White Northerners asserted they fought to suppress a rebellion against the legitimate national government and to preserve the Union.

Significantly, it was the slaves themselves who demonstrated their own relevance. From the earliest days of the conflict, men and women in bondage never doubted the war was about them. For many Northern troops, the war was their first personal encounter with the "peculiar institution," and they did not like what they saw. Union officers also realized that slaves were a military asset for the Confederacy. Slaves could dig entrenchments, deliver supplies, and provide personal service to the Southern army, as well as keep the plantation system functioning despite the absence of so many white men who had gone off to war. Therefore, giving refuge to escaped slaves was double gain for the Union; it deprived the Confederacy of their services while at the same time making their labor available to Northern forces.

It took the crafty administrative brain of General Benjamin F. Butler to formalize what quickly became an informal policy of giving sanctuary to escaped slaves. Butler, overseeing the occupation of Union-controlled areas in coastal Virginia, realized the slaves' military value. What he devised to avoid confronting the issue of slavery directly was to declare slaves entering Union lines to be "contraband of war." In other words, because they likely would be used to support a rebellion against the legal government of the United States, the duly authorized agent of that government—the Union army—could seize the slaves as contraband (i.e., illicit property) and refuse to return them to their disloyal owners.

## The First and Second Confiscation Acts

Other Union commanders quickly copied Benjamin Butler's contraband policy, and it became the basis for the First Confiscation Act passed by the U.S. Congress in the summer of 1861. This legislation made slaves used in support of the Confederacy subject to seizure. Federal officials quickly interpreted the First Confiscation Act to mean that not only did federal officials in the rebellious states have the authority to confiscate the slaves of disloyal owners, but also that those slaves could be put to work for wages in support of the Union. The First Confiscation Act also was evidence of growing sentiment in the North in favor of ending slavery. But like most Republicans, President Abraham Lincoln was no abolitionist and was loath to confront slavery. He merely wanted slavery confined to the states where it already existed, with no possibility for its expansion into the western territories—the Free Soil position. Lincoln was loath to abandon this stance early in the Civil War because he feared alienating the four remaining Union slave states: Maryland, Delaware, Kentucky, and Missouri. Lincoln also hoped that if his government did not embrace emancipation, he might encourage the rebellious states to end their insurrection by showing them slavery would be safe within the Union if they returned to it.

Yet, as the war dragged on through the remainder of 1861 and into 1862, events increasingly made Abraham Lincoln's position untenable. The trickle of contraband slaves into Union lines in 1862 became a torrent as Northern forces occupied increasingly large amounts of the South. Congress responded to the growing numbers of contraband slaves in the South by passing the Second Confiscation Act in July 1862. This law built on the First Confiscation Act by actually freeing the slaves of disloyal owners. So no longer were slaves who reached Union-controlled territory from the Confederacy in limbo merely as confiscated property—under this law, they became free.

In passing the Second Confiscation Act, Congress also was responding to increasing sentiment in the North in favor of emancipation. As the casualties and costs mounted from the fighting, conciliatory sentiments toward the Confederacy evaporated and the significance of slavery in the war became increasingly apparent. Many people in the North came to believe that if the Union was ever to be restored, to be truly healed, it must be as a nation without slavery.

## The Emancipation Proclamation

During the summer of 1862, Lincoln's position on slavery was changing. By spring of 1862, he had already proposed federal support for the state-implemented emancipation in the Border States, which would be gradual and where loyal slaveholders would be compensated. Neither Delaware, Kentucky, Maryland nor Missouri accepted in 1862 the idea of gradual compensated emancipation. By July, the president told his cabinet privately that he planned to issue a proclamation freeing the slaves in the rebellious states. However, he also took their advice to delay a public announcement until the Union won a significant victory on the battlefield, so that the pronouncement would not appear as a desperate measure. This victory finally came on September 17, 1862, at the Battle of Antietam, when Union forces stopped a Confederate invasion of Maryland.

Shortly thereafter, on September 22, Lincoln issued what became known as the Preliminary Emancipation Proclamation. This proclamation threatened that unless the seceded states rejoined the Union by the end of 1862, Lincoln would issue a decree freeing the slaves in those states. No states acted on Lincoln's offer. So on January 1, 1863, he signed the final Emancipation Proclamation. As critics have pointed out, this pronouncement did not immediately free a single slave. It exempted not only the loyal slave states but also those areas of the Confederacy then under Union occupation (a gesture by Lincoln to encourage Union sentiments). It is also true that Lincoln embraced emancipation more from expediency than principle. His main aim continued to be to save the Union and as far as slavery was concerned, he was prepared to do whatever it took to achieve that goal.

## Black Military Service

The commitment of the Union to emancipation was further bolstered by the recruitment of black men into the Union army. The recruitment of black soldiers began in a limited fashion in late 1862 and accelerated considerably after Lincoln signed the final Emancipation Proclamation. From 1863 on, the Union army became an army of liberation, and freedom for the slaves became tied to Union success on the battlefield.

Not only did the nearly 179,000 black soldiers who served bolster the Union cause, but also their very existence undermined slavery. The most common excuse for excluding black men from military service before the Civil War was that they were not citizens. When military necessity for the Union prompted their recruitment, reversing the logic gave all black men a powerful claim to both freedom and citizenship. When blacks later claimed suffrage and other citizenship rights, they often cited the service of black soldiers in the Union army to strengthen their case.

## The Thirteenth Amendment

The widespread recruitment of black soldiers in the Border States undermined slavery. Maryland and Missouri bowed to this reality, emancipating slaves on their own in late 1864 and early 1865, respectively. Unionist governments in Arkansas, Louisiana, and the new state of West Virginia also freed their slaves by the end of 1864. Delaware and Kentucky, however, stubbornly clung to slavery even after the final Confederate surrender in the spring of 1865.

It was the resistance of Delaware and Kentucky, plus uncertainty, that statutory law or executive orders concerning emancipation were beyond reversal that prompted the Thirteenth Amendment to the U.S. Constitution. The amendment simply stated, "Neither slavery nor involuntary servitude, except as a punishment for crime whereof the party shall have been duly convicted, shall exist within the United States, or any place subject to their jurisdiction." The amendment passed the U.S. Senate with the required two-thirds majority in April 1864 but was unable to pass the House of Representatives due to lack of Democratic support. After key Union victories in the fall of 1864 and Lincoln's reelection in November of that year, the House finally approved the amendment in January 1865, and by the end of the year, it had been ratified by the states.

## Liquidation of Slavery

The actual end of slavery, in particular locales, varied from place to place. In some locations, owners bowed to the inevitable and freed their slaves with the arrival of the Union army. In other places, it was necessary for army officers or agents of the Freedmen's Bureau to inform slaves of their liberation. Some slaveholders, especially on isolated plantations, tried as long as possible to hide the news. This proved difficult to accomplish, however, especially as the prospect of their liberation long preceded the arrival of Union forces, and slaves determinedly sought out any news that might herald approaching freedom. With the prospect of freedom, slaveholders often were forced to bargain with their slaves to retain their labor, even before Northern troops actually reached their locale. The end of slavery, of course, begged the question of what would replace it. It was here that the work of Reconstruction began in earnest.

*Donald R. Shaffer*

**See also:** Confiscation Acts; Howard, Oliver Otis (1830–1909).

## Further Reading

Berlin, Ira, Barbara J. Fields, Steven Miller, and Joseph P. Reidy, eds. *Free at Last: A Documentary History of Slavery, Freedom, and the Civil War.* New York: The New Press, 1992.

Berlin, Ira, Barbara J. Fields, Steven Miller, Joseph P. Reidy, and Leslie Rowland. *Slaves No More: Three Essays on Emancipation and the Civil War.* Cambridge: Cambridge University Press, 1992.

Guelzo, Allen C. *Lincoln's Emancipation Proclamation: The End of Slavery in America.* New York: Simon and Schuster, 2004.

Klingaman, William K. *Abraham Lincoln and the Road to Emancipation, 1861–1865.* New York: Viking, 2001.

Vorenberg, Michael. *Final Freedom: The Civil War, the Abolition of Slavery, and the Thirteenth Amendment.* Cambridge: Cambridge University Press, 2001.

## AIKEN, D. WYATT (1828–1887)

A Democratic politician during Reconstruction and leading agricultural reformer, David Wyatt Aiken of South Carolina was born in Winnsboro, South Carolina, on March 17, 1828, to two immigrants from County Antrim, Ireland, David Aiken and Nancy Kerr. He graduated from South Carolina College in 1849 and began farming near Winnsboro in 1852. Aiken immediately became interested in agricultural improvement, and in 1855, he was one of the founding members of the State Agricultural Society. Aiken became involved in Democratic politics and served with the Seventh South Carolina Regiment during the Civil War.

During Reconstruction, Aiken continued his antebellum efforts to cultivate agricultural practices in the South and thus improve the lot of the white farmer. For Aiken, this required finding a means to control black labor in the absence of slavery. Aiken warned against overreliance on cotton and turned to growing small grains, clover, and other crops at his "Coronaca" plantation in Abbeville County. In 1869, Aiken helped reorganize the old State Agricultural Society into the State Agricultural and Mechanical Society and encouraged the new body to do more to educate farmers. As part of that effort, he became a correspondent, and later editor and owner, of the Rural Carolinian from 1869 to 1877.

Aiken's most significant work for agricultural improvement was his role as an organizer for the Patrons of Husbandry (the Grange), a fraternal organization for white farmers. Aiken had never left politics, serving as a representative in the South Carolina House of Representatives from 1864 to 1866.

Aiken gained seat in the U.S. House of Representatives from upstate's Third District via the infamous 1876 campaign; he served until 1887. His greatest legacy was his ultimately successful fight to get the Bureau of Agriculture raised to a cabinet-level department. That occurred in 1889, but Aiken had died on April 6, 1887, of complications arising from a fall a year earlier.

*Bruce E. Baker*

*See also:* Labor Systems; Redemption.

## Further Reading

Pritchard, Claudius Hornby Jr. *Colonel D. Wyatt Aiken, 1828–1887: South Carolina's Militant Agrarian.* Hampden-Sydney, VA: privately printed, 1970.

## AKERMAN, AMOS TAPPAN (1821–1880)

A lawyer from Georgia and U.S. attorney general during the presidency of Ulysses S. Grant, Amos Tappan Akerman used his federal office to aggressively prosecute members of the Ku Klux Klan and to protect the civil rights of African Americans in the South.

Akerman was born February 23, 1821, in Portsmouth, New Hampshire. After attending Dartmouth College, he moved to Georgia, studied law, and became a member of the Georgia bar in 1850. He set up law practices in Clarkesville and Elberton. A devout Presbyterian, Akerman married Martha Rebecca Galloway in 1864; the couple had seven children. Although opposed to secession, Akerman served in the Georgia State Guard during Sherman's march through the state. He joined the Republican Party after the war and became federal district attorney for the state in 1869.

A year later, to the surprise of many, President Ulysses S. Grant offered Akerman the job of U.S. attorney general. With his new position, Akerman assumed charge of the newly created Justice Department. Akerman's greatest challenge lay in the violent political force of the Ku Klux Klan in the South. In 1871, upon Akerman's recommendation, President Grant suspended the writ of habeas corpus in nine counties in Piedmont, South Carolina. Federal marshals arrested hundreds of suspected Klan members, and Akerman's legal team prosecuted scores of Klan leaders in federal court. Akerman's dedication in protecting civil and political rights attracted criticism from some of Grant's cabinet members, and corporate railroad interests also lobbied against him. Pressure forced President Grant to request his resignation in December 1871. Akerman returned to Cartersville, Georgia, where he had resettled his family in early 1871. He continued to practice law until his death from rheumatic fever on December 21, 1880.

*Kimberly R. Kellison*

**See also:** Grant, Ulysses S. (1822–1885).

A Republican lawyer from Georgia, Amos T. Akerman served as U.S. attorney general under President Grant, heading the newly formed Justice Department. He directed the joint Justice-War Department assault on the Ku Klux Klan in 1871. (Library of Congress)

### Further Reading

Akerman, Robert H. "Amos Tappan Akerman," in Kenneth Coleman and Charles Stephen Gurr, eds., *Dictionary of Georgia Biography*. Vol. 1. Athens: University of Georgia Press, 1983, pp. 8–10.

McFeeley, William S. "Amos T. Akerman: The Lawyer and Racial Justice," in J. Morgan Kousser and James M. McPherson, eds.,

*Region, Race, and Reconstruction: Essays in Honor of C. Vann Woodward.* New York: Oxford University Press, 1982, pp. 395–415.

# ALABAMA

Alabama faced the chaos and uncertainty of the post–Civil War world in much the same way as other defeated Confederate states: fear and suspicion, exhilaration and misery, weariness and triumph blended together as whites and blacks moved forward into the unknown. While not as stricken as the states of Virginia, South Carolina, or Georgia, Alabama had seen significant physical devastation, the disruption and liberation of its main labor pool, and the death or maiming of some 70,000 of its citizens. As with its sister states, Reconstruction in Alabama featured significant change, tremendous controversy, and, ultimately for black Alabamians, deep disappointment.

The greatest threat facing Alabama in the immediate aftermath of war was economic collapse. The war—and the Confederacy's self-imposed embargo on cotton—wreaked havoc on the state's economy. In 1865, landed whites had no labor and emancipated blacks (now free after the Thirteenth Amendment) lacked a means of survival. In March 1865, Congress had created the Bureau of Refugees, Freedmen, and Abandoned Lands; this served as both a stopgap measure for the moment and a means of establishing momentum for a free-labor wage system; General Wager Swayne was appointed assistant commissioner for Alabama and was entrusted with distributing food, medicine, tools, and instruction to destitute blacks and whites. He and his bureau agents also created "contracts" for a new labor system, working as neutral arbiters to get white landowners and black laborers to settle on mutual terms for services rendered. Urgency increased through 1865 and into 1866, as Freedmen's Bureau rations and disbursements ran out or were discontinued. Making matters worse, thousands of freed black men, women, and families who had left to find relatives, works, or simply enjoy the freedom to move found themselves penniless and starving; by spring 1866, blacks began migrating back to their former plantations as the planting season loomed. Both planters and labors recognized that cooperation was necessary for survival, but many factors spoiled any chance of equity. For one, despite the efforts by Bureau agents to encourage a wage-labor system, Alabama whites simply did not have cash to pay their workers. In addition, blacks found wages peculiar and open to easy fraud, and their unfamiliarity with the system exacerbated these. As a result, the sharecropping method of labor contracting appeared early in Alabama.

Laborers and landowners negotiated the division of crops early in the year, then at harvest time blacks (and some whites) took their share of the harvest and sold it as they pleased. Sadly, revenue rarely matches expenses, and the black community found itself caught in a cycle of debt that would persist until after World War II. Another frustrating economic venture—again typical across the Reconstruction South—involved railroad development. Many states, especially while under Republican rule, saw transportation as a good investment, as railroads would lure industrial enterprise into the state, and even link inland production centers with coastal shipping. But a combination of inept entrepreneurs and unscrupulous politicians and financiers merely threw Alabama into debt; through the 1870s, both Republican and Democratic regimes posted enormous bonds designed to spur railroad construction. By Redemption in 1875 no more than a few hundred miles of rail resulted, while Alabama defaulted on nearly $30 million in payments due. Not until the late 19th century would Alabama see significant industrial and infrastructure growth.

As with every Confederate state except Tennessee, Alabama passed through two distinct phases of Reconstruction: one under the supervision of President Andrew Johnson, and the second under the statutes passed by the Republican Congress. Reconstruction ended earlier in Alabama than some other Southern states, as political power passed back to Democratic white Conservatives by 1875. The ebb and tide of change can be seen in Alabama's three Reconstruction constitutions, first under Presidential Reconstruction to reestablish much of the prewar situation (1865), the second instigated by Republicans under Congressional (or Radical) Reconstruction to empower black Alabamians (1868) and finally a third (1875) which restored control to the so-called Bourbons and initiated the removal of African Americans from political and economic power.

On June 21, 1865, President Johnson appointed Lewis E. Parsons of Talladega as provisional governor of Alabama, who was charged with supervising a constitutional convention that would rewrite the Alabama Constitution, abolish slavery and repudiate secession, and elect new officers at the state and federal levels. The convention that met in September ratified the Thirteenth Amendment, thus abolishing slavery, but went no further with regard to recognizing black rights. The convention established electoral plans and suffrage requirements (along prewar lines), which were soon implemented; within weeks new officers had been elected, with Robert M. Patton chosen as governor and two Unionists—Lewis E. Parsons and George S. Houston—as U.S. senators. Nonetheless, Alabama's chosen federal senators and representatives would never take seats in Congress. Republicans in Washington, concerned about the high number of Democrats and former confederates elected to offices across the South under President Johnson's plan, refused to seat the members-elect.

In an effort to juggle presidential prerogative, local and state authorities and still protect the newly freed African Americans, Congress developed the Fourteenth Amendment. This provided citizenship to blacks, guaranteed equality under the law and basic civil rights, and offered a "carrot-and-stick" that would disfranchise former confederates in proportion to disfranchised black males; this was an effort to encourage Southern states to give black men the right to vote. Alabama's political leaders, with no federal representation in Congress, agreed with President Johnson that such an amendment was unconstitutional—partly because the federal government had never ruled on voting before, and partly because Southern states (like Alabama) should not be required to ratify something they had no role in creating. As a result Alabama rejected the amendment. Facing an obstructionist president and a less-than-penitent white South, Republicans in Congress cast aside compromise and assumed control of Reconstruction.

In March 1867, Congress passed the first of four Reconstruction acts, completely restructuring the political and social framework for the 10 former Confederate states that rejected the amendment (Tennessee ratified it, and was readmitted to the Union). Alabama was placed under the Third Military District, initially commanded by General John Pope, a no-nonsense "radical" general (later replaced by George Meade). The army could remove (and did remove) any appointed or elected officials and nullified laws passed under the Johnson constitution and its legislature. General Pope then supervised a new constitutional convention, based upon universal male suffrage—by summer, more blacks were registered to vote in Alabama than whites. In October 1867, black males voted in Alabama for the first time, joining white allies in sending 100 delegates to Montgomery, of whom 96 were carpetbag and scalawag Republicans, and 18 of whom were black. This group gathered and produced a revolutionary constitution for Alabama, granting voting and office-holding rights to white and black Alabamians, and granting economic and educational rights to blacks and women.

These victories were not easy or unanimous. Severe differences divided this new Alabama Republican Party. Many whites had reservations about extending suffrage to blacks, and others wanted greater restrictions on former confederates. Differences emerged along racial lines and between natives and carpetbaggers. Even regional lines were polarized, with northern Alabamians rooted in yeomanry and uninterested in the plantation and labor interests of Southern whites. In fact, blacks resented the fact that the first slate of Republican officials were all white, which may have accounted for a decline in registration in early 1868. These fissures would weaken the party as Reconstruction progressed.

Another threat—Conservative white Democrats—nearly scuttled the new constitution with shrewd electoral maneuver. Under Congress's Reconstruction Act, the 1868 Constitution had to be ratified by public referendum with 50 percent of the registered voters approving. So Alabama Conservatives registered in full force, then voted "no" or simply did not vote; as a result, the referendum failed to garner approval. As a result, according to the new law, it had failed. Congress quickly realized its mistake and passed a new Reconstruction act, that called for 50 percent of those voting to affirm passage (not 50% registered). Although Johnson vetoed the act and protested violently, Congress overrode the veto, and the new Alabama Constitution—which had a vast majority of those voting support it—went into effect. On June 25, 1868, Congress readmitted Alabama to the Union; the state ratified the Fourteenth Amendment a month later.

With an influx of carpetbaggers and a large, enthusiastic African American voting base, Republicans dominated elected offices for the next four years. Republicans controlled the state legislature, including electing 27 black legislators, placing William H. Smith in the governor's chair, and sending three blacks—Benjamin Turner of Selma, James T. Rapier of Montgomery, and Jeremiah Haralson of Dallas County—to Congress. Alabama Republicans were progressive and energetic, but ill-prepared for the demands of the new economic and political climate. They advocated railroad construction, canal building, and a new public school system (that included blacks), but lacked the revenue or experience to fund or operate any of these initiatives successfully. Charges of corruption plagued the party and infighting only made matters worse.

By 1870, these cracks were having an impact, as the Conservatives were able to challenge Republicans in the state election. Relying on fraud, violence through the Ku Klux Klan, and Republican divisions, Democrats captured the governorship. Robert Lindsay took over from William Smith in a controversial election, but the Republicans retained control of the legislature.

The 1872 season showed similar strains in the party, an increase in Klan violence, and new Democratic scare tactics, including warnings that the whites was facing extinction through "integration" of the races. This time a Republican managed to secure the governor's position—local Alabamian David P. Lewis from Huntsville—while the legislature was mired in controversy. Election returns showed fraud on both sides, with a strong element of terrorism and violence coming from Democratic forces. Each party claimed victory and seated its own legislature, until the U.S. attorney general recognized the Republican house and ordered the Democratic group to disband.

Through racist messaging, Klan violence, and internal discipline, by 1874, Alabama Democrats were simply more united than the Republicans on the issue of race and in their opposition to continued federal Reconstruction. In the state elections of 1874, Conservative whites took total control, winning the governorship and both houses of legislature. On November 24, George S. Houston was inaugurated as governor, restoring Democratic, white, home rule to Alabama.

The Redeemer government moved swiftly to consolidate power and undo the changes of the past decade. By 1875 another constitutional convention was in session, featuring 80 Democrats and a smattering of 12 Republicans, 4 of whom were black. The 1875 Constitution insinuated voting restrictions into state law, pulled back from internal improvements and public education, and passed lien laws that would cripple poor farmers—white and black. These issues and others, such as reduced property taxes, favored the Bourbon planter elite, the same group who had led Alabama to the brink of destruction 15 years earlier. This constitution set the stage for the 1901 Constitution, which combined racist hatred of the Jim Crow era with opposition to Farmers' Alliances (as seen in the Populist movement) to create a reactionary, antidemocratic document that restricted power to the Bourbons and a few new industrialists.

Alabama during Reconstruction earns a mixed review. While some progressive whites and blacks promoted racial equality, industrial development, public education, and equality under law, many Alabamians (and outside opportunists) embraced selfish greed, petty jealousies, racist bigotry, and even murder, preventing the state from moving forward. Ultimately, the temporary victories of Reconstruction were buried by generations of white supremacist militancy, Jim Crow prejudice, state's rights idolatry, and one-party rule.

*Richard Zuczek*

**See also:** Ku Klux Klan (KKK); Labor Systems.

## Further Reading

Fleming, Walter Lynwood. *Civil War and Reconstruction in Alabama*. New York: The McMillan Company, 1905.

Kolchin, Peter. *First Freedom: The Responses of Alabama's Blacks to Emancipation and Reconstruction*. Tuscaloosa: University of Alabama Press, 2008.

McMillan, Malcolm Cook. *Constitutional Development in Alabama, 1791–1901: A Study in Politics, the Negro, and Sectionalism*. Spartanburg, SC: The Reprint Company, 1978.

Noe, Kenneth, *The Yellowhammer War: The Civil War and Reconstruction in Alabama*. Tuscaloosa: University Alabama Press, 2014.

Rogers, William Warren, and Leah Rawls Atkins. *Alabama: The History of a Deep South State*. 2nd ed. Tuscaloosa: University of Alabama Press, 2010.

Schweninger, Loren. "Black Citizenship and the Republican Party in Reconstruction Alabama." *Alabama Review* 29 (April 1976): 83–103.

Storey, Margaret. *Loyalty and Loss: Alabama's Unionists in the Civil War and Reconstruction*. Baton Rouge: Louisiana State University Press, 2004.

## ALCORN, JAMES LUSK (1816–1894)

James Lusk Alcorn was a Republican governor of Mississippi and a U.S. senator during Reconstruction. Born in Illinois on November 4, 1816, Alcorn's family moved to Kentucky soon after his birth. Admitted to the Kentucky bar in 1836, Alcorn practiced law briefly before moving to the rich alluvial Mississippi Delta and becoming a wealthy lawyer-planter. During the late 1840s and 1850s, Alcorn served as a Whig in the state legislature, and when Abraham Lincoln won the presidential election of 1860, Alcorn served as a Union delegate in the state convention called to consider the question of secession. When it became clear that Mississippi would leave the Union, he announced that he would vote for the secession ordinance. Appointed as a brigadier general of state troops, he only served briefly before resigning and returning to his plantation.

After the Civil War, Alcorn was elected to the U.S. Senate by the state legislature under President Andrew Johnson's plan of presidential Reconstruction. The Republican Congress, however, refused to seat Alcorn and the other representatives from the former Confederate states. When Congress assumed control of Reconstruction policy, Alcorn supported black political equality and helped organize the state's Republican Party. In 1869, following a second vote that finally approved the new state constitution, Alcorn won the governorship due to heavy support from black voters.

Alcorn promised to protect black rights and to provide public education for both races, although the school system he helped establish was racially segregated. His appointments to office reflected a prejudice against Northern newcomers, known as carpetbaggers, and especially those who supported Senator Adelbert Ames, a Radical Republican. Alcorn believed that by appointing former Union Whigs and Moderates, Southern whites might support his administration. Despite his moderate policies, Alcorn failed to obtain a broadly based following for the Republican Party; by late 1870, the rise of the Ku Klux Klan made this clear. Senator Adelbert Ames and other Radicals demanded that Governor Alcorn seek federal intervention to put down the Klan, but Alcorn unsuccessfully pushed for creation of a state military to stop the violence. He was more successful at running for the U.S. Senate, and he resigned as governor to take his seat in late 1871. When his rival, Ames, won the Republican nomination for governor in 1873, Alcorn returned home, bolted the regular state party, and announced that he would run as a reform Republican. His effort to gain the support of Democrats backfired and most black voters also refused to support him, and Ames won the election. Alcorn continued in the Senate until 1877, after which he returned to his plantations in the Mississippi Delta. He died on December 19, 1894, at his home in the Delta.

*William C. Harris*

**See also:** Carpetbaggers; Civil Rights; Congressional Reconstruction; Enforcement Acts (1870, 1871, 1875); Jim Crow Laws; Presidential Reconstruction; U.S. Army and Reconstruction.

## Further Reading

Harris, William C. The *Day of the Carpetbagger: Republican Reconstruction in Mississippi*. Baton Rouge: Louisiana State University Press, 1979.

Pereyra, Lillian A. *James Lusk Alcorn: Persistent Whig*. Baton Rouge: Louisiana State University Press, 1966.

Sansing, David G. "Congressional Reconstruction," in Richard Aubrey McLemore, ed., *A History of Mississippi*. Vol. 1. Hattiesburg: University and College Press of Mississippi, 1973, pp. 571–589.

## AMERICAN MISSIONARY ASSOCIATION (AMA)

The American Missionary Association (AMA), founded in September 1846, supported the abolition of slavery. The association sent missionaries to Africa, Egypt, Hawaii, Ireland, Jamaica, the Sandwich Islands, and Siam to monitor living conditions. In the United States, missionaries labored in Kentucky, Missouri, North Carolina, and the Northwest. In the early years of the Civil War, the AMA collected and distributed clothing, food, and medicine to Southern slaves in areas liberated by the Union army. The AMA also pushed education, as when Rev. Lewis C. Lockwood conducted schools in the Virginia war zone in late 1861. By 1863, schools had been established in the District of Columbia, Virginia, South Carolina, the Sea Islands, and Memphis, Tennessee. Focusing on Port Royal, South Carolina, as an early showplace of what could be achieved, 31 AMA teachers operated 14 schools with more than 1,000 students. Not only interested in teaching basic literacy and math skills, the missionaries also hoped to spread Christianity, inculcate middle-class values and morality, encourage a strong work ethic, and stimulate civic virtue.

Paternalism often tinged missionaries' behavior as they demanded that blacks assimilate their bourgeois values about work, sexuality, gender, and the family. They also encouraged blacks to pattern their religious practices after Northern Protestant churches and become less emotional and more formalized. The missionaries believed that education would ensure real freedom for the freedpeople; as with many American reformers, they often viewed schools as a panacea for all societal woes. As the war ended in April 1865, many Northern benevolent societies competed against each other instead of uniting. The Bureau of Refugees, Freedmen, and Abandoned Lands Freedmen's Bureau, established in March 1865, attempted to unite and direct the efforts of various organizations; despite receiving nearly $4 million from the Bureau, the AMA never fully allowed coordination or direction.

The AMA confronted enormous obstacles in its efforts to remake the South. AMA laborers often encountered violence, intimidation, and ostracism by local whites who considered them meddlesome and self-righteous. Schoolhouses were burned, and teachers were unable to secure lodging. School funding always proved problematic, with AMA speakers canvassing the North and England for donations. Despite these challenges, the AMA's most significant and lasting contribution occurred in the creation of a Southern school network. By 1867, more than 400 AMA teachers labored in the South, teaching nearly 40,000 students in day and night schools and more than 18,000 students in Sabbath schools. A constant shortage of properly qualified teachers spawned creation of secondary and teacher training schools that included Fisk University in Nashville, Tennessee; Hampton Institute in Richmond, Virginia; Atlanta University in Atlanta, Georgia; Tougaloo University in Mississippi; Avery Institute in Charleston, South Carolina; Berea College in Berea, Ohio; Dillard University in New Orleans, Louisiana; Howard University in Washington, D.C.; Huston-Tillotson College in Austin, Texas; and Talladega Institute in Talladega, Alabama.

*Randy Finley*

**See also:** Education.

### Further Reading

"The American Missionary Association and the Promise of a Multicultural America: 1839–1954," http://www.amistadresearchcenter.org.

DeBoer, Clara Merritt. *His Truth Is Marching On: African Americans Who Taught the Freedmen for the American Missionary Association, 1861–1877*. New York: Garland Publishers, 1995.

Jones, Jacqueline. *Soldiers of Light and Love: Northern Teachers and Georgia Blacks, 1865–1873*. Athens: University of Georgia Press, 1992.

McFeely, William S. *Yankee Stepfather: General Oliver Otis Howard and the Freedmen*. New Haven, CT: Yale University Press, 1968.

McPherson, James M. *The Abolitionist Legacy: From Reconstruction to the NAACP*. Princeton, NJ: Princeton University Press, 1975.

Richardson, Joe M. *Christian Reconstruction: The American Missionary Association and Southern Blacks, 1861–1890*. Athens: University of Georgia Press, 1986.

# AMES, ADELBERT (1835–1933)

Adelbert Ames, Union general, Reconstruction senator, and governor of Mississippi, was born October 21, 1835, in Rockland, Maine. A strong student, Ames received an appointment to the U.S. Military Academy at West Point in 1856 and graduated in May 1861. At the First Battle of Bull Run, Ames was seriously wounded, yet continued to issue orders until he collapsed; in 1893, his actions earned him the Congressional Medal of Honor. Ames fought in numerous battles in the eastern theater, and by the end of the war, Ames had been brevetted to major general. In spring 1865, he served with occupation forces in North Carolina, and later was transferred to South Carolina. In the Carolinas, Ames became increasingly sympathetic to the plight of the freedpeople. After a brief trip overseas, Ames reported to his new command in Mississippi in 1867.

The Military Reconstruction Acts of 1867 divided the former Confederate states into five military districts, and Ames was assigned to the Fourth Military District covering Mississippi and Arkansas. In 1868, Ames was appointed Provisional Governor. He readily used federal troops to protect the rights of African Americans, removed numerous Democrats from state offices, and published an order allowing African Americans to serve on juries. White Democrats fiercely opposed Ames's policies, but Mississippi completed its Reconstruction process in 1870, with Radical Republicans capturing control of the state legislature. Republican legislators proceeded to elect two U.S. senators: Hiram R. Revels, the first African American seated in the U.S. Senate, and Adelbert Ames. Ames resigned from the army and left for Washington, but faced a Senate investigation over the legitimacy of his candidacy. Senators debated whether a military governor with dubious claim to Mississippi citizenship could hold office. Ultimately, the Senate seated Ames, who during this period had met and fallen in love with Blanche Butler, daughter of Union general and Massachusetts congressman Benjamin F. Butler. The two married in July 1870 in Lowell, Massachusetts. In 1871, the Mississippi legislature elected former Republican governor James L. Alcorn to succeed Hiram R. Revels as U.S. senator. A native Mississippian, Alcorn drew political support from Conservative Republicans and some white Democrats.

Alcorn and Ames soon clashed over a variety of issues. In the Senate, they publicly debated the extension of the Enforcement Acts. Alcorn disclaimed the need for military intervention to break the power of the Ku Klux Klan, while Ames demanded greater federal assistance. In 1873, both Alcorn and Ames sought the Republican nomination for

Adelbert Ames, a Union general during the war, dominated Mississippi's Reconstruction politics. A Radical Republican, he served as U.S. senator and governor until he resigned under threat of impeachment in 1876. (Library of Congress)

governor. Ames secured the nomination, leading Alcorn to run as an Independent. Radical Republicans carried the election for Ames. Inaugurated in January 1874, the governor promoted compulsory public education, cuts in state funding for railroads, more equitable codes of taxation, and agricultural diversification. Ames had always been unpopular with most white Mississippians, who increasingly resorted to violence to seize political control from Republicans. In 1875, in what became known as the Mississippi Plan, whites formed gun clubs and used violence to keep Republicans from the polls. In Vicksburg, a full-scale race riot ensued; Ames appealed to the president for troops and began to organize an African American militia, but election returns revealed that Democrats had captured the state legislature. Ames addressed the new legislature in January 1876, labeling them an illegitimate body; Democrats responded by drafting 11 impeachment charges against the governor. On March 29, 1876, Ames resigned as governor of Mississippi, in exchange for the dismissal of all charges.

The Ames family left Mississippi in 1876 and, after traveling a bit, settled down in Tewksbury, Massachusetts. When the Spanish-American War began in 1898, Ames returned to his military roots by volunteering; as brigadier general he participated in the siege of Santiago, Cuba. On April 12, 1933, at the age of 97, he died at his winter home in Ormand, marking the death of the last surviving Civil War general.

*Kimberly R. Kellison*

***See also:*** Congressional Reconstruction; Pardons; Redemption; Republicans, Radical.

## Further Reading

Ames, Blanche. *Adelbert Ames, 1835–1933: General, Senator, Governor.* New York: Argosy-Antiquarian Ltd, 1964.

Current, Richard. *Three Carpetbag Governors.* Baton Rouge: Louisiana State University Press, 1967.

King, Benson Harry. "The Public Career of Adelbert Ames, 1861–1876." Ph.D. dissertation, University of Virginia, 1975.

# AMNESTY PROCLAMATIONS

Several amnesty proclamations were issued during the Civil War and Reconstruction. The first one, Abraham Lincoln's Proclamation of Amnesty and Reconstruction, was published on December 8, 1863, and clarified on March 26, 1864. The second, Andrew Johnson's, was promulgated on May 29, 1865. Johnson issued a third on September 7, 1867, a fourth, on July 4, 1868, and a fifth on December 25 of that year. Congress also passed several declarations of amnesty, the first as part of the Confiscation Act of July 16, 1862, the second, of the Fourteenth Amendment, and a third specific Amnesty Act in 1872. Not until 1896 were all restrictions on former Confederate leaders removed.

Although Lincoln's and Johnson's proclamations have often been compared, they were very different. Also called the Ten Percent Plan, Lincoln's amnesty act was a wartime measure, designed to bring about the return to loyalty of as many confederates as possible. Relying on the presidential pardoning power authorized by the U.S. Constitution as well as congressional legislation for the same purpose, he provided for full pardon for all persons who had participated in the rebellion, with restoration of all rights of property, except for slaves. Six exceptions to this amnesty existed: civil or diplomatic agents of the Confederacy, any person who had left judicial positions in the United States to aid the Confederacy, all Confederate officers above the rank of colonel in the army or lieutenant in the navy, all who left seats in Congress to join the Confederacy, all who resigned commissions in the U.S. Army or Navy, and all who had mistreated black soldiers or their officers in U.S. service. As soon as 10 percent of the 1860 voters of the seceded states had taken the oath, the State could reestablish a state government. On March 26, 1864, Lincoln clarified the proclamation by exempting from it all those who were prisoners at the time they took the oath and authorized civil and military officers to register the oath.

In spite of its original popularity, the proclamation soon ran into opposition, especially among the Radical Republicans. The 10 percent provision and the alleged failure to provide for complete emancipation came in for particular criticism. In July, Congress passed the so-called Wade-Davis Bill offering a more stringent plan. It required an oath of 50 percent of the voters of 1860 before a state could be restored, but it admitted only those able to take an ironclad oath to any ensuing elections; it also abolished slavery. Lincoln pocket-vetoed the proposal, but the amnesty and Reconstruction issue was not settled prior to his assassination. However, both Louisiana and Arkansas had reestablished governments under Lincoln's policy, although neither had been recognized by Congress.

Because the war was over when Andrew Johnson issued his proclamation, he did not need to woo insurgents, and it was necessarily different. Believing as he did that the states had never left the Union, despite their secession, he was anxious to restore them as quickly as possible. In addition, he wanted to keep the South a "white man's country." Thus, the proclamation offered full pardon to all those willing to take an oath of loyalty to support the Constitution and the Union and the wartime proclamations concerning slavery, much in the same manner as his predecessor—but there was no provision for any percentage necessary to reestablish a state. There were 14 exemptions, including all those who were covered by the previous proclamation, as well as all Confederate governors; all who left the United States to help the Confederacy abroad; all who engaged in the destruction of U.S. commerce on the high seas or from Canada; all who violated their oath of amnesty in accordance with the proclamation of December 8, 1863; and all those whose property was worth more than $20,000. Special application for pardon, however, might be made by any of the exempted persons. Additional proclamations of September 7, 1865; July 4, 1868; and December 25, 1868, reduced the list of exemptions and finally ended them altogether, although this proclamation was ineffectual because of the provisions of the Fourteenth Amendment. As Congress was not in session at the time of Johnson's original proclamation, its provisions were speedily carried out. By December, all Southern states except Texas had completed the Johnson process of Reconstruction. The president had freely granted pardons to the exempt classes, so that leading former confederates, including Vice President Alexander H. Stephens, were elected to prominent positions, even membership in Congress. Moreover, the Johnson legislatures passed stringent Black Codes, virtually remanding the blacks to a status similar to slavery.

Congressional Republicans universally opposed Johnson's approach. Not only did Johnson's plan seem to undo most of the gains of the Civil War, but the dominance of the Republican Party itself appeared to be in danger. Should the Southerners, now almost all members of the Democratic Party or Conservatives, be admitted to Congress, they could combine with their Northern allies and seize control of the government. Consequently, Congress appointed a Joint Committee on Reconstruction to begin constructing a new policy, and refused to admit any of Johnson's' Southern representatives and senators. Congressional Republicans tackled the amnesty issue via the Fourteenth Amendment, which disfranchised and disbarred from office all former officers of the United States who had joined the Confederacy, but provided for a possible amnesty for them by a vote of two-thirds of both houses. Congress also exercised its pardon power pardon in a special Amnesty Act of May 22, 1872, which left only members of the 36th and 37th Congress, military, naval, and judicial officers, and heads of departments and foreign ministers of the Confederacy still barred from office holding. During the next decades, individual pardons were extended to most of these, until Congress finally repealed the restrictions altogether in 1896. Considering the overall effect of the amnesty policy after the Civil War, it is evident that federal treatment of former adversaries was comparatively mild. The only persons executed were the commandant of Andersonville prison and those implicated in the assassination of Abraham Lincoln; even Jefferson Davis, the Confederate president, was allowed to resume his writing after a short prison term. In comparison with the punishments meted out by other countries after victory in civil wars, the United States comes off very well indeed.

*Hans L. Trefousse*

**See also:** Congressional Reconstruction; Presidential Reconstruction; Republicans, Radical.

## Further Reading

Belz, Herman. *Reconstructing the Union: Theory and Policy during the Civil War*. Ithaca, NY: Cornell University Press, 1969.

Dorris, Jonathan T. *Pardon and Amnesty under Lincoln and Johnson*. Chapel Hill: University of North Carolina Press, 1953.

Hesseltine, William B. *Lincoln's Plan of Reconstruction*. Chicago: Quadrangle Books, 1967.

McKitrick, Eric. L. *Andrew Johnson and Reconstruction*. Chicago: University of Chicago Press, 1960.

Trefousse, Hans L. *Andrew Johnson: A Biography*. New York: W. W. Norton, 1989.

# ARKANSAS

At the end of the Civil War—in which more than 5,000 Arkansans died, 110,000 slaves gained their freedom, and more than $30 million worth of property was destroyed—Arkansas faced staggering political, economic, and social challenges. State officials had to renegotiate readmission into the Union with the federal government. Planters clashed with newly empowered politicians, many of whom hailed from the North and included African Americans, to gain political mastery. Economically, planters wondered how to regain the labor supply while freedpeople tested the limits and meaning of freedom.

By the end of 1863, the Union army controlled almost all of the strategically important points in Arkansas. President Abraham Lincoln recommended leniency for readmission to the Union with his Ten Percent Plan. Excluding high-ranking civil and military Confederate officers, the proposal created a new state government when 10 percent of those who voted in 1860 swore allegiance to the Union and agreed to abolish slavery. In January 1864, delegates met in Little Rock, drafted a new constitution, and soon after elected Isaac Murphy as the new governor. The newly elected legislature chose Elisha Baxter and William Fishback as U.S. senators. Although Lincoln accepted the new regime as legitimate, Republicans in Congress refused to recognize the two senators.

President Lincoln's assassination on April 14, 1865, changed Reconstruction in Arkansas and throughout the South. With the less able Andrew Johnson as the new president, Arkansas quickly fell prey to political factions: the legislature imposed a second loyalty oath that required voters to prove their loyalty to the "Lincoln" state government, hoping to bar many former confederates. In the October 1865 election, anti-Murphyites, calling themselves Conservatives, made an impressive showing, and further increased their number in the state legislature that following August. Meeting in November, they dominated the legislature and refused to allow blacks to vote, run for office, serve on juries, marry whites, or receive state funds for schools. As with every former Confederate state except Tennessee, they also rejected the Fourteenth Amendment. But Conservative dreams of restoring the antebellum South evaporated in 1866, as Radical Republicans gained control of Congress. They attacked President Johnson's leniency toward confederates, and they lambasted his indifference toward Black Codes and race riots. Radicals in Congress passed three Reconstruction acts from May to July 1867, which placed Arkansas in the Fourth Military District, with Mississippi. E.O.C. Ord, commander of the Fourth Military District, disbanded the previous state legislature and, with Governor Murphy's support, called for a November 1867 referendum to decide whether Arkansas would hold a new constitutional convention. The referendum succeeded with overwhelming black support, and the constitutional convention convened on January 7, 1868, in Little Rock. On February 1, 1868, the convention passed the new constitution that afforded male suffrage to all men over 21 years of age, regardless of race; opposed interracial marriages; allowed blacks to serve in government offices, on juries, and in the militia; ordered the legislature to fund school systems for students regardless of race; and established a state university.

Democrats loathed this new constitution and intimidated black and white Unionists from voter registration. The Ku Klux Klan, a paramilitary organization appearing in Arkansas in late 1867 to deter black registration and voting, whipped, shot, and killed political enemies and often burned their homes and churches. Despite violence and intimidation, voters ratified the new constitution in April 1868, chose Powell Clayton as the new governor, and elected Republicans to Congress and state offices. When the newly elected legislature ratified the Fourteenth Amendment, Congress officially readmitted Arkansas to the Union on June 22, 1868. Inaugurated on July 2, 1868, Republican governor Powell Clayton, a Union cavalry officer from Pennsylvania, intended to restore law and order to Arkansas. Violence escalated as the 1868 presidential campaign approached, with more than 200 blacks and Unionists murdered. Ulysses Grant defeated Democratic contender Horatio Seymour in Arkansas and nationally, and the state elected a Republican congressional delegation.

On November 4, 1868, the day after the presidential election, Clayton imposed martial law and divided Arkansas into four military districts. He used Union troops and black Arkansas militiamen to restore order; by early 1869, the Klan had been suppressed. In April 1869, a group of Republican insurgents, calling themselves "liberals" and led by Lieutenant Governor James Johnson, opposed Clayton. Both wings tossed political accusations, and through a series of messy coincidences a truce resulted by spring 1871 with Clayton in the U.S. Senate, an ally Ozra Hadley in the state house, and Johnson assuming Arkansas's secretary of state. Political infighting continued with a new generation. Republican Joseph Brooks, an Iowa Methodist minister, replaced Johnson as the leader of the anti-Clayton "liberals." He opposed Elisha Baxter, who had served on the state Supreme Court. The gubernatorial election of 1872 was marred by electoral fraud, with Baxter coming out on top. But following months of investigations and accusations, in early 1874, a Pulaski County circuit judge overturned the election and certified Brooks the winner, setting off the "Brooks-Baxter War." Each faction quickly assembled a militia, and squabbling ensued. Fearing all-out rioting, President Grant ordered Brooks's forces to disband, reinstated Baxter as governor, and selected Brooks as postmaster of Little Rock.

As in other rebellious Southern states, the Civil War destroyed much of Arkansas's economic infrastructure and left the economic in shambles. The labor status of Arkansas's 110,000 freedpeople remained a mystery, while white planters worried about securing labor for their cotton crop. Federal Freedmen's Bureau agents arrived in 1865, surveyed the labor supply, and began meeting with planters and freedpersons to negotiate labor contracts. Cotton seemed to both blacks and whites their best bet to gain economic security. Agreements became more streamlined in 1866 and established the system of sharecropping as landowners and laborers each received half of the crop at harvest. Bankers extended credit to both landowners and tenants, as all expected great profits from the 1866 crop, but heavy spring flooding and a subsequent summer drought caused less than half of the cotton crop to be baled in October. This economic catastrophe hit freedpeople and small-scale white farmers especially hard. The fall harvest produced less than two-thirds of the anticipated crop. Increasingly mired in debt, large-scale planters borrowed large sums of money in 1867 and 1868 from Northern capitalists. With each year, farmers sank deeper in debt, becoming more dependent on cotton. By 1874, the price of cotton had fallen to 11 cents per pound. Both whites and blacks plunged into a perennial debt that lasted, with few exceptions, until World War II. The federal government tried to assist Southern states—and impoverished Americans—with its share of economic plans. In 1866, President Johnson signed the Southern Homestead Act, which opened up 46 million acres of land in Alabama, Florida, Louisiana, Mississippi, and Arkansas. Of the 16,395 claims made in Arkansas under the Southern

Homestead Act, only 44 percent (10,807) were completed. African Americans in Arkansas entered approximately 1,000 of these original claims, with 25 percent completing their entries. Beginning in 1867, Radical Republicans took a turn at initiating economic growth. State leaders such as scalawag Edward Gantt and carpetbagger governor Powell Clayton hoped to induce industries to the region by building state-funded railroads, but the low-lying terrain of much of the state made laying track difficult. Radicals also hoped to lure immigrants to Arkansas by offering 160-acre farms to anyone who paid a nominal filing fee. Although more than 30,000 immigrants moved into Arkansas during Reconstruction, most stayed only briefly and moved on to Texas. Tied to economics was education. To enact the Radical agenda of better schools, roads, and hospitals, the state legislature raised property taxes (paid by whites who owned nearly all property), which provided political fuel for Conservatives who promised lower taxes during campaigns. Despite these attempts, by the end of Radical Reconstruction in 1875, Arkansas stayed yoked to the ups and downs of the cotton market. To the degree that freedom hinged on economic success and opportunities, most Arkansas blacks and whites remained slaves to poverty and debt.

As Reconstruction ended, much in Arkansas returned to prewar patterns: planter control, dependency on cotton, white supremacy, and poverty for the masses of whites and blacks. However, many fundamental changes had occurred. Schools and churches for blacks appeared throughout Arkansas. Black marriage was legal, and black families could not be broken apart. Although it was not—as blacks had dreamed—the Day of Jubilee, slavery had ended, and freedom—halting and undefined as it was—had begun.

*Randy Finley*

*See also:* Assassination of Abraham Lincoln (1865); Bureau of Refugees, Freedmen, and Abandoned Lands.

## Further Reading

Crouch, Barry, and Donaly E. Brice. *Cullen Montgomery Baker: Reconstruction Desperado*. Baton Rouge: Louisiana State University Press, 1997.

DeBlack, Thomas A. *With Fire and Sword: Arkansas, 1861–1874*. Fayetteville: University of Arkansas Press, 2003.

Finley, Randy. *From Slavery to Uncertain Freedom: The Freedmen's Bureau in Arkansas, 1865–1869*. Fayetteville: University of Arkansas Press, 1996.

"Freedmen's Bureau Online," http://www.freedmensbureau.com/arkansas/.

Moneyhon, Carl H. *The Impact of the Civil War and Reconstruction in Arkansas: Persistence in the Midst of Ruin*. Baton Rouge: Louisiana State University Press, 1994.

"Persistence of the Spirit: African-American Experiences in Arkansas," http://www2/aristotle.net/persistence/.

## ASHLEY, JAMES M. (1824–1896)

James Ashley was born in Pittsburgh, Pennsylvania, on November 14, 1824. In his youth, Ashley worked as a boat clerk on the Ohio and Mississippi Rivers. But law was his passion;

Ashley passed the bar in 1849; moved to Toledo, Ohio; and entered politics as a Republican. More abolitionist that his comrades, Ashley entered Congress in 1859, played a significant part in the passing of the Thirteenth Amendment in 1865, and became an outspoken critic of President Andrew Johnson.

Ashley envisioned an ideal nation, one based on absolute racial equality. This put him at odds with much of his party and of course the president, Andrew Johnson. The only difference between Johnson's perception of antebellum and postbellum America was the abolition of slavery; civil and political rights for freedpeople held no place. But for Ashley, Congressional Reconstruction was severely flawed also. First, according to Ashley, his Republican colleagues were wrong when they argued that the Military Reconstruction Act guaranteed that newly emancipated slaves were to have all the necessary rights to lead productive and economically independent lives. What made black independence impossible was that African Americans still had no power rooted in landownership. Black Americans therefore remained dependent on either renting land owned by whites or working for their former masters. Both scenarios connoted a restoration of antebellum labor system and labor code founded on white racial superiority.

To create a more equal society, Ashley openly sought the removal of President Andrew Johnson, on the grounds that Johnson abused his presidential powers by refusing to provide black Americans with civil rights and political access—what Ashley called a bill of rights. More Moderate Republicans were lukewarm on impeachment, arguing that no actual crime had been committed; Ashley claimed that Johnson's abuse of power, violation of public trust, and neglect of duty authorized Congress to impeach the president. Ashley also reasoned that Johnson's outdated, racist view of the Constitution impeded America's development. Creating racial equality was central for the United States to secure a strong economic future. Only with social and economic rights could African Americans fully contribute to the American economy.

Despite his fanatical crusade against President Johnson, James M. Ashley's ideas of equal racial representation and economic opportunity proved that America was capable of following an emerging political trend. He was at the forefront of those who believed African Americans should participate in the American lifestyle and have the chance to prosper evenly with whites. Irresponsible American politicians negated Ashley's model, and pursued policies that denied black Americans proper civil and political rights until the second half of the 20th century.

*Gerardo del Guercio*

*See also:* Black Suffrage; Field Order No. 15; Joint Committee on Reconstruction; Presidential Reconstruction; Stevens, Thaddeus (1792–1868).

## Further Reading

Foner, Eric. *Free Soil, Free Labor, Free Men: The Ideology of the Republican Party before the Civil War.* New York: Oxford University Press, 1970.

Horowitz, Robert F. *Great Impeacher: A Political Biography of James M. Ashley.* New York: Brooklyn College Press, 1979.

Kahn, Maxine B. "Congressman Ashley in the Post–Civil War Years." *Northwest Ohio Quarterly* 36 (Summer, Autumn 1964): 116–33, 194–210.

# ASSASSINATION OF ABRAHAM LINCOLN (1865)

John Wilkes Booth shot President Abraham Lincoln on Good Friday, April 14, 1865. Vice President Andrew Johnson and Secretary of State William H. Seward were supposed to be assassinated at the same time; Seward was severely wounded, but Booth's accomplice who was to kill Johnson, George A. Atzerodt, lost his nerve. The death of Lincoln and the survival of Johnson affected Reconstruction in profound ways. The conspirators' original plot involved kidnapping Lincoln and taking him south to be held for a ransom advantageous to the Confederacy. The conspirators included Booth, an actor; Atzerodt, a carriage painter and ferryman; John H. Surratt Jr., a confederate courier; David E. Herold, a pharmacist's clerk; Lewis Paine (or Payne, who also used the alias Lewis Thornton Powell) and Samuel Arnold, former Confederate soldiers; and Michael O'Laughlin, a feed-store clerk. The group met at the Washington, D.C., boardinghouse of Mary Surratt, John's mother.

After the fall of Richmond and the surrender of Robert E. Lee's army, the kidnap plot was no longer viable. Booth's decision to assassinate Lincoln may have been an independent decision at the last-minute development, perhaps even on the morning of April 14. With a few advance preparations and his connections as an actor, Booth was able to enter the presidential box during the performance. He shot Lincoln in the head and jumped over the railing onto the stage, shouting *Sic semper tyrannis* ("thus ever to tyrants," the motto of Virginia). He made his way to a waiting horse, despite a broken leg caused by catching his spur in a flag draped near the president's box. President Lincoln, mortally wounded, was taken across the street to the Peterson House, where he died at 7:22 the following morning. The War Department initiated a massive manhunt for Booth and Herold (who had assisted in his escape) which ended on April 26, when they were cornered in a Virginia tobacco barn. Herold surrendered, but Booth was shot and died shortly after. Agents of the federal government rounded up hundreds of suspects, but finally focused on eight: Herold, Atzerodt, Paine (who had seriously wounded Secretary of State Seward), Mary Surratt, Samuel Mudd (who set Booth's leg), Arnold, O'Laughlin, and Edward Spangler, a Ford's Theatre handyman. These eight were tried and found guilty by a controversial military commission; Herold, Atzerodt, Paine, and Mary Surratt were hanged on July 7, while the other four were sentenced to life imprisonment at Fort Jefferson, off the coast of Florida. O'Laughlin died in 1867, and Johnson ordered the others to be freed in early 1869.

Lincoln's assassination affected Reconstruction in several ways. It immediately caused a tremendous cry for vengeance against the South in general and against the conspirators in particular, resulting in a trial of questionable fairness. The hanging of Mary Surratt was especially controversial, partly because she was a woman, and partly because she had not participated in the plot in any significant way. Also, Johnson's ascendancy to the presidency brought an executive more rigid in his beliefs than Lincoln had been. In addition, and despite early indications, Johnson approached the South leniently and he had no interest or sympathy for the freedpeople. While no one knows what would have followed the Civil War had Lincoln lived, in all probability Lincoln would have dealt with Southern—and Northern—opposition more flexibly, and would have shown greater concern for the plight of former slaves.

*Glenna R. Schroeder-Lein*

On April 14, 1865 (Good Friday) John Wilkes Booth shot President Lincoln, after the plan to capture him—and ransom him for Confederate independence—fell apart. Lincoln's death elevated Southerner Andrew Johnson to the presidency, adding to the confusion of Reconstruction. (Library of Congress)

*See also:* Democratic Party; Johnson, Andrew (1808–1875); Lincoln, Abraham (1809–1865); Republicans, Radical.

## Further Reading

Guelzo, Allen C. *Fateful Lightning: A New History of the Civil War and Reconstruction.* New York: Oxford University Press, 2012.

Hanchett, William. *The Lincoln Murder Conspiracies.* Urbana: University of Illinois Press, 1983.

Leonard, Elizabeth D. *Lincoln's Avengers: Justice, Revenge, and Reunion after the Civil War.* New York: W. W. Norton, 2004.

Turner, Thomas Reed. *Beware the People Weeping: Public Opinion and the Assassination of Abraham Lincoln.* Baton Rouge: Louisiana State University Press, 1982.

# B

## BANKS, NATHANIEL P. (1816–1894)

Nathaniel P. Banks was a central figure in Abraham Lincoln's plans for Reconstruction. He demonstrated tremendous talent as Speaker of the House in the Massachusetts legislature, was elected as a representative to the U.S. Congress in 1853, and by 1855 had taken control as Speaker of the House. He returned to Massachusetts to serve as governor in 1858, but when the Civil War broke out Lincoln appointed Banks major general of U.S. volunteers. While ill-prepared to assume such high rank, he quickly proved his worth by securing federal control over Maryland, a key victory since the U.S. Capital could have resided in a seceding state.

In 1862, Banks was ordered to occupy the Shenandoah Valley, but Confederate general Thomas J. Jackson took advantage of Banks's inexperience and soundly defeated Bank's Union forces. Recognizing that the general's political skills surpassed his military ones, Lincoln sent Banks to federal-occupied Louisiana, to replace the heavy-handed administration of Benjamin Butler. Banks needed finesse to cajole citizens of the Confederate state to renounce secession and swear loyalty to the Union. Undeterred by stiff resistance, Banks began compiling a list of voters who had taken loyalty oaths, and once he had hit Lincoln's "ten percent" mark, the general ordered two elections in early 1864: one for governor, lieutenant governor, and several other state offices, and the second election for delegates to a constitutional convention. Together, the two elections formed the basis for a new state government, the Free State of Louisiana, which both Banks and Lincoln hoped would gain the approval of the U.S. Congress for readmission to the Union.

Voters selected Georg Michael Hahn governor, and the convention they seated created a document that was forward-looking, given the standards of the day. It abolished slavery, and left the door open for extending the vote to African Americans. Banks was less successful in continued military exploits, and his Red River campaign of spring 1864 ended in disaster. In fall of 1864, Lincoln recalled Banks to Washington to lobby Congress to readmit Louisiana; with Confederate defeat imminent, Congress had no intention of allowing any of Lincoln's "10 Percent" states easy readmission. Disappointed, Banks left Louisiana for good, and moved back to Massachusetts. He went on to serve six more terms in the U.S. House of Representatives, but had little impact on national policy.

*James G. Hollandsworth Jr.*

**See also:** Amnesty Proclamations; Presidential Reconstruction; Republicans, Moderate.

## Further Reading

*Debates in the Convention for the Revision and Amendment of the Constitution of the State of Louisiana.* New Orleans, LA: W. R. Fish, 1864

Fitzgerald, Michael W. *Splendid Failure: Postwar Reconstruction in the American South.* New York: Ivan R. Dee Publishers, 2008.

Foner, Eric. *Reconstruction Updated Edition: America's Unfinished Revolution, 1863–1877.* Reprint, New York: Harper Collins, 2014.

Hepworth, George H. *The Whip, Hoe, and Sword: The Gulf-Department in '63.* Boston: Walker, Wise & Co., 1864.

Hollandsworth, James G. *Pretense of Glory: The Life of General Nathaniel P. Banks.* Baton Rouge: Louisiana State University Press, 1998.

McCrary, Peyton. *Abraham Lincoln and Reconstruction: The Louisiana Experiment.* Princeton, NJ: Princeton University Press, 1978.

# BINGHAM, JOHN A. (1815–1900)

John Armor Bingham was congressman, leader of Moderate Republicans during Reconstruction, and author of Article 1 of the Fourteenth Amendment.

Bingham was born in Mercer, Pennsylvania, on January 21, 1815 to Hugh and Esther Bailey Bingham. In the 1820s and 1830s young Bingham shifted back and forth between Ohio and Pennsylvania, for school, due to family issues, and in pursuit of a newspaper career. As his reputation grew so did his antislavery feelings and his interest in politics and the law. By 1841, Bingham had been admitted to both the Pennsylvania and Ohio bar, and he had moved into Whig politics. Now living in Cadiz, Ohio, in the mid-1850s, Bingham joined other antislavery Whigs and Democrats in forming the new Republican Party in Ohio.

In 1854, Bingham won election to Congress, and continued to serve as Ohio's representative from the Twenty-first Congressional District until his district was eliminated in 1862. Elected as the representative of the Sixteenth Congressional District in 1864, Bingham continued in Congress until 1872. During the Civil War, Bingham pushed for the confiscation of Confederate property and advocated that the army not return escaped slaves. As a member of the House Judiciary Committee, he vigorously advocated the emancipation of all slaves and managed the bill that admitted the western counties of Virginia as the new state of West Virginia. Also, in late April 1865, Secretary of War Edwin Stanton appointed him chief investigator into the assassination of Abraham Lincoln, and President Andrew Johnson appointed him as special judge advocate in the trial of the conspirators.

During Reconstruction, Bingham emerged as one of the leading members of Congress and the Moderate wing of the Republican Party, playing an influential role on the Joint Committee on Reconstruction, the committee Congress created in 1865 to recommend legislation for completing the restoration process. Believing Radical Republicans to be impractical, Bingham attempted to work with President Andrew Johnson until it became apparent that the president would not compromise on legislation to protect former slaves. Bingham originated the idea of a constitutional amendment to ensure that all citizens had federal protections for their inalienable rights, what ultimately became the Fourteenth Amendment. By late 1867, Bingham had joined the radical forces, supporting expansion of military reconstruction. While he initially opposed Johnson's impeachment, he turned after Johnson fired Secretary of War Stanton in violation of the Tenure of Office Act, even serving as chairman of the impeachment managers for the House of Representatives impeachment trial.

In 1872, after eight terms in Congress, Bingham lost his nomination to a Liberal Republican challenger, Lorenzo Danford. In 1873, President Ulysses S. Grant appointed him U.S. minister to Japan, a position he held until he served in that capacity until 1885, returning unofficially in 1895 to negotiate the Formosa question between Japan and China. Bingham died in Cadiz, Ohio, on March 19, 1900.

*Roberta Sue Alexander*

***See also:*** Congressional Reconstruction; Presidential Reconstruction; Republicans, Moderate; Trumbull, Lyman (1813–1896).

John A. Bingham, a Moderate Republican from Ohio, authored the Fourteenth Amendment and served as chairman of the prosecution during President Johnson's impeachment trial. (Library of Congress)

## Further Reading

Aynes, Richard L. "The Continuing Importance of Congressman John A. Bingham and the Fourteenth Amendment." *Akron Law Review* 36 (2003): 589–616.

Beauregard, Erving. *Bingham of the Hills: Politician and Diplomat Extraordinary*. New York: Peter Lang, 1989.

Benedict, Michael Les. *The Impeachment and Trial of Andrew Johnson*. New York: Norton & Company, 1973.

Curtis, Michael Kent. "John A. Bingham and the Story of American Liberty: The Lost Cause Meets the 'Lost Clause'." *Akron Law Review* 36 (2003): 617–70.

Riggs, C. Russell. "The Antebellum Career of John A. Bingham: A Case Study in the Coming of the Civil War." Ph.D. dissertation, New York University, 1958.

# BLACK CODES

The Black Codes were part of a complex web of postwar restraints designed to maintain economic and social control over former slaves. The Black Codes originated in 1865 and 1866, as Southern lawmakers met to modify their state constitutions under

President Andrew Johnson's Reconstruction program. Mississippi legislators passed the first Black Code in November 1865; this became the prototype for similar legislation throughout the South. Whites insisted that the Black Codes recognized the blacks' freedom: codes allowed the freedmen to own property, testify in courts, sue and be sued, and marry other blacks. In reality, state Black Codes functioned to keep the former slaves at work and tied to the land—in a condition as close to bondage as possible. Mississippi's Black Codes mandated that the freedpeople "have lawful home or employment," yet stipulated that they could not lease or rent land outside towns or cities. It required them to sign labor contracts, and those who broke their contracts were liable to arrest. It empowered probate courts to apprentice black children "whose parent or parents have not the means, or who refuse to provide and support said minors," thus creating a pool of ready servants.

Mississippi's "Act to Amend the Vagrant Laws of the State" defined "vagrants" broadly—to include idle blacks—and those who failed to pay their fines after five days were hired out at auction to recoup the fine and court costs. In a broadly discriminatory supplementary act, Mississippi's Black Code also forbade freedmen, with exceptions, from carrying "firearms of any kind, or any ammunition, dirk or bowie knife." The act included many other prohibitions for blacks, ranging from making insulting gestures to ministering the Gospel without license. Although other states modeled their Black Codes after Mississippi's, one state after another applied special racial proscriptions to its freedpeople. South Carolina, for example, included among vagrants "those who are engaged in representing publicly or privately, for fee or award, without license, any tragedy, interlude, comedy, farce, play, or similar entertainment, exhibition of the circus, sleight-of-hand, wax-works, or the like." An ordinance in St Landry Parish, Louisiana, required blacks to carry passes to enter the parish, and they could not be absent from their employers after 10:00 p.m. While the Texas Black Code guaranteed the freedpeople the right to choose their employers, it stipulated "but when once chosen, they shall not be allowed to leave their place of employment, until the fulfillment of their contract, unless by consent of their employer, or on account of harsh treatment or breach of contract on the part of the employer." Texas law required the black employee to "obey all proper orders of his employer," and he or she was liable for fines if proven disobedient. Talking back, swearing, neglecting duty, leaving the farm without permission, and entertaining visitors during work hours—such infractions might be tolerated on the part of white workers, but they were strictly forbidden in the case of the freedpeople. Such provisions, not surprisingly, led to a firestorm of protest in the North.

The Black Codes outraged Radical Republicans and Moderate Northerners alike who interpreted them accurately as evidence of white Southerners' unwillingness to accept emancipation's full meaning. Upon returning from his 1865 fact-finding tour of the South, for example, General Carl Schurz denounced the Black Codes as extensions of the old slave codes. Commenting on South Carolina's Black Code, the editor of the *New York Tribune* remarked that under it "involuntary servitude will exist for the punishment of no crime except the old crime of having a black skin." The Black Codes signified white Southerners' ongoing commitment to slavery, to white supremacy, and their determination to circumscribe the legal status of the freedpeople. In response, Congress passed the Civil Rights Act in 1866 and the Fourteenth Amendment (1868) to outlaw such racial discrimination and protect the freedpeople from the neo-slavery represented in the notorious Black Codes. Sadly, the spirit of the Black Codes only went into remission; these racist laws provided foundation for the labor contracts, vagrancy legislation, lien laws, convict labor statutes, and debt peonage laws enacted by the Southern states following Redemption and the end of Reconstruction.

*John David Smith*

*See also:* Abolition of Slavery; Congressional Reconstruction; Labor Systems.

## Further Reading

Egerton, Douglas R. The *Wars of Reconstruction: The Brief, Violent History of America's Most Progressive Era*. New York: Bloomsbury Press, 2014.

Fitzgerald, Michael W. *Splendid Failure: Postwar Reconstruction in the American South*. New York: Ivan R. Dee Publishers, 2008.

Fleming, Walter L. *Documentary History of Reconstruction. 2 vols. 1906–1907*. Reprint, New York: McGraw-Hill, 1966.

Harris, William C. *Presidential Reconstruction in Mississippi*. Baton Rouge: Louisiana State University Press, 1967.

Smith, John David. *An Old Creed for the New South: Proslavery Ideology and Historiography, 1865–1918*. Westport, CT: Greenwood Press, 1985.

Wilson, Theodore B. *The Black Codes of the South*. Tuscaloosa University of Alabama Press, 1965.

# BLACK SUFFRAGE

First implemented by congressional legislation in 1867 and then nationalized by the Fifteenth Amendment in 1870, the enfranchisement of African American men (but not women) represented the most revolutionary reform of the Reconstruction era. The granting of voting rights to the freedmen separated African Americans' post-emancipation experience from their counterparts in Latin American nations in the 19th century.

## Emancipation and Wartime Demand for Suffrage

The Civil War proved to be pivotal in abolishing slavery and subsequently creating the opportunity for blacks to win voting rights. The Republican Party had envisioned neither when the war began in April 1861, but as time passed unexpected forces created momentum for black suffrage. As the war wore on, the federal government, and its Commander in Chief Abraham Lincoln, took bolder and bolder actions to suppress the rebellion. Among these was the Emancipation Proclamation, which took effect on January 1, 1863; under this executive order, African Americans could enlist in the Union army. Eventually, about 200,000 African American men served in the Union army and navy. Another 300,000 served as laborers for the Union throughout the war. Black participation in the Union war effort laid the foundation for their demand for suffrage after the war. In addition, some Republican leaders recognized that freedpeople constituted the only loyal population that the Republican Party could rely on for postwar Reconstruction.

## Presidential Reconstruction

In the first phase of Reconstruction—the Presidential Reconstruction period between 1863 and 1866—black suffrage was not on the agenda. Lincoln's first Reconstruction plan, known as the "Ten Percent Plan" of 1863, was based upon the prewar voting population of the Southern states; since no Southern blacks could vote before the Civil War, they were excluded from the process. African Americans protested the white-only Reconstruction program by holding national meetings in the North and sending leading Southern blacks to Washington to lobby for the vote. After meeting black ambassadors, Lincoln wrote to the military governor of Louisiana that the state consider enfranchising black soldiers and "intelligent" blacks because these people could help the Union "to keep the jewel of liberty within the family of freedom" (nothing came from the advice). Andrew Johnson continued the white-only Reconstruction policy, although under changed circumstances: Lincoln's plan served an expedient wartime objective, establishing a pro-Union state government in the Union-occupied South, while Johnson assumed power after the war had ended. Now ex-confederates were hoping to restore the prewar political and social order, and Johnson had no intention of interfering.

## Initial Congressional Reactions

Many Republican Conservatives were in line with the Presidential Reconstruction plan, viewing Reconstruction as no more than the restoration of the original constitutional national framework, minus slavery. Moderates, the majority of the party, sought national protections for the basic rights of the freedmen but were reluctant to enfranchise ex-slaves, fearing it would backfire and hurt the party in North. However, Radical Republicans saw Reconstruction as an opportunity to uproot the Southern ruling elite, and to build a new South ruled by the free labor Republicanism and market economy. They saw the freedmen as the party's only ally in promoting such reforms. Black enfranchisement was also necessary to protect the interests of freedmen, as economic and social freedom could only come if blacks could vote and hold office. Thus, Radicals insisted that black suffrage be made a prerequisite for the readmission of the ex-Confederate states. A combination of Southern and executive folly pushed back suffrage to the center of discussion. The Black Codes, passed by Southern states in 1865 and 1866, enraged Republicans of all sorts, who united to pass the Civil Rights Act of 1866—and then repass it over President Johnson's veto. Republicans then modified the Constitution to create a greater legal environment beyond the President's reach, via the Fourteenth Amendment. The second section of the amendment stipulated that if a state denied its adult male citizens the right to vote, its representatives to the House of Representatives would be reduced in proportion. The Southern states would be heavily punished by losing representation in the House for withholding suffrage of freed men; but northern states could continue to disfranchise their black citizens with little impunity since the Northern black population was too small to make a real difference in the proportionate calculation of a state's representation in the House. More important, this set an awesome precedent, as the federal government now moved into the realm to regulating suffrage conditions. Republicans quickly applied this new national power: between December 1866 and February 1867, Congress enfranchised black men in the District of Columbia and unorganized federal territories, and made impartial suffrage—equal voting rights for adult male citizens regardless of color—a precondition for the admission of Nebraska and Colorado.

## Congressional (Radical) Reconstruction

The midterm elections of 1866 ushered in a two-thirds majority for Republicans in both houses of Congress, creating a veto-proof environment that allowed Republicans to begin dismantling Johnson's Reconstruction structure. Starting in March 1867, Congressional acts repealed existing presidential directives and ordered the making of new state constitutions in 10 former Confederate states (Tennessee was exempted because it chose to ratify the Fourteenth Amendment). Congress mandated that freedmen participate in electing delegates to state constitutional conventions, and that new state constitutions incorporate universal manhood. Under the congressional program, about 735,000 blacks and 635,000 whites were registered in the 10 unreconstructed states. The new state constitutional conventions produced the most democratic state constitutions since the founding of the nation as they adopted universal suffrage, public schools for both blacks and whites, and state-funded services for the poor and disabled. African Americans' participation in Congressional Reconstruction was instrumental in the South's adoption of the Fourteenth Amendment, a requirement by Congress. With the ratification of the Fourteenth Amendment in 1868, seven states including Alabama, Arkansas, South Carolina, North Carolina, Georgia, and Louisiana were readmitted into Congress. Virginia, Mississippi, and Texas were readmitted, respectively, in 1869 and 1870. In 1870, Hiram Revels of Mississippi was seated in the Senate as the nation's first black senator. In the next 30 years, altogether 22 African American men were elected to Congress from the South. Another 1,400 held public offices at the state and local governments during Reconstruction. Between 1867 and the early 1870s, interracial democracy was an American reality.

## The Making of the Fifteenth Amendment

The mandate for black enfranchisement in the South came from the Military Reconstruction Acts; thus the former Confederate states were more progressive (arguably under coercion) than their Northern counterparts. This raised the issue of black suffrage in the North, and even intensified the debate over women's suffrage. Northern states, however, continued to vote down black suffrage proposals; Ulysses S. Grant's slim victory (a plurality of 300,000 out of 5.7 million votes) in the 1868 election, combined with Democrats' victories in six non-Confederate states (Oregon, New Jersey, New York, Delaware, Maryland, and Kentucky) alarmed Republicans about their precarious control of the political world. Republicans also recognized the necessity of securing black voting rights on a more permanent basis, since the new constitutions (created under the Reconstruction Acts) could evaporate once former Confederate states were readmitted. To address these concerns, Republicans proposed the Fifteenth Amendment in early 1869. A host of proposals emerged, but ultimately Republicans adopted a compromise version that forbade states to deny citizens the right to vote on grounds of race, color, or previous condition of servitude; by March 30,1870, the Fifteenth Amendment became part of the Constitution. Largely a work of the Moderate Republicans, the amendment did not affirmatively guarantee voting rights to African Americans; it simply prohibited states from denying voting rights for racial reasons. It did not grant voting rights to women, and continued to allow states to disfranchise citizens with literacy, residency, and nativity qualifications. However, it affirmed and nationalized the practice of black voting as first implemented in 1867, effectively overrode northern and western states' power to exclude blacks from political process, and gave Congress the power to enforce black suffrage in the years to come.

## Enforcing the Fifteenth Amendment

Rather than afford blacks protection and security, Black suffrage led to intensified violence and harassment. White paramilitary organizations, such as the Ku Klux Klan and the Knights of the White Camelia, posed the most direct challenge to voting rights in the South. Southern states lacked either resources or willingness to enforce voting privileges, so beginning May 1871, the Republican Congress launched an enforcement campaign. Within a year, Congress had enacted three Enforcement Acts to bolster the Fifteenth Amendment. These laws put the exercise of voting rights by U.S. citizens (as defined by the Fourteenth Amendment) under the protection of federal government and provided severe penalties against state officials, as well as private citizens, for using force, bribery, or intimidation to obstruct citizens from registering or voting. These laws also established federal mechanisms for enforcement, including having federal district courts try enforcement case; allowing the president to use U.S. military to assist civilian authorities; and creating the Department of Justice in 1870. Enforcement peaked with the election of 1872 and Grant was reelected in a landslide. The vigor of enforcement declined soon after, partly due to an economic recession that struck in 1873 and the rise of the Liberal Republican movement. The national tone shifted as well. The Supreme Court's decision in *United States v. Reese* (1876), declared two sections of the May 1871 enforcement "insufficient." In *United States v. Cruikshank* (1876), the Court deemed other federal enforcement laws defective. Democrats regained control of the House in 1874, and blocked any further legislation.

## The Coming of Disfranchisement

The final blow came from the disputed 1876 presidential election. As part of the so-called Compromise of 1877, Republican candidate Rutherford B. Hayes received the disputed electoral votes (and thus the White House), but the federal troops were withdrawn from the statehouses in Louisiana and South Carolina in April 1877. The Republican governments in those two states collapsed, completing the process of Democrats' "redemption" of all Southern states. Systematic disfranchisement of African Americans in the South had already begun, proceeded through the 1880s, and peaked in the 1890s. Elaborate voting restrictions, such as poll taxes and literacy tests, disfranchised African American men across the South. The few blacks who managed to register to vote were further curtailed by the white primary, which restricted the participation in Democratic Party primary elections only to whites—and in the South, the Democratic Party was virtually the only party. The Fifteenth Amendment remained virtually unenforced by the federal government until the passage of the Voting Rights Act of 1965. The implementation of black suffrage during Reconstruction, however, remained a powerful example of interracial democracy that inspired generations of blacks and whites in their fight for equality in the 20th century.

*Xi Wang*

**See also:** Compromise of 1877; Elections of 1876; Presidential Reconstruction; Redemption.

## Further Reading

Benedict, Michael Les. *A Compromise of Principle: Congressional Republicans and Reconstruction, 1863–1869.* New York: W. W. Norton, 1974.

Gillette, William. *The Right to Vote: Politics and the Passage of the Fifteenth Amendment.* Baltimore: The Johns Hopkins University Press, 1965.

Goldman, Robert M. *"A Free Ballot and a Fair Count": The Department of Justice and the Enforcement of Voting Rights in the South, 1877–1893.* New York: Fordham University Press, 2001.

Goldman, Robert M. *Reconstruction and Black Suffrage: Losing the Vote in Reese and Cruikshank.* Lawrence: University Press of Kansas, 2001.

Holt, Thomas. *Black over White: Negro Political Leadership in South Carolina during Reconstruction.* Urbana: University of Illinois Press, 1977.

Kaczorowski, Robert J. *The Politics of Judicial Interpretation: The Federal Courts, Department of Justice, and Civil Rights, 1866–1876.* 1985. Reprint, New York: Fordham University Press, 2005.

Keyssar, Alexander. *The Right to Vote: The Contested History of Democracy in the United States.* New York: Basic Books, 2000.

Kousser, J. Morgan: *Colorblind Injustice: Minority Voting Rights and the Undoing of the Second Reconstruction.* Chapel Hill: University of North Carolina Press, 1999.

Perman, Michael. *Struggle for Mastery: Disfranchisement in the South, 1888–1908.* Chapel Hill: University of North Carolina Press, 2001.

Wang, Xi. *The Trial of Democracy: Black Suffrage and Northern Republicans, 1860–1910.* Athens: University of Georgia Press, 1997.

# BLACK TROOPS (U.S. COLORED TROOPS) IN THE OCCUPIED SOUTH

The U.S. Colored Troops (USCT), part of the volunteer Union army, consisted of black troops who served during the war and early Reconstruction. Approximately 180,000 former slaves and free black men from the North and South served in all theaters of the Civil War, and many served as occupation forces across the South. While black men were not admitted into the Union army in the war's first year, they were accepted in 1862, and were actively recruited from 1863 through the end of the war. Black soldiers in the USCT were not equal to their white counterparts: they served in segregated units under white officers; could not become officers until late in the war; were paid less than white troops; received inferior food, equipment, and medical care; and at first

Members of the 4th U.S. Colored Troops (U.S.C.T.), African American soldiers comprised over 10 percent of the Union army. Following the war, many held key political and social positions in the South. (Library of Congress)

were confined to noncombat tasks such as work details and guard duty. Black troops also faced greater risks than white troops, since if captured they were sold into slavery, tried for insurrection and executed, or summarily killed. Yet they (and many abolitionist white allies) argued for the right to fight, and key 1863 battles such as Port Hudson and Fort Wagner validated black troops' effectiveness and bravery in combat. In June 1864, black troops won another victory when the U.S. Congress equalized pay between black and white soldiers. The experience men gained as soldiers equipped many for leadership roles after the war, including serving in politics, suffrage leagues, churches, and business ventures. Service for the nation helped blacks lay claim to full citizenship rights in the reconstructed nation.

After Confederate defeat, the Union army (including the USCT) served as an army of occupation in the South. White regiments were often mustered out earlier than black regiments, because white regiments had been formed earlier in the war. Nearly 85,000 black soldiers remained in the Union army at war's end, comprising more than one-third of the federal occupying force in the South. In the aftermath of the Civil War, the Union army provided the only source of order in the war-torn South; the army and the USCT enforced law, distributed rations to needy civilians, cleared away rubble, and begin the physical rebuilding of the South. Black Union soldiers often inspired former slaves, and black soldiers working in cooperation with the Bureau of Refugees, Freedmen, and Abandoned Lands (the Freedmen's Bureau) encouraged local freedpeople to form civic organizations, mutual assistance societies, schools, and political leagues to press for rights. Black troops also protected communities of former slaves, discouraging white Southerners from attacking blacks or coercing them into conditions that resembled slavery. Yet this very presence also proved hostile to defeated former confederates. To former confederates, black Union troops as occupying forces symbolized the complete destruction of the Southern social order, and utter defeat of the Confederate cause. Plantation owners argued that the presence of black soldiers disrupted the black labor force by giving blacks ideas about rights and equality. Some responded by trying to discredit black troops as disorderly, vicious, or incompetent, and called on army officials to remove black troops. Others harassed USCT outright, which led to violence. Shootings, beatings, and ambushes increased across the South, climaxing in the Memphis Riot (1866), which resulted in the deaths of 46 blacks. In 1866, ranking U.S. general Ulysses S. Grant decided that removing black soldiers might ease tensions. Most black regiments were relocated to coastal forts where they interacted with few civilians or were sent to western posts.

The worthy service of black soldiers during the Civil War and Reconstruction ensured a place for black troops in the regular U.S. Army. In July 1866, the U.S. Congress reorganized the regular army, creating two black cavalry regiments, the Ninth and Tenth Cavalry, and four black infantry regiments. The black regiments served mainly in the West, where they became known as Buffalo Soldiers. For black soldiers, army service staked a claim to full equality, yet the reality of the army also reflected many of the disappointments blacks confronted in the aftermath of the Civil War, as black troops in Reconstruction faced discrimination and hostility. Like Reconstruction itself, service in the USCT was full of both great promise and tragically unfulfilled hopes.

*Chandra Miller Manning*

*See also:* U.S. Army and Reconstruction.

## Further Reading

Berlin, Ira, Joseph P. Reidy, and Leslie S. Rowland, eds. *Freedom: A Documentary History of Emancipation, 1861–1867. Series II. The Black Military Experience.* New York: Cambridge University Press, 1982

Glatthaar, Joseph T. *Forged in Battle: The Civil War Alliance of Black Soldiers and White Officers.* New York: The Free Press, 1990.

Hahn, Steven. *A Nation under Our Feet: Black Political Struggles in the Rural South from Slavery to the Great Migration.* Cambridge, MA: Harvard University Press, 2003.

McRae, Bennie J. Jr. "Freedom Fighters: United States Colored Troops." Website [Online July 2004], http://www.coax.net/people/lwf/data.htm.

Miller, Steven F. Freedmen and Southern Society Project. Website [Online July 2004] http://www.history.umd.edu/Freedmen/home.html.

Smith, John David, ed. *Black Soldiers in Blue: African American Troops in the Civil War Era.* Chapel Hill: University of North Carolina Press, 2002.

## BLAIR, FRANCIS P., SR. (1791–1876)

Patriarch of the powerful Blair family of Missouri, Francis Preston Blair participated in the rise of the Democratic and Republican parties, served as advisor to three presidents, and witnessed the decline of his—and his family's—power and influence. Born in Abingdon, Virginia, Blair moved to Kentucky while still quite young. He met and married Violet Gist and the couple had five children, including Montgomery (1813–1883) and Francis

Jr. (1821–1875), both of whom became prominent national figures during the Civil War. By the 1820s, Blair was involved in law, publishing, and banking. In the 1820s, he supported Henry Clay, but shifted allegiance to Andrew Jackson and Democratic Party. Blair's understanding of finance, law, and communication made him a national spokesperson for the new party. Although the family moved to Missouri, Blair moved to Washington with the Jackson administration, and built his estate, "Silver Spring" outside the capital (the genesis of the modern city there). In 1830, he started the Washington Globe as the administration's official mouthpiece. A member of Jackson's unofficial "kitchen cabinet," Blair helped establish the Congressional Globe (now the Congressional Record), which reports the debates of Congress. By the 1850s, as sectional tensions over the spread of slavery took center stage, Blair's affiliation with the Democratic Party began to fray. With the family and its interests now tied to Missouri, the issue of slavery and westward expansion held critical significance for Blair.

In 1854, Blair led the charge to create the Missouri Republican Party, and backed the relatively unknown Abraham Lincoln in the 1860 election. In the secession crisis of 1861, Missouri—which permitted slavery—teetered on the edge, with Blair and his sons playing critical roles in keeping the state in the Union. They were rewarded accordingly: Montgomery became postmaster general, Francis Jr. (Frank) became a Union general, and their father again assumed the role of advisor to the president. As the war progressed, Blair supported Lincoln's wartime Reconstruction efforts, with Blair believing the war was to secure the Union and, perhaps, to decide the issue of slavery; those seeking black equality or Confederate retribution were "extremists." His support of the executive transferred to Johnson after Lincoln's assassination; Blair knew Johnson, as the Tennessean had been in the Senate when Montgomery was in the House of Representatives; in fact both Blair and his son, Montgomery, served as witnesses when Johnson was sworn in at the Kirkwood House on April 15, following Lincoln's death. Other ties bound the men: both men hailed from slave states, both were staunch Unionists, both were originally Democrats, and both believed the ending of the war had settled the most pertinent issues. Unfortunately, the new president, steeped in stubbornness and conservatism, only received encouragement from Blair, which did nothing for Johnson's relationship with the North or Congress. Blair had three interrelated goals: help Johnson protect his Reconstruction agenda, help rebuild the Northern Democratic Party, and push the favorite son, Frank, into national greatness (many saw Frank as presidential material). In 1866, Blair was a driving force behind the failed National Union Movement, and later allied with New Yorker Horatio Seymour in the latter's presidential bid in 1868 (with Frank Jr. as Seymour's running mate). Ironically, this did more harm than good, as Johnson had who naively sought the nomination, and Frank's hostile, venomous attacks on Congressional Reconstruction earned the party more enemies than friends. When Johnson left the White House in March 1869, the Blair family found itself without influence and without position. Blair straddled homes in Missouri and Maryland, but after Frank Jr. suffered a stroke, the father's health declined as well. Frank never fully recovered, and died from an accident in 1875; the elder Blair died the following year.

*Richard Zuczek*

**See also:** Amnesty Proclamations; Black Suffrage; Democratic National Convention (1868); Elections of 1864; Elections of 1868; Presidential Reconstruction; U.S. Army and Reconstruction.

## Further Reading

Parrish, William E. *Frank Blair: Lincoln's Conservative*. Columbia: University of Missouri Press, 1998.

Schroeder-Lein, Glenna, and Richard Zuczek. *Andrew Johnson: A Biographical Companion*. Santa Barbara, CA: ABC-CLIO, 2001.

Smith, Elbert B. *Francis Preston Blair*. New York: Free Press, 1980.

Smith, William Ernest. *The Francis Preston Blair Family in Politics*. 2 vols. 1933. Reprint, New York: Da Capo Press, 1969.

# BOURBONS

The term "Bourbons" (also called "redeemers") refers to a political group of white Southerners who "redeemed" their state's governments during the 1870s by ousting the Republican Reconstruction governments. In general, they sought to reestablish the racial and social hierarchy of the antebellum South. "Bourbons" began as a derogatory term, by which opponents likened white Southerners to the Bourbon kings of France, who returned to power following the defeat of Napoleon in 1815. Comprised of Southern Democrats, 90 percent of the group's membership included former Confederate government officials and veterans; most represented the antebellum Southern elite, but some were simply economic opportunists interested in bringing industrialization to the New South. Regardless of identity, the Bourbons united on goal: retrench the South in its antebellum social policies and negate the social and political changes implemented by Reconstruction governments. These policies gave former slaves unprecedented political power in the former white hegemony. Outnumbering their white counterparts in some states, African Americans became a valuable and influential group in the American political process.

The Bourbons passed legislation in their respective states that derailed Republican agendas and nullified freedmen's newfound civil rights. The Bourbons also sought to cripple the former slaves by sabotaging their economic opportunities, by increasing the obligations of black tenant farmers and sharecroppers to white landowners. During roughly two decades of power, they regained political and social control of all of the Southern states, held one-third of the seats in Congress, and introduced industrialization in the New South. For many Bourbons, retrenchment also meant lower taxes, so many public services eroded. In Texas, for example, free public education ended completely, and in other states illiteracy rates increased as a result of Bourbon policies.

*Jennifer Coates*

*See also:* Compromise of 1877; Democratic Party; Gun Clubs; Jim Crow Laws; Ku Klux Klan (KKK); Labor Systems; Red Shirts; White League.

## Further Reading

Hart, Roger. *Redeemers, Bourbons, and Populists*. Baton Rouge: Louisiana State University Press, 1975.

Richter, William L. *The ABC-CLIO Companion to American Reconstruction, 1862–1877.* Santa Barbara, CA: ABC-CLIO, 1996.

Trefousse, Hans L. *Historical Dictionary of Reconstruction.* Westport, CT: Greenwood Press, 1991.

Woodward, C. Vann. *The Origins of the New South, 1877–1913.* Baton Rouge: Louisiana State University Press, 1971.

# BOUTWELL, GEORGE S. (1818–1905)

Statesman, lawyer, and memoirist, George Sewall Boutwell spent 60 years in political service at the local, state, and federal levels. Boutwell, the son of a farmer, was born in Brookline, Massachusetts. After an unexceptional youth, he became interested in politics and gained attention by writing newspaper commentaries encouraging collaboration between antislavery Democrats and Free Soilers. In 1842, he was elected to the Massachusetts House of Representatives, and in 1850 was elected governor. He participated in the Republican convention that nominated Abraham Lincoln for president, and in 1861 Lincoln appointed him the first commissioner of Internal Revenue.

From 1863 until 1869, Boutwell represented Massachusetts in the U.S. House of Representatives. A leader among Radical Republicans, Boutwell matched Thaddeus Stevens's commitment to black civil rights and universal suffrage; he drafted early versions of the Fourteenth and Fifteenth Amendments, was a guiding member of the House Judiciary Committee, and in 1867, authored the first report to initiate impeachment hearings against President Johnson. When the impeachment trial became a reality in 1868, Boutwell briefly served as chair of the impeachment managers, but fellow Republicans replaced him with the more Moderate representative John A. Bingham for strategic purposes.

The new president, Ulysses S. Grant, appointed Boutwell secretary of the treasury in 1869. Boutwell took measures to cut the enormous postwar debt, and overhauled the department's collection procedures and personnel. On September 24, 1869—a date referred to by the press of the time as "Black Friday"—Boutwell followed orders from President Grant and released $4 million into the gold market in order to block speculators Jay Gould and James Fisk from cornering the gold market. Boutwell's unquestioning support for the gold standard later contributed to the temporary demonetization of silver (or the "Crime of 1873"). Businesses were ruined by the ensuing panic, and these affairs contributed to a growing lack of faith in the Grant administration. Boutwell's memoirs of his years in office were completed and released in 1902. He died in Groton, Massachusetts, in 1905.

*Michelle LaFrance*

**See also:** Ames, Adelbert (1835–1933); Congressional Reconstruction; Presidential Reconstruction; Sherman, John (1823–1900); White League.

## Further Reading

Benedict, Michael Les. *A Compromise of Principle: Congressional Republicans and Reconstruction, 1863–1869.* New York: W. W. Norton & Co., 1974.

Bogue, Allan G. *The Earnest Men: Republicans of the Civil War Senate.* Ithaca, NY: Cornell University Press, 1981.

Boutwell, George S. *Reminiscences of Sixty Years in Public Affairs.* New York: McClure, Phillips and Co., 1902.

Trefousse, Hans L. *The Radical Republicans: Lincoln's Vanguard for Racial Justice.* New York: Knopf, 1969.

# BROOKS-BAXTER WAR (ARKANSAS)

This 1874 clash between two contending Republican governors effectively ended Reconstruction in Arkansas. Republicans came to power in Arkansas following the adoption of the constitution of 1868, whose ironclad oath denied the franchise to ex-confederates. In the first state elections, former Union brigadier general Powell Clayton was elected governor. His term witnessed the defeat of the Ku Klux Klan, the groundwork for a state system of public education, the expansion of railroads, and the creation of the state's university. But Clayton had trouble holding the various elements of his party together. Mountain Unionists ("scalawags") were not enthusiastic about higher taxes or railroads they would never see, and blacks felt excluded from government positions. Republicans who had issues with Clayton unified under the banner of Liberal Republicans and, by 1872, made a run for the governor's position. They coopted many Conservatives by promoting universal suffrage, which meant extended voting to former confederates.

By the time of the gubernatorial election, Clayton had been elected senator, but his faction of the party nominated native Unionist Elisha Baxter of Batesville, a Union veteran and local judge. The Liberals were represented by former Methodist minister Joseph Brooks, who supported both civil rights for former slaves and reinstatement of privileges to former confederates. After an election marred by massive fraud, Baxter was declared the winner. Brooks turned to the courts, but made little headway until March 1874 when Governor Baxter's actions called into question the legality of railroad grants—the economic centerpiece of Republican Reconstruction. With that, Senator Clayton decided that Baxter had to go, and he engineered Baxter's removal through a circuit court ruling. Brooks, accompanied by an armed force of about 20 men, seized the state house and expelled Baxter. Abandoned by most Republicans, Baxter was embraced by the Democrats, and both sides began organizing vigilante militias. Federal infantry arrived in Little Rock to separate the forces, although a few scattered incidents did result in casualties. Outside of the town, where no federal forces operated, extensive fighting cost perhaps as many as 300 lives, the most violent single episode being the Brooks forces attack on Baxter militia aboard the steamer *Hallie.*

In Washington, legal maneuvering continued by advocates of both Baxter and Brooks. Baxter called the legislature into special session, a move President Grant supported and Brooks opposed, and also called for a new convention to draft a new state constitution. On May 13, 1874, the legislature assembled and two days later President Grant officially recognized Baxter as governor. During the summer, the convention wrote the easily adopted constitution of 1874 that restored voting rights to ex-confederates and weakened the powers of the governor. Joseph Brooks was mollified by being appointed U.S. postmaster in Little Rock, but died in 1877. Elisha Baxter declined the gubernatorial nomination under the new constitution; he died in 1899.

*Michael B. Dougan*

*See also:* Arkansas.

## Further Reading

Dougan, Michael B. *Arkansas Odyssey: The Saga of Arkansas from Prehistoric Times to Present*. Little Rock, AR: Rose Publishing Co., 1994.

Harrell, John M. *The Brooks and Baxter War: History of the Reconstruction Period in Arkansas*. St Louis: Slawson Printing Co., 1893.

Moneyhon, Carl. *The Impact of the Civil War and Reconstruction on Arkansas: Persistence in the Midst of Ruin*. Fayetteville: University of Arkansas Press, 2002.

Woodward, Earl F. "The Brooks and Baxter War in Arkansas, 1872–1874." *Arkansas Historical Quarterly* 30 (1971): 315–36. See also http://www.oldstatehouse.com.

# BROWN, JOSEPH EMERSON (1821–1894)

Joseph Brown, Civil War governor, Reconstruction scalawag, and U.S. senator, was born in South Carolina on April 15, 1821. He attended Yale University Law School and settled in Georgia in 1847 to commence his legal career. Elected to the state Senate in 1849, Brown emerged as a Democratic leader. His investments in real estate, mineral rights, and railroads soon made him very wealthy. When the Democratic Convention of 1857 deadlocked over a choice for governor, they nominated Brown, who won easily. Reelected in 1859, he warned about the dangers of the new Republican Party and abolitionist agitators. Believing that Lincoln's election meant the end of the Southern way of life, he urged secession in January 1861.

Once war began, Governor Brown set the standard for supporting the Confederacy but opposing the Confederate central government. By war's end his state lay in ruins—courtesy of General Sherman—and he sat in prison, arrested by order of President Andrew Johnson. Pardoned in September 1865, Brown supported Johnson's moderate approach to Reconstruction, but he also advocated for black civil rights and even backed the Fourteenth and Fifteenth Amendments. In 1867, he approved moving the state capital to Atlanta, where he represented scores

Governor of Georgia during the Civil War, Joseph E. Brown was a vocal critic of Confederate president Jefferson Davis. After the war, Brown joined the Republican Party, supported black rights, and advocated reconciliation. (Library of Congress)

of prominent businessmen. As Radical Reconstruction took hold, he encouraged Conservative whites to accept the end of slavery, but also cautioned blacks not to push too fast for change. By 1868, he openly embraced Republicans and even stumped the state for Ulysses Grant in the 1868 presidential contest. Georgia fell back under control of Conservative Democrats earlier than other states—1870—and the party extended an offer for Brown to rejoin the home party. Respected and wealthy, Brown assumed a U.S. Senate seat in 1880 and served until 1890. He died on November 30, 1894.

*Randy Finley*

*See also:* Democratic Party; Georgia.

## Further Reading

Cimbala, Paul. *Under the Guardianship of the Nation: The Freedmen's Bureau and the Reconstruction of Georgia*. Athens: University of Georgia Press, 1997.

Davis, William C. *The Union That Shaped the Confederacy: Robert Toombs and Alexander Stephens*. Lawrence: University of Kansas Press, 2001.

Parks, Joseph H. *Joseph E. Brown of Georgia*. Baton Rouge: Louisiana State University Press, 1977.

Roberts, Derrell C. *Joseph E. Brown and the Politics of Reconstruction*. Tuscaloosa: University of Alabama Press, 1973.

# BROWNLOW, WILLIAM G. ("PARSON") (1805–1877)

William Gannaway Brownlow, Methodist preacher, Whig newspaper editor, Southern Unionist, and Reconstruction governor of Tennessee, was born in 1805 in Wythe County, Virginia. Orphaned at age 11 and raised by relative, Brownlow apprenticed as a carpenter before having an "experience" that caused him to become a Methodist minister. In 1836, he settled in East Tennessee and became editor of a Whig newspaper. He was acerbic and sarcastic, and denounced his enemies with great vehemence, be they Baptists, Catholics, Democrats, immigrants, abolitionists, or secessionists.

In the sectional crisis of the 1850s, Brownlow rejected secession and vowed fidelity to the Union. His Unionism was not based on antislavery principles (he was an outspoken defender of slavery) but instead his belief that sectional troubles was the work of extremists—scheming, self-interested Southern politicians and fanatical Northern abolitionists. Like the other states of the Upper South, Tennessee remained predominantly Unionist even after Abraham Lincoln's election in 1860. But with the outbreak of war in April 1861, public sentiment in Middle and West Tennessee went over to secession (where plantation slavery was more predominant) and the state seceded in June. East Tennessee held firm to its Unionism, however, with Brownlow playing a leading role. In fact, a Unionist convention held in Greeneville in June 1861 petitioned the now-Confederate state government to allow East Tennessee to become its own state—Franklin. That did not occur, and after a brief period of conciliation Nashville cracked down, arresting Brownlow and exiling him north. When a Union army invaded East Tennessee in the fall of 1863, Brownlow returned to Knoxville, reestablished his newspaper, and resumed his anti-Confederate editorials. He quickly emerged as a leader of the state's Radical Unionists, who favored dealing harshly with secessionists and abolishing slavery. In January 1865, with Tennessee firmly under Union army control, a convention met in Nashville to set in motion the state's political restoration; in March 1865, Brownlow was elected governor.

Tennessee had a distinctive Reconstruction experience. As a fully functioning loyalist entity already operating at war's end, Tennessee was unaffected by Johnson's Reconstruction program. Moreover, in July 1866, the Tennessee legislature ratified the Fourteenth Amendment to the Constitution, and Congress readmitted the state to the Union. But readmission did not mean peace, and Brownlow's tenure as governor was controversial from the start. The legislature that convened with Brownlow was solidly Radical, and denied the vote to all who had supported the Confederacy. But loopholes granted suffrage to former Unionists who had confederate leanings, which concerned Brownlow. In 1866, the legislature gave Brownlow control over voter registration, which he manipulated to keep many Conservative Unionists as well as ex-confederates from the ballot box. In early 1867, he made his most controversial move yet, pushing black suffrage through the legislature. Brownlow, who remained a white supremacist at heart, took this step for purely partisan reasons, knowing that the blacks would vote Radical. Tennessee thus became the first Southern state to fully enfranchise black men. At the same time, in order to ensure Radical control of polling places and protect black voters, the legislature created the State Guard, a militia composed of black and white men loyal to Brownlow. These measures assured Brownlow an easy reelection in August 1867 and another Radical-dominated legislature, but they also provoked fierce resistance from his enemies. By mid-1867, political violence was widespread, much of it led by the Ku Klux Klan, which had originated in Pulaski, Tennessee, in 1866. Brownlow suspended civil law, called his militia into action, and managed to keep the state Republican for the 1868 presidential election.

As tensions tore at Tennessee, Brownlow cast about for other positions, coveting a U.S. Senate seat. In February 1869, when one became vacant, the legislature gave it to him; as soon as he resigned the governorship, the Radical party in Tennessee succumbed to internal factionalism, Conservative violence, and election fraud. In the August state elections, Conservatives swept Brownlow's allies from power, "redeeming" the state and ending Reconstruction in Tennessee's. In poor health, Brownlow managed to serve out his term in the Senate, but he retired to Knoxville in 1875, where he continued to live until his death in 1877.

Historians are critical of Brownlow's governorship. His manipulation of ballots and voter registration was indefensible, and the state government he presided over was riddled with corruption. Nevertheless, his administration modernized the public school system, and provided for black education, black civil rights, and black suffrage. Although Brownlow supported most of these measures for expediency not ideology—and although most programs were gutted by "redeemers" after they secured control—Brownlow's four year rule can be remembered as a time of unparalleled progress for black Tennesseans.

*Stephen V. Ash*

***See also:*** Black Suffrage.

## Further Reading

Ash, Stephen V., ed. *Secessionists and Other Scoundrels: Selections from Parson Brownlow's Book.* Baton Rouge: Louisiana State University Press, 1999.

Coulter, E. Merton. *William G. Brownlow: Fighting Parson of the Southern Highlands.* Knoxville: University of Tennessee Press, 1999.

Kelly, James C. "William Gannaway Brownlow." *Tennessee Historical Quarterly* 43 (1984): 25–43, 155–72.

# BRUCE, BLANCHE KELSO (1841–1898)

Blanche K. Bruce was a black political leader and the first African American to serve a full term in the U.S. Senate. Born a slave in Farmville, Virginia, he may have been the son of his owner. He was comparatively well treated as a youngster and was taught to read and write by the same tutor who instructed his master's white son. Bruce was taken to Missouri as an adult, and managed to escape to Kansas in 1861. He returned to Missouri during the war years, where he opened a school for black children.

Following Confederate defeat, Bruce relocated to Mississippi and by 1867 had become active in Republican politics. Well spoken, charming, and intelligent, he gained a reputation for moderation that garnered him the respect of blacks and whites. He was on compatible terms with many Democrats, including L.Q.C. Lamar. He emerged as Bolivar County's chief power broker, where he served as sheriff, superintendent of education, tax collector, and editor of the *Foreyville Star*. With the support of Governor Adelbert Ames, the Mississippi legislature elected Bruce to the U.S. Senate in 1874, and he served from 1875 to 1881. He supported federal aid for railroads, opposed the Chinese Exclusion Act of 1878, and called for a more just policy toward American Indians. He spoke bluntly against the Back-to-Africa movement, and just as harshly against the upsurge of white violence as Democrats sought to redeem Mississippi in 1875. Bruce remained in

Born a slave in Virginia, Blanche K. Bruce became an influential moderate Republican in Mississippi's Reconstruction politics. Bruce was the first African American to serve an entire term in the U.S. Senate. (Library of Congress)

Washington after his Senate term expired, serving in the Treasury Department on-and-off until his death in 1898.

*William C. Hine*

**See also:** Ames, Adelbert (1835–1933); Mississippi.

## Further Reading

Foner, Eric. *Reconstruction Updated Edition: America's Unfinished Revolution, 1863–1877*. Reprint, New York: HarperCollins, 2014.

Gatewood, Willard B. *Aristocrats of Color: The Black Elite, 1880–1920*. Bloomington: Indiana University Press, 1990.

Harris, William C. "Blanche K. Bruce of Mississippi: Conservative Assimilationist," in Howard N. Rabinowitz, ed., *Southern Black Leaders of the Reconstruction Era*. Urbana: University of Illinois Press, 1982, pp. 3–38.

Urofsky, Melvyn. "Blanche K. Bruce: United States Senator, 1875–1881." *Journal of Mississippi History* 29 (1967): 118–41.

Wharton, Vernon Lane. *The Negro in Mississippi 1865–1890*. Chapel Hill: University of North Carolina Press, 1947.

## BULLOCK, RUFUS B. (1834–1907)

The only Republican governor of Georgia until 2002, New York-native Rufus Brown Bullock's saga is one of opportunism, morality, and malignance. Known to many only through the vindictive portrait found in Margaret Mitchell's *Gone with the Wind*, Bullock was actually a well-intentioned, if egotistical, Northern proponent of the New South. Born in 1834 in Bethlehem, New York, Bullock grew up in Albion, where he soaked up the progressive local environment and adopted the abolition cause. By the early 1850s, he had married Rhode Island-native Elizabeth Salisbury; they moved to Philadelphia, and in 1856 or 1857 to Augusta, Georgia, to take advantage of the burgeoning telegraph and railroad business developing in the state. Bullock was torn during the secession crisis; he remained a staunch Unionist but was also loyal to his adopted state. He stayed in Georgia when the state seceded, and (perhaps to avoid persecution) accepted a position in the Confederate army's quartermaster corps where his technical and business skills made him supervisor of telegraph operations.

Although distraught when the war ended, Bullock had no deep association with slavery or the Confederate cause, so he was able to see opportunity in the mayhem. He held doubts about President Andrew Johnson's rapid restoration program, for he calculated that a prosperous new Georgia—and a new South—could only rise from the ashes of the Confederacy if Southerners embraced significant social, political, and economic changes. In addition, his reformist Yankee upbringing challenged the morality and practicality of ignoring the freedpeople's needs. Therefore, as congressional Republicans wrestled control of Reconstruction from the president, Bullock migrated into politics. Following the passage of the Military Reconstruction Acts in 1867, Bullock served in the state's constitutional convention that convened in December, and supported both the new liberal constitution and the initiative to move the state capital to Atlanta.

Military authorities arranged for spring 1868 legislative and gubernatorial elections, with Rufus Bullock as the Republican candidate and former Confederate general John B. Gordon representing white Conservatives. Bullock won by a small margin. As governor, Bullock tackled two tasks: fulfill the requirements for Georgia's readmission to the Union and rebuild the state's shattered economy. He was ultimately successful at both, although at great personal cost. He quickly embarked on an expensive series of loans and borrowing to begin rebuilding the state's infrastructure and communications network. His connections brought a great deal of money into the state, for constructing a new capital city, rebuilding railroads, laying telegraphs, and building bridges and canals. The money also caused scandal and accusations, and certainly there was corruption and misuse; Margaret Mitchell's prejudiced portrait of Bullock in her novel *Gone with the Wind* pays particular attention to alleged corrupt dealings by the governor, but the momentum he initiated, merging public and private interests into a common progressive venture, outlived his tenure as governor.

Governor Bullock's other mission fared less well. At first, prospects for readmission seemed good; the state ratified a new constitution and the Fourteenth Amendment in the April 1868 election, and in June, Congress readmitted Georgia to the Congress. But a backlash occurred in the summer with the appearance of the Ku Klux Klan (tied to John B. Gordon) and a rise in political violence. The 1868 presidential campaign increased tensions, and the inflammatory statements made by Democratic vice presidential nominee Francis P. Blair Jr. encouraged opposition to Congress's measures. In a stunning turn of events, Conservatives coopted some Moderates in the legislature, and in September 1868 they declared black membership illegal; they then nullified the election of 28 African American members and expelled them. The legislature then refused to ratify the Fifteenth Amendment the following spring. Bullock risked his political future, took matters into his own hands, and traveled to Washington to see the new president.

Bullock had an unusual request of President Ulysses S. Grant—remand Georgia to military supervision—effectively kick the state back out of the Union. Incredibly, the Grant administration concurred, and in December 1869, placed Georgia back under military supervision. Third District Commander Alfred Terry reassembled the original 1868 legislature, and together Bullock and Terry evaluated the credentials of all assembly members; many were ousted. In February 1870, this legislature nullified antiblack measures, ratified the Fifteenth Amendment, and reapplied for readmission. In July, Congress readmitted Georgia to the Union, again. Due to the chaos in the recent electoral cycle, state leaders decided to start anew with elections in December 1870—and these resulted in a Democratic victory. Some say that Bullock's gamble—placing the state back under military control—backfired; the incoming legislature was a hostile one, and rumors of impeachment proceedings spread quickly. Although the specifics remain a mystery, Bullock resigned in October and moved the family back north. The Democratic legislature met in November, and in a special election chose Conservative James M. Smith as Georgia's governor. But it was not over for Bullock: he was arrested in 1876, and returned to Georgia to face charges of malfeasance and fraud. He was acquitted, and strangely, opted to stay in Atlanta. He became one of the city's most prominent citizens—a living symbol of the trials, tribulations, and finally, the rise of a new Georgia. Bullock became president of the city's first cotton mill and of a loan company, served on many public and industrial boards, and was president of the Atlanta Chamber of Commerce. In declining health, Bullock and his wife returned to Albion, New York, in 1903, and he died there in 1907.

*Richard Zuczek*

*See also:* Congressional Reconstruction; Elections of 1868; Presidential Reconstruction; Provisional Governors; Redemption; U.S. Army and Reconstruction.

## Further Reading

Drago, Edmund L. *Black Politicians and Reconstruction in Georgia: A Splendid Failure.* Baton Rouge: Louisiana State University Press, 1982.

Duncan, Russell. *Entrepreneur for Equality: Governor Rufus Bullock, Commerce, and Race in Post-Civil War Georgia.* Athens: University of Georgia Press, 1994.

Nathans, Elizabeth Studley. *Losing the Peace: Georgia Republicans and Reconstruction, 1865–1871.* Baton Rouge: Louisiana State University Press, 1969.

## BUREAU OF REFUGEES, FREEDMEN, AND ABANDONED LANDS

The Bureau of Refugees, Freedmen, and Abandoned Lands, commonly known as the Freedmen's Bureau, was a branch of the U.S. War Department created at the end of the Civil War to oversee the South's transition from slavery to freedom. Often considered the first federal social welfare agency, the Bureau was involved in a vast array of activities through the end of 1868, when its responsibilities were significantly curtailed, until its June 1872 closing. Although it represented an unprecedented expansion of federal authority, it was nonetheless envisioned as a temporary expedient rather than a long-term solution; in addition, the Bureau never received the resources sufficient to fulfill its broad mandate. While former slaves viewed the Bureau as their main ally in the postwar South, the Bureau earned the animosity of most white Southerners and the opposition of President Andrew Johnson. The Bureau dramatically improved the lives of thousands of freedmen and indigent whites during the immediate postwar years, but it did not fulfill all the responsibilities with which it was entrusted.

The origins of the Freedmen's Bureau lay in the efforts of the War Department, Treasury Department, and various Northern benevolent organizations to address the disruption of Southern civilian life during the Civil War. Fugitive slaves who had fled to federal lines—as the Union army gained Confederate territory—required humanitarian aid, as did white Southern Unionists driven from their homes. Throughout the Union-occupied South, thousands of former slaves worked under federally sponsored free-labor arrangements on abandoned and confiscated plantations, while thousands more, especially the families of black soldiers and military laborers, lived and worked within the confines of contraband camps, and "freedmen's villages." Even before the war had ended, congressional Republicans considered the need for a federal agency to oversee the process of transition throughout the South. The first bill appeared in December 1863, but conflict between the departments of War and Treasury stalled passage; not until early 1865, with Union victory imminent, did an agreement emerge to locate the Bureau within the War Department.

On March 3, Congress passed the bill, which President Abraham Lincoln immediately signed, creating the Freedmen's Bureau. The 1865 Freedmen's Bureau bill established within the War Department "bureau of refugees, freedmen, and abandoned lands" that was charged with the supervision and management of abandoned lands and "the control of all subjects relating to refugees and freedmen from rebel states." The Bureau was to be headed by a commissioner appointed by the president, who was authorized to appoint assistant commissioners to head the Bureau in the ex-Confederate states. The legislation empowered the secretary of war to issue provisions, clothing, and fuel for the relief of destitute refugees and freedmen. It also authorized the commissioner, under the president's direction, "to set apart, for the use of loyal refugees and freedmen," abandoned and confiscated land within the insurrectionary states, stipulating that "every male citizen" could rent up to 40 acres of such land for three years with an option to purchase at any time during this period.

The first and only Freedmen's Bureau commissioner was General Oliver Otis Howard, a graduate of Bowdoin College and West Point and a distinguished Civil War veteran who had lost his right arm in battle. An avowed Christian, Howard's missionary zeal and connections to Freedmen's Relief Societies earned him the moniker "Christian General" and made him an obvious choice for the position.

Howard's first task was to appoint assistant commissioners for the Southern states, but since Congress allocated no money for the Bureau, Howard relied mostly upon army personnel for staffing. Like Howard, most Bureau officials saw themselves as engaged in the reform mission to remake the South upon a free-labor basis. Idealistic, they believed that over time former slaveholders and freedmen would see the benefits of a labor system based upon mutual consent and the freedom to contract, rather than upon coercion. Most Bureau officials also naively believed that freedmen and their former masters would quickly overcome slavery's bitter legacy. Although the administrative structure of the Bureau varied from state to state, in general states were divided into districts and subdistricts and were administered by a hierarchy of officials that included assistant commissioners, civilian and military superintendents, and agents. In addition to army personnel, the Bureau employed white Southerners—either civilian officials or private citizens—as agents. Nonetheless, the Bureau was chronically understaffed, with no more than 900 men serving at any one time, and with individual agents responsible for thousands of square miles of territory.

Because the Freedmen's Bureau had been charged with responsibility for "all subjects" relating to freedmen and refugees, little lay beyond its scope. In establishing a workable system of free labor for the South, Bureau agents oversaw the signing of labor contracts between employers and freedmen; mediated labor disputes; saw that freedmen received their due compensation; established systems of public health and medical care; and even supplied transportation to former slaves trying to reunite families. The Bureau also assisted needy whites; in fact, more than a quarter of the approximately 20 million rations issued went to whites. Two particularly important Bureau functions involved law enforcement and education. Commissioner Howard and his Bureau agents were firmly committed to the principle of equality before the law.

Throughout the South, however, freedmen not only found themselves subject to violence by whites, but they were also denied access to justice under state governments created by President Johnson's Reconstruction program. In response, the Bureau instituted its own court system as a means of securing impartial justice; Howard estimated that Bureau courts annually heard more than 100,000 complaints. Nonetheless, doubts about the constitutionality of military courts during peacetime—especially after the U.S. Supreme Court's decision in the 1866 *Milligan* case—caused Bureau officials to focus their efforts on securing freedpeople justice in civilian courts. The other major initiative was education; for Howard and many Bureau officials, education was central to black progress. The Bureau established its own system of schools, sometimes working with missionary societies such as the American Missionary Association.

The federal government and the (usually) white, female teachers sent South by the missionary societies embraced their duty to teach basic literacy and middle-class values—such as punctuality, sobriety, and the dignity of labor—all essential for competing in the capitalist marketplace. By 1869, the Bureau operated some 3,000 schools, with a total enrollment of more than 150,000 students. The Bureau helped lay the foundations of public education in the South, perhaps its most important long-term accomplishment.

The Freedmen's Bureau was also involved with a number of other organizations that assisted former slaves. Several "normal" (teacher training) schools and universities—such as the Hampton Normal and Industrial Institute at Hampton, Virginia, and Howard University in Washington, D.C. (which was named after the commissioner)—received Bureau's assistance and established the foundations of the historically black colleges.

Perhaps the Bureau's most important assignment, and its greatest failure, involved land redistribution. Congressional Republicans charged the Bureau with managing abandoned and confiscated land in the South, and it directed the president and the commissioner to make such land available to freedmen. Land redistribution was key to restructuring Southern society by dismantling the plantation system and providing at least some freedmen with the land essential to economic independence in an agricultural system. With the wartime abandonment of farms and plantations, and due to various confiscation measures enacted by Congress, by war's end the federal government controlled nearly 900,000 acres of land and 5,000 town lots, almost all of which were transferred to the Freedmen's Bureau. But significant black land ownership did not materialize. First, since Congress never provided the Bureau any funding, Howard had hoped to sell and rent property to subsidize the Bureau; without money, former slaves were unlikely tenants. President Johnson also blocked land redistribution; in his amnesty proclamation of May 1865, Johnson restored property rights to pardoned ex-confederates. Confusion developed as pardons continued, but many former confederates returned to their land only to find former slaves already raising crops. Commissioner Howard tried to circumvent the president's actions, but Johnson held firm and in Circular No. 15 Howard ordered that land controlled by the Bureau must be returned to pardoned ex-confederates. As broad as Circular No. 15 was, Howard argued it did not apply to land that fell under General William T. Sherman's Special Field Order No. 15—a January 1865 wartime directive that had granted freedmen 40-acre plots along coastal South Carolina and Georgia. By mid-1865, some 40,000 freedmen had gained possessory title to almost a half-million acres of "Sherman lands." President Johnson, however, declared that Circular No. 15 did apply; in October he ordered Howard to oversee personally the restoration of this land to whites, and to convince freedmen there to sign labor contracts if they wanted to remain. Despite his reservations and significant black resistance, Howard complied with the order.

The Freedmen's Bureau was controversial from birth. Radical Republicans envisioned the Bureau as the key to remaking Southern society. Moderate Republicans recognized the temporary need for the Bureau but expressed concerns over increasing federal authority. Members of the Democratic Party, North and South, objected to the expansion of federal power, and its alleged bias in supporting a particular social group. Freedmen regarded the

Bureau as their ally in fending off white violence, while white Southerners protested its very existence. In 1866, as Republicans began to unite around opposition to Johnson's Reconstruction agenda, Congress passed the Civil Rights Act and a new Freedmen's Bureau bill, which continued the Bureau and expanded its powers. Not only did Johnson veto the bill, but he also issued a scathing veto message that condemned the Bureau as an unconstitutional expansion of federal authority. The president then authorized an investigation into the Bureau, hoping to discredit the entire agency. Congressional Republicans responded with another Bureau bill, which—due to Johnson's skill at alienating more and more Republicans—they easily passed over another Johnson veto.

With passage of the 1867 Military Reconstruction Acts, the Bureau lost much of its identity in favor of the new military districts. Through 1868, as states secured readmission, Bureau responsibilities transferred to civilian governments. In order to keep the Bureau operating through the elections of 1868, Congress extended its existence until January 1, 1869, after which date all Bureau operations ceased except for the education and claim divisions. In 1870, educational activities were terminated, and in June 1872 Congress discontinued the Bureau entirely.

*John C. Rodrigue*

**See also:** Civil Rights; Confiscation Acts; Contraband, Slaves as; Edisto Island, South Carolina; Elections of 1866; Field Order No. 15; Joint Committee on Reconstruction; Howard, Oliver Otis (1830–1909); Ku Klux Klan (KKK); Labor Systems; Port Royal Experiment; Southern Homestead Act (1866); U.S. Army and Reconstruction.

## Further Reading

Bentley, George R. *A History of the Freedmen's Bureau*. Philadelphia: University of Pennsylvania Press, 1955.

Carpenter, John A. *Sword and Olive Branch: Oliver Otis Howard*. Pittsburgh: University of Pittsburgh Press, 1964.

Cimbala, Paul A. *Under the Guardianship of the Nation: The Freedmen's Bureau and the Reconstruction of Georgia, 1865–1870*. Athens: University of Georgia Press, 1997.

Cimbala, Paul A., and Randall M. Miller, eds. *The Freedmen's Bureau and Reconstruction: Reconsiderations*. New York: Fordham University Press, 1999.

Egerton, Douglas R. *The Wars of Reconstruction: The Brief, Violent History of America's Most Progressive Era*. New York: Bloomsbury Press, 2014.

Fitzgerald, Michael W. *Splendid Failure: Postwar Reconstruction in the American South*. New York: Ivan R. Dee Publishers, 2008.

Foner, Eric. *Reconstruction Updated Edition: America's Unfinished Revolution, 1863–1877*. Reprint, New York: HarperCollins, 2014.

Guelzo, Allen C. *Fateful Lightning: A New History of the Civil War and Reconstruction*. New York: Oxford University Press, 2012.

Howard, Oliver Otis. *Autobiography of Oliver Otis Howard*. 2 vols. New York: The Baker & Taylor Co., 1908.

McFeely, William S. Yankee. *Stepfather: General O. O. Howard and the Freedmen*. New Haven, CT: Yale University Press, 1968.

## BUTLER, BENJAMIN FRANKLIN (1818–1893)

Congressman, Union general, and Reconstruction commander, Benjamin Butler was born in Deerfield, New Hampshire, and educated in Maine before moving to Massachusetts for his law practice. Butler gravitated toward the Democratic Party, and served in the state house and the state senate in the 1850s. Devoted to the Union, Butler sought a command in the federal volunteer army when the Civil War began. President Abraham Lincoln, who wanted support for the war across party lines, offered the Democrat an appointment as a volunteer major general in 1861. This marked a turning point, as Butler would transition from Democrat to Radical Republican over the next few years. In the war, Butler held a series of assignments, having to do more with politics than combat. After an initial posting in Maryland, Butler was sent to the coast of Virginia and at Fort Monroe, where he enunciated his controversial "contraband of war" policy, declaring that slaves were enemy property to be confiscated by the army.

Later in 1861, Butler led Union forces in engagements at Big Bethel, Virginia, and Hatteras Inlet, which led his most important assignment of the war—commanding the army expedition intended to occupy New Orleans and to begin wartime Reconstruction in Louisiana. Butler's army of 10,000 soldiers occupied New Orleans in May 1862. The general was determined to reestablish Louisiana's ties with the Union and replace Confederate with federal governance. Butler interpreted loyalty broadly, and trampled on Southern sensibilities as a result: it became illegal to insult Union soldiers or the U.S. flag (Butler ordered the execution of William Mumford, a local gambler who had torn the flag from atop a federal building); women who insulted Union soldiers were arrested as prostitutes; Conservative newspapers were shut down and churches closed until pro-Confederate messages ended. Conservatives replied, and accused the general of trading with confederates and stealing personal belongings, including silverware (the derogatory "Spoons Butler" derives from this). Meanwhile, the general took steps to clean up the city streets and reduce diseases. He inaugurated programs to feed the destitute, and replaced Confederate currency with

A powerful Massachusetts Democrat, Benjamin Butler received a general's commission by President Lincoln. Mediocrity and controversy marred Butler's wartime performance. After the war he shifted to the Republican Party, where as a senator from Massachusetts he ardently opposed President Johnson. (Library of Congress)

federal money in business and government transactions. Butler replaced pro-confederate politicians with pro-Union office holders, including the mayor of New Orleans. The general arranged Louisiana's first electoral steps under Lincoln's wartime Reconstruction plan, including elections for Congress, won by Michael Hahn and Benjamin Flanders, both long-time Louisiana residents now supporting the Republican Party. Unfortunately, the Lincoln administration sensed the pressure building against Butler, and reassigned him in December 1862. He commanded the army of the James in 1864 near Richmond, but delivered a lackluster performance.

After the war, Butler returned to politics—and to Congress—this time as a Republican. He served four terms in Congress, later switching back to the Democratic Party. In 1882, he switched back to the Democrats to be elected governor of Massachusetts.

*Joseph G. Dawson III*

*See also:* U.S. Army and Reconstruction.

## Further Reading

Dawson, Joseph G., III. *Army Generals and Reconstruction, Louisiana 1862–1877*. Baton Rouge: Louisiana State University Press, 1982.

Hearn, Chester. *When the Devil Came Down to Dixie: Ben Butler in New Orleans*. Baton Rouge: Louisiana State University Press, 1998.

Trefousse, Hans L. *Ben Butler: The South Called Him Beast!* New York: Twayne, 1957.

# C

## CAIN, RICHARD HARVEY (1825–1887)

Richard Harvey Cain was a black abolitionist, minister, editor, Republican state senator, and congressman from South Carolina. Born free in Greenbrier County, Virginia, Cain moved to Ohio and became an African Methodist Episcopal (AME) minister. As an abolitionist, Cain worked with Frederick Douglass, and supported the African Colonization Society's efforts to promote emigration to Africa in the late 1850s. He attended Wilberforce University in Ohio before relocating to a church in Brooklyn during the Civil War. Once the Civil War began, the AME focused on relief operations and education, and in 1864 Cain opened a series of freedmen's schools in Washington, D.C.

In May 1865, the Reverend Cain was transferred to Charleston, South Carolina, as superintendent of the AME Church missionary activities there. Through his efforts, the AME Church became the largest black Methodist denomination in the state by 1877. In 1866, Cain purchased a Republican newspaper, the *South Carolina Leader*, and became editor of the state's first black newspaper. Renamed the *Missionary Record*, Cain's newspaper covered the usual topics, but served primarily as a voice promoting freedmen's interests. The Reverend Cain is often considered the consummate preacher-politician. He participated in the November 1865 Colored Peoples Convention in Charleston, where blacks protested against racial strictures in the 1865 South Carolina Constitution and demanded equal civil rights.

Under Congressional (Radical) Reconstruction in 1867, Cain laid the groundwork for the state Republican Party, and was elected a delegate to the 1868 state constitutional convention. He led an unsuccessful effort to secure federal loans to assist freedpeople in buying land; its failure drove Cain to convince the convention to create a state land commission to assist small farmers and the landless. South Carolina was the only state to create such an agency, although its usefulness is still debated. The Reverend Cain served a term in the state senate (1868–1870) and two terms in Congress (1873–1875 and 1877–1879). After Reconstruction, the Reverend Cain encouraged black Carolinians to seek a future in Africa and he assumed a leadership role in the Liberian Exodus Movement 1877–1878, based in Charleston. In 1880, he was elected an AME bishop with responsibility for Louisiana and Texas. He died on January 18, 1887, in Washington, D.C.

*Bernard E. Powers Jr.*

**See also:** Abolitionists; Churches; South Carolina.

## Further Reading

Foner, Eric. *Freedom's Lawmakers: A Directory of Black Officeholders during Reconstruction.* New York: Oxford University Press, 1993.

Hildebrand, Reginald. *The Times Were Strange and Stirring: Methodist Preachers and the Crisis of Emancipation.* Durham, NC: Duke University Press, 1995.

Holt, Thomas. *Black over White: Negro Political Leadership in South Carolina during Reconstruction.* Urbana: University of Illinois Press, 1977.

Powers, Bernard E. " 'I Go to Set the Captives Free': The Activism of Richard Harvey Cain, Nationalist Churchman and Reconstruction-Era Leader," in Randy Finley and Thomas A. De Black, eds., *The Southern Elite and Social Change.* Fayetteville: University of Arkansas Press, 2002, pp. 34–52.

# CARDOZA, FRANCIS L. (1837–1903)

Francis L. Cardoza was a black minister, educator, Republican secretary of state, and state treasurer in Reconstruction South Carolina. Born free in Charleston to a wealthy Jewish merchant and a free black woman, as a youth Cardoza attended private schools for free blacks. He pursued ministerial education at the University of Glasgow and later studied in Presbyterian seminaries in London and Edinburgh. In 1864, he returned to the United States, was ordained a congregational minister, and accepted a pastorate in New Haven, Connecticut. In June 1865, following the end of the Civil War, Cardoza joined the American Missionary Association, to promote freedmen's education. He returned to Charleston to help establish the Avery Normal Institute, a private school for black Charlestonians. Given the relationship between freedmen's education and the political environment, Cardoza was soon swept into politics. During Presidential Reconstruction, he openly criticized the discriminatory nature of South Carolina's new constitution and its Black Codes. With the advent of Congressional domination, the landscape changed. Cardoza was a founding member of the state's Republican Party and president of the Union League. In the Constitutional Convention of 1868 he served as chairman of the education committee, guiding the state to its first publicly financed statewide school system. Elected secretary of state in April 1868, Cardoza became the first black elected to statewide office in South Carolina history. He was elected state treasurer in 1872, and held the position until 1877.

Despite some radical tendencies, Cardoza had a reputation as a Moderate, reform-minded politician. When corruption crept into the state land commission, he resigned from its advisory board and (as secretary of state) commenced an investigation, ultimately reorganizing the entire agency. His integrity as treasurer so angered some legislators that they considered impeachment, a plot thwarted by a coalition of reform Republicans and Democrats. Cardoza was a close advisor to carpetbag governor Daniel Chamberlain, the reform Republican governor elected in 1872 and re-elected in 1874. Despite Republican reformers' best efforts, Democratic Conservative's use of the "shotgun plan" in 1876 redeemed the state, and the subsequent Compromise of 1877 ended Reconstruction in South Carolina. Retribution against Republican officials resulted in the arrest of many Reconstruction politicians, including Cardoza. Ironically, he was convicted of corruption while treasurer; he was subsequently pardoned in 1879. Francis Cardoza moved back north, and lived out his life in Washington, D.C., working for the Treasury Department and as a high school principal. He died on July 22, 1903.

*Bernard E. Powers Jr.*

**See also:** American Missionary Association (AMA); Black Suffrage.

## Further Reading

Bleser, Carol K. *The Promised Land: The History of the South Carolina Land Commission, 1869–1890.* Columbia: University of South Carolina Press, 1969.

Foner, Eric. *Freedom's Lawmakers: A Directory of Black Officeholders during Reconstruction.* Oxford: Oxford University Press, 1993.

Foner, Eric. *Reconstruction Updated Edition: America's Unfinished Revolution, 1863–1877.* Reprint, New York: HarperCollins, 2014.

Holt, Thomas. *Black over White: Negro Political Leadership in South Carolina during Reconstruction.* Urbana: University of Illinois Press, 1977.

Powers, Bernard E. Jr. "Francis L. Cardoza: An Early African American Urban Educator," in Roger Biles, ed., *The Human Tradition in Urban America.* Wilmington, DE: Scholarly Resources, 2002, pp. 37–52.

Underwood, James L., and W. Lewis Burke. *At Freedom's Door: African American Founding Fathers and Lawyers in Reconstruction South Carolina.* Columbia: University of South Carolina Press, 2000.

# CARPETBAGGERS

"Carpetbagger" was a pejorative nickname applied to white Northerners who moved South during or after the Civil War, most of whom were Republicans. The term first appeared in Alabama newspapers in late 1867, and by mid-1868 was in national use. The negative portrayal was central to the white South's depiction of Republicans as the dregs of Northern society, swarming over South like hungry locusts, their meager belongings stuffed in woolen carpetbags (a form of duffel bag). Corrupt and vindictive, these adventurers and opportunists came South to impose "Negro-Carpetbag rule," rob poor defeated whites, loot public treasuries, and sow decades of racial discord.

Although historians long ago disproved the myth, it remains embedded in popular culture, in large part due to books-turned-Hollywood film, such as *Birth of a Nation* (1915) and *Gone with the Wind* (1939). While some carpetbaggers were corrupt, as a group they were no worse than their Democratic enemies or politicians in the North. Some carpetbaggers, Mississippi governor Adelbert Ames and South Carolina governor Daniel H. Chamberlain are good examples, earned reputations for honesty. In North Carolina, even Judge Albion W. Tourgée's Democratic enemies conceded that he was fair, honest, and able. But there were bad apples: George E. Spencer, U.S. senator from Alabama, and Louisiana governor Henry Clay Warmoth had shady reputations, ranging from bribery and accepting gifts to buying votes and outright stealing.

Ironically, the historical record indicates the opposite, and reveals a positive image of these Northern transplants. Most carpetbaggers were young men in their 20s and 30s who

A Thomas Nast caricature depicting a "carpetbagger." This derogatory term applied to Northerners who came south after the war; Southerners claimed such persons were mere fortune-hunters, bent on taking advantage of the region's political and economic chaos. (Bettmann/Corbis)

had served in the Union army during the Civil War, many as officers in the U.S. Colored Troops. Most settled in the South *before* Congressional Reconstruction, so had little intention of a political career. They came to fill legitimate needs or pursue noble reforms, with backgrounds in business, law, medicine, and educators. Many came as Freedmen's Bureau agents. They were well educated, often with college backgrounds, and brought to the South capital and business know-how severely lacking in a former plantation-slave economy.

With the advent of Congressional Reconstruction, the Northerners' education, experience, and general concern for improving freedmen's lives made them as leaders of the new Southern Republican Party. Although they numbered no more than a few hundred men in any state, between 1867 and 1877, carpetbaggers held public offices of every description across the former Confederacy. They served as state legislators, judges, sheriffs, and governors; overall, carpetbaggers held about one-fourth of the public offices in most of the Reconstruction states. A total of 10 governors were carpetbaggers, 17 carpetbaggers served in the U.S. Senate and 44 in the U.S. House of Representatives.

As a group, carpetbaggers were practical men of affairs who combined self-interest and reform as they guided new state constitutions. They were a modernizing, progressive influence in the South, advocating state-supported public schools and state penitentiaries; promoting railroads, canals, and harbor clearance; and ridding the South of public whipping posts, imprisonment for debt, and other outdated practices. They backed liberalized divorce laws and separate property rights for married women. Above all, they supported civil and political rights for blacks.

The carpetbaggers' moment was brief. Southern Democrats did not simply seek to remove Republicans from office; they sought to destroy the Republican Party as an entity and remove from social and political power its members, be they carpetbaggers, blacks, or scalawags (native Southern Republicans). To this end, Democratic Conservatives employed fraud, assassination, torture, and extortion. From 1874 to 1876 Conservative Southern whites terrorized carpetbaggers, scalawags, and blacks across the Deep South. In one particularly egregious case, the Louisiana White League murdered six carpetbaggers in Red River Parish, Louisiana—four of the victims were members of the Twitchell family from

Vermont. Shot six times, the head of the family, Marshall H. Twitchell, survived after the amputation of both arms. Democrats who controlled the private wealth of the Southern states—the plantations, banks, and businesses—used economic power against Republicans. Under such pressures, by the mid-1870s, Republican regimes splintered into factions pitting scalawags against carpetbaggers, blacks against whites, and carpetbaggers against carpetbaggers. Republican governments lasted longest in state with higher black percentages, as the carpetbag-black alliance proved the most resilient. Hence, Congressional Reconstruction in Mississippi lasted until 1875, and the Republican regimes in Louisiana, South Carolina, and Florida lasted until the Compromise of 1877.

When Reconstruction ended, many carpetbaggers returned North. Former Mississippi governor Adelbert Ames made a fortune in Massachusetts through business investments and mechanical inventions (notably pencil sharpeners and fire-engine ladders). South Carolina governor Daniel H. Chamberlain became a prominent member of the New York City bar, while Albion W. Tourgée also settled in New York City and wrote a best-selling novel, *A Fool's Errand* (1879), a semi-autobiographical account of a North Carolina carpetbagger. Mentioned above, Marshall H. Twitchell became an American consul to Canada, and busted a Spanish spying operation in Montreal during the Spanish-American War. His autobiography remained in storage for two generations before being published as *Carpetbagger from Vermont: The Autobiography of Marshall Harvey Twitchell* (1989). A few transplants remained in their adopted region: Powell Clayton became an Arkansas railroad president, a business promoter, and the owner of a 40,000-acre plantation on the Arkansas River. He wrote about his Reconstruction experience in *The Aftermath of the Civil War in Arkansas* (1915). Henry Clay Warmoth remained active in Louisiana business and politics, and from 1890 to 1893 was collector of the Port of New Orleans. His *War, Politics and Reconstruction: Stormy Days in Louisiana* (1930) is one of the best political memoirs of the period.

*Ted Tunnell*

**See also:** Ames, Adelbert (1835–1933); Chamberlain, Daniel Henry (1835–1907); Twitchell, Marshall H. (1840–1905); Warmoth, Henry Clay (1842–1931).

## Further Reading

Current, Richard N. *Those Terrible Carpetbaggers*. New York: Oxford University Press, 1988;

Foner, Eric. *Reconstruction Updated Edition: America's Unfinished Revolution, 1863–1877*. Reprint, New York: HarperCollins, 2014.

Hume, Richard L. "Carpetbaggers in the Reconstruction South: A Group Portrait of Outside Whites in the "Black and Tan" Constitutional Conventions." *Journal of American History* 64 (1977): 313–30.

Powell, Lawrence N. "The Politics of Livelihood: Carpetbaggers in the Deep South," in J. Morgan Kousser and James M. McPherson, eds., *Region, Race, and Reconstruction*. New York: Oxford University Press, 1982, pp. 315–47.

Tunnell, Ted. *Crucible of Reconstruction: War, Radicalism and Race in Louisiana, 1862–1877*. Baton Rouge: Louisiana State University Press, 1984.

Tunnell, Ted. *Edge of the Sword: The Ordeal of Carpetbagger Marshall H. Twitchell in the Civil War and Reconstruction*. Baton Rouge: Louisiana State University Press, 2001.

## CHAMBERLAIN, DANIEL HENRY (1835–1907)

Carpetbag governor of South Carolina from 1874 to 1877, Daniel Chamberlain was the ninth of 10 children born to Eli Chamberlain, a farmer in West Brookfield, Massachusetts. He entered Yale College in 1859, and although tempted to "bear a hand in this life-or-death struggle for the Union and for Freedom," he remained at Yale, graduating in 1862. Admitted to Harvard Law School, he withdrew after a year and joined the Fifth Massachusetts Cavalry, a black regiment, as a lieutenant. When his service ended in December 1865, he moved to Charleston, South Carolina, to settle the affairs of a friend, but remained and took up cotton planting. At this time South Carolina society and politics were in chaos, as defeat turned to Presidential Reconstruction, which then gave way to congressional control and the rise of the Southern Republican Party.

Congress's 1867 Military Reconstruction Act required the calling of a constitutional convention based on universal manhood suffrage, but while that meant black males now comprised 60 percent of South Carolina's voters, few men in the state possessed both the education and the experience to rewrite a constitution. With his education, abolitionist credentials and legal mind, Chamberlain earned a seat at the 1868 constitutional convention and impressed his colleagues—and even the Democratic press—with his intelligence and ability. Following the writing and ratification of the new constitution, Chamberlain was elected state attorney general; he served from 1868 to 1872. This position also made him a member of the three-person state financial board, his most controversial role during Reconstruction. He was deeply implicated in the board's over-issue of state bonds and in its use of a corrupt financial agent. It is somewhat less clear whether Chamberlain himself benefited from any of these frauds. After failing to garner the Republican gubernatorial nomination in 1872, Chamberlain pursued his law private, but re-entered politics to counter the state's (and the party's) national reputation for corruption and financial disorder. Chamberlain won the governorship in 1874, and immediately embarked on reform. He replaced incompetent officeholders, cleaned out fraudulent agencies, and vetoed spending bills. He increasingly won praise from Moderates of both parties—and condemnation from hardliners in his own, especially after overturning the legislature's appointments to three judgeships in 1875. Under fire from members of his own party, Chamberlain was vulnerable and Conservative Democrats seized the opportunity. A series of riots and shootings during the campaign of 1876—largely between Republican black militia and Democratic "gun clubs"—forced the governor to call for federal aid. This revealed the weakness of his administration, incensed white Carolinians, and unified the Democratic Party behind former Confederate General Wade Hampton III. The campaign witnessed a Democratic onslaught of murder, harassment, intimidation, and fraud; in the fall, both parties claimed victory, with Chamberlain and Hampton each being sworn by respective allies. At the street level it came down to force, with Hampton's army of "red shirts" amassed against units of federal infantry protecting Chamberlain in the Columbia State House.

Confusion at the state level mirrored confusion at the national level, which remained uncertain until the so-called Compromise of 1877. In April 1877, a special commission afforded disputed electoral votes (including some from South Carolina) to Republican President Rutherford B. Hayes. He abandoned his predecessor's activist Southern policy, and ordered federal troops to not interfere in state politics. Without federal support Chamberlain had no choice but to resign, telling his Republican supporters, "To-day—April 10,

1877—by the order of the President whom your votes alone rescued from overwhelming defeat, the Government of the United States abandons you, deliberately withdraws from you its support, with the full knowledge that the lawful government of the State will be speedily overthrown." Soon after, Chamberlain left South Carolina for New York, where he prospered as a lawyer. By the end of his life, he adopted the wrongheaded scientific attitudes of the time, embraced the Democratic Party, and consorted with white supremacists rather than reform-minded proponents of equality.

*Hyman Rubin III*

*See also:* Carpetbaggers; South Carolina.

## Further Reading

Allen, Walter. *Governor Chamberlain's Administration in South Carolina.* New York: G. P. Putnam's Sons, 1888.

Current, Richard N. *Those Terrible Carpetbaggers.* New York: Oxford University Press, 1988.

Fowler, Wilton B. "A Carpetbagger's Conversion to White Supremacy." *North Carolina Historical Review* 43, no. 3 (1966): 286–304.

Simkins, Francis B., and Robert H. Woody. *South Carolina during Reconstruction.* Chapel Hill: University of North Carolina Press, 1932.

Zuczek, Richard. *State of Rebellion: Reconstruction in South Carolina.* Columbia: University of South Carolina Press, 1996.

# CHANDLER, ZACHARIAH (1813–1879)

A leading Radical Republican and U.S. senator from Michigan, Zachariah Chandler was born in Bedford, New Hampshire. After local schooling and working at various jobs, he migrated to Michigan in 1833. In Detroit, he established a successful dry goods store and invested in road-building; politics, however, was his major career interest. Elected in 1851 as Whig mayor of Detroit, Chandler moved to the more radical wing of the party, embracing abolition, supporting the Underground Railroad and abolition, and heatedly opposing to the Kansas-Nebraska Act of 1854. He assumed an early leadership role in the infant Republican Party, and in 1857 was elected to the U.S. Senate; he remained until 1875.

As a senator during the Civil War, he pushed aggressive military operations against rebels and their property, and early on linked ended slavery to saving the Union. Creator of the Joint Select Committee on the Conduct of the War, he criticized both General George McClellan's military moderation and President Abraham Lincoln's wartime Reconstruction plan. Chandler called for more substantial change, including voting rights and grants of land for African Americans (the so-called 40 acres and a mule). The source of land was obvious: confiscate the property of Confederate leaders. It was no surprise Chandler clashed early and often with President Andrew Johnson; he advocated his removal from office, and voted "yea" in the unsuccessful conviction effort that followed Johnson's impeachment.

Chandler's political career involved more than Reconstruction. Not straying far from his Whig-Republican roots, he supported higher tariffs and the creation of national banks, trusting that federal aid was necessary for economic growth. Chandler lost his senate seat in the 1874 election, but President Ulysses S. Grant appointed him secretary of the interior. He has been praised highly for his reforms within the Bureau of Indian Affairs.

A successful business person—his estate exceeded $2 million—he also possessed high ideals, as expressed in his abolitionism and nationalism. He believed that civil rights, federal authority, moral force, and economic nationalism all worked for the greater good. This perspective made the failure of Reconstruction an especially bitter disappointment.

*Donald K. Pickens*

**See also:** Congressional Reconstruction; Field Order No. 15; Johnson, Andrew (1808–1875); Joint Select Committee on the Conduct of War; Presidential Reconstruction.

## Further Reading

Harris, Wilmer C. *Public Life of Zachariah Chandler, 1851–1875.* Lansing: Michigan Historical Commission, 1917.

Williams, T. Harry. *Lincoln and the Radicals.* Madison: University of Wisconsin Press, 1941.

[No Author.] *Zachariah Chandler: An Outline Sketch of his Life and Public Services.* Detroit: Post and Tribune Co., 1880.

## CHASE, SALMON PORTLAND (1808–1873)

Born in Cornish, New Hampshire, the eighth child in a family of 11, Salmon Portland Chase's parents, Ithamar, a glassmaker, and Janette, also ran a tavern. His father died when Chase was nine and for economic reasons the family moved to Ohio. There Chase lived with his uncle, Philander Chase, an Episcopal bishop from whom Chase developed a strong sense of self-discipline, and a concern for religious and social obligations. Twin energies— limitless ambition and a burning desire to do good—shaped his entire life. Chase graduated from Dartmouth in 1826, and moved to Washington D.C. to study law, but relocated to the expanding West in hopes of greater opportunity. He soon became successful—financially, politically, and socially—in Cincinnati; his private life was ridden with death and sadness, which spurred him on to perform great deeds publicly.

Chase joined the American Sunday School Union in 1837, and soon became a vital part of the antislavery crusade. He gained attention for defending fugitive slaves and slaves brought North by owners, arguing state statutes, not the constitution, defined slavery, thus such persons became free—an interesting foreshadowing of the Dred Scott argument 20 years later. He joined the abolitionist Liberty Party in 1841, migrated to the Free Soil Party by the late 1840s, and entered the U.S. Senate in 1849. There he led the fight against the Kansas-Nebraska Act, which helped him solidify his leadership in the new Republican Party. He returned to Ohio, was elected governor in 1855, and hoped that the presidential nomination might be his in 1856. When the bid went to John C. Fremont, Chase returned to the Senate, but his gaze still fell upon the White House; he was deeply disappointed when a relatively junior Abraham Lincoln won the nomination—and the election—in 1860. Despite some bitter feelings, Chase defended Lincoln's refusal to compromise during the secession crisis; his loyalty and background earned him the secretary of the treasury position in 1861. Chase's contributions were extraordinary.

He ranks second to Alexander Hamilton in creating a significant public fiscal policy, and only behind Lincoln and Secretary of War Edwin Stanton for his contribution to winning the war.

As secretary, he improved collection of taxes and insisted on honesty and weeded out any hint of corruption. He forced paper money as legal tender through Congress and by 1863 had established a national banking system. His system of bonds and loans avoided wartime inflation, and kept taxes low while still paying for the war.

Nor did he abandon his reforming spirit: He was ahead of Lincoln in moving toward freeing the slaves and thereby changing the dynamic of the Civil War. Chase pushed Lincoln toward emancipation without reference to colonization or compensation. Always mindful of religious context for human action, Chase placed "In God we trust" on

Salmon P. Chase, one of the earliest and most prominent Republicans, served as secretary of the treasury during the war, and Chief Justice of the United States during Reconstruction. (Library of Congress)

the new greenbacks. But his relationship soured as the 1864 election approached, as Chase still pined for the White House; in June 1864, Chase left the Lincoln's cabinet. Yet within six months, Lincoln appointed Chase chief justice of the U.S. Supreme Court. The appointment illustrated the centrality of Chase's role in the events and policies of the day. In 1866, in *Ex parte Milligan*, he upheld that if civil courts were functioning, military courts could not. In the *Texas v. White* case in 1869, he ruled that the Union was inviolable, upholding the view that the rebel states never left the Union. Perhaps his most interesting role came during the impeachment and trial of President Andrew Johnson. As Chief Justice, he sat as judge in the proceedings, which riveted the nation's attention. His legal acumen and fairness, in a viciously intense political climate, reflected his honesty and his genuine sense of justice. Never achieving his ultimate goal of president, Chase nonetheless occupied a central role in the events of Civil War and Reconstruction. He died in New York City on May 7, 1873.

*Donald K. Pickens*

**See also:** Lincoln, Abraham (1809–1865); Supreme Court.

## Further Reading

Blue, Frederick J. *Salmon P. Chase: A Life in Politics.* Kent, OH: Kent State University Press, 1987.

Chase, Salmon P. *Diary and Correspondence of Salmon P. Chase.* New York: Da Capo Press, 1971.

Hart, A. B. *Salmon Portland Chase.* Boston: Houghton Mifflin, 1909.

Niven, John. *Salmon P. Chase: A Biography.* New York: Oxford University Press, 1995.

Smith, Donnal V. *Chase and Civil War Politics.* Columbus, OH: The F. J. Heer Publishing Co., 1931.

# CHURCHES

Churches played a central role in the Civil War and Reconstruction afterward. Northern denominations extended missionary aid to the freedpeople, and Northern churches emerged from the war proclaiming the United States a redeemer nation on a holy mission. On the other hand, white Southern churches became rallying points for a defeated people needing a sense of common purpose. White Southern ministers figured prominently in the cult of the "Lost Cause," which cast the Confederacy as a noble enterprise and the Confederate soldier as the embodiment of Christian character. Blacks, meanwhile, abandoned biracial churches in the South to create their own churches, which became the foundations of black political leadership and community. The major Protestant denominations (Baptists, Methodists, and Presbyterians) that had split before the war over slavery and related theological issues remained divided during, and in part because of, Reconstruction.

During and after the war, Northern churches linked religion with relief. The U.S. Sanitary Commission and the Christian Commission—the principal Union agencies developed during the war to provide support for war widows, orphans, and wounded soldiers—grew out of and relied on Protestant churches for resources and recruits. The millions of Bibles, religious tracts, and pamphlets that they distributed during the war put a religious stamp on the conflict: war was a test of faith and holy national purpose, thus so too must be the efforts to bind up the nation's wounds.

The Northern churches' special interest was promoting Reconstruction through education. During and after the war, the Protestant religious press called for educational aid to the freedpeople, and individual churches and denominations sponsored schools, supplied and paid teachers, and distributed countless Christian reading materials to evangelize among whites and blacks. Best known among such ministries were the Quaker-run freedmen's schools in the South Carolina sea islands, some of which continued well into the 20th century. Virtually every Protestant denomination set up schools. The United Presbyterian Church in North America, for example, established a Freedmen's Mission in 1863, and the U.S. Presbyterian Church appointed a Committee for Freedmen in 1865—from which Presbyterians founded and maintained black industrial and teacher-training schools in several Southern states. Especially active was the American Missionary Association (AMA), which carried its antebellum and wartime antislavery energy into Reconstruction. The AMA first did so as part of the Port Royal Experiment in South Carolina, but its principal and most enduring contributions were establishing more than 500 schools for blacks in every former Confederate state. Northern churches and the AMA often worked in hand with the Freedmen's Bureau, which combined free labor ideology with evangelical interest in setting up, staffing, and supplying schools. Northern missionaries in the South established Sunday schools, a practice adopted by many Southern white churches to instill respect for authority in their youth and to revitalize their communities with their own lessons in morality, Christian discipline, and the basics of reading, writing, and arithmetic. The Catholic Church lent some support, but a swelling tide of diverse Catholic immigrants diverted the church's attention to northern cities. Independent action by the freedpeople paralleled activity by white churches.

Eager to assert their freedom, blacks left biracial Baptist and Methodist congregations to form their churches free of any white oversight. The African Methodist Episcopal (AME) Church, the largest and most powerful black denomination, evangelized vigorously among the freedpeople, and encouraged and underwrote new churches; but their quest for autonomy convinced many Southern blacks to start independent congregations rather than affiliate with the Northern-based AME Church. Black churches provided both spiritual and practical benefits: black churches were the meeting place for the black community in every locale; churches operated schools, sponsored social events, established mutual aid associations, burial societies, and literary organizations. Preachers stressed self-reliance and moral order as the path to spiritual and temporal salvation, delivering a powerful messianic message that echoed in black politics. Churches served as the venues for political debate and political mobilizing, with ministers pounding home the duty to vote. Some ministers used their speaking and organizational skills, and their stature in the black community, to enter politics directly. Richard H. Cain in South Carolina, Henry M. Turner and Tunis G. Campbell in Georgia, and James D. Lynch in Mississippi were prominent minister-politicians, a few of the more than 100 black ministers who won election to Southern legislatures. The political relationship between black churches and the Republican Party made them targets of terrorist groups like the Ku Klux Klan. Vigilantes burned churches, assassinated and kidnapped ministers, and terrorized members to snuff out political activism.

White Southern churches also provided for physical relief and spiritual renewal. Many white communities were intent on rebuilding the physical structures damaged or destroyed during the war, while also rebuilding the shattered spiritual and social lives. Men crippled by wartime injuries and disease found it hard to explain their sacrifice, and women left widowed or abandoned doubted the old truths about God as a protecting father and their men as Christian patriarchs. The white churches responded by restoring community through worship, a full array of social services, Sunday schools, and programs to bring families together in the church. Women gained new authority by engaging in church-sponsored reform efforts, such as temperance and orphan relief, and running fund drives to support church renovations and veterans' needs. White Southern churches also entered politics, objecting to the unholy Republican-controlled "black and tan" legislatures, and insisting on a racial order consistent with biblical "truths." Many white Southern clergymen took up the "Lost Cause" by arguing that God had not forsaken the South in allowing Northern victory; rather, the argument went, He was chastising the South for its sins of selfishness, which had undercut the noble Confederate experiment in independence. Ministers likened the South to the Israel of old, thereby encouraging white Southerners that, as God's "chosen people," they could escape this temporary exile of Reconstruction by acting right in politics and public life. Central to this myth-making was the deification of the Confederate soldier, especially Robert E. Lee, and the construction and consecration of monuments, gravesites, and other public reminders of what Christian duty demanded. The public involvement of ministers and church club women in rituals celebrating the Lost Cause ideology, such as Confederate Memorial Day, bound church and state in "redeeming" the South from Republican rule.

Sadly, by the end of the century, Northern white churches had abandoned the "mission" of Reconstruction, and had adopted the racist trend of sectional reconciliation that emphasized the nobility of the white Civil War soldier (regardless of uniform), ignored slavery as the war's cause, and criticized Reconstruction as a mistake. What did not change were the distinctions among the white and black churches that flowed from Reconstruction, and the role of black churches in social and political life. These attributes persisted into the 20th century to re-emerge during the modern civil rights movement.

*Randall M. Miller*

**See also:** Bureau of Refugees, Freedmen, and Abandoned Lands; Cain, Richard Harvey (1825–1887); Lost Cause; Lynch, James D. (1839–1872); Redemption.

## Further Reading

Blum, Edward J. *Reforging the White Republic: Race, Religion, and American Nationalism, 1865–1898*. Baton Rouge: Louisiana State University Press, 2005.

Cimbala, Paul A., and Randall M. Miller, eds. *The Freedmen's Bureau and Reconstruction: Reconsiderations*. New York: Fordham University Press, 1999.

Dvorak, Katharine L. *An African American Exodus: The Segregation of Southern Churches*. Brooklyn, NY: Carlson Publishing, 1991.

Friedman, Jean E. *The Enclosed Garden: Women and Community in the Evangelical South, 1830–1900*. Chapel Hill: University of North Carolina Press, 1985.

Howard, Victor B. *Religion and the Radical Republican Movement 1860–1870*. Lexington: University Press of Kentucky, 1990.

Jacoway, Elizabeth. *Yankee Missionaries in the South: The Penn School Experiment*. Baton Rouge: Louisiana State University Press, 1980.

McMillen, Sally G. *To Raise Up the South: Sunday Schools in Black and White Churches, 1865–1915*. Baton Rouge: Louisiana State University Press, 2001.

Miller, Randall M., Harry S. Stout, and Charles Reagan Wilson, eds. *Religion and the American Civil War*. New York: Oxford University Press, 1998.

Stowell, Daniel W. *Rebuilding Zion: The Religious Reconstruction of the South, 1863–1877*. New York: Oxford University Press, 1998.

Walker, Clarence E. *A Rock in a Weary Land: The African Methodist Episcopal Church during the Civil War and Reconstruction*. Baton Rouge: Louisiana State University Press, 1982.

Wilson, Charles Reagan. *Baptized in Blood: The Religion of the Lost Cause, 1865–1920*. Athens: University of Georgia Press, 1980.

# CIVIL RIGHTS

From its founding, the United States has always been a culture of rights. Such language, in the European natural law tradition, informs America's founding documents, especially the Declaration of Independence and the Bill of Rights of the U.S. Constitution. Prior to the Civil War and Reconstruction, the individual states were the keepers of the large share of these civil liberties. The national government did not often interfere in the states' civil matters. In other words, our modern conception of civil rights, which includes the active national protection of, and the ability of groups to claim, rights in the event of their violation by states or by private parties, did not exist. The Bill of Rights was thus a very limited set of guarantees, having little to do with how people experienced their daily lives.

The Civil War and Reconstruction transformed how Americans thought about rights, and transformed the federal government's role regarding those rights. But in order for civil rights to acquire any real meaning, the idea that a group of people (namely African Americans) could even claim rights first needed legitimizing. In antebellum America, such notions existed in astonishingly few quarters. The Fugitive Slave Law of 1850 and the 1857 *Dred Scott v. Sanford* case had made clear that black people had no rights whatsoever in the minds of the most white Americans. So war and Reconstruction released an intellectual revolution, one that changed America's existing culture in such a way that civil rights became a legitimate, supportable issue. The startling shift in thinking about slavery within the Republican Party between 1861 and 1865 was an example of this phenomenon.

In early 1861, Congress was ready to approve a constitutional amendment to protect slavery; within months that support had eroded. Congress in 1862 repealed the Fugitive Slave Law, abolished slavery in the District of Columbia, and allowed the Union army to confiscate slaves. President Lincoln's Emancipation Proclamation was immensely important, as it defined the nature of the war and allowed black enlistment. By late 1864, whites were backing a constitutional amendment outlawing slavery. This evolution exemplified the shift in thought regarding rights, even something as basic as the right to life, to own one's labor, and to be a free human being—not someone's property.

## Republicans, Congress, and Protecting Rights

The Thirteenth Amendment, ratified in 1865, set into law the notion that civil rights might be something African Americans could claim; the second article of the amendment clearly stated that, "Congress shall have the power to enforce this article by appropriate legislation." So Congress would provide the necessary protections, so African Americans could be free. Race, civil rights, and an assertive national government were now connected. In 1866, in response to the restrictive Black Codes passed by Southern states, Congress passed the Civil Rights Act of 1866, which for the first time defined citizenship in national terms, entitling American citizens to certain rights. Among these was the ability to make and enforce contracts; to bring lawsuits in court; to hold, conduct, and defend personal property; and to seek legal action in federal court against those who violated these rights. While symbolically important, its impact proved minimal in practice. Congress then went further, fearing that a less-progressive body could react on promises. The result was the Fourteenth Amendment to the Constitution, ratified in 1868. The amendment sought to solidify the spirit found in the Civil Rights Act by embedding protection in the U.S. Constitution itself, rather than in a law that could be nullified by some future court. In effect, the Fourteenth Amendment overturned the *Dred Scott* decision, expanding national citizenship and changing the traditional relationship between the national government, the states, and individuals; from this point forward individual were citizens of the nation first and foremost, of their state only secondarily. The amendment mandated that no state could make or enforce any law which abridged rights of citizens of the United States; states could not deprive a person of life, liberty, or property without due process of law nor could a state deny a person within its jurisdiction equal protection of the laws.

## Enforcement Acts and the Courts

Republican supporters argued that the amendment gave Congress the right to ensure the civil rights of American citizens. As a result, Congress followed with more specific legislation to curtail the widespread violation of African American rights through economic coercion, fraud, violence, and intimidation. In 1870 and 1871, Congress passed three Enforcement Acts, designed to stop Ku Klux Klan terrorism. In addition to helping stomp out the vigilante organization, the acts made individual acts of violence and conspiracy federal crimes, laying further groundwork for the modern meaning of civil rights. Whereas earlier legislation provided protection against state interference with civil rights, now Republicans expanded national government authority to include the acts of private individuals. Yet just as quickly the Supreme Court began undermining the implications of civil rights legislation: in the *Slaughterhouse* decision of 1873, the court ruled that the Fourteenth Amendment protected only those rights specifically emanating from national, rather than state, citizenship; the states retained their authority over the vast majority of civil rights that African Americans might experience in their daily lives. In 1876, based upon the limited definition of citizenship proposed in *Slaughterhouse*, the court further narrowed national authority in *United States v. Cruikshank*. The court decided that the Fourteenth Amendment's Enforcement Acts applied only to violations by states and *not* by individuals. Reflecting a growing acceptance of blacks as second-class citizens, the court effectively rendered the national government powerless to protect black civil rights.

## The Civil Rights Act of 1875

With the revolutionary possibilities of Reconstruction evaporating, Congress enacted potentially one of the most far-reaching pieces of civil rights legislation in U.S. history—although in practice the act had little value. The Civil Rights Act of 1875, passed largely in homage to Senator Charles Sumner (who died in 1874) made racial discrimination and exclusion in public accommodations illegal, providing for "full and equal" use of inns, theaters, and public transportation. The act also stipulated that race could not be a factor in jury selection. But African Americans shouldered the burden of enforcing the Civil Rights Act of 1875, for they needed to pursue violations in the federal courts. Few tried; those who did found the court bureaucracy too confusing, too backlogged, or too racist. Following an all-too-familiar pattern, the Supreme Court in the Civil Rights Cases of 1883 struck down nearly all aspects of the act, leaving only the jury section.

## Looking Ahead

The conception of civil rights created during the Reconstruction era largely endures to this day. By the end of Reconstruction, as formal recourse for their grievances and claims evaporated, African American activists kept the idea alive, while the masses of black Americans

(North and South) maintained the social institutions of family and church so crucial to the practice of Reconstruction politics. That the modern civil rights movement (1954–1965) emanated from black social institutions on the local level should come as no surprise—in many cases, the creation and cultivation of those institutions coincided with the intellectual construction of civil rights in America, an innovative way of thinking about African Americans—and all American citizens—and their relationship to the national government that was fashioned during the Reconstruction era.

*Peter A. Kuryla*

**See also:** Civil Rights Act of 1866; Civil Rights Act of 1875; Enforcement Acts (1870, 1871, 1875).

## Further Reading

Cortner, Richard C. *The Supreme Court and the Second Bill of Rights: The Fourteenth Amendment and the Nationalization of Civil Liberties.* Madison: University of Wisconsin, 1981.

Du Bois, W.E.B. *Black Reconstruction: An Essay toward the Part Which Black Folk Played in the Attempt to Reconstruct Democracy in America, 1860–1880.* New York: S.A. Russell, 1956.

Dworkin, Ronald. *Taking Rights Seriously.* Cambridge, MA: Harvard University Press, 1977.

Foner, Eric. *Reconstruction Updated Edition: America's Unfinished Revolution, 1863–1877.* Reprint, New York: HarperCollins, 2014.

Green, Robert P., ed. *Equal Protection and the African American Constitutional Experience: A Documentary History.* Westport, CT: Greenwood Press, 2000.

Hahn, Steven. *A Nation under Our Feet: Black Political Struggles in the Rural South from Slavery to the Great Migration.* Cambridge, MA: Harvard Belknap, 2003.

Hyman, Harold. *A More Perfect Union: The Impact of the Civil War and Reconstruction on the Constitution.* New York: Knopf, 1973.

Kaczorowski, Robert: *The Politics of Judicial Interpretation: The Federal Courts, Department of Justice, and Civil Rights, 1866–1876.* Dobbs Ferry, NY: Oceana, 1985.

# CIVIL RIGHTS ACT OF 1866

In the aftermath of the American Civil War, emancipated slaves in the South faced an uncertain future and occupied an uncertain status. Presidents Abraham Lincoln and then Andrew Johnson hoped that the defeated Confederate states would attempt to integrate African Americans into Southern society as free persons. When white Southerners failed to do so—and the notorious Black Codes proved this—Congress acted to secure basic civil and legal rights for the millions of emancipated slaves. The earliest of these efforts was the Civil Rights Act of 1866.

In December 1865, Republicans in control of the U.S. Congress created a 15-member Joint Committee on Reconstruction, which was made up of 6 senators and 9 representatives. This committee drafted the Civil Rights Act of 1866, which, for the first time, defined national citizenship and provided citizenship to anyone born or naturalized in the United States (the act did not apply to non-taxed Native Americans). Prior to the law, defining the rights of citizens was the sole prerogative of the states. The act overturned the South's Black Codes, which severely limited the legal and economic freedom of blacks after the Civil War, by restricting the ability to make contracts, to own property, and, in some instances, even to marry. The act was also a direct repudiated the 1857 case of *Dred Scott v. Sanford*, which denied citizenship to blacks, both slave and free. The 1866 act defined certain minimum legal rights of citizenship, including the right to serve on juries, to sue, to give evidence at trial, to make contracts, to serve as a witness, and to own private property, and provided a right to due process. Congress passed the act in March 1866, with unanimous Republican support in the House of Representatives and the support of all but three Republican senators. But President Johnson never accepted the idea of providing full citizenship to African Americans and vetoed the act, sending a hostile message back to Congress that further unified Republicans, many of whom found the act to be a reasonable, even conservative. The Republicans responded by passing law over the president's veto on April 9, 1866, the first significant piece of legislation passed over a presidential veto in American history. The concern over future battles with the president (and possibly the Supreme Court), led to the Fourteenth Amendment, which included similar language and ideals. The amendment was adopted by the Congress and sent to the states for ratification two months after the Civil Rights Act, on June 13, 1866.

The Civil Rights Act not only defined basic civil and legal rights but also provided for federal enforcement of those rights. Under the legislation, Congress gave the states concurrent jurisdiction over civil rights, except for the power to regulate the rights named in the act on the basis of race, color, or previous condition of servitude. Those found violating the law were subject to fines and imprisonment in federal court. Moreover, the army and navy were given the power to enforce the act. After his veto was overturned, President Johnson remained openly opposed to the act; the executive branch did little to enforce the legislation, removed army commanders who did, and vigorously campaigned against the ratification of the Fourteenth Amendment, all of which contributed to Congress's move to impeach and remove the President in 1868.

*Daniel W. Hamilton*

**See also:** Abolition of Slavery; Bureau of Refugees, Freedmen, and Abandoned Lands; Congressional Reconstruction; Emancipation Proclamation (1863); Presidential Reconstruction.

## Further Reading

"Kramer, L. D., L. G. Sager, J. E. Fleming, A. S. Greene, R. J. Kaczarowski, A. Saiger, and B. C. Zipursky. Symposium: 'Theories of Taking the Constitution Seriously Outside the Courts.'" *Fordham Law Review* 73 (2005): 1415.

# CIVIL RIGHTS ACT OF 1875

The Civil Rights Act of 1875 was the last civil rights statute of the Reconstruction period. Before its enactment, the country had added three amendments to the U.S. Constitution, and Republican congressional leaders had passed several enforcement measures to combat antiblack discrimination and violence. Senator Charles Sumner introduced the bill, and his death in March 1874 prompted colleagues to push its passage as a form of tribute to the influential Radical Republican from Massachusetts. The senator had previously proposed the bill every year since 1870, arguing that the Thirteenth and Fourteenth Amendments authorized federal protection for black civil rights, including access to such public, quasi-public, and private accommodations as schools, inns and theaters, churches, and cemeteries. Sumner called private racial discrimination a "badge of slavery" and was prohibited by the Thirteenth Amendment.

But by the mid-1870s, the country had tired of Reconstruction, and commitment to black rights had faded; nevertheless, respect for Sumner and Republicans' desire to appeal to black voters after the Democratic victories in the 1874 state and congressional elections energized the party (albeit briefly). Still the act that Congress passed in 1875 fell short of Sumner's goals, excluding such controversial areas as schools and cemeteries. The statute, titled "An act to protect all citizens in their civil and legal rights", stipulated that all Americans should have equal access to such public accommodations as inns and theaters, public conveyances on land or water, and places of amusement in general. It prohibited racial discrimination in the selection of federal and state juries, and gave the federal courts exclusive jurisdiction over both civil and criminal cases arising under the law. Many Americans in both the North and South opposed it as a dangerous expansion of federal power into private affairs. In 1880, in *Ex parte Virginia and Strauder v. West Virginia*, the U.S. Supreme Court upheld the jury section, but sections 1 and 2 (dealing with public accommodations) were voided in 1883 in the Civil Rights Cases. These cases, five cases from California, Kansas, Missouri, New Jersey, and Tennessee, tested the application of section 5 of the Fourteenth Amendment, and involved innkeepers, theater owners, and a railroad. By an 8 to 1 vote, the Court declared that the Fourteenth Amendment limited only official state action, not private action. In addition, the Court cited that although the Thirteenth Amendment prohibited slavery and its "badges," denial of access to a hotel, restaurant, or railroad car was not a reinstitution of slavery. The Court's narrow interpretation of the Fourteenth Amendment severely limited the provision's usefulness in battling racial discrimination over the next century. As a result, Congress did not pass another public accommodations bill until 1964; this time framed on Congress's Commerce Power.

*Claudine L. Ferrell*

*See also:* Civil Rights; Jim Crow Laws.

## Further Reading

Donald, David. *Charles Sumner and the Rights of Man*. New York: Knopf, 1970.

Gillette, William. *Retreat from Reconstruction, 1869–1879*. Baton Rouge: Louisiana State University Press, 1979.

# CLAYTON, POWELL (1833–1914)

Union general and Reconstruction governor of Arkansas (1868–1871), Powell Clayton was born on August 7, 1833, in Bethel County, Pennsylvania, to John and Ann (Clarke)

Originally from Pennsylvania, Powell Clayton rose to the rank of general in the Union army. He remained in the South after the war, and as a Republican dominated Arkansas politics as governor and U.S. senator. (Library of Congress)

Clayton. He attended Partridge Military Academy in Pennsylvania, and then studied civil engineering before moving to Kansas in 1855. A Unionist and Northern War Democrat during the secession crisis, he joined the Leavenworth Light Infantry (United States) and rose to the rank of brigadier general by the Civil War's end. Finishing the war in Arkansas, he settled on a plantation near Pine Bluff, and married Adaline McGraw, the daughter of a Confederate major. Clayton did not enter politics until the beginning of Congressional Reconstruction, drawn by interest in the Radical Republican's program. Under the 1867 Reconstruction Acts the state held a constitutional convention, which drew up a new constitution to enfranchise blacks, disfranchise former confederates, and recognize the Thirteenth Amendment to the U.S. Constitution. New state elections were held, and Clayton was elected "carpetbag" governor in 1868.

Clayton's tenure met with stiff resistance and made significant improvement. His greatest challenge was law and order, as the Democratic Party, and its political action arm the Ku Klux Klan, used violence and extortion to reimpose antebellum social and political trappings. Clayton built on a base of loyal mountain residents and newly enfranchised freedmen, and fought the Klan to a standstill; he even survived an assassination attempt.

Clayton's government established Arkansas's first a public education system and funded railroad construction. By the end of the decade, state Liberal Republicans in Arkansas turned against both President Ulysses S. Grant and Governor Clayton and allied themselves with the Democrats to wrest control away from the governor. Clayton manipulated legislator's terms to retain hold of the state, then earned a Senate seat and moved to Washington in 1871. His structure suffered under the Brooks-Baxter War in 1874, but incredibly Clayton remained in charge of federal appointments and positions in Arkansas until his retirement in 1912. Among his later perks was appointment as ambassador to Mexico, serving from 1897 to 1905. Clayton was by far one of the ablest and most effective of the Republican Reconstruction governors. His memoir, *The Aftermath of the Civil War in Arkansas* (1915), is a straightforward defense of his actions, based on research from documents and newspapers.

*Michael B. Dougan*

***See also:*** Black Suffrage; Carpetbaggers; Constitutional Conventions; Military Reconstruction Acts (1867–1868); Union League of America; U.S. Army and Reconstruction.

## Further Reading

Burnside, William H. *The Honorable Powell Clayton*. Conway: University of Central Arkansas Press, 1991.

Clayton, Powell. *The Aftermath of the Civil War in Arkansas*. New York: Neale, 1915.

Donovan, Timothy P., Willard B. Gatewood Jr., and Jeannie M. Whayne, eds. *The Governors of Arkansas: Essays in Political Biography*. Fayetteville: University of Arkansas Press, 1995.

## COLFAX, SCHUYLER (1823–1885)

Congressman and later vice president of the United States, Colfax brought little leadership and much questionable behavior to his political career. Born on March 23, 1823, to working-class parents in New York City, Colfax entered the workforce as a clerk. After his father's death his mother remarried and the family moved to New Carlisle, Indiana. Colfax grew interested in politics. Elected county auditor in 1841–1849, he moved to South Bend. For nearly 20 years, he operated a newspaper that turned into an effective instrument for Whigs and, later, Republicans.

He was elected to the House of Representatives, and served from 1855 to 1869. Although Speaker of the House for nine years, he developed no major legislation, but was a loyal party man who backed his supporters. Colfax was a safe addition to the Republican's Ulysses S. Grant ticket in 1868, but his tenure was soon mired in scandal and corruption. A great benefactor of financial support from railroads, he used a railroad pass as a natural benefit of his position. He and financier Jay Cooke were close associates, and it was little surprise Colfax into the infamous Credit Mobilier scandal. He was open about his interests, and felt no shame in accepting gifts from lobbyists. Perhaps hearing rumors of legal action, Colfax left government service in 1873 (although never charged with a violation). In Indiana, he remained popular, often touring as a lecturer. He died on January 13, 1885, during a speaking tour. Not a reformer or moralist Radical, he was more typical of the Gilded Age's politician as spoilsman.

*Donald K. Pickens*

Schuyler Colfax, congressman from New York, served as Speaker of the House and vice president during Ulysses S. Grant's first presidential term. (Library of Congress)

*See also:* Grant, Ulysses S. (1822–1885).

## Further Reading

Morgan, H. Wayne. *The Gilded Age*. Syracuse, NY: Syracuse University Press, 1963.

Smith, Willard H. *Schuyler Colfax: The Changing Fortunes of a Political Idol*. Indianapolis: Indiana Historical Bureau, 1952.

Summers, Mark W. *Party Games: Getting, Keeping, and Using Power in Gilded Age Politics*. Chapel Hill: University of North Carolina Press, 2004.

# COMMAND OF THE ARMY ACT (1867)

In 1866, Republicans in Congress began to unify against President Andrew Johnson and his conservative approach to Reconstruction. The Executive opposed even the most meager of efforts to protect freedpeople; his intransigence energized congressional efforts to take matters into their hands. In early 1867, Congress passed a series of acts to limit the power of the president. The Command of the Army Act, passed on March 2 as a provision attached to the Army Appropriations Act, was one such measure. First, the act defined the residence of the general of the army at the nation's capital—a minor condition, but one that would put the general of the army in close proximity to the workings of the government, specifically Congress. Next, it required that any order issued to the U.S. Army be done through the general in chief; the president, who was the commander in chief, was denied the right to issue commands directly to the nation's military. As the army was largely responsible for enforcing many Reconstruction directives, congressional Republicans wanted to be sure to control all communications—and they believed that the general in chief, Ulysses S, Grant, was on their side. In order to further constrain the president, the act also specified that the general in chief could not be removed temporarily or permanently by presidential initiative alone—the Senate had to approve any such changes. In addition to limiting presidential authority, Congress also required that any militia in the former Confederate states, with the exception of Arkansas and Tennessee, be immediately dissolved. In 1868, when President Johnson found himself facing impeachment, the ninth Article of Impeachment (the charges) claimed he violated the Command of the Army Act by directly communicating with military commanders in the South.

*Heidi Amelia-Anne Weber*

**See also:** Bureau of Refugees, Freedmen, and Abandoned Lands; Congressional Reconstruction.

## Further Reading

Chambers, John Whiteclay, III. "The Military and Civil Authority," in John E. Jessup and Louise B. Ketz, eds., *Encyclopedia of the American Military*. Vol. 3. New York: Charles Scribner's Sons, 1994.

Dawson, Joseph G., III. "Reconstruction and American Imperialism," in John E. Jessup and Louise B. Ketz, eds., *Encyclopedia of the American Military*. Vol. 2. New York: Charles Scribner's Sons, 1994.

Fitzgerald, Michael W. *Splendid Failure: Postwar Reconstruction in the American South.* New York: Ivan R. Dee Publishers, 2008.

Fleming, Walter L. *Documentary History of Reconstruction.* Vol. 1. Cleveland, OH: The Arthur H. Clark Company, 1906.

Foner, Eric. *Reconstruction Updated Edition: America's Unfinished Revolution, 1863–1877.* Reprint, New York: HarperCollins, 2014.

## COMPROMISE OF 1877

Shrouded in myth and controversy, the Compromise of 1877 is generally cited as marking the end of Reconstruction. The event culminated in a February 26, 1877 meeting in the Wormley Hotel in Washington, D.C., where leading Republicans allegedly promised to abandon Southern Reconstruction if Southern Democrats conceded disputed electoral votes in the 1876 presidential election; in effect, Republicans traded the South for the White House, and Rutherford B. Hayes became president. The truth is both more and less complicated.

The Compromise of 1877 grew out of the confused presidential election of 1876, which coincided with Southern Democrats' attempt to retake control of the three Southern states still in Republican hands: Florida, Louisiana, and South Carolina. In the national contest, Democrat Samuel J. Tilden, the governor of New York, won the popular vote, but when uncontested state electoral votes were counted, Tilden had received 184 votes, one short of election. Four states submitted disputed votes: Oregon (one vote) and the three Southern states (Florida, four; Louisiana, eight; and South Carolina, seven). Republican nominee Rutherford B. Hayes, the governor of Ohio, needed all of the disputed votes to secure election. Democrats and Republicans in the three Southern states leveled charges and countercharges of intimidation, corruption, and violence. Indeed, white terrorists had prevented thousands of blacks from voting, and both ballots and ballot boxes were stolen. But it was unclear to which candidate the states' electoral votes should go, and the Republican Senate and Democratic House could not reach any agreement.

As a result, on January 29, 1877, Congress created a special Electoral Commission, which included five members of the House of Representatives, five of the Senate, and five of the Supreme Court. By party, the breakdown was seven Republicans, seven Democrats, and one neutral, the nonpartisan Justice David Davis of the Supreme Court. But in uncanny stroke, Davis accepted election to the U.S. Senate from Illinois; he left the commission and was replaced by Justice Joseph P. Bradley, who leaned toward the Republicans. The Electoral Commission announced, in an 8 to 7 decision, that Florida's votes should go to the Republican Hayes. It reached the same conclusion for both Louisiana and South Carolina. With Tilden unable to get the single vote needed, the Democrats sought to delay the official congressional count with a filibuster. Here the party itself divided over strategy and long-term goals: some prominent Democrats had been assured by Republicans that Hayes would not use federal power to support Republican governments in the South, allowing the return of "home rule" to that region. These Democrats refused to cooperate in the filibuster, preferring the end of federally enforced Reconstruction and the protection of black rights to control of the presidency. Then Hayes sweetened the deal by promising to support a Southern-based transcontinental railroad, federal funds for the rebuilding of levees on the Mississippi River, and the appointment of a Southerner as postmaster general. Allegedly in negotiations at the Wormley Hotel, Democrats agreed in return to obey the three new constitutional amendments. As a result, the Democrats' filibuster strategy collapsed, and on March 2, 1877, the electoral count was announced, with Hayes winning by a 185 to 184 vote. The Compromise and Hayes's presidency were the result of the North's growing apathy toward continuing violence and political turmoil in the former Confederate states. The goal of equal opportunity and racial equality before the law had to wait another century; political Reconstruction was over.

*Claudine L. Ferrell*

*See also:* Redemption.

## Further Reading

Polakoff, Keith Ian. T*he Politics of Inertia: The Election of 1876 and the End of Reconstruction*. Baton Rouge: Louisiana State University Press, 1973.

Roseboom, Eugene H., and Alfred E. Eckes Jr. *A History of Presidential Elections: From George Washington to Jimmy Carter*. 4th ed. New York: Macmillan, 1979.

Simpson, Brooks D. *The Reconstruction Presidents*. Lawrence: University Press of Kansas, 1998.

Woodward, C. Vann. *Reunion and Reaction: The Compromise of 1877 and the End of Reconstruction*. Boston: Little, Brown, 1951.

# CONFISCATION ACTS

During the Civil War, the U.S. Congress, in the First and Second Confiscation Acts, enacted sweeping confiscation programs designed to seize the private property of enemy citizens. These measures demonstrated two significant shifts on the part of the federal government and the North in general: a growing acceptance of an expanded, aggressive war effort, and an increasing understanding of the centrality of slavery to the Confederate war effort, and the war itself.

In August 1861 Congress passed the First Confiscation Act, authorizing the federal government to seize the property of those participating directly in the rebellion. Ten months later, in July 1862, the increasingly influential faction called Radical Republicans pushed Congress into passing the much broader Second Confiscation Act. This permitted federal officials to seize any personal property of anyone taking up arms against the government, anyone aiding or offering aid to the rebellion, or any property being used to support the rebellion. This effectively meant that U.S. military forces could legally seize any property of any who even recognized the legitimacy of the Confederacy. Despite the general wording, everyone knew the property at the heart of these acts: slaves.

These measures revealed contradictory attitudes within the North. First, the idea of confiscation itself reflected a developing radicalism in the North. Although the seizing of Confederate property was not new, the intended nature of the property (slaves) was. Since confederates insisted that the Southern African American population was property, Radicals in Congress used their definitions against them. Thousands of slaves had already self-emancipated themselves, fleeing plantations and towns and heading toward the invading Union armies. Some generals embraced these "contrabands" as a practical way of damaging the South. After all, with such a large portion of the white male population under arms, the Confederacy depended on the labor of slaves. Although primarily involved in agriculture, slaves also worked in the mines; built roads, railroads, and bridges; and even constructed forts and defenses. Defining them as "property" used to aid in the rebellion allowed federal officers to seize them without crossing the sensitive line of freeing slaves. With the coming of the Emancipation Proclamation on January 1, 1863, federal officials no longer needed any pretense or subterfuge; emancipation was direct and obvious.

Yet, in other ways, federal confiscation policy showed a conservative side of Union efforts. When compared to the American Revolution, with the exception of slaves, very little Confederate property was actually confiscated. In the Revolution, a great deal of Loyalist (or Tory) property was seized permanently, without compensation or legal recourse. In the Civil War, acts of Union confiscation were carefully registered, bureaucratically handled, and even frequently compensated. The grandest threat of confiscation never occurred—the Radical's demand that plantations be taken from confederates and divided among the freed-people. Even such obvious actions as seizing abandoned homesteads were only temporary; nearly all lands and homes were returned to their former owners in the years after the war. Despite claims of "total war" and allegations of horrors committed by invading generals, when it came to the confiscation of enemy property, the Union war machine restrained itself. Confiscation revealed core conceptual differences surrounding the competing rights of property, the demands of citizenship, and the prerogatives of sovereign power. Even as war raged, confiscation policy prompted fundamental questions about the basis of private property, the nature of the U.S. Constitution, and the relationship of individual property rights to the needs of the state.

*Daniel W. Hamilton*

**See also:** Abolition of Slavery; Amnesty Proclamations; Field Order No. 15; Loyalty Oaths; Pardons; Port Royal Experiment; Southern Claims Commission (SCC); U.S. Army and Reconstruction.

## Further Reading

"An Act to Confiscate Property Used for Insurrectionary Purposes." *U.S. Statutes at Large* 319 (1861): 12.

"An Act to Suppress Insurrection, to Punish Treason and Rebellion, to Seize and Confiscate the Property of Rebels, and for Other Purposes." *U.S. Statutes at Large* 589 (1862): 12.

Grimsley, Mark. *The Hard Hand of War: Union Military Policy towards Southern Civilians, 1861–1865*. New York: Cambridge University Press, 1995.

McPherson, James M. *Abraham Lincoln and the Second American Revolution*. New York: Oxford University Press, 1991.

# CONGRESSIONAL RECONSTRUCTION

Reconstruction, the process of restoring the former Confederate states to the Union following the Civil War, proceeded in two distinct phases—Presidential Reconstruction and Congressional Reconstruction. Congressional Reconstruction refers to the stage of that process when Congress, rather than Presidents Abraham Lincoln and Andrew Johnson, directed policy.

## Presidential Efforts

Even as the Civil War raged, Northerners debated the future of the seceded states. In 1863, President Lincoln outlined his plan for restoring the former Confederate states to the Union. His Ten Percent Plan offered liberal amnesty and a rapid process for states (and their citizens) to prove their allegiance and rejoin the federal Union. Many Moderate Republicans supported Lincoln's program, but a growing section of Radical Republicans sought to punish white Southerners and guarantee black civil and even political rights.

While Moderates and Republicans disagreed on Reconstruction policy, they did agree that Congress needed to play a role; therefore, they countered with a plan of their own, the Wade-Davis Bill, which presented more stringent demands upon the former confederates. An impasse developed, as Lincoln pocket-vetoed the bill, and Congress refused to admit the representatives from states organized under Lincoln's plan. In the spring of 1865, the debate shifted significantly, in two ways: first, the war ended, removing wartime expediency (and the executive's wartime powers) as a crutch for presidential control; second, an assassin's bullet changed the players in the debate. Now War Democrat Andrew Johnson of Tennessee sat in the White House. Like Lincoln, Johnson favored a quick restoration with lenient terms. In May 1865, without Congress in session, Johnson outlined a plan that restored civil and political rights to most ex-rebels; recognized the Lincoln-sponsored governments of Arkansas, Louisiana, Tennessee, and Virginia; and appointed provisional governors in the remaining seven unreconstructed states. These governors were to oversee the drafting of new constitutions and the electing of new state and federal officials. The results seemed to ignore the reality of Confederate defeat: some states refused to ratify the Thirteenth Amendment, many passed Black Codes to restrict black civil rights, and nearly all elected high-ranking Confederate civil and military officials to state and federal offices.

## Congress Asserts Itself

In December 1865, Congress refused to seat the new Southern delegates and insisted on revising Johnson's program. Congress created a Joint Committee on Reconstruction to examine all future action on restoration. The party remained divided: Radicals continued to push for Confederate punishment and civil rights for the freedmen, while Moderates sought basic civil rights for the blacks, but not the right to vote. In early 1866, Moderates courted Johnson with a relatively harmless Freedmen's Bureau Bill and a Civil Rights Act. Both measures passed Congress easily, but the president shocked everyone by vetoing both. Moderate and Radical Republicans united to override the veto of the Civil Rights Act and to pass a new Freedmen's Bureau Bill.

## Congressional Reconstruction: First Phase

Driven together by Johnson's (and the white South's) opposition, Republicans acknowledged that the president would defy any legislation they proposed. Therefore, the Joint

Committee on Reconstruction proposed amending the Constitution; in June 1866, the Fourteenth Amendment passed both houses of Congress as a compromise between the Radicals and Moderates. The amendment essentially became the Republican peace treaty for the Confederacy. To protect blacks, it defined all native-born and naturalized persons as citizens and prohibited states from denying any person equal protection under the law. Also, while blacks were not granted suffrage, any state that withheld the vote from adult male citizens would have its congressional representation reduced proportionally. The amendment also presented various disqualification criteria relating to support of the Confederacy. But for the amendment to become part of the Constitution, it needed approval from three-fourths of the state, including some former Confederate states. Johnson called on Southern states to reject the amendment; ironically, Johnson's home state of Tennessee ratified it in July 1866, and Congress allowed it to reenter the Union. Undaunted, Johnson embarked on a speaking tour of the Northeast and Midwest to drum up support for his policies and his new National Union Party. The so-called Swing around the Circle was a disaster; Johnson depicted Republicans as traitors, openly argued with the crowds, and pointedly criticized individual lawmakers by name.

Johnson's antics, his obstruction of the Fourteenth Amendment, and reports coming from Memphis and New Orleans about deadly race riots, convinced Northern voters that the president's policies had failed. The Republicans swept the elections of 1866, gaining a huge majority in Congress, capable of easily overriding any veto. Republicans won all Northern gubernatorial contests, and controlled every northern state's legislature. Johnson's bid for a new Conservative coalition collapsed, and Republicans took charge of Reconstruction.

## Congressional Reconstruction: Second Phase

Before the Fourteenth Amendment could be adopted, at least some of the unreconstructed states had to ratify it; that would certainly not happen under Johnson's existing governments. So, Congress embarked on a program designed to remove those structures and establish loyal, orderly— and hopefully Republican—governments in their place. The first step toward this was the Military Reconstruction Act. Passed in March 1867, over the president's veto, the law declared that the 10 Johnson state governments were provisional only, and divided them into 5 military districts, each commanded by a major general. Congress authorized the army to supervise the registration of all male voters, including blacks but excluding whites who would be barred under restrictions in the Fourteenth Amendment. Voters would elect delegates for new state conventions where they would frame new constitutions providing for black suffrage and barring prominent ex-rebels from holding state and federal offices. Once Congress approved the new constitutions, elections for state and national office would follow, and the new legislatures would be required to ratify the Fourteenth Amendment. States would then be readmitted, and Reconstruction would then end. To prevent presidential interference, Congress passed two statutes of questionable constitutionality: the Command of the Army Act, which required Johnson to issue all orders to the army through the general in chief of the army, Ulysses S. Grant, and the Tenure of Office Act, which forbade the president to remove certain officeholders without the Senate's consent. Obstruction by former confederates moved Congress to increase the army's authority in the Second Reconstruction Act (also March 1867), and when Johnson's Attorney General Henry Stanbery issued a ruling that limited military authority in the South, Congress simply passed another Military Reconstruction Act (July 1867), declaring the army's supremacy over Southern civilian governments. White Southerners tried to derail the new constitutional conventions through a loophole in the original Reconstruction Act, which mandated that a majority of registered voters was needed to affirm the new constitutions; by coercing enough voters to stay home, passage of the constitutions could be prevented. Congress closed the loophole by passing the Fourth Military Reconstruction Act in March 1868, which specified that ratification of the constitutions required a majority of those actually voting, not registered. By June 1868, six states—Alabama, North Carolina, South Carolina, Arkansas, Louisiana, and Florida—had approved constitutions, elected government officials, ratified the Fourteenth Amendment, and rejoined the Union.

## Impeachment

Johnson could not prevent the Republicans from legislating their program, but he could impede their progress. For instance, as commander in chief, he appointed Conservative generals to administer the five military districts. Radicals recognized Johnson would never relent, and some advocated his removal from office. The first attempt occurred in January 1867, when the House authorized the Judiciary Committee to investigate the possibility of impeachment. However, despite Radical arguments that the president's actions constituted an abuse of power, Moderates insisted that officials could only be impeached for indictable crimes. Deterred but not defeated, Radicals launched another impeachment effort in August 1867, after Johnson suspended Secretary of War Edwin Stanton and replaced generals Philip H. Sheridan and Daniel E. Sickles with less-energetic officials. Moderates again held back, noting that Johnson's suspension of Stanton occurred when Congress was in recess, so technically it did not violate the Tenure of Office Act. The Radicals forced a House vote on impeachment, but without Moderate support, the resolution failed, 108 to 57. Johnson again proved to be his own worst enemy. Determined to rid himself of the "suspended" Stanton, the president removed him in February 1868, and replaced him with Adjutant General Lorenzo Thomas. Since the Senate was in session, and Stanton had been formally removed, Radicals claimed Johnson had defiantly violated the Tenure of Office Act. This time, the Moderates voted with the Radicals, and the president was impeached by a party-line vote of 126 to 47 on February 24, 1868. Oddly, after the impeachment vote, House prosecutors, known as managers, drew up 11 charges against the president. Eight dealt with his alleged violation of the Tenure of Office Act, one accused the president of violating the Command of the Army Act, one accused Johnson of bringing Congress into public disrepute, and the final article drew together a hodgepodge of charges from the previous ten.

Johnson's talented legal team claimed that he had committed no crime in testing the constitutionality of the Tenure of Office Act, and they argued that even if the act were constitutional, it did not apply to Stanton, who had been appointed by Lincoln.

Although even Moderate Republicans despised Johnson, many feared his removal would set a dangerous precedent, opening the door for future Congresses to a president who disagreed with their policies. Moderates also distrusted radical Benjamin Wade, president *pro tem* of the Senate and next in line to the presidency (no new vice-president was selected after Lincoln's assassination). Using intermediaries, Johnson and the Moderates worked toward a compromise. The president stopped denouncing Congress, and stopped interfering with the Reconstruction Acts. While Stanton's removal stuck, Johnson appointed the acceptable General John M. Schofield as secretary of war. On May 16, 1868, the trial concluded and the vote on removal was called: on the 11th article of impeachment, the Senate voted 35 to 19. All 12 Democrats and 7 Moderate Republicans voted against removal. With a two-thirds majority (36 votes) needed to remove the president from office, Johnson had been saved by one single vote. Votes on Articles 2 and 3 on May 26 had the same result, and the impeachment managers conceded defeat.

With his meager victory in hand, Johnson spitefully defied Congress during his last months in office. He vetoed Reconstruction bills that the Republicans easily overrode and delivered speeches critical of the Radicals. Naively, he clung to the hope that the Democratic Party would nominate him for president in 1868. However, the party threw its support behind New York governor Horatio Seymour, leaving Johnson as a president without a party.

## Congressional Reconstruction: Third Phase

While the nation focused on the duel between Johnson and Congress, Reconstruction marched forward. Hundreds of thousands of black Southerners registered to vote, while many whites refused to participate. A coalition of blacks, Southern white Republicans (known to their confederate neighbors as "scalawags"), and recent Northern transplants or "carpetbaggers" united to direct the proceedings at the conventions. The progressive constitutions produced granted universal manhood suffrage, provided for statewide public schools, and often disqualified a small percentage of ex-confederates from voting and holding office. By mid-1868, North Carolina, South Carolina, Florida, Alabama, Arkansas, and Louisiana had ratified new constitutions and elected new officials. The new legislatures promptly ratified the Fourteenth Amendment, and the states rejoined the Union. Georgia, Texas, Virginia, and Mississippi followed by 1870. The national election of 1868 served as a referendum on Republican Reconstruction policy. Although Republican Ulysses S. Grant easily defeated his Democratic challenger, Horatio Seymour, in the Electoral College, had it not been for black votes in the South, Grant would have lost the popular vote. Republicans scrambled to strengthen the party; they drafted the Fifteenth Amendment to the Constitution in February 1869 which nationalized black voting rights. Republicans reasoned that their survival depended on increasing their voter base beyond the South itself. As some had warned, this backfired, with Republicans losing support in the North because of the combination of black suffrage, the increasing pro-business stance of the party, and growing evidence of corruption. As a result, securing political control of the South became more important than ever, just as the Southern party began to fracture.

Tensions between Northerners and Southerners and between blacks and whites, together with the extreme hostility among white Southerners, divided the party in various elections. Between 1869 and 1874, seven states returned to white Democratic control: Virginia, North Carolina, Tennessee, Alabama, Georgia, Texas, and Arkansas. The growth of the Ku Klux Klan and similar groups accelerated the collapse of the Southern Republican coalition. Using intimidation and violence, these groups prevented many Southern Republicans, especially blacks, from voting, and drove many Northerners out of the South. Except in Arkansas, North Carolina, and Tennessee, the Republican state militias were incapable of stopping the violence; Republican governments turned to Washington for help, and Congress responded with the Enforcement Acts in 1870–1871. These acts protected a citizen's right to vote, outlawed groups such as the Klan, and authorized the president to use military force to enforce the law. While controversial, use of the military to protect voters helped Grant secure presidential victory in 1872 against an alliance of "Liberal Republicans"— bolters tired of Reconstruction and Republican scandals—and Democrats. The 1872 split was no anomaly; the party's momentum had begun to lag, and an economic recession in 1873 returned control of Congress to the Democrats. Republicans managed to push the Civil Rights Act of 1875, a sweeping measure which outlawed racial segregation but lacked an enforcement support. Idealistic and toothless, it was the last piece of Reconstruction legislation. That same year, Democrats in Mississippi combined economic pressure with open violence to win control of their state.

The presidential election of 1876 brought down the final curtain on Reconstruction. Republican candidate Rutherford B. Hayes ran against Democrat Samuel Tilden of New York. Although Tilden won the popular vote, fraud and violence left the electoral votes of South Carolina, Florida, and Louisiana in dispute. Congress created a special Electoral Commission to decide the votes—and thus the presidency. Republicans and Democrats struck a deal, known as the Compromise of 1877. This arrangement stipulated that if the Democrats agreed not to challenge the Commission's report, which gave all votes to Hayes, then Republicans would remove the remaining federal troops from the South and not interfere with new Democratic state governments. Without federal support, the remaining Republican state governments in the South collapsed, and Democrats gained control of all former Confederate states. White "redeemers" wrote new state constitutions, quickly established laws to segregate the black population and nullify their voting, and dismantled many of the progressive social reforms and institutions created under Reconstruction.

Historians continue to debate the success of Reconstruction. The two Republican goals following the Civil War of protecting black civil rights and promoting a Southern Republican Party had failed. During the first half of the 20th century, the South was a rigidly segregated society dominated by an all-white Democratic Party. Yet Republicans accomplished much. The educational impact of Reconstruction survived, as did the legacy of black churches founded under Republican protection. More important, Reconstruction created a significant precedent, that the federal government had the authority to guarantee equality under the law. Unfortunately, it would take another century, until the civil rights movement, before blacks would enjoy the promises of the Fourteenth and Fifteenth Amendments.

*John D. Fowler*

**See also:** Abolition of Slavery; Bureau of Refugees, Freedmen, and Abandoned Lands; Memphis Riot (1866); New Orleans Riot (1866); Redemption; U.S. Army and Reconstruction.

## Further Reading

Belz, Herman. *Reconstructing the Union: Theory and Policy during the Civil War*. Ithaca, NY: Cornell University Press, 1969.

Egerton, Douglas R. *The Wars of Reconstruction: The Brief, Violent History of America's Most Progressive Era*. New York: Bloomsbury Press, 2014.

Fitzgerald, Michael W. *Splendid Failure: Postwar Reconstruction in the American South*. New York: Ivan R. Dee Publishers, 2008.

Foner, Eric. *Reconstruction Updated Edition: America's Unfinished Revolution, 1863– 1877*. Reprint, New York: HarperCollins, 2014.

Gillette, William. *Retreat from Reconstruction: A Political History, 1867–1878*. Baton Rouge: Louisiana State University Press, 1979.

Perman, Michael. *The Road to Redemption: Southern Politics, 1869–1879*. Chapel Hill: University of North Carolina Press, 1984.

Richardson, Heather Cox. *The Death of Reconstruction: Race, Labor, and Politics in the Post—Civil War North, 1865–1901*. Cambridge, MA: Harvard University Press, 2001.

Stampp, Kenneth M. *The Era of Reconstruction, 1865–1877*. New York: Vintage Books, 1965.

Trelease, Allen W. *White Terror: The Ku Klux Klan Conspiracy and Southern Reconstruction*. New York: Harper & Row, 1971.

# CONSTITUTIONAL CONVENTIONS

The Military Reconstruction Acts, passed by the U.S. Congress in early 1867, required that Southern states revise their constitutions before they could be readmitted into the full privileges of statehood. Voting for delegates to these conventions was based on universal male suffrage, so for the first time in American History, the federal government dictated voting policy, and that dicta allowed black males to both vote and hold office. Black males turned out and supported Republican candidates for these conventions in huge numbers. In many places, Democratic Conservatives boycotted the elections entirely. As a result, these conventions were typically controlled by Radicals and they included significant, though by no means overwhelming, representation from the African American community. White Northerners comprised about one-sixth of the delegates, white Southerners the majority, and Southern blacks the rest. Only in South Carolina and Louisiana did blacks make up a majority of members. White Conservatives heaped condemnation upon the conventions—and their resulting constitutions—but changes made to state constitutions were well within the contemporary traditions of state governance. The most radical change enshrined in the new constitutions was equality before the law for all citizens, but none of the constitutions mandated social integration nor did any enact land redistribution. After new constitutions were written, public referendums validated them; again based upon universal male suffrage, every new constitution passed. Finally, still operating under the Military Reconstruction Acts, each Southern state held new elections for state and federal officials. Congress then accepted the new constitution, allowed representatives and senators back into Congress, and remanded state powers back to civil officials.

The constitutional conventions addressed three major areas of state administration: voting regulations, rules regarding office holding, and general social policies. Foremost among the changes insisted upon by Congress was the enfranchisement of black men. Also of great interest was the disfranchisement of ex-confederates, urged on by Unionist white Southerners but rarely supported by black delegates. In several states, Republican delegates increased popular access and reduced the power of prewar political elites. For instance, constitutions repealed qualifications for office-holding (such as property-holding) and reduced the sway of plantation districts over upland or mountain areas (which had ostracized many poorer whites). South Carolina also gave voters the power to elect the governor, state officers, and presidential electors.

New governments also addressed some of the social problems that confronted the postbellum South. Of paramount importance was establishing public school systems, to educate former slaves and the white population; Southern states did not maintain systems of public education in the antebellum period. Although unpopular, these delegates established new taxes and land sales in order to generate the revenue for schools. Education did not mean equality; only in New Orleans and parts of South Carolina were schools racially integrated. Outside of their policy initiatives, the constitutional conventions mobilized African Americans and Republicans. The process of forging the coalitions to lead Southern Republican governments began in the halls of these conventions. Yet hindsight also allows us to identify the fault lines hidden in these coalitions. Black delegates focused on civil rights, access to the vote, land, and fair labor policies; Northern white Republicans looked ahead to economic development, and Southern white Republicans sought an increased voice but a racial status quo. For white Conservatives, the conventions focused opposition to black and Republican political activism. Conservative delegates opposed the new constitutions from their inception, and worked to defeat the constitutions at the polls. Boycotts of the ratification elections used a loophole to derail the process, until Congress allowed ratification to be based upon a majority of voters, not a majority of those registered.

Ultimately, the constitutions were progressive but not revolutionary. Despite the intensity of opposition from Conservative whites, most of the constitutions lasted a full generation, testimony to their effectiveness and to their essentially moderate nature. By the end of the century, however, Southern states embarked on a process of further erasing the gains of Reconstruction.

*Aaron Sheehan-Dean*

***See also:*** Black Suffrage.

## Further Reading

Donald, David H. *The Politics of Reconstruction, 1863–1867*. Baton Rouge: Louisiana State University Press, 1965.

Franklin, John Hope. *Reconstruction after the Civil War*. Chicago: University of Chicago Press, 1964.

Hyman, Harold. *A More Perfect Union: The Impact of the Civil War and Reconstruction on the Constitution*. New York: Knopf, 1973.

# CONTRABAND, SLAVES AS

By fleeing bondage during the Civil War, slaves initiated both emancipation and Reconstruction; fugitives who escaped to Union army lines were known as contrabands. The name arose from the phrase "contraband of war," the name for enemy property confiscated during wartime. Defining slaves as contraband was a bit of legal trickery that allowed army officers to emancipate them without undermining federal policy that did not yet embrace abolition.

The contraband saga began in May 1861, when three slaves fled to Union general Benjamin Butler's lines at Fortress Monroe, Virginia. The runaways' owner, a confederate officer, demanded their return, but Butler refused on grounds that the slaves had been building fortifications for the Confederacy, so were contraband subject to confiscation. Congress validated Butler's actions with the Confiscation Acts.

Contraband slaves in Culpeper, Virginia. Before President Lincoln moved toward emancipation, army officers began confiscating slaves as "contraband," claiming slaves aided the Confederate war effort and thus could be seized. It was a way of using legal loopholes to liberate, and utilize, slaves before emancipation became lawful. (Library of Congress)

By late 1862, with numbers growing, fugitives were directed into contraband camps run by the Union army, often with the assistance of organizations like the American Missionary Association and later the Bureau of Refugees, Freedmen, and Abandoned Lands (the Freedmen's Bureau). In camps, former slaves worshiped, founded schools and organizations, and labored for the army and themselves. Some of these camps were confiscated plantations; instances in which slaves leased land directly, such as Davis Bend, Mississippi, were promising experiments in free labor, but evaporated when President Andrew Johnson returned land to former confederates.

The impact of defining slaves as contraband was mixed. Since it allowed army officers to free slaves while sidestepping moral questions, contraband policy emancipated many slaves earlier than otherwise would have been the case. Contraband policy also created opportunities, which slaves eagerly seized, to play active roles in the war. Yet, by defining fugitives as property, contraband policy perpetuated questions about slaves' status and rights, which affected Reconstruction goals and policies. This narrow practical rationale behind contraband policy robbed emancipation of a secure ideological foundation capable of supporting and sustaining racial progress.

*Chandra Miller Manning*

***See also:*** Bureau of Refugees, Freedmen, and Abandoned Lands; Confiscation Acts.

## Further Reading

Berlin, Ira, Barbara J. Fields, Thavolia Glymph, Joseph P. Reidy, and Leslie S. Rowland, eds. *Freedom: A Documentary History of Emancipation, 1861–1867. Series I, Volume 1. The Destruction of Slavery*. New York: Cambridge University Press, 1985.

Gerteis, Louis S. *From Contraband to Freedman: Federal Policy toward Southern Blacks 1861–1865*. Westport, CT: Greenwood Press, 1973.

Hahn, Steven. *A Nation under Our Feet: Black Political Struggles in the Rural South from Slavery to the Great Migration*. Cambridge, MA: Harvard University Press, 2003.

# D

## DAVIS, EDMUND J. (1827–1883)

Edmund Jackson Davis was born in St Augustine, Florida on October 2, 1826. His family moved to Texas in the 1840s, where Davis practiced law and served as a district court judge. A Unionist, he opposed secession in 1860–1861 and by 1862 had fled the state to avoid persecution. He visited Washington, D.C., and received permission from the War Department to raise a Union cavalry regiment of Texas refugees. He organized the First Texas Cavalry, United States, at New Orleans and eventually rose to the rank of brigadier general. It was Davis who received the surrender of Confederate forces in Texas on June 12, 1865.

Following the war, Davis opposed President Andrew Johnson's program of Reconstruction, convinced that only black suffrage would sustain loyal governments in the South. The triumph of the Conservatives, a loose coalition of former secessionists and Unionists who supported the president, relegated Davis and his kind to background roles. Following the creation of the Johnson-phase constitution, he ran unsuccessfully for a seat in the state senate. As Congress pushed Johnson aside, Davis migrated back toward politics, joining the state's Republican Party in 1867 and securing a seat in the new constitutional convention. There, he became associated with the group that came to be known as the Radicals, who supported black suffrage and the extension of civil rights to the African American freedmen while restricting the political rights of former confederates. The Radical program confronted a hostile majority, composed of a coalition of Conservatives and Conservative Republicans led by Johnson's provisional governor, Andrew J. Hamilton. The Radicals did secure black male suffrage, but only minimum guarantees of civil rights, and little else. Following the convention, Davis and Hamilton squared off for governor, with Davis eeking out a victory in an election marred by violence and fraud. As governor, Davis created a state police force, added additional state courts, and established a statewide public school system, which he considered critical to helping the freedmen and poor whites of the state. Davis's legislative program had little chance to mature, as Conservative Republicans and Democrats joined together to charge the governor with tyranny and suppressing the will of the majority; they argued that Davis's government did not represent the majority, and that its taxes were unjust. As with many Reconstruction governments, expenses did increase, largely due to new services; for the most part Davis's administration was honest and avoided the fraud that tainted Republican regimes elsewhere. Nonetheless, Davis's opponents used their claims to foster a "Taxpayers' Convention" that produced court challenges to state taxes and a private boycott of paying taxes that caused operational problems across the state.

The tax issue blocked efforts to attract wider support, while immigration from across the South expanded numbers hostile to the Radicals. When Davis ran for reelection in 1873, Republicans already had lost their majorities in the state legislature. In the 1873 gubernatorial election, Democratic challenger Richard Coke handily defeated Davis.

The pattern of political chaos typical of Southern states in the 1870s now spread to Texas. At first Davis accepted the election results, but then Republicans challenged the election on a technicality, and the state Supreme Court declared the results void in a decision known as the *Semicolon* Case. Davis concluded that he had to sustain the court, and his stand produced a crisis in January 1874, when the legislature reassembled. Davis refused to recognize the legislature, but it met anyway, ignored him, and inaugurated Coke. Davis called for federal assistance, but President Grant and the national party turned a deaf ear; fearing further violence, Davis stepped down.

Davis continued to be active in the state's Republican Party after 1874. He chaired the state executive committee and ran unsuccessfully for governor and for Congress. He stayed true to his basic principles, such as when he refused an appointment as collector of customs at Galveston, because he opposed the reconciliation approach of President Rutherford B. Hayes. Davis supported himself through these years by practicing law in Austin, where he died on February 7, 1883.

*Carl H. Moneyhon*

**See also:** Education; Military Reconstruction Acts (1867–1868); Presidential Reconstruction; Redemption; U.S. Army and Reconstruction.

## Further Reading

Gray, Ronald Norman. "Edmund J. Davis: Radical Republican and Reconstruction Governor of Texas." Ph.D. dissertation, Texas Tech University, 1976.

Moneyhon, Carl H. "Edmund J. Davis in the Coke-Davis Election Dispute of 1874: A Reassessment of Character." *Southwestern Historical Quarterly* 100 (1996): 131–45.

## DAVIS, JEFFERSON FINIS (1808–1889)

Jefferson Davis, the president of the Confederate State of America, was born in Kentucky, the 10th and last child in his family (hence his middle name "finis"). Davis attended schools in Kentucky and Mississippi, then Transylvania University, and finally West Point, where he graduated in 1828. He resigned from the U.S. Army in 1835, and married Sarah Knox Taylor, the daughter of his commanding officer, Zachary Taylor. They moved to Davis's new plantation, "Brierfield," in Mississippi where Sarah soon died, probably of malaria, and Davis suffered aftereffects of the illness for the rest of his life. He married Varina Howell in 1845; the couple eventually had six children.

Davis became interested in politics and was elected to Congress as a Democrat in 1845. On July 4, 1846, Davis resigned his seat to serve as colonel of the First Mississippi Volunteers in the Mexican American War. As a war hero, Davis was elected to the U.S. Senate from Mississippi; he favored slavery's expansion and vigorously opposed the Compromise of 1850. In 1853, Franklin Pierce selected Davis as his secretary of war. In 1857, Davis was again elected to the Senate, where he served until Mississippi seceded in January 1861.

In February 1861, representatives of the first six seceded states chose Davis as the provisional president of the new Confederacy; later Davis was elected to a six-year term. While some considered him the best person available, his qualities were ill-suited for head of state—especially an amorphous collection of states heading toward war. He did not accept criticism, discharged those who disagreed with him, showed favoritism and excessive loyalty to friends, was extremely inflexible, and was often in ill health.

Captured in the waning days of the war on May 10, 1865, Davis spent two years imprisoned at Fortress Monroe, Virginia. Secretary of War Edwin M. Stanton and Judge Advocate General Joseph Holt tried to link Davis to the assassination of Abraham Lincoln. It became evident that the testimony against Davis was perjured, and it was difficult to determine a realistic charge

Jefferson F. Davis, former senator from Mississippi and secretary of war, served as the Confederacy's only president. Ill-tempered, stubborn, and in poor health, many blame his leadership for the Confederacy's defeat. (Library of Congress)

on which to try Davis; the indictment against him was dropped and Davis was released in December 1868.

After his release, Davis tried his hand at several business ventures, but these were unsuccessful and his family lived in genteel poverty, eventually at "Beauvoir," a home in Biloxi, Mississippi, given to him by a friend. He wrote his memoirs, the two-volume *Rise and Fall of the Confederate Government* (1881); while not a financial success, these helped begin the Lost Cause myth that romanticized the Confederacy and downplayed slavery and racism in its founding. Davis died in New Orleans of pneumonia on December 6, 1889.

*Glenna R. Schroeder-Lein*

**See also:** Amnesty Proclamations; Republicans, Radical.

## Further Reading

Cooper, William J. Jr. *Jefferson Davis, American.* New York: Vintage, 2000.
Davis, William C. *Jefferson Davis: The Man and His Hour.* New York: HarperCollins, 1991.

## DELANY, MARTIN R. (1812–1885)

Martin R. Delany was a black abolitionist, Union army recruiter, and political activist in Reconstruction South Carolina. Born free in Charles Town, Virginia, Delany grew to manhood in Pittsburgh, Pennsylvania, and in 1850, briefly undertook medical studies at Harvard University. As an abolitionist in the 1840s, Delany published *The Mystery*, the first black newspaper west of the Alleghenies, and coedited *The North Star*, with Frederick Douglass. As a black nationalist, Delany believed that African Americans possessed a unique destiny and promoted emigration to Africa. The Civil War transformed Delany's activism, as he began recruiting blacks for the famous Massachusetts Fifty-Fourth and Fifty-Fifth Regiments. He was commissioned a major in the U.S. Army and was its first black commissioned officer. During the war Delany worked in South Carolina as a Freedmen's Bureau agent on Hilton Head and other sea islands. His greatest disappointment was that most confiscated planter land was restored, leaving the former slaves landless.

A free black before the war, Martin R. Delany, studied medicine at Harvard, encouraged emigration back to Africa, and became the first black commissioned officer in the U.S. Army. As an influential leader in Reconstruction South Carolina, Delany criticized carpetbaggers for monopolizing political power. (Getty Images)

In Reconstruction, Delany never held a major political office, but was a political force in South Carolina. Following the Military Reconstruction Acts, Delany cautioned blacks against aggressively pursuing political office under the new 1868 State Constitution, hoping to avoid alienating whites. When so-called scalawags and carpetbaggers came to dominate the offices, Delany then urged black men to pursue their fair share of offices, proclaiming that black people required their own leaders. Soon three blacks were elected congressmen, one as lieutenant governor, and one to the state supreme court. Delany openly criticized white Republicans, whom he claimed were corrupt and selfserving. Thus, he broke with Radicals in the early 1870s, supporting reform-minded Liberal Republicans and warming to Moderate Democrats. In 1874, he ran unsuccessfully for lieutenant governor on the Independent Republican ticket, headed by a Democrat.

In the election of 1876, Delany had moved even further; he supported Wade Hampton, the Conservative Democratic candidate for governor, having concluded that black rights could best be preserved by Southern aristocrats, rather than by white Republicans who faced a limited future in the South. Conservatives praised his pragmatism, while many black and white Republicans saw him as a traitor to his race. But his hopes of racial conciliation were ultimately dashed with Redemption and the end of Reconstruction; he returned to his earlier strategy of African emigration. In 1877–1878, he organized the Charleston-based Liberian Exodus Movement, which promised blacks a better future in West Africa. Financial difficulties ended this effort after a single voyage in 1878. Martin Delany eventually left South Carolina for Wilberforce, Ohio, where he resided until his death on January 24, 1885.

*Bernard E. Powers Jr.*

*See also:* Bureau of Refugees, Freedmen, and Abandoned Lands; Stevens, Thaddeus (1792–1868).

## Further Reading

Foner, Eric. *Freedom's Lawmakers: A Directory of Black Officeholders during Reconstruction*. New York: Oxford University Press, 1993.

Holt, Thomas. *Black over White: Negro Political Leadership in South Carolina during Reconstruction*. Urbana: University of Illinois Press, 1977.

Painter, Nell I. "Martin R. Delany: Elitism and Black Nationalism," in Leon Litwack, and August Meier, eds., *Black Leaders of the Nineteenth Century*. Urbana: University of Illinois Press, 1991

Ullman, Victor. *Martin R. Delany: The Beginnings of Black Nationalism*. Boston: Beacon Press, 1971.

# DEMOCRATIC NATIONAL CONVENTION (1868)

The Democratic Party's 10th national convention convened in the newly built Tammany Hall in New York City, on July 4, 1868. The Democrats were in disarray. Internal disagreements stretching back to the Civil War still plagued them as they faced a presidential election. They were firm in their opposition to Republican reconstruction policies in the South, but uncertain about a candidate, and were heavily divided over the emerging issue of paper money. Many Western Democrats favored the continued circulation of the paper greenbacks that the government had issued during the war. They demanded that a law be passed mandating the repayment of government bonds in these greenbacks, not solely in gold, as "hard money" banks and bondholders wanted. The Conservative hard money bloc of mostly Eastern Democrats strongly disagreed. They believed that specie (actual metal) was the only proper medium of commercial activity. To them, paper greenbacks were inflationary and threatening to a prosperous economy.

Still, there was some hope. Their Republican opponents were in turmoil, split over the future direction of Reconstruction policy; they had failed to oust President Andrew Johnson through impeachment proceedings, and recently the Democrats had won a number of important state elections. Also, the appearance of delegates from the readmitted Southern states offered promise of electoral gains in the former Confederacy.

On the opening day, the delegates chose Horatio Seymour, the former governor of New York, as the convention's permanent chairman. Committees were quickly organized and the meeting turned to address its two main tasks: the party's platform, and selecting candidates for president and vice president. The platform came first. Despite the differences in the party, the Resolutions Committee found common ground, demanding the restoration to the Union of Southern states still under radical domination; amnesty for those who held high office in the Confederate states during the war; and the abolition of the Bureau of Refugees, Freedmen, and Abandoned Lands. On monetary matters, the committee called for paying off the public debt "in the lawful money of the United States," including, it was clear, if not directly stated, the government-issued greenbacks.

Balloting for candidates for president and vice president began on July 7. The convention adopted the party's traditional two-thirds rule, the vote of 205 of the delegates present (not only those voting) would be necessary for a successful nomination. Prior to the convention, President Andrew Johnson retained naïve hopes that he might yet receive the nomination. But from the beginning, George Pendleton of Ohio, once a Peace Democrat opposed to the war and now the leader of the soft money forces, led the field. His vote totals never approached the needed two-thirds mark. The Conservative wing had not settled on any one candidate and supported several different possibilities but no one had the necessary support. The convention settled into a repetitive cycle of voting, trying different candidates, and delegates switching from one name to another. After three days, and 18 ballots, the party was still unable to agree. Then, Ohio withdrew Pendleton's name and on the 22nd ballot, swung its votes from Pendleton to Seymour. The ex-governor protested, but the delegates persisted and states fell in line; Seymour was unanimously nominated on that ballot. The convention then chose as the vice presidential nominee Francis P. Blair Jr., a former Civil War general from an old Democratic family. Now living in Missouri, he was strongly supported by Southern delegates for his outspoken stance against Reconstruction. The convention adjourned on July 9, with mainstream Democrats about the fall. The stakes were high: the country's monetary policy, the fate of Reconstruction, and the future of African Americans hung in the balance. But the mass of voters were not yet through with the South and the potential of Reconstruction, choosing instead the Republicans and Ulysses S. Grant.

*Joel H. Silbey*

**See also:** Congressional Reconstruction; Elections of 1868; Grant, Ulysses S. (1822–1885); Military Reconstruction Acts (1867–1868).

## Further Reading

Franklin, John Hope. "Election of 1868," in Arthur M. Schlesinger Jr., ed., *History of American Presidential Elections, 1789–1968*. New York: Chelsea House, 1971.

Mitchell, Stewart. *Horatio Seymour of New York*. Cambridge, MA: Harvard University Press, 1938.

Silbey, Joel H. *A Respectable Minority: The Democratic Party in the Civil War Era*. New York: W. W. Norton, 1977.

Unger, Irwin. *The Greenback Era: A Social and Political History of American Finance, 1865–1879*. Princeton, NJ: Princeton University Press, 1964.

# DEMOCRATIC PARTY

Since their consolidation as a party under Andrew Jackson in the 1820s, Democrats had carved out an ideological focus that stressed limited federal government intervention in economic affairs, and into the lives of American citizens. Their strict view of the U.S. Constitution and laissez-faire drew popular support from the lower Midwest's Southern-born citizens, from growing urban centers where Irish Catholics were becoming a significant, and from traditionally antigovernment farmers and shopkeepers elsewhere in the North. By mid-century, Democrats ardently opposed the Whig Party's federal intervention into the economy, its high tariff policies, and its banking system. As the national Whigs evolved into the regionally based Republicans, Democrats focused more and more on the preservation of slavery and the plantation economy.

Although many equated Democrats with Southerners and secessionists (since the Democratic Party dominated the South), the party's appeal in the North remained solid even after the war began; a small group of "War Democrats," argued that Americans had to rise above partisan differences and support the Union. These actively supported the Lincoln administration, and even included some fringe Southerners, such as Vice President Andrew Johnson of Tennessee. Peace Democrats ("Copperheads" to their enemies) challenged the war and its costs, and—to them—it is unacceptable disruption of American society. A third group of Democrats claimed to be "legitimate" critics of the Republican Party, but supporters of the war effort. Thus even excluding the extremist Southern members who broke from the Union, the Democratic Party was beset by internal strife. As the war progressed and the Lincoln administration took more aggressive measures, Democrats of all sorts grew agitated over the growth of federal power, the growth of executive power, and the increased focus on blacks and their place in the nation. Republicans withstood wartime challenges easily, taking advantage of their opponents' divisions, and labeling Democrats as treasonous, cowardly "copperheads," who were indifferent to the Union's survival and sacrifices. Republicans successfully retained power in a series of wartime elections, culminating in Lincoln's defeat of Democratic general George B. McClellan in 1864.

As the Civil War ended, the Democratic Party faced an uncertain future. With many of its national leaders tainted by secession, war, and defeat, it seemed forlorn and hopeless. Yet Democratic Party leaders displayed great confidence, believing the worst was over. Abraham Lincoln's aggressive centralization policies and abolitionist tilt reenergized the party faithful. With the war over, and the Thirteenth Amendment forever settling the issue of slavery, Americans had (in the words of Democratic New York governor Horatio Seymour), "closed our lips upon the questions of the past." Democrats looked forward to building a new agenda, a new South, and a new party. But Republicans were not ready to move on; they continued to denounce Democrats, reminding voters of the Peace Democrats' efforts to undermine the Union war effort. Certainly, evidence of the white South's refusal to accept the results of the war—in particular the harsh treatment of freedpeople and the memorializing of former confederates—further damaged Democrats' image. The lenient Reconstruction policy of Andrew Johnson caused a reaction against the Democrats in the early postwar years. Northern voters reacted against the Democrats in state and congressional elections in the Northern states in 1865 and 1866, delivering states and the federal government fully over to Republican control. With the coming of Congressional Reconstruction in 1867, Democrats were both brushed aside from power and provided with weapons to utilize in their struggle: the party focused on the un-American aspects of military control, black dominance, and political corruption. In effect, their arguments after the war mirrored their arguments during the war; they stood by their strict constitutional conservatism and refusal to accept the changes wrought by war and legislated by Republicans and the newly freed blacks. Many a Democratic newspaper, North and South, bore the words: "The Constitution as it is; the Union as it was."

In 1867, Democrats made significant gains due to Republicans pushing black suffrage in several Northern states. The Democrats won a number of statewide elections, and mobilized voters to defeat black suffrage amendments to Northern state constitutions. The Republican response included finding less vulnerable means of solidifying political power and black rights (i.e., the Fourteenth and Fifteenth Amendments) and restraining the Democrats' national leader, who happened to be president. By late 1867, Republicans had begun impeachment efforts against the president, who was actively encouraging Democratic resistance to the Reconstruction measures. But by late spring 1868, Radical failure to remove the president encouraged Democrats and worried Republicans. This helps explain their choice for presidential nominee, the politically inexperienced Ulysses S. Grant, the nation's greatest war hero. The Democrats' effort in the presidential election of 1868 was energetic but misplaced; former governor Horatio Seymour of New York brought a mix of support and concern, but Frank Blair Jr., the vice presidential choice, was an intemperate hothead who embarrassed the party with his wild rejection of Reconstruction. Grant and the Republicans, assisted by the newly enfranchised Southern black vote (under the Reconstruction Acts) assumed control of the White House.

After the election of 1868, the Democratic Party was in angry confusion. It continued to be the nation's minority party, unable to wrest control from its opponents. Some leaders argued for changed direction and a different focus in their policies, which came to be called a "New Departure." In other words, they should, while still hostile to Reconstruction in their public stance, focus more and more on issues of government corruption and federal monetary policy. The final ratification of the Fifteenth Amendment in 1870 seemed to mark a transition point; the policy issue of black male suffrage was now settled by constitutional amendment. Certainly events in the South remained unsettled and unstable, as white resistance and violence only continued to increase, particularly with the growth of the Ku Klux Klan in the early 1870s.

Yet for Northerners, other topics competed for attention. Many cultural tensions, hidden during the war, reemerged; Republicans in Northern states were pushing for the prohibition of alcohol, instituting school curricula reforms, and demanding religious instruction, which Irish Catholics considered an attack on their values. New Departure Democrats also saw allies in a growing, vocal band of dissident Republicans called Liberal Republicans, who criticized Grant's inept appointments, culture of scandal, and interventionist approach toward the South. For the election of 1872, they formed a third party to contest the presidential race, joined by many New Departure Democrats who believed this offered a distasteful, but effective, means of regaining power. The Democrats' national convention adopted the Liberals' platform and endorsed its nominee, the eccentric (and longtime anti-Democratic) newspaper editor Horace Greeley.

The effort at fusion failed miserably, and Grant won re-election by a larger margin than four years earlier. Republicans "waved the bloody shirt"—a political metaphor for dredging up the horrors and sacrifices of the Civil War—and the Democrat's role in it. In 1872,

Republicans added further meaning to the bloody shirt, since white and black Republicans faced deadly violence across the former Confederacy at the hands of vigilante Conservative groups. The Liberal call for reform had its adherents but could not overcome the larger national attitude outward preserving—and possibly expanding—the gains from the Civil War. The Democratic Party seemed to be going backward.

Events during Grant's second term finally provided opportunity for Democrats to reverse their declining fortune. In 1873, the nation plunged into a recession; the Panic of 1873 left thousands jobless and shattered the stock market. Economic suffering brought the currency issue to prominence once again, with Democrats arguing that an inflationary policy—adding money to circulation—would stimulate the economy. They attacked the "Crime of '73," when Congress ended the coinage of silver, and called for the continued used of greenbacks. Conditions led to significant Democrats gain in 1874: 169 Democrat seats in the House of Representatives (up from 88), shifted control of the House to Democrats for the first time in 15 years. They also added 10 additional Democratic senators; a substantial gain, but Republicans still controlled the upper house. As the presidential election of 1876 approached, Democrats believed that they had finally had a winning combination as cries of "Grantism" (ineptitude and political corruption) and a failing economy sounded across the nation. They finally offered a unifying candidate of experience and charisma, Samuel J. Tilden, a Democrat from New York.

Tilden held to a conservative social and political perspective and had demonstrated his reform credentials by prosecuting the notorious "Boss" William Tweed in New York City, who had served as a national model for corruption and fraud. Tilden faced off against Republican Rutherford B. Hayes of Ohio. The election was extremely close. Tilden arguably won a majority of the popular vote, and the larger number of electoral votes, but the confused and questionable results from several Southern states, threw the numbers—and thus results—into disarray. After months of discussion and debate, a special Electoral Commission gave the disputed electoral votes, and thus the election, to the Republican Hayes. As part of this "Compromise of 1877," the Republicans retained the presidency, but Democrats gained as well. The agreement allowed them to regain control over the remaining Southern governments, and the last of the former Confederate states were "redeemed." They also demonstrated their resiliency without losing their ideological soul, and climbed back from near extinction to electoral parity with the Grand Old Party—a significant feat indeed.

*Joel H. Silbey*

**See also:** Black Codes; Compromise of 1877; Democratic National Convention (1868); Elections of 1864; Elections of 1866; National Union Movement (1866); Redemption; U.S. Army and Reconstruction.

## Further Reading

Gambill, Edward. *Conservative Ordeal: Northern Democrats and Reconstruction, 1865–1868.* Ames: Iowa State University Press, 1981.

Gillette, William. *Retreat from Reconstruction, 1868–1879.* Baton Rouge: Louisiana State University Press, 1979.

Mitchell, Stewart. *Horatio Seymour of New York.* Cambridge, MA: Harvard University Press, 1938.

Polakoff, Keith I. *The Politics of Inertia: The Election of 1876 and the End of Reconstruction*. Baton Rouge: Louisiana State University Press, 1973.

## DOUGLASS, FREDERICK (CA. 1818–1895)

Frederick Douglass, former slave, abolitionist, and orator, was born into slavery along the shores of Maryland. He was the son of a white man, of whom he knew nothing, and a slave woman, who died when he was a child. Relatives reared him, until he was sold as a child to the Auld family of Baltimore. In the Auld home he learned in secret to read and write, first via Hugh Auld's wife and later by bribing other white children. As a teenager, Douglass was sold to a brutal plantation owner, and later he worked on the Baltimore shipyards. In 1838, he escaped to New York City. There, Douglass changed his last name from Bailey to Douglass to avoid slave catchers. Within a month, Douglass married Anna Murray, a freed slave he had met in Baltimore.

Douglas settled in New Bedford, Massachusetts, and began participating in abolitionist activities and became well known through his slave narratives. He also contributed to abolitionist newspapers, *The Liberator* and *The National Anti-Slavery Standard*. Prominent abolitionists William Lloyd Garrison and Wendell Phillips encouraged him to join the abolitionist speaking circuit. Douglass became involved in the American Massachusetts Anti-Slavery Society, which sent him on speaking tours across the United States and Great Britain. Shortly thereafter, Douglass wrote his *Narrative of the Life of Frederick Douglass, an American Slave, Written by Himself*. Completed in 1845, this was one of the first narratives written by a slave rather than a white abolitionist. His popularity brought risks: he had to flee to Great Britain to avoid capture, since his book made him well recognized throughout the country. Finally, in 1846, two friends from England raised more than $700 to pay for Douglass's freedom, and he returned to the United States. By 1848, he had begun publishing his own anti-slavery newspaper, *The North Star*, which was later renamed *Frederick Douglass' Paper*. He also attended the first women's rights convention in Seneca Falls, New York.

Born a slave, Frederick Douglass escaped from bondage and became the preeminent African American abolitionist. He dedicated his entire life to the cause of black civil and political rights. His several autobiographies remain brilliant commentaries on the black experience of the 19th century. (Library of Congress)

During the Civil War, President Abraham Lincoln consulted Douglass regarding options for assimilated slaves into the rest of the population. By 1862, Douglass had become one of Lincoln's trusted advisors, and he assisted in helping recruit African Americans for Union regiments. He campaigned tirelessly for the rights of blacks to enlist in the Union army and for emancipation and abolition. With the coming of abolition and the assassination of Lincoln, Douglass fell out of favor. President Andrew Johnson, a staunch Unionist but no friend of black Americans, distrusted Douglass and wanted nothing to do with him. During Congressional Reconstruction he became editor of *The New National Era*, a short-lived newspaper in Washington, D.C., which chronicled the progress of African Americans in the United States. In 1872, he served as a presidential elector at large for New York, and his support of presidential candidate Benjamin Harrison earned him the position of consul general to the Republic of Haiti. He resigned the post a year later, in protest of American businessmen who engaged in dishonest practices. In 1881, he wrote his final autobiography, *The Life and Times of Frederick Douglass*, which accounted for his post-slavery experiences. Douglass died in 1895 from a heart attack at his home in Washington, D.C.

*Mary J. Sloat*

**See also:** Abolition of Slavery; Black Suffrage; Black Troops (U.S. Colored Troops) in the Occupied South; Military Reconstruction Acts (1867–1868); Presidential Reconstruction; U.S. Army and Reconstruction.

## Further Reading

Andrews, William L. "Frederick Douglass, Preacher." *American Literature* 54, no. 4 (1982): 592–97.

Dillon, Merton L. *The Abolitionists: The Growth of a Dissenting Minority*. DeKalb: Northern Illinois University Press, 1974.

Martin, Waldo E. Jr. *The Mind of Frederick Douglass*. Chapel Hill: University of North Carolina Press, 1985.

Ray, Angela G. "Frederick Douglass on the Lyceum Circuit: Social Assimilation, Social Transformation?" *Rhetoric and Public Affairs* 5, no. 4 (2002): 625–47.

# DUNN, OSCAR JAMES (CA. 1821–1871)

Oscar J. Dunn was a black political leader in Louisiana who served as lieutenant governor from 1868 until his death in 1871. Born in New Orleans to a free woman of color, he learned to read, write, and play violin; before the Civil War, he taught music, worked as a barber, and was apprenticed as a plasterer. After the federal capture of New Orleans in 1862, he joined a regiment of black Union troops raised in Louisiana. Toward the end of the war, Dunn actively advocated not only abolition but also black suffrage.

He worked with both the Freedmen's Bureau and the Freedman's Savings and Trust Company, and held a variety of New Orleans city offices following the advent of Radical Reconstruction in 1867. When Republicans nominated Henry Clay Warmoth for governor, he chose Dunn for lieutenant governor. He was elected in April 1868, the first black in U.S. history to hold such office.

Although a member of Warmoth's administration, Dunn and other Louisiana Republicans clashed with the governor over his appointing of white Conservatives to office and his weak support for black civil rights and black political appointments. By 1870, the Louisiana Republican Party had fractured, with Dunn emerging as a leading figure in the anti-Warmoth or "Custom House" faction. When Warmoth left the state to recuperate from an injury in 1871, Dunn, as acting governor, seized the opportunity and removed a number of Warmoth loyalists from office. Dunn reigned in the party convention later that year, and his faction ejected Warmoth and his supporters from the Republican Party. By late 1871, Custom House Republicans even considered uniting with Democrats to impeach Warmoth, but this plan stalled when Dunn died unexpectedly on November 22 from what was called congestion of the brain. His sudden death sparked rumors that he had been poisoned, but no valid evidence has ever surfaced. His funeral was said to be one of the largest ever held in New Orleans, and so affected the state that it brought a temporary truce to the state's political infighting; even Warmoth, who would be eventually impeached, was among the pallbearers.

*John C. Rodrigue*

**See also:** Bureau of Refugees, Freedmen, and Abandoned Lands; Congressional Reconstruction; Democratic Party; Freedmen's Relief Societies; Pinchback, Pinckney Benton Stewart (1837–1921); Presidential Reconstruction.

## Further Reading

Foner, Eric. *Freedom's Lawmakers: A Directory of Black Officeholders during Reconstruction.* Rev. ed. Baton Rouge: Louisiana State University Press, 1996.

Perkins, A. E. "Oscar James Dunn." *Phylon* 4 (1943): 105–21.

Taylor, Joe Gray. *Louisiana Reconstructed: 1863–1877.* Baton Rouge: Louisiana State University Press, 1974.

# E

## EDISTO ISLAND, SOUTH CAROLINA

Located between Charleston and Beaufort on the South Carolina coast, Edisto Island became a focal point for the distribution of land to freedmen following the Civil War. Responding to a request by African American leaders in Savannah, Georgia, Gen. William T. Sherman issued Special Field Order No. 15 in January 1865. This order set aside a 30-mile wide strip of land along the Atlantic Coast from Charleston to Florida's St. Johns River (which had been abandoned by white owners during the war) for settlement by former slaves. The assistant Freedmen's Bureau commissioner, Gen. Rufus Saxton, distributed the land in 40-acre tracts; Freedmen received a possessory title to the land, and in some cases, they received mules and horses that had been seized by Sherman's troops. By June 1865, 40,000 freedpeople had settled on land that included James Island, Edisto Island, and Hilton Head (all in South Carolina), and Sapelo and St. Simon's Islands in Georgia.

White owners objected forcefully and appealed directly to President Andrew Johnson that their land be returned. In September, Johnson ordered the commissioner of the Bureau of Refugees, Freedmen, and Abandoned Lands, Gen. Oliver Otis Howard, to issue Circular 15, which restored lands occupied by freedmen to the original owners. Howard traveled to Edisto Island in October and spoke to a crowd of perhaps 1,000, explaining that they had to abandon the land. A committee composed of Henry Brown, Ishmael Moultrie, and Yates Sampson told Howard that they must have land to be truly free. They spoke eloquently of their generations of toil and their sufferings at the hands of whites, but Howard had his orders. The committee also petitioned Johnson, reminding the president that they had "always [been] true to the Union" and that they were prepared to pay for the land. While Johnson was a Unionist who had supported abolition and the Thirteenth Amendment, he was also a former slaveholder who believed support for black rights was unfair and unconstitutional. At a time when even most Republicans rejected the idea of land confiscation, Johnson was far too racist and too conservative to entertain the notion of giving white land to blacks. As a result, the president issued scores of pardons to former confederates, which restored their political rights and their property—including land. Some freedmen retained their land, but only if they possessed valid titles; in those few cases property rights favored African Americans. Although the precise number remains unclear, most freedmen on Edisto Island—and elsewhere on the coast—did not retain their land. Some moved on, while others remained, only to work again for white landowners.

*William C. Hine*

*See also:* Amnesty Proclamations; Congressional Reconstruction; Contraband, Slaves as; Labor Systems; Port Royal Experiment; Presidential Reconstruction; Republicans, Radical; Stevens, Thaddeus (1792–1868).

## Further Reading

McFeely, William S. *Yankee Stepfather: General O.O. Howard and the Freedmen.* New York: W.W. Norton, 1968.

Oubre, Claude F. *Forty Acres and a Mule: The Freedmen's Bureau and Black Land Ownership.* Baton Rouge: Louisiana State University Press, 1978.

# EDUCATION

Universal education was one of the most significant and permanent achievements of Reconstruction. This was made possible by government and military intervention and a profusion of individuals, churches, religious organizations, and benevolent societies. African Americans themselves lent a considerable hand to these efforts. Advancements, such as the establishment of a never-before-seen Southern public school system for blacks and poor whites, private schools, and black colleges and universities, permanently altered the Southern landscape. But despite the high hopes of the philanthropists, education did not remedy the social, economic, and political ills of post-slavery life.

Prior to the Civil War, education in the South was a luxury enjoyed by wealthy landowners and their families. Education generally included private tutoring, music and dance lessons, English, history, and instruction in plantation management. Planters owned extensive private libraries to supplement this individual schooling. Many of their sons attended colleges or universities, often in Europe or the North.

With a sparse and decentralized population—due to the vast tracks of agricultural land—there was neither money for nor a concentrated population for a public school system. The majority of yeomen (small farmers), as well as poor whites in the isolated mountainous regions, were illiterate. Most Southern states had laws that forbade slaves from receiving an education. Preexisting free black communities, which established their own schools or followed a form of education similar to the wealthy landowners, were other, minor, exceptions. Consequently, education was another way that the great landed communities maintained their dominance over the lower levels (black and white) in this strict class system.

Education for the masses of former slaves was a revolutionary development that began during the war. Even before abolition and victory, throngs of individuals and groups swarmed into the South to educate blacks. The American Missionary Association (AMA) funded teachers' salaries and purchased buildings. Some blacks preferred to establish private schools rather than attend public schools, with impoverished parents eagerly paying the tuition to support schools taught and owned by blacks. Moreover, blacks themselves raised significant funds to build schools and pay teacher salaries. Churches and benevolent aid societies (both secular and religious) from the North and South were instrumental in the establishment of new schools. They often worked with federal aid, in particular the Bureau of Refugees, Freedmen, and Abandoned Lands, which supplied buildings, while private individuals and organizations paid for teaching supplies and salaries. Within Congress, black and white politicians campaigned for more and better schools, colleges, and universities for blacks. The Morrill Act of 1890 provided funds from the sale of federal lands to states willing to establish separate land-grant colleges for blacks. Alcorn A&M in Mississippi, Florida A&M, Southern University in Louisiana, and Tuskegee Institute in Tennessee were among those schools created.

Religious organizations, both black and white, produced more black colleges and universities during Reconstruction than in any other period in America's history. The AMA founded Atlanta University in Georgia, Fisk University in Tennessee, Talladega College in Alabama, Tougaloo College in Mississippi, and Hampton Institute in Virginia, which also accepted American Indians. White Methodists set up Clark College in Georgia, and Claflin University in South Carolina, and white Baptists funded such schools as Atlanta Baptist College, later known as Morehouse College, in Georgia and Shaw University in North Carolina. The African Methodist Episcopal Church established both Allen University in South Carolina and Morris Brown College in Georgia. Many of the elite black men and women of this period attended these schools.

Despite the proliferation of schools in the South, education was not without its obstacles and problems. Blacks were subjected to violence, rioting, beatings, and killings. Other obstacles included a lack of funding, inferior school buildings and classrooms, inadequate supplies, and outdated books. Moreover, white teachers at black schools were paid less than at white schools, and black teachers in general were paid even less. Black schools received another blow when the Freedman's Bureau ended most of its operations in 1870. Moreover, when Conservative Southern whites "redeemed" their states, ending Reconstruction, they cut taxes and refused to fund black public schools. Without federal and state assistance, schools suffered tremendously.

Many of the problems faced by blacks in society at large were reflected in the new educational system. Believing blacks unfit to govern themselves, whites insisted on controlling, funding, and teaching black schools themselves. Reflecting the class ideas and racism of the antebellum period, many whites saw black education as irrelevant given their social class and economic areas of pursuit. The popular curriculum of the period promoted middle-class ethics based upon racist ideas geared toward limiting blacks to occupations in agriculture, industry, and service rather than empowering blacks to improve their station.

Despite these significant shortcomings, a burgeoning population of black scholars, inventors, doctors, and professionals appeared. Yet, education did not alleviate the social, economic, and political problems confronting blacks. Southern whites—indeed, most white Americans—did not change their racist views. In fact, they kept blacks in a state not far from slavery by taking away their civil rights and liberties through Jim Crow laws; hoarding wealth and positions of power; and maintaining dominance through political control, racist court systems and law enforcement, and outright violence. Regardless of these difficult circumstances, education enabled blacks to govern themselves, to maintain self-sustaining communities, to stimulate positive change, and to contribute to the nation.

*Gladys L. Knight*

**See also:** Bourbons; Douglass, Frederick (ca. 1818–1895); Edisto Island, South Carolina; Freedmen's Relief Societies; Port Royal Experiment; Redemption; U.S. Army and Reconstruction.

## Further Reading

Anderson, James D. *The Education of Blacks in the South, 1860–1935.* Chapel Hill: University of North Carolina Press, 1988.

Butchart, Ronald E. *Northern Schools, Southern Black Schools, and Reconstruction.* Westport, CT: Greenwood Press, 1980.

Gatewood, Willard B. *Aristocrats of Color: The Black Elite, 1880–1920.* Bloomington: Indiana University Press, 1990.

Richardson, Joe M. *Christian Reconstruction: The American Missionary Association and Southern Blacks, 1861–1890.* Athens: University of Georgia Press, 1986.

# ELECTIONS OF 1864

The presidential election of 1864 took place amid a destructive and frustrating war, which substantially affected everything about the contest and shaped the nation's political agenda for years afterward.

Both Democratic and Republican parties were beset by internal divisions as the election approached. In 1861, a small group of War Democrats had thrown their support to the administration and its policies in order to preserve the Union. That support had eroded over years of war, with many Northern Democrats appalled by President Abraham Lincoln's expansion of presidential powers, callous approach to civil rights during wartime, and support for widening the war with his Emancipation Proclamation. But Democratic leaders disagreed over how to voice their opposition to Republican Party.

Many believed that they should support the war effort as necessary to restore the Union but use their assistance as a way to exert control over Republican attempts to enlarge the scope of federal power or wage war against slavery. Their mantra was strict construction and no social revolution: "The Constitution as it is, the Union as it was." Another wing, the so-called Peace Democrats, turned against any pragmatic concessions on the war. They believed that continuing it was an error and called for a truce before greater damage to the nation, its values, and its institutions occurred.

These two main party wings brought these arguments to the 1864 national convention in Chicago in late August. They came to an uneasy compromise, adopting a so-called peace platform which, while calling for the Union to be restored and applauding the nation's soldiers for their bravery, branded the war a failure and severely condemned the administration's actions on the home front. This message was accompanied by the nomination of Gen. George McClellan, who supported the war but opposed the Republicans' expansion of its aims and its prosecution, including confiscation, emancipation, and the suspension of civil liberties by Lincoln. The vice presidential candidate, George Hunt Pendleton, came from the Democrats' peace wing.

The Republicans also had their problems. But in contrast with the Democrats, a growing bloc in the Republican Party believed that Lincoln was too moderate and hesitant. These politicians and generals, who earned the title Radicals, pushed the administration to embrace emancipation and implement policies designed to aid former slaves in their transition to freedom. In truth, Lincoln felt it prudent to follow a more restrained course in the hopes of maintaining national unity and winning support from outside the Republican

Party. So at Lincoln's prodding, and with party support, leaders actually changed the name of the party to the National Union Party for the campaign. Some Radicals resisted, and there was a threat of a split in the party; cooler heads prevailed and the grumbling components fell into line. At their national convention in Baltimore in early June, Lincoln's support proved much too strong for the dissidents and he was easily renominated. To exhibit the broadness of the party and attract more moderate support, delegates selected a War Democrat, Andrew Johnson of Tennessee, as the Union Party's vice presidential nominee. It was a risk, as he could have lured many more voters or alienated many more: although a prewar slaveholder, he violently opposed secession and was the only senator from a Confederate state to remain in Congress.

Once the campaign began, internal party divisions faded as the desire to win took over. Their respective campaign organizations staged rallies and speeches and published pamphlets and partisan newspapers. At the outset, the Democrats seemed to have the edge, for the campaign

GRAND, NATIONAL UNION BANNER FOR 1864.
LIBERTY, UNION AND VICTORY.

Currier & Ives print depicting the 1864 Union Party ticket of Abraham Lincoln and Andrew Johnson. Replacing "Republican" with "Union" was intended to draw support and begin reconciliation, but the choice of a Southerner for vice president would have vast ramifications. (Library of Congress)

was taking place at the bleakest point of the war. The Union's failure to defeat the rebellion led to growing war weariness, and McClellan constantly played on the administration's failures. Democratic leaders also appealed to racism and the Constitution and believed that the country would reject emancipation and the uplifting of the freed blacks at the expense (they argued) of white Americans. The Republicans had their weapons, as well. Lincoln's political managers played down the administration's controversial policies and instead focused on the Democrats' ambiguity about the war.

McClellan, who supported the war in his acceptance letter, was simply a tool of the peace wing of the party; these "Copperheads" conspired with Southern sympathizers to undermine the war effort, provoke resistance to the draft, but and even work with Confederate agents to undercut the Union's strength. In short, Democrats were allies of "Dixie, Davis and the Devil."

For a time, even Lincoln believed that he would lose and told his cabinet so. But in summer the war news grew better, culminating in Admiral David G. Farragut's seizure of Mobile Bay, Gen. Philip H. Sheridan's brilliant campaign in the Shenandoah Valley, and

Gen. William T. Sherman's capture of Atlanta. These victories energized Republican support and convinced many undecided voters that success was at hand. Just as important, and very meaningful for understanding the war, was the role of the soldier's vote. Northern states mobilized voting campaigns, army units allowed furloughs so soldiers could vote, and some states even allowed soldiers to vote from the field. Over the voting days in late October and early November, almost 4 million votes were cast with the Republicans winning 2.2 million of them, about 55 percent of the total, and 212 electoral votes from 22 states. Interestingly, those who bore the brunt and suffered the most—the soldiers—went overwhelmingly for Lincoln and the continued prosecution of the war. The Democrats had substantial popular support: 1.8 million voters had chosen them, but they remained a minority, winning only three states and 21 electoral votes. The Republicans, waving the banner of the Union and denouncing Democratic treason, had proved to be too much for them.

*Joel H. Silbey*

*See also:* Abolition of Slavery; Confiscation Acts; Contraband, Slaves as; Presidential Reconstruction; Republicans, Moderate; Wade, Benjamin Franklin (1800–1878).

## Further Reading

Donald, David. *Lincoln*. New York: Simon and Schuster, 1995.

Hyman, Harold M. "Election of 1864," in Arthur M. Schlesinger Jr, ed., *History of American Presidential Elections, 1789–1968*. New York: Chelsea House, 1971, 1155–78.

Silbey, Joel H. *A Respectable Minority: The Democratic Party in the Civil War Era*. New York: W. W. Norton, 1977.

Waugh, John. *Reelecting Lincoln: The Battle for the 1864 Presidency*. New York: Crown, 1997.

# ELECTIONS OF 1866

The fall congressional elections in 1866 marked a watershed in the history of Reconstruction. The elections pitted the name, policy, and party of the president, Andrew Johnson, against the Moderate and Radical Republicans. At stake was control of the U.S. Congress and quite possibly the entire Reconstruction program.

Reconstruction occurred all across the country, in households and courtrooms, in the planter's fields, and in the state legislatures. But the federal government would play the pivotal role. Its resources, its vision, its power and authority could make or unmake the future. Since the middle of the war, Reconstruction had largely been a presidential prerogative, since Abraham Lincoln was acting as commander in chief and the country was at war. The end of the war coincided with the end of his life, allowing Southern Unionist and War Democrat Andrew Johnson into the presidency. But with the war over, the environment changed rapidly; many in the North wanted to assure the fruits of victory, the dominance of the Republican Party, and the role of Congress. Johnson, however, acted in contradictory ways, wielding power as if the war was still going on, yet treating Democrats, the military, and former confederates as if peace were indeed at hand. By late 1865, Republican skepticism grew in the face of Johnson's leniency toward former rebels, his liberal attitude towards reinstating

Southern states, and his indifference towards the black codes erected by legislatures. When, in 1866, Moderate Republicans sought compromise via such proposals as the Civil Rights bill, Freedmen's Bureau bill, and Fourteenth Amendment, Johnson's hostile rejections drove Moderate Republicans into the Radical camp. Johnson's acerbic speeches, his antagonistic veto messages, and growing violence in the South—including the Memphis riot and capped by the New Orleans riot on July 30—convinced many Northerners that the president was out of touch with the changes wrought by war. Presidential Reconstruction had failed to assist the freedpeople, had failed to bring real peace, and had to instill and reinforce loyalty in the white South. This set the stage for the 1866 fall elections, which would determine which party controlled Congress and therefore the Reconstruction of the Union.

In order to defend his program and stave off Republican assaults, Johnson launched a new political party. Taking the name of the broad-based party Lincoln created for 1864, Johnson and his advisors announced their National Union Party in the summer of 1866. Johnson banked on support from Democrats and hoped to lure Northerners suspicious of Radical Republican's ambitious agenda—especially with respect to black rights. At a convention in Philadelphia in August, pro-Johnson Conservatives from around the nation gathered to applaud the Union veterans, criticize the Radical Republicans, and cheer on Johnson. Nicknamed the "arm-and-arm" convention because of wartime rivals arriving with arms linked to show unity, delegates promoted Johnson's message of reconciliation, peace, and stability. The Republicans countered with two conventions, one in Philadelphia in September and the other later in Pittsburgh. These showed divisions in the party, in particular over black suffrage, but did little to either bolster the Republican effort or hamper it. Most Republicans walked a middle road, endorsing certain black civil rights but rejecting proposals for suffrage or land confiscation. In the end, the president, his program, and white Southerners were their own worst enemies. Johnson's ill-fated "Swing around the Circle" speaking tour made more enemies than friends. Johnson's obstinate behavior and continuous reports of violence in the South were proof enough that the president and his program had failed.

The fall elections began in September and ended in November. With many of the Southern states still out of the Union, the elections were primarily a Northern and border-state contest. Along with the elections for national office, many states also had state seats up for grabs. Unfortunately for the president and his National Union Movement, election reports brought only disappointment. Turnout was the highest of a congressional off-year election between 1858 and 1874—and this too helped the Republicans. Republican candidates swept the field and increased their number in both houses of the national legislature. The balance of power in Congress—and the federal government—shifted dramatically, with anti-Johnson forces seizing significant majorities in the House and in the Senate. The 40th Congress would be in effect "veto proof" if members voted by party block, since the Republican Party now constituted more than two-thirds of the House and the Senate and could override any veto. In theory, Congress could pass legislation at will.

To prevent presidential interference and strike while momentum was at hand, the sitting Congress called the new Congress-elect into session in March 1867, immediately after the 39th had closed (rather than wait for fall). This prevented Johnson from acting on his own, without Congress in session, as he had done in 1865 when he issued his amnesty proclamation and reconstruction plan. Therefore, Reconstruction, in many respects, began anew in the spring of 1867, with a Republican-dominated Congress dictating policy. So began the period alternately called Congressional, Military, or Radical Reconstruction.

*Richard Zuczek*

*See also:* Amnesty Proclamations; Black Codes; Bureau of Refugees, Freedmen, and Abandoned Lands; Civil Rights Act of 1866; Command of the Army Act (1867); Congressional Reconstruction; Elections of 1864; Joint Committee on Reconstruction; Loyalty Oaths; Military Reconstruction Acts (1867–1868); Pardons; Provisional Governors; Race Riots; U.S. Army and Reconstruction.

## Further Reading

Benedict, Michael Les. "The Politics of Reconstruction," in John F. Marszalek and Wilson D. Miscamble, eds., *American Political History: Essays on the State of the Discipline.* Notre Dame, IN: University of Notre Dame Press, 1997.

Schroeder-Lein, Glenna, and Richard Zuczek. *Andrew Johnson: A Biographical Companion.* Santa Barbara, CA: ABC-CLIO, 2001.

Trefousse, Hans L. *Andrew Johnson: A Biography.* New York: W. W. Norton and Co., 1989.

# ELECTIONS OF 1867

Beginning in September and stretching into November, the fall state elections of 1867 presented complex, and even contradictory, aspects of Reconstruction. Unlike the rather clear-cut elections of 1866, or the presidential years of 1868 and 1872, the elections of 1867 occurred at the state level and involved a wider variety of players, issues, stages—and even results. In general, however, the results emboldened the Democratic Party and confused the Radical Republicans. The elections of 1867 also differed from other Reconstruction campaigns in that there were really two separate sets of elections under way—one in the North and one in the South.

In the South, the former Confederate states were going through the process imposed by Congress via the Military Reconstruction Acts of March 1867. Under these acts the U.S. Army oversaw voter registration, which included African American males and excluded many former confederates; supervised voting for a constitutional convention; and supervised the election of delegates for this convention. Details of the Southern state elections are covered in state entries elsewhere in this encyclopedia. Taken as a whole, the fall elections did represent a real political revolution, as for the first time, on large scale, black men voted in the United States. Not surprising, the Republican Party scored overwhelming triumphs in all former Confederate states. Neither attempts by white Conservatives to stop the conventions by abstaining nor President Andrew Johnson's Amnesty Proclamation of September 7 (which removed political disabilities from many former confederates) could stop Republican victory. New constitutions were followed by new elections for state legislatures and state offices—most of which went to Republicans. From the perspective of black and white members of the new Southern Republican Party, the Congressional phase of Reconstruction seemed to be off to a successful start.

Things were different in the North. Again, these were state elections, without federal positions at risk, with voters focused upon municipal, county, and state offices, including their legislatures and governors. Historically, Republicans did better on major, national issues that drew solid party voting, whereas Democrats did better when the topics were local and diverse, without an overriding national theme. Such was the case in 1867.

Of course, no election could completely ignore Reconstruction, but topics that related to the Reconstruction program took on state characteristics and local meaning.

For instance, black suffrage was on the ballot in Ohio, Kansas, and Minnesota; the proposals failed in all three states, as did many Republicans who advocated them. In other states, talk of black equality and land confiscation lost Republicans votes and seats. The exact reasons for the backlash are unclear. In some cases, Moderate voters recoiled from extremist proposals. Sometimes other topics crowded in with Reconstruction, such as ethnic demographics that pit the "Yankees" of the Republican Party against the growing number of Irish and Germans who went solidly Democratic. In Massachusetts and New York, the item of chief concern seemed to be prohibition and liquor laws. In some developing western states, the central issue was agitation for—or against—government aid to large railroad companies. National finance also mobilized Democrats, as the battle over monetary policy set soft-money Democrats against hard-money Republicans. Across the North, the party of Lincoln suffered its worst losses since before the Civil War, with Democrats taking possession of most state legislatures; most governors' offices; and many judicial, county, and local positions. This introduced an interesting political dynamic, with the federal government securely in the hands of Republicans, but Democrats in control of the Northern states.

For contemporaries, the Northern results seemed to offer an array of lessons. Democrats took the results as a true reflection of the American electorate (unlike in the South, where "military tyranny" imposed Republican rule) and encouraged the party to continue stressing items that seemed to be working: anti-disfranchisement, anti–black suffrage, and pro-inflation (or soft money). At the national level, no one was more pleased than President Johnson, who did not fully appreciate the local flavor of the election and saw it instead as vindication of his policies. He believed Radicals were on the run—and some argue these developments convinced him to push harder, as in removing Secretary of War Edwin Stanton. Some Democrats (including Johnson) saw the elections as a positive omen, forecasting presidential success in 1868.

By and large, Republicans saw the Democratic resurgence as a rebuke, a warning against going too far too fast. Many Republicans moved more toward the political center, wary of political experiments. Although Johnson forced their hand into impeachment, one sees their conservatism in his acquittal. Certainly the choice of a lukewarm Ulysses S. Grant for the Republican nomination in 1868 also reflected this. Even the capstone to the Reconstruction program, the Fifteenth Amendment, captured this sensitivity; the language is negative (banning specific discriminations) not positive (actually granting voting rights), taking care to allow loopholes for Northern states.

*Richard Zuczek*

**See also:** Alabama; Arkansas; Edisto Island, South Carolina; Elections of 1868; Field Order No. 15; Florida; Fourteenth Amendment (1868); Georgia; House Judiciary Committee; Louisiana; Loyalty Oaths; Mississippi; National Union Movement (1866); North Carolina; Pardons; Port Royal Experiment; Presidential Reconstruction; South Carolina; Southern Homestead Act (1866); Stevens, Thaddeus (1792–1868); Sumner, Charles (1811–1874); Tenure of Office Act (1867); Texas; Union League of America; Virginia.

## Further Reading

Benedict, Michael Les. "The Politics of Reconstruction," in John F. Marszalek and Wilson D. Miscamble, eds., *American Political History: Essays on the State of the Discipline*. Notre Dame, IN: University of Notre Dame Press, 1997.

Benedict, Michael Les. "The Rout of Radicalism: Republicans and the Election of 1867." *Civil War History* 18 (December 1972): 334–44.

Foner, Eric. *Reconstruction Updated Edition: America's Unfinished Revolution, 1863–1877*. Reprint, New York: HarperCollins, 2014.

Leppner, Paul. *The Third Electoral System, 1853–1892: Parties, Voters, and Political Cultures*. Chapel Hill: University of North Carolina Press, 1979.

# ELECTIONS OF 1868

The first presidential election since the Civil War, the election of 1868 continued many of the same debates seen four years earlier. In particular, arguments swirled over the expansion of the national government and the racial initiatives of the Republican Party, controversies that had been aired since the outbreak of the Civil War in 1861.

Republican Party leaders were split over their strategy. Some argued that they had pushed too far, and that the 1867 losses indicated that the party should moderate its policies. Of greatest concern was the Northern opposition to black suffrage. The Radical wing disagreed; Reconstruction in the South was not complete, as whites remained defiant, while blacks faced violence, economic hardship, and civil discrimination. It seemed Moderates won out: at the Republican National Convention in Chicago in May, the delegates unanimously chose Ulysses S. Grant as their candidate. His platform declared that black suffrage was a state-level question, at least in the states that had not seceded from the Union, and his mantra, "let us have peace," seemed to imply a less aggressive relationship to the former Confederate states. Speaker of the House Schuyler Colfax of Indiana became his running mate, defeating the Radical senator Ben Wade.

The Democratic Party had its own problems. The party was still weak and disorganized. Although a Democrat currently held the presidency, Republicans had taken full control of Congress in the elections of 1866. Democrats still reeled under the banner of treason and civil war, and despite the vast numbers of Northern Democrats who had supported the war effort, still carried the burden of secession and defeat. But the state elections of 1867 seemed a positive omen, and Republicans' inability to remove President Johnson from office showed the party was mortal. Democratic leaders intended, therefore, to push ahead on the themes of restoration, excessive Republican radicalism, and resistance to black rights.

But like their rivals, the Democrats were also divided. There were sharp divisions over federal monetary policy, with westerners pushing to continue wartime federal use of national banknotes ("greenbacks") that had been issued during the conflict. This "soft-money" group argued expanding the money in circulation would boost a weak economy, while fiscally Conservative Democrats in the East supported specie (metallic money) as the only legal circulating medium. At the Democratic Convention in New York, held in the newly completed Tammany Hall on July 4, the soft-money leader, George Hunt Pendleton of Ohio, took the early lead for the nomination, but hard-money Conservatives did their best to block him. For a time, some favored Chief Justice Salmon P. Chase, a former Democrat who helped found the Republican Party; as chief justice, his fair handling of Johnson's impeachment trial impressed Democrats. As for the incumbent Johnson, his dreams of being the party nominee only added to the portrait of a man out-of-touch with a changing nation. He found no significant support for his nomination. Finally, the

Conservatives fixed on Horatio Seymour, wartime governor of New York and critic of the Abraham Lincoln administration. After much debate and dealing, Seymour earned the nomination on the 22nd ballot. Frank Blair Jr., of Missouri, a former Republican and Civil War general from a once-prominent Democratic family, was selected for vice president.

The Democrats focused on the failure of, and revolutionary tumult caused by, Republican Southern policies. In the words of the April 14, 1868 issue of the *New York World*, the platform was "1. Opposition to Congressional usurpation. 2. Opposition to Negro supremacy. 3. Immediate restoration of the unity and peace of the nation." The Republicans predictably counterattacked by waving the "bloody shirt," emphasizing the violence in the South, allegedly aimed at reversing the results of the war, and Seymour's alleged support of the draft rioters in New York City in 1863. Republicans also went after Blair for his pro-Southern, anti-Reconstruction stance, which called on former confederates to resist Republican efforts in the South.

In the end, Republicans won their third straight presidential election, albeit with reduced margins. They captured 26 states with 214 electors and 52.7 percent of the popular vote to the Democrats' 80 electors and just over 47 percent of the votes cast. Eight (of eleven) reconstructed states of the former Confederacy participated in the election, with the Republicans winning six of them. However, the Democrats gained 42 seats in the House of Representatives, rebounding from their disastrous totals of two years before. They had not won the presidency nor regained control of Congress, but the results still gratified many Democrats and startled Republican leaders. Still, memories of the Civil War, and at least some support for protecting blacks rights, continued to ensure Republican dominance.

*Joel H. Silbey*

*See also:* Presidential Reconstruction; Republicans, Moderate; Republicans, Radical.

## Further Reading

Franklin, John Hope. "Election of 1868," in Arthur M. Schlesinger Jr., ed., *History of American Presidential Elections, 1789–1968*. New York: Chelsea House, 1971, pp. 1247–1300.

Mitchell, Stewart. *Horatio Seymour of New York*. Cambridge, MA: Harvard University Press, 1938.

Unger, Irwin. *The Greenback Era: A Social and Political History of American Finance, 1865–1879*. Princeton, NJ: Princeton University Press, 1964.

# ELECTIONS OF 1876

Many regard the U.S. presidential election of 1876 as the most controversial in American history. The Democratic Party nominee, Samuel J. Tilden, won more popular votes that Republican Party nominee Rutherford B. Hayes but did not win the required number of votes in the Electoral College. Complicating matters were 20 disputed electoral votes from Oregon, Florida, Louisiana, and South Carolina. Congress was compelled to create an unprecedented Electoral Commission to address the deadlock, which, after much negotiation and secrecy, chose Rutherford B. Hayes as the 19th president of the United States.

Banner depicting the rival tickets in the 1876 presidential election. Although the Democrat Tilden received more votes, a special commission named Republican Hayes the winner, generating the "compromise of 1877" controversy. (Library of Congress)

By 1876, Americans were anxious to replace President Ulysses S. Grant. Many blamed him for the Panic of 1873 and the ensuing depression, and his administration was notorious for its scandals and corruption. By 1876, the Democrats had regained political power in all but three Southern states—Louisiana, South Carolina, and Florida—by ruthlessly intimidating Southern Republicans and violently stamping out black suffrage. Thus, the Democrats represented a formidable challenge to the Republicans. For their part, the Republicans were desperate to keep the Democrats out of the presidency. Both parties were prepared to win at any cost. Ohio governor Rutherford B. Hayes narrowly won the Republican Party nomination. Hayes was an attorney, Civil War hero, and governor who had earned a reputation as a reformer. The Democratic Party was nearly unanimously in favor of New York governor Samuel J. Tilden, an eminent lawyer with many railroad companies as clients. Tilden too had a reform background, recognized for challenging the powerful Tammany Hall organization and prosecuting William M. "Boss" Tweed. A third party challenge arose from the Greenback Labor Party, which nominated New York's Peter Fenimore Cooper for president. Cooper had a striking background as a philanthropist and proponent of the American Indian reform movement. The other parties, too small to pose a significant challenge, included the Prohibition Party, the American National Party, and the Communist Party.

The election of 1876 was a hotly contested race. Both the Democratic and Republican nominees promoted reform and the end of Reconstruction; both rallied an equally large number of supporters. Tilden garnered 4,288,546 votes. Hayes lagged behind him with

4,034,311 votes, and Cooper was third with 75,973. Thus, Tilden was the decisive winner in popular voting, but the situation was far from clear in terms of the Electoral College votes. Tilden had 184 electoral votes to Hayes's 165. The 20 remaining votes were in dispute. Outraged by the outcome, the Republicans argued that the Democrats had intimidated and bribed blacks in those Southern states, thereby taking votes that should have gone to Hayes. The Democrats retorted by accusing the Republicans of tampering with ballots in Florida. Evidence indicates, in fact, that both parties bought votes in Florida, Louisiana, and South Carolina.

Once Oregon went for Hayes, the 19 contested votes in the three Southern states still remained. Florida had four electoral votes, Louisiana eight, and South Carolina seven, just enough to put Hayes over the top if he had them all. All three states presented dual electoral votes to Congress, one from the official election supervisory agency and the other from the carpetbag Republicans. The supervisory agency showed Tilden ahead in the popular vote in those states, but the Republicans nullified many Democratic ballots, claiming that the Democrats had committed fraud and used violence.

The Electoral Commission of 1877 was Congress's response to the election crisis. Its objective was to decide each of the 19 disputed votes. In a still-controversial series of deals collectively called the "compromise of 1877," the Commission and the rival parties reached an agreement that brought an end to the presidential impasse. The specifics of those promises remain in dispute, but historians do know that the Commission awarded all disputed electoral votes to Hayes, and eventually Democrats in Congress accepted the decision. In exchange, Republicans agreed to withdraw federal troops from the South, end Reconstruction, and provide support for Southern railroads. Two days prior to inauguration day, Congress awarded the 19 remaining disputed votes to Hayes, giving him a total of 185 electoral votes, one more than Tilden.

In general, Hayes had a successful term. He attacked corruption in the federal government, grappled with civil-service reform, and brought about an end to the depression caused by the Panic of 1873. However, the withdrawal of federal support and law enforcement in the South left African Americans and their Southern Republican allies unable to defend themselves against the heinous crimes of disfranchisement, discriminatory laws, and violence. Thus, the election marked the end of any serious, federally sponsored reconstruction efforts for nearly a century.

*Gladys L. Knight*

**See also:** Gary, Martin Witherspoon (1831–1881); Gun Clubs; Hampton, Wade, III (1818–1902); Kellogg, William Pitt (1830–1918); New South; Nicholls, Francis Redding Tillou (1834–1912); Packard, Stephen B. (1842–1922); Redemption; Shotgun Plan; U.S. Army and Reconstruction; Wells, James M. (1808–1899); White League.

## Further Reading

Dickerson, Donna L. *The Reconstruction Era: Primary Documents on Events from 1865 to 1877.* Westport, CT: Greenwood Press, 2003.

Morris, Roy. *Fraud of the Century: Rutherford B. Hayes, Samuel Tilden, and the Stolen Election of 1876.* New York: Simon & Schuster, 2003.

Polakoff, Keith Ian. *The Politics of Inertia: The Election of 1876 and the End of Reconstruction.* Baton Rouge: Louisiana State University Press, 1973.

## ELLIOTT, ROBERT B. (1842–1884)

Robert Brown Elliott was a talented African American who rose from obscurity to positions of considerable political power as one of the leading Republicans in South Carolina.

Although Elliott claimed to have been born in Boston on August 11, 1842, to parents from the West Indies, his biographer concludes that he was more likely born in Liverpool and arrived in Boston shortly after the Civil War. Somewhere, though probably not Eton College as he claimed, Elliott received a first-rate classical education, as his political speeches demonstrated. What does appear certain about his early years is that by 1867, he was working as a typesetter in Boston when he heard of an opportunity to move to Charleston, South Carolina, to join Richard H. Cain on the staff of a Republican newspaper, the *South Carolina Leader*.

Arriving as a black carpetbagger in South Carolina in March 1867, Elliott threw himself into political activity. Under the environment of the Military Reconstruction Acts, Elliott helped organize the Union League for the state, and then served as a delegate to the 1868 Constitutional Convention. He was elected to the South Carolina House of Representatives later that year and served through 1870. In the legislature Elliott became one of the most powerful Republicans, serving as assistant adjutant general in 1869 and launching the controversial state militia. In 1870, Elliott was elected to the U.S. House of Representatives, where he served two terms and was widely noted for his speaking ability and his determination to protect African Americans from violence and discrimination. Elliott's most celebrated speech was delivered on January 6, 1874, in support of the bill that became the Civil Rights Act in 1875.

Elliott resigned his seat in Congress in 1874 and returned to South Carolina to fight the corruption that was weakening the Republican Party. Elliott cooperated with carpetbagger Daniel H. Chamberlain to push the corrupt governor of South Carolina, Franklin J. Moses Jr., out of political life. Elliott was elected to the South Carolina House of Representatives in 1874 and became the speaker. In the chaotic election of 1876, he ran unsuccessfully for attorney general. With white Conservatives forcing their way back into power, Elliott recognized his political days for the state were numbered; he accepted a federal job as a customs official in Charleston, and by 1881, he had transferred to New Orleans. He died of malaria there on August 9, 1884.

*Bruce E. Baker*

*See also:* Bourbons; Congressional Reconstruction; Scalawags.

### Further Reading

Lamson, Peggy. *The Glorious Failure: Black Congressman Robert Brown Elliott and the Reconstruction in South Carolina.* New York: W. W. Norton, 1973.


## ENFORCEMENT ACTS (1870, 1871, 1875)

In an effort to safeguard and fortify Reconstruction, Congress passed a great deal of legislation in the years between 1867 and 1875. The Fourteenth and Fifteenth Amendments represent capstones to this effort, but these met with considerable opposition in the South. As a result, congressional Republicans sought other ways to enforce and guarantee civil rights for African Americans.

Among these tools were a series of measures called Enforcement Acts, four of which were passed in 1870 and 1871, with a fifth measure failing in 1875. For many historians, the 1875 attempt to pass a fifth enforcement act (along with the 1875 Civil Rights Act) represented the closing of congressional Reconstruction.

The four laws passed in 1870 and 1871 were criminal codes designed to protect blacks' rights to vote, serve on juries, hold political office, and receive equal protection under the law. The first act, passed on May 31, 1870, was titled "An Act to Enforce the Right of Citizens of the United States to Vote in the Several States of this Union, and for Other Purposes." Focusing on the Fifteenth Amendment, it targeted private and public actions. It prohibited state election officials from enforcing discriminatory laws and from using force, intimidation, or bribery to prevent men from voting because of their race. It prohibited private citizens from combining and using force, intimidation, or violence to deny others their right to vote. Violators faced fine and imprisonment. The statute also reenacted the Civil Rights Act of 1866 using both the Fourteenth Amendment and Fifteenth Amendment as its constitutional base. In a path-breaking step, it also applied federal penalties to private individuals. Violations of the law were to be handled by the Department of Justice, newly created in 1870, and tried in federal courts.

The next two Enforcement Acts, of July 14, 1870, and February 28, 1871, expanded the number of federal election supervisors, especially for cities with more than 20,000 in population, an indication that Republican concerns extended to Democratic-dominated Northern cities as well as to Southern rural areas. Passed on April 20, 1871, the fourth act, also known as the Ku Klux Klan Act, once again addressed discrimination within state laws as well as private conspiracies. Its title reveals its constitutional base: "An Act to Enforce the Provisions of the Fourteenth Amendment to the Constitution of the United States and for other Purposes." The act made it a federal crime to conspire and to disguise one's self in order to deny others the equal protection of the laws. Such restrictions on private action provoked debate in Congress over the intent and reach of all three Reconstruction amendments. The statute authorized the president to suspend the writ of habeas corpus, declare martial law, and employ federal troops in affected areas. Under its authority, in October 1871, President Ulysses S. Grant suspended the writ in nine counties of South Carolina. Use of the statute to attack Klan activity in that state, as well as Mississippi, North Carolina, and Tennessee, was undermined by many problems, including a lack of funds and federal troops, intimidation of officials, and uncertain commitment by federal enforcement and judicial officers.

With several Southern states already back in the hands of white Conservatives, Republicans in Congress recognized that Redemption swept away many of the positive changes. Furthermore, the national elections of 1874 marked a watershed, for the Democratic Party had regained control of Congress. Thus, the lame-duck Republican Congress recognized this might be their last opportunity to provide federal protection for besieged Southern Republicans. Long advocated by Radical Republican Massachusetts senator Charles Sumner—who had recently passed away—and Benjamin Butler, the movement for a new enforcement act followed the March passage of the Civil Rights Act of 1875. Designed to protect equal rights and freedom of access to public facilities such as hotels, railroads, restaurants, and theaters, the Civil Rights Act included all persons, regardless of race. The law also prohibited the exclusion of blacks from jury duty. A clause stipulated that it was a criminal offense to deny entrance at public places to any person, regardless of race; as a result, another enforcement measure seemed a natural. The enforcement bill provided additional resources and authority for supervising elections, and even allowed the president to suspend the writ of habeas corpus, not seen since 1871 (that provision had been revoked by Congress in 1872). Some Republicans believed this act was vital to protecting Southern voters, key for the upcoming elections of 1876.

Unfortunately, Republicans had already begun to drift from their party and their agenda, and many were tired of the Reconstruction muddle. Northerners in general had grown indifferent to the plight of Southern blacks, especially in light of tales of Southern corruption and the national recession since 1873. There was little enthusiasm for an additional act to enforce existing legislation. Sensing that the fervor over protecting Southern Republicans had burnt out, longtime Republican congressman and Speaker of the House James G. Blaine offered that it might be better to "lose the South and save the North," than end up losing both. Oddly, against his advice, the House did pass the measure, but it failed in the Senate. The last effort in the 19th century to provide federal enforcement was dead, and for blacks in particular, and Reconstruction in general, it seemed clear that congressional interest was as well.

As another indicator of the climate, the very next year the Supreme Court delivered two landmark decisions that stopped federal enforcement in its tracks. In *United States v. Reese* and *United States v. Cruikshank*, the Court severely curtailed the scope of the Fourteenth and Fifteenth Amendments and the federal government's jurisdiction. Later in *United States v. Harris* and the Civil Rights Cases, decisions delivered in 1883, the Court largely overturned the government's entire enforcement foundation. Just as it had expanded, the federal government's authority contracted and left millions to the whims of hostile state governments, discriminatory businesses, and prejudiced private individuals.

*Claudine L. Ferrell and Heather Duerre Humann*

**See also:** Black Suffrage; Bourbons; Congressional Reconstruction; Grant, Ulysses S. (1822–1885); Gun Clubs; Jim Crow Laws; Republicans, Liberal; Suffrage; U.S. Army and Reconstruction.

## Further Reading

Foner, Eric. *Reconstruction Updated Edition: America's Unfinished Revolution, 1863–1877*. Reprint, New York: HarperCollins, 2014.

Kelly, Alfred H., Winfred Harbison, and Herman Belz. *The American Constitution: Its Origins, Growth, and Development*. 6th ed. New York: W. W. Norton, 1983.

Swinney, Everette. *Suppressing the Ku Klux Klan: Enforcement of the Reconstruction Amendments, 1870–1877*. New York: Garland, 1986.

Williams, Lou Falkner. *The Great South Carolina Ku Klux Klan Trials, 1871–1872*. Athens: University of Georgia Press, 1996.

# F

## FESSENDEN, WILLIAM PITT (1806–1869)

Congressman, senator, and leader of the Moderate Republicans in the Senate, William Pitt Fessenden was born in Boscawen, New Hampshire, but moved to practice law in Portland, Maine. He became a state legislator, and in 1841 a one-term member of Congress. In so ruggedly Democratic a state, he could not have expected to rise higher, and, indeed, was defeated in later efforts to win the congressional seat. Then, in the early 1850s, the quarrels over liquor prohibition and the expansion of slavery ripped the Democratic Party apart. In the political confusion, Whigs and anti-Nebraska Democrats had the votes to put Fessenden into the Senate in 1854. They were not disappointed; switching to the Republican Party almost at once, he held the seat until his death in 1869.

From his first address, a denunciation of the Kansas-Nebraska bill, he became a senator that colleagues listened to and admired. He served on the Finance Committee during the war and made important contributions to wartime banking and tax legislation. He briefly held the position as Abraham Lincoln's secretary of the treasury in 1864 (following Salmon Chase's departure) but returned to the Senate in 1865. There, he was central among the architects of Congressional Reconstruction. He chaired the Joint

William Pitt Fessenden, Moderate Republican senator from Maine. He cast one of the "nay" votes at President Johnson's impeachment trial. (Library of Congress)

Committee on Reconstruction that repudiated Andrew Johnson's Southern policy, yet voted for his acquittal during the impeachment trial; fear of diminishing the presidency, coupled with a desire to block Radical Ben Wade from moving into the presidency, motivated his not-guilty vote. At his death in the fall of 1869, he was still widely respected and admired for his fairness, political skill, and moderation.

*Mark W. Summers*

***See also:*** Presidential Reconstruction.

## Further Reading

Jellison, C. A. *Fessenden of Maine: Civil War Senator.* Syracuse, NY: Syracuse University Press, 1962.

# FIELD ORDER NO. 15

On January 16, 1865, three months before Appomattox, Union general William T. Sherman issued his famous Special Field Order No. 15. This order set aside "the islands from Charleston south, the abandoned rice-fields along the rivers for thirty miles back from the sea, and the country bordering the St. John's River, Florida," for the exclusive settlement of slave refugees. Sherman instructed General Rufus Saxton to grant each head of a black family not more than 40 acres of land and to "furnish . . . subject to the approval of the President of the United States, a possessory title." By June 1865, Saxton reported that approximately 40,000 blacks had settled on about 400,000 acres of land on what became known as the Sherman Reservation. Sherman authorized Saxton to loan the black families farm animals—decrepit creatures too broken down for military service. These presumably were the "mules" intended to work the proverbial "forty acres."

As the freedmen and women moved to occupy the land, in the summer and fall of 1865, President Andrew Johnson overturned Sherman's order. Johnson pardoned former confederates and ordered the restoration of all property except that sold under a court decree (and of course slaves).

Subsequent events—creation of the Bureau of Refugees, Freedmen, and Abandoned Lands (the Freedmen's Bureau) in March 1865 and the passage of the Southern Homestead Act in June 1866—further complicated the role of the federal government in distributing land and farm animals to the freedpeople. In fact, the Freedmen's Bureau was authorized to lease, not to grant outright, "not more than forty acres" of abandoned or confiscated lands to freedmen with the option to "purchase the land and receive such titles thereto as to the United States can convey." The Homestead Act set aside public land in Alabama, Arkansas, Florida, Louisiana, and Mississippi, for purchase by the freedpeople for a five-dollar fee. The available land, however, was generally of inferior quality and the freedmen lacked sufficient capital to purchase implements and to farm the land properly. When, in 1876, Congress repealed the Homestead Act, blacks cultivated only several thousand acres, mostly in Florida.

Denying any role in misleading the freedmen and women in the Field Order No. 15, Sherman later recalled that "the military authorities at that day . . . had a perfect right to grant the possession of any vacant land to which they could extend military protection, but we did not undertake to give a fee-simple title; and all that was designed by these special field orders was to make temporary provisions for the freedmen and their families during the rest of the war, or until Congress should take action in the premises." Sherman added that Secretary of War Edwin M. Stanton had approved his field order.

Although some Radical Republicans, including Thaddeus Stevens and George W. Julian, supported confiscation of Southern plantations with hopes of reforming the South's social and economic system, most 19th-century Americans held private property too sacred to endorse wide-scale land redistribution.

Nonetheless, the slogan "forty acres and a mule" remains a rallying cry for reparationists, a symbol of the heartfelt hopes and dreams of many African Americans. Since Reconstruction, debates over the meaning of Sherman's Field Order No. 15 have fueled demands for reparations by blacks and their white allies. Proponents of reparations have argued that the government reneged on its wartime pledge to compensate the ex-slaves with land and farm animals. Reparationists continue to cite "forty acres and a mule" as justification for their appeals for a broad range of compensation—from cash payments to tax credits—for the descendants of America's 4 million black slaves.

*John David Smith*

**See also:** Amnesty Proclamations; Contraband, Slaves as; Pardons.

## Further Reading

Bentley, George R. *A History of the Freedmen's Bureau.* Philadelphia: University of Pennsylvania Press, 1955

Oubre, Claude F. *Forty Acres and a Mule: The Freedmen's Bureau and Black Land Ownership.* Baton Rouge: Louisiana State University Press, 1978

Sherman, William T. *Memoirs of General William T. Sherman. By Himself. In Two Volumes.* New York: D. Appleton and Co., 1875.

## FIFTEENTH AMENDMENT (1870)

The Fifteenth Amendment was proposed in 1869 and ratified in 1870. It consists of two sections. The first section prohibits federal and state governments from denying or abridging U.S. citizens the right to vote "on account of race, color, or previous condition of servitude." The second section empowers Congress to enforce the amendment. Simply put, the amendment removed race as voting barrier for American citizens and enabled African Americans, including both ex-slaves in the South and disfranchised free blacks in the North, to participate in the American political process. Together with the Thirteenth Amendment (which abolished slavery) and Fourteenth Amendment (which established birthright citizenship and national protection of civil rights), the Fifteenth Amendment is now seen by historians as part of America's constitutional reinventions of the Reconstruction era that profoundly transformed the meaning and practice of American democracy.

In spite of African Americans' demands and agitation for equal suffrage during and after the Civil War, black suffrage was not included on the agenda of the phase of Presidential Reconstruction (1863–1866). Both presidents Abraham Lincoln and Andrew Johnson, in their Reconstruction plans, limited the participation in reconstructing the postwar state governments to whites. By nationalizing black men's right to vote after the Civil War, the Fifteenth Amendment nationalized the practice of black enfranchisement that began in the South under the Military Reconstruction Acts of 1867. But black enfranchisement in the South challenged black disfranchisement in the North and West, where 21 states still excluded free black citizens from voting. To rid the party of its ideological awkwardness and moral hypocrisy and to secure black suffrage on a more permanent constitutional basis, Republicans, who were a majority in both houses of Congress, proposed to nationalize black suffrage, but the party again was divided on how to construct the amendment. Several proposals were advanced, varying from an affirmative pronouncement of voting rights being conferred to all adult male American citizens to simply prohibiting denying citizens voting rights on a racial basis. Eventually, the prohibition version—the most conservative version—was chosen and agreed upon. The rationale for this version had to do with preserving the original separation of powers between federal and state governments. States had retained the power to prescribe qualifications for voters. And that power, in the understanding of many Moderate Republicans should not be completely removed.

Thus, the final wording of the Fifteenth Amendment did not directly confer voting rights to any U.S. citizens; it prevented federal or state governments from denying voting rights to citizens on a racial basis. In other words, the amendment conferred upon U.S. citizens the right not to be denied the right to vote because of race. States could still use other mechanisms or qualifications to deprive citizens the right to vote. During the period of black disfranchisement in the 1880s and 1890s, Southern states used such devices as poll tax, literacy test, and white primary to virtually end African American voting.

The ratification of the Fifteenth Amendment went relatively quickly, compared with the ratification processes of the other two Reconstruction amendments. Western states like Nevada ratified the amendment only after they were assured that they could continue to use nativity to exclude undesirable groups like the Chinese from voting. Radical Republicans had attempted to include the right for blacks to hold offices, and some even pushed for including women, but these issues were set aside.

After federal enforcement declined and the South experienced "redemption" in 1877, black disfranchisement emerged as the norm in the South well into the 1960s. The Fifteenth Amendment was sparsely enforced yet remained a constitutional principle; not until the civil rights movement would the issue of black voting again gain national attention.

*Xi Wang*

***See also:*** Enforcement Acts (1870, 1871, 1875); Fourteenth Amendment; Republicans, Radical; Suffrage.

## Further Reading

Foner, Eric. *Reconstruction: America's Unfinished Revolution, 1863–1877*. New York: Harper and Row, 1988.

Gillette, William. *The Right to Vote: Politics and the Passage of the Fifteenth Amendment.* Baltimore, MD: Johns Hopkins University Press, 1965.

Goldman, Robert M. *Reconstruction and Black Suffrage: Losing the Vote in Reese &Cruikshank.* Lawrence: University Press of Kansas, 2001.

Keyssar, Alexander. *The Right to Vote: The Contested History of Democracy in the United States.* New York: Basic Books, 2000.

Wang, Xi. *The Trial of Democracy: Black Suffrage and Northern Republicans, 1860–1910.* Athens: University of Georgia Press, 1997.

# FLORIDA

Florida's Reconstruction officially began on May 20, 1865, when Confederate officials surrendered to the Union army at the state capital of Tallahassee. The state and its 140,000 residents managed to emerge from the Civil War without witnessing the destruction of property and the great loss of life that her sisters in the Confederacy endured. At the end of hostilities, approximately 15,000 Floridians lost their lives on the battlefield, with Tallahassee as the only Southern capital to escape invasion during the war. This lack of federal presence meant that unlike some other states, there was no wartime Reconstruction.

Florida's first effort at Reconstruction began with Andrew Johnson's May 29, 1865, amnesty proclamation. In accordance with the proclamation, William Marvin, Johnson's appointed provisional governor of Florida, called for statewide elections for the purpose for selecting delegates for a constitutional convention. Fifty-four delegates gathered in Tallahassee and drafted a document fitting the requirements of Johnson's proclamation; the new constitution nullified Florida's ordinances of secession, repudiated the Confederate debt, and abolished slavery; but in all other aspects, it mirrored the states previous constitution. It did not allow for black suffrage, and continued to count African Americans as three-fifths of a white person for the purpose of representation in the state assembly. By December 1865, Florida had selected representatives to Congress, and elected one of the state's former Supreme Court justices and Whig, David S. Walker, as governor.

Ironically, many of the problems that Walker and the state faced during his brief two-year term as Florida's chief executive resulted from his efforts to ensure tranquility in the state. For instance, the legislature passed Black Codes and laws prohibiting vagrancy, possession of firearms, stealing, and breaking labor contracts. Similar statutes provided for the involuntary apprenticeship of African American children and limitations on the ex-slaves' ability to seek redress for grievances in the state court system. Despite the many obstacles preventing Florida's freedpeople from enjoying the full measure of freedom, they eagerly pushed the boundaries of their new rights. With the assistance of the Bureau of Refugees, Freedmen, and Abandoned Lands, the state's African American population began to take an active interest in politics. They joined groups such as the Union League and Lincoln Brotherhood which served as political training grounds for many of Florida's future African American leaders.

The opportunity of these leaders to participate in the political process came quickly. After Congress passed the Military Reconstruction Act in March 1867, the U.S. Army supervised a new series of elections for yet another redrafting of Florida's Constitution. Held in November 1867, this was the first statewide election open to the state's African American population. However, extending suffrage to many men who had been former slaves initiated much of the political turmoil and charges of corruption that plagued Florida during the Reconstruction. Many Democrats, refusing to acknowledge the legitimacy of any convention that had the participation of former slaves, stayed away from the polls on Election Day. In addition, the unity enjoyed by Florida Republicans from the end of the war to the onset of Congressional Reconstruction disintegrated into two factions, the radicals or "Mule Team" and a group of Moderates and Conservatives known in some circles as Union Republicans. The "Mule Team" earned its name because of the two mules that pulled their wagon as they campaigned throughout the state. Their radical, uncompromising message of political and social equality appealed greatly to the state's African American population, but at the same time, frightened many native Floridians and Republicans alike. In response to this fear, Union Republicans, led by future governor Harrison Reed, created a coalition of Republicans and Democrats by placing emphasis on the economic reconstruction of the state rather than its social issues; an approach that enjoyed the support of many of Florida's wealthier citizens as well as the approval of President Johnson. When the constitutional convention convened in Tallahassee on January 20, 1868, these divisions had not been reconciled, and the convention broke apart; radicals drafted their document, but more than half of the convention's delegates met in a rump convention where they drafted a more conservative document. Likewise, this new assembly, under Harrison Reed, drafted new rules that resulted in the dismissal of radical delegates for not being Florida residents. Ultimately, Congress accepted the constitution drafted by the rump convention, despite the fierce debate by the radicals over the legitimacy of the process that created it.

Although Florida's new constitution was one of the most progressive in the history of the state, it differed from the Radicals' document in very significant ways. Whereas the Radicals' constitution required all officeholders to take a loyalty oath and prohibited ex-confederates from holding state office, the ratified constitution placed no such restrictions on former supporters of the Confederacy. The radicals favored making most state and local officials elected, but the new document gave the governor the power to appoint individuals to these offices. Last, the new constitution limited the number of representatives each county could have in the state assembly to four, regardless of its population. The last provision had a dramatic effect on the state's African Americans because it diminished their voting strength in counties where they were the most populous. This allowed, in effect, a third of the state's actual population to control the entire state legislature.

With the ratification of the new constitution, this tenuous alliance between Moderate Republicans and Democrats quickly disintegrated. Harrison Reed, who had been instrumental in the drafting and ratification of the document, served as Florida's first governor under Congressional Reconstruction. However, political infighting, violence, and rumors of scandal marked his tenure as governor. By the time Reed's term in office expired in 1872, the state legislature had initiated impeachment proceedings against him on four different occasions.

Despite losing much of their political power because of the constitution, Florida's African Americans made some gains during the Reed administration. Two of the most notable include Josiah T. Walls, an ex-slave and Union soldier who became Florida's first African American congressman in 1870, and Dartmouth graduate Jonathan C. Gibbs, who became secretary of state. However, most of their political gains occurred in the cities and towns, where they served in positions that lay outside of the governor's considerable power of patronage. Throughout the state, African Americans served as city aldermen, in law enforcement, and on city councils.

Not all Floridians welcomed these political gains, and some responded violently toward African Americans and Republicans throughout the state. Gibbs, himself the target of several assassination plots, attributed more than 1,800 deaths to violence from groups such as the Ku Klux Klan during his first three years as secretary of state. The violence finally subsided with the passage of the Enforcement Acts in 1870 and 1871; by this time, many African Americans had become reluctant to seek political office, vote, or even remain in the state. The Republican Party was able to retain control of the executive branch in 1872 with the election of Ossian B. Hart, a Florida Unionist and former slave owner, as governor. However, the Democrats made gains during the election that would only increase until they recaptured the state four years later. By 1875, the party's strength was sufficient to maintain segregation in public schools, despite the best efforts of the radicals in the legislature. The party's momentum from the two previous elections carried on to the presidential election of 1876. In a highly contested election that had national as well as state ramifications, the Democrats successfully elected George F. Drew, a Northerner, as governor. But the voting irregularities that caused Florida's involvement with the presidential election also affected Drew's election; many argued that the Republican candidate, Marcellus Stearns, had won the election. In a decision that had national implications, Florida Democrats chose to challenge the returns of the gubernatorial, but not the presidential, election. Consequently, when the state ruled Drew the victor of the 1876 election, its decision not to recount presidential returns delivered the state's four electoral votes to Republican Rutherford B. Hayes. The inauguration of Drew marked Florida's "redemption," the end of Republican control of the state and of the Reconstruction process.

Although Florida suffered from many of the problems that plagued other Southern states during the period, including economic hardship, election fraud, and violence, many positive changes occurred under Republican rule. The 1868 Constitution, in addition to ushering the state back into the Union, extended democracy to both whites and African Americans and gave the state the responsibility for educating its citizens.

*Learotha Williams Jr.*

**See also:** Compromise of 1877; Shotgun Plan; White League.

## Further Reading

Richardson, Joe M. *The Negro in the Reconstruction of Florida, 1865–1877.* Tallahassee: Florida State University, 1965.

Shofner, Jerrell H. *Nor Is It over Yet: Florida in the Era of Reconstruction, 1863–1877.* Gainesville: University Press of Florida, 1974.

## FORREST, NATHAN BEDFORD (1821–1877)

Born in Tennessee, Nathan Bedford Forrest moved with his family to Mississippi in 1834, and there became responsible for the entire family after his father's death. Retaining his estates there, he later relocated back to Memphis, where he became quite wealthy as a planter and slave trader.

Forrest enlisted in the Confederate army in June 1861 and soon climbed the ranks, partly due to a natural military ability (he had no formal military training or education) and partly

Confederate general and brilliant military tactician, Nathan Bedford Forrest's reputation suffered from the April 1864 Fort Pillow massacre, which left over 200 black Union soldiers dead. Evidence indicates Forrest played a leading role in the growth of the Ku Klux Klan, perhaps even serving as its imperial grand wizard. (Library of Congress)

due to wealth—he could equip and supply entire cavalry units, and so became an officer automatically. At the head of mounted troops, Forrest saw extensive service in the western theater, and his simple-if-mythical slogan, "Get there first with the most," accurately summed his audacity and primitive cunning. Unfortunately, these are often overshadowed by the controversy surrounding the attack on Fort Pillow in April 1864, which was followed by the massacre of 231 black soldiers who had surrendered; to this day, his role in the alleged atrocity remains unclear.

As the Civil War drew to a close, Lt. Gen. Forrest considered prolonging the struggle via guerrilla means, but opted to surrender his command and return to his plantation in Mississippi. Forrest sought to revive his plantation, even going into partnerships with former Union officers and contracting with black labor on decent terms. A shrewd businessman, Forrest created a system that delivered relatively high wages, but bound them to himself through the contracts they signed with him; many became deeply indebted to him. Nevertheless, Forrest continued to struggle with financial instability and personal uncertainty. His wartime association with the "massacre" at Fort Pillow still festered, and at one point he even posted a $10,000 bond for a treason trial that never took place. He gained some solace when President Andrew Johnson granted him a presidential pardon in 1868 (due to his rank and wealth, Forrest had to petition directly). Continued economic difficulties compelled him to expand beyond the plantation; he lent his name to a grocery business, served briefly as president of the Planters' Insurance Company, and supervised the construction of the Memphis and Little Rock Railroad.

Although he had vowed to remain peaceful and loyal, Forrest could not resist involvement in political affairs in his state and region. Believing that Radical Republicans—in particular Governor William G. "Parson" Brownlow in Tennessee—were abusing power, he joined the Democratic Party effort to restore home rule. As a result, Forrest became involved in an organization known as the Pale Faces, and then with the Ku Klux Klan. Publicly, Forrest denied being a member of the secret society much less its leader, as some accused, but during congressional interviews he expressed intimate knowledge of its operations. In fact, one of the Klan's original cofounders confirmed that when the organization grew sufficiently large, it required a strong leader and the members turned to the cavalry chieftain as grand wizard. This likely happened at a meeting in Nashville in April 1867. Under Forrest's leadership, the Klan grew and expanded dramatically. Whenever his business associations took him into neighboring states, it was more than coincidental that the first public notices for the Klan would appear in local newspapers. Yet the Klan's nature worked against a central authority, and the rigidly demanding ex-soldier could not exert real control over the wide-ranging secret society. In addition, the growing attention of the federal government and the departure of his Tennessee nemesis Brownlow to the U.S. Senate convinced Forrest that the Klan was no longer a useful tool. Forrest ordered the Klan to disband in early 1869.

Despite his order, Klan activity continued and the organization came under greater scrutiny. Forrest turned his energies instead to railroad finance, in particular the Selma, Marion and Memphis Railroad, of which he was president. Struggling through investment challenges and economic crises, he finally relinquished the presidency on April 1, 1877, and refocused his energies on farming, leasing President's Island near Memphis.

In his declining years, Forrest attended reunions and continued to run his landholdings. In 1875, he experienced a religious conversion, but his health and finances continued to deteriorate. He died in Memphis on October 29, 1877.

*Brian S. Wills*

**See also:** Abolition of Slavery; Amnesty Proclamations; Bourbons; Congressional Reconstruction; Enforcement Acts (1870, 1871, 1875); Redemption; White League.

## Further Reading

Henry, Robert Selph. *"First with the Most" Forrest.* Indianapolis: Bobbs-Merrill, 1944.
Hurst, Jack. *Nathan Bedford Forrest: A Biography.* New York: Alfred A. Knopf, 1993.
Wills, Brian Steel. *A Battle from the Start: Life of Nathan Bedford Forrest.* New York: HarperCollins Publishers, 1992.

## FOURTEENTH AMENDMENT (1868)

With the abolition of slavery by the Thirteenth Amendment in 1865, questions immediately appeared regarding the status of freedpeople in the South. Legal and extralegal restrictions in the Southern states severely limited freedmen's economic rights and gave the former slaves few if any social or political rights. The former Confederate states were also indifferent to violence against blacks. In addition, with the abolition of slavery ending the Three-Fifths Compromise, Southern strength in the House of Representatives and the Electoral College was even stronger after the Civil War than before (blacks counted as a full person now, although they received no rights or privileges).

In response to the changes wrought by war, Republicans in Congress moved to define the freedom created by the Thirteenth Amendment. Within the Republican Party, Radicals hoped to define the rights, liberties, and status of all Americans, protecting them through federal power while maintaining state-based federalism. Along with many other Northerners, they expected to secure the war's results (preservation of the Union and abolition of slavery) from future modification or challenge. Much of this was present in the Civil Rights Act of 1866, which President Andrew Johnson vetoed on March 27, 1866;

this event prompted a constitutional amendment that would make the act's definition of black civil equality (largely economic) safe from presidential reach and from reversal by a later Congress. It would also define the Republicans' plan for Reconstruction, as the approaching 1866 congressional elections gave them the opportunity to challenge Johnson and the plan he initiated in May 1865. In April 1866, the Joint Committee on Reconstruction considered a five-part proposal that included provisions on black civil rights, the enfranchisement of blacks after 1876, penalties for restricting black suffrage, repudiation of Confederate debts, and congressional power to enforce the amendment. The proposal also required former Confederate states to ratify the amendment in order to be readmitted to Congress.

As passed by Congress, the Fourteenth Amendment was a compromise that followed this general structure. It added to the Constitution the Radical Republicans' vision of a nation centered on equal rights, protected by national power. However, the Radical desire for black suffrage and for disfranchisement of former confederates was tempered by the belief that suffrage was a privilege, not a right of citizenship. The first section's vague and general language never mentions race but does provide the U.S. Constitution's first definition of national citizenship: all born or naturalized in the United States (except American Indians) were citizens. State citizenship would no longer determine national citizenship, overturning Chief Justice Roger Taney's denial of black citizenship in *Dred Scott v. Sanford*. The section also prohibited a "State" from depriving any "person" (as distinct from citizens, so meant to include foreigners) "life, liberty, or property without due process of law." It concluded by prohibiting denial of the "equal protection of the law" to any "person within its jurisdiction." Whether all congressional framers and backers of these provisions viewed them as prohibiting discrimination against blacks in all aspects of life (political, economic, and social), some Radicals with abolitionist backgrounds certainly did.

If section 1 generally satisfied Radicals, section 2 fell far short of their goals. Many Radicals saw voting as a requirement for functional citizenship but the amendment made only a half-step in an area that was constitutionally and traditionally under state control. The North's opposition to black suffrage undoubtedly led to the elimination of a black suffrage provision; instead, section 2 stipulated that states that denied suffrage to any of its adult male citizens faced a proportional loss of representation in Congress. The threat turned out to be a hollow one as, by the end of the century and well into the 1900s, adult black males were consistently denied suffrage through various state and private practices. Section 3 was a response to President Andrew Johnson's policies, which permitted Southern states to fill state and national offices with antebellum and former Confederate leaders. The amendment removed from voting and officeholding anyone who had held political or military office before the Civil War, and then had fought for or aided the Confederacy (Congress could remove the restriction through a two-thirds vote, which it soon did for most former confederates). Section 4 answered a question linked both to the war's impact on the nation's economy and to views of the South's secession. It invalidated all ideas that the Confederacy had actually existed, by stipulating that debts or other financial obligations resulting from the South's secession would not be honored by the national or state governments. In addition, slave owners could not receive compensation for slaves lost through the war or through emancipation. Finally, section 5 gave Congress "the power to enforce" the preceding four provisions by "appropriate legislation." This expansion of the national government's power, along with a parallel provision in section 2 of the

Thirteenth Amendment, marked the greatest increase in Congress's power in the Constitution's 77 years of existence.

Congressional passage of the Fourteenth Amendment came on June 11, 1866. Ratification required approval by three-quarters of the states, but there was no specific guarantee that ratification by an ex-Confederate state would bring readmission (Congress tabled a provision to readmit seceded states that ratified the amendment in July). Yet, following Tennessee's ratification of the amendment in July, Congress quickly seated the state's eight representatives and senators. The remaining 10 seceded states shared Andrew Johnson's opposition to the Fourteenth Amendment, and refused to ratify it; opposition centered on the third section's "restrictions" and on Johnson's optimism that Northern public opinion would demand a more moderate policy. To the white South's disappointment, the fall elections of 1866 demonstrated the opposite. Republicans seized control of both houses of Congress and took over Reconstruction.

Congress's Military Reconstruction Act of March 2, 1867 voided the governments established under Johnson and temporarily arranged the 10 former Confederate states into 5 military districts. The act also mandated black male suffrage in those states (and only those states), a partial remedy for the amendment's indirect suggestion in section 2. In addition, Congress now required the states to ratify the Fourteenth Amendment or remain in constitutional limbo, unrepresented in Congress. This requirement for ratification raised questions about the amendment's constitutionality, since Article V of the U.S. Constitution made ratification a state's decision, yet now ratification was a requirement under the Reconstruction Act. It took nearly a year since passage to secure the approval of 22 states. On July 20, 1868, Secretary of State William Henry Seward announced the amendment's ratification. Eight former Confederate states had ratified the Fourteenth Amendment (in this order): Tennessee, Arkansas, Florida, North Carolina, Louisiana, South Carolina, Alabama, and Georgia. Once obstructing the amendment was moot, Mississippi, Texas, and Virginia added their approval. (Interestingly, Kentucky did not approve the amendment until a century later, in 1976; recall that Kentucky had not seceded.)

The Fourteenth Amendment's impact during Reconstruction was limited; declining interest in the status of blacks and the continuing preference for a limited national government undercut serious action. Nonetheless, the Fourteenth Amendment (and the Fifteenth Amendment, ratified in 1870) formed the base for federal protection of civil rights, bolstered in 1870 and 1871 by the Enforcement Acts and the 1875 Civil Rights Act. For instance, prosecutions of Klansmen and antiblack violence often occurred under the Fourteenth Amendment and its enforcement measures. But that intensity burned out quickly, partly due to Northern indifference and party due to increased Supreme Court attention.

The Court interpreted the amendment very narrowly in the Slaughterhouse Cases (1873) and *United States v. Cruikshank* (1876), which left most rights under state control and limited the reach of the amendment unless denial of rights was motivated by race. As the 19th century ended, a final Supreme Court ruling confirmed the restrictions on the Fourteenth Amendment. If its framers had intended that social equality be covered by section 1, *Plessy v. Ferguson* (1896) cancelled that application for more than half a century. The Court defended the need to allow states to distinguish between groups (such as whites and blacks); as a result, the regrettable doctrine of "separate but equal" entered the Fourteenth Amendment's history.

*Claudine L. Ferrell*

*See also:* Amnesty Proclamations; Black Codes; Congressional Reconstruction; Jim Crow Laws; Ku Klux Klan (KKK); New South; Pardons; Presidential Reconstruction; Trumbull, Lyman (1813–1896).

## Further Reading

James, Joseph B. *The Ratification of the Fourteenth Amendment.* Macon, GA: Mercer University Press, 1984.

Maltz, Earl M. *Civil Rights, the Constitution, and Congress, 1863–1869.* Lawrence: University Press of Kansas, 1990.

Meyer, Howard N. *The Amendment that Refused to Die: Equality and Justice Deferred: A History of the Fourteenth Amendment.* Rev. ed. Lanham, MD: Madison Books, 2000.

Nelson, William E. *The Fourteenth Amendment: From Political Principle to Judicial Doctrine.* Cambridge, MA: Harvard University Press, 1988.

# FREEDMAN'S SAVINGS AND TRUST COMPANY

The Freedman's Savings and Trust Company, also known as the Freedman's Bank, was a private savings bank chartered by Congress in 1865 primarily for the benefit of African Americans. After initial success, it was forced to close in 1874 as a result of careless oversight, outright fraud, and the financial Panic of 1873. The bank's collapse, and the consequent losses suffered by thousands of small depositors, came to symbolize the nation's betrayal of the freedmen and the larger failure of Reconstruction.

The bank was born of the Civil War and emancipation. Freedmen working under free labor arrangements in Union-held areas had lacked a place to secure their earnings, while various military departments had created agencies for black veterans to deposit their bounties and pay. Recognizing the need for an interstate branch banking system to provide these services after the war, Congress chartered The Freedman's Savings and Trust Company on March 3, 1865, the same day it established the Bureau of Refugees, Freedmen, and Abandoned Lands (the Freedmen's Bureau). The Freedman's Bank was the first interstate branch bank since Andrew Jackson killed the Second Bank of the United States during the 1830s.

The charter named 50 citizens to a board of trustees. Mainly New Yorkers, the trustees included some of the nation's most prominent businessmen, a number of whom also served on the boards of various Freedmen's Relief Societies. In fact, however, many trustees were listed as figureheads, and most had little involvement in bank affairs. Moreover, while the charter seemed to detail the bank's operations, it made insufficient provisions to guarantee that the bank would be run on sound business and banking principles.

The charter originally specified a minimum-risk investment strategy, since the Freedman's Bank was intended as a nonprofit, mutual savings bank owned by the depositors. There were no stockholders, initial capitalization, or authorization to make loans. Upon receiving deposits, the bank would retain as much as one-third for operating expenses and invest the rest in safe government securities. Profits were to be returned to the depositors as interest. The bank was envisioned as part of the larger mission to remake the South upon a free-labor basis and to inculcate in former slaves the values necessary to compete within capitalist society. By encouraging freedmen to save their earnings, reformers believed, the bank would help instill in them thrift, industry, and frugality, enabling them to acquire property and enter the American economic mainstream.

Originally headquartered in New York City, the Freedman's Bank started small but grew quickly. There were 10 branches by the end of 1865 and 22 by 1867. Eventually, the bank operated 34 branches in every Southern state, Washington, D.C., and several Northern states that had cities with significant black populations. Although such rapid expansion contributed to some organizational and operational difficulties, the bank proved popular among former slaves and even attracted a small number of white clients. By 1870, the bank held some 23,000 active accounts and $1.6 million in deposits, and by 1874, more than 61,000 accounts and almost $4 million had been deposited. During its nine-year life, the bank handled a total of more than 100,000 accounts and more than $50 million in deposits. The large majority of depositors were individuals with small accounts. The bank accepted deposits of as little as five cents to encourage freedmen to save. Larger individual accounts, though uncommon, were held in such cities as New Orleans and Charleston, South Carolina, which hosted an antebellum free-black elite. Black churches, schools, businesses, and mutual aid and benevolent associations also accounted for an important part of the bank's business. Hundreds if not thousands of individual depositors, representing thousands more freedmen, purchased land, homes, or businesses with the money they had saved at the bank.

Although there was no official connection between the bank and the Freedmen's Bureau, the two organizations overlapped considerably. Local bureau offices and branch banks often shared the same building, bureau agents served as bank cashiers and on branch advisory boards, and higher-ranking bureau officials sat on the board of trustees. Although the Freedmen's Bureau commissioner, General Oliver Otis Howard, played no official role in the bank and was not directly involved in its affairs, he nonetheless envisioned the bank as one among a host of organizations and institutions, including schools, hospitals, and freedmen's aid associations that were centered around the bureau and worked for the freedmen's advancement.

Despite the bank's growth, heavy operating expenses and the desire to produce larger dividends prompted bank officials—who were always overwhelmingly white, although some blacks served as trustees or on branch advisory boards—to seek other sources of revenue. In 1870, they persuaded Congress to amend the charter to permit the bank to lend money. Although limited to investing in real estate securities, bank officials soon began to make large, unsecured loans and to speculate in a number of unauthorized ventures, thus transforming the bank's mission from philanthropy and racial uplift to the pursuit of profit. With its headquarters having been relocated to Washington, D.C., the bank now fell under the control of Henry Cooke, brother of Civil War financier Jay Cooke. Cooke was a full partner in, and the Washington agent of, the financial house of Jay Cooke and Company. The Freedman's Bank began investing heavily in Washington real estate and construction companies, as the city was experiencing a population boom, and it even undertook selling the bonds of Jay Cooke's Northern Pacific Railroad. Moreover, the bank loaned large sums—without sufficient collateral—to companies in which bank officials or trustees held financial interests.

By 1873, a major part of the bank's assets were invested not in government securities but in real estate and unsecured loans to railroads and other companies. The inability of Jay Cooke and Company to market its Northern Pacific Railroad bonds brought about the house's collapse, precipitating the Panic of 1873 that caused hundreds of businesses nationwide to fail. Facing bankruptcy, bank officials undertook a number of measures in late 1873 and early 1874 to reassure nervous depositors, including naming Frederick Douglass as president in March. Congress passed a bill in June to keep the bank alive, but confidence in it had been lost as depositors continued to withdraw funds. On July 2, 1874, the board of trustees voted to close the bank for good. When the bank closed, it owed just under $3 million on 61,144 accounts, about half of which were for less than $50. The main office had only $400 in U.S. bonds, and the branches had only $31,689 in cash. Freedmen throughout the South received the news of the bank's closing first with alarm and then resignation. Before closing the bank, the trustees appointed a committee to collect the bank's assets and repay depositors. It did so until 1881, when Congress, finding further mismanagement, abolished the commission and transferred the bank's affairs to the federal comptroller of the currency. Between 1875 and 1883, five dividends were paid totaling 62 percent of the bank's indebtedness. Of 61,131 eligible depositors, only 29,996—fewer than half—sent their passbooks as required to receive the first dividend. They received a total of $555,360.08, or an average of $18.51. With each subsequent dividend, the number of claimants declined, so that by the time the last formal dividend was paid, only 17,893 of the more than 61,000 original depositors received the full 62 percent.

The failure of the Freedman's Bank provided political ammunition for the Democratic Party and contributed to disillusionment and a sense of betrayal among the freedmen. For years afterward, individual members of Congress argued, to no avail, that the federal government had an obligation to repay the depositors in full. The comptroller of the currency continued to recoup the bank's assets, and between 1899 and 1919, under congressional authority, dividends were paid to depositors and their descendants who could prove that they had not received the full 62 percent of their deposits. In 1919, the affairs of the bank were closed for good.

*John C. Rodrigue*

**See also:** Abolition of Slavery; American Missionary Association (AMA); Black Troops (U.S. Colored Troops) in the Occupied South

## Further Reading

Fleming, Walter L. *The Freedmen's Savings Bank: A Chapter in the Economic History of the Negro Race*. Chapel Hill: University of North Carolina Press, 1927.

McFeely, William S. *Yankee Stepfather: General O. O. Howard and the Freedmen*. New Haven, CT: Yale University Press, 1968.

Osthaus, Carl R. *Freedmen, Philanthropy, and Fraud: A History of the Freedman's Savings Bank*. Urbana: University of Illinois Press, 1976.

## FREEDMEN'S RELIEF SOCIETIES

During Reconstruction, a network of charitable organizations known as Freedmen's Relief Societies sought to guide and assist former slaves in their transition to freedom. These groups provided food and other material aid, helped build schools and churches, and worked to facilitate freedpeople in finding a meaningful place in the political and economic order that arose in the U.S. South following the Civil War. Many relief workers came from religious background and had been active in abolitionism before the war, but others were soldiers, businessmen, and politicians. These men and women did much to help the freed African Americans, especially in terms of alleviating their worst suffering and establishing the beginnings of an education system. They proved less successful in helping former slaves acquire land and in establishing true equality in the Reconstruction South.

The beginnings of the Freedmen's Relief Societies can be found during the Civil War. Early in the conflict, areas of the South with large concentrations of slaves came under Union control. The most famous place was the Sea Islands region of coastal South Carolina and Georgia. Owners fled on the arrival of Union forces, leaving behind thousands of slaves. Abolitionists in the North proved eager to travel south to assist these contraband slaves. A contingent of 50 plantation agents, as well as teachers, clergy, and doctors, under the leadership of Edward L. Pierce, a Boston lawyer appointed by Treasury secretary Salmon P. Chase, came to the Sea Islands in spring 1862. These "Gideonites" were the vanguard of an aid movement directed at former slaves whose activities would continue into Reconstruction and in some forms, especially education, for decades thereafter.

After the war, education became the dominant activity of the Freedmen's Relief Societies. The Bureau of Refugees, Freedmen, and Abandoned Lands, a federal agency established in March 1865, took over the massive task of providing material relief for former slaves and war refugees. The bureau encouraged private organizations, such as the American Missionary Association, and numerous other religious and secular groups to channel their relief efforts into building schools and providing teachers for former slaves.

Within four years, these groups had established thousands of schools in the Southern states, serving hundreds of thousands of students. While the leadership of the Freedmen's Relief Societies was almost invariably men, the service providers on the ground during Reconstruction often were women. Indeed, a classic image of this period in the South is the Yankee schoolmarm, gently but energetically instructing and guiding her black pupils. While there is much truth to this picture, it conceals the fact that many of the women in the aid movement were activists as well as teachers, and their efforts involved more than simply education. Indeed, some women saw assisting freedpeople as a vehicle by which they might advance reform more generally and improve the status of women in American society by giving them a voice in the formulation of public policy. Without the contribution of women, the efforts of the Freedmen's Relief Societies in the South during Reconstruction, especially in terms of education, would not have been possible. They provided much of the personnel on the ground, translating the good intentions of Northern philanthropic groups into actual results.

Blacks were not only beneficiaries of the Freedmen's Relief Societies but also significant contributors. Free blacks in the North, starting during the Civil War, hastened to assist their brethren in the South. Elizabeth Keckley, seamstress to Mary Todd Lincoln, founded the Contraband Relief Association in 1862 to provide aid for slaves seeking refuge in Washington, D.C. Black Northerners, such as Charlotte Forten, worked as part of the Port Royal Experiment in South Carolina as teachers. Not surprisingly, the efforts of these Northern blacks in the South extended into Reconstruction. The African Civilization Society, led by Richard H. Cain, a clergyman in the African Methodist Episcopal Church, sought to educate former slaves and encourage racial pride. Cain and his organization believed that blacks from the North were better teachers for blacks in the South since they had greater cultural affinity than white Northerners and were less judgmental. Their approach and beliefs put them somewhat at odds with white-run organizations, especially those with more racist inclinations.

The activities of these aid groups continued on a smaller scale after the end of Reconstruction, mostly centered in the field of education. White Southerners had resented greatly the activities of the Freedmen's Relief Societies in the South, correctly seeing them as undermining white supremacy. Likewise, in the 1870s, Northern interest in the plight of former slaves waned and it became necessary for aid organizations to scale back their efforts. This goal accounts for the rise of the industrial education for blacks in the South, emphasizing practical skills and moral rectitude over classical education and political activism. By the end of the 19th century, the radical abolitionism of the Gideonites that had characterized the Freedmen's Relief Societies at their beginning had given way to the racial accommodation of the Tuskegee Institute and Booker T. Washington.

*Donald R. Shaffer*

*See also:* Edisto Island, South Carolina; Howard, Oliver Otis (1830–1909); Labor Systems; Redemption; Republicans, Radical; U.S. Army and Reconstruction.

## Further Reading

Butchart, Ronald E. *Northern Schools, Southern Blacks, and Reconstruction: Freedmen's Education, 1862–1875.* Westport, CT: Greenwood Press, 1980.

Faulkner, Carol. *Women's Radical Reconstruction: The Freedmen's Aid Movement.* Philadelphia: University of Pennsylvania Press, 2004.

Richardson, Joe M. *Christian Reconstruction: The American Missionary Association and Southern Blacks, 1861–1890.* Athens: University of Georgia Press, 1986.

# G

## GARRISON, WILLIAM LLOYD (1805–1879)

William Lloyd Garrison, white abolitionist, journalist, and social reformer, was born on December 10, 1805, in Newburyport, Massachusetts. A radical on issues of slavery and race during most of his career, Garrison became more conservative during the Civil War and Reconstruction.

Abijah Garrison abandoned the family in 1808, plunging it into poverty and stiffening his wife Frances's resolve to instill a Christian conscience in her children—including William. In 1818, he became an apprentice in the office of the *Newburyport Herald* and was soon editing for newspapers all over the Boston area. Regarding himself as a "universal reformer," he wrote against the consumption of alcoholic beverages, Sunday mail delivery, lotteries, war, and racial oppression. When he met Benjamin Lundy, a white Quaker abolitionist, Garrison shifted his focus to abolition. At first, Garrison advocated gradual abolition and supported the American Colonization Society, but by 1829, when he moved to Baltimore to work with Lundy's newspaper, Garrison began to advocate immediate emancipation without expatriation. In Baltimore, Garrison saw the brutality of slavery firsthand, and became a more determined advocate of African American rights. He undertook peaking tours across the Northeast to promote immediate abolitionism and began publishing *The Liberator* in January 1831. He declared in the first issue, "I am in earnest—I will not equivocate—I will not excuse—I will not retreat a single inch, and I will be heard." Dependent on black financial contributions and subscribers, *The Liberator* became the leading American abolitionist newspaper of the 1830s. In 1833, he led in the formation of the American Anti-Slavery Society (AASS). Garrison's moral views and Nat Turner's 1831 Virginia slave revolt shaped the society's rejection of violent means and its tactic of appealing to the conscience of slaveholders and other Americans. It contended that slaveholding was a sin and a crime and African Americans had a right to equality in the United States.

By 1835, the AASS, which represented a tiny minority of Northerners, had undertaken massive efforts which produced an anti-abolitionist and antiblack reaction. Congress refused to receive petitions about slavery, and mobs attacked Garrison and other abolitions across the North. The intensity of the reaction convinced Garrison that slavery had so corrupted American society that abolition alone could not redeem it. To avoid God's wrath, the nation required fundamental reform; Garrison and his closest associates became anarchists, refusing to vote or hold elective office. They maintained that the U.S. Constitution

An outspoken abolitionist, William Lloyd Garrison operated the *Liberator*, the leading antislavery newspaper. (National Archives)

was a proslavery document. Garrison also opposed organized religion as superstitious, proslavery, and corrupting. Decrying patriarchal oppression, he even supported the fledgling women's movement. Most immediatists believed Garrison's approach alienated allies; after several years of turmoil, the AASS shattered in 1840.

Starting in 1842, Garrison maintained that only dissolution of the Union could save Northerners from the sin of slavery. But he was not as impractical as his critics believed: he condemned the tiny Liberty Party and accurately sensed the Free Soil Party, formed in 1848, and the Republican Party, formed between 1854 and 1856, as indications that Northerners were becoming more antagonistic to slavery.

With war coming in April 1861, Garrison contradicted his earlier views on nonviolence and became a strong supporter of President Abraham Lincoln's forceful effort to preserve the Union. Like other immediatists, he urged Lincoln to make emancipation a goal of the war and to enlist black troops. Strangely, he defended Lincoln's Moderate pace against those who advocated more rapid progress toward emancipation and black rights. In 1863 and 1864, he disagreed when his immediatist colleague Wendell Phillips and some Radical Republicans advocated providing land to former slaves, black suffrage, and an extended postwar military occupation of the former Confederacy.

In May 1865, believing that he and other abolitionists had achieved their goal, he called on the AASS to disband; many members rejected his proposal, so he and most of his Massachusetts colleagues withdrew from the organization. Following the ratification of the Thirteenth Amendment in December 1865, he ceased publication of *The Liberator*.

Garrison naively assumed that former slaves could advance themselves without national intervention, but as events demonstrated that white Southerners would return most African Americans to slavery in all but name, he became more supportive of national government action to protect the freedpeople. But he was not a prominent figure in the debate over Reconstruction. He moved into a period of semi-retirement by the late 1860s, while still speaking and writing on prohibition, women's rights, a more enlightened policy toward American Indians, and black civil rights. He died in New York City on May 24, 1879.

*Stanley Harrold*

***See also:*** Black Codes; Congressional Reconstruction; Presidential Reconstruction.

## Further Reading

Mayer, Henry. *All on Fire: William Lloyd Garrison and the Abolition of Slavery.* New York: St Martin's Press, 1998.

McPherson, James M. *The Struggle for Equality: Abolitionists and the Negro in the Civil War and Reconstruction.* Reprint, Princeton, NJ: Princeton University Press, 2014.

Merrill, Walter M. *Against Wind and Tide: A Biography of William Lloyd Garrison.* Cambridge, MA: Harvard University Press, 1965.

Stewart, James Brewer. *William Lloyd Garrison and the Challenge of Emancipation.* Arlington Heights, IL: Harlan Davidson, 1992.

Thomas, John L. *The Liberator: William Lloyd Garrison, A Biography.* Boston: Little Brown, 1963.

# GARY, MARTIN WITHERSPOON (1831–1881)

Known as the "Bald Eagle of Edgefield" because of his personality and appearance, Martin Witherspoon Gary played a primary role in helping the South Carolina Democratic Party reassert political control during Reconstruction.

Born on March 25, 1831, in Cokesbury, South Carolina, Gary attended South Carolina College from 1850 to 1852 but transferred to Harvard University, graduating in 1854. Gary returned to South Carolina, established a law practice in Edgefield and in 1860 won election to the state legislature. A strong advocate of secession and already a cavalry colonel in the South Carolina militia, Gary enlisted in the Confederate army as an infantry captain in Wade Hampton's Legion. He participated in major battles including First and Second Manassas, Antietam, Fredericksburg, and Chickamauga, ending the war as a major general.

After the war, Gary resumed his legal practice in Edgefield. Under the Republican governments, Gary grew more restless and less patient, and increasingly advocated aggressive tactics to oust black and white Republicans from office. By the mid-1870s politics was his focus, as he rolled out his "Edgefield Plan" to support Democratic candidates through fraud, voter intimidation, and vigilante action; some attribute "vote early, vote often" to him, and while proof is lacking, it is accurate in its depiction of his win-at-any-cost attitude. Gary portrayed the struggle for control of the state in stark, even extremist language, speaking of war, revolution and even survival. In 1876, Gary adamantly refused fusion with carpetbag, scalawag, and African American Republicans, and opposed any efforts at compromise. Gary headed the violent and ultra-conservative "Straight-out" faction of the Democratic Party in support of Wade Hampton III's successful gubernatorial election.

Once Democrats regained power, Gary was elected state senator in consecutive terms (1876–1878; 1878–1880) but many Democrats, including Wade Hampton, began to distance themselves from Gary's racial extremism. As a result he lost his bid for the U.S. Senate in 1877 and 1879 and became increasingly antagonistic toward his fellow Democrats. In 1880, Gary returned to Edgefield, where he died in 1881.

*Kimberly R. Kellison*

**See also:** Chamberlain, Daniel Henry (1835–1907); Compromise of 1877; Congressional Reconstruction; Elections of 1876; Grant, Ulysses S. (1822–1885); Gun Clubs; Redemption; Shotgun Plan; U.S. Army and Reconstruction.

## Further Reading

Bailey, N. Louise, Mary L. Morgan, and Carolyn R. Taylor. *Biographical Dictionary of the South Carolina Senate, 1776–1985*. Vol. 1. Columbia: University of South Carolina Press, 1986.

Egerton, Douglas R. *The Wars of Reconstruction: The Brief, Violent History of America's Most Progressive Era*. New York: Bloomsbury Press, 2014.

Zuczek, Richard. *State of Rebellion: Reconstruction in South Carolina*. Columbia: University of South Carolina Press, 1996.

# GEORGIA

The Reconstruction of Georgia (1865–1871) began in May 1865, with the end of the Civil War and the surrender of Georgia's Confederate governor, Joseph E. Brown. President Andrew Johnson's appointment of James Johnson as provisional governor initiated the presidential Reconstruction process.

Governor Johnson oversaw the election of delegates to a convention which met in Milledgeville in October 1865. Two men dominated the proceedings: Charles Jones Jenkins was the presiding officer and Herschel V. Johnson was chairman of the committee on business. The convention's delegates developed a new constitution that repealed the Ordinance of Secession and abolished slavery. Another task was the repudiation of the state's war debt, which became the most difficult issue to resolve; only the threat of non-readmission convinced delegates to repudiate the debt. State elections followed in November, with Jenkins as the only candidate for governor.

In December, the Georgia General Assembly ratified the Thirteenth Amendment but also enacted legislation that regulated freedmen's rights and opportunities. While President Johnson believed that Georgia was ready for readmittance, Republicans in Congress thought differently. The Congress exercised its right to validate its members and rejected all the Johnson governments from the former Confederate states. This launched a period of attempted compromise on the part of congressional Republicans, who sought protection for freedpeople in the South through the Civil Rights Act of 1866 and a renewed Freedmen's Bureau bill. President Johnson vetoed both bills and showed marked indifference to Southern violence, thereby unifying the North and the Republicans and opening the door to Republican control of Congress in the fall elections.

In March 1867, Congress passed the Military Reconstruction Act, which divided the South into five districts, each governed by an army general who supervised the execution of the acts. Georgia was part of the Third Military District, governed by Gen. John Pope, who registered eligible black and white voters in advance of a convention for a new constitution. In protest, Jenkins traveled to Washington and filed a petition before the Supreme Court for an injunction against the enforcement of the Reconstruction Act. The courts dismissed his petition in May of that year.

Jenkins conceded the loss and issued an address to the people of Georgia that advised them to avoid tensions and violence in the state. Georgia blacks organized a black Republican Party in May 1867 that focused on forming alliances with white Republicans. In October and November 1867, an election was held for delegates to a constitutional convention that met from December 1867 to March 1868. The convention drafted a new constitution for Georgia, which included black suffrage, the establishment of free public schools, the move of the seat of state government from Milledgeville to Atlanta, and numerous other changes. Statewide voters—now including black males—ratified the constitution and elected a new governor, Republican candidate Rufus Bullock. In July 1868, the Georgia Assembly ratified the Fourteenth Amendment, inaugurated Governor Bullock to a four-year term, and was formally incorporated to the Union.

No sooner did Georgia rejoin the Union than state Conservatives began seeking ways to reduce the impact of Reconstruction and the role of blacks. Some opposition grew from within the Republican Party, as scalawags, Southern-born members of the party (often staunch Unionists or even opponents of the Confederacy) held significant influence in the Georgia Assembly and began to influence other whites to oust black legislators who had recently gained political status. Another development aimed at reducing black voice was the Ku Klux Klan, a terrorist organization that conducted brutal, violent attacks against blacks who sought political or social equality. The Klan was blamed for the murder of Georgia Radical George W. Ashburn, a staunch Republican and advocate for blacks' civil rights. In September 1868, the black Republican Party planned to hold a rally in a small Georgia town known as Camilla. Prior to the scheduled event, a confrontation between blacks and whites led to the killing of 12 blacks and the injuring of several whites. Known as the Camilla Massacre, this was one of many incidents during this period that was indicative of the precarious nature of blacks' social and political status.

In an effort to finance public education, Republican politicians implemented a poll tax. When it became evident that the poll tax would disfranchise black voters, Governor Rufus Bullock suspended it, but Democratic leaders had realized its power in controlling voting. Some months later, in 1869, Congress passed the Fifteenth Amendment, which prohibited voting discrimination based on race. This amendment was ratified in 1870, but allowed a great many loopholes, including the poll tax. In December 1870, a combination of Republican infighting and white violence allowed Georgia Conservatives to win a sizeable victory in the General Assembly; when the new legislature convened in fall 1871, Conservatives reinstated the poll tax, which reduced the black vote significantly.

Another sign of Reconstruction unraveling was the demise of Bullock. Bullock's advocacy for blacks garnered him much of the black Republican support, but it alienated some Moderate Republicans and alienated Conservatives in the state. In 1871, the assembly moved to impeach the governor, but Bullock resigned in October 1871 rather than battle the Democratic legislature. Upon his resignation, Bullock warned Georgians that if they voted for leaders who ignored the Fourteenth Amendment and Fifteenth Amendment, then they risked never being able to incorporate the South into the mainstream of the United States.

Although historians usually use 1877 as the end of Reconstruction, Reconstruction ended for Georgians with the election of both a Democratic governor (James Smith) and a Democratic legislature in January 1872. While some elements of the Republican federal and state program remained, a major political, social, and economic restructuring of the state did not occur.

*Kijua Sanders-McMurtry*

***See also:*** Presidential Reconstruction; Race Riots; Redemption; Union League of America.

## Further Reading

Cimbala, Paul. *Under the Guardianship of the Nation: The Freedmen's Bureau and the Reconstruction of Georgia, 1865–1870.* Athens: University of Georgia Press, 1997.

Drago, Edmund. *Black Politicians and Reconstruction in Georgia.* Baton Rouge: Louisiana State University Press, 1982.

Fitzgerald, Michael W. *Splendid Failure: Postwar Reconstruction in the American South.* New York: Ivan R. Dee Publishers, 2008.

Wetherington, Mark. *Plain Folks Fight: Civil War and Reconstruction in Piney Woods, Georgia.* Chapel Hill: University of North Carolina Press, 2005.

# GORDON, JOHN B. (1832–1904)

John Brown Gordon, Confederate major general and postwar politician, was born in Georgia on February 6, 1832. He attended the University of Georgia but left that institution early to study law. Gordon entered the Civil War as a captain and rose in the ranks through arduous service that included a severe wounding at Antietam and participation in major campaigns of the Eastern Theater in the war. After Gen. Robert E. Lee's surrender at Appomattox Court House, it was Gordon, leading the defeated Confederate ensemble, who offered the return salute to one given by Union general Joshua Lawrence Chamberlain.

Confederate general, U.S. senator, and postwar governor of Georgia, John B. Gordon is widely understood to have been a major force behind Georgia's Ku Klux Klan. (National Archives)

Following the conflict, Gordon returned to Atlanta. He resumed his law practice and later became president of the Atlanta branch of the Southern Life Insurance Company of Memphis. As many former Confederate leaders-turned-businessmen, he could not avoid being drawn into politics. In 1868, as a Democrat, he ran unsuccessfully for the governorship of Georgia against Republican Rufus B. Bullock. He attended the Democratic National Convention in New York City that year as well. About the same time, and coinciding with a visit to Georgia by former Confederate general Nathan Bedford Forrest, Gordon became involved with the Georgia Ku Klux Klan, reputedly holding the post of Grand Dragon. In testimony before a congressional investigating committee in 1871, both Forrest and Gordon defended the organization—while denying membership in it—as existing solely for self-protection. Gordon's popularity remained high among white Conservatives, and when Democrats took control of the legislature in fall of 1872, they selected Gordon for the U.S. Senate. He held that seat from 1873 until 1880 and again during 1891–1897; during 1876–1877, he played a key role in helping to break the political impasse created by the disputed presidential election.

Gordon interspersed his time in the Senate with work in the private sector and two terms as governor of Georgia (1886–1890). He was part of a Democratic clique that supported a commercialized and industrialized New South. Gordon completed his wartime memoirs, *Reminiscences of the Civil War*, in 1903, shortly before dying in Miami, Florida, on January 9, 1904.

*Brian S. Wills*

*See also:* Compromise of 1877; Congressional Reconstruction; Enforcement Acts (1870, 1871, 1875); Grant, Ulysses S. (1822–1885); Redemption.

## Further Reading

Bartley, Numan V. *The Creation of Modern Georgia*. Athens: University of Georgia Press, 1983.

Eckert, Ralph Lowell. *John Brown Gordon: Soldier, Southerner, American*. Baton Rouge: Louisiana State University Press, 1989.

Tankersley, Allen P. *John B. Gordon: A Study in Gallantry*. Atlanta: Whitehall Press, 1955.

# GRANT, ULYSSES S. (1822–1885)

Ulysses S. Grant rose to command all federal armies by the end of the American Civil War and became president of the United States from 1869 to 1877. Grant's still-controversial role in the politics of Reconstruction cannot be understood apart from his role in the winning of the Civil War.

Born Hiram Ulysses Grant in Point Pleasant, Ohio, on April 27, 1822, Grant was the son of Jesse Root Grant and Hannah Simpson Grant. With his father active in Whig politics, young Grant earned an appointment to the U.S. Military Academy in 1839; there he changed his name to Ulysses Simpson Grant, for reasons that have never been entirely clear. For the rest of his life, he went by the name of Ulysses Simpson Grant, giving rise to his famous nicknames—"U.S." Grant, or "Sam" Grant, which eventually linked him by name to Unconditional Surrender, Uncle Sam, and the United States. Upon graduation in June 1843, he was commissioned as a second lieutenant in the infantry and assigned to duty at Jefferson Barracks, outside of St Louis, Missouri, where he met his future wife, Julia Dent.

When Congress declared war on Mexico in 1845, Grant distinguished himself as a combat leader; his grasp of movement and planning were especially remarkable. Grant accompanied Taylor's army to Monterey and later transferred with his regiment, the Fourth Infantry, to the command of Gen. Winfield Scott. Under Scott, Grant's talents again stood out; his coolness under fire and skills as a strategist were evident at such battles as Molino del Rey and Chapultepec.

After the war, Grant returned to the United States, where his first order of business was to marry Julia. The Grants' marriage was a happy one which produced four children, and Julia remained a stabilizing influence on Grant throughout his life. The peacetime army, however, brought boredom and monotony; rumors of Grant's drinking and alleged alcoholism date from this period. In 1854, on the Oregon frontier without his family, he resigned from the army, almost certainly under the threat of court-martial for drunkenness. For the next five years he struggled to support his family by farming (on a plot donated by an uncle) and engaging in a variety of petty commercial operations. All of these ventures failed, so in the spring of 1860, he moved his family to Galena, Illinois, to work in his father's leather store.

In April 1861, when news spread that President Abraham Lincoln had called for volunteers, Grant reenlisted in the army. In Galena, he quickly organized a volunteer company of infantry; by June he had been given command of the Twenty-first Illinois Infantry Regiment and a commission as a colonel in the Union army. By fall 1861, his actions in Missouri earned him the rank of brigadier general. In the spring of 1862, his grander operational approach—using a combination of naval and army forces on the rivers to sweep into the Confederacy—had borne fruit. In February 1862, he captured forts Henry and Donelson on the Tennessee and Cumberland Rivers and forced the "unconditional surrender" of Confederate general Simon B. Buckner. Grant's victories were often costly—such as at Shiloh in April 1862—and laborious, as in the eight months it took to seize Vickburg, the so-called Gibraltar of the Mississippi. After the fall of Vicksburg and the securing of the Mississippi in July 1863, Grant turned his attention eastward. He joined the Union forces in East Tennessee, drove the Confederate army of Tennessee back into Georgia, and unleashed his prized subordinate, Gen. William T. Sherman, on Georgia. Such audacity and success convinced Lincoln to name Grant commanding general of all Union armies and earned him a promotion to lieutenant general. Grant moved east in the spring of 1864 to personally supervise a new campaign against Robert E. Lee's army of Northern Virginia. In a series of spectacular and costly battles in the spring and summer of 1864, Grant and Lee fought the final great act of the Civil War. In the end Grant forced Lee into a siege stretching from Richmond to Petersburg, and in April 1865, Confederate defenses finally cracked. Grant's forces pursued the remnants of Lee's fleeing army to its final surrender at Appomattox Court House.

Confederate defeat, followed by the assassination of Lincoln, made Grant the most popular figure in the country. This strained his relationship with Lincoln's successor, Andrew Johnson. In late 1865, at Johnson's request, Grant toured the defeated South. In his public report, Grant believed that ex-confederates accepted defeat and abolition. Johnson promptly used Grant's report to support his program of pardon and amnesty, which many Republicans in Congress opposed. At the time, many congressmen felt betrayed by what they interpreted as Grant's support for Johnson. But the relationship did not last; mirroring the shift among many Moderate Republicans, Grant grew suspicious of Johnson's policies in the summer and fall of 1866, as the president refused any compromise and showed callous indifference to the suffering of former slaves in the South. When the congressional elections of 1866 gave Republicans a "veto proof" majority in both houses of Congress, Grant faced an awkward situation: his commander in chief was determined to thwart the will of Congress. Grant had to negotiate an uneasy existence, as the Military Reconstruction Acts of March 1867 handed supervision of Reconstruction over to the army—and thus to Grant. In August 1867, perhaps in an attempt to win over Grant, Johnson appointed him interim secretary of war after Johnson removed Edwin M. Stanton. Johnson's act and Grant's acceptance outraged the Republican Congress, which saw this as a deliberate violation of the Tenure of Office Act. As a result, in 1868, Congress initiated impeachment proceedings, and Grant hurriedly stepped back toward the Republican camp, returning Stanton's office to him upon the Senate's advice. Now Grant faced an irate president who felt betrayed by his senior general. This cemented Grant's ties to the Republican Party and forever severed his relation with Johnson. Impeached but not removed, Johnson spent 1868 battling Congress, dreaming of Democratic nomination for president, and trading barbs with his senior army commander.

The relationship between Johnson and Grant grew even more awkward over the summer of 1868, as it became clear Johnson was a man without a party—and Grant was the golden boy of the Republicans. He easily won nomination as president, and in November 1868 defeated his Democratic opponent, former New York governor Horatio Seymour, on the campaign slogan, "Let Us Have Peace." Grant's record as president from 1869 to 1877 has been as fiercely debated as the history of Reconstruction itself, and for nearly the same reasons. To many Americans at the time, particularly Northerners who supported the war and African Americans, his ascent to the highest office of the land heralded an era of just and lasting civil peace to match a previous era of strife and civil war. To others, particularly white Southerners who had fought for the Confederacy, his election represented a hated Yankee determination to oppress a prostrate South and establish the humiliations of "negro domination" and "bayonet rule" over Southern states. Using an unprecedented array of federal powers enacted under congressional (or radical) Reconstruction, Grant made the greatest effort of any American president before the 1960s to enforce civil rights and political opportunity for African Americans. He worked well with congressional Republicans to create a structure for protecting rights and promoting change. Under his tenure, ratification of the Fifteenth Amendment in 1870 outlawed voting discrimination on the basis of race. The passage of the Enforcement Acts of 1871 and 1872 put legislative teeth into the promise of the amendment, by making it a federal crime to conspire to prevent voting, and authorizing the suspension of the writ of habeas corpus in extreme cases of lawlessness. The creation of the Department of Justice during his administration gave the federal government the means to pursue legal cases against white supremacist violence. From 1870 through 1872, Grant wielded these powers in what became, in effect, a counterinsurgency campaign to break the power of the Ku Klux Klan across the South. While many in the South (and a growing number in the North) criticized his heavy hand and his use of the military, Grant's success in ensuring free access to the ballot for blacks ensured his 1872 reelection against the New York newspaper editor Horace Greeley.

But Greeley's defeat masked the real impact of the Liberal Republican, anti-Grant movement. A growing faction within the Republican Party had split with Grant over a number of issues, including his ill-considered scheme to annex Santo Domingo, civil service reform, signs of corruption, and his use of the military in the South. This last point alienated more and more Northerners, who were appalled at rumors of Southern Republican corruption and questioned the legitimacy of using federal forces to bolster helpless regimes. The uproar was so great that when Mississippi governor Adelbert Ames requested that Grant send federal troops to supervise elections in Mississippi in 1875, Grant's cabinet warned him against it. Without federal aid, Mississippi Republicans lost the state elections in November, and white supremacists seized the state legislature, impeached the black lieutenant governor, and forced Ames to resign. Across the South, black and white Republicans found themselves on the defensive, and so did the Grant administration. In a series of decisions from the Slaughterhouse Cases in 1873 to the *Cruikshank* decision in 1876, the Supreme Court ruled against expansive readings of federal power in the Fourteenth and Fifteenth Amendments, narrowing the authority of the Justice Department. Scandals undercut the Grant administration's reputation, and while Grant himself was never personally implicated, his secretary of war, William W. Belknap, and his personal secretary both resigned under accusations of malfeasance and profiteering. In 1873, a bank panic led to a stock market collapse and a run on banks that produced a five-year depression. In an incredible turn of events, the Democrats regained control of the House of Representatives in the mid-term elections of 1874.

Yet despite all of these difficulties, Grant's personal popularity remained enormous. Some Republicans even wanted him to run for an unprecedented third term in 1876. Grant refused, and devoted his remaining time in office to ensure that the disputed presidential election between Samuel Tilden and Rutherford B. Hayes did not spill over into another civil war. After overseeing the semi-secret inauguration of Hayes, the eventual Republican winner, at the White House in March 1877, he and Julia departed Washington for a two-year trip around the world.

Grant's triumphant return, and Hayes's decision not to seek a second term, made him a popular choice for president again in 1880. The campaign reached a climax on the 36th ballot of the Republican National Convention, when James Garfield, who had also served as a volunteer general during the Civil War, won the nomination.

Grant's return to private life was reminiscent of his return to private life after his first war. He moved his family to New York and invested his life savings in a brokerage partnership with Frederick Ward; unsupervised and unskilled, Ward's speculative investments crashed in the Wall Street panic of 1884 and the Grants lost everything. Desperate to pay his debts and support his family, and knowing he had contracted cancer of the throat from a lifetime of cigar smoking, Grant turned to writing the book that ultimately vindicated his public life. His *Personal Memoirs of Ulysses S. Grant* has been critically acclaimed as the finest military memoir ever written by an American; some claim it the greatest military memoir since Julius Caesar.

Grant's memoir contains virtually no commentary about Reconstruction or his difficult years as president. Written with a bluntness and clarity that reflected his technique in penning military order, his prose remains attractive to this day; it proved so popular and spellbinding that some believed it ghostwritten by his friend Mark Twain. Those familiar with Grant's pithy dispatches during the war, however, immediately recognize that at the end of his life, Grant had regained that certainty of expression that had characterized his triumphant conduct of Union strategy in the Civil War. Grant did not live to see his memoir's success; suffering through incredible agony in his final days, struggling to complete his last chapter, Grant died just days after finishing his conclusion.

*James K. Hogue*

**See also:** Black Suffrage; Command of the Army Act (1867); Congressional Reconstruction; Elections of 1866; Elections of 1868; Elections of 1876; Presidential Reconstruction; Redemption; Republicans, Radical.

## Further Reading

Gillette, William. *Retreat from Reconstruction, 1868–1879*. Baton Rouge: Louisiana State University Press, 1979.

Simon, John Y. *The Papers of Ulysses S. Grant*. 26 vols. Carbondale: University of Southern Illinois Press, 1967–ongoing.

Simpson, Brooks D. *Let Us Have Peace: Ulysses S. Grant and the Politics of War and Reconstruction, 1861–1868*. Chapel Hill: University of North Carolina Press, 1991.

# GREELEY, HORACE (1811–1872)

Born in 1811 in Amherst, New Hampshire, to a poor family, Horace Greeley became one of the most powerful American figures of the 19th century. A small, eccentric man with a moon face and a fringe of white whiskers who embraced a wide variety of reforming causes, Greeley was easy to lampoon, but anyone who underestimated him made a mistake. From his position as editor of the enormously powerful *New York Tribune*, Greeley became an important voice in American politics from the accession of John Tyler to the presidency to the anti-Ulysses S. Grant campaign of 1872, in which Greeley was a presidential candidate.

Trained as a printer as a boy, Greeley moved to New York City in 1831. Ten years later, he started publication of the *New York Tribune*, which he designed to promote moral, intellectual, and political knowledge. Refusing to print police reports and unscrupulous advertisements, Greeley dedicated his paper to Whig policies and a reform agenda that included labor cooperatives, support for women's rights, and antislavery. In his determination to stop the spread of slavery and develop the country with free labor, Greeley demanded that Northerners hold the line against Southern attempts to control the nation, and he hailed the birth of the Republican Party with enthusiasm. Although not a strong supporter of Abraham Lincoln in 1860, he helped the Illinois lawyer win the Republican nomination as he considered other candidates unelectable. During the Civil War, Greeley was frustrated with what he considered to be Lincoln's lackluster prosecution of the war. In August 1862, Greeley published "The Prayer of Twenty Millions," demanding that the president embrace emancipation as a war aim. Confronted with an attack from such a prominent Republican, Lincoln responded to Greeley with the now-famous reply that defended his goal of saving the Union, and that freeing slaves, or not freeing slaves, would only be part of that policy.

With the end of the war, Greeley believed the nation could now forward economically without the hampering weight of slavery. As soon as Gen. Robert E. Lee surrendered to Grant at Appomattox Court House, Greeley called for "Magnanimity in Triumph," urging the country forward to a triumphant future. Greeley held to this course even after the assassination of Lincoln and ultimately joined others in protesting the continued imprisonment of Jefferson Davis without trial. In fact, Greeley was one of 20 men who guaranteed Davis's bail. Not surprisingly, Greeley initially supported Andrew Johnson's conciliatory policy but had a change of heart over the president's lack of support for black civil and economic rights.

Nor did Greeley completely agree with Radical Republicans, who he believed preyed upon fears and memories to secure votes. Hoping that Grant would bring order and honesty to the Republican Party, Greeley backed him for the presidency in 1868. He grew disgusted quickly, seeing Grant as a weak figure surrounded by scoundrels. Scandals among top administration insiders, aggressive annexation schemes by the State Department, and inconsistent policies toward Southern Republican governments drove a wedge between the newspaperman and the president. A full break occurred in 1871 with Greeley's publication of "Political Problems in South Carolina," in which the editor claimed

Horace Greeley, owner of the *New York Tribune*, was a lifelong reformer and abolitionist. He unsuccessfully ran for president as leader of the Liberal Republican movement in 1872. (Library of Congress)

that Carolina Republicans were creating taxation and patronage systems designed to bribe blacks into voting Republican—thus keeping carpetbaggers in power. Only a Republican with a long history of battling for black rights could have criticized Grant in this way. His editorial encouraged Southern Democrats and made many Northerners to think twice about the goals of the Southern Republican Party.

Greeley's attacks on the Republican administration dovetailed with complaints from other reformers, concerned about Republican corruption and apparent attempts to secure party dominance at any cost. These critics organized as the Liberal Republican Party in 1872, hoping to lure reform Republicans and Moderate Democrats into an alliance that could seize the presidency. The Liberal Republicans insisted on the Southern acceptance of the Reconstruction amendments to the U.S. Constitution, called for pardons for former confederates who had been disfranchised, and demanded civil service reform and an end to government corruption. At their Cincinnati Convention, delegates gave the presidential nomination to Greeley, and the following month, the Democratic Party endorsed the platform and candidates. Greeley proved a poor campaigner, and his public record opened him easily to all sorts of attacks and spoofs. Worse, the alliance with the Democrats hurt the reformers, as memories of war—and continued accounts of hostility in the South—lost more votes that it garnered. Grant, despite the failings of his administration, remained a popular figure, and won reelection easily. Greeley, drained by the campaign and distraught by the recent death of his wife, fell into depression and died soon after the election, on November 29, even before all votes had been counted.

*Heather Cox Richardson*

**See also:** Abolitionists; Abolition of Slavery; Amnesty Proclamations; Congressional Reconstruction; Fifteenth Amendment (1870); Fourteenth Amendment (1868); Labor Systems; Moses, Franklin J. Jr. (1838–1906); New Departure; Presidential Reconstruction; Republicans, Radical; Thirteenth Amendment (1865).

## Further Reading

Greeley, Horace. *Recollections of a Busy Life*. New York: J. B. Ford, 1868.

Richardson, Heather Cox. *The Death of Reconstruction: Race, Labor, and Politics in the Post–Civil War North*. Cambridge, MA: Harvard University Press, 2001.

Van Deusen, Glyndon. *Horace Greeley: Nineteenth-Century Crusader*. Philadelphia: University of Pennsylvania Press, 1953.

# GRIMES, JAMES W. (1816–1872)

Republican senator James Wilson Grimes was born in Deering, New Hampshire, on October 20, 1816, the youngest of eight children. He graduated from Dartmouth College in 1836 and moved west to practice law in the "Black Hawk Purchase"—land that eventually became Michigan, Wisconsin, the Dakotas, and Iowa. When the Iowa Territory was formed in 1838, he served as a delegate on the territorial assembly, as well as Burlington City solicitor and justice of the peace. Once Iowa became a state in 1846, Grimes served in the legislature and in 1854 was elected governor. Although Iowa was a Democratic state, Grimes was a Whig, respected for his fairness and moderation. An advocate of "free soil," he transitioned into the new Republican Party, and moved to the U.S. Senate in 1859; he was reelected in 1865.

Secession and the war years tested Grimes's moderation. He participated in the spring 1861 convention to find a compromise solution to the secession crisis and avoid war.

As a Moderate Republican and potential swing voter, Grimes became one of the power brokers in the Senate, often wooed by the Radical Republicans. At first, like many Moderates, he supported President Andrew Johnson; also like many Moderates, the president's 1866 vetoes of the Freedmen's Bureau Bill and the Civil Rights Bill drove a wedge between them. As Congress developed an alternate plan for Reconstruction, Grimes took a seat on the Joint Committee on Reconstruction, an important place for a voice of moderation. He supported, although with reservations, the 1867 Military Reconstruction Acts, but openly argued that the Tenure of Office Act—which Radicals used to impeach Johnson—did not cover Secretary of War Edwin Stanton; hence Johnson did not violate the Act. Grimes's stance worried Radicals during the impeachment trial, for they knew the vote for conviction would be close.

In May 1868, with the nation fixated on the president's trial and with party pressure intensifying, Grimes suffered an attack of paralysis (possibly from a minor stroke). As a telling sign of the political climate, Radical Republicans and their newspapers rejoiced, hoping this would keep him from voting. Yet on May 16, when the Senate convened for its first vote, Grimes arrived on a stretcher; Chief Justice Salmon P. Chase even waived chamber the rules so the senator could vote without standing. As expected, Grimes voted "not guilty," one of the seven so-called Republican "recusants" who voted not guilty. The results were the same for each article called, and the Senate failed to convict and remove the president; Johnson would finish his term.

The reasons for Grimes's "not guilty" vote are clear. There were personal issues involved, for everyone knew that Grimes hated Radical Benjamin Wade, who would succeed Johnson if the president were removed. More important, Grimes's sincere belief in fairness and moderation drove his vote. Interviewed soon after the Senate adjourned as High Court of Impeachment, Grimes stated, "I can not [*sic*] agree to destroy the harmonious working of the Constitution for the sake of getting rid of an unacceptable President. Whatever may be my opinion of the incumbent, I can not [*sic*] consent to trifle with the high office he holds. . . . However widely, therefore, I may and do differ with the President respecting his political views and measure, and however deeply I have regretted, and do regret the differences between himself and the Congress of the United States, I am not able to record my vote that he is guilty of high crimes and misdemeanors by reason of those differences" (*Harper's Weekly*, June 6, 1868).

Already ill at the trial, Grimes became an immediate target of Republican retribution (as did all "recusants"). He never recovered his health, and suffered a more debilitating stroke in 1869. He resigned his Senate seat and moved abroad for two years. Not long after returning to the United States his heart failed, and he died on February 7, 1872. Grimes was buried in Aspen Grove Cemetery in Burlington, Iowa.

*Michelle Mellon*

**See also:** Civil Rights; Congressional Reconstruction; Elections of 1866; Fessenden, William Pitt (1806–1869); Presidential Reconstruction.

## Further Reading

"Biographical Directory of the United States Congress, 1774–Present," http://bioguide .congress.gov/scripts/biodisplay.pl?index¼ G000475.

Foner, Eric. *Reconstruction Updated Edition: America's Unfinished Revolution, 1863–1877*. Reprint. New York: HarperCollins, 2014.

"The Iowa Official Register, Iowa History Project: The Nativity of the Pioneers of Iowa," http://iagenweb.org/history/ Pioneer%20Nativity.htm.

Roske, Ralph J. "The Seven Martyrs?" *American Historical Review* 64 (January 1959): 323–30.

"Virtual American Biographies: James Wilson Grimes," http://www.famousamericans.net/ jameswilsongrimes/.

# GUN CLUBS

Gun clubs, also known as "rifle clubs" or "sabre clubs," were an important element of the Democratic paramilitary organizations active during Reconstruction. Although many Deep South states saw the appearance of gun clubs in the 1870s, South Carolina served as the center of activity. Gun clubs reflected the historical tendency toward extralegal violence in the South, the evolution of terrorist organizations during Reconstruction, and ultimately the lack of legitimacy of the Southern Republican governments.

When the Republicans in Congress passed the Military Reconstruction Act in March 1867, it placed the South under military supervision, and disbanded all existing state militias. Once states had been readmitted under congressional Reconstruction, many federal restrictions were lifted, including the ban on militias. In South Carolina, carpetbag governor

Robert K. Scott reorganized South Carolina's militia in 1869 on an integrated basis; however, many native whites refused to serve with blacks, and instead formed all-white companies such as the Carolina Rifles of Charleston. The state refused to acknowledge these as legal, so to dodge state (or perhaps federal) trouble these clubs altered their description from militia units to "social clubs." While they did sponsor dances, parties, picnics, and parades, they also procured weapons, drilled regularly, and even had uniforms. The gun clubs tended to be led by prominent white citizens, including Andrew Pickens Butler and C. Irvine Walker. When the Ku Klux Klan appeared in the late 1860s and early 1870s, the federal government, and in particular the Ulysses S. Grant administration, responded with an active intervention policy to enforce the Fourteenth Amendment and Fifteenth Amendment. The demise of the Klan encouraged the growth of gun and saber clubs as a less obvious form of paramilitary organization. More serious proliferation began in earnest in 1874; waning federal interest and growing state Republican problems convinced Democrats that an opportunity to regain control had arrived. By some accounts, gun and saber clubs numbered in the hundreds by early 1876, serving as pockets of political mobilization and communication as the Democratic Party repaired its organization. The clubs also presented an efficient and experienced means of intimidating and harassing local Republicans, black and white.

So as the 1876 campaign began, Wade Hampton and the Democratic Party already had an extensive network of gun clubs that could turn their hands to electioneering. These organizations formed the basis of the Red Shirts, an amalgamation of clubs from across the state, which harassed and intimidated Republican voters and candidates. Governor Daniel H. Chamberlain issued an order disbanding all gun clubs in October 1876, but the gun clubs simply fell back on the fiction of their purely social purpose. For example, the Allendale Rifle Club renamed itself the Allendale Mounted Baseball Club and continued its activities without pause. Taking its cue from the so-called Mississippi Plan in the neighboring state, these private military forces staged parades and rallies, and appeared at Republican functions to intimidate their political adversaries. Most contemporaries and historians agree that the armed presence of these large organizations had a powerful effect on the election. That impact was not restricted to curtailing the Republican vote; it also sent a message to the North that the Republicans had no real legitimacy with white natives in the state. Moreover, it was clear the state government had no monopoly on force, a key to enforcing the law and providing public order.

But the work of the Red Shirts and the gun clubs did not end with the election, as both parties claimed fraud and both parties claimed victory. Through the fall and winter, thousands of rifle club members converged on the state capital in Columbia. These groups claimed to be protecting Democrats who were contesting the election results, but they also pressured white and black Carolina Republicans. Black militia units were no match for former Confederate soldiers, so using state force was out of the question. Only the presence of the U.S. Army protected Chamberlain and his government; so for months, Columbia sat in the grip of a tense standoff. Finally, a decision in Washington that gave the presidency to Republican Rutherford Hayes also gave the state house to Democrat Wade Hampton. Under the so-called Compromise of 1877, the new president removed federal troops from the Southern capitals; Hampton and his gun club army stood unopposed, and Chamberlain's Republican administration had no choice but to capitulate.

*Bruce E. Baker*

*See also:* Carpetbaggers; Compromise of 1877; Congressional Reconstruction; Elections of 1876; Hampton, Wade, III (1818–1902); Ku Klux Klan (KKK); Redemption; Red Shirts.

## Further Reading

Egerton, Douglas R. *The Wars of Reconstruction: The Brief, Violent History of America's Most Progressive Era.* New York: Bloomsbury Press, 2014.

Fitzgerald, Michael W. *Splendid Failure: Postwar Reconstruction in the American South.* New York: Ivan R. Dee Publishers, 2008.

Zuczek, Richard. *State of Rebellion: South Carolina during Reconstruction.* Columbia: University of South Carolina Press, 1996.

# H

## HAHN, GEORG MICHAEL DECKER (1830–1886)

Michael Hahn, U.S. congressman and governor of Unionist Louisiana during the Civil War, played a prominent role among Unionists in wartime New Orleans and in Louisiana's Republican Party during Reconstruction.

Born in Germany on November 24, 1830, he emigrated as a small child with his widowed mother and siblings to the United States, eventually settling in New Orleans around 1840. Orphaned in 1841, he attended local schools and received his law degree in 1851 from what is today Tulane University. A pro-Union Democrat before the war, he opposed secession, and after New Orleans fell to federal forces in 1862, he helped organize Unionists and worked closely with federal military officials. He became a Republican, vigorously endorsing emancipation and the policies of President Abraham Lincoln; under Lincoln's wartime Reconstruction operation in 1863, he briefly represented Louisiana in the U.S. Congress. Returning to New Orleans, he helped write the state's 1864 Constitution abolishing slavery, and that same year, he was elected governor under Lincoln's Ten Percent Plan. He resigned in early 1865 upon his election to the U.S. Senate, but Congress never seated those elected under Lincoln's plan.

Following Lincoln's assassination, Hahn, not surprisingly, opposed the Reconstruction policies of President Andrew Johnson. He was part of the group that attempted to reconvene a constitutional convention to enact black suffrage; he nearly died from a gunshot wound suffered at the New Orleans riot of July 30, 1866 that resulted when the convention tried to meet. Undeterred, he became manager and editor of the *New Orleans Republican* in 1867, which he used to mobilize local Republicans as congressional Reconstruction took root. In 1872, Hahn moved to his sugar plantation in St Charles Parish, but he remained involved in politics. He was elected to the state legislature in 1872, 1874, and 1876. In 1878, became superintendent of the U.S. Mint at New Orleans; and from 1879 to 1885, he served as a federal district judge in Louisiana. In 1880, he founded the *New Orleans Ledger* to support Republican candidates and was elected to Congress in 1884 from the heavily Democratic Second Congressional District.

Hahn died in Washington, D.C., on March 15, 1886, before completing his term, and he was buried in Metairie, Louisiana. Although considered a Moderate Republican, Hahn was nonetheless a principled defender of black civil rights. Even his political opponents came to admire his physical courage, strength of conviction, and personal integrity.

*John C. Rodrigue*

*See also:* Amnesty Proclamations; Banks, Nathaniel P. (1816–1894); Butler, Benjamin Franklin (1818–1893); Presidential Reconstruction; Race Riots; Suffrage; Wells, James M (1808–1899).

## Further Reading

McCrary, Peyton. *Abraham Lincoln and Reconstruction: The Louisiana Experiment.* Princeton, NJ: Princeton University Press, 1978.

Simpson, Amos E., and Vaughan B. Baker. "Michael Hahn, Steady Patriot." *Louisiana History* 13 (1972): 229–52.

Taylor, Joe Gray. *Louisiana Reconstructed: 1863–1877.* Baton Rouge: Louisiana State University Press, 1974.

# HAMPTON, WADE, III (1818–1902)

Wade Hampton, a wealthy Confederate general, dominated South Carolina politics in the 1870s, and led the forces of "Redemption" which overthrew Republican rule in 1876.

Born into one of the wealthiest planter clans in the South, Hampton turned his attention to managing extensive family estates in South Carolina and Mississippi after graduating from South Carolina College in 1836. Elected to South Carolina's General Assembly in 1852 and 1858–1861, Hampton took a Moderate tone. He opposed efforts to reopen the transatlantic slave trade and even questioned the independent secession of his state in 1860. Once South Carolina seceded, however, he accepted a colonel's commission, personally raising and financing "Hampton's Legion," a unit comprising six companies of infantry, four companies of cavalry, and a battery of artillery. During the Civil War, he rose to the rank of lieutenant general, assuming command of Gen. Robert E. Lee's cavalry following the death of J.E.B. Stuart. By the time the Confederacy fell, he had lost his wealth and his slaves, seen his plantations burned, and been wounded five times.

Hampton returned to South Carolina in 1865 as the gallant and beloved hero and faced a movement to elect him governor under President Andrew Johnson's restoration

A former Confederate general, Wade Hampton III helped overthrow the Reconstruction government of South Carolina. He became the state's governor in 1877. (Library of Congress)

policy. Hampton deferred to another Moderate, James L. Orr, believing that the selection of an ex-Confederate general might inflame Northern hostility. Instead, Hampton concentrated on salvaging his family's agricultural empire. In 1868, with debts topping $1 million, he declared bankruptcy and consigned his shattered property to creditors. By this time, Hampton's moderation had begun to fade, as the realities of Radical reconstruction took hold across the South. "If we had known you were going to back with bayonets the carpetbagger, the scalawag, and the negro in their infamous acts," he later told President Ulysses S. Grant, "we would never have given up our arms!" Thousands of other white Carolinians felt likewise, engulfing the state in a reign of Ku Klux Klan terror. In 1868, when Republican carpetbag governor Robert K. Scott enlisted Hampton's assistance, the former general's public call for the "preservation of order" resulted in a sharp reduction in violence. While no fan of the Republicans or their new social system, Hampton—a once wealthy, well educated, stoical Episcopalian conservative—always put moderation and order first. Given the bloody vengefulness of the Red Shirt campaign during the election of 1876, it is easy to forget Hampton's moderating mission. Unlike Edgefield's Martin W. Gary, who served under Hampton in the Civil War and who masterminded the Red Shirt strategy that put Hampton in the governor's chair that year, Hampton's Bourbonism featured restraint—"force without violence," in his phrase—and racial accommodation—but not political or social equality. Such rhetoric drew some African Americans to the conservative cause, but did little to restrain white gun clubs eager to settle scores and reassert dominance.

But by 1876, Hampton was the veteran, the glorious war hero, and the Democratic candidate for governor, making him responsible for the violence and terrorism that murdered and intimidated African American citizens in the state. The former officers of his Confederate Hampton Legion directed the Red Shirt campaign across the state. Republican dedication and willpower, devoid of support from Washington, were no match for the planning, brutality, and thoroughness of Hampton's campaign. Carpetbag governor Daniel H. Chamberlain disputed the state's election results, but his cries fell on deaf ears. With the so-called Compromise of 1877 taking effect, Hampton, Gary, and their gun clubs took power in the spring of 1877.

Once in power, Hampton and his cronies (many of whom were high-ranking Confederate veterans and landholders) displayed little in the way of political vision. They threw Republican appointees out of office, prosecuted Republican officials, and developed a more onerous crop lien law in 1878. By the time Hampton was sent to the U.S. Senate in 1879, he had done much to reestablish planter hegemony in South Carolina and turn back the clock on race relations. Hampton's success presented a serious setback for the state's black and white agricultural working class, setting the stage for regressive social and economic policies for decades to come.

*Vernon Burton*

***See also:*** Black Troops (U.S. Colored Troops) in the Occupied South; Bourbons; Civil Rights; Congressional Reconstruction; Jim Crow Laws; Military Reconstruction Acts (1867–1868); Presidential Reconstruction; Race Riots; U.S. Army and Reconstruction.

## Further Reading

Drago, Edmund L. *Hurrah for Hampton! Black Red Shirts in South Carolina during Reconstruction.* Fayetteville: University of Arkansas Press, 1998.

Egerton, Douglas R. *The Wars of Reconstruction: The Brief, Violent History of America's Most Progressive Era.* New York: Bloomsbury Press, 2014.

Jarrell, Hampton M. *Wade Hampton and the Negro: The Road Not Taken.* Columbia: University of South Carolina Press, 1949.

Wellman, Manly W. *Giant in Gray: A Biography of Wade Hampton of South Carolina.* New York: Charles Scribners' Sons, 1949.

Williams, Alfred B. *Hampton and His Red Shirts: South Carolina's Deliverance in 1876.* Charleston, SC: Walker, Evans, and Cogswell, 1935.

# HANCOCK, WINFIELD SCOTT (1824–1886)

A professional army officer, Winfield Scott Hancock commanded troops in Louisiana during Reconstruction. A native of Pennsylvania, Hancock was born in Montgomery Square to a respected attorney and his wife. After graduating from the U.S. Military Academy in 1844, Hancock saw frontier service, fought in the Mexican War, and although a devout Democrat remained with the Union during the Civil War. He established an excellent record as a leader in battle, distinguishing himself at Antietam (1862) and for his gallant stand against "Pickett's Charge" at the Battle of Gettysburg (1863), where he was badly wounded. By the end of the war, he was accorded a hero's status in the North and was one of only five major generals in the regular army in 1866.

As Reconstruction opened, Hancock was serving in the West but was recalled by President Andrew Johnson when Congress passed the Military Reconstruction Acts in March 1867. When Congress divided the South into five military districts, Johnson found innovative ways to obstruct Congress by using his presidential authority to name the commanding generals—and he sought the most Moderate men possible. As a high-profile Democrat, Hancock was an obvious choice, and Johnson assigned him to command the Fifth Military District (Louisiana and Texas) in November 1867. As Johnson had hoped, Hancock seized the opportunity in Louisiana to try to reverse the policies of his predecessors, generals who vigorously enforced congressional acts. Hancock used his authority under the acts to remove officeholders and appoint replacements to vacant positions and most of his appointees were Democrats. Hancock also stopped appointing African American men on juries and discouraged black males from registering to vote.

On November 20, 1867, Hancock issued his hallmark political statement embodied in his General Order No. 40. Announcing that whenever possible, civilian officials' decisions should take priority over military rulings, Hancock's General Order No. 40 undercut military government authorized in the Military Reconstruction Acts and his own authority in supervising the operation of local, county (parish), and state governments.

Hancock's actions came to the attention of General Ulysses S. Grant in Washington, D.C., who drew an imaginary protective line around the Republican city council of New Orleans, headquarters of the Fifth District. When Hancock wanted to replace some of the councilmen, Grant blocked the move, prompting Hancock to seek a transfer out of Louisiana. Grant gladly accommodated his request.

Hancock was significant as a Reconstruction commander for several reasons. The general spoke or acted for many Conservative army officers (such as George Meade) who opposed Republican Reconstruction policies. Ironically, his support for Johnson won him so many supporters that he was even considered for the Democratic nomination for president in 1868—which of course Johnson coveted. Yet despite his clear opposition to the national policy and congressional law, Hancock was not punished, demoted in rank, or sent to isolated outposts; to the contrary, he remained in the army as a major general.

In the postwar years, Hancock made no secret of his presidential aspirations. He might have made a good choice for the Democrats to counter the Republicans' nomination of Grant for the election of 1868, and likewise could have pitted his creditable military record against the incumbent in 1872. Instead, the Democrats eschewed the war hero and placed their hopes on New York governor Horatio Seymour and newspaperman Horace Greeley, respectively, neither of whom had served in the military during the war. Hancock was again passed over in 1876, this time for New York governor Samuel Tilden, who was also not a veteran. Finally, in 1880, Hancock was finally nominated for president by the Democrats, narrowly losing the election to the Republican nominee, James A. Garfield, a former Union volunteer general. Hancock remained on active duty until his death at Governors Island, New York.

*Joseph G. Dawson III*

*See also:* Black Suffrage; Congressional Reconstruction; Elections of 1876; Republicans, Liberal; U.S. Army and Reconstruction.

## Further Reading

Dawson, Joseph G., III. *Army Generals and Reconstruction: Louisiana, 1862–1877.* Baton Rouge: Louisiana State University Press, 1982.

Jordan, David M. *Winfield Scott Hancock: A Soldier's Life.* Bloomington: Indiana University Press, 1988.

Richter, William L. *The Army in Texas during Reconstruction.* College Station: Texas A&M University Press, 1987.

# HAYES, RUTHERFORD BIRCHARD (1822–1893)

Rutherford B. Hayes, 19th president of the United States, was born in Delaware, Ohio, the posthumous son of Rutherford Hayes and Sarah Birchard Hayes. He was educated at Kenyon College and Harvard Law School. He settled in Cincinnati, where he became a successful attorney and served as city solicitor from 1858 to 1861. In politics, he was an antislavery Whig who defended fugitive slaves.

During the Civil War, Hayes served as colonel of the Twenty-Third Ohio Volunteer Infantry Regiment, both in West Virginia and the Shenandoah Valley. Wounded several times, he rose to the rank of major general. Elected as a Republican to Congress in 1864, he refused to leave military service while the war was still going on; he did not take his seat in the House of Representatives until late in 1865. A Moderate Republican, he opposed President Andrew Johnson, and in 1867, was elected governor of Ohio, though the legislature fell to the Democratic Party. Hayes was reelected two years later but lost a bid to return to Congress in 1872. In 1875, however, he managed to defeat the inflationist William Allan for governor, thus winning an unprecedented third term.

Republican Rutherford B. Hayes became president in 1877. The election of 1876 involved so much controversy that he was eventually selected by special commission, as part of the "compromise of 1877." (Library of Congress)

At the 1876 Republican National Convention, the leading candidates— James G. Blaine, Oliver Morton, and Roscoe Conkling—could not muster majorities. Hayes emerged as a compromise candidate for the Republicans, with William Wheeler of New York as his running mate. The platform pledged equal rights for all, including women, the speedy resumption of specie payments, and the separation of powers. Because of the corruption during Ulysses S. Grant's presidency, Hayes's reputation for honesty made him an attractive candidate. Hayes's opponent was New York governor Samuel J. Tilden, who had established a record as a reformer by smashing the notorious Tweed Ring. With two such candidates, the election was bound to be close, and the result was one of the most disputed elections in American history.

Although most of the Southern states had already been "redeemed" by the Conservatives and Democrats, Florida, South Carolina, and Louisiana still had Republican governments. In the election, Hayes received 165 undisputed electoral votes, and Tilden had 184. For election, 185 were necessary, so that 20 disputed votes from the three Southern states (one was disputed in Oregon because of a technicality) would decide the presidency. The Republicans, who controlled the Senate, maintained that the presiding officer of that body ought to decide which votes were legitimate, but the Democrats, in control of the House, objected. The result was the creation of a Joint Electoral Commission, with three Republican and two Democratic senators, three Democratic and two Republican representatives, and one Republican and one Democratic Supreme Court justice, with an independent justice, presumably David Davis. Davis, however, was elected to the Senate, so Justice Joseph P. Bradley of New Jersey, a Republican, took his place. As a result, the commission, by a party vote of 8 to 7, decided for Hayes, with 185–184 electoral votes.

When the Democrats threatened a filibuster that would prevent the inauguration, a series of negotiations and compromises moved the process forward. Hayes was inaugurated on March 5, although he lacked a popular majority (4,300,590 were cast for Tilden, and 4,036,298 for Hayes). Yet, he always believed he had been honestly elected because of the number of black voters denied the vote in the three states.

The Hayes presidency was controversial from the beginning—opponents called him "your fraudulency" or "Rutherfraud." Instead of appointing any of his rival candidates to the cabinet, he chose reformers such as William Evarts, who had defended Andrew Johnson, and Carl Schurz, who had bolted in 1872 with the formation of the Liberal Republicans, as well as a Southerner, David M. Key. Hayes's most controversial action was his withdrawal of the federal troops from the Southern state houses, which allowed Democrats to oust the last of the Republican governments; of course, many claim the "Compromise of 1877" required the removal in exchange for the presidency. Personally devoted to black welfare and civil rights, he sought promises from Southerners to treat African Americans well, a promise that was soon forgotten after Daniel H. Chamberlain had to give up the governorship of South Carolina and Stephen B. Packard that of Louisiana. To the end of his life, however, Hayes actively supported black education by working with the Slater Fund and the Peabody Foundation. In addition, he vetoed several Democratic attempts to repeal the Enforcement Acts by riders to appropriation bills.

His other challenge was civil service reform. Bitterly opposed by regular Republicans, this change was introduced in some departments, particularly in Carl Schurz's Department of the Interior, but it encountered real difficulty in New York, where Roscoe Conkling's machine sought to resist efforts to remove its supporters in the Customs House. For more than a year, the Senate refused to confirm Hayes's appointment of successors to Collector Chester A. Arthur and naval officer Alonzo B. Cornell, until Hayes finally prevailed.

His final difficulty was the economic problem created by the Panic of 1873. Confronted with railroad strikes in the summer of 1877, Hayes sent federal troops upon the request of various state governors. These did not have to go into action, but the measure has been criticized as an antilabor policy by the administration. At the time, however, it was considered perfectly justified, and not until the turn of the century did the Theodore Roosevelt government adopt a more equitable attitude toward strikes.

Always having advocated a one-term presidency, Hayes did not run for reelection, but his administration had been successful enough to make possible the victory of James A. Garfield as his successor. Hayes enjoyed a lengthy retirement devoted to his favorite causes, such as help for black education. He died at Fremont, Ohio, in 1893.

*Hans L. Trefousse*

*See also:* Redemption.

## Further Reading

Davison, Kenneth E. *The Presidency of Rutherford B. Hayes*. Westport, CT: Greenwood Press, 1972.

Hoogenboom, Ari. *Rutherford B. Hayes: Warrior and President*. Lawrence: University Press of Kansas, 1995.

Trefousse, Hans L. *Rutherford B. Hayes*. New York: Henry Holt, 2002.

# HOLDEN, WILLIAM WOODS (1818–1892)

William Woods Holden was North Carolina's provisional governor under President Andrew Johnson's plan of Reconstruction and its Republican governor during Congressional Reconstruction.

Holden was the illegitimate son of Thomas Holden and Priscilla Woods; he lived with his father and his wife until at age 17 he became a typesetter on a Raleigh newspaper. In 1843, he became editor and proprietor of the *North Carolina Standard*, the voice of the state Democratic Party; his political influence grew quickly. In 1858, he sought his party's nomination for governor but was defeated by John W. Ellis, which created a division in the party. After Abraham Lincoln's election in 1860, Holden led the constitutional Union or Moderate party that advocated a "wait and watch" policy toward the antislavery president. The Union party in February 1861 checked the secessionist effort to take the state out of the Union, but after Fort Sumter and Lincoln's call for troops to suppress the rebellion, Holden reversed his position and called on North Carolinians to resist the president's "gross usurpation" of power. He served as a delegate to the state convention in May that took North Carolina out of the Union and into the Confederate states.

Barely a year into the war, Holden was bitterly criticizing the state Democratic and Confederate administrations for discriminating against old Union men in their military appointments and other policies. The adoption of conscription by the Jefferson Davis government gave Holden additional cause for denouncing Confederate authorities.

Holden organized the Conservative Party in 1862 and secured the election of Zebulon B. Vance as governor. When Holden organized a peace movement in the state in mid-1863, staunch confederates charged that he was giving aid and comfort to their enemies and encouraging desertions from the army. In early 1864, he proposed that a state convention meet to seek peace in cooperation with other Southern states. He also announced his candidacy for governor against Vance, who had broken with Holden over war issues. Vance easily won the election.

One month after the war, Johnson appointed Holden provisional governor of the state to launch the process of civil reorganization under his plan of Reconstruction. As required by Johnson, Holden called a state convention to invalidate the secession ordinance, abolish slavery, and repudiate the Confederate debt. He achieved these tasks, but also used his office to deny presidential pardons to his old political enemies, including former governors Zebulon B. Vance and William A. Graham. In fall 1865, Holden ran for governor against Jonathan Worth, the candidate of the Vance-Graham faction. He lost in a close election, and when Johnson did not support his complaints about former confederates taking charge, he began drifting toward national Republicans.

When congressional Republicans passed the Military Reconstruction Acts in March1867, Holden cast his lot with the Republicans and used his *North Carolina Standard* to help organize the party in the state. He argued that North Carolinians must put the Civil War behind them, accept the new political reality in the nation, and save the state from further ruin. Holden announced his acceptance of black civil rights and even black male suffrage, and the ratification of the Fourteenth Amendment to the U.S. Constitution— all requirements by Congress before North Carolina could be readmitted to the Union. In April 1868, Holden, with a large number of blacks and some white voting for him, was elected governor by a vote of 92,235 to 73,593 over his Conservative (Democratic) Party opponent; Republicans also won control of the General Assembly and the other state offices.

In July, Holden took the oath of office as governor and military rule ended, but the efforts of the Republican administration to advance progressive policies like a comprehensive system of public education for both races soon went awry. A large majority of the white citizens, encouraged by Holden's old rivals Vance and Graham, never accepted the legitimacy of the new biracial political order. Conservatives seized every opportunity to discredit the Republicans. State aid to complete the statewide railroad system and the scandals associated with it offered a fertile field for their attacks, although Holden was never directly implicated in any wrongdoing. Worse than financial abuse was the threat that Reconstruction posed to white supremacy, which led to intimidation and violence against the Holden regime and its supporters. By 1869, violent bands known generically as the Ku Klux Klan had emerged in the state. At first Holden issued proclamations calling for peace and citizen action, but by late 1869 and early 1870, Klan violence intensified, and Holden secured the passage of a bill that gave him the authority to proclaim a state of insurrection and call out the state militia. After several high-profile assassinations, in February 1870, Holden declared a state of insurrection and asked President Ulysses S. Grant for troops. Grant refused to intervene and advised the governor to use his own resources, but Holden feared the mostly black militia were no match for the Klan. But the approaching election in August for seats in the General Assembly guaranteed the violence would not abate. The final straw for Holden occurred in May, when John W. Stephens, a Republican state senator, was murdered in the Caswell County courthouse. In response the governor raised a force of 670 men in western North Carolina under the command of Col. George W. Kirk, who had commanded a Union regiment during the Civil War, and dispatched it to Alamance and Caswell counties to suppress the Klan. Not a shot was fired in the so-called Kirk-Holden War, though minor incidents occurred. More than 100 Klansmen were arrested and confined, with Holden hoping to hold military trials. But Holden had overreached, and a federal district court—backed by Grant—denied confinement and ordered all suspects handed over to civil courts for trial.

The reaction to the Kirk-Holden War and the military arrests pushed Conservatives' anger to new heights and Democrats took control of the legislature in the August 1870 election. With a 2 to 1 majority in the General Assembly, Conservatives moved to impeach and remove Holden from office. In his annual message to the General Assembly, Holden promised to cooperate with the legislature in measures "to promote the prosperity and happiness of our people." The time for conciliation, however, had passed. On December 19, the House of Representatives voted eight articles of impeachment against the governor, most of which charged him with raising an illegal military force and wrongfully directing it to arrest and hold civilians. Holden answered the charges by claiming that he had acted to protect the citizens of the state from "insurgents," and he had intended to surrender the Klansmen to the regular courts after order had been restored. On March 22, 1871, the North Carolina Senate rendered its verdict: Holden was found guilty and removed from office, the first governor in American history to suffer this indignity.

After a brief period of "exile" in Washington to escape possible court action against him, Holden returned to Raleigh in 1872. The next year, Grant appointed him postmaster of Raleigh, a position he held until his removal by President James A. Garfield in 1881. Although he made peace with many of his old political foes, including Vance, Holden spent his post-Reconstruction years attempting in vain to obtain a reversal of the impeachment verdict. In North Carolina historical lore, he is the villain of the Reconstruction era.

*William C. Harris*

**See also:** Amnesty Proclamations; Black Suffrage; Redemption.

## Further Reading

Harris, William C. *William Woods Holden: Firebrand of North Carolina Politics*. Baton Rouge: Louisiana State University Press, 1987.

Raper, Horace W., and Thornton W. Mitchell, eds. *The Papers of William Woods Holden*. Raleigh: North Carolina Division of Archives and History, 2000.

Trelease, Allen W. *White Terror: The Ku Klux Klan Conspiracy and Southern Reconstruction*. New York: Harper and Row, 1971.

# HOUSE JUDICIARY COMMITTEE

The U.S. House of Representatives has the constitutional authority to impeach federal officials, if necessary. During Reconstruction, many Republicans believed President Andrew Johnson deserved to be impeached (and even removed, the potential following and more extreme step) because they disagreed with his policies, thought he interfered with the law, or abused his power. The House of Representatives referred all resolutions pertaining to the impeachment of Johnson to its Judiciary Committee, which conducted investigations to determine whether Johnson had actually done impeachable offenses.

The Judiciary Committee, as of January 1867, consisted of nine members, all lawyers by profession. Four of them were Moderate Republicans, including committee chairman James F. Wilson (Iowa), Frederick E. Woodbridge (Vermont), Daniel Morris (New York), and Francis Thomas (Maryland). George S. Boutwell (Massachusetts), Thomas Williams (Pennsylvania), Burton C. Cook (Illinois), and William Lawrence (Ohio) were Radical Republicans, while Andrew J. Rogers (New Jersey) was the only member of the Democratic Party. Although there had been considerable talk about impeachment earlier, on January 7, 1867, Republican James M. Ashley (Ohio) introduced the first resolution to impeach the president. The committee began secret investigations immediately. The issues under investigation included whether Johnson had improperly corresponded with former Confederate president Jefferson Davis, had sold offices, had made illegal appointments of provisional governors in the South, had improperly taken money from the U.S. Treasury, and had illegal dealings with some railroads. The committee interviewed several cabinet members, Judge Advocate General Joseph Holt, and various disappointed office seekers. However, none of these witnesses produced much relevant information.

Because the new Congress took their seats on March 4, 1867, several members of the Judiciary Committee changed. Republican John C. Churchill (New York), and Democrats Charles A. Eldredge (Wisconsin) and Samuel S. Marshall (Illinois) replaced Morris, Rogers, and Cook. The reorganized committee continued fishing for some impeachable private or political offense that Johnson might have committed. Witnesses testified about Johnson's veto messages, pardons, appointments, the New Orleans riot, the government's failure to try Jefferson Davis, and other issues. However, the committee still found no impeachable offense and voted to adjourn on June 3, 1867.

Johnson proved to be his own worst enemy when in August he suspended Secretary of War Edwin M. Stanton and removed army district commanders Philip H. Sheridan and Daniel E. Sickles (who were vigorously enforcing Reconstruction acts). When the committee met, for a fourth time, in November 1867, they finally recommended impeachment by a narrow 5 to 4 votes. Wilson, Woodbridge, Eldredge, and Marshall opposed impeachment. Williams, who wrote the majority report, charged Johnson with a number of offenses, including pardoning traitors, causing the New Orleans riot, and defying Congress. Although Wilson and Woodbridge believed that Johnson had done the things charged, they did not agree that these were impeachable offenses.

On December 5, 1867, Boutwell introduced the impeachment resolution in the House. Many members believed that Johnson could not be impeached unless he had committed an indictable crime. Because there was no evidence that Johnson had done so, the members defeated the resolution by a vote of 108 to 57. Then, Johnson again did something to provoke a shift in sentiment against him: in February 1868, he removed Stanton as secretary of war, allegedly in violation of the Tenure of Office Act. John Covode (Pennsylvania) quickly presented an impeachment resolution to the House. This time, however, the House bypassed the Judiciary Committee and referred the resolution to the Joint Committee on Reconstruction, chaired by Radical Republican Thaddeus Stevens. The committee approved, the House agreed, and on February 24, 1868, the impeachment proceedings began. The Judiciary Committee as a whole had no further involvement with Johnson's impeachment and trial, although Wilson, Boutwell, and Williams served as impeachment managers—the "prosecution" in the offense against the president.

*Glenna R. Schroeder-Lein*

*See also:* Amnesty Proclamations; Congressional Reconstruction; Presidential Reconstruction.

## Further Reading

Trefousse, Hans L. *Impeachment of a President: Andrew Johnson, the Blacks, and Reconstruction.* Knoxville: University of Tennessee Press, 1975.

# HOWARD, OLIVER OTIS (1830–1909)

A Union general during and after the Civil War, Oliver Otis Howard served during Reconstruction as commissioner of the War Department's Bureau of Refugees, Freedmen, and Abandoned Lands, commonly known as the Freedmen's Bureau. Although Howard was genuinely committed to black education and to the economic advancement and civil rights of African Americans, his record as Freedmen's Bureau commissioner was one of mixed success.

Howard was born on November 8, 1830, in Leeds, Maine. He attended Bowdoin College but then received an appointment to the U.S. Military Academy at West Point. He graduated in 1854 and decided to remain in the military. After fighting the Seminoles in Florida, Howard returned to West Point as an instructor in 1857. While in Florida, Howard had undergone a religious conversion experience and became an avowed Christian and served as an informal chaplain at West Point. By 1860, he contemplated leaving the military for the ministry, but the outbreak of the Civil War convinced him to stay in the army. During the war, Howard earned the nickname "Christian General" for his religious zeal. By the end of 1861, he had

Union general Oliver Otis Howard served as the first, and only, commissioner of the Freedmen's Bureau (1865–1872). Howard University in Washington, DC, is named for him. (National Park Service)

achieved the rank of brigadier general, and during the next two years he participated in nearly all the major battles of the Army of the Potomac. He lost his right arm during the Peninsula Campaign of the spring of 1862 and returned to command at Antietam, Fredericksburg, Chancellorsville, and Gettysburg.

The following fall 1863, Howard was transferred to the western theater, and he later commanded the Army of the Tennessee in William T. Sherman's campaign through Georgia and the Carolinas.

Following the Confederate surrender, Secretary of War Edwin M. Stanton offered Howard the position of commissioner of the recently created Freedmen's Bureau. Building upon wartime relief and freedmen's aid efforts, and recognizing the need for a federal agency to oversee the South's transition from slavery to freedom, in March 1865, Congress had created the Freedmen's Bureau as a branch of the War Department. Howard's missionary sense of purpose, antislavery credentials, and distinguished combat record, made Howard a leading candidate for the commissioner's job. President Andrew Johnson approved the appointment, and Howard became Freedmen's Bureau commissioner in May 1865.

Howard faced vast challenges in his position. Congress had bestowed upon the bureau a daunting task. It was responsible for implementing free labor in the South, distributing federally controlled land to the freedmen, establishing schools, providing aid and relief to wartime refugees and to the destitute of both races, maintaining systems of public health, adjudicating disputes and securing justice, and providing many other essential services in the war-ravaged South. To fulfill these tasks, the bureau initially received no fiscal appropriation of its own and was chronically understaffed. Despite its broad mandate, moreover, the bureau was generally regarded as temporary, causing many white Southerners and other opponents to resist its authority. Howard himself reflected the contradictions of the bureau's mission to remake Southern society. Recognizing that the former slaves required some form of assistance while emerging from centuries of servitude, he also subscribed to 19th-century free labor ideology, which emphasized individual initiative and the supremacy of the capitalist marketplace, and he feared the creation of a class of permanent dependents. Howard also displayed an almost naive faith in human nature, and he often seemed oblivious to the nuances of Reconstruction politics, in which he, as head of the controversial Freedmen's Bureau, was inevitably embroiled.

Perhaps Howard's greatest challenge was Johnson's opposition. Subscribing to an essentially conservative vision of Reconstruction, Johnson did not foresee a fundamental overturning of Southern society, and he believed that the Freedmen's Bureau represented an unconstitutional expansion of federal authority. In particular, Johnson objected to the reallocation of abandoned and confiscated land for free people's use.

Although Johnson's Amnesty Proclamation of May 1865 restored almost all property rights to pardoned ex-confederates, the legal status of bureau-held land remained unclear, and Howard instructed bureau agents not to return such land to its former owners. The president nullified the order, and had Howard issue a second order specifying that bureau-controlled land be returned to pardoned former confederates.

Johnson also resorted to other tactics, both overt and subtle, in his war on the Freedmen's Bureau. He pressured Howard to dismiss assistant commissioners (heads of the bureau in the Southern states), such as Rufus Saxton of South Carolina, who were too radical in their political views and who advocated too strongly the interests of the freedmen. In a major strategic error, in February 1866, Johnson vetoed the Freedmen's Bureau Bill, which authorized extending the bureau's existence beyond the originally imposed one-year time limit (after the end of hostilities). That spring, Johnson also ordered an official investigation clearly intended to discredit the bureau. Congress subsequently passed two laws in July continuing the bureau for another two years (overriding a second veto) and providing it a separate appropriation.

Notwithstanding the many challenges it faced and the numerous disadvantages it suffered, the Freedmen's Bureau under Howard dramatically improved the lives of thousands of freedmen and indigent whites during the immediate postwar years. With passage of the Military Reconstruction Acts in 1867, however, the bureau lost much of its independent identity within the War Department, and Howard relinquished most of his authority to the military district commanders. As Southern states gained readmission to the Union, the bureau surrendered most of its responsibilities to the civilian governments, although Congress enacted one final law extending the bureau until after the elections of 1868. At the end of that year, the bureau ceased all operations except for its educational work and the securing of black veterans' bounty claims, which continued until 1872, when the bureau was finally closed.

Education had been of particular importance to Howard, and he was instrumental in Congress's 1867 chartering of historically black Howard University in Washington, D.C., which was named after him. He served as president of the school from 1869 to 1873 (while still bureau commissioner) and continued to be involved in its affairs for the rest of his life. Although the school was not affiliated with the Freedmen's Bureau, an accident during its construction resulted in an 1870 congressional investigation that exonerated Howard but found much inefficiency and misappropriation of funds within the bureau. Moreover, irregularities surrounding the paying of veterans' bounties led to a military court of inquiry in 1874 that again absolved Howard of wrongdoing. That same year, the Freedman's Savings and Trust Company (the Freedman's Bank) failed, a victim of poor oversight and the financial Panic of 1873. Although not officially part of the Freedmen's Bureau, the bank was closely identified with it, and the bank's demise further clouded Howard's and the bureau's reputations.

In 1874, Howard returned to active duty in the Pacific Northwest, and he led the 1877 campaign that captured Chief Joseph and the Nez Perce Indians. He served briefly as superintendent of West Point during the early 1880s, was promoted to major general in 1886, and held several other commands until his retirement in 1894. Howard settled in Burlington, Vermont, and remained active in religious and educational endeavors. He published his autobiography in 1908, and he died on October 26, 1909, in Burlington, where he was buried.

*John C. Rodrigue*

**See also:** American Missionary Association (AMA); Black Codes; Black Troops (U.S. Colored Troops) in the Occupied South; Churches; Civil Rights Act of 1866; Congressional Reconstruction; Democratic Party; Edisto Island, South Carolina; Field Order No. 15; Freedmen's Relief Societies; Grant, Ulysses S. (1822–1885); Labor Systems; Port Royal Experiment; Presidential Reconstruction; Republicans, Moderate; Republicans, Radical; Southern Homestead Act (1866); Trumbull, Lyman (1813–1896); U.S. Army and Reconstruction.

## Further Reading

Bentley, George R. *A History of the Freedmen's Bureau.* Philadelphia: University of Pennsylvania Press, 1955.

Carpenter, John A. *Sword and Olive Branch: Oliver Otis Howard.* Pittsburgh: University of Pittsburgh Press, 1964.

Howard, Oliver Otis. *Autobiography of Oliver Otis Howard.* 2 vols. New York: The Baker & Taylor Co., 1908.

McFeely, William S. *Yankee Stepfather: General O. O. Howard and the Freedmen.* New Haven, CT: Yale University Press, 1968.

# HUMPHREYS, BENJAMIN GRUBB (1808–1882)

Born on August 26, 1808, in Claiborne County, Mississippi, Benjamin Grubb Humphreys was one of 13 children. He attended preparatory schools in both Kentucky and New Jersey. He was admitted to West Point in 1825, but after a Christmas frolic that turned into a student riot, he was expelled in May 1827.

Back in Mississippi, Humphreys studied law, married, and assisted in managing the family's plantation. An antebellum Whig, Humphreys was elected to the lower house of the state legislature in 1837. Two years later, he served a term as state senator. After that, he retired from politics and devoted himself to his agricultural interests, his second wife, and their growing family. Reentering politics in the crisis atmosphere of 1860, he ran unsuccessfully as an outspoken Unionist candidate for Mississippi's secessionist convention. As with many Southern Unionists, once the state voted for secession, Humphreys stood with the Confederacy.

Compiling a distinguished record in the field, Humphreys commanded at Gettysburg, then accompanied James Longstreet to Georgia and Tennessee, returning to the Shenandoah Valley in 1864, where he was seriously wounded. By that time a brigadier general, he spent the next several months recovering. Just before the war's end, he was appointed to the command of a new, experimental unit composed exclusively of slaves. The conflict concluded, however, before his command was activated.

Returning to Mississippi, Humphreys quickly involved himself in the postwar politics of the state. As prewar Unionist, he fit the mold of Moderates President Andrew Johnson envisioned as implementing his restoration policy for the former Confederate states. Following Johnson's provisional phase, Humphreys was elected governor on October 2, 1865, along with a host of other antebellum Whigs who swept Mississippi's congressional elections and the state legislature. Humphreys saw himself as a voice of moderation and reunion, which may have been true by antebellum standards—but as with the president, those standards no longer applied. He supported and defended the state's new Black Codes, and seemed indifferent to the state's growing reputation for racial violence. As conditions for the freedpeople deteriorated, Humphreys and federal military forces (such as the Freedmen's Bureau) came into conflict more often. Paralleling this were developments in Washington; Johnson's growing problems with Congress ultimately led to the Radical Republican emergence, and the coming of Congressional Reconstruction. The passage of the 1867 Reconstruction Acts meant the end of Humphreys, who was removed by federal soldiers.

Humphreys essentially retired from elective politics after 1868, but he became a respected leader in Mississippi's new Conservative Party. He returned to his plantation, Lucknow, outside Port Gibson, where he practiced law and dabbled in the insurance business. He died there in 1882.

*Martin J. Hardeman*

**See also:** Military Reconstruction Acts (1867–1868); Presidential Reconstruction; U.S. Army and Reconstruction.

## Further Reading

Harris, William. *Presidential Reconstruction in Mississippi*. Baton Rouge: Louisiana State University Press, 1967.

Rainwater, Percy L., ed. "The Autobiography of Benjamin Grubb Humphreys." *Mississippi Valley Historical Review* 21 (1934): 231–54.

Warner, Ezra. *Generals in Gray: Lives of Confederate Commanders*. Baton Rouge: Louisiana State University Press, 1959.

# HUNNICUTT, JAMES WALTER (1814–1880)

James Walter Hunnicutt, Baptist minister, newspaper editor, Unionist, and Radical Republican, was born in South Carolina in 1814. Despite his South Carolina birth, Hunnicutt called Virginia home for most of his life. In 1848, Hunnicutt launched the *Christian Banner* newspaper in Fredericksburg, Virginia, but during the secession crisis and Civil War, however, Hunnicutt's opinions clashed with the town's pro-Confederate majority. His outspoken unionism ultimately forced Hunnicutt to flee in the summer of 1862.

Confederate defeat brought Hunnicutt home, and he quickly became the state's leading Radical Republican. In October 1865, he launched the *New Nation*, which he used to criticize President Andrew Johnson's conciliatory Reconstruction policy. Hunnicutt believed the president's strategy placed Virginia's restoration in the hands of former confederates who mistreated black and white Southern Unionists. His defense of blacks' civil rights defined Hunnicutt's Reconstruction career. Through the *New Nation*, Hunnicutt advocated black suffrage as well as the redistribution of occupied lands to blacks. His commitment to these issues distinguished the editor as the most radical Republican in Virginia, and strained his relationship with his Moderate Republican colleagues. As the party worked to establish a solid organization in Virginia, Hunnicutt had strong support among the African American population and more urban areas where many Northern migrants congregated; in the countryside, white Virginians viewed his ideas with disdain.

The conflict within the Virginia Republican party came to a head in 1867. Drawing upon his broad support among black Virginians, Hunnicutt sought the Republican nomination for governor in the 1868 election. In April, a convention dominated by Hunnicutt and his black supporters drafted a radical platform that shocked Moderate Republicans. They met in a second convention in August, determined to derail Hunnicutt's candidacy. When Moderates secured the nomination, Hunnicutt's political influence started a steady decline. The editor's efforts later that year to disfranchise former confederates sealed his political fate; months of economic and political pressure by opponents forced the *New Nation* out of business in 1868.

Renewed factional fighting among the Republicans in the early 1870s sparked a brief comeback and one last run for public office, but Hunnicutt failed to secure support. Disappointed with both his personal defeat and the disintegration of Radical Reconstruction overall, Hunnicutt left public view and retired to Stafford County. He died in 1880.

*Steven E. Nash*

**See also:** Congressional Reconstruction; Presidential Reconstruction; Republicans, Liberal; Scalawags.

## Further Reading

Lowe, Richard. *Republicans and Reconstruction in Virginia, 1856–1870.* Charlottesville: University Press of Virginia, 1991.

Olsen, Otto H., ed. *Reconstruction and Redemption in the South.* Baton Rouge: Louisiana State University Press, 1980.

Taylor, Alrutheus A. *The Negro in the Reconstruction of Virginia.* Washington, DC: The Association for the Study of Negro Life and History, 1926.

# I

## IMPEACHMENT MANAGERS

The impeachment managers were, in effect, the prosecution at the Senate trial of President Andrew Johnson. Chosen from their peers in the House of Representatives, these men were expected to take the 11 articles of impeachment and convince the U.S. Senate that these offenses warranted conviction and removal from office.

The House selected seven Republicans to serve as managers. The chair was John A. Bingham of Ohio. The most vocal and extreme of the mangers were Thaddeus Stevens of Pennsylvania and Benjamin F. Butler of Massachusetts. Other members were former general John A. Logan of Illinois, George Boutwell of Massachusetts, Thomas Williams of Pennsylvania, and James F. Wilson of Iowa. All presented solid Republican credentials, as there was no need for neutrality here; although charges of partisanship will forever taint the impeachment vote and the Senate vote, the impeachment managers were deliberately selected to present a powerful, convincing case against Johnson. Ultimately, they failed.

The trial, which began on March 30, 1868, and lasted until May 26, 1868, represented an unprecedented event in American political history, so the managers had no training or guidelines to follow. Although every manager was a lawyer, questions and disagreements over how to proceed led to dissension in the team, and a poor showing at the trial. Stevens, the most forceful and famous of the seven, had become seriously ill (he never did recover) and this deprived the committee of his contribution; most orations and arguments were left to Rep. Butler, who many found just as antagonistic but far less talented. Newspapers spoofed his performance almost daily and pro-Republican presses called for a replacement. The managers also called witnesses, although the nature of the charges left little of fact unknown and provided no real rationale for witnesses. The managers frequently called for changes in rules and objected to various components of Johnson's defense counsel's tactics.

Many forces converged to undercut the managers' case against Johnson. The articles of impeachment were themselves weak, especially those hinging upon the dubious Tenure of Office Act. The Senate trial was presided over by Chief Justice Salmon P. Chase, who accommodated no horseplay or antics; he was neutral, or even pro-Johnson, in his interpretations of the rules of order, so the managers received no assistance from him. Johnson's five-man defense counsel was exceptional, boasting two former attorneys general (Reverdy Johnson and Henry Stanbery) and a former Supreme Court justice (Benjamin R. Curtis).

Managers and defense counsel presented their final statements in the last week of April and first week of May. Voting was scheduled for May 12, 1868, but was postponed until

May 16. Managers and other Republicans watched in horror as the Senate acquitted Johnson of Article XI by a vote of 35 to 19, one vote shy of the two-thirds necessary for conviction. Voting commenced on Article II on May 26, with exactly the same result. The managers had failed to convince the Senate that President Johnson was guilty of "high crimes and misdemeanors." The Senate as high court adjourned, and the position of impeachment manager evaporated.

Butler, however, was not finished. Butler, and perhaps other managers, thought the result impossible and the margin too curious. Certain that Johnson was acquitted as a result of foul play, Butler convinced the House to allow the managers to act as an impromptu investigating committee. They charged that Republican senators had been bribed by Johnson, and especially targeted Edmund Ross of Kansas (even though his Moderate leaning was well documented). Butler issued subpoenas, called witnesses, interviewed scores of people, and even confiscated bank records, telegrams, and mail. In the end, he was unable to find any evidence of bribery; Johnson served out the rest of his presidential term.

*Richard Zuczek*

**See also:** Congressional Reconstruction; Democratic Party; House Judiciary Committee; Joint Committee on Reconstruction; Presidential Reconstruction; Republicans, Radical; Stanton, Edwin M. (1814–1869).

## Further Reading

Benedict, Michael Les. *The Impeachment and Trial of Andrew Johnson*. New York: W. W. Norton and Co., 1973.

Schroeder-Lein, Glenna, and Richard Zuczek. *Andrew Johnson: A Biographical Companion*. Santa Barbara, CA: ABC-CLIO, 2001.

Trefousse, Hans L. *Impeachment of a President: Andrew Johnson, the Blacks, and Reconstruction*. Knoxville: University of Tennessee Press, 1975.

## IMPEACHMENT OF ANDREW JOHNSON (1868)

A three-year struggle between President Andrew Johnson and the Moderate and Radical Republicans in Congress over the extent and direction of Reconstruction culminated in 1868 with the impeachment of the president. The Republican Party was dedicated toward protecting the civil rights of the newly freed African Americans and preventing the ex-confederates from reassuming power in the South. Johnson's strict constructionist view of the U.S. Constitution, his determination to prevent a social revolution in his native South, and his desire to build a new Conservative Party from a coalition of white Southerners, Northern Democrats, and Conservative Republicans led to a clash with Congress.

In May 1865, Johnson announced his plan for restoring the Southern states to the Union. Like his predecessor Abraham Lincoln, he wanted a lenient peace, and, also like his predecessor, he offered a blanket pardon for virtually all former rebels. The ex-Confederate states then needed only to organize constitutional conventions where they would renounce secession, repudiate all debts incurred during the war, and abolish slavery. Elections for state and national offices would follow, the new legislatures would ratify the Thirteenth

Amendment, and the restoration process would end with the readmission of the states.

Initially, many Conservative Republicans in Congress supported the president's plan. But the situation had changed from the wartime years of Lincoln. The Confederacy had been defeated, and the emergency powers of the presidency evaporated. Making matters worse was the behavior and attitude of the former confederates. Under Johnson's plan, state after state established restrictive laws known as the Black Codes to hold the former slaves in subordinate economic and social positions, and Johnson's elections resulted in former Confederate military and civilian leaders heading to Congress. Congress refused to seat the former rebels sent to Washington and established a Joint Committee on Reconstruction to study the situation in the South. Wanting to play an active role in reconstructing the South, Congress passed two bills in 1866 to support the freedpeople.

Andrew Johnson, the first American president to be impeached by the House of Representatives. The Senate, however, failed to convict and remove him. (Library of Congress)

The Freedmen's Bureau Bill expanded the agency's operations, and the Civil Rights Bill extended citizenship to blacks and essentially nullified the Black Codes. Not only were these measures resisted by white Southerners, they were resisted by Johnson as well. He viewed them as unnecessary and unconstitutional, and he vetoed both. Congress overrode his veto of the civil rights bill and subsequently passed another Freedmen's Bureau bill. Republicans in Congress then went further, passing the Fourteenth Amendment to enshrine those same rights in the Constitution directly, granting black citizenship, nullifying the Black Codes, and restricting the political influence of ex-confederates. Defiantly, Johnson urged the Southern states to not ratify the measure. The elections of 1866 served as a litmus test in the North, as Johnson battled the Republicans for control of Congress. Republicans won a huge majority in both houses of Congress and assumed control of the Reconstruction process.

Now able to override any presidential veto, Congress passed the Military Reconstruction Act in March 1867, beginning Congressional (or Radical) Reconstruction.

Johnson vetoed this Military Reconstruction Act and also two subsequent acts designed to clarify and strengthen it. The Republican majority in Congress overrode his vetoes easily. However, under his authority as commander in chief and in an effort to slow or redirect the congressional intent, Johnson appointed Conservative officers, such as Winfield Scott Hancock, to command the military districts, and removed zealous officers.

While some Radical Republicans called for Johnson's removal, their more Moderate colleagues sought to curtail his power through two laws of questionable constitutionality. A provision of the Army Appropriations Act of 1867 required the president to issue all orders to army commanders through the general in chief of the army, Ulysses S. Grant. The Radicals hoped Grant could exercise a controlling influence over Johnson. The most direct challenge to presidential authority was the Tenure of Office Act, under which an official appointed with the Senate's consent remained in office until the Senate approved a successor. Ostensibly intended to protect patronage offices, the law, in reality, was designed to prevent the removal of Secretary of War Edwin M. Stanton, a Radical in Johnson's inherited Cabinet.

Even with these attempts to restrict Johnson's impact on Reconstruction, the president retained a considerable capacity to obstruct congressional efforts. Radicals had launched impeachment efforts as early as 1867, but Moderates insisted that the president could only be removed from office for committing indictable crimes. Perhaps encouraged by this reasoning, Johnson took advantage of a loophole in the Tenure of Office Act, which permitted the president to remove and appoint officials while the Senate was in recess. Once reconvened, the Senate would then decide to support or reject the president's actions. Johnson waited until Congress adjourned and suspended Stanton in August 1867. He then persuaded Grant to assume the position of interim secretary of war.

Johnson surmised that Grant's status as a war hero would prevent the Radicals from forcing the general's removal. Grant had urged the president not to suspend Stanton, but he accepted the appointment. This time, the Radicals in the House were able to force a vote on impeachment. In December 1867, the House defeated the measure 108 to 57. But now Congress had reconvened, and Senate had to decide whether to reject or uphold Johnson's suspension of Stanton. The Senate rejected Johnson's rationale for Stanton's suspension; Grant vacated the office and turned it back to its former occupant.

Foiled in his attempt to use Grant's prestige to rid himself of Stanton, the president challenged Congress directly by removing Stanton (not suspending him), this time while the Senate was in session. Congress erupted, and when Republican senators urged Stanton to ignore the order, he barricaded himself in the War Department and refused to leave.

Johnson's obvious disregard of the terms of the Tenure of Office Act convinced even Moderate Republicans that he would oppose all congressional requirements in the Reconstruction process. Therefore, on February 24, 1868, the House voted to impeach the president along a strict party-line vote of 126 to 47; Johnson became the first president to be impeached. So eager were the Republicans to remove Johnson that they voted to impeach the president before drawing up formal charges. The House then created a committee of prosecutors known as impeachment managers that included Radicals such as Thaddeus Stevens, George Julian, Benjamin Butler, John Logan, and George Boutwell. Finally, the House produced 11 articles of impeachment. The first eight dealt with Johnson's attempt, in violation of the Tenure of Office Act, to remove Stanton and to appoint a successor without the Senate's consent. The ninth article charged Johnson with trying to persuade the army commander in the District of Columbia to violate the command provisions of the 1867 Army Appropriations bill (Command of the Army Act) by accepting orders directly from the president. The tenth article accused the president of harboring resentment against Congress, and the final "omnibus" article essentially drew together all the charges of the previous 10.

Impeachment, a formal declaration that the president has violated the law or abused power, did not automatically remove the president from office. Once impeached by the House of Representatives, the president now faced trial in the Senate. The Senate trial began March 30, 1868, and continued with interruptions for two months. This protracted process worked in the president's favor by cooling the passions that had climaxed with his attempted removal of Stanton. Johnson's defense counsel included some of the leading lawyers in the country: Henry Stanbery, the attorney general; William M. Evarts, a future attorney general under Johnson and secretary of state under President Rutherford B. Hayes; and Benjamin R. Curtis, a former justice of the Supreme Court. During the trial, these men demonstrated a good deal more legal acumen than did the House's impeachment managers. Johnson's team based its defense on three arguments: that a government official can be impeached only for criminal offenses that would be indictable in ordinary court; that Johnson had committed no crime by seeking to remove Stanton and testing the constitutionality of the Tenure of Office Act; and that because the act applied only to cabinet officers "during the term of the president by whom they may have been appointed," it did not apply to Stanton, who had been appointed by Lincoln.

The impeachment managers challenged this line of defense, asserting that because Johnson was serving out Lincoln's term, the Tenure of Office Act did cover Stanton. To allow the president to disobey a law to test it in court would set a dangerous precedent. Finally, whether or not Johnson was guilty of any crime, impeachment was a political rather than criminal process.

Regardless of the charges, everyone understood that Johnson was being tried for his three years of relentless opposition to the Republican Reconstruction program. Although Moderate Republicans abhorred Johnson, many feared his removal would pave the way for future parties with a two-thirds congressional majority to remove any president who disagreed with their proposals. The constitutional balance of power would be destroyed. Moderates also distrusted radical Benjamin Wade, president *pro tem* of the Senate and next in line for the presidency (no vice president had been selected). Using intermediaries, Johnson and the Moderates worked toward an understanding. The president gave no more speeches or interviews denouncing Congress, and he promised to enforce the Military Reconstruction Acts. Johnson also appointed the highly respected general John M. Schofield as secretary of war. On May 16, 1868, the Senate voted on the 11th article of impeachment, 35 to 19. All 12 Democrats and 7 Moderate Republicans voted against conviction and removal. With a two-thirds majority needed to remove the president from office, Johnson had been saved by a single vote. Votes on Articles 2 and 3 on May 26 ended in the same result, forcing the impeachment managers to concede defeat. As these were the most legitimate and valid articles, failure to reach conviction meant Johnson would survive. So too did the constitutional balance between the president and Congress.

*John D. Fowler*

**See also:** Bureau of Refugees, Freedmen, and Abandoned Lands; Elections of 1868; Presidential Reconstruction.

## Further Reading

Benedict, Michael Les. *The Impeachment and Trial of Andrew Johnson.* New York: W. W. Norton and Co., 1973.

McKitrick, Eric L. *Andrew Johnson and Reconstruction*. Chicago: University of Chicago Press, 1960. Reprint, New York: Oxford University Press, 1988.

Trefousse, Hans L. Impeachment *of a President: Andrew Johnson, the Blacks, and Reconstruction*. Knoxville: University of Tennessee Press, 1975. Reprint, New York: Fordham University Press, 1999.

# J

## JENKINS, CHARLES J. (1807–1883)

Best known as the first elected governor of Georgia after the Civil War, Charles Jones Jenkins was also the last governor to take residence in the governor's mansion in Milledgeville, Georgia.

Charles Jones Jenkins was born on January 6, 1805, in Beaufort District, South Carolina. He moved with his family to Jefferson County, Georgia, in 1816. Jenkins took up law and in 1830 was elected to the Georgia House of Representatives. The following year he became attorney general of the state of Georgia. Jenkins was often the Speaker of the House when the Democratic Party was in the majority in the legislature and remained active in the legislature during the period between 1836 and 1850. Jenkins became a state senator in 1856 and later, during the Civil War, he was appointed by Governor Joseph E. Brown as a justice of the Georgian Supreme Court.

In June 1865, President Andrew Johnson appointed James Johnson provisional governor of Georgia, charged with overseeing a new constitution and the election of new officials. The convention gathered in Milledgeville, in October 1865. Jenkins worked with Herschel V. Johnson to manage this convention of nearly 300 delegates. Herschel Johnson acted as the presiding officer while Jenkins held the office of chairman of the committee on business. His role in the convention positioned him well for the executive post, and Jenkins was elected governor that fall. Jenkins immediately began working to resolve the state budget crisis and address other issues of restoration, including the ratification of the Thirteenth Amendment to the U.S. Constitution. He made great strides with the state budget, restored the Western and Atlantic Railroad, and persuaded the Georgia legislature not to ratify the Fourteenth Amendment, which Congress required for readmission to the Union. The rejection of this amendment by every former Confederate state except Tennessee was the beginning of the end of Andrew Johnson's program, and with it Georgia's Conservative efforts toward Reconstruction.

In 1867, the U.S. Congress revoked the legitimacy of the governments in most of the Southern states under the Military Reconstruction Acts. The Southern states were divided into five military districts. Alabama, Florida, and Georgia were all placed in the Third Military District. Jenkins traveled to Washington, D.C., to enter a petition before the Supreme Court for an injunction against the enforcement of the Reconstruction Act that authorized military control in his state. Jenkins also refused to have Georgia pay the state funds that were ordered by the federal government for a constitutional convention. He protested the federal government's mandate that $40,000 in state funds be used to pay for this convention. Some accounts report that Jenkins protested payment for this convention because it was racially integrated; other accounts note that Jenkins believed that the proceedings were illegal and was concerned about Georgia's recently stabilized budget.

Due to his continued squabbling over the Reconstruction Acts, Jenkins was removed from office in January 1868. The military reconstruction of Georgia was supervised by Gen. John M. Pope, who installed Gen. Thomas H. Ruger as military governor in 1868. Rufus B. Bullock was appointed provisional governor of Georgia in January 1868 and was inaugurated as the official governor in July of the same year. Jenkins fled the state, and took records of the governor's office along with the seal of the executive department. He also removed state funds and deposited the funds into a New York bank account. Jenkins toured Europe and later fled to Nova Scotia until Reconstruction fervor died down in Georgia. He returned to Augusta, Georgia, in the early 1870s, and gave all of the state property in his possession to then governor James M. Smith.

Jenkins was a popular governor because of his resistance to Congressional Reconstruction. In 1872, he received two electoral college votes for the vice presidency of the United States because of the death of the Liberal Republican candidate, Horace Greeley, who had been endorsed by the Democratic party. For a while, Jenkins retired to private life, but in 1877, following Redemption and the return to conservative rule, he became the chair/president of the Georgia Constitutional Convention. Jenkins died on June 14, 1883. Jenkins County, Georgia, was named in his honor in 1905.

*Kijua Sanders-McMurtry*

*See also:* Amnesty Proclamations; Black Codes; Presidential Reconstruction.

## Further Reading

Fitzgerald, Michael W. *Splendid Failure: Postwar Reconstruction in the American South.* New York: Ivan R. Dee Publishers, 2008.

James, Joseph. "Southern Reaction to the Proposal of the Fourteenth Amendment." *Journal of Southern History* 22, no. 4 (November 1956): 477–97.

McCrary, Royce, ed. "The Authorship of the Georgia Platform of 1850: A Letter by Charles J. Jenkins." *Georgia Historical Quarterly* 54 (Winter 1970): 585–90.

Thompson, Mildred. *Reconstruction in Georgia.* Freeport, NY: Books for Library Press, 1915. Reprint, 1971.

## JIM CROW LAWS

Following the Civil War, and with it the abolition of slavery, a large body of custom and law developed across the South that was meant to regulate relations between African Americans and whites. They were collectively referred to as Jim Crow, a term taken from the name of a popular prewar minstrel character that appeared in blackface. While their main aim was to enforce racial segregation, Jim Crow also represented a pervasive—and invasive—system designed to instill a sense of inferiority in black Southerners. It prevented them from marrying across racial lines, attending the same schools as whites, and accessing on an equal basis

"Jim Crow" represented the social segregation between blacks and whites across the South. This photo, from the 1930s, depicts a young boy at a "black" water fountain in North Carolina. (John Vacha/FPG/Getty Images)

all manner of public services and facilities. These codes placed humiliating restrictions on blacks throughout their lives, and even after their deaths, as Southern cemeteries were segregated as well. Note that Jim Crow largely referred to social and economic issues, not political access; although an elaborate—and effective—system of disfranchisement grew up parallel to Jim Crow, segregation itself did not directly involve voting.

While precursors to Jim Crow can be found in the prewar North and in the treatment of free blacks in the South before the Civil War, the postwar system's origins lay in Reconstruction. It was in the confusion of this period that its early outlines are visible, as the people of the South struggled to establish a new racial order to replace slavery. White Southerners greatly resented slavery's end and during Presidential Reconstruction sought to return blacks as close to slave status as possible through the Black Codes. These laws restricted blacks to working as agricultural laborers or domestic servants and even permitted their arrest if they refused to work for whites. Both blacks and their white supporters in the North, especially Radical Republicans in the U.S. Congress, vigorously opposed the Black Codes; these codes drove Radicals to guarantee blacks citizenship and equality through the Civil Rights Act of 1866 and soon thereafter through the Fourteenth Amendment to the U.S. Constitution.

Despite the activities of Congress aimed at insuring racial equality in the South, informal segregation appeared in the region from the earliest days following the Civil War. In part, this de facto or customary segregation merely reflected the very real divide between the two races that had existed even under slavery, and persisted and even grew under free-dom. During Reconstruction, blacks carved out for themselves an existence independent of whites. Blacks established their own churches, reunited their families, and resisted attempts by former owners to place black children under forced apprenticeships. Many would have also established an independent black economy, with former slaves farming for themselves, except for their failure to obtain land during Reconstruction.

Indeed, the priority of blacks during Reconstruction seems less to insist on racial integration, but simply on obtaining access to the public facilities and formal equality under the law.

A good example of informal segregation during Reconstruction was in education. Most places in the South did not have public schools prior to the Civil War. Hence, the priority of state and local governments during this period was to establish public school systems, with black parents eager to have their children attend school. The integration of such schools did not appear to have been a significant concern. Both white and black parents seemed to have assumed their children would attend separate schools. In fact, of all the school systems that appeared in the South during Reconstruction, only the one in New Orleans is known to have integrated schools, and its experiment in interracial education came to an abrupt end in 1874, when the schools' operations were disrupted by white rioters.

Despite the widespread existence of informal segregation, a formal—legally mandated—Jim Crow system did not appear until after Reconstruction. While black Southerners apparently acquiesced to many forms of informal segregation during Reconstruction, as long as they had access to the public facilities and services they desired, they and their white allies during Reconstruction opposed formalizing segregation as a part of the law. Indeed, they fought for formal equality. The Civil Rights Act of 1875 outlawed racial discrimination under federal law in the access and use of trains, hotels, and other public facilities. Yet, to get this act through Congress, its supporters had to remove any effective enforcement provisions from the law. So it was never truly implemented and became invalid in 1883, when the Supreme Court ruled it unconstitutional. So formal segregation—characterized by laws formally distinguishing between the races—started after the end of Reconstruction. The first state to enact such a statute was Tennessee, which segregated its railway cars in 1882. Under its railroad law, blacks were prohibited from riding in the first-class railroad cars even if they purchased a first-class ticket. Other Southern states quickly followed Tennessee's lead and through the 1880s and the decades that followed, enacted their own laws segregating railroads and other public facilities. These laws would be given the blessing of the Supreme Court in *Plessy v. Ferguson* (1896), where all but one justice ruled that racial segregation was constitutional as long as the facilities for whites and blacks were equal. The "separate but equal" doctrine provided a legal fiction that continued to justify the very real inequalities of Jim Crow in the U.S. South for the next six decades, until a reversal started in 1954 with the decision in *Brown v. Topeka Board of Education*.

It should be noted that one other significant aspect of Jim Crow was established during Reconstruction. Racial segregation in the South ultimately was made possible not only by the law but also the willingness of white Southerners to use extralegal violence to enforce it. The law and economic pressure kept most blacks subordinated, but for serious transgressions, beatings and even murder became the all-too-common response. Lynching, or extralegal public torture and execution, was the most extreme sanction meted out to those persons who violated Jim Crow. In the heyday of the practice, between 1889 and 1946, almost 4,000 black Southerners met their end in lynching at the hands of white mobs. Although many of these resulted from alleged rape accusations, the horrible practice of lynching was a community's reaction to perceived violations of the larger context of Jim Crow—racial subordination and obedience. White violence was certainly not new, as seen in the Ku Klux Klan, gun clubs, and the horrid array of race riots perpetrated by whites against blacks during Reconstruction. Extralegal violence was just another, if particularly gruesome, aspect of Jim Crow, which—like informal segregation—also was identifiable during Reconstruction.

*Donald R. Shaffer*

**See also:** Enforcement Acts (1870, 1871, 1875); Race Riots; Redemption; Tourgée, Albion Winegar (1838–1905); *United States v. Cruikshank* (1876).

## Further Reading

Litwack, Leon F. *Trouble in Mind: Black Southerners in the Age of Jim Crow*. New York: Alfred A. Knopf, 1998.

McPherson, James M. *The Struggle for Equality: Abolitionists and the Negro in the Civil War and Reconstruction*. Reprint, Princeton, NJ: Princeton University Press, 2014.

Williamson, Joel. *The Crucible of Race: Black-White Relations in the American South since Emancipation*. New York: Oxford University Press, 1984.

Williamson, Joel. *A Rage for Order: Black-White Relations in the American South since Emancipation*. New York: Oxford University Press, 1986.

Wormser, Richard. *The Rise and Fall of Jim Crow*. New York: St. Martin's Press, 2003.

# JOHNSON, ANDREW (1808–1875)

Andrew Johnson became the 17th president of the United States (1865–1869) following John Wilkes Booth's assassination of Abraham Lincoln on April 14, 1865. Johnson faced the immediate challenge of restoring the former Confederate states to the Union. His constitutional and social conservatism and ambition led to an immediate clash with congressional Republicans, and a savage political struggle over the Reconstruction process erupted. As a result, Johnson became the first U.S. president to be impeached, escaping conviction in his Senate trial when Republicans failed by one vote to garner the required two-thirds majority.

Johnson was born in Raleigh, North Carolina, on December 29, 1808. His parents were poor, illiterate, and landless laborers who worked for a local inn. Widowed, his mother apprenticed Andrew to James J. Selby, a tailor. It was in Selby's shop that the future president learned to sew and also to read. After five years with Selby, Andrew abruptly fled the community because an adolescent prank landed him in trouble with the law. He drifted for several years before settling in Greeneville, Tennessee, in 1827. There, Johnson opened a tailor shop and shortly thereafter married Eliza McCardle. He earned a comfortable living and eventually purchased a farm and a few slaves. Andrew and Eliza had five children—two daughters, Martha and Mary, and three sons, Charles, Robert, and Andrew Jr. ("Frank").

Johnson's burning ambition steered him into politics. His later career colored what was an incredible political life, as he held nearly every elected office possible: in 1829, he became alderman; in 1834, mayor; in 1835, state representative; in 1841, state senator; and in 1843, served the first of five terms in the U.S. Congress. Johnson was drawn to Andrew

Jackson's Democratic Party by its support for laboring classes and its anti-elite ideology. At the national level, as a Southern Democrat, he backed the party's stance on limited federal spending, low tariffs, the annexation of Texas, and the subsequent Mexican War. Johnson also supported the institution of slavery. Although he owned a few slaves, most people in his home region of East Tennessee did not. Therefore, slavery was not a major issue to his constituents or to him, but, like many whites in his adopted region of Appalachia, Johnson resented the wealth and political power of the planter class. Always the champion of the lower classes, he sponsored a homestead bill granting poor white farmers free public land. Although he guided the resolution through the House, it failed to attract enough support in the Senate.

In 1853, when Whigs altered his congressional district, he won the first of two consecutive terms as Tennessee's chief executive. As governor, he established a state library and a state-supported public school system. In 1857, the Tennessee general assembly selected him for the U.S. Senate. As a senator, Johnson directed most of his energy (unsuccessfully) to securing his beloved homestead act. As the secession crisis developed in 1860, Upper South states such as Tennessee supported the Constitutional Union Party's candidate, John Bell.

In the wake of Abraham Lincoln's victory, the Deep South threatened secession. Johnson delivered a powerful speech in the Senate on December 18, 1860, denouncing disunion and declaring himself loyal to the United States. Two days later, South Carolina seceded, quickly followed by the rest of the Deep South. In February 1861, Johnson gave another impassioned address against secession, and in the spring of that year, he returned to East Tennessee determined to prevent his home state from joining the exodus. He and other Unionists failed; in a June 1861 referendum, Tennessee joined the Confederacy, and Johnson fled his home to avoid capture by rebel authorities. He defiantly remained in the U.S. Senate, refusing to acknowledge Tennessee's decision—the only senator from a Confederate state to do so. His devotion to the Union made him a Northern celebrity and the chief spokesman for the so-called War Democrats who supported Lincoln.

By early 1862, federal forces had regained control of much of Middle and West Tennessee, and in March, Lincoln appointed Johnson military governor of the state with the rank of brigadier general of volunteers. Lincoln hoped that Johnson's old popularity would enable him to restore civil government and hasten a return to the Union. Johnson believed that a handful of ardent rebels had coaxed the majority of the state's populace into seceding. In reality, however, the majority of Tennesseans actually supported the Confederacy and considered Johnson a traitor. For the next three years, the governor alternately punished and cajoled the state's rebels in an attempt to root out secessionist support.

Prior to the election of 1864, Republicans and War Democrats united to form the National Union Party. The fused party nominated Lincoln for president and Johnson as his running mate. Johnson was an expedient choice. He was a Southerner, a leading War Democrat, and a devout Unionist. In November, the Lincoln-Johnson slate was elected in a huge electoral college victory. Only six weeks after the inauguration, however, John Wilkes Booth assassinated Lincoln, thrusting Johnson into the presidency.

Johnson brought a wealth of experience to the office of the presidency, and he needed all his acumen to tackle the monumental tasks of restoring the Union, rebuilding the South, and determining the place of the former African American slaves in American society. Like Lincoln before him, Johnson favored a quick restoration with lenient terms. He formally recognized Lincoln's wartime Reconstruction governments of Arkansas, Louisiana, Tennessee, and Virginia, reconstructed under Lincoln's so-called Ten Percent Plan. Then, in May 1865, he issued two proclamations that outlined his Reconstruction plan. The first granted amnesty to most former confederates, while the second specifically with the restoration of North Carolina but became the model for the remaining unreconstructed states. Johnson appointed provisional governors—often native Unionists, such as himself—and required that they organize state constitutional conventions to draft new constitutions to abolish slavery, repudiate state debts incurred under the Confederacy, and nullify ordinances of secession. Elections could then be held for state and federal officials. Once the new state legislatures ratified the Thirteenth Amendment, martial law would end, federal troops would be withdrawn, and the states could resume their place in the Union.

From the outset, white Southerners manipulated Johnson's program. Some states refused to ratify the Thirteenth Amendment, others repealed rather than nullified their secession ordinances, and many balked at repudiating the Confederate debt. The new state legislatures also passed a series of laws known as the Black Codes to restrict black civil rights. Perhaps most brazen, the states elected high-ranking ex-Confederate civil and military leaders to political offices. Frustrated, Johnson decided to ignore such actions because he hoped to merge white Southerners, Northern Democrats, and Conservative Republicans into a new national conservative party led by him.

In December 1865, displeased with the results of Johnson's efforts, Congress refused to seat the new Southern congressmen and created a Joint Committee on Reconstruction to study the situation in the South. Hoping to cooperate with the president, in 1866, Moderate Republicans proposed two bills, one extending the life of the Bureau of Refugees, Freedmen, and Abandoned Lands, and the other voiding the Black Codes and providing civil protection and support Southern blacks needed. Although both the Freedmen's Bureau Bill and the civil rights bill passed easily, the president shocked and angered Moderate Republicans by vetoing both. They responded by using their two-thirds congressional majority eventually to override Johnson's vetoes and formulate their own plans for Reconstruction.

Johnson believed in classic Jacksonian Democratic principles, including white supremacy, small government, and support for common laborers. He would not support Republican goals of protecting the rights of Southern blacks and had no issue with local populations electing ex-confederates to office. Therefore, the Joint Committee on Reconstruction proposed the Fourteenth Amendment to the U.S. Constitution, which passed both houses of Congress in June 1866 and essentially became the Republican peace terms for the defeated Confederacy. For the amendment to become part of the Constitution, it needed a three-fourths vote of approval from the states, including some former Confederate states—which Congress considered out of the Union. Johnson argued this was hypocrisy, as Southern states were denied the benefits of being represented in Congress, yet were required to ratify the amendment. Although any Southern state that ratified the Fourteenth Amendment would be restored to the Union, Johnson actively discouraged the Southern states from approving the amendment.

To Johnson's dismay, his home state of Tennessee ratified it in July 1866 and became the first Confederate state to reenter the Union. Undaunted, Johnson embarked on a speaking tour of the northeastern and Midwestern states to drum up support for his policies, influence the 1866 elections, and promote his new, Conservative, National Union Movement and party. Although this "Swing around the Circle," as he called it, began favorably, he quickly encountered unruly and hostile crowds. The president made matters worse by engaging in arguments with hecklers and denouncing certain Republicans as traitors. Newspapers and cartoonists lambasted the president, while Radicals attacked both Johnson and his Democratic supporters as the true traitors to the Union. Making matters worse for the president, major race riots in Memphis (May) and New Orleans (July), coupled with the former Confederate states' resistance to the Fourteenth Amendment, persuaded Northern voters that Johnson's policies could not be trusted to guarantee what many called the "fruits of victory." As a result, Republicans achieved overwhelming victories in the elections of 1866 and took full control of Congress.

As Johnson's bid for a new Conservative coalition collapsed, Congressional Reconstruction entered a more radical phase in which the Republicans prepared to force the recalcitrant South into submission. The Military Reconstruction Act of spring 1867, passed over the president's veto, declared that the 10 Johnson-supported state governments were provisional and divided them into five military districts, each subject to a major general. The army would supervise the registration of all male voters, including blacks (but excluding former confederates who were barred under the Fourteenth Amendment), who would elect delegates to participate in state conventions to write new constitutions. Once Congress approved the new constitutions, elections for state and national offices would follow, new legislatures would ratify the Fourteenth Amendment, and the states would resume their normal situation.

Johnson remained obstinate, and he used his authority as commander in chief of the armed forces to interfere with the Republican program. He firmly believed that these acts were unconstitutional expansions of congressional and federal power, and inappropriate—even prejudicial—as they supported one social group (freed blacks) over another (Conservative whites). Hamstrung by a veto-proof Congress, Johnson removed zealous generals and appointed Conservative ones to slow the Republican's process. To curtail the president's power, Congress passed two statutes of questionable constitutionality. The Command of the Army Act, a rider to the 1867 Army Appropriations Act, required Johnson to issue all orders to subordinate army commanders through the general-in-chief of the army, Ulysses S. Grant. The Radicals hoped Grant could serve as a controlling force over Johnson's actions. The most direct challenge to presidential authority, however, was the Tenure of Office Act, which authorized an official appointed with the Senate's consent to remain in office until that body approved a successor. This law was designed to prevent the removal of Secretary of War Edwin Stanton, a Radical in Johnson's inherited cabinet. Johnson vetoed the Tenure of Office Act and considered vetoing the Army Appropriations Act. However, he signed this bill, allowing the army to receive its funding, yet sent in a formal written protest regarding the Command of the Army provision.

In August 1867, perhaps testing Congress's mettle, Johnson suspended Secretary of War Stanton and removed generals Philip H. Sheridan and Daniel E. Sickles, two of the most fervent enforcers of the Reconstruction Acts. But since Johnson suspended Stanton during congressional recess, many Republicans refused to challenge the president. Of course, Congress had to approve the suspension when it reconvened. As expected, Congress refused to concur with the suspension—at which point Johnson went even further, and formally removed Stanton from office altogether. Johnson claimed this was an attempt to test the constitutionality of the law, but everyone knew it was another battle in a war over control of Reconstruction—and in effect, the federal government.

The Senate objected to the removal, and the House, claiming the president had violated the law, voted to impeach Johnson by a party-line vote of 126 to 47 on February 24, 1868. Johnson's obstinance and reactionary attitude brought him the dubious distinction of being the first U.S. President to be impeached. House prosecutors, known as impeachment managers subsequently proffered 11 charges against the president, called "articles of impeachment." Most dealt with his apparent violation of the Tenure of Office Act, while others involved his relations with the army and Congress.

Once impeached, the issue then passed to the Senate for a formal trial, with the chief justice, Salmon P. Chase, presiding. If convicted the president would be removed from office. But while impeachment may have seemed easy, it was not; Republicans only succeeded on their third try. Removing a president would prove even harder. Johnson's able legal team claimed that he had committed no crime in testing the constitutionality of the Tenure of Office Act. They argued that even if the Act was constitutional, it did not apply to Stanton, who had been appointed by Lincoln, not Johnson. Smartly, they also convinced Johnson to stay quiet and stay away from the trial; his hot temper and aggressive style made more enemies than friends. Although Moderate Republicans abhorred Johnson, many feared a dangerous precedent. His removal could pave the way for future parties with a two-thirds congressional majority to remove any president who disagreed with them. The constitutional system of checks and balances could be destroyed. Moderates also distrusted radical Benjamin Wade, president *pro tem* of the Senate and next in line to the presidency (no one had replaced Johnson as vice president). Using intermediaries, Johnson and the Republican Moderates worked toward an understanding. The president gave no more speeches or interviews denouncing Congress, promised to enforce Reconstruction Acts, and appointed the well-respected Gen. John M. Schofield as the new secretary of war. On May 16, 1868, the Senate voted on the 11th article of impeachment, 35 guilty to 19 not guilty. All 12 Democrats and 7 Moderate Republicans voted against conviction and removal. With a two-thirds majority needed to remove the president from office, Johnson had been saved by a single vote. Votes on Articles 2 and 3 on May 26 had the same result, leading the managers to concede defeat and adjourn the proceedings.

During his final months in office, Johnson did not adhere to the spirit of the accommodation and again defied Congress by vetoing Reconstruction bills and delivering speeches critical of the Radicals. Perhaps Johnson felt encouraged by the Republicans' inability to remove him. Congress, in return, largely ignored him, and routinely passed legislation over his vetoes; Republicans knew he was politically crippled, and the end of the impeachment drama coincided with the Republican National Convention, which nominated Ulysses S. Grant for president; surely Republicans felt confident in victory come November. On the other hand, Johnson naively clung to the hope that the Democratic Party would nominate him for president in 1868; there was no chance of this occurring (the 1866 defeat sealed it earlier): The man who had won election to nearly every position in American democracy would never be elected to its highest office.

After leaving the White House in 1869, Johnson, who did not attend Grant's inauguration, returned to Tennessee where he remained obsessed with politics. Unsuccessful attempts to land a congressional seat in 1869 and 1872 did not deter this lifelong politician. Finally elected to the U.S. Senate in 1875, Johnson became the only president to serve in the Senate after leaving the presidency. On March 5, 1875, during a special session of the Senate, he took his seat to the applause of many Conservative senators. When the Senate recessed, Johnson returned to Tennessee and suffered a paralytic stroke four months later. He died on July 31, 1875, and was buried in Greeneville. Befitting his devotion to the Union, mourners wrapped Johnson in an American flag; alternate accounts have a copy of the Constitution in his hand, while others place it under his head.

Johnson remains as enigmatic today as during his lifetime. A Southern slaveholder, he risked his career, all his possessions, and even his life in support of the Union. A savvy and successful career politician, his skills and cleverness failed him when he needed them the most. Clearly racist and stubbornly Conservative, it has been argued that his opposition directly contributed to Republican unity—and as a result, a much broader and more progressive Reconstruction program. Certainly a product of 19-century Southern mores, he was a man of principle who was blindly devoted to his narrow definition of constitutional, democratic government. His ultimate legacy is yet to be determined.

*John D. Fowler*

**See also:** Democratic National Convention (1868); Presidential Reconstruction; Race Riots; U.S. Army and Reconstruction.

## Further Reading

Benedict, Michael Les. *The Impeachment and Trial of Andrew Johnson*. New York: W. W. Norton, 1973.

Castel, Albert E. *The Presidency of Andrew Johnson*. Lawrence: Regents Press of Kansas, 1979.

Graf, LeRoy P., Ralph W. Haskins, and Paul H. Bergeron, eds. *The Papers of Andrew Johnson*. 16 vols. Knoxville: University of Tennessee Press, 1967–2000.

McKitrick, Eric L. *Andrew Johnson and Reconstruction*. Chicago: University of Chicago Press, 1960. Reprint, New York: Oxford University Press, 1988.

Sefton, James E. *Andrew Johnson and the Uses of Constitutional Power*. Boston: Little, Brown, 1980.

Trefousse, Hans L. *Andrew Johnson: A Biography*. New York: Norton, 1989.

Trefousse, Hans L. *Impeachment of a President: Andrew Johnson, the Blacks, and Reconstruction*. Knoxville: University of Tennessee Press, 1975. Reprint, New York: Fordham University Press, 1999.

## JOINT COMMITTEE ON RECONSTRUCTION

Following the assassination of President Abraham Lincoln and the surrender of the last Confederate armies, Andrew Johnson asserted his authority as chief executive and commander in chief and assumed the task of reconstructing the Union. Beginning with his Amnesty Proclamations in May, the new president imposed criteria upon the former Confederate states that—in his mind—prepared them to reclaim their place in Congress and the federal Union. Congress had not been in session since May, so Johnson had a free hand in deciding what the former Confederate states and the former confederates themselves had to do, or not do, for readmission. A Conservative Southern Unionist, Johnson's focus (like his predecessor's) had been preserving the Union; having accomplished that, he cared little for the plight of freedpeople, black rights, or complaints about former confederates.

Over the summer, Northerners in general and Republicans in particular grew concerned about the lack of transformation in the South. Even before Congress reconvened in December 1865, many Republicans had decided to challenge the president's approach, partly due to their desire to reshape Southern social and political patterns, their interest in protecting freedpeople, and their belief that such an unprecedented undertaking required some congressional voice. In December, the Southern representatives and senators elected under Johnson's plan, many of them former Confederate officers and civilian officials, reported to Washington. Congress faced a choice. It could accept the president's verdict that the states were ready to resume their place in the federal system, ending federal power over the states and placing Southern states' internal affairs off limits to Congress. Congress's other option—one exercised earlier during Abraham Lincoln's attempt at Presidential Reconstruction—was to refuse to seat the Southerners under Article I, Section 5 of the Constitution. This provision grants Congress power to rule on the qualifications of its own members. Congress chose the latter, and excluded the representatives of the former Confederate states when the clerk of the House, Edward McPherson, called roll on December 4, 1865. Having signaled its break with the president, now Congress asserted its constitutional role in, and responsibility for, Reconstruction by establishing the Joint Committee of Fifteen on Reconstruction. The committee's task was to investigate and report on conditions in the former Confederate states. The committee, proposed by Pennsylvania representative Thaddeus Stevens, a member of the Radical Republican faction in the party, was composed of nine members from the House and six from the Senate. Three were from the Democratic Party, and the rest were Republicans. The majority of the committee was made up of Moderate Republicans, including its chair, the respected Maine senator William Pitt Fessenden. Other Republican members included John Bingham of Ohio, Roscoe Conkling of New York, and George Boutwell of Massachusetts; among the Democrats was Reverdy Johnson of Maryland.

During the early months of 1866, the committee listened to witnesses who spoke both of the postwar problems and successes in the South, especially those related to the newly freed African Americans. Most testimony pointed to harassment and mistreatment by Southern whites who opposed federal authority, black freedom, and any form of equal civil rights. With exceptions, testimony painted a picture of an unrepentant South, a place still obsessed with slavery and local control. The committee's final report, issued in June 1866, reflected this picture and argued for further and more thoroughgoing Reconstruction. It found civil rights to be insecure, stable government and equal representation lacking, and those who had led the rebellion were back in power. What Johnson found most appalling was the report's idea of "forfeited rights"; that is, the Southern states had never left the Union but through their actions had forfeited their political rights in it. These rights could be restored only through congressional, not presidential, action.

Relations between Congress and the president deteriorated in early 1866, as Johnson alienated Moderates by vetoing both the Civil Rights Act and the Freedmen's Bureau Bill. The committee sought to secure change via legislation beyond the president's control—a constitutional amendment. The Fourteenth Amendment, drafted in the spring of 1866, addressed black citizenship and rights, the status of the Confederate debt, the growth of Southern political strength following the demise of slavery and its three-fifths clause, and the selection of ex-confederates for political office in the South. The amendment was submitted to the Southern states that summer. Committee member John Bingham proposed making ratification a guarantee of readmission; Radicals, who wanted to avoid limiting their opportunity for remaking the South and protecting blacks and the party, refused, so that Congress still had the flexibility to operate as it saw fit.

The committee was reconstituted in late 1866, but Stevens's efforts to have it continue even longer failed in the next session. Overwhelming Republican victories in the elections of 1866, and growing party unity brought on by Johnson's obstinacy, nullified the need for the committee. Congress itself directly took control of Reconstruction, made clear in the Reconstruction Acts of 1867.

*Claudine L. Ferrell*

**See also:** Amnesty Proclamations; Congressional Reconstruction.

## Further Reading

Foner, Eric. *Reconstruction Updated Edition: America's Unfinished Revolution, 1863–1877*. Reprint, New York: HarperCollins, 2014.

Kendrick, Benjamin B. *The Journal of the Joint Committee of Fifteen on Reconstruction, Thirty-Ninth Congress, 1865–1867*. New York: Columbia University and Longmans, Green, 1914.

Trefousse, Hans L. *Reconstruction: America's First Effort at Racial Democracy*. Malabar, FL: Krieger, 1999.

# JOINT SELECT COMMITTEE ON THE CONDUCT OF THE WAR

The Joint Select Committee on the Conduct of the War was a technically bipartisan (though heavily Radical Republican) committee, made up of three senators and four members of the House of Representatives. Congress established the committee in December 1861, in response to Union military failures, especially the recent defeat at Ball's Bluff. A sense existed that the administration was not pursuing the war effort with enough tenacity and particular generals were too sympathetic to their Confederate enemies.

The original committee members were senators Benjamin F. Wade (Ohio, Republican), the chairman, Zachariah Chandler (Michigan, Republican), and Andrew Johnson (Tennessee, Democrat), as well as representatives George W. Julian (Indiana, Republican), John Covode (Pennsylvania, Republican), Daniel Gooch (Massachusetts, Republican), and Moses Odell (New York, Democrat). When Johnson became military governor of Tennessee in March 1862, he resigned from the Senate and was replaced on the committee by Joseph Wright (Indiana), who was succeeded by Benjamin F. Harding (Oregon), and finally, Charles R. Buckalew (Pennsylvania), all Democrats. Later, when Covode ran for governor rather than for reelection to the House, he was succeeded by Benjamin F. Loan (Missouri, Republican) in January 1864.

Over the course of the war, the committee investigated many things, such as the causes of certain battle defeats, the behavior and competence of particular generals, alleged rebel atrocities after First Manassas (Bull Run) and later Fort Pillow, and potential corruption in military supply contracts. Overall the committee possessed great zeal but little knowledge. None of the committee members (with the exception of Loan at the end) had any military background whatsoever nor did they think that they needed to learn anything about military activity. They believed that military success depended upon common sense and proper politics, so they opposed West Point–trained generals, particularly harassed generals who were members of the Democratic Party (such as George B. McClellan), and pushed the careers of Republican generals like John C. Fremont and Benjamin F. Butler, even though they were poor performers. The committee also advised President Abraham Lincoln, who followed their counsel only if it already suited his purposes. While some of the committee's investigations were useful and may have improved the morale of the Northern civilians and soldiers, the committee generally had a negative effect. Its failure to understand the realities of warfare encouraged unrealistic ideas about what a general and an army might accomplish in battle. The committee's political emphasis encouraged factions rather than cooperation and unfairly damaged the reputation of several generals.

When Andrew Johnson became president following Lincoln's assassination in April 1865, Johnson's former committee colleagues were pleased because they expected him to be tougher toward the South than Lincoln seemed to be. As military governor of Tennessee, Johnson failed confederates, shut down presses and churches, and allegedly said "treason is a crime, and must be made odious." Committee members Wade, Julian, and Chandler promptly visited Johnson hoping to become his political advisors. At first, members were encouraged, as Johnson seemed to support a more stringent readmission process. However, when it became evident that Johnson would be even more lenient toward the South than Lincoln, Wade, Julian, and Chandler became some of his most outspoken critics. The Committee on the Conduct of the War permanently adjourned on May 22, 1865.

*Glenna R. Schroeder-Lein*

**See also:** Congressional Reconstruction; Presidential Reconstruction; U.S. Army and Reconstruction.

## Further Reading

Foner, Eric. *Reconstruction Updated Edition: America's Unfinished Revolution, 1863–1877.* Reprint, New York: HarperCollins, 2014.
Tap, Bruce. *Over Lincoln's Shoulder: The Committee on the Conduct of the War.* Lawrence: University Press of Kansas, 1998.

# JULIAN, GEORGE WASHINGTON (1817–1899)

A leading Radical in the Republican Party, George Washington Julian was a reformer his entire life. Born in Centerville, Indiana, his father died in 1823, and Julian was raised by his devout Quaker mother. By the age of 18, Julian began his legal studies and developed his interest in politics. In 1845, as a Whig, he was elected to the Indiana legislature.

Julian was a deeply religious man who believed that slavery was a moral evil and its existence retarded the civil liberties all men. This drove Julian to the Free Soil Party and their motto of "free soil, free speech, free labor, and free men." In 1849, Julian was elected to the House of Representatives, where he opposed the measures collectively known as the Compromise of 1850, and especially the components related to the Fugitive Slave Act. This measure was a horror to him, and he even represented runaway slaves in the Indiana courts in the 1850s. Early during the Civil War, Julian urged President Abraham Lincoln to

Indiana representative George Washington Julian. A Radical Republican and reformer, Julian advocated emancipation and black rights, and openly pushed for the removal of President Johnson. (Library of Congress)

see the conflict as an issue of slavery versus freedom. As a member of the powerful Joint Select Committee on the Conduct of the War, Julian tried to remove Gen. George McClellan, a leading Democrat who seemed reluctant to engage the enemy. Julian welcomed the Emancipation Proclamation, which for him meant abolitionism had become part of the Union war effort.

Julian's commitment to abolitionism was part of a larger vision of reform and social justice, which became even clearer during Reconstruction. He advocated confiscating Confederate planter's land for the freed African Americans, who could then work their own land. Displeased with Lincoln's cautious policies, he recognized that President Andrew Johnson's accession to the presidency was a disaster for progressive reform. Pressing for land and suffrage for the freedmen, Julian was an early voice calling for Johnson's impeachment and removal. Disappointed by failure to remove Johnson from the White House, Julian took comfort in his leadership role in the passage of the Southern Homestead Act (1866).

Defeated in his re-election bid for Congress, Julian joined the Liberal Republican crusade for the election of 1872. Following that disaster, he campaigned (unsuccessfully) on behalf of Samuel J. Tilden in the disputed election of 1876. After practicing law for several years, Julian became surveyor general for New Mexico under President Grover Cleveland. There, he fought against the land interests of railroads and speculators. On the eve of the 20th century, Julian died in Irvington, Indiana, his hometown.

*Donald K. Pickens*

*See also:* Abolition of Slavery; Civil Rights; Presidential Reconstruction; Republicans, Radical; Suffrage.

## Further Reading

Stampp, Kenneth M. *Indiana Politics during the Civil War*. Indianapolis: Indiana Historical Bureau, 1949.

Trefousse, Hans L. *The Radical Republicans, Lincoln's Vanguard for Racial Justice*. Baton Rouge: Louisiana State University Press, 1968.

# K

## KELLOGG, WILLIAM PITT (1830–1918)

William Pitt Kellogg was a carpetbagger who served as U.S. senator (1868–1872) and as governor (1873–1877) of Louisiana during Congressional Reconstruction. A native of Vermont, Kellogg moved with his family in the 1840s to Illinois, where he taught school and read law. He was admitted to the bar in 1853, and in 1856, he helped found the Illinois Republican Party. Appointed by President Abraham Lincoln as chief justice of the Nebraska Territory, he resigned to fight in the Civil War and eventually commanded a Union cavalry brigade. In April 1865, Lincoln named him collector of customs in New Orleans, a position he used to build the Louisiana Republican Party. Kellogg held this post until July 1868, when the Louisiana legislature, under the Congressional Reconstruction program, elected him to the U.S. Senate. Kellogg resigned from the Senate in November 1872, having been nominated Republican candidate for governor of Louisiana.

The election of 1872 in Louisiana was among the most controversial in the state's history. Intimidation and violence against blacks characterized the campaign, and fraud marred the election. Both Kellogg and Democratic gubernatorial candidate John D. McEnery claimed victory. In January 1873, separate inaugurations were held, and Democratic and Republican majority legislatures convened. Louisiana endured the spectacle of rival state governments until May 1873, when President Ulysses S. Grant recognized Kellogg as governor. The Kellogg administration never overcame the circumstances of its birth, and the large majority of white Louisianans rejected Kellogg. Democrats and other white Conservatives engaged in tax strikes (they refused to pay taxes, shutting down many services and state functions); civil insurrection and violence increased, and Louisiana became the site of some of Reconstruction's worst race riots, including the massacres of black and white Republicans at Colfax (April 1873) and Coushatta (August 1874). In 1874, the paramilitary terrorist group known as the White League forcibly ousted Kellogg, and only the intervention by federal troops restored his administration; Kellogg even survived an assassination attempt. Finally, a Democratic legislature impeached Kellogg in early 1876, though the Republican state senate refused to convict. Kellogg did not run for reelection in 1876, but he was elected to the U.S. Senate as part of the Compromise of 1877. In 1883, he won election to the U.S. House of Representatives. When his term expired in 1885, Kellogg retired from public office and moved to Washington, D.C., where he died on August 10, 1918. He is buried in Arlington National Cemetery.

As governor, Kellogg implemented a number of reforms, including lowering taxes and public expenditures, funding and reducing the state debt, and making government more efficient, all important measures during the economic depression of the 1870s. Yet his term was hampered by fierce white opposition, owing to the circumstances surrounding his election, his appointing of blacks to key offices, and his general support for black civil rights. Kellogg was no saint; he hurt the Republicans by engaging in bribery and other corrupt practices associated with 19th-century Louisiana politics—a luxury that he and his party could ill afford.

*John C. Rodrigue*

**See also:** Black Suffrage; Democratic Party; Elections of 1876; Nicholls, Francis Redding Tillou (1834–1912); Packard, Stephen B. (1842–1922); Pinchback, Pinckney Benton Stewart (1837–1921); Race Riots; Redemption; Twitchell, Marshall H. (1840–1905); U.S. Army and Reconstruction; *United States v. Cruikshank* (1876); Warmoth, Henry Clay (1842–1931).

## Further Reading

Gonzales, John E. "William Pitt Kellogg, Reconstruction Governor of Louisiana, 1873–1877." *Louisiana Historical Quarterly* 29 (1946): 394–495.

Keith, Lee Anna. *The Colfax Massacre: The Untold Story of Black Power, White Terror, and the Death of Reconstruction.* New York: Oxford University Press, 2009.

Lonn, Ella. *Reconstruction in Louisiana after 1868.* New York: G. P. Putnam's Sons, 1918.

Taylor, Joe Gray. *Louisiana Reconstructed: 1863–1877.* Baton Rouge: Louisiana State University Press, 1974.

# KENTUCKY

When Confederate armies surrendered in spring 1865, Kentucky officially stood as a "border state," a loyal state—albeit one with slavery—that had never left the Union. As a full member of that Union, it did not face the Reconstruction process affecting the former Confederate states. So instead, it found itself in a nebulous, confusing, and uncertain status after Appomattox.

Oddly, both Northerners and Southerners viewed it more as a former Confederate state than a Union one—and with some justification. Kentucky had representatives at the Confederate Congress and a star on the Confederate flag; yet the state contributed two times as many soldiers to the Union cause as to the Confederate. In an oft-quoted statement written six decades after the conflict's end, one historian concluded that Kentucky "waited until after the war was over to secede from the Union." If the state did not experience full Reconstruction, it certainly went through what could be termed "readjustment." The South, under full Reconstruction, viewed Kentucky as the spokesman for its interests. In turn, Kentucky's actions and reactions to postwar events suggest how the South might have reacted without Reconstruction. A very different Kentucky emerged from that era than had existed at the start of the Civil War.

One of the largest slave states in population, wealth, and importance, and with a natural defense line at the Ohio River, Kentucky had been a sought-after prize for both governments at the start of the Civil War. Legend has it that early in the conflict, Abraham Lincoln (who was born in Kentucky) told his cabinet, "I certainly hope God is on our side. But I must have Kentucky!" Badly divided—for it would be truly "The Brothers' War" in Kentucky—the state first chose neutrality for a period of four months. Devoted to both the Union and slavery, Kentucky abandoned neutrality and indicated its intention to remain part of the United States. Pro-confederates organized their own government, and many slaveholding Unionists turned against the Lincoln administration after the Emancipation Proclamation. The state, however, remained in the Union.

Strangely, following the defeat of the Confederacy, the less numerous former confederates and Confederate sympathizers dominated politics, winning the next six governorships. Those leaders faced the harsh reality of rebuilding after the war. A good prewar educational system stood in shambles, and the economy remained crippled. While the state suffered less than some from rampaging rival armies, horrific guerrilla warfare had raged unchecked for four years; after the war, violence continued, making rural areas dangerous for white and black alike.

The greatest change in postwar Kentucky concerned not economics but race relations. Almost one in every five Kentuckians had been an enslaved person in 1861. In fact, the state had furnished some 23,000 black soldiers to the Union cause—the second highest number of any state. Various federal laws and general orders had declared those soldiers and their families to be free, an action Kentucky refused to recognize. The state's highest court declared such actions unconstitutional in December 1865, and the legislature refused to ratify any of the Reconstruction amendments. By the time of the ratification of the Thirteenth Amendment in December 1865, only Kentucky and Delaware still retained slavery. The system died hard in the state. Newspapers filled with dire concerns of racial revolution, black control, and military rule. Resulting Ku Klux Klan violence matched or exceeded similar acts in Deep South states, and at least 100 lynchings occurred in a four-year period. Some blacks formed protective hamlets in rural areas, while others migrated to the relative safety of Kentucky's more urban areas or to other states. Such opposition to black rights resulted in martial law, which lasted until October 1865. As late as 1873, George A. Custer and the Seventh Cavalry served in the state to help control rampant Klan activity.

Opposition to black rights manifested itself in legal actions as well. In 1866, the legislature banned racial intermarriage and forbade blacks to testify in cases against whites. The state also set up a separate, racially segregated school system but not until 1874 would it really function, and not until eight years after that would the funds from both white and black taxes be merged into a common pool for redistribution. A rare exception to the growing segregation was Berea College, which offered biracial education (this ended in 1908, when the U.S. Supreme Court, in *Berea College v. Kentucky*, forced the school to expel its black students). The racial violence, restrictive rights, and educational deficiencies brought limited federal involvement in Kentucky, in the form of the Freedman's Bureau. It started in the state in December 1865 and continued operations in some form until 1871. Kentucky protested that the agency could only operate in states formerly in rebellion, but to no avail. Its 369 schools, staffed mostly by black teachers, educated nearly 19,000 students, despite opposition that in a one-year period included 20 murders, 18 other shootings, 11 rapes, and 270 further acts of violence. Yet, despite all the opposition, blacks won several victories, including a successful fight to resist the segregation of streetcars in Louisville. They had already won the greater battle of developing strong communities as free people. Widows with school-age children could vote for school trustees, for example.

Change did occur in Kentucky politics. The chaos of the conflict left uncertainty about several questions as peacetime elections began. The first major test of the political scene came in the 1867 gubernatorial and legislative elections. Since Kentucky had never left the Union, the Military Reconstruction Acts did not apply, so the black male population was not enfranchised as it was in 10 former Confederate states. In the campaign, three groups vied for votes. All sought to win over the old ex-Whigs and the ex-Unionists from both prewar parties. The Union Party (Radical Republicans) openly supported the Congressional Reconstruction program and the federal amendments, and stressed their Union ties. Opponents tried to tar them with radicalism and supporting black rights. The Democratic Party, in turn, openly rejected further support for blacks. Opponents termed them unrepentant rebels, and the party's candidate's son had been killed fighting for the Confederate army. A third group, the Conservative Union Party, tried to take a more Moderate stance and unite the Unionist ex-Whigs under its banner. That attempt to re-form a new alliance failed, the third party died, and the Democrats dominated for the next three decades. In 1867, they won 113 of 138 legislative seats; in a special governor's race the next year, the party won 80 percent of the popular vote. The Democrats had forged a fragile coalition of former confederates, some ex-Whigs, a few old Unionists angered by racial issues, and of course the more Conservative prewar Democrats.

Republicans got the rest, including the black male voters—who could not vote until ratification of the Fifteenth Amendment in 1870. Even when the Republicans put forth their best candidate, John Marshall Harlan, he lost out in 1871 to ex-Whig Preston Leslie, 126,455 to 89,299 (Harlan later became a progressive Supreme Court justice, offering brilliant dissents in the Civil Rights Cases (1883) and *Plessy v. Ferguson* (1896). Four years later Harlan lost to former Confederate colonel James B. McCreary, 130,026 to 94,236. The lack of a large black population, combined with the cultural alliance with the former Confederate states, drove Kentucky toward becoming part of the Solid South.

Yet, despite all the postwar changes, people of both races and both sexes went on with their lives, growing the new burley tobacco, making a hard living on farms, and seeking education for their children. They viewed a state unencumbered by debt but one that devoted too little support for social and public services. They observed a commonwealth that displayed wealth in its cities and horse farms, but more commonly presented a people suffering from a poverty of the spirit. They saw a Kentucky in change, yet unchanging.

*James C. Klotter*

**See also:** Black Suffrage; Bureau of Refugees, Freedmen, and Abandoned Lands; Civil Rights; Fourteenth Amendment (1868); Freedmen's Relief Societies; U.S. Army and Reconstruction.

## Further Reading

Coulter, E. Merton. *The Civil War and Readjustment in Kentucky*. Chapel Hill: University of North Carolina Press, 1926.

Harrison, Lowell H., and James C. Klotter. *A New History of Kentucky*. Lexington: University Press of Kentucky, 1997.

Lucas, Marion B. *A History of Blacks in Kentucky: From Slavery to Segregation, 1760–1891.* Frankfort: Kentucky Historical Society, 1992.

Webb, Ross. *Kentucky in the Reconstruction Era.* Lexington: University Press of Kentucky, 1979.

## KIRK-HOLDEN WAR (1869–1870)

Named for George W. Kirk, a Civil War colonel who commanded Union troops in east Tennessee and western North Carolina, and William W. Holden, the Republican governor of North Carolina, the Kirk-Holden War represented a desperate effort to end a reign of terror that had cost the lives of leading Republicans and intimidated countless white and black voters between 1869 and 1870. Although successful in ending Klan activity in central North Carolina, the Kirk-Holden War represented the high-water mark of Republican rule in North Carolina during Reconstruction. While the Kirk-Holden War helped destroy the Ku Klux Klan in central North Carolina, it also brought the impeachment of Holden.

Founded in Tennessee following the Civil War, the Ku Klux Klan became the extralegal political arm of the Democratic Party in many of the former Confederate states. In 1867, following the passage of the Military Reconstruction Act and the advent of Congressional Reconstruction, the combination of black suffrage and political activity by native scalawags and Northern carpetbaggers completely ousted white Democrats from political power. As this Southern Republican Party grew, the Ku Klux Klan evolved into a terrorist organization aimed at wresting political control away from the infant Southern Republican Party. At first, Holden tried to curtail Klan violence through persuasion. In October 1869, when he threatened to declare a state of insurrection in Lenoir and Jones counties, local Klan activity operations nearly ceased. The Republican state legislature followed the governor's lead and passed a law making it illegal to appear disguised in public for the purpose of violence or intimidation. Holden also cultivated support within troubled communities. He appealed to white Conservatives' desire for stability and beseeched them to convince Klansmen to disband. These efforts helped restore peace in several troubled counties.

Alamance and Caswell counties, however, defied the governor's attempts to negotiate peace. White Republicans went out of their way to appease the Democrats in each county but failed to placate the Klansmen. In both counties, night riders tormented white and black Republicans continuously. Conciliation's failure in Alamance and Caswell forced Holden to confront the Ku Klux Klan directly. In late 1869, state senator T. M. Shoffner, a Republican from Alamance County, introduced legislation to expand the state's ability to deal with the violence. The proposed legislation authorized the governor to suspend the writ of habeas corpus and to employ state militia against the Klan in counties where the civil authorities were ineffective (although the habeas corpus clause was stricken from the act as passed). For Shoffner, the legislation's impact was personal. If not for a warning delivered by a disaffected Klan leader, Shoffner might have found himself at the wrong end of a gun rather than in a new home in Indiana.

Matters in Alamance and Caswell came to a head following the murders of two high-profile Republicans in the spring of 1870. Under a tremendous amount of pressure to restore order, the governor issued a proclamation offering rewards for the capture of the assassins. Holden also made a plea for federal assistance. President Ulysses S. Grant, however, felt that North Carolina's problems were its own and offered Holden no support. Since conciliation had failed and the federal government would not help, the governor decided it was time, and called out the militia. Deciding to employ the militia was only the first step, since Holden had to find reliable men to fill its ranks. Realizing that forces drawn from the counties surrounding Alamance and Caswell would probably include many of the Klansmen he sought to defeat, Holden turned to the western counties. He hoped that many of the former Unionists in the state's mountain counties would rally once again to suppress rebellious elements in the state. Although initial command over state forces was given to Col. William J. Clarke, a Northerner living in New Bern, it passed to George W. Kirk after Clarke left to secure supplies in the nation's capital. The east Tennessean commanded troops in the Carolina mountains during the Civil War and Holden hoped that his presence would lure his former soldiers into the ranks again. Kirk's popularity, coupled with the promise of regular army pay, brought 670 men between the ages of 15 and 70 into the ranks in late June and early July 1870. Once Holden declared Alamance and Caswell in a state of insurrection, Kirk's militia began arresting suspected Klansmen in the troubled counties almost immediately. The arrest nearly 100 suspected Klansmen had the effect Holden intended. Night riding in Alamance and Caswell halted, allowing Holden to resume negotiations to end the violence. Conservative residents, frustrated by violence but afraid to speak out against the terror organization, seized the opportunity to work for the Klan's demise.

Nevertheless, success failed to ease the pressure on the governor and his militia. Both found themselves in trouble with the law. The state Supreme Court's issuance of writs of habeas corpus for Kirk's prisoners presented Holden with a dilemma. Turning over his prisoners threatened to undermine the success already achieved, but refusing would give credence to the charges that he abused his authority. Adding to the governor's woes was the fact that Kirk was busy collecting confessions, but was unprepared to present that evidence in court. Trapped in a predicament of his own making, Holden chose to ignore the court and move forward with his plan to try the prisoners before a military tribunal.

Most of the detainees never made it to a military court. With their appeals to the state judicial system stymied by the governor, the alleged Klansmen appealed to a federal judge in Salisbury. Although sympathetic to Holden's efforts, the federal judge issued a writ of habeas corpus for the accused men, who ironically had claimed that their rights to due process guaranteed by the Fourteenth Amendment had been violated. Using an amendment to free the Klansmen—which Holden himself supported as a guarantee of blacks' political and civil rights—made it painfully clear that the governor had overplayed his hand. His militia disbanded on September 21, 1870.

Holden's opponents refused to let the matter dissipate with the militia. Recognizing that the state government did not possess the authority it claimed, Klan violence and intimidation increased again and kept hundreds of Republican voters from the polls late that summer. The August elections allowed Holden's opponents to capture a majority in the state legislature. The new legislators—many of whom historians suspect had ties to the Ku Klux Klan—filed eight charges against Holden and initiated impeachment proceedings. Holden responded to charges of violating the state constitution by mobilizing the militia and declaring a state of insurrection by presenting Kirk's evidence of the danger posed by the Klan. Holden's antagonists were unimpressed. The legislature voted 36 to 13 for impeachment on March 22, 1871. Their action removed Holden from office and also barred him from holding state political office again. More important, their political revenge against Holden marked the fall of the Republicans and the "redemption" of North Carolina as Democrats took control—virtually ending Republican influence in the state for the next generation.

*Steven E. Nash*

**See also:** Black Suffrage; Enforcement Acts (1870, 1871, 1875); Race Riots; U.S. Army and Reconstruction; White League.

### Further Reading

Escott, Paul D. *Many Excellent People: Power and Privilege in North Carolina, 1850–1900.* Chapel Hill: University of North Carolina Press, 1985.

Fitzgerald, Michael W. *Splendid Failure: Postwar Reconstruction in the American South.* New York: Ivan R. Dee Publishers, 2008.

Harris, William C. *William Woods Holden: Firebrand of North Carolina Politics.* Baton Rouge: Louisiana State University Press, 1987.

Zuber, Richard L. *North Carolina during Reconstruction.* Raleigh, NC: State Department of Archives and History, 1969.

## KU KLUX KLAN (KKK)

The Ku Klux Klan (KKK) was an organization dedicated to restoring political and social power to white Conservative Democrats in the South after the Civil War. It became the counterrevolutionary vehicle for the Democratic Party, through which extralegal means could be employed to thwart the Reconstruction agenda of Radical Republicans, Unionist scalawags, carpetbaggers, and their African American allies. At its height, the Klan served as the military manifestation of the struggle for "home rule," as well as a breeding ground for intimidation and violence, having transformed from a largely fraternal organization with limited numbers and goals into a secret society that spanned the South and demonstrated the willingness to employ all the weapons at its disposal to achieve its ends.

Begun in Pulaski, Tennessee, in early 1866, by six former Confederate officers, the organization at first served as a source of amusement and an opportunity to recall wartime connections for the ex-soldiers. The first order of business was to decide upon a name and establish the rules and rituals. The early members settled on a hybrid of Greek (*kuklos* or "circle") and English (clan). The rules and rituals took some time to compose and reflected the relatively innocuous nature of the organization at this point in its existence. The initial practices of the Klan amounted to little more than harmless pranks, but success in mild forms of intimidation became infectious and Klan activities grew more audacious and aggressive. Nevertheless, the founders and early leaders touted the secret society as essentially benevolent in nature, providing assistance to whites in need and serving a self-anointed local, as well as internal, policing role. In this way, it harkened back to the slave patrols and other community-sponsored outfits that enforced black subordination before the war. Proponents of the organization insisted that its membership consisted of former confederates who had served honorably, and other leading citizens.

The Klan's military heritage was unmistakable in its chain of command and structural hierarchy. The "Invisible Empire," commanded by a grand wizard, was subdivided into realms (statewide organizations led by a Grand Dragon), dominions (congressional districts under a grand titan), provinces (counties commanded by a grand giant), and local dens (headed by a grand cyclops). Since the founders and most of the members were veterans, it made sense that these descending units and offices corresponded to those found in the military. It also reflected a cultural propensity and tradition of secret order and rites, such as those found in the popular Masonic Order of the time. A "Prescript" or constitution established the nature and purposes of the organization, its authorship attributed to former Confederate general George W. Gordon, an attorney in Pulaski who also served as a key Klan leader. By the end of 1866, the KKK in Tennessee had spread statewide. In April 1867, the leadership met in Nashville at the Maxwell House hotel to give the organization greater cohesion. At about the same time, it received its most famous recruit—and future leader— when former Confederate cavalry general Nathan Bedford Forrest joined its ranks and, according to some, assumed the office of grand wizard. Forrest had vowed to remain quietly at home when the war ended until he felt the actions of wartime Unionist and postwar governor William G. "Parson" Brownlow against former confederates and Democrats in the state prompted him to become active in response.

Under Forrest's leadership, the Klan grew exponentially. Using his contacts in his railroad construction and insurance ventures, Forrest worked to expand the organization into neighboring states and throughout the South. Often he met on business matters with ex-confederate colleagues such as John B. Gordon, who then subsequently became central figures in establishing and leading Klan activities in their states. Forrest also benefited from friendly newspapers that included notices or editorialized favorably on the secret society's behalf. In 1867, as the Republican Reconstruction program implemented black suffrage, the KKK turned its attention to the political arena. At first, the organization employed mostly nonviolent tactics in an attempt to persuade African Americans to vote Democratic, largely on the antebellum assumption that they would view their former masters as most closely associated with their best interests. When this did not occur, frustrated whites turned increasingly to force, or at least the threat of force, to obtain the same result—prevent blacks from participating in the political process. Thus, the KKK sought to influence political affairs and restore the social order to something approximating the prewar status quo. To this end, Klan members targeted the secret Republican clubs known as Union Leagues (also called Loyal Leagues), whose membership included blacks and Unionists. The Klan played an important but as it turned out not very decisive role in the presidential election of 1868 between Democrat Horatio Seymour and Republican Ulysses S. Grant. In Georgia, Klan forces also failed to elect Democrat and Klan leader John B. Gordon over Republican Rufus Bullock. At the same time, William W. Holden, originally appointed as provisional governor by President Andrew Johnson, became North Carolina's first Republican governor. Yet, the organization enjoyed some successes in its home state of Tennessee when Brownlow left the statehouse to take up a seat in the U.S. Senate and his successor, DeWitt Clinton Senter, proved more amenable to the former confederates and Democrats there. In North Carolina, Holden employed the militia under Col. George W. Kirk to battle continuously with Klan forces in his state before finally being impeached and removed from that office in 1871.

Yet, by this point in its development, the KKK was also becoming an organization that no central authority, even one as determined and dynamic as Forrest, could control. Although this became a common and convenient subterfuge—such as when Klan members wanted to deny violence and intimidation in their ranks by attributing such activities to renegade elements—it was sufficient to encourage Forrest to dissociate himself from the organization. Consequently, in early 1869, the grand wizard sent out an edict for members to destroy their regalia. Although the Klan officially disbanded, it by no means disappeared and in some areas became even more abusive in methods. In South Carolina, in particular, the Klan seemed especially well organized and active. Continuing Klan violence prompted the U.S. Congress to pass Enforcement Acts in 1870 and 1871 to counteract the terrorist organization; President Grant utilized these measures when he suspended habeas corpus and sent federal forces (both army and Justice Department marshals) into South Carolina in the early 1870s, ending Klan violence there. Congress also called prominent leaders believed to be associated with the organization, including Forrest and Gordon, to testify in Washington. In their descriptions of the secret society, offered despite their denial of membership in the Klan, such leaders demonstrated considerable knowledge and detail concerning it.

Despite the celebratory images, the stereotypes, and the heated rhetoric of "Lost Cause" adherents, the KKK was not solely responsible for the undoing of Reconstruction but it clearly aided in the endeavors of white Southern Conservative Democrats to return to power and helped to reestablish a social system of white supremacy in the South. The gun clubs of the mid-1870s used many of the same tactics, but had no need for secrecy or disguise because the North had become so indifferent to the Southern Republican plight. The Klan returned to public attention in the 1910s and 1920s (the cross-burning, anti-Semitic, xenophobic Klan developed here) and again in the 1960s, but the Reconstruction Klan clearly remained an inspiration for these later versions, as evidenced by Thomas Dixon's novel *The Clansman*, which served as the source for D. W. Griffith's silent film *The Birth of a Nation* (1915), and the words and action of the Jim Crow segregationists of the civil rights era.

*Brian S. Wills*

**See also:** Congressional Reconstruction; Kirk-Holden War (1869–1870); Race Riots; U.S. Army and Reconstruction; White League.

## Further Reading

Chalmers, David M. *Hooded Americanism: The History of the Ku Klux Klan*. New York: Doubleday & Co., 1965.

Foner, Eric. *Reconstruction Updated Edition: America's Unfinished Revolution, 1863–1877*. Reprint, New York: HarperCollins, 2014.

Horn, Stanley F. *Invisible Empire: The Story of the Ku Klux Klan, 1866–1871*. Boston: Houghton Mifflin, Co., 1939.

Trelease, Allen W. *White Terror: The Ku Klux Klan Conspiracy and Southern Reconstruction*. New York: Harper & Row, 1971.

Wade, Wyn Craig. *The Fiery Cross: The Ku Klux Klan in America*. New York: Simon & Schuster, 1987.

# L

## LABOR SYSTEMS

Union victory and the destruction of slavery did not solve the riddle of labor in the South. Abolition meant that the slaves of the South were now free laborers, a condition codified by the Thirteenth Amendment (1865), which abolished slavery entirely and prohibited labor systems based on "slavery or involuntary servitude." But Southern whites, especially former slave owners, were reluctant to treat blacks with the necessary to forming contracts between mutually consenting parties; more common were racist attitudes that viewed the African American freedpeople as naturally inferior. On the other hand, among the freedpeople, the habits and work discipline of a modern wage-labor force were unknown, and unsurprisingly, most former slaves sought self-sufficiency for themselves and their families rather than entering into contracts or market-oriented relationships—especially with their old masters.

The basis of the Southern economy both before and after the Civil War was the production of agricultural commodities, chiefly cotton. Before the war, most cotton was produced on farms or plantations by black slaves working under the supervision of white owners. As a labor system, slavery had meant that workers toiled only because of the constant threat—and often, reality—of violence; that is, a form of extra-economic compulsion. By contrast, in the Northern and Western states, laborers were "free," which is to say that the work they performed was part of a reciprocal exchange (e.g., tasks for wages) governed mainly by market incentives and the laws of contract. During the early years of Reconstruction, military officers working under the auspices of the Federal Bureau of Refugees, Freedmen, and Abandoned Lands, or the Freedmen's Bureau, supervised the labor arrangements that emerged in various Southern localities. There was no escaping a simple reality: white landowners needed labor, and the freedpeople needed jobs. At first, the most common means of reaching labor agreements with the former slaves was to contract with them as groups, often in "squads" composed of loosely allied families and individuals. Attempts were made to pay these squads cash wages on a semi-regular basis—weekly or monthly—but the lack of capital among white landowners made such payments impossible to sustain. In their place, a variety of arrangements emerged across the South by the late 1860s, which deferred of cash wages in favor of a portion of the crop. This was the genesis of the sharecropping system that dominated Southern agriculture until the 1950s.

Though not a uniquely American form of labor system—sharecropping had many historical antecedents—its form in the postwar South had particular features that were well adapted to the regional context. As a substitute for a system of cash wages, sharecropping

**193**

seemed to benefit both parties. The deferral of compensation meant that white planters could productively employ the only capital they had left—the land—without the need for monetary reserves, and as freedpeople impelled the further evolution of sharecropping away from the gang labor common to the squad system toward contracts with individual households, they grew reconciled to sharecropping's ability to approximate the ideal of independent farming that most held dear. Still, sharecropping fully satisfied no one: landowning capitalists would have preferred more leeway for regulating and disciplining "their" laborers; freedpeople would have preferred to own their own land to use as they saw fit.

If this was "free labor," then it was a peculiar form at best. Sharecropping's main shortcomings appeared in the need for seasonal agricultural credit that could provide for the day-to-day needs of workers until the annual harvesting and marketing of the crop. Although some planters took an active role in provisioning their tenants over the course of the year, the same lack of liquid capital that kept them from paying regular cash wages made it difficult for most to obtain goods from Northern markets for distribution to their workforces. As a result, a third party, the independent furnishing merchant with ties to outside capital, arose during Reconstruction when the numbers of so-called country stores (many were actually located in or served as the basis of small towns) grew tremendously throughout the South. Although white landowners greatly resented the intrusion of these merchants into their customary positions of community power (many of them were Northern migrants, and often Jewish as well), the situation proved even worse for the sharecroppers. Many found themselves forced into long-term debt to the furnishing merchant as a result of high interest rates, as well as shortfalls due to poor harvests, low crop prices, or both. Laborers fell into debt, and as a result lost mobility, crop choice as investors and merchants dictated life; these forces a form of debt peonage—restoring many African Americans to a condition disturbingly similar to slavery.

This makeshift, inefficient labor system, gestated and born during Reconstruction, plagued the Southern economy for decades to come. Like slavery, sharecropping was never the exclusive labor system of the South—it coexisted with other steps on the "agricultural ladder," from cash renting to farm ownership. It did, however, constitute the dominant mode of production, and as such, it exerted a determinant influence on the relationships in those around it. There were other forms of labor control in the postwar South: perhaps the most notorious was the convict-lease system, which was gaining popularity by the 1870s. Also, similarities to other labor systems then arising in the mining towns of the West could be found in the new cotton mill villages of the lower Atlantic seaboard, where displaced white rural workers—men, women, and children—were transformed into factory operatives under conditions of company paternalism.

In the North, the workforce still remained surprisingly rurally dispersed immediately after the war, but the trend was clearly toward its increasing concentration in urban areas, especially after labor's ranks were augmented by the waves of immigration that picked up steam during the late Reconstruction era. As the manufacturing sector grew in importance during the postwar years, there were crucial efforts to further institutionalize the nascent organized labor movement, but with mixed results. Partisan politics intruded on attempts to build and sustain the National Labor Union led by William H. Sylvis; the Knights of Labor, founded in 1869, would enjoy brief success in the late 1870s. The future of the American labor movement was in the attempt to organize craft unions by particular trades during Reconstruction, though most of these were wiped out by the Panic of 1873. However, throughout the many strikes of the 1870s, which culminated in the great strike wave of 1877, a community-oriented consciousness settled in among workers; yet they remained divided by ethno and religious conflicts, so union actions tended to remain spontaneous, unfocused, and vulnerable to disruption.

*Scott P. Marler*

**See also:** Freedmen's Relief Societies; Southern Homestead Act (1866); Stevens, Thaddeus (1792–1868); U.S. Army and Reconstruction.

## Further Reading

Jaynes, Gerald David. *Branches without Roots: The Genesis of the Black Working Class in the American South, 1862–1882.* New York: Oxford University Press, 1986.

Montgomery, David. Beyond *Equality: Labor and the Radical Republicans, 1862–1872.* New York: Alfred A. Knopf, 1967.

Ransom, Roger L., and Richard Sutch. *One Kind of Freedom: The Economic Consequences of Emancipation.* 2nd ed. New York: Cambridge University Press, 2001.

## LINCOLN, ABRAHAM (1809–1865)

Abraham Lincoln, the 16th president of the United States, in his first inaugural address on March 4, 1861, announced his intention to preserve the government and to restore the seceded states to the Union. Lincoln never recognized the legitimacy of secession or the government of the Confederate states. He reasoned that individuals, not states, had rebelled and thereby had overturned republican forms of government in the South as guaranteed by the U.S. Constitution. When the war began in April 1861, Lincoln believed that it was his constitutional responsibility as commander in chief to suppress the armed rebellion and restore legitimate, loyal governments in the Southern states.

Lincoln favored a large measure of self-reconstruction that would be led by a nucleus of Southern Unionists. Lincoln's first effort toward Reconstruction occurred in western Virginia. With his encouragement, Unionists in this area met at Wheeling in June 1861, and created the Restored Government of Virginia. They selected Francis H. Pierpont as governor, elected two U.S. senators, and called for the popular elections of three congressmen. Lincoln approved, and Congress seated the senators and representatives from the Pierpont government, which in 1862 became the state of West Virginia. The Restored Government of Virginia then moved to Alexandria within Union lines; after Robert E. Lee's surrender, Pierpont assumed control in Richmond. In 1868, he was removed by Gen. John M. Schofield under Congressional Reconstruction.

Tennessee served as a different test case. Although it too offered a large Unionist contingent, restoration proceeded very differently. Early in the war, Lincoln sought to liberate the Unionists of East Tennessee and pressed his military commanders to launch campaigns into the area. Not until early 1862 did federal forces successfully penetrate the state, and Lincoln dispatched Senator Andrew Johnson to Middle Tennessee to begin the process of Reconstruction. Appointed military governor of the state, Johnson refused to hold state elections until Unionists in East Tennessee were liberated and could prevent rebels from overwhelming the new government. Lincoln also had to placate Johnson and East Tennessee

Unionists by exempting all of the state from the Emancipation Proclamation (although these Unionists, and Johnson, later supported abolition). By early 1865, with the state firmly under federal control, a state convention of Unionists abolished slavery and formed a government under William G. "Parson" Brownlow. It was not until after the war that Tennessee sent representatives to Congress.

Lincoln also appointed military governors for North Carolina, Louisiana, and Texas. After federal forces occupied northeastern North Carolina in March, Lincoln sent Edward Stanly, a former congressman, to New Bern to begin the process of civil reorganization in the state. Stanly, however, made little progress toward Reconstruction, and when the president issued his Emancipation Proclamation, he resigned. Lincoln did not appoint a replacement. After New Orleans fell to federal forces in May 1862, Lincoln appointed Col. George F. Shepley, under the overall command of Gen. Benjamin F. Butler, as military governor of the city and directed him to seek the restoration of civil government and hold elections for two congressmen in the occupied districts. Only after much prodding on the president's part were two representatives elected, and in early 1863, they were seated to serve out the remaining days of the congressional term. Lincoln's appointment of Andrew Jackson Hamilton for Texas proved fruitless, mainly because the Union controlled only a coastal sliver of the state. However, after the war, President Andrew Johnson appointed Hamilton provisional governor of Texas.

Lincoln's policy of using military governors and Unionists changed as the Union war effort turned for the positive. Following federal military successes at Gettysburg, Vicksburg, and Chattanooga in 1863, Lincoln became more optimistic. On December 8, 1863, he issued the Proclamation of Amnesty and Reconstruction, also called the Ten Percent Plan. His plan granted amnesty to the great majority of Southerners who took an oath of future loyalty to the Union, the Constitution, and the proclamations and laws regarding slavery. Certain classes of Confederate officials and those who had mistreated prisoners of war were excluded from amnesty for the time being. In the second part of his proclamation, Lincoln outlined a method to restore the state governments to the Union. He indicated that when one-tenth of those eligible to vote in the 1860 presidential election had taken the oath of allegiance, citizens could "re-establish a State government which shall be republican" in character. The president did not explain why the ten-percent plan was chosen, but, eager to get the process under way, he probably believed that while the war raged, this percentage constituted a "tangible nucleus" to launch loyal state governments. He required that these new governments affirm the abolition of slavery and provide for the education of young blacks.

Lincoln's December 8, 1863 proclamation resulted in a flurry of Reconstruction activity in federal-occupied areas, although the process was not completed in any state during the war. Louisiana became the centerpiece of the president's new initiative. In early 1864, a loyal government was elected, but a group of prominent New Orleans blacks visited Washington and urged the president to consider enfranchising black males. Lincoln refused to impose such criteria on a state, but wrote to the new governor, Michael Hahn, that perhaps "some of the colored people may not be let in—as, for instance, the very intelligent, and [soldiers]. . . . But this is only a suggestion, not to the public, but to you alone." Louisiana did not extend suffrage to African Americans in its new.

When the war stalemated during the summer of 1864, restoration policy shifted again. This time, Lincoln's political stock plummeted, and Radical Republicans, joined by other Lincoln opponents, secured the passage of the Wade-Davis Reconstruction bill, designed to substitute a stringent Reconstruction policy for the president's lenient plan. Lincoln pocket vetoed the measure, but congressional Republicans retaliated, refusing to seat the representatives from so-called Lincoln governments. After Lincoln won reelection in fall of 1864, he directed his efforts toward securing an early peace on his mild terms—the surrender of the rebel armies, restoration of the Union, and emancipation. In his classic second inaugural address, Lincoln closed with the plea, "With malice toward none; with charity for all; with firmness in the right, as God gives us to see the right, let us strive on to finish the work we are in; to bind up the nation's wounds; to care for him who shall have borne the battle, and for his widow, and his orphan—to do all which may achieve . . . a lasting peace."

On April 11, three days before his tragic death, Lincoln made his final public statement on Reconstruction. It was also his last speech. Though some historians disagree, it seems probable that Lincoln had not changed his fundamental policy of self-Reconstruction controlled by Southern Unionists, and not by the federal government. He announced that the differences among the loyal people regarding "the mode, manner, and means of reconstruction" had caused "additional embarrassment," and, with Louisiana in mind, Lincoln admitted that he would have preferred that "the elective franchise" were "conferred on the very intelligent [blacks], and on those who serve our cause as soldiers." Nowhere in this address, however, did he suggest that he would impose black suffrage or civil rights legislation upon Louisiana or any Southern state. He did indicate that "it may be my duty to make some new announcement to the people of the South." With the war ending, Lincoln probably was thinking about a declaration extending temporary military control to states where no loyal governments existed, a purpose that became clearer when he met with his cabinet three days later. A second meeting on a proposal along this line was scheduled for April 18. By then Lincoln was dead, and the meeting was never held; Vice President Andrew Johnson would take charge of restoring the Southern states.

*William C. Harris*

**See also:** Assassination of Abraham Lincoln (1865); Black Codes; Elections of 1864; Presidential Reconstruction.

## Further Reading

Belz, Herman. *Reconstructing the Union: Theory and Policy during the Civil War*. Ithaca, NY: Cornell University Press, 1969.

Cox, La Wanda. *Lincoln and Black Freedom: A Study in Presidential Leadership*. Columbia: University of South Carolina Press, 1981.

Foner, Eric. *Reconstruction Updated Edition: America's Unfinished Revolution, 1863–1877*. Reprint, New York: HarperCollins, 2014.

Harris, William C. *With Charity for All: Lincoln and the Restoration of the Union*. Lexington: University Press of Kentucky, 1997.

## LINDSAY, ROBERT B. (1824–1902)

Robert B. Lindsay was one of the more troubled Democratic governors of the Reconstruction era, perhaps most famous for presiding over the unraveling of Alabama's ambitious railroad subsidy program.

Robert Burns Lindsay, born in Scotland in 1824, entered politics as a Democratic legislator from the Tennessee Valley in the 1850s. In the presidential campaign of 1860, Lindsay supported Stephen Douglas and opposed secession. He took "a slight part in the rebellion" and was "never much of a soldier." In reluctantly Confederate north Alabama, this political profile was popular, and after a brief dalliance with Reconstruction, he emerged as a Moderate leader in the Democratic Party, relatively untainted by sectional extremism.

In 1867, the Alabama Republican Party ascended to power under the Military Reconstruction Acts, with the state readmitted to the Union in 1868. Republican William H. Smith was the first governor elected under Congressional Reconstruction, and he ran again in 1870. In November 1870, Lindsay challenged Smith and claimed a narrow victory over the incumbent. After several weeks of tension and near-violence, a court decision in Lindsay's favor placed the Moderate Democrat in office.

As Lindsay assumed office, a fiscal crisis immediately ensued. In January 1871, the Alabama and Chattanooga Railroad defaulted on its state-endorsed bonds, and Lindsay discovered that his predecessor had signed some half a million dollars in unauthorized securities. Lindsay refused to honor the extralegal bonds, and he declined to pay anything for months without full investigation. His stand on principle and law paralyzed the largest railroad in the state leading to its bankruptcy; this undermined the financing of all the other projects under construction in the state. With the coming of the Panic of 1873, most of the endorsed lines went bankrupt, taking the state government with them. The railroad imbroglio also damaged the governor's personal reputation. When the state government took over the failing Alabama & Chattanooga line, the previous management lavishly bribed Lindsay's best friend in an attempt to regain control of the company. The governor may or may not have been involved, but his reputation was compromised, and militant Democrats pressed for more wholesale repudiation of the tainted company's bonds. Furthermore, Alabama's financial crisis closed the public schools for a year, further damaging an educational system just trying to regain its footing. As a result of these difficulties, the party rejected Governor Lindsay's bid for renomination; the Democrats went on to lose the governorship in the next election.

Despite his difficulties, Lindsay's administration had its victories. Lindsay openly discouraged Ku Klux Klan terrorism, for fear the federal government would intervene (rather, apparently, than for reasons of morality). These avowals may have contributed to the decline in Klan activity over the course of his administration.

Soon after leaving office, Lindsay suffered an attack of paralysis. He resumed law practice at a limited level, but he took no further interest in politics. He remained an invalid until his death in Tuscumbia, Alabama, in 1902.

*Michael W. Fitzgerald*

**See also:** Amnesty Proclamations; Carpetbaggers; Education; Fourteenth Amendment (1868); Johnson, Andrew (1808–1875); Parsons, Lewis E. (1817–1895); Republicans, Radical.

## Further Reading

Fitzgerald, Michael W. *Splendid Failure: Postwar Reconstruction in the American South.* New York: Ivan R. Dee Publishers, 2008.

Fitzgerald, Michael W. "Wager Swayne, the Freedmen's Bureau, and the Politics of Reconstruction in Alabama." *Alabama Review* (July 1995): 188–218.

Owen, Thomas M. *History of Alabama and Dictionary of Alabama Biography*. 4 vols. Chicago: S. J. Clark, 1921.

Summers, Mark W. *Railroads, Reconstruction, and the Gospel of Prosperity: Aid under the Radical Republicans, 1865–1877*. Princeton, NJ: Princeton University Press, 1984.

# LOST CAUSE

The "Lost Cause" is the name given to a romanticized interpretation of the Civil War and Reconstruction, which seeks to salve the Southern conscience at the expense of both historical accuracy and African Americans. The movement gained definitive shape in the 1880s, mostly through the writings of Civil War veterans, especially former Confederate general Jubal Early. The interpretation, or memory, consists of a set of beliefs that justified the Confederate side of Civil War. Over the late 19th and early 20th centuries, this memory became ritualized, institutionalized, and was often expressed in quasi-religious terms in the South.

The cult of Lost Cause is characterized by an intense focus on the past and is closely connected to the creation of organizations like the Southern Historical Association, the United Daughters of the Confederacy, and the United Confederate Veterans. The Lost Cause consists of four central tenets. First, white Southerners fought the Civil War as a defense of the political philosophy of states' rights. This offers an elegant philosophical justification for the violence committed during the war. Second, Union victory can be explained via the North's overwhelming numerical advantages, both in terms of supplies and soldiers. This explanation ignores all historical contingency during the war and paints a picture of the antebellum South as an innocent rural region set upon by a greedy industrial Northern giant. Third, the Confederacy reflects the true Christian society. In this account, Robert E. Lee, Stonewall Jackson, and even confederate women stand as saints and martyrs, while Northerners are represented as money-worshipping Yankees whose greed blinds them to the necessity of spiritual humility, and ultimately, salvation. Finally, the Lost Cause largely ignores slavery, or when it must confront the system it treats it as a benevolent institution. African slaves were lucky to have had the opportunity to be brought to America where they were introduced to Christianity and kindly masters instead of dwelling in pagan barbarism in Africa. The antebellum South is presented as a lost time of near perfection—a utopia for white people, and, when black people are considered at all, a decided improvement over their fortunes had they remained in Africa. The centrality of slavery to the Civil War, and the institution's inhumane, immoral, and repressive aspects, are left out entirely.

Although the Lost Cause is typically identified with the Civil War, it extends easily to explain the period of Reconstruction. The interpretation of Reconstruction continues the picture of innocent, noble Southern whites, greedy scheming Northerners, and incompetent blacks. The rise of Republican governments in the South is regarded as an unholy alliance between greedy Northern carpetbaggers, a few wicked white Southern scalawags, and gullible freedmen. These governments are portrayed as uniformly disastrous and hopelessly corrupt. Redemption by white Conservatives—a term with religious overtones—is thus regarded as an improvement for both the white Southerners whose rights were denied by

Radical Republicans and, ultimately, a boon to the South, because with men of good character returned to office, the future of the South would be safe once again.

The Lost Cause emerged at a time—the 1880s—when white Southerners bristled under Northern economic dominance of their region, but when both regions sought national reunion. In its time, the Lost Cause helped perform much of the work of reconciliation by explaining the war as a test of wills among honorable white men. Both sides could take pride in their heroism, while ignoring the causes and outcomes. Once Reconstruction had ended, the nation looked toward issues capable of unifying whites, including American Indian wars, westward expansion, and even overseas imperialism via the war with Spain. At home, white supremacy was an obvious bond. At the same time, Civil War veterans' reunions were becoming more and more popular; both former Yankees and Rebels, wittingly or not, embraced the Lost Cause just as they embraced each other, former enemies, now all Americans. The Lost Cause received its most dramatic articulation in *The Birth of a Nation*, D. W. Griffith's 1915 film about the effects of black rule on the South. Based upon the Thomas Dixon novel *The Clansman*, the film's characterization of dangerous, ignorant blacks, deceitful Northern whites, and victimized Southern whites typifies the treatment that Lost Cause adherents attributed to Reconstruction. The film's popularity around the country demonstrated the eagerness with which Northern whites accepted the same myths. For anxious white Northerners contending with the rise of corporations and labor unions, the influx of immigrants, and the instability of rapid urban growth, the idyllic vision of the plantation South represented the tranquility and control they desperately sought in their own lives.

The Lost Cause interpretation was vigorously contested by African Americans like Frederick Douglass and later W.E.B. Du Bois. Douglass campaigned throughout the remainder of his life, as did many black veterans, insisting on the centrality of slavery as a cause of the war and on abolition as its most important outcome. In 1935, Du Bois published his *Black Reconstruction*, which represented both a rebuttal to the Lost Cause, and an alternative reading, of the whole experience of Reconstruction. In Du Bois's view, the lower classes of the South, white and black, missed a crucial opportunity to build a more equitable society in the wake of war. The work of Douglass and Du Bois continues to this day. Despite the outpouring of scholarship on the Civil War era, a few dominant ideas continue to influence popular conceptions of the period. Among these are the importance of states' rights as the prime justification of the war, the inevitable superiority of a modern urban industrial North, and a blameless, honorable white South. Modern incarnations of the Lost Cause no longer portray slavery as the positive good that postbellum Southern scholars did, but they do this primarily by removing the whole issue from view. The importance of slavery to the antebellum Southern economy is denied or ignored, as is its relevance to the war. The centrality of race to the experience of Reconstruction is thus lost as well, leaving a curiously truncated and inaccurate interpretation of the period as one of a noble lost cause.

*Aaron Sheehan-Dean*

***See also:*** Bourbons; Congressional Reconstruction; Ku Klux Klan (KKK); New South.

## Further Reading

Foster, Gaines. *Ghosts of the Confederacy: Defeat, The Lost Cause, and the Emergence of the New South*. New York: Oxford University Press, 1987.

Gallagher, Gary W., and Alan T. Nolan, eds. *The Myth of the Lost Cause and Civil War History*. Bloomington: Indiana University Press, 2000.

Wilson, Charles R. *Baptized in Blood: The Religion of the Lost Cause, 1865–1920*. Athens: University of Georgia Press, 1980.

# LOUISIANA

President Abraham Lincoln implemented some of Reconstruction's earliest steps in Louisiana, and the state was one of the last in the American South to retain a Republican governor in the 19th century.

Louisiana, home to the South's largest city and gateway to its largest river, was an early target for Union forces during the Civil War. In April 1862, Gen. Benjamin F. Butler led the federal military expedition that occupied New Orleans, and under his controversial guidance, Louisiana began renewing its ties to the Union. Lincoln had high hopes that Louisiana would provide a positive example of his Presidential Reconstruction policy, one that might be applied to the rest of the Confederacy. Lincoln's plan of restoration hoped to shorten the war by inviting Southern states back to the Union under lenient terms. Although Butler and a sequence of other officers, notably Gen. Nathaniel P. Banks, compiled administrative accomplishments, it was difficult to reconstruct Louisiana as long as the Civil War continued and more than half of Louisiana was outside federal control. Despite these handicaps, wartime military governors and Unionists put through some reforms, including drafting a new state constitution that abolished slavery, holding elections for the U.S. Congress, and setting up a new system of public education open to black and white students in New Orleans.

From 1862 to 1877, Louisiana served as a laboratory for political, social, and military experiments. The state demonstrated bitter partisanship and factionalism within its Republican and Democratic parties. In 1860, Louisiana's population was about 49 percent African American. Therefore, it was logical for blacks to hold office during Reconstruction on the local, parish (county), and state levels, indicating that the status of African Americans would change in the South and the nation. Louisiana also displayed a distressing amount of violence, as former confederates responded to the new society produced by defeat and Reconstruction.

From 1862 on, Louisiana's Republican factions seldom agreed on a unified course of action. These disagreements meant that their opponents (including Democrats, Conservative Unionists, ex-confederates, and some disaffected Republicans) gained their political footing and sometimes exploited openings created by the Republicans' factionalism. The strongest faction was the so-called Custom House Ring. In the building on Canal Street in New Orleans where the federal government collected the customs duties (tariffs), the Ring dominated the city, which was serving as the state capital. The Ring consolidated behind the regular wing of the national Republican Party and supported President Ulysses S. Grant. Leaders of the Ring included U.S. marshal Stephen B. Packard, U.S. senator William P. Kellogg, U.S. customs official James F. Casey, brother-in-law of Grant's wife, and Oscar J. Dunn, a leading black politician. Both Lincoln and Grant depended partly upon Southern state leaders who had opposed secession and remained loyal to the Union—men stigmatized by the Democrats as being scalawags.

Most scalawags were not Louisiana natives, but the most prominent had resided in the state for decades and had established themselves in respectable professions and agricultural pursuits. They included Joshua Baker, an engineer and judge born in Kentucky and residing in Louisiana since 1822; Michael J. Hahn, born in the German state of Bavaria and residing in Louisiana since 1840; and Benjamin F. Flanders, a railroad executive born in New Hampshire and a Louisiana resident since 1843. Another was Louisiana-native James Madison Wells, one of the state's controversial politicians of the postwar period. All of them held the office of governor during Reconstruction and three held other offices: Flanders was mayor of New Orleans; Hahn was a state legislator; and Wells was federal surveyor of customs at New Orleans. Within a few years, peer pressure from other Southern whites and bitter politics undercut some scalawags' careers. Republicans began to turn to leaders from outside the state. Carpetbaggers were Northern men who moved to the South during or after the war, sometimes bringing their families with them. Opponents of Reconstruction not only condemned and vilified the carpetbaggers, but they also created a derisive negative label that smeared them during Reconstruction and ever since. However, detailed research by historians demonstrates a variety of motives, backgrounds, and actions by these settlers from the North. For example, originally from Vermont, William Pitt Kellogg entered politics in Illinois and served in an Illinois regiment during the war. Kellogg was elected U.S. senator and then Louisiana governor, and anti-Reconstruction forces attempted to overthrow his administration in street fighting in 1874. Stephen Packard, a Union army veteran from Maine, held the patronage post of U.S. marshal for Louisiana. He wielded considerable political influence and was nominated as the Republican candidate for governor in the contested election of 1876.

Because they were from out of state, politicians like Kellogg and Packard were easy targets for Democrats to stigmatize as carpetbaggers, but Marshall H. Twitchell was another type. A heroic soldier with the Vermont brigade during the war, Twitchell encouraged several members of his family to settle with him in north Louisiana. There, the Twitchells not only entered into business enterprises, but they also crusaded for black civil, political, and economic rights. Twitchell tried to indicate his attachment to his new state by marrying the daughter of a local dignitary, but to his enemies Twitchell personified Reconstruction's social, political, and economic changes. Unknown assailants murdered seven members of Twitchell's family and severely wounded him, shooting him down in broad daylight and leaving him for dead. Distraught and crippled, he returned to Vermont. Among the most significant carpetbaggers was Henry Clay Warmoth, a former Union officer from Missouri who was elected Louisiana governor, serving from 1868 to 1872. A flamboyant and powerful politician, Warmoth proposed a list of expensive state construction projects, appeared to foster an integrated public school system, worked with African American politicians, and seemed to support black suffrage. On the other hand, he let black civil rights slide and slipped over toward the Democrats, opposing President Grant and the Custom House faction. Consequently, Warmoth failed to unify Louisiana's Republican Party and opponents in the state house of representatives impeached him in 1872, but he remained a Louisiana resident until his death in 1931. Warmoth's impeachment suspended him from office and opened the way for an African American governor.

Louisiana had one of the largest pools of educated free and enslaved blacks in the United States before the Civil War. Born free in New Orleans, Oscar J. Dunn, gained recognition and gradually moved up in the Republican Party. Nominated as lieutenant governor, Dunn ran on Warmoth's ticket in 1868. Upon his election, Dunn became Louisiana's most influential African American political official. Suddenly, however, on November 22, 1871, Dunn died of an uncertain physical ailment. Promptly, replacements lined up, and Republican leaders decided that Dunn's office had to be filled by another African American. One possibility was state senator Caesar C. Antoine, a member of the state constitutional convention of 1867–1868. Antoine later served as Kellogg's lieutenant governor. Another prospect was Dunn's sharpest competitor, Pinckney Benton Stewart Pinchback. Born a slave in Georgia, Pinchback had worked as a riverboat steward and served in two federal military units, including as a captain in one. In politics, Pinchback also had held a seat in the 1867–1868 constitutional convention with Antoine and then was elected state senator. In December 1871, his senate colleagues picked Pinchback to complete Dunn's term. A year later, Pinchback understood that Warmoth was suspended from office while awaiting trial in the state senate, and thus for 35 days, he became the only African American governor of a state during Reconstruction (and the only black governor in the United States until Douglas Wilder was elected governor of Virginia in the late 20th century).

Although they tried, Democrats neither persuaded high-profile African American leaders to leave the Republican Party nor rallied the black vote—in part, at least, because of the Democrats' consistent use of violence during Reconstruction. By 1876, a few blacks had been intimidated or bribed into voting for Democrats, but employing violence and threats of violence against white and black Republicans offset the claims by ex-confederates that they would provide the best political home for freedmen and their families. The threat of violence could not be removed by either federal officials, such as U.S. marshals, federal attorneys, and the U.S. Army, or by state or local officers, including the Metropolitan Police (actually, what amounted to the Louisiana state militia), district attorneys, or county sheriffs. Ex-confederates and their supporters could strike almost any time against Republican businessmen and their investments; schoolteachers and their schools (including ones enrolling black pupils); church leaders and houses of worship; and politicians, including mayors, town councilmen, sheriffs, judges, and state legislators. All Republicans, including businessmen, teachers, ministers, officeholders, and independent-minded farmers who were African Americans, became symbols of Reconstruction's new social, economic, and political order.

Spectacular incidents of violence undermined the whole process of Reconstruction. One of the worst was the New Orleans riot of July 30, 1866, in which dozens of people were killed and injured. Although the situation was ominous before the riot, the U.S. Army failed to take steps to prevent violence. City policemen failed to suppress the riot and instead became rioters themselves. Ironically, when combined with other factors, such as the opposition by President Andrew Johnson to recharter the Bureau of Refugees, Freedmen, and Abandoned Lands (Freedmen's Bureau) and the proposed Fourteenth Amendment to the U.S. Constitution, the New Orleans riot contributed to the willingness of congressional Republicans to pass the Military Reconstruction Acts of 1867. Numerous other violent incidents marred Louisiana's record, some carried out by vigilantes belonging to the White League and the Knights of the White Camellia, groups similar to the Ku Klux Klan. Among them were the actions of armed whites who murdered several black leaders in St Landry Parish in October 1868. In April 1873, at the town of Colfax, named for Schuyler Colfax, Grant's vice president, in Grant Parish, named for the president himself, an organized group of whites attacked the parish courthouse, resulting in more than 100 deaths or injuries, mostly to black men. In the town of Coushatta in Red River Parish in August 1874, as many as 1,000 White Leaguers detained several Republicans, including a deputy U.S. marshal.

Although they let the marshal go, the Leaguers murdered their other unarmed captives, including Homer Twitchell. Perhaps the most spectacular and well-organized violence occurred in September 1874 in New Orleans. Ex-confederates and supporters of the defeated Democratic candidates in the gubernatorial election of 1872 sought to overthrow Governor Kellogg, and nearly succeeded. Raging street battles pitted the Republicans' Metropolitan Police (led by former Confederate general James Longstreet) against the White League under former Confederate colonel David Penn; by the time the army arrived, dozens had been killed and injured.

Taken together, such events showed the willingness of Conservative whites to employ domestic disorder on a large scale to block or cancel out the reforms of Reconstruction, including black male suffrage, holding office, serving in the militia, owning land, and serving on juries, and black children attending public schools. As a result of the violence, by the mid-1870s, many black and white Louisiana Republicans restrained or ended their reform activities, left office, and even moved out of the state.

Interestingly, a series of court cases arising in Louisiana not only undercut Republican efforts in the state but also hindered the program at the national level. The *Slaughterhouse* Cases (1873) grew out of a dispute over a monopoly granted to a New Orleans meat-processing business, but the real issue related to the Fourteenth Amendment's vital citizenship rights clauses. The Supreme Court's decision restricted the reach of federal authorities to protect citizens' rights under the amendment, placing the burden of that protection back on the states. In another case, after white vigilantes attacked the courthouse in Colfax, several of them were arrested, including William Cruikshank. He was one of four whites convicted of murder. He appealed, and in *United States v. Cruikshank* (1876), the Supreme Court concluded that Cruikshank had been improperly indicted: he could have been indicted for violating the rights of black citizens, but the case had focused on murder, which falls under state, not federal, jurisdiction. This ruling made it nearly impossible for the federal government to uphold the terms of the Fourteenth Amendment and the ensuing Enforcement Acts.

Back in Louisiana, by 1876, the Democrats' methodical applications of intimidation and violence in Louisiana resulted in chaos during the presidential election. Towns and parishes that had recorded heavy votes for President Grant in 1868 and 1872 recorded few or no votes for Republican Rutherford B. Hayes. Democrats called their tactics "bulldozing" which produced results so close—and so disputed—that Louisiana's Democrats and Republicans claimed victory. James Madison Wells and Louisiana's Republican returning board (the state election commission) certified the victory of Packard, with Caesar Antoine planning to continue serving as lieutenant governor. They were inaugurated. The Democrats again rejected the certified results. Democrats arranged for another returning board to award victory to former Confederate general Francis R. T. Nicholls, and inaugurated him. Again, Louisiana had dual governments.

The outcome of the presidential vote bore directly on the state election. Deciding the presidential outcome required establishing a special Election Commission, which declared Hayes the winner via the Compromise of 1877. As part of the deal, Hayes retracted the army's support for Packard, placing the Democratic gubernatorial candidate, Nicholls, in office; this brought the traditional period of Reconstruction to a stunning conclusion. Yet for a decade after 1877, vestiges remained of the changes brought by Reconstruction. William Kellogg was elected to another term in the U.S. Senate in 1876, held his seat against a challenge, and then won election to the U.S. House of Representatives from 1883 to 1885. Louisiana voters elected four other Republicans to the U.S. House between 1877 and 1891, including Michael Hahn, who died in office in 1886. Scattered across the state, a handful of Republicans held office. But for African Americans, no such twilight existed; Democratic "Redeemers" (who had "redeemed" the state for their party) resorted to violence against blacks—including lynching—to assert white supremacy, discourage agitation, and reduce political voice. Soon social segregation, in the form of Jim Crow, and punitive economic measures would eliminate most of the gains made during Reconstruction.

*Joseph G. Dawson III*

**See also:** Amnesty Proclamations; Compromise of 1877; Congressional Reconstruction; Race Riots; Redemption.

## Further Reading

Current, Richard N. *Those Terrible Carpetbaggers*. New York: Oxford University Press, 1988.

Lane, Charles. *The Day Freedom Died: The Colfax Massacre, the Supreme Court, and the Betrayal of Reconstruction*. New York: Paperbacks, 2009.

Taylor, Joe Gray. *Louisiana Reconstructed, 1863–1877*. Baton Rouge: Louisiana State University Press, 1974.

Tunnell, Ted. *Crucible of Reconstruction: War, Radicalism, and Race in Louisiana, 1862–1877*. Baton Rouge: Louisiana State University Press, 1984.

Tunnell, Ted. *Edge of the Sword: The Ordeal of Carpetbagger Marshall H. Twitchell in the Civil War and Reconstruction*. Baton Rouge: Louisiana State University Press, 2001.

Vandal, Gilles. *Rethinking Southern Violence: Homicides in Post–Civil War Louisiana, 1866–1884*. Columbus: Ohio State University Press, 2000.

Vincent, Charles. *Black Legislators in Louisiana during Reconstruction*. Baton Rouge: Louisiana State University Press, 1986.

# LOYALTY OATHS

Loyalty oaths appeared during the Civil War to ensure citizens remained loyal. They were instituted after the war as a means of regulating political participation as former rebel states rejoined the Union.

Abraham Lincoln's attorney general, Edward Bates, suggested that all federal employees take oaths of allegiance; by the second week of the Civil War loyalty tests began. Led by a Republican congressman, John F. Potter, a five-member committee investigated who had refused to take the oath. On August 6, 1861, Lincoln made it a requirement that all federal and prospective federal employees take a loyalty oath. The oath affirmed future loyalty to the government and Constitution of the United States.

Although not mandated, similar oaths became expected for many involved with government activity. Newspaper correspondents had to take oaths before they were allowed to accompany federal forces, and Americans abroad had to take oaths to renew visas and passports. In 1862, Lincoln signed into law the ironclad oath test, a more stringent measure. This required that all appointed or elected persons—except the president and vice president—to any U.S. government office, be it civil, military, or naval, take an oath attesting to past loyalty as well, meaning they never bore arms against the Union, and pledging future loyalty to the Union. In December 1863, when Lincoln presented his Ten Percent Plan for Reconstruction, he included an amnesty oath pardoning those former confederates who pledged future loyalty to the Union. His program also authorized the creation of state and local governments in those states, once 10 percent of the white male population (who had voted in 1860) took the oath and pledged to support the Constitution and all federal laws regarding slavery—including emancipation and the institution's impending abolition.

A growing sect of Radical Republicans in Congress opposed the leniency of the president's plan. As an alternative to Lincoln's proposal, in 1864, congressional Republicans introduced the Wade-Davis bill, which required use of the "ironclad oath" which required future support of the Constitution (as under Lincoln's plan) but also a profession of past support. In other words, anyone who had supported the Confederacy, resigned a commission in the U.S. government or its military, or in any way aided the rebellion was automatically disqualified from voting or holding office. Lincoln, seeking a speedy reconciliation, pocket-vetoed the bill to prevent its operation.

Following the assassination of Lincoln, Andrew Johnson, at first, seemed to offer hope to the more radical elements in the party. Although a Southern Democrat, Johnson's position as a War Democrat since 1864 and his unswerving loyalty to the Union encouraged other Republicans. As military governor of Tennessee during the war, Johnson followed a hard line toward confederates, so Radicals believed Johnson would support them in using the ironclad oath to keep former rebels out of office. However, now the war was over and the Union preserved, so the emergency had passed. Johnson's approach to Reconstruction was at least as lenient as Lincoln's, and he included something very much like Lincoln's amnesty oath in his own program. Johnson's 1865 amnesty proclamations were broad and inclusive, and those excluded (largely high-ranking officials and the wealthy) were allowed to petition directly to the president for pardons; nearly all were speedily granted.

When the elections of 1866 delivered Congress firmly into Republican hands, it was the Republicans' turn to set the tone. The Military Reconstruction Acts in 1867 swept most former Confederates aside, and the U.S. Army, charged with enforcing these new Reconstruction measures, used severe oaths to eliminate former rebels from the political arena. As a result, Republican carpetbaggers, scalawags, and newly enfranchised African American males seized control of most Southern states. In 1868, the ratification of the Fourteenth Amendment nationalized the issue of loyalty and softened the blow. The amendment largely removed the oath from the scene and replaced it with a carrot-and-stick approach, as former confederates would be disqualified at a rate equal to the disqualification of black males— an attempt to cajole states into allowing black suffrage outside of congressional pressure. Finally, upon Southern states' readmission to the Union, the issue of loyalty was subsumed back into the local sphere. Congress did not dictate that a readmitted state needed to measure the loyalty of its citizens, and so most states dropped the issue altogether.

*Catherine Anyaso*

**See also:** Amnesty Proclamations; Black Suffrage; Civil Rights; Congressional Reconstruction; Constitutional Conventions; Democratic Party; Joint Committee on Reconstruction; Pardons; Presidential Reconstruction; Republicans, Liberal; Republicans, Moderate; Suffrage.

## Further Reading

Hyman, Harold M. *Era of the Oath: Northern Loyalty Tests during the Civil War and Reconstruction*. Philadelphia: University of Pennsylvania Press, 1954.

# LYNCH, JAMES D. (1839–1872)

James D. Lynch was among the throng of black leaders from the North who migrated to the South during Reconstruction. In Mississippi, Lynch established himself as an influential educator, speaker, minister, editor, and politician. He worked diligently to advance the issues he believed were critical to black advancement—spiritual well-being, education, political rights, and economic opportunity. His early death, at the age of 33, deprived black Mississippians of one of their greatest advocates.

Lynch was born on January 8, 1839, in Baltimore, Maryland. He was raised in relative freedom. His mother was a former slave, but her husband had purchased her freedom. Lynch's father made his living as a merchant and a minister. When he was 13, Lynch's parents sent him to Kimball Union Academy in Meriden, New Hampshire, one of the few schools in the region that accepted blacks. Two years later, Lynch was forced to leave due to financial hardship. Uncertain what to do with his life, Lynch moved to New York, where he taught for a time in Long Island, and studied for the ministry in Brooklyn.

In 1862, Lynch moved to Baltimore, where he ministered at Waters Chapel Church and married Eugenia Rice. With the war raging and thousands of slaves fleeing to freedom, Lynch and others like him headed south to help in any way they could. In South Carolina and Georgia, Lynch ministered to several black regiments and helped establish schools for black children. In Savannah, Georgia, he delivered a moving speech at a meeting attended by black leaders, Secretary of War Edwin Stanton, and Gen. William T. Sherman. He spoke boldly in support of racial integration, captured the attention of African Methodist Episcopal (AME) Church leaders and freedpeople alike. Bewildered and unequipped for life in liberty, blacks flocked to Lynch, who seemed a symbol of what they could attain. He captivated them with his oratorical style and exhorted them with messages of hope and optimism.

In 1866, Lynch and his family moved to Philadelphia, Pennsylvania, where he edited the *Christian Reader*, a publication for the AME Church. Longing to recommit to his previous work with the former slaves, Lynch and his family relocated to Mississippi. By moving back to the South, Lynch gave up a promising ministerial career in the North.

Lynch quickly became a political and spiritual giant in Mississippi. Within a year of his return to the South, he had acquired 6,000 black members and established 20 meeting houses. Blacks walked for miles to hear him speak. Lynch used his influence to emphasize the need for education and to cultivate black voting power. He believed the Republican Party was the best advocate for blacks. He actively worked to help organize the Mississippi Republican Party, contributing greatly to its mass black support. With the coming of Congressional Reconstruction, white Republicans took notice and elected him vice president of the first state party convention in the fall of 1867. Lynch's political career gained momentum when he established the *Colored Citizen Monthly*, which he used to promote his views and kept blacks well informed. By the end of 1869, Lynch was one of the most prominent black politicians in the state, although he also maintained his commitment to the church.

In politics, Lynch held Moderate views and was more inclusive than some Radical colleagues. Whereas the Radical Republicans wanted to exclude the former confederates from political roles, Lynch endorsed black suffrage but did not support Confederate disfranchisement; indeed, he believed all males should vote. Whereas the local white Conservatives wanted to limit black freedom and political power, Lynch espoused black rights and equality. As a result, he toiled to win not only black support but to convert white Conservatives. Lynch also endorsed black economic power, pushing for black landowning and opposing sharecropping.

A young, black outsider, Lynch accomplished an extraordinary amount in a short period. He helped manage public lands, enabling Mississippi to allocate lands for schools, and in other ways, helped move Mississippi toward its first free public school system. Lynch held numerous positions as well, including Freedmen's Bureau state assistant, superintendent for education, a member of the Mississippi Board of Education, and secretary of state for Mississippi in 1869 and 1871. Following his second stint as secretary of state, he served as a delegate to the National Republican Convention in 1868. Although he did not obtain his party's nomination for Congress, he campaigned in Indiana for the Grant-Wilson ticket. Upon his return to Mississippi in late 1872, Lynch died unexpectedly from a bronchial infection and Bright's disease.

Lynch was the first known black leader in Mississippi to be buried alongside other state dignitaries in the all-white Greenwood Cemetery in Jackson, Mississippi. The Republican-dominated state legislature appropriated $1,000 toward a monument in his honor. During the Jim Crow era, whites challenged the presence of Lynch's remains in the segregated cemetery. Members of the Ladies Auxiliary Cemetery Association were granted permission to remove his remains and the monument erected in his honor. However, the organization never followed through, and James D. Lynch and his monument remain at Greenwood Cemetery today.

*Gladys L. Knight*

***See also:*** Bureau of Refugees, Freedmen, and Abandoned Lands; Carpetbaggers; Contraband, Slaves as; Democratic Party; Edisto Island, South Carolina; Elections of 1868; Field Order No. 15; Freedmen's Relief Societies; Labor Systems; Military Reconstruction Acts (1867–1868); Port Royal Experiment; Republicans, Moderate.

## Further Reading

Harris, William C. *The Day of the Carpetbagger: Republican Reconstruction in Mississippi.* Baton Rouge: Louisiana State University Press, 1979.

Morris, Robert C. *Reading, 'Riting, and Reconstruction: The Education of Freedmen in the South, 1861–1870.* Urbana: University of Chicago Press, 1981.

Walker, Clarence. *A Rock in a Weary Land: The African Methodist Episcopal Church during the Civil War and Reconstruction.* Baton Rouge: Louisiana State University Press, 1982.

Wharton, Vernon Lane. *The Negro in Mississippi.* Chapel Hill: University of North Carolina Press, 1947.

# LYNCH, JOHN R. (1847–1939)

John Roy Lynch, the first black congressman from Mississippi, Reconstruction historian, lawyer, soldier, and businessman, was one of the most distinguished leaders of the Reconstruction and post-Reconstruction eras.

Born near Vidalia, Louisiana, on September 10, 1847, on his father's plantation, Lynch remained a slave until the Civil War. His white father and slave mother also had at least two other children. In 1863, the young slave escaped to Union lines, working in military camps and later as a waiter on a naval vessel. After the war, with Natchez occupied by Union troops, he was able to get his only formal education, attending night school for four months until the school closed. He furthered his education by reading on his own and listening to the lessons at the white school across the alley from the photographic studio where he worked and eventually managed.

With the coming of the Republican Party to the South—following the passage of the Military Reconstruction Acts in 1867—Lynch began to move into politics. It seemed a logical progression: aristocratic in appearance, slender, with a light complexion and impressive oratorical skills, Lynch seemed a natural African American leader. As Mississippi crafted its new government under Congressional Reconstruction, Lynch campaigned for black civil rights and the new state constitution. Impressed with the young man's abilities, Governor Adelbert Ames appointed Lynch a Natchez justice of the peace. After serving for a year, Lynch entered the Mississippi legislature in 1870 as the representative from Adams County, where he served for three terms. Although blacks represented a minority in the state house of representatives and Lynch was only in his mid-20s, he was elected speaker in 1873. Democrats and Republicans, whites and blacks, praised his intelligence, his speaking abilities, and his impartiality. Indeed, one Democratic Party member admitted that there were few who could exceed Lynch's skills as a stump speaker. As a state legislator, Lynch introduced legislation attempting to declare the Ku Klux Klan illegal, to establish a university for blacks, and to provide for integrated seating in public transportation. He also fought against the convict-lease system and urged the governor to request federal troops to counter violence in Mississippi.

In November 1872, citizens of Mississippi's Sixth Congressional

A former slave, John R. Lynch served as congressman from Mississippi during and after Reconstruction. He later wrote a balanced history of the period, *The Facts of Reconstruction*, intended to counter many racist claims. (Library of Congress)

District elected Lynch to the U.S. Congress, choosing him over the white Republican incumbent, L. W. Pearce and then over his Democratic opponent, Judge Hiram Cassidy. Taking his seat in December 1873, Lynch entered as the youngest member of the 43rd Congress, the first black congressman from Mississippi, and only one of 22 blacks to serve in Congress between 1870 and 1901. Reelected to the 44th Congress, Lynch was the only Republican to win a congressional seat from Mississippi for that term, narrowly defeating Democrat Roderick Seal, a prominent antebellum politician and Confederate war hero. While in Congress, Lynch worked in many ways to ensure fair elections and a life for all free of intimidation. For example, he spoke forcefully for the enactment of stronger enforcement legislation to protect equal rights in the South and worked energetically for the passage of the Civil Rights Act of 1875, which banned discrimination in public accommodations (but later declared unconstitutional by the U.S. Supreme Court in the Civil Rights Cases of 1883).

However, Lynch could not survive the white Mississippians' "redemption" techniques of violence, intimidation, and corruption; he lost, in November 1876, by 4,000 votes to Confederate general James R. Chalmers, who had commanded the troops at the Fort Pillow massacre. Although he appealed to Congress, charging the Democrats with fraud, the Democratic majority on the House Committee on Elections refused to consider his case. In November 1880, Lynch again ran for Congress against Chalmers. In another close contest, Lynch was declared the loser, only after the Democratically controlled election board threw out thousands of votes. This time, the Republican majority in Congress listened to Lynch's charges of fraud and, on April 27, 1882, voted to seat him. In this, his last term in Congress, he introduced bills attempting to ensure honest elections, to provide relief for orphans, and to reimburse depositors who had lost money in the Freedman's Savings and Trust Company. After losing by narrow majorities in his 1882 and 1884 bids for Congress, Lynch retired from elective politics. Throughout his congressional career, he had been one of the most influential blacks in the country, frequently consulting with presidents Ulysses S. Grant and James A. Garfield.

Returning to Natchez as a private citizen, Lynch engaged in banking and agricultural and real estate ventures, eventually owning several plantations in the Natchez area. Politically, he served as chair of the Republican State Executive Committee from 1881 to 1892, advocating fusion of Mississippi's Republicans with Independent Populists, and as a delegate from Mississippi to five Republican national conventions. Lynch passed the Mississippi bar in 1896, and practiced in the state and in Washington, D.C.

In 1898, at the age of 51, he embarked on a new career as an officer in the U.S. Army, answering President William McKinley's call for black officers at the start of the Spanish American War. Serving as a paymaster, Lynch traveled to Cuba, Haiti, other Caribbean islands, and the Philippines. Upon his retirement from the army in 1911 with the rank of major, Lynch married Cora E. Williamson of Chicago and moved to Chicago, resuming his law practice.

More importantly, Lynch took up the task of correcting what he saw as the errors historians were making regarding Reconstruction. In 1913, he published *The Facts of Reconstruction*, attacking the histories of James Ford Rhodes, William A. Dunning, and their students. Writing that his goal was "to bring to public notice those things that were commendable and meritorious" during Reconstruction, Lynch denied the Dunning school's story of greedy carpetbaggers, corrupt scalawags, and ignorant blacks. Rather, he detailed his experiences in Mississippi, contending that the Southern Reconstruction governments accomplished a great deal of good, broadened democracy, and were neither corrupt nor inept. He continued this fight against historical distortion when he published articles in the *Journal of Negro History* in 1917 and 1918, later published in 1922 as a book titled *Some Historical Errors of James F. Rhodes*. Arguing against Rhodes's claim that illegal election methods were needed to overthrow "Negro domination," Lynch demonstrated that Republicans, not blacks, dominated. Further, he contended, the Reconstruction governments were the only governments in the South to ever have a truly Republican form of government. At his death, he was writing his *Reminiscences of an Active Life*; in 1970, this was edited and published by John Hope Franklin and the University of Chicago Press. Those reminiscences detail Lynch's life, including his struggles to win elections in the face of white hostility and fraud and his role in Reconstruction politics. Lynch died in Chicago on November 2, 1939, at the age of 92. He was buried in Arlington National Cemetery with full military honors.

*Roberta Sue Alexander*

***See also:*** Constitutional Conventions; Contraband, Slaves as; White League.

## Further Reading

Franklin, John Hope. "John Roy Lynch: Republican Stalwart from Mississippi," in *Race and History: Selected Essays, 1938–1988*, 250–266. Baton Rouge: Louisiana University Press, 1989.

Lynch, John R. *The Facts of Reconstruction*. New York: The Neale Publishing Co., 1913.

Lynch, John R. *Reminiscences of an Active Life*. Edited with an introduction by John Hope Franklin. Chicago: University of Chicago Press, 1970.

# MARVIN, WILLIAM (1808–1899)

William Marvin became provisional governor of Florida in 1865 and oversaw the state's first effort to restore its formal relationship with the Union after the Civil War. Under his tenure, Florida drafted its first postwar constitution, ratified the Thirteenth Amendment, and elected new members to Congress. Marvin was also elected as one of Florida's senators under Presidential Reconstruction, although he never served because of the 39th Congress's refusal to seat the representatives of states reconstructed under Andrew Johnson's Reconstruction program.

William Marvin was born on April 14, 1808, in Fairfield Herkimer County, New York, and spent most of his early years deeply involved in the Methodist Church. In 1830, he abandoned what had become a growing passion for the ministry, deciding instead to pursue a career in law. Marvin enjoyed much early success as a lawyer and later as a judge. In 1835, Andrew Jackson appointed him to the post of district attorney for the Southern district of Florida. This appointment led to him later becoming involved in Florida politics, serving in the state's territorial assembly, constitutional convention, and, ultimately to his active participation in the drafting of what would be Florida's first constitution in 1845.

After the defeat of the Confederacy, President Andrew Johnson appointed Marvin provisional governor on July 13, 1865. As governor, Marvin encouraged Florida's white citizens to accept defeat and abolition. He openly embraced the idea of African American citizenship and civil rights but stopped short of extending suffrage to blacks.

In addition to his overseeing Florida's readmission to the Union under Presidential Reconstruction, Marvin oversaw the applications for pardons submitted by ex-confederates excluded under Johnson's amnesty proclamations. Marvin's lenient attitude toward these men, in addition to his calls for reconciliation and rapid restoration, led to the state assembly electing him to represent Florida in the U.S. Senate. However, when he arrived in Washington, D.C., and presented his credentials, congressional Republicans denied him and other Southern representatives their seats. This was Marvin's last major political act on behalf of Florida. He returned to the state but became disillusioned with Reconstruction and especially the specter of African Americans voting. Marvin left Florida during the 1880s and retired to Skaneateles, New York, where he died in 1899.

*Learotha Williams Jr.*

*See also:* Black Codes; Black Suffrage; Carpetbaggers; Civil Rights; Congressional Reconstruction; Democratic Party; Joint Committee on Reconstruction.

## Further Reading

Shofner, Jerrell H. *Nor Is It over Yet: Florida in the Era of Reconstruction, 1863–1877.* Gainesville: University Presses of Florida, 1974.

# MARYLAND

During the Civil War, the border slave state of Maryland remained loyal to the Union, and as such—a slave state that was not part of the Confederacy—Reconstruction here was unique, relatively brief, and largely self-determined. Throughout the war and its aftermath, the divided loyalties of Marylanders complicated efforts at providing security to the state's newly freed slaves and also compromised attempts to legislate suffrage (the right to vote) to black males. A considerable minority of white Marylanders had supported the Confederacy; some 20,000 had taken up arms against the Union. Their return to the state and the anger of many Marylanders over their changed circumstances shaped the state's postwar political, economic, and racial course until the restoration of control to the Democratic Party in 1867.

As with other areas under Union control, Reconstruction began in Maryland even before the Civil War ended. In the summer of 1864, during a period when the Unionist Republican Party (also called Unconditional Unionists) controlled the legislature, leaders of that organization rewrote the state constitution. The most significant measure of this new constitution emancipated Maryland's 87,189 slaves, some of whom had already emancipated themselves by serving in the Union army and navy and by fleeing the farms and plantations where they had been enslaved. Dealing with the kind of issues that would confront other Southern states in the late 1860s, Maryland's Constitution of 1864 also reapportioned the state legislature by basing representation on white, not total, population. The archaic earlier arrangement had given disproportionate power to slaveholding planters in Southern Maryland and on the Eastern Shore, where more than 80 percent of the state's slaves lived. Maryland also had one of the largest free black populations in the United States; under the new constitution they would be counted for apportioning of legislative seats, although they could not vote. The new constitution also established registration procedures for prospective voters. It required a loyalty oath intended to disfranchise those white Marylanders who had supported the Confederacy. Democrats—who constituted one-third of the 1864 convention—voted against the final version of the state constitution. They specifically opposed emancipation, hoping that slavery could somehow survive. In a preview of the racial attitudes that made Maryland's Reconstruction so brief, Democrats raised the specter of what they called a loathsome "amalgamation, equality and fraternity" with blacks. The campaign for ratification of this new constitution merged with the national election of 1864. Thus, the fate of President Abraham Lincoln, the Unionist candidate for governor, Thomas Swann, and the new constitution all rolled together. Only the favorable soldier's vote saved the Maryland Constitution.

When the war ended five months later, the return of Maryland's soldiers to civilian life was not an easy one. There were clashes between former Confederate and Union soldiers.

Former slaves moved about the state and into the District of Columbia in efforts to find family members. These early years of Reconstruction were further complicated by the deterioration of relations between the races. In the summer of 1866, whites in Anne Arundel County invaded a black religious meeting and assaulted worshippers. Blacks attempting to establish schools during the postwar period found their efforts impeded by a state government that refused to apply taxes collected from blacks for black schools. There were assaults on black schoolteachers and instances of the burning of black schools. In Baltimore, white caulkers refused to work alongside blacks, just as whites refused to sit by blacks in the city's public transportation facilities. In their efforts to re-exert control over the African American community, many Maryland whites tried to return blacks to a virtual form of slavery by means of an apprenticeship system. By 1867, more than 3,000 black minors had been bound over to their former masters. The state's version of the Black Codes required that blacks be employed, outlawed black testimony against whites, and sought to restrict travel, but these discriminations were contested in state courts after Congress passed the Civil Rights Act of 1866. Agriculture and attending labor issues were among the most pressing problems in Maryland. The Bureau of Refugees, Freedmen, and Abandoned Lands (the Freedmen's Bureau) operated in Maryland as in other Southern states, to negotiate work contracts with planters for former slaves requiring reasonable wages and housing. In time, these arrangements followed the sharecropping contracts emerging in the post–Confederate South that bound blacks to the land for a return of part of the crop, but there were efforts to establish Maryland's blacks as landowners as well. In Maryland's version of the failed forty-acres-and-a-mule policy, the Freedmen's Bureau in St. Mary's County set aside land where for over a year, 500 blacks successfully farmed 3,000 acres abandoned by previous owners who had moved to the Confederacy during the war. However, this was only a temporary arrangement and a mirror of what took place throughout the state (and much of the South) when the owners came back to the state and received amnesty from President Andrew Johnson: these "government farms" reverted to white planters. By 1880, nearly two-thirds of all Maryland's black farmers were sharecroppers, about 10 percent were tenant farmers, and less than a quarter owned their own land.

Among the changes for blacks was the proliferation of segregated schools, some funded by private groups. Maryland Quakers were especially active in this cause through the Baltimore Association for Moral and Educational Improvement of Colored People, which helped set up more than 100 schools throughout the state, along with a school to train black teachers. During this period of readjustment, there were significant economic changes.

Baltimore, the commercial center of the state, now became a railroad center more dependent on the transportation of wheat, corn, and fertilizer than cotton and tobacco. The manufacture of clothing and the canning industry also emerged as essential enterprises, and the state's most important railroad, the Baltimore and Ohio, spurred the development of ancillary iron foundries.

Governor Thomas Swann, who took office in 1865, supported emancipation but opposed—like most Marylanders—the black suffrage that was crucial to protect the rights of former slaves. Swann became the chief agent of a coalition of Democrats and Conservative Unionists intent on returning the state to those who intended to preserve the system of white domination and political control by former slaveholding counties. Recognizing the power of the Democrats in Maryland, in 1866, he appointed registrars who supported the claims of former confederates that they should be allowed to vote. He praised Andrew Johnson and his lenient program of restoration (even though it did not apply directly to

Maryland) and denounced the divided Unconditional Unionists. Even that faction's efforts to "wave the bloody shirt," an effective campaign cry for Republicans in other states, could not prevent the Democrats returning to control in Maryland.

By 1867, the Democrats led by Swann—who now had switched parties—controlled 60 percent of the state legislature, a domination that continued into the 20th century. Now Maryland's political future belonged to a political party that played on white voters' racism to seize and maintain political power. Once in power, the Democrats wrote a new constitution in 1867 that omitted the oaths that had restricted ex-confederates from holding office.

In the election of 1868, Maryland supported the Democratic presidential candidate Horatio Seymour, as Marylanders of both parties continued to oppose the Fifteenth Amendment, which enfranchised black males. Under the national amendment, blacks began voting in local elections in 1870, but as a minority, they never became a solid base for the Republican Party or reached the 20 percent they represented in the general population. With the government firmly in the hands of the Democratic Conservatives, Maryland's future was under the control of those who believed in a white man's government.

*Jean H. Baker*

**See also:** Bourbons; Churches; Congressional Reconstruction; Education; Field Order No. 15; Fourteenth Amendment (1868); Jim Crow Laws; Labor Systems; Loyalty Oaths; Pardons; Presidential Reconstruction; Redemption.

## Further Reading

Baker, Jean H. *The Politics of Continuity: Maryland Political Parties from 1858–1870.* Baltimore, MD: Johns Hopkins University Press, 1970.

Fuke, Richard. *Imperfect Equality: African Americans and the Confines of White Racial Attitudes in Post-Emancipation Maryland.* New York: Fordham University Press, 1999.

## McCARDLE, EX PARTE (1868)

One of the earliest and most controversial of the Reconstruction court cases, *Ex parte McCardle* was a significant victory for Congressional Reconstruction and, some argue, a serious setback for the federal government's balance of powers.

William McCardle, editor of the *Vicksburg Times*, was an outspoken critic of the Military Reconstruction Act, passed in 1867. In that year, McCardle was arrested by the U.S. Army in Mississippi after writing and publishing articles critical of Congressional Reconstruction. He was held in custody by the military, awaiting a trial by a military commission. While detained, McCardle sought a writ of habeas corpus, claiming that his arrest and detention under the Military Reconstruction Act was unconstitutional. His claim was denied in the district court, so McCardle appealed to the Supreme Court under the Habeas Corpus Act of 1867. The Court agreed to hear the case and denied a motion to dismiss for lack of jurisdiction brought by other branches of the government.

After hearing that this motion to dismiss was denied, Radical Republican leaders in Congress feared that the Supreme Court might declare the Military Reconstruction Act unconstitutional. This legislation formed the backbone of Congressional Reconstruction, and such a move could dismantle the entire Reconstruction program. As it had done earlier in battles with President Andrew Johnson, Republicans acted to protect their authority over the Reconstruction process. In March 1868, the Congress passed a bill repealing the Habeas Corpus Act, under which McCardle had appealed to the Supreme Court. This deprived the Supreme Court of jurisdiction over the case. As expected, Johnson vetoed the bill, but Congress passed it over his veto.

The Court, already examining the case, reacted strangely. In its decision, handed down on April 12, 1868, the Court acknowledged the actions of the Congress and dismissed McCardle's case on the grounds for lack of jurisdiction. In his opinion, Chief Justice Salmon P. Chase held that congressional withdrawal of the Court's jurisdiction was not unconstitutional, falling under Congress's power under Article III of the Constitution. Others, then and now, disagreed, claiming that Chase, a Radical Republican, was protecting the Reconstruction program; but Chase's balance—even anti-Radical behavior—during the impeachment trial works against this theory. Regardless, the move did set a dangerous precedent for congressional activity. Those who see an unnecessary—or even unconstitutional—expansion of congressional power equate this victory over the Court as equal to Congress's victory over the executive, in the impeachment of Johnson. For the time being, no one could challenge the Republicans in Congress.

*Daniel W. Hamilton*

**See also:** Milligan, Ex parte (1866).

## Further Reading

*Ex parte McCardle*, 74 U.S. 506 (1868)

Kutler, Stanley. *Judicial Power and Reconstruction Politics.* Chicago: University of Chicago Press, 1968.

# MEMPHIS RIOT (1866)

The Memphis riot constituted some of the worst urban bloodshed in American history and typified ethnic violence that occurred in the trying times following abolition.

War, emancipation, and abolition had brought enormous cultural shocks to Tennessee, as it had to all former Confederate states. Freedpersons flooded into Nashville, Memphis, and other urban areas. In the South, liberated blacks had never concentrated in neighborhoods of their own; now their shantytowns became the state's first African American ghettos. Before the war, Memphis had fewer than 4,000 blacks, living among whites as a subordinate caste who could not threaten white supremacy. Former Confederate whites, returning after hiding in the countryside, were aghast at what they saw. According to a Union army census conducted in mid-1865, some 16,509 freedpersons lived in greater Memphis, including nearby President's Island. The figure represented a 400 percent increase since 1860 and more than half of the city's overall population of 27,703. Nearly one-third of blacks were children or individuals too old or sick to work, many existing on assistance provided by the Bureau of Refugees, Freedmen, and Abandoned Lands.

No matter what the newcomers did, older residents resented them. Able-bodied persons of color competed for work on the levees and wharves and in the depots, taking

The burning of a Freedmen's schoolhouse during the Memphis Riot of 1866. The riot helped convince Republicans that President Johnson would not protect blacks or enforce their rights. (Library of Congress)

previously "white" jobs, and depressing wages through their sheer numbers. These blacks enjoyed tangible success. By early 1866, they possessed 8 churches and owned 500 hacks, various stores, several saloons, fruit stands, lunchrooms, and sponsored a Colored Barbers' Association. Although the state still prohibited the education of African Americans, by late 1865, there were 22 black schools with 1,101 pupils in daily attendance, not including 1,549 black soldiers at Fort Pickering's regimental schools. Given the South's desperate postwar economic conditions, the many white refugees in the city, and the thousands of Irish immigrants seeking employment, many deeply resented black economic advancement. Equally haunting to whites was the mythical, racist specter of a criminal, even violent, free black underclass. In a society that had always feared runaway slaves and slave rebellions, there were now young, free, African American men, some with no employment or families. Lacking other alternatives and opportunities, some did turn to crime.

Added to the social and economic disorder was the culture of Memphis itself. Confederate flags flew defiantly and Southerners insulted Yankees and freedpersons alike. The city's police force was afforded no training, and the officers wore no uniforms—only badges. They were permitted to drink, gamble, and loiter while on duty. They were certainly not pleased when African American elements of the Union army arrived in Memphis. Altercations between black troops and white Memphis policemen became routine during the spring of 1866 and exploded into mayhem from May 1 to May 3.

On May 1, 1866, in Memphis, a street brawl erupted among several policemen and a group of blacks recently discharged from the U.S. Army. The disturbance quickly escalated into a full-scale battle between the police department, overwhelmingly Irish immigrants, and virtually all African Americans wearing Union blue in the downtown area. Around nightfall, the former soldiers took refuge in Fort Pickering, near South Street, the site of the brawl. White federal troops, who had been occupying the city since the Civil War, disarmed and detained them. Meanwhile, frenzied white mobs began a 40-hour reign of terror that lasted, until the afternoon of May 3. Their target was South Memphis, a low-income biracial community that had grown rapidly after slavery's death in Tennessee. The fury of the gangs killed 46 blacks, wounded between 70 and 80 others, robbed at least 100, severely beat 10 more, raped 5 women of color, and burned to the ground 89 African American residences, 4 churches, and 12 schoolhouses. The crowds killed no whites but, on May 3, after the predatory bands had wearied, one white man was murdered by another for drinking in a saloon with a black acquaintance. Two whites—a fireman and a policeman—died in the Tuesday afternoon street battle. The local press gave these casualties vastly disproportionate publicity.

Irish police and fire personnel made up more than half of the mobs' participants. Other rioters were native born and included artisans, shopkeepers, and professionals. They enjoyed more than the tacit support of the city's white upper class. Indeed, prominent rioters included the judge of the recorder's court, the editor of the city's leading racist newspaper—the *Daily Avalanche*—and the attorney general of Tennessee.

Most historians agree that these and other atrocities wholly discredited President Andrew Johnson's program of Presidential Reconstruction, helped the Radical Republicans sweep the congressional elections of 1866 and take a veto-proof majority to Washington, and set in motion a process that led ultimately to President Andrew Johnson's impeachment and Senate trial.

Although demography, tension, hysteria, and other factors probably made some sort of confrontation in South Memphis inevitable, the violence of May 1 was not spontaneous. The date chosen was more than a coincidence. It was the day after the last black troops in the city had been discharged and became civilians. As soon as these men lost their Union Army status, they were vulnerable, viable targets.

*James G. Ryan*

**See also:** Black Codes; Congressional Reconstruction; Labor Systems; Militias; National Union Movement (1866).

## Further Reading

Brown, Richard Maxwell. *Strain of Violence: Historical Studies of American Violence and Vigilantism*. New York: Oxford University Press, 1975.

Fitzgerald, Michael W. *Splendid Failure: Postwar Reconstruction in the American South*. New York: Ivan R. Dee Publishers, 2008.

Hardwick, Kevin R. " 'Your Old Father Abe Lincoln Is Dead and Damned': Black Soldiers and the Memphis Race Riot of 1866." *Journal of Social History* 27 (Fall 1993): 109–28.

Rable, George C. *But There Was No Peace: The Role of Violence in the Politics of Reconstruction*. Athens: University of Georgia Press, 1984.

Ryan, James G. "The Memphis Riots of 1866: Terror in a Black Community during Reconstruction." *Journal of Negro History* 62, no. 3 (July 1977): 243–56.

Waller, Altina L. "Community, Class and Race in the Memphis Riot of 1866." *Journal of Social History* 18 (Winter 1984): 233–46.

# MILITARY GOVERNORS

For Reconstruction efforts during the Civil War and after, the title of military governor was applied to civilians appointed to hold volunteer army commissions, or civilian administrators with the authority to act directly on behalf of the federal government. After Union troops began occupying areas in some of the Confederate states, President Abraham Lincoln appointed men to the position of military governor. In each case, Lincoln neglected to spell out the specifics of military governors' authority. Instead, the president was interested to see what his appointees would do with the poorly defined office, how well they would cooperate with the senior Union general in the state, and in what ways the military governors could advance the executive's vision of wartime Reconstruction—empowering loyal Unionists, cajoling repentant rebels, reuniting the state with the nation, and, later, upholding emancipation.

Significant among military governors was Andrew Johnson, posted in Tennessee. An obvious choice for the job, Johnson, a prominent member of the Democratic Party, had been elected to every important office in Tennessee, including the legislature and governor, and had served in the U.S. House of Representatives and U.S. Senate. Most important, he was a staunch Unionist, the only U.S. senator from a so-called seceded state to retain his seat in Congress. By March 1862, when Union troops had gained control of portions of western and central Tennessee, Lincoln announced that Johnson would lead Reconstruction efforts there. Johnson took actions that set the tone and precedents for other military governors to follow. Generous toward loyal Unionists and vicious toward rebel secessionists, he required all government appointees to swear a loyalty oath to the U.S. Constitution, demanded that newspaper editors act loyal to the Union or have their papers closed, dismissed several ministers of the gospel for preaching in support of the Confederacy.

As Johnson tested the reach of his office in Tennessee, other military governors failed to equal his actions. Previously a member of Congress from Missouri, John S. Phelps accepted Lincoln's assignment as military governor of Arkansas in July 1862. Like Johnson, Phelps held the rank of volunteer brigadier general in the Union army. However, after five months, he exercised little authority, failed to gain the support of Gen. Samuel Curtis and could claim no real progress in Reconstruction. In December, Lincoln canceled Phelps's commission when he went back to Missouri. Meanwhile, Lincoln hoped that pro-Union sentiment would resurface in North Carolina. He designated Edward Stanly as military governor, but unlike his approach with Johnson and Phelps, he neither asked Congress to approve his appointment nor made him a volunteer general. Opposed to abolition, Stanly balked at Lincoln's Emancipation Proclamation and did not get much help from Union troops, who made little headway into the interior of the state and had to be satisfied with enclaves on the coast. Few Carolina Unionists came forward to help Stanly, whose ineffectual administration lost credibility after Zeb Vance was elected Confederate governor in August 1862. When Stanly left office, Lincoln appointed no replacement.

While Phelps and Stanly floundered, Lincoln turned to another state—Louisiana. George F. Shepley first served as a subordinate to Major General Benjamin F. Butler, senior officer in the Union's Department of the Gulf and controversial commander of federal troops that had occupied New Orleans since May 1862. Lincoln made Shepley, a lawyer from Maine and volunteer brigadier general, military governor in June, thus splitting the responsibilities of department commander and military governor. Shepley was soon overshadowed by Butler's replacement, Maj. Gen. Nathaniel P. Banks, who arrived in December. Having held prominent offices, including governor of Massachusetts and speaker of the U.S. House of Representatives, Banks gained a volunteer army commission. Banks controlled circumstances dealing with the status of the freedmen and worked toward an acceptable labor system for the former slaves. Governor Shepley attended to arranging elections, including choosing members for the U.S. House of Representatives and, in March 1864, the first successful gubernatorial election was held in a state under wartime military government with the selection of Michael Hahn.

Even in the postwar period, the military governor usually remained subordinate to the senior army commander in the states. For example, Benjamin F. Flanders acted as military governor in Louisiana from June 1867 to January 1868 and answered to Gen. Philip Sheridan. Subsequently, Gen. Winfield S. Hancock held authority over military governor Joshua Baker. The military governor of Texas, Andrew Jackson Hamilton, had been appointed a brigadier general in the Union army in November 1862 by President Lincoln. Strongly pro-Union, like Flanders and Baker, Hamilton had been unable to take his job because federal forces were limited to small enclaves on the Texas coast. Confirmed by President Andrew Johnson, Hamilton became provisional governor of Texas in June 1865 but resigned his volunteer army commission. Hamilton held office until a former confederate, James W. Throckmorton, was elected in August 1866.

*Joseph G. Dawson III*

**See also:** Amnesty Proclamations; Presidential Reconstruction.

## Further Reading

Dawson, Joseph G. III. *Army Generals and Reconstruction: Louisiana, 1862–1877*. Baton Rouge: Louisiana State University Press, 1982.

Harris, William C. *With Charity for All: Lincoln and the Restoration of the Union*. Lexington: University of Kentucky Press, 1997.

Maslowski, Peter. *Treason Must Be Made Odious: Military Occupation and Wartime Reconstruction in Nashville, Tennessee, 1862–1865*. Millwood, NY: KTO Press, 1978.

Sefton, James E. *The United States Army and Reconstruction, 1865–1877*. Baton Rouge: Louisiana State University Press, 1967.

## MILITARY RECONSTRUCTION ACTS (1867–1868)

The operational legislation that formally inaugurated Congressional Reconstruction, the Military Reconstruction Acts thoroughly reorganized the state governments of the former Confederate states. They collectively marked a turning point in Reconstruction policy, when

Moderate Republicans and their Radical colleagues joined forces to overturn the restoration program set in motion by President Andrew Johnson. The acts also set several unique precedents in American history, including the assumption by the federal government of issues traditionally under state jurisdiction, the imposition of black voting on a large scale, and a dangerous juggling of American civil–military relations, when the national legislature deliberately turned over to the military authority never before surrendered by civil officers.

Since the end of 1865, and increasingly through 1866, the president and the Republican majority in Congress had been at odds over the situation in the former Confederate states, the former rebels inhabiting them, and the former slaves just recently freed. Johnson's vetoes of the Moderate Civil Rights Act and the Freedmen's Bureau bill, his hostile veto messages, and his attempt to undermine Congress through a third-party movement collectively forged a consensus against him. These events combined to deliver Congress over to the Republican Party in the fall 1866 elections. On March 2, 1867, both houses passed the first of four Military Reconstruction Acts, to "[p]rovide for the More Efficient Government of the Rebel States." Passed on March 2, March 23, and July 19, 1867, and March 11, 1868, the Military Reconstruction Acts can be viewed collectively. Johnson believed that the laws were not only unnecessary but also unconstitutional, and he vetoed each of them. Congress overrode his veto each time. Because Tennessee had ratified the proposed Fourteenth Amendment to the U.S. Constitution, Tennessee was not covered by the terms of the acts, nor were Missouri and Kentucky, states that during the war had seats in the Confederate Congress and stars on the Confederate flag, but had never formally seceded.

According to the acts, the state and local governments of the 10 other former Confederate states, including the governments created by Johnson, were declared "provisional" and placed within five military districts. Temporarily, 10 state governments lost their legal standing, but the governments themselves were not ousted. Serious consideration was never given to actually redrawing (or renaming) the states, as some Radical Republicans wanted. Virginia comprised the First Military District, and North Carolina and South Carolina were included in the Second District. Alabama, Georgia, and Florida formed the Third District; the Fourth District contained Mississippi and Arkansas; and Texas and Louisiana made up the Fifth District. Each district was commanded by a brigadier general, appointed by Johnson and possessing far-reaching powers. The commanders could fill vacant offices, remove officials, and determine which courts could operate. Of course, it was extraordinary— Democrats said "radical"—for American army officers to have these powers over civil officials; while neither war nor martial law existed, congressional Republicans claimed the federal government could hold these states in the "grasp of war" until it had secured the "fruits of victory."

Securing those fruits also fell to the district commanders. Within each district, the commanders began the readmission process by supervising voter registration (heretofore a state right) and calling for constitutional conventions that would draft new state constitutions. Congress required that adult black males be permitted to vote for delegates to the constitutional conventions, the first national decree affecting state voting and the first large-scale implementation of black suffrage in America (a few New England states had allowed restricted black voting before the Civil War). The acts granted the military latitude to decide who could register, and many former confederates were banned from participating. Moreover, these new state constitutions would grant freedmen the right to vote, again sweeping aside the rights of the states to determine voter qualification. Once the conventions drafted new constitutions, they would be approved or rejected by the voters in an election supervised and certified by the army, again with black men voting. The army would supervise additional elections for all state and local offices, including governor and both houses of the legislature, as well as U.S. congressmen and senators. The new state legislature was also required to ratify the Fourteenth Amendment.

Reconstruction would be concluded in that state, all federal officeholders would take their seats, and all powers and authority would return to the elected civil authorities; presumably the army would depart.

These federal laws made the U.S. Army the agent of social and political change in the South, and these changes had implications for the rest of the nation. In many ways, the Military Reconstruction Acts were radical because Congress called on the U.S. Army to enforce the laws' terms. In reality, Congress had nowhere else to turn. The Republicans could not rely on agents of the Treasury Department, or a handful of U.S. marshals, to carry out national Reconstruction policy. The Justice Department did not even fully exist as a separate entity until 1870. No combination of federal agencies could accomplish all of the steps required by the acts. Further, both as a result of the wartime occupation and through the efforts of the Bureau of Refugees, Freedmen, and Abandoned Lands (a War Department agency), the army was already in position to execute and supervise the legislation. Only the army possessed the personnel (the leaders and enough units) dispersed across the South to carry the administrative load.

The Reconstruction acts temporarily replaced state rights with federal directives. It was unclear how former confederates might react to this new approach. Soon enough, some white Conservatives realized that by acting individually or in groups they might forestall the changes that Republicans sought, including black men participating in politics. Relying on the terms of the Congressional Reconstruction Acts, the generals began to carry out the expectations of the Republican majority. Assigned on March 11, 1867, Johnson's choices for district commanders were John M. Schofield (First District), Daniel E. Sickles (Second District), John Pope (Third District), E.O.C. Ord (Fourth District), and Philip H. Sheridan (Fifth District). Except for Sickles, a former Democratic Party politician and volunteer army officer, the original district commanders were professional officers from the regular army and had not held political office. As general in chief, Ulysses S. Grant watched all Reconstruction developments closely. Committing the army to enforce civil rights, he ordered district commanders to protect former slaves and made sure that his subordinates arrested anyone accused of committing crimes against soldiers or Freemen's Bureau agents. All of the district commanders removed civil officials, including governors of Louisiana, Texas, Virginia, and Georgia. Gradually, one by one, the former Confederate states completed the requirements and were readmitted between 1868 and 1870.

Reconstruction under the Military Reconstruction Acts may be termed a procedural success: The army and its officers guided all 10 affected states through the requirements. Military dictatorship never developed, no army atrocities occurred, and generals eagerly handed power back to civilians once Congress's terms had been fulfilled. For a brief time, the former Confederate states had progressive state constitutions, universal male suffrage, and vibrant state Republican parties. Successfully implemented, no one could vouch for their success once federal supervision dissipated and the army departed.

The acts had other impacts as well. While Congress's orders were reshaping the South, the methods and attitudes of four district commanders (Schofield, Sickles, Pope, and Sheridan) displeased Johnson, and he removed them, generating resentment among many Republicans. Combined with Johnson's opposition to the Civil Rights Act, the Fourteenth

Amendment, and the Freedmen's Bureau, his removal of generals contributed to Republicans' willingness to support his impeachment in February 1868.

*Joseph G. Dawson III*

**See also:** Amnesty Proclamations; National Union Movement (1866); Presidential Reconstruction; Trumbull, Lyman (1813–1896).

### Further Reading

Dawson, Joseph G. III. *Army Generals and Reconstruction: Louisiana, 1862–1877*. Baton Rouge: Louisiana State University Press, 1982.

Foner, Eric. *Reconstruction Updated Edition: America's Unfinished Revolution, 1863–1877*. Reprint, New York: HarperCollins, 2014.

Sefton, James E. *The United States Army and Reconstruction, 1865–1877*. Baton Rouge: Louisiana State University Press, 1967.

## MILITIAS

The militia system during Reconstruction was one of the most controversial organizations of the post-Civil War period in the South. Created by Southern Republicans to suppress paramilitary challenges to their new state governments, state militias were partisan law enforcement bodies. Moreover, Southern state militias recruited large numbers of African Americans, earning the organization its enduring epithet: "Negro militia." This term is misleading, however, as many whites volunteered as well, although blacks and whites served in segregated units. Nonetheless, most white Southerners denounced the militia just as they despised the Republicans for granting suffrage to the former slaves.

Militias were an attempt by newly formed Republican governments to combat the violence aimed at their party and its constituents. Soon after the war had ended, white Conservatives turned to violence to enforce traditional codes of behavior and levels of social status. The coming of black suffrage under the Reconstruction Acts furthered tensions, and soon violence went from ad hoc and individual to organized and semi-military, as in groups such as the Ku Klux Klan. Since Republican governments could not trust many native whites, the local black male population seemed the only resource for creating a law enforcement unit. Across the former Confederate states, the so-called black militias were chartered, armed, and trained. Oddly enough, Southern Republicans actually proved reluctant to field militia units. Concerns over cost militated against organizing a militia. A militia force of any meaningful size could be very expensive, and Republican administrations were usually short on revenue. Most important, Republican officials recognized that very few militiamen (excepting perhaps veterans of the war) could stand against former Confederate soldiers. Some even feared that using a "Negro militia" would unleash a race war that would destroy Southern society. As a result, executive use of state militias was uneven (they never came into existence at all in Georgia and Virginia) and often marred by indecisiveness.

The first use of state militia occurred in Tennessee in 1867. Governor William G. Brownlow rightly believed that bands of ex-confederates were planning to disrupt the state election that year.

Determined to protect this important political event, Brownlow mobilized the Tennessee State Guard, a militia force that comprised 1,900 men. A majority of these militia volunteers were white Unionists, but about a quarter of the recruits were blacks. Throughout the spring and summer of 1867, the governor deployed his troops to more than 30 "rebellious" counties where they maintained the peace despite a few instances of violence. Republicans won the election in a landslide. Later in the year, Brownlow successfully used the state guard a second time during the mayoral election in Nashville, where the state militia helped thwart an extralegal attempt by opponents of Reconstruction to seize power in the capital. In both operations, the Tennessee State Guard conducted itself with a high degree of discipline and restraint, thereby setting an admirable standard for other reconstructed states to imitate.

From 1868 to 1872, Reconstruction militias battled a wave of terror unleashed by the Ku Klux Klan. Actually a generic term for a host of rebel vigilante outfits, the Klan posed a serious threat to the authority of the Republican Party and the safety of its largely black constituency. In several states, Republican governors raised militias to combat the Klan menace. Arkansas governor Powell Clayton launched the boldest anti-Klan campaign.

Declaring martial law in 15 counties, Clayton deployed the Arkansas State Guard, a force of some 2,000 men (60% black). Over a four-month period beginning in November 1868, Clayton's militia thrashed the Klan, killing several night riders in open skirmishes and arresting dozens more. In January 1869, Brownlow reorganized his militia for a showdown with the Klan in Tennessee. Between February and May, the Tennessee State Guard (this time an all-white force of 1,600 men) occupied nine counties in the middle and western parts of the state. Unlike events in Arkansas, however, there were few violent confrontations. Apparently under instructions from Grand Wizard Nathan B. Forrest, Klan dens in Tennessee prudently went underground and avoided contact with the state militia. Nonetheless, until it was disbanded in the summer of 1869, the Tennessee State Guard neutralized Klan terrorism simply by being in the field. The following year, Governor William H. Holden declared war on the Klan in North Carolina. Between June and August, an all-white force of 600 militiamen hunted the Klan in the most terror-plagued counties of the state. In making more than 100 arrests, the militia briefly suppressed the Klan in North Carolina. Finally in 1871, Governor Edmund J. Davis of Texas conducted one of the most effective anti-Klan operations of the Reconstruction period. In addition to raising 3,500 mostly black volunteers for the Texas militia, Davis also utilized a mostly white state police of 200 mounted troopers, which he used as his principal strike force against the Klan. Texas law enforcers arrested more than 1,000 perpetrators and, for a couple of years, subdued ex-confederate vigilantism.

Elsewhere in the South, Republican administrations proved incapable of stopping the Klan. The governors of Alabama, Florida, Louisiana, and Mississippi all threatened to use their state militias against the Klan, but for various reasons they never actually mobilized their forces, preferring instead to call on the federal government for conditional assistance. Governor Robert K. Scott of South Carolina, however, heeded his constituents' cry for help and, in 1870, raised the largest militia force of the Reconstruction period. In all, some 20,000 blacks mustered into service (whites refused to join). Although the state adjutant general managed to arm only about half the volunteers, the state's Conservative whites criticized what they considered a "Negro insurrection." Klan units in up-country South Carolina skirmished with the militia throughout the early months of 1871, mauling several black companies in a series of bloody engagements. Convinced that a race war was imminent, Scott placated the white populace by ordering all of his militia units to disarm and disband. Scott's actions amounted to a capitulation that white Southerners would not soon forget.

After the Klan, the Southern white insurgency became more sophisticated. Ex-Confederate officers reorganized the various "klans" into political armies under centralized leadership. Instead of indiscriminate terror, these new paramilitary forces instigated policies of selective intimidation and violence, fully aware that most Republicans would hesitate to use their "Negro militia." For those Republican administrations that still held political power in the 1870s, the state militia became a last line of defense. Governor Davis went down fighting in Texas. Disputing the fairness of the 1873 gubernatorial election, he and a company of black militiamen barricaded themselves in the statehouse. As a white paramilitary force, the Travis Rifles, prepared to storm the building, President Ulysses S. Grant urged Davis to stand down. The governor complied, and the militia story in Texas came to an abrupt end. In Louisiana, the demise of the militia was just as inglorious. The most spectacular clash of arms occurred in New Orleans. In September 1874, the paramilitary White League marched into the city and overthrew the Republican government. The Louisiana State Militia, ironically under former Confederate general James A. Longstreet, contested this usurpation. With 3,000 black militiamen (augmented by about 400 Metropolitan Police), Longstreet confronted as many as 8,000 White Leaguers. Like the black militia of South Carolina, the Louisiana militia was no match for the Confederate veterans. In a matter of minutes, the White League routed the militia and took over the city. U.S. soldiers eventually arrived and restored order, but the credibility of the militia was destroyed.

White Liners in Mississippi and Red Shirts in South Carolina conducted similar operations in those states. Following a spate of racial violence in the summer and fall of 1875, Governor Adelbert Ames put Mississippi on a war footing, but his efforts were mostly a bluff. Although he armed three companies of militia (two black), Ames never deployed the units for fear of race war. Instead, he pleaded in vain for federal assistance, while paramilitary White Liners intimidated black voters and swept the state elections in November. Not long thereafter, Republicans in South Carolina succumbed to the Red Shirt movement. Although disbanded by Scott in 1871, a few black militias retained their weapons and their confidence, sparring with former rebels from time to time. By the election of 1876, however, Red Shirt formations were ready to eliminate this last vestige of Republican power. In bloody incidents at Hamburg and Ellenton, white vigilantes shot down black militiamen who had either surrendered or were unarmed. These atrocities facilitated Democratic efforts to steal the state election through fraud and intimidation.

In evaluating the effectiveness of the militia, the paradox of law enforcement during Reconstruction is unmistakable. In using the militia, Republicans incurred charges of military oppression; in not using the militia, Republicans betrayed a weakness that ex-confederates were all too ready to exploit. In the end, Southern Republicans never found the right mixture of conciliation and coercion. Nevertheless, in at least four states—Arkansas, North Carolina, Tennessee, and Texas—the state militia temporarily staved off ex-Confederate opposition to civil government and provided some protection to the freedmen. It is telling that Democrats, on regaining political power in those states, immediately repealed all militia legislation. Had all Republican governors used their militias aggressively, regardless of the risk of race war, or had the militia remained active longer in the states where it did achieve results, the white paramilitary organizations that helped bring down Reconstruction may have never developed into such serious threats. In any event, the militia arguably offered Southern Republicans their best means both for retaining their hold on power and for making Reconstruction work at the state level.

*Ben H. Severance*

**See also:** Race Riots; Redemption.

## Further Reading

Baenziger, Ann Patton. "The Texas State Police during Reconstruction: A Reexamination." *Southwestern Historical Quarterly* 72, no. 4 (April 1969).

Fitzgerald, Michael W. *Splendid Failure: Postwar Reconstruction in the American South.* New York: Ivan R. Dee Publishers, 2008.

Rector, Charles J. "D. P. Upham, Woodruff County Carpetbagger." *Arkansas Historical Quarterly* 59, no. 1 (Spring 2000).

Severance, Ben H. *Tennessee's Radical Army: The State Guard and Its Role in Reconstruction, 1867–1869.* Knoxville: University of Tennessee Press, 2005.

Singletary, Otis A. *Negro Militia and Reconstruction.* New York: McGraw-Hill Book Co., 1957.

Trelease, Allen W. *White Terror: The Ku Klux Klan Conspiracy and Southern Reconstruction.* Baton Rouge: Louisiana State University Press, 1971.

## MILLIGAN, EX PARTE (1866)

This landmark Supreme Court case considered the constitutionality of military arrests and trials during and after the Civil War. In an opinion handed down in December 1866, the court held that military trials were unconstitutional when the civil courts were open. This was a rebuke to the Abraham Lincoln administration, which suspended the writ of habeas corpus, and the U.S. Congress, which sanctioned Lincoln's actions in the Habeas Corpus Act of 1863.

The decision involved the arrest of Lambdin Milligan in Indiana in 1864 for serving in a secret organization supportive of the Confederacy. Milligan, a lawyer active in the Democratic Party, and two others were tried by military tribunal, convicted of treason, and sentenced to death. Lincoln postponed the execution, but after Lincoln's assassination, President Andrew Johnson ordered that the hanging take place. Milligan sought a writ of habeas corpus from a federal circuit court in Indiana, asking for a civilian trial on the grounds that, as a civilian, the military commission had no jurisdiction over him. The court divided on the question of whether a federal court could hear appeals from military trials, and the case was sent to the Supreme Court.

The Court, in a unanimous opinion written by Justice David Davis asserted, "The Constitution of the United States is a law for rulers and people, equally in war and in peace, and covers with the shield of its protections all classes of men, at all times, and under all circumstances." The Court ruled that Milligan was wrongfully convicted by a military court because civil courts remained open in Indiana, and that the military had not followed the procedures set forth in the Habeas Corpus Act for military trials. The Court's ruling was a critical moment for the elaboration of American civil liberties in wartime, limiting military jurisdiction over civilians. Importantly, however, Milligan was not issued until after the war, and the Supreme Court did not find military arrests and trials unconstitutional during the Civil War itself.

*Daniel W. Hamilton*

**See also:** Amnesty Proclamations; Congressional Reconstruction; *McCardle, Ex parte* (1868); Pardons.

### Further Reading

*Ex parte Milligan*, 71 U.S. 2 (1866).
Kutler, Stanley. *Judicial Power and Reconstruction Politics*. Chicago: University of Chicago Press, 1968.
Neely, Mark. *The Fate of Liberty: Abraham Lincoln and Civil Liberties*. New York: Oxford University Press, 1991.

# MISSISSIPPI

Mississippi's Reconstruction period began in 1865 and ended in 1876. The Reconstruction governors were William Sharkey (1865), Benjamin Humphreys (1865–1868), Adelbert Ames (1868–1870; 1874–1876), J. L. Alcorn (1870–1871), and R. C. Powers (1871–1874). Mississippi was the first former Confederate state to hold its Reconstruction convention in 1865. However, the results were disastrous, as unrepentant white Mississippians blatantly opposed even the minimal changes President Andrew Johnson requested. Moreover, they enacted Black Codes, severely limiting the civil rights of the African American community. Eleven years later, Conservative Mississippians successfully defeated the state Republicans, and life reverted to a state not far removed from the antebellum period. Jim Crow laws replaced the former slave codes, and blacks were disfranchised, denied basic civil rights, subjected to horrible violence, and remanded to a sharecropping system that resembled slavery. More than ever, Mississippians relied on an agrarian lifestyle based on cotton and resisted industrialization.

The Civil War reached Mississippi in 1862. There were a total of 16 official battles in Mississippi, plus scores of skirmishes and lesser confrontations. The war's impact on Mississippi was similar to other Southern states: as Union armies advanced, slavery disintegrated as slaves fled the plantations. Some 17,000 freedmen joined the Union forces, fighting against their former owners. Beyond this, slaves and former slaves in Mississippi received little attention or assistance during the war, or during the Presidential Reconstruction process under Abraham Lincoln. The war ended for Mississippi when Gen. Richard Taylor surrendered in 1865.

Johnson's restoration plan was designed to quickly and quietly unite the former Confederate states and their Northern brethren. In 1865, Mississippi's governor, Charles Clark (1863–1865), and two other leaders, William L. Sharkey and William Yerger, traveled to Washington to determine what Johnson expected from them. The president only agreed to meet with the men unofficially. At this meeting, Johnson established Sharkey as Mississippi's provisional Reconstruction governor. He dictated that Mississippians must take loyalty oaths to the Union and choose delegates for a constitutional convention, which would abolish slavery, nullify secession and the Confederate debt, and ratify the Thirteenth Amendment. Mississippi's Reconstruction convention met in August 1865. The results of the convention would make or break Johnson's reputation, particularly with members of the Republican Party in Congress who were beginning to question his program. But Mississippians decided to follow their own constitution (written in 1832) and disregarded many of Johnson's instructions. They did, however, recognize the abolition of slavery. Following the convention, newly elected governor Benjamin Humphreys gave a speech that reflected Mississippian's opinions in regard to Reconstruction. In the speech, Humphreys argued for Southern white control over Mississippi's social, economical, and political destiny.

To appease Northerners, he affirmed Mississippi's commitment to provide education and protection to blacks. The new state legislation met in November 1865, and set out to put Humphreys's speech into law. The laws created were known as the Black Codes: blacks could not sue or be sued; they could only serve as witnesses in cases concerning other blacks; they could not own weapons, drink to intoxication, preach without a license, or be found without employment. Unemployed blacks—called vagrants—could be arrested and then auctioned off to an employer. Johnson's plan had failed in Mississippi and soon would prove equally weak in other Southern states. Through fall 1865 and winter 1866, Congress gradually stepped in to take charge over the process of Reconstruction, realizing that no significant change, and certainly no significant progress, would occur under Johnson's leadership.

Congress—and the North in general—was in the hands of Republicans, many of whom were dedicated to a complete upheaval of the South's economic, social, and political system. These so-called Radicals wanted to rebuild Mississippi, not as it was, but as it could be, unfettered by slow progress and slavery. They wanted to bestow full rights on blacks, create a Southern Republican Party, and move the South toward industrialization and real democracy. At the end of 1865, Congress rejected the congressional delegation Mississippians had chosen to represent the state in Washington. This began the Republican's break with the president, which intensified through 1866 as the branches struggled over control of Reconstruction policy. The fall 1866 elections decided a winner, as Northerners delivered a stunning rebuke to the executive and voted in a veto-proof Congress dominated by Republicans. Radical (or Congressional) Reconstruction started the following spring with the first Military Reconstruction Act, which divided the former Confederate states into districts under army control. Mississippi and Arkansas constituted the Fourth Military District, under Gen. E.O.C. Ord. Under his supervision, and in accordance with the Reconstruction Acts, blacks and whites registered to vote, formed a constitutional convention and drafted a new constitution, and elected new state and federal officers. Many former confederates were barred from participation, while former slaves and Northerners forged a new Republican Party.

B. T. Montgomery, Blanche Kelso Bruce, Hiram Rhodes Revels, and John R. Lynch were among the prominent black politicians in Mississippi during Reconstruction. B. T. Montgomery was a prosperous planter and business manager for Joseph and Jefferson Davis. He was the first black to hold state office, serving as justice of the peace at Davis Bend. Bruce and Revels were U.S. senators. Revels was the first black senator, serving from 1870 to 1871. Bruce served in the Senate from 1874 to 1881. Lynch, a native Louisianan, was elected to the legislature in 1870 at only 22, and later chosen as speaker of the House. He served a total of six years in Congress, after which he practiced law and rose to the rank of major in the military. In his later years, he wrote books on Reconstruction, providing a unique and enlightening perspective on one of America's most turbulent periods.

The first governing body under Congressional Reconstruction met in 1868 and wrote a new state constitution. This constitution mandated public schools for all children in the state. The Republican-controlled legislature also set up Alcorn University, which was the black counterpart of the University of Mississippi. They made improvements to the judicial system, renovated public buildings, built state hospitals, and abolished racial discrimination laws. In 1869, they passed legislation allowing ex-confederates to be admitted into office while also securing black suffrage. Republicans raised state taxes to finance these progressive projects. Largely based on landholdings, these taxes fell disproportionately on the whites who controlled the land. Also, because taxes did not cover all of these expenses, government borrowing put Mississippi into greater debt.

White Mississippians, accustomed to the traditional system of scant taxes and minimal state involvement in their affairs, were outraged. Making matters worse, murmurings of scandal and corruption were prevalent and often legitimate. Humiliated and furious over the state of affairs, Conservative Mississippians engaged in aggressive tactics, referred to as the Mississippi or Shotgun Plan, to overthrow the Republican government. As early as 1871, whites successfully ran Republicans out of office in Meridian, but federal troops intervened and restored them to power. A similar situation occurred in Vicksburg three years later. In 1875, whites murdered 30 teachers, church leaders, and Republican officials. Race riots broke out throughout the state. During this period, James Z. George and L.Q.C. Lamar masterminded the George-Lamar plan. Their objective was to seize political power by overtaking vacant seats in the legislature and Congress. Once in office, they planned to remove Republican governor Adelbert Ames, a former Union general, and the Republicans by impeachment.

In the summer of 1875, white members of the Democratic Party, representing the former landowner class of antebellum Mississippi, took up arms against the state government, convinced that Republicans were divided, that blacks were intimidated, and that the federal government was indifferent. Ames, a former Union general, considered forming a militia comprised of black troops. Democrats warned that black troops would trigger race riots. Ames sought the help of President Ulysses S. Grant, urging him to send federal troops. Grant, already overwhelmed with problems of his own, denied the request and refused to send help. Ames reconsidered using black troops, but abandoned his plans when Democratic leaders promised, in return, a peaceful election. Ames did not use state troops on Election Day, November 3, 1875. However, the election was not entirely peaceful, as one black man was killed and several others wounded at Port Gibson. Democrats set up guards, and even cannons, at polls, and escorted some at other locations. The greater portion of Mississippi had already been subdued by Election Day and presented no threat to the Conservatives. Having used violence—and the threat of violence—to attain power, once in office the Democrats set out to unseat their opponents, secure white supremacy, and disfranchise blacks. In 1876, Democrats impeached the lieutenant governor, a black man named A. K. Davis. Ames and his state superintendent, hoping to avoid the same fate, vacated their positions. The executive offices, like the legislative, were now in the hands of Conservative whites once again. Mississippi's Redemption was complete.

Mississippi Democrats then began their own Reconstruction. Through various illegal and nefarious methods, by 1882, the number of black politicians had been reduced to 11. At the Constitutional Convention of 1890, Democrats met specifically to remove black politicians from the Mississippi political scene. In 1890, there were only six remaining blacks in the legislature, and only one in attendance at the convention. Democrats also worked to inhibit industrialization and to formulate many ordinances designed to hinder blacks, including the rigging of voting requirements to keep blacks from voting. For example, voters had to prove literacy and residency, loopholes that served to disfranchise African American males but still fell within the legal bounds of the Fifteenth Amendment. Despite advancements in education and efforts to strengthen black political power, and voting and civil rights, Mississippi, as a whole, resisted change, and reverted as closely as possible to the social life, economics, and politics of the Old South. Mississippians embraced their agricultural cotton economy more than ever before. They replaced the former slavery system with Jim Crow, sharecropping, and tenancy for blacks and former white yeomen farmers. Lynchings and other acts of racial violence were rampant. Blacks, unlike those in other states, did not relocate to other locations. Reconstruction in Mississippi had failed.

*Gladys L. Knight*

**See also:** Black Troops (U.S. Colored Troops) in the Occupied South; Bourbons; Civil Rights Act of 1866; Contraband, Slaves as; Elections of 1876; Fourteenth Amendment (1868); Labor Systems; U.S. Army and Reconstruction; White League.

## Further Reading

Bolton, Charles C. "Farmers without Land: The Plight of White Tenant Farmers and Share-croppers." Mississippi Historical Society, http://mshistory.k12.ms.us/features/feature50/farmers.htm (Accessed September 2005).

Fitzgerald, Michael W. *Splendid Failure: Postwar Reconstruction in the American South.* New York: Ivan R. Dee Publishers, 2008.

Harris, William C. *The Day of the Carpetbagger: Republican Reconstruction in Mississippi.* Baton Rouge: Louisiana State University Press, 1979.

Skates, John Ray. *Mississippi: A Bicentennial History.* New York: Norton, 1979.

Wharton, Vernon Lane. *The Negro in Mississippi.* Chapel Hill: University of North Carolina Press, 1947.

## MOSES, FRANKLIN J., JR. (1838–1906)

Scalawag governor of South Carolina from 1872 until 1874, Moses was born Franklin Israel Moses Jr., in Sumter District, South Carolina. Although from a prominent Jewish family, Moses Jr. eventually became a vestryman in the Episcopal Church. He entered South Carolina College in 1853, but left without obtaining a degree. Originally a secessionist, Moses served as secretary to Francis W. Pickens, the state's governor during the Civil War.

Moses served the Confederacy during the war; in fact, it was reputedly Moses who raised the Confederate flag over Fort Sumter in April 1861. After the war, he edited the Democratic *Sumter News* and served as a secretary to the 1866 state constitutional convention, in which white South Carolinians under Andrew Johnson's restoration program attempted to rejoin the Union while changing their state as little as possible. From 1866 forward, however, Moses became increasingly alienated from the more Conservative former confederates that surrounded him, and his editorials grew increasingly sympathetic to Congress's view of Reconstruction.

In 1867, when Congress overrode Johnson's veto of the Military Reconstruction Acts, Moses, now openly a Republican, won election as a delegate to the new constitutional convention. Moses emerged as a champion of the Republican Party and of the poor, speaking several times in favor of debtor relief and poor relief. After the convention, Moses was elected to the state House of Representatives from Sumter, and in that body, he was elected speaker. By his own later admission, he used that position to extort bribes from other officials.

He also built up a powerful political network that helped elect him governor in 1872. As governor, Moses demonstrated the same concern for the poor and the same practical competence that he had demonstrated in the convention but also the same tendency toward corruption. Moses called for reform of the sharecropping system and the crop lien laws and brought some relief from the debt created by the Robert K. Scott administration. The legislature repudiated part of the debt and funded another part, thus bringing the state's indebtedness down to a level it could maintain. In other Southern states, it was not until Redemption—the return of native white Democrats to power—that this work was achieved.

On the other hand, Moses continued to use his official position to enrich himself—or more precisely, to keep afloat, since he lived far beyond his means. For example, in 1873, he purchased the Hampton-Preston mansion, which had been home to two of South Carolina's wealthiest families. To support his extravagant lifestyle, Moses signed fraudulent warrants on the Governor's Contingent Fund, and he was alleged to have sold pardons to criminals. In 1874, with the national Republican Party calling for the South Carolina party to reform, Moses was not renominated for governor. His friends in the legislature elected him to a circuit judgeship in 1875, but he was prevented from taking office by the new governor, carpetbagger Daniel H. Chamberlain.

After the overthrow of the Republican state government following the so-called Compromise of 1877, Democrats set out to expose the criminal actions of their predecessors to help justify their seizure of power. Moses, certainly among the guiltiest, aided in this effort by providing evidence against himself and many of his former associates. After admitting his mistakes to the Democratic legislators, Moses left South Carolina for the North.

He was later arrested and jailed for petty crimes in Massachusetts, Chicago, and Detroit. He finally settled in Winthrop, Massachusetts, where he died on December 11, 1906, asphyxiated by gas from a stove; it has never been determined whether his death was an accident or suicide.

*Hyman Rubin III*

**See also:** Black Suffrage; Congressional Reconstruction; Democratic Party; Labor Systems; Presidential Reconstruction; Republicans, Liberal.

## Further Reading

"Moses, Franklin J." In *Dictionary of American Biography*. New York: Charles Scribner's Sons, 1935.

Perman, Michael. *The Road to Redemption: Southern Politics, 1869–1879*. Chapel Hill: University of North Carolina Press, 1984.

Simkins, Francis B., and Robert H. Woody. "Franklin J. Moses, Jr., Scalawag Governor of South Carolina, 1872–74." *North Carolina Historical Review* 10 (April 1933): 111–32.

Simkins, Francis B., and Robert H. Woody. *South Carolina during Reconstruction*. Chapel Hill: University of North Carolina Press, 1932.

# N

## NAST, THOMAS (1840–1902)

Political cartoonist Thomas Nast helped to shape the way the public viewed important issues of his day. While best remembered for his Reconstruction-era political cartoons, he is also associated with creating the elephant as a Republican Party symbol and the popular image of Santa Claus as described in Clement Moore's Christmas poem.

Born in Germany in 1840, Nast moved with his family to the United States in 1846. By age 16, he was working as an illustrator for *Frank Leslie's Illustrated Newspaper*. In the summer of 1862, he became a staff artist for *Harper's Weekly*. Both President Abraham Lincoln and Gen. Ulysses S. Grant praised him for his contributions to the war effort and ultimate Union victory in the Civil War.

During Reconstruction, Nast's work had a similar impact. More of a Radical Republican than he might admit, Nast articulated through his work the ideals, as he saw them, of the Republican Party. His great talent was to produce cartoons that featured individuals whom the readers of the day could recognize and characterizations that they readily understood.

Nast's most potent targets were political figures, former Confederate leaders, and Southern institutions. He particularly delighted in excoriating President Andrew Johnson by depicting him as an inhumane tyrant, a Roman emperor sacrificing victims in the arena or on the chopping block with indifferent ease. His drawings could border on the grotesque, especially when depicting Southern violence toward Republicans and freedpeople. An expert at heaping scorn on opponents of progressive change, he also used his art to applaud federal successes,

Thomas Nast, the political cartoonist from *Harper's Weekly*. He used his drawings to attack racism, violence, and political corruption. (National Archives)

Thomas Nast, the influential political cartoonist for *Harper's Weekly*, used his art to oppose violence, political corruption, and civil rights abuses. This cartoon, regarding the presidential election of 1864, criticized the Democratic Party's peace platform. (Library of Congress)

and unabashedly approved of African American civil rights, black suffrage, and equal education.

He turned the same power of his pencil in support of Ulysses S. Grant and against his Democratic Party opponent Horatio Seymour in 1868, and the bolting Horace Greeley, in 1872. Seymour's features played brilliantly into Nast's hands as he twisted the candidate's hair into horns, while Greeley's hat and white coat became the trademarks of that campaign.

Whether depicting the "crocodile tears" of those who sought to accommodate with the defeated South, the platitudes of politicians over the graves of fallen Union veterans, the elevation of ex-confederates over blacks who had served the Union or suffered as slaves, or the excesses of race riots and the Ku Klux Klan, Nast pursued his artistic efforts with zeal and determination. He became a powerful advocate for reform in New York City by exposing the scandals associated with Tammany Hall's Democratic Tweed Ring. Many directly credit his drawings with helping to topple William M. "Boss" Tweed and his cronies from power.

Nast's collaboration with *Harper's* ended in 1886. He freelanced and then undertook a diplomatic post in Ecuador, but held it for only six months when he contracted yellow fever and died on December 7, 1902.

*Brian S. Wills*

***See also:*** Elections of 1868; Republicans, Liberal.

## Further Reading

Hess, Stephen, and Sandy Northrop. *Drawn & Quartered: The History of American Political Cartoons.* Montgomery, AL: Elliott and Clark Publishing, 1996.

Keller, Morton. *The Art and Politics of Thomas Nast*. New York: Oxford University Press, 1968.

Paine, Albert Bigelow. *Thomas Nast: His Period and His Pictures*. New York: Macmillan, 1904.

## NATIONAL UNION MOVEMENT (1866)

The National Union Movement was an attempt by President Andrew Johnson to protect his Reconstruction policy by crafting a new political party. Called the National Union Party, this movement would bring together Democrats, Conservative and possibly Moderate Republicans, and others alienated by the aggressive tone of the Republican Party. Johnson hoped the party would seize Congress in the fall 1866 elections, and even open the door for his presidential run in 1868.

A seasoned politician, Johnson recognized by the summer of 1866 that he and his program were in trouble. His self-proclaimed defense of white culture, federalism, and the U.S. Constitution—made clear in his antagonistic veto messages for the Civil Rights Act and the Freedmen's Bureau Bills the previous spring—had driven many Moderate Republicans into the Radical camp. Even worse, continued violence against former slaves and Unionists in the South, and the incomprehensible arrogance displayed by former confederates, shifted the North against Johnson as well. To promote his program of swift reconciliation, Johnson needed a Congress that would work with him, and even envisioned (perhaps naively) his own election as president.

His vehicle for securing control of Congress was a new political party. Unlike the 20th century with its entrenched two-party system, party politics were much more fluid and dynamic in the 19th century. Politicians saw entire parties come and go and may have belonged to several during their political career; some Radical Republicans may have begun as Whigs, dallied with the Nativists/Know-Nothings, spent time in the Free Soil or perhaps Liberty parties, all before joining the new Republican Party. The idea of a new party was therefore not unknown, and Johnson made the initiative more attractive by reaching back to the war years. In 1864, at the height of the war, Abraham Lincoln and his Republican Party had created a new organization for the presidential contest, the National Union Party. With Union as its platform, it opened its arms to all manner of members, including War Democrats such as Andrew Johnson. Harkening back to the unifying message of "The Union" to curry broad-based cross-party appeal, in June 1866, Johnson and his advisors announced a call for a National Union Convention to meet in Philadelphia in August. This marked the opening shot in the battle for control of Congress. Certainly, his base was with the Democratic Party and other Conservatives, but his appeal had to capture the North. To gain Northern votes, Johnson's advisors—including navy secretary Gideon Welles, Treasury secretary Hugh McCulloch, Senator James R. Doolittle, and the Bennetts, father–son owner-publishers of *the New York Herald*—positioned the party as a protector of the Constitution, white opportunity, and traditional American state's rights federalism.

The movement and the campaign formally opened with the National Union Convention in Philadelphia on August 14, 1866. Called by reporters the "Arm-in-Arm Convention," the spectacle began with a procession of dignitaries led by Governor James L. Orr of South Carolina and Darius Couch of Massachusetts, who entered the hall walking arm in arm. The symbolism was, of course, deliberately concocted, as the former slaveholder from the state that seceded first was an unlikely chum of a decorated Union general. For two days, conventioneers from states North and South blasted the Republican's financial plan, the national bank, the tariffs, and most important the various Reconstruction items that overturned traditional state's rights, dangerously elevated ignorant freedpeople, and opened the door for federal tyranny. On August 16, as the convention closed, delegates passed resolutions of gratitude to veterans for saving the Union, and in support of Johnson's restoration program.

The Republicans countered with two conventions, one in Philadelphia in September and the other later in Pittsburgh. The party, like all parties, had its internal differences, but could easily find common cause in what they opposed: Johnson's refusal to reform the South. Republicans on campaign did not need to propose what they would do; they merely directed voters' attention to what Johnson had done—and what he had not. Johnson inadvertently assisted the Republican effort, by embarking on one of the most dysfunctional campaign trips of all time. His ill-fated "Swing around the Circle" speaking tour made more enemies than friends, and engendered greater hostility among Northern voters and Moderate politicians.

Johnson's obstinate behavior and continuous reports of violence in the South were proof enough that the president and his program had failed. Voters flocked to the polls beginning in September, and by November, all understood that the next Congress would be firmly in the hands of Republicans. The elections of 1866 not only spelled doom for the short-lived National Union Party, but they also sealed the fate of Johnson's restoration program.

*Richard Zuczek*

*See also:* Amnesty Proclamations; Civil Rights; Congressional Reconstruction; Democratic National Convention (1868); Elections of 1868; Memphis Riot (1866); New Orleans Riot (1866); Pardons; Presidential Reconstruction; Race Riots.

## Further Reading

Benedict, Michael Les. "The Politics of Reconstruction," in John F. Marszalek and Wilson D. Miscamble, eds, *American Political History: Essays on the State of the Discipline.* Notre Dame, IN: University of Notre Dame Press, 1997, pp. 54–107.

Schroeder-Lein, Glenna, and Richard Zuczek. *Andrew Johnson: A Biographical Companion.* Santa Barbara, CA: ABC-CLIO, 2001.

Trefousse, Hans L. *Andrew Johnson: A Biography.* New York: W. W. Norton and Co., 1989.

## NATIONAL UNION PARTY (1864)

The National Union Party was a name adopted by Republicans for the election of 1864 to broaden their appeal, hoping to capture War Democrats.

Francis P. "Frank" Blair Jr. of Missouri was already gathering Unionists, whether Republican or Democrat, into a single party as early as 1861. Pro-Union coalitions quickly spread across the North, and by the fall elections of 1862, they could be found in every state still in the North. Many members were Democrats who supported the Union but had difficulty with other Republican agenda items; but on preserving the Union they stood shoulder to shoulder with Republicans. In addition to the Blair family, the party attracted such prominent Democrats as Stephen Douglas and Tennessee senator Andrew Johnson. Much to the disgust of the Radical Republicans, President Abraham Lincoln soon urged the Republican Party to organize under the National Union Party name. He wanted very much to capture the Unionist vote of both parties.

The Republican national party evidently did not use the name any earlier than October 1863. In the spring of 1864, with the war effort stalling, some disgruntled Radical Republicans had considered replacing Lincoln as the presidential candidate. When the National Union Party convention met in Baltimore in June 1864, there was some movement to replace the current vice president, Hannibal Hamlin, with a War Democrat to broaden the party's appeal.

The National Union Party made it possible to have Abraham Lincoln, a Republican, as presidential candidate and Andrew Johnson, a Democrat, running for vice president on the same ticket. As a senator from Tennessee, he had vigorously opposed secession in 1860 and 1861, and was the only senator from a seceding state to remain in Congress after his state had left the Union. In March 1862, Lincoln had appointed Johnson military governor of Tennessee, a post involving difficult duties, which Johnson generally handled with competence. In addition, Johnson had harshly denounced Southern traitors and urged their punishment. As a result, he not only appealed to War Democrats, but to many Republicans as well.

After the victory of Lincoln and Johnson in November 1864, Republicans dropped the National Union Party name almost immediately, but the effect of the name was significant: Not only might it have helped Lincoln and the Republicans win, but it also drastically affected the course of Reconstruction. When Lincoln was assassinated only six weeks into his second term, his successor was not a Republican but a Democrat who ultimately had very different ideas from most of the Republicans. The National Union Movement of 1866, while resurrecting the same name and attempting a similar coalition strategy, was actually a party of Democrats trying to win alliance with some Conservative Republicans.

*Glenna R. Schroeder-Lein*

*See also:* Presidential Reconstruction.

## Further Reading

Fehrenbacher, Don E. "The Making of a Myth: Lincoln and the Vice-Presidential Nomination in 1864." *Civil War History* 41 (December 1995): 273–90.

Waugh, John C. *Reelecting Lincoln: The Battle for the 1864 Presidency*. New York: Crown, 1997.

# NEW DEPARTURE

The New Departure was the political embodiment of the Democratic Party's acceptance of the Civil War settlement. This development was long in coming, for despite white Southerners' postwar assurances, their acceptance had reservations and contradictions. They admitted that they had been beaten, but many did not acknowledge having actually surrendered; violence, obstructionism, political maneuvering, and legal objections all indicated that many ex-confederates rejected the results of the war. Not until the early 1870s did some Democratic factions accept the changes wrought by war.

At the war's end, many former confederates accepted the abolition of slavery grudgingly, meted out rights to the former slaves in skimping measure, denounced federal civil rights laws as unconstitutional intrusions, pronounced peacekeeping military forces as tyrannical satraps, declared the Military Reconstruction Acts unlawful, and denied that African American males could be made voters or that any government based on black suffrage would stand.

Some Northern Democrats argued even that amending the U.S. Constitution was unconstitutional, if its provisions went against the spirit of the original document—which, they argued, any intrusion on the states' rights to define citizenship or protect slavery did. Diehards declared that if the Southern governments were not legal enough to be represented in Congress, as Radical Republicans claimed, then they could not be legal enough to ratify the Thirteenth Amendment and Fourteenth Amendment and put them into the Constitution. The culmination came in the 1868 Democratic National Convention, which declared the Reconstruction policies and the Southern Republican governments unconstitutional.

By the time the Fifteenth Amendment had passed in 1870, some Southern Democrats had begun making their peace with what now seemed a new status quo. They appealed for black votes, and even endorsed black candidates when no white Conservative had any chance of winning. The drawing power of their favorite issue, Negro suffrage, vanishing rapidly, Northern Democrats wanted desperately to change the subject. The New Departure became their vehicle. Politics should make a "departure" to living issues and current problems: high taxes, high tariff rates, corporate giveaways and privileges, and government corruption. Led by Clement Vallandigham, Ohio's foremost Peace Democrat, the party in the Buckeye State embraced the New Departure in 1871. By 1872, the party not only accepted parts of Reconstruction policy as its platform but gave the most concrete proof of a change of heart by making a lifelong enemy, Republican editor Horace Greeley, their 1872 presidential candidate.

This odd marriage of Republican bolters under the Liberal Republican flag and Democrats seeking a "new departure" had potential. The New Departure took away some Republican appeal up north, but more importantly it gave Southern Democrats the rhetorical cover for campaigns returning them to power. While at the national level the regular Republicans and President Ulysses S. Grant easily won reelection in 1872, the shift in politics split the Republicans in the South, removing them from power in Virginia, Missouri, and Tennessee as early as 1869, and in all of the Upper South by 1874.

The New Departure had two main effects. For most, the New Departure concession was more illusion than reality. Democrats promised to abide by the amendments, but defined their scope so narrowly that they undercut the intentions of the laws. White Southerners appealed for black votes to get into power, but once in power they modified state constitutions and used local intimidation to disfranchise the blacks.

The second impact of the New Departure related to Republicans: it merged with the Liberal Republican movement in the North and added momentum to Republican Moderates weary of upholding Southern Reconstruction governments, tired of war issues and black rights, and determined to shift to issues of corruption, administration, and finance.

*Mark W. Summers*

***See also:*** Bourbons; Presidential Reconstruction; Redemption.

## Further Reading

Gaston, Paul. *The New South Creed: A Study in Southern Mythmaking.* New York: Knopf, 1970.

Grossman, Lawrence. *The Democratic Party and the Negro: Northern and National Politics, 1868–1892*. Urbana: University of Illinois Press, 1976.

Perman, Michael. The *Road to Redemption: Southern Politics, 1869–1879*. Chapel Hill: University of North Carolina Press, 1984.

# NEW ORLEANS RIOT (1866)

The race riot in New Orleans, Louisiana, was one of two riots in the summer of 1866 that undermined Moderate Republicans' faith in President Andrew Johnson's Reconstruction efforts. Following only two months after a deadly, antiblack riot in Memphis, Tennessee, the July riot was especially damaging for Johnson, because it occurred in a state that was supposedly reconstructed and ready for readmission into the Union under the president's restoration plan. For many Northern voters, the riots fueled their rejection of Johnson's National Union Party candidates in the fall elections of 1866.

Louisiana's history during the Civil War and Reconstruction periods was replete with political infighting and racial tensions. The 1866 riot grew out of the continuing battles over political power and black suffrage. Governor James Madison Wells, a wealthy planter before the war, had been a Unionist, but after the war he allowed former confederates to vote in an effort to build a political base. As a result, Conservatives soon controlled both the legislature and most parish (county) governments. The state Democratic Party openly opposed black suffrage, which Wells believed in, and so the governor tried to reconvene President Abraham Lincoln's wartime reconstruction convention to enfranchise blacks and disfranchise former confederates—a "turning-back-the-clock," which very few (even few Republicans) thought was legal.

Seeking to prevent the "rump" convention of white and black delegates from meeting and forcing black suffrage on an unwilling state, a mob of armed whites, mostly poor, young men, attacked the two dozen delegates and their 200 black supporters as they marched to their meeting site, as they sought shelter in the convention hall, and as they fled waving white flags. The New Orleans police, which had a history of harassing and intimidating blacks, joined rather than restrained the mob. The local commander of federal troops, who had incorrect information about the convention's meeting time, failed to use the 800 troops until the riot was well underway; when he arrived two hours later he imposed martial law and the mob dissipated.

Over three dozen delegates and marchers were dead, all but three of whom were black. Among the dead was Anthony P. Dostie, the radical former state auditor who whites feared had been inciting blacks to use violence. More than 200 were injured in the attacks, in attempting to escape, or because they were in the wrong place at the wrong time. The attackers suffered only one dead and two dozen injured. Gen. Philip H. Sheridan, whose military district included Louisiana, reported that the police were responsible for the slaughter. His telegrams to Washington, D.C., reporting on the riot provided newspapers with detailed descriptions of the horrific ordeal and the murder of innocent civilians.

President Johnson had no direct link to the violence, but his Reconstruction plan ignored the safety and security of African Americans in the South, and he was currently pushing states to reject the Fourteenth Amendment, which prohibited states from denying the equal protection of the laws. Strangely, Secretary of War Edwin M. Stanton, a Radical, did not show the president a pre-riot telegram from the local army commander, requesting instructions on handling growing tensions. Thus, Conservatives blamed the Radicals for the event, with some even claiming Stanton conspired to make Johnson look culpable. A congressional investigation team of two Republicans and one Democrat divided along party lines in ascribing responsibility for the riot. Ultimately, voters—and history—blamed white Southerners and President Johnson, leading to a unified Republican Party that soon wrestled control of Reconstruction from the executive.

*Claudine L. Ferrell*

**See also:** Civil Rights Act of 1866; Militias; National Union Movement (1866); Presidential Reconstruction; Race Riots; U.S. Army and Reconstruction.

## Further Reading

Hollandsworth, James G. *An Absolute Massacre: The New Orleans Race Riot of July 30, 1866.* Baton Rouge: Louisiana State University Press, 2001.

Rable, George C. *But There Was No Peace: The Role of Violence in the Politics of Reconstruction.* Athens: University of Georgia Press, 1984.

Riddleberger, Patrick W. *1866: The Critical Year Revisited.* Carbondale: Southern Illinois University Press, 1979.

# NEW SOUTH

The New South referred to the post-1877 period, after "redemption," when white Conservatives in the South attempted to recover from the changes wrought by Civil War, Congressional Reconstruction, and Radical Republican control. Some states moved forward with progressive initiatives in industrialization and in agricultural development, while most moved backward in the areas of social development and African American rights.

Prominent Southern journalists such as Henry Grady of the *Atlanta Constitution* and Richard Edmonds of the *Manufacturers' Record* pushed for Southern white rule, sectional reconciliation, and racial separation. Southern and Northern bankers, merchant planters, and industrialists found support and (in some places) investment as states tried to reform single-crop plantation economies. What the New South did not do was challenge old racisms or systematic methods of siphoning wealth and power from the underprivileged classes, including yeomen (small farmers) and poor whites. As one might expect, African Americans suffered the most during this period. Despite the experience of emancipation and reconstruction, blacks were at the mercy of Southern white Conservatives, who obliterated black civil rights and their political power, assailed them with violence, and reduced them to abject poverty. At the heart of the New South remained an economy, government, and social life based on the old system of white supremacy.

By 1877, the Bourbons or Redeemers (Southern white Conservatives) had reclaimed political control for native whites throughout the South. The Bourbons differed from state to state but largely consisted of old planters, wealthy bankers, merchant planters, and a few industrialists. Once in power, however, Southern Conservatives were split as to what to do next. Some wanted to go back to life as it used to be in the Old South (or antebellum South), a life based on agriculture and slavery. The prominent "cash crops" were tobacco, rice, sugar, and cotton. Little else was grown for export. Cotton was the most sought-after crop because it was the cheapest to grow, and the most profitable. On the other hand, it exhausted the land (although not as swiftly as tobacco), required a great deal of labor and land, and had lost its value during the war: The Confederacy's self-imposed embargo (designed to solicit foreign help) backfired, and many foreign customers turned to new sources. Other Southerners realized that progress required change; Southerners needed money to resuscitate their war-ravaged communities; the time of slavery was over, and they needed to modify their economy for the new reality.

Rather than succumb to the absolute industrialism of their neighbors in the North, Southerners incorporated industry into their agrarian way of life. In doing so, they solved an old problem. In the antebellum South, landowners had relied upon the North for transportation and processing. Now, states and individuals invested in ships, new roads, and railroad systems, to allow planters to trade directly with the North and with European markets. They also built factories and mills to prepare their crops, thus controlling the prices and production themselves. Southern whites constructed new cotton mills, tobacco factories, and wool and rayon mills. These factories led to the development of new towns, and semi-urban areas began to appear across what had been a sparely populated agrarian region. The labor force consisted of former yeomen farmers and poor whites; blacks were rarely permitted to work in factories, and very few lived in the towns. The mill owner provided each town with a company store, a church, houses, and other amenities of life. He paid the salaries of all the constituents in the town, including the police and preacher, as well as the workers. While poor whites eagerly embraced the opportunity, yeomen farmers were reluctant to give up their classic independence and self-reliance; many had no choice, because of debts accrued during the war and increased taxes during Reconstruction. Not surprisingly, the South during this time did not experience the onslaught of foreign immigration, labor complaints and strikes, and urban industrial turmoil that shocked the North. Wealthy Southerners exploited lower-class whites just as landowners had exploited their slaves, and class divisions were as rigid as ever. Southern industry and economy bloomed under these conditions.

Increased access to markets, new factories and mills, and technological experimentation helped encourage the development of agriculture and related new ideas for making money. Cotton eventually regained its status as a profitable source of income for the South, helped by new fertilizers, alternating crop rotations, and expanding the product to new fields in Texas and Oklahoma. Other experiments in agriculture yielded more varieties of tobacco and sugarcane, and many planters ventured into nuts, grains, fruits, and vegetables; Mississippi established creameries and Tennessee supplied poultry. Recognizing the national expansion in population and the coming of the Industrial Revolution, Southerners prospered from rich sources of minerals, lumber, and oil; the iconic image of Appalachian iron and coal mining began here, as did the birth of Birmingham, Alabama, as a center of steel production. Texas, Oklahoma, Louisiana, Arkansas, Kentucky, West Virginia, and Tennessee sunk oil wells as the nation's need for fuel and lubricants accelerated.

How to secure labor after the abolition of slavery was the chief concern of planters and large landholders. The New South inaugurated systems of tenant farming and sharecropping. Tenant farmers (tenant, as in "renter") paid landowners for the right to grow crops on a piece of property owned by another. They might have their own livestock and tools, and made enough profit to pay their rent. Tenant farmers were largely comprised of members of the antebellum yeoman class, who before the war lived independently, growing enough food to feed themselves and their families on land they owned. Sharecroppers were different. Lacking and money—or perhaps even tools—they farmed land for the landowner, in exchange for a share of crops which they sold on their own. Many former slaves—and their descendants—tended to be sharecroppers.

Both systems were barely above unfree labor, as the tenant farmer and sharecropper stayed indebted to the landowner, from whom they received the credit needed to purchase goods, seeds, even food. Tenants and croppers were often forced to work until they paid off their debt. Moreover, blacks and whites rarely accumulated enough money to pay off their debts or purchase property, and so became tied to the land and the landowner. All of these groups—including the landholders themselves—fell under the power of the newest class in the economic chain, the merchants and bankers. Merchants and bankers provided loans to landowners, who possessed the plots legally, but had little in the way of disposable income or liquid cash (another reason paying workers with a "share" of the "crop" made sense). Loan rates were exorbitant, and could range from 40 to 100 percent of the amount of the loan. As a result, merchants and bankers repositioned themselves at the top of the economic pyramid in the New South.

The objectives of the Bourbons were to eradicate the region's debt, maintain their own economic interests, and protect white dominance. Like politicians of the Old South, leaders of the New South claimed they sought a government with limited powers—a "laissez-faire" government—which left things largely alone; this was really a myth, as both in the Old and New South leaders used the government to restrict African American rights and promote planter economic interests. They did not want a government that intervened directly into their affairs, especially with regard to taxes—since they carried the brunt of that expense. As a result, Bourbons drastically cut state taxes, which had a devastating impact on the schools established during Reconstruction.

The Bourbons achieved many of their goals. H. H. Riddleberger organized the Readjuster Party, whose main concern was to reduce the South's debt, which had mounted to a total of more than $140 million. The party was able to repudiate most of this debt. Nevertheless, the Bourbons showed no consideration for the impoverished classes, the laborer, or black rights. This focus is still debated, as to whether it was a selfish class action or a necessary approach for the good of the region at large.

Certainly the biggest political losers were African Americans. Southern white Conservatives throughout the region established an array of discriminatory tests and requirements and even rewrote state constitutions, all to disfranchise black voters. Many whites would be eliminated as well, prompting some states and localities to construct the "grandfather clauses," provisions that exempted voters from tests if their grandfathers had voted. This would preserve the white electorate but erase the black one.

There were challenges, of course. In 1875, the Farmer's Alliance formed in Texas to provide a voice for oppressed farmers. Although not a political party, many members of the Farmer's Alliance eventually joined a political movement, the Populist Party. The Populist Party (or the "People's Party," as it was also called) was the most significant political opposition to the Bourbons, and one of the most exciting third-party developments in American political history. Established in the 1890s, the Populists represented a mass number of disempowered farmer. Although predominately white, the Populists did extend some support and protection to blacks. The reigning white Democratic Conservatives defeated the Populists in the 1894, 1896, and 1898 elections by means of ballot fraud, violence, and intimidation. They also purchased speakers and votes. The Populist Party collapsed in 1896, partly due to the numerous defeats, and partly by aligning with Democrats on the "white line," preferring to support an all-white government. Southerners were adamantly opposed to returning to the mixed-race governments, which had occurred during Radical Reconstruction.

Not a coincidence, also in the 1890s, Mississippi, South Carolina, and Louisiana enacted laws and new constitutions to exclude blacks from voting. Starting in 1900, five more states would institute similar laws. These laws, along with violence and intimidation, reduced the number of black politicians to almost nothing in state and federal governments.

Blacks were the hardest hit by the retrenchment of the New South. After Reconstruction, neither the federal nor state governments offered blacks any protection or support. During slavery, some masters would at least provide protection for their property. Blacks had now attained emancipation and education, but as a whole, they remained landless, impoverished, and vulnerable to oppressive laws and violence. Just between 1889 and 1918, there were 3,000 lynchings in the South and the North. There were positive developments, such as education, the right to marry, and the flourishing of black churches. With the exception of designated "black only" facilities, blacks could go where they pleased. As a result, large numbers of blacks from the South moved north in search of more and better opportunities. Some went west to be cowboys or joined the army as "Buffalo soldiers." Others moved to larger and more progressive Southern towns, spurred by the hope that life was more than the weary moil of sharecropping and the threat of violence. Some blacks even migrated to Africa and set up colonies, such as Liberia.

Black communities also avoided the problems inherent in the rise of the Jim Crow system of segregation, one of the most notorious aspects of the New South. Although many white and black Republicans had hoped to endow blacks with full rights and equal opportunities, Conservative whites created a world of forced separation under Jim Crow laws. Under these laws, stores, parks, hospitals, theaters, bus stations, and restaurants were divided into sections for either "whites only" or "blacks only." More often than not, "black only" facilities and sections were inferior to the white ones. Whites insisted upon separation because they believed blacks and whites should not mingle and could never coexist peaceably. The ideology of the South, born and bred in slavery and white supremacy, needed physical, tangible, observable signs of white dominance and black subordination. Jim Crow laws were the simplest way of reflecting that relationship.

Blacks responded to hostility, repression, and oppression in many ways. With more than 1 million members, the Colored Farmer's Alliance was one of the largest black organizations in U.S. history. Another, the National Association for the Advancement of Colored People, founded in 1909, became a powerful organization that rose to challenge racism in the South and abroad.

*Gladys L. Knight*

**See also:** Ku Klux Klan (KKK); Labor Systems; Race Riots; White League.

## Further Reading

Ayers, Edward L. *The Promise of the New South: Life after Reconstruction.* New York: Oxford University Press, 1992.

Crockett, Norman L. *The Black Towns.* Lawrence: Regents Press of Kansas, 1979.

Woodward, C. Vann. *Origins of the New South, 1877–1913*. Baton Rouge: Louisiana State University Press, 1951.

Wright, Gavin. *Old South, New South: Revolutions in the Southern Economy since the Civil War*. Baton Rouge: Louisiana State University Press, 2005.

## NICHOLLS, FRANCIS REDDING TILLOU (1834–1912)

Francis R. T. Nicholls was the governor of Louisiana whose term from 1877 to 1880 marked the end of Congressional Reconstruction in the state. He later served a second term as governor and as a justice on the state supreme court.

Born in Donaldsonville, Louisiana, on August 20, 1834, Nicholls graduated from the U.S. Military Academy at West Point in 1855, but resigned his commission in 1856 to practice law. At the beginning of the Civil War, Nicholls enlisted in the Confederate army and eventually rose to brigadier general. He lost an arm at Winchester in 1862 and a foot at Chancellorsville in 1863 and fulfilled administrative duties for the rest of the war. Following the war, Nicholls resumed his law practice and for most of Reconstruction avoided politics, but in 1876, he decided to run for governor, and "all that was left" of him won the Democratic Party's nomination.

A double-amputee from his Confederate service, Francis Redding Tillou Nicholls became governor of Louisiana in 1877, when the "compromise of 1877" abandoned the Republican state government. (Library of Congress)

The 1876 state and presidential elections in Louisiana were rife with intimidation, vote fraud, and violence, especially against the state's black population, and both Nicholls and Republican gubernatorial candidate Stephen B. Packard claimed victory. Rival legislatures convened in early 1877, and the state's presidential electoral votes were disputed between Democrat Samuel J. Tilden and Republican Rutherford B. Hayes. The Compromise of 1877 gave Hayes the presidency while recognizing Nicholls and the Democratic legislature, thereby "redeeming" Louisiana from Republican rule.

Although Nicholls was personally honest and displayed the patrician's concern for the public good, his notoriously corrupt administration inaugurated the era of Bourbon rule in Louisiana that lasted well into the 20th century. The Louisiana State Lottery Company—a private corporation operating as a state-chartered monopoly and shielded by state treasurer Edward A. Burke—openly bribed state legislators and other public officials, while other aides operated, and profited from the state's infamously brutal convict-lease system. Fiscally conservative, Nicholls cut taxes and social services, including education; and although he eschewed the racial extremism of other Conservatives, he was nonetheless firmly committed to white supremacy. Yet, Nicholls's opposition to the lottery and to other excesses of Bourbon rule made him many enemies, and when Louisiana Conservatives met in 1879 to write a new constitution, Nicholls's term was shortened by one year. Opposition to the lottery continued to grow, however, and Nicholls was elected governor again in 1888 on an anti-lottery platform.

After his term as governor ended, Nicholls served as chief justice of the Louisiana Supreme Court from 1892 to 1904 and as an associate justice from 1904 until his retirement in 1911, years that saw legal segregation and black disfranchisement implemented in the state. Nicholls died on January 4, 1912.

*John C. Rodrigue*

***See also:*** Black Suffrage; Elections of 1876; Jim Crow Laws; Redemption; Suffrage.

## Further Reading

Hair, William Ivy. *Bourbonism and Agrarian Protest: Louisiana Politics, 1877–1900.* Baton Rouge: Louisiana State University Press, 1969.

Taylor, Joe Gray. *Louisiana Reconstructed: 1863–1877.* Baton Rouge: Louisiana State University Press, 1974.

# NORTH CAROLINA

The postwar period offered North Carolina a ripe opportunity for change because of the war's heavy toll on the state. Among the last states to leave the Union, North Carolina made a profound contribution to the Confederacy. More than 120,000 white North Carolinians served in the Confederate army, which exceeded the number of soldiers from any other Southern state. More than 40,000 of these sacrificed their lives for the cause, but secession's cost could not be measured in blood alone.

The surrender of Ft. Hatteras on the state's east coast provoked an early effort to restore North Carolina to the Union. President Abraham Lincoln appointed Edward Stanly, a former state politician, as military governor, and directed him to begin moving the state toward restoration in the Union. Stanly proved a disappointment. He had tenuous control over a small area around New Bern in the eastern coastal region but no power over the rest of the state. Even more problematic, Stanly steadfastly refused to evolve with the Union war effort. The rapid growth of New Bern's black population—which doubled during the war's first two years—amplified Stanly's discomfiture with the policies of a president drifting toward emancipation. In May 1862, he closed schools established for slaves because educating blacks violated state law. When Lincoln signed the Emancipation Proclamation on January 1, 1863, the military governor realized that he could not restore his native state to the Union as it existed in 1860. His resignation two weeks later ended wartime Reconstruction in North Carolina.

Lincoln's death and Confederate general Joseph E. Johnston's surrender at Durham Station placed the South's future in the hands of Andrew Johnson. On May 29, 1865, Johnson initiated his Reconstruction policy and appointed as North Carolina's provisional governor William W. Holden, the controversial newspaper editor and peace leader routed by fiery Zebulon Vance in the state's 1864 gubernatorial election. The president ordered the new governor to convene a meeting to draft a new state constitution consistent with emancipation and the other consequences of Union victory. Holden complied quickly and scheduled an election for delegates to a constitutional convention, which opened in October 1865. When the convention finally adjourned in June 1866, it had created the office of lieutenant governor and set white population rather than county wealth as the basis of representation in the legislature. Popular focus, however, was on its dealings with the war's aftershocks. Resolutions repealing secession and abolishing slavery passed with little difficulty. Much more divisive was the resolution introduced by Thomas Settle Jr., a Democrat who later denounced the Confederacy and joined the peace movement, to repudiate the state's war debt. Many North Carolinians feared that the debt's negation would deliver a fatal blow to the beleaguered state banks and public schools. A majority of the delegates resolved to table the proposal without acting on it, but Johnson's insistence on the debt's negation forced the delegates' compliance. The constitution itself did not survive the controversy; it was defeated by popular referendum in August 1866.

While obeying the president's directives, Holden simultaneously cultivated a political base that might keep him in the governor's mansion beyond his provisional term. One way in which he molded support was through presidential pardons. As Johnson's handpicked governor, Holden had significant influence over the executive pardons of leading confederates and others excluded from a general amnesty granted by the president. The provisional governor backed the petitions from many former secessionists but ignored applications filed by high-ranking Conservatives and former Unionist Whigs who he feared could defeat him in a popular election; so he supported their continued disqualification from public office and disfranchisement from voting.

The provisional governor's labors produced a loose political coalition that can best be described as "anti-Confederate." At its core, the provisional governor's support derived from the state's consistent Unionists and peace supporters. They also hoped to garner the votes of poorer whites resentful of wartime policies, such as conscription and the tax-in-kind, which leveled a heavy burden on them and their families. Some upper-class white men also joined the anti-confederates because they felt that resistance to the war's consequences would only intensify Northern demands for reunion. All that held the anti-confederates together was bitterness lingering from the war and a belief that Johnson's lenient Reconstruction policy was the best settlement term they could expect.

The anti-confederates opposed the Conservatives for the first time in an organized manner as white North Carolinians chose new state officials in December 1865. Attention focused on the gubernatorial election, pitting Holden against state treasurer Jonathan Worth of the Conservative Party. His public opposition to secession coupled with his dutiful service during the war made him the perfect foil to Holden's outspoken wartime opposition. Despite being relatively unknown in the western part of the state, Worth rode an overwhelming majority in the eastern and Piedmont counties to victory. Allies of the provisional governor won control of the state legislature, but their leader's defeat was a setback.

Black North Carolinians faced an even more unsettled future. Concerned that the freedmen were unprepared for the responsibility of citizenship, Holden, as provisional governor, called for a system to control the freedpeople who white believed were unprepared for freedom. State legislators responded by passing the Black Codes. The commission advocated placing the former slaves on a level comparable to antebellum free blacks. As enacted, the codes included vagrancy laws, apprenticeship standards, and other provisions that limited civil rights and directly discriminated against the state's black population. In particular, the legislature wrestled with blacks' legal rights. Four days of debate centered on black citizens' rights in civil courts. Legislators decided ultimately to allow black testimony in legal disputes between blacks, but never in cases involving a white person. Juries would also remain lily-white under the new statutes.

Black North Carolinians found an ally in the Bureau of Refugees, Freedmen, and Abandoned Lands. Created during the war's final months to oversee the South's transition from a slave to free labor society, the Freedmen's Bureau (as it was popularly known) provided the former slaves with rations, clothing, and legal protection. They supervised the chaotic labor system and negotiated contracts between whites and blacks, protected the former slaves' wages in contests with white employers, and assisted black schools. After the Black Codes passed, most agents' work consisted of legal matters. Wherever civil courts were interrupted or blacks' rights were denied, the bureau intervened to guarantee justice to the freedmen. In some cases, this entailed acting as legal counsel, but more frequently it involved hearing the black testimony barred by state law.

Black North Carolinians pursued a more radical agenda at a state convention in October 1866. Organized ostensibly to promote education, this convention called for political and economic rights. No longer willing to wait for whites—a majority of whom opposed the extension of basic rights to the freedpeople—to come around, the representatives called for universal male suffrage. Even more galling to Conservative whites, the assembly aligned itself with Northern Radical Republicans. Blacks had lost whatever faith they had in their white neighbors and looked increasingly to the bureau and the federal government for help. Delegates applauded Congress's approval of the Freedmen's Bureau Bills and the Civil Rights Act, as well as the proposed Fourteenth Amendment assuring equal protection under the law to all Americans regardless of color. This more radical tone foreshadowed the future of Reconstruction in North Carolina.

Worth accepted emancipation as a consequence of defeat, but despised the social redefinition it engendered. Like many members of the antebellum white ruling class, Worth wanted to restore North Carolina to the Union swiftly to maintain the power of the former property-holding white elite. He fought tirelessly with federal authorities that stood in the way of that goal, especially the Freedmen's Bureau. Agents across North Carolina observed and occasionally overturned civil decisions where the state disallowed black testimony. Worth defended the civil courts vigorously in disputes with the Freedmen's Bureau. When the agent in Buncombe County reversed the conviction of a freedman for assaulting a white man, the judge resigned in protest. The governor was livid. Worth believed that bureau interference threatened to cripple state courts by alienating its "best" judges.

Attempts to restore the antebellum status quo encountered another obstacle when Congress submitted the Fourteenth Amendment to the states for ratification. The amendment's extension of due process to blacks aggravated many white North Carolinians. Worth could not stop the amendment's passage, but he and his party refused to sanction it. The legislature adhered to the popular mood, and President Johnson's advice, and rejected the amendment. For his role, Worth converted his opposition to the amendment into electoral success. He easily defeated Alfred Dockery, a reluctant candidate selected by Holden, to win a second term in 1866. Rejection of the Fourteenth Amendment by every former Confederate state, except Tennessee, convinced Congress that the South remained unrepentant and unprepared to resume its responsibilities in the Union. In March 1867, Republicans passed the Military Reconstruction Acts creating military districts out of the defeated states. North and South Carolina comprised the Second Military District headed first by Maj. Gen. Daniel Sickles and later by Maj. Gen. E.R.S. Canby; primary duties were to supervise voter registration—which would include blacks—and the creation of a new state constitution that recognized black suffrage.

Black men's inclusion on the voter rolls contributed to another political shift. After their pitiful showing in the 1866 elections, the remnants of the anti-confederates assembled in Raleigh to assess their political future. When they emerged from Holden's office, they announced the creation of North Carolina's Republican Party. More importantly, their alignment with the national Republicans meant that they had adopted a new strategy. State Republicans abandoned their earlier opposition to blacks' political participation and actively recruited them into the party. The military authorities worked with the Freedmen's Bureau and state Republicans to register voters white and black, prepare a new constitution, and schedule new state elections. In particular, it was the constitution of 1868 that defined military Reconstruction. Denounced by Conservatives due to its control by black and white Republicans, the new constitution enacted significant change to the original 1776 state document that had only been amended once, in 1835. Beyond the creation of new offices like the lieutenant governor, the constitution was most noted for its Democratic reforms. It reallocated membership in the legislature based on population instead of wealth and increased the number of elective offices markedly. Both local officials and state judges were to be chosen by the people.

Tensions ran high during the 1868 campaign season. Conservatives opposed the constitution as the product of black political domination and Republican rascality, but their efforts to defeat it failed. Not only did the constitution pass but also the Conservatives' old nemesis Holden won his first regular term as governor. Dismayed with their inability to overcome the Republicans, the Conservatives cast about for a new direction. Around 1869, the Ku Klux Klan, which began as a social organization in Tennessee, entered the state. Klan terrorism threatened to undermine the Republican administration. At first Holden tried to negotiate an end to the violence, but atrocities in Alamance and Caswell counties in 1870 forced the governor to implement martial law and organized a militia under the command of George W. Kirk. The militia suppressed the Klan in both counties, but overzealous militiamen led to cries of "tyranny" by the Conservatives. Worse, federal judges issued writs for the release of prisoners Holden was holding for military trial. The so-called Kirk-Holden War ended with the release of prisoners and the disbanding of the militia.

Amid Holden's struggles with the Klan, North Carolinians went to the polls on August 4, 1870. The Klan's campaign of intimidation, plus Holden's alienating of many Moderates, delivered the state legislature to the Conservatives. Once in office, they charged Holden with abuse of authority and on March 22, 1871, impeached and removed him from office.

Holden's permanent departure from politics destroyed neither the Ku Klux Klan nor the Republican Party. Although Kirk's men quelled the disturbance in Alamance and Caswell, the organization's activities soared after Holden's political downfall. Major attacks and scores of killings motivated Congress to pass the Enforcement Acts in 1871, which empowered President Ulysses S. Grant to use federal troops to restore order. More important, it gave the president the authority to suspend the writ of habeas corpus. Federal forces arrested hundreds of suspected Klansmen and indicted more than 1,400 men. Randolph A. Shotwell, a newspaper editor in western North Carolina, received the harshest sentence handed out under federal law—six years in prison and a $5,000 fine—for his role as Rutherford County's Klan leader.

Despite the violence, state Republicans continued to persevere. Lieutenant Governor Todd R. Caldwell stood for reelection on his own after serving the remainder of Holden's term; he won the 1872 election by only 2,000 votes out of nearly 200,000 ballots cast, and Conservatives retained the legislature. Since the governor was now largely powerless, the legislature turned to reshaping the state. In 1875, Conservatives summoned delegates to Raleigh to revise the constitution. The convention banned secret societies (including both the Ku Klux Klan and the Republican Union League), limited legislators' expenses, segregated public schools, and banned interracial marriages. The convention also rescinded some 1868 reforms, by taking away direct election of local officials.

Reconstruction finished with a bang in North Carolina as two of the state's most powerful politicians squared off in the 1876 gubernatorial election. After deferring the nomination in 1872, Civil War governor Zeb Vance accepted the Democratic nomination—the Conservatives formally united with the national Democratic Party in 1876—four years later. Opposing him was Settle, who had served on the state legislature and Supreme Court since the 1865 Convention. The candidates crisscrossed the state, engaging in dozens of high-profile debates. Vance blamed Republicans for corruption, and criticized Carolinians for betraying their race by aligning with Northern Radicals to impose black "domination" on white Carolinians. Settle countered by making Vance's Confederate past a point of contention. He accused the war governor of enacting policies that discriminated against poor whites during the Civil War. Considering the emotional nature of the issues, the contest was remarkably peaceful. When the votes were tallied, however, the Conservatives had crushed the Republicans, winning the governorship a majority in the legislature, and seven out of eight congressional seats.

This clash of political titans ended Reconstruction in North Carolina. The Democrats regained the governorship, the last piece of the state government they needed to regain complete control of the state's power apparatus. For most of the next century, the Democrats controlled the state government, but Reconstruction revolutionized the disposition of power in the state. As a result of the Civil War and Reconstruction, lower-class whites and blacks possessed greater access to power than ever in the state. Black voters played a critical role in elections and party politics, while also asserting greater personal control over their lives and their families than ever before. The Republican Party also remained a fixture from that point on, although with varying degrees of influence. Prior to the Civil War, power rested firmly in the hands of a propertied white elite. Vance's election seemingly marked a resurgence of that class, but circumstances had changed. Power was more accessible for all levels of society than ever before. For that reason, Reconstruction was a pivotal period in North Carolina's history.

*Steven E. Nash*

***See also:*** Amnesty Proclamations; Bourbons; Enforcement Acts (1870, 1871, 1875); Jim Crow Laws; National Union Party (1864); New South; Presidential Reconstruction; Redemption; U.S. Army and Reconstruction.

## Further Reading

Alexander, Roberta Sue. *North Carolina Faces the Freedmen: Race Relations during Presidential Reconstruction, 1865–67*. Durham, NC: Duke University Press, 1985.

Escott, Paul D. *Many Excellent People: Power and Privilege in North Carolina, 1850–1900*. Chapel Hill: University of North Carolina Press, 1985.

Harris, William C. *William Woods Holden: Firebrand of North Carolina Politics*. Baton Rouge: Louisiana State University Press, 1987.

McKinney, Gordon B. *Zeb Vance: North Carolina's Civil War Governor and Gilded Age Political Leader*. Chapel Hill: University of North Carolina Press, 2004.

Zuber, Richard L. *Jonathan Worth: Biography of a Southern Unionist*. Chapel Hill: University of North Carolina Press, 1965.

Zuber, Richard L. *North Carolina during Reconstruction*. Raleigh: North Carolina State Department of Archives and History, 1969.

# O

## ORR, JAMES L. (1822–1873)

James Lawrence Orr was born in Pendleton District, South Carolina, near the upcountry town of Anderson. He attended the University of Virginia briefly, read law in South Carolina, and began practicing in Anderson in 1843. Orr also took up planting, and edited *The Anderson Gazette*. Orr served in the South Carolina House of Representatives from 1844 to 1848 and the U.S. House of Representatives from 1849 to 1859, including a stint as Speaker of the House from 1857 to 1859. He consistently advocated industrialization and economic diversification for South Carolina, and pushed for more political clout for the upcountry portion of the state.

Although a secessionist in the early 1850s, Orr grew unsure of the best way to protect Southern society. By July 1860, he cautiously advocated secession in the event of a Republican president but against South Carolina seceding alone. Following the election of Abraham Lincoln, he attended the South Carolina Secession Convention in December 1860 and supported secession. In 1861, Orr organized and commanded a Confederate regiment known as Orr's Rifles, and later served in the Confederate Provisional Congress and the Confederate Senate.

After the Confederacy's surrender, Orr quickly seized the opportunity to play a role in South Carolina politics. When President Andrew Johnson set forth his restoration program in May 1865, Orr became a delegate to South Carolina's September convention, and that October narrowly defeated Confederate cavalry hero Wade Hampton for governor, even though Hampton refused his own nomination. Johnson's appointed provisional governor, Benjamin Perry, stepped aside, and Orr was inaugurated on November 29.

As governor, Orr demonstrated the moderation he had shown in the antebellum period. Although he signed into law the legislature's Black Codes, he later urged lawmakers to modify them and successfully urged Gen. Daniel Sickles to suspend their enforcement. He also advocated qualified suffrage for black men, fearing (fairly prophetically) that the state's failure to act would result in the federal government imposing universal male suffrage.

Despite his efforts at moderation, Orr's policy was not progressive enough for the Republican-controlled Congress. In December 1865, Congress refused to seat South Carolina's newly elected members, and later insisted that former Confederate states ratify the Fourteenth Amendment before being readmitted to the Union. Orr agreed with President Johnson, that this demand was unconstitutional and degrading to the South, and so advocated rejection of the amendment. In March 1867, Congress passed the first two Military

A native South Carolinian, James L. Orr was a moderate in politics who opposed secession and supported minimal black rights. He served as the state's governor from 1865 to 1868. (Library of Congress)

Reconstruction Acts, requiring the former Confederate states to hold new constitutional conventions under universal male suffrage and to ratify the Fourteenth Amendment. Orr became, in effect, a provisional governor, supervised by the U.S. Army, until a new state constitution went into operation.

Under Congressional Reconstruction, the Republican Party gained control of the state. After the April 1868 elections, Orr gave up the governor's seat to a former Union general, carpetbagger Robert K. Scott, formerly of Ohio. Orr then joined the state's Republican Party, believing that native whites must do so to retain their leadership of South Carolina. The Republican legislature gave him the judgeship of the eighth South Carolina judicial circuit, which he held from 1868 to 1870. Many native white Democrats, however, now considered him a scalawag—a traitor. By 1872, Orr had grown disgusted with the scandals afflicting the Republican regime in the state and turned his back on the party. In December of that year, President Ulysses S. Grant appointed Orr as minister to Russia. Weakened by a persistent cold and the Russian winter, he died in St Petersburg on May 6, 1873, at the age of 50. He was buried in Anderson.

*John (Rod) Andrew Jr.*

*See also:* Amnesty Proclamations; Civil Rights Act of 1866; Presidential Reconstruction.

## Further Reading

Leemhuis, Roger P. *James L. Orr and the Sectional Conflict*. Washington, DC: University Press of America, 1979.

Sobel, Robert, and John Raimo, eds. *Biographical Directory of the Governors of the United States*. Westport, CT: Meckler Books, 1978.

# P

## PACKARD, STEPHEN B. (1842–1922)

Stephen B. Packard, an influential Republican carpetbagger in Reconstruction Louisiana, was born in North Auburn, Maine. Packard served as a captain in the Twelfth Maine Volunteer Infantry Regiment in the Civil War. After the war, he set up a law practice in New Orleans, and by 1868 became a fixture in the state's Republican Party. Despite (or perhaps because of) Democratic Party criticisms, his prominence increased, and in 1871, President Ulysses S. Grant appointed him U.S. marshal in Louisiana. As federal marshal, Packard picked his deputies and assigned them throughout the state.

During the 1870s, Packard led the so-called Custom House Ring within the state Republican Party and wielded considerable influence without holding elective office. Basing his faction in the federal Custom House in New Orleans, then the state's capital, the marshal opposed Republican governor Henry Clay Warmoth, who had been elected under the Congressional Reconstruction program in 1868. In fact, Packard pushed for Warmoth's impeachment. When the state legislature removed Warmoth in 1872, an African American, Lieutenant Governor P.B.S. Pinchback, served out the last few days of Warmoth's term.

In the 1872 gubernatorial campaign, Packard acted as campaign manager for Republican candidate William Pitt Kellogg. When Kellogg was elected governor, Packard served as the chairman of the Republican Party's state central committee. Four years later, in 1876, he ran for his first major office as the Republican nominee for governor. His opponent, former Confederate general Francis T. Nicholls, campaigned on a platform of "redemption," or "returning the state to white, Democratic, home rule." Both parties used fraud, intimidation, and violence in one of the worst elections in Louisiana and American history. Both parties claimed that their candidate had won the governorship, but the state's official Returning Board, dominated by Republicans, favored Packard; Democrats created their own board that endorsed Nicholls. This impasse produced a bizarre result: Packard and Nicholls were both inaugurated in separate ceremonies, leaving the choice of who would be governor up to the next president of the United States—Democrat Samuel J. Tilden or Republican Rutherford B. Hayes—but the presidency was also in doubt due to the controversial national election of 1876. Congress created an extraordinary federal electoral commission to determine the outcome of the disputed national election. In the meantime, in February 1877, an unidentified assassin unsuccessfully tried to murder Packard.

As a part of the complex bargaining that produced the so-called Compromise of 1877, the Republican Hayes became president and recognized Nicholls as Louisiana's governor.

Packard had little choice but to capitulate. As a consolation, Hayes appointed Packard to serve as U.S. consul in Liverpool, England.

*Joseph G. Dawson III*

*See also:* Constitutional Conventions; Military Reconstruction Acts (1867–1868).

### Further Reading

Dawson, Joseph G. *Army Generals and Reconstruction: Louisiana, 1862–1877.* Baton Rouge: Louisiana State University Press, 1982.

Taylor, Joe Gray. *Louisiana Reconstructed, 1863–1877.* Baton Rouge: Louisiana State University Press, 1974.

## PARDONS

During the Civil War and Reconstruction, Abraham Lincoln, Andrew Johnson, and Congress issued several amnesty proclamations to those who had been part of the Confederacy. An amnesty is a blanket forgiveness that removes any restrictions on a person's abilities

As a result of the war, Presidents Lincoln and Johnson, and the U.S. Congress, barred many Confederates from participating in politics. Persons of high rank or wealth needed to appeal directly to the Executive for a pardon, as seen in this sketch. (Library of Congress)

or qualifications. Pardons are directed more toward a specific individual than an entire group. Like an amnesty, a pardon forgives some past indiscretion, and allows the recipient to reclaim the rights and privileges of citizenship. After the war, former confederates faced the possibility of land confiscation and voting and office-holding prohibitions, making individual pardons critically important. Also like amnesty, the issue of pardons—who held the ultimate authority in dispensing them, who should receive them, and what criteria should be used in that judgment—became a hotly debated topic between the president and Congress.

Presidents Lincoln and Johnson held many similar views, including the belief that the Union and its states were indestructible. Thus, the war was between people, and people were disloyal, not the political entities or the states. Also, both believed that the U.S. Constitution conferred pardoning power on the president, so it was he who held ultimate authority in issuing pardons. As the war drew to a close, Lincoln sought a way to cajole confederates, speed an end to the war, and create a way to return as many states to the Union as possible.

On December 8, 1863, Lincoln issued his Proclamation of Amnesty and Reconstruction, also called the Ten Percent Plan. The proclamation provided a full pardon to all those who had participated in the rebellion except Confederate civil or diplomatic agents, those who left the judiciary to aid the Confederacy, all Confederate officers above the rank of colonel in the army or lieutenant in the navy, all who left congressional seats to join the Confederacy, all who resigned federal army or navy commissions, and all who had mistreated black troops or their officers. It allowed seceded states to reestablish governments after 10 percent of the voters had taken a loyalty oath. The Radical Republicans opposed Lincoln's amnesty proclamation and introduced the Wade-Davis bill in 1864, which required 50 percent of the voters to take an ironclad oath before a state could be readmitted (an ironclad oath required the swearing of past loyalty as well as future loyalty, thus many ex-confederates were denied any chance at amnesty except through direct, individual pardon).

The struggle between the executive office and the legislative branch continued when Andrew Johnson was sworn into office. On May 29, 1865, Johnson issued his own Proclamation of Amnesty and Reconstruction. His proclamation was similar to Lincoln's, providing full pardon to those who took the loyalty oath but did not provide a percentage necessary to reestablish statehood. His proclamation included all the exemptions provided in Lincoln's proclamation and added exemptions for all Confederate governors, those who aided the Confederacy abroad, all who destroyed U.S. commerce at sea and from Canada, those who violated the amnesty oath provided for in the December 8, 1863, proclamation, and all those who owned more than $20,000 worth of property. Additional proclamations in 1865 and 1868 eventually abolished all the exemptions; in 1868, the Supreme Court ruled the ironclad oath unconstitutional.

The specific issue of pardons generated as much controversy as the broader amnesty. All those who found themselves in the "exceptions" under Johnson's plan could apply for a pardon from the president directly. This led to pandemonium in the pardon office and State Department, as thousands of applications flowed in—often assisted via a blossoming "pardon broker" industry that shepherded the paperwork through the byzantine governmental bureaucracy. Johnson granted pardons so freely that critics charged the exception clauses had no weight whatsoever; critics claimed they were merely designed to feed Johnson's ego by forcing former high-ranking officials to grovel at the president's feet, entirely dependent on his goodwill for a restoration of civil, political, and property rights.

In 1867, as Congressional Republicans wrestled control of the Reconstruction process away from Johnson, the impact of Johnson's pardons became murky. Although the states were placed under military and congressional supervision, Johnson believed this did not nullify the effect of an executive pardon, and he continued to issue pardons. When the bulk became too massive, he resorted to more sweeping gestures, such as his amnesty proclamations in 1868. Congressional Republicans used the U.S. Army in the South and the Fourteenth Amendment to counter some of the president's liberal pardoning tendency, as the amendment disfranchised some former confederates, and the on-scene military commanders were empowered to remove or deny office to civilians. But once states were readmitted to the Union, Congress had little ability to bar former confederates from their rights. Southern Republicans, who could agree in theory with the idea of punishing traitors and eliminating political opposition found the reality much different. In fact, many black and white Republicans in the South realized the need to reconcile with former rebels and developed local alliances that would outlast fleeting federal support.

Complex and unprecedented, the topic of postwar pardons touches on the nature of the citizen, the relationship between Congress and the president, the definition of treason and criminal, and even the nature of the Union itself. It was one more feature of the Reconstruction period that made the era one of the most contentious and interesting in American history.

*Catherine Anyaso*

**See also:** Black Suffrage; Civil Rights; Congressional Reconstruction; Constitutional Conventions; Democratic Party; Joint Committee on Reconstruction; Presidential Reconstruction; Republicans, Liberal; Suffrage.

## Further Reading

Dorris, Jonathan T. *Pardon and Amnesty under Lincoln and Johnson.* Chapel Hill: University of North Carolina Press, 1953.

Hyman, Harold M. *Era of the Oath: Northern Loyalty Tests during the Civil War and Reconstruction.* Philadelphia: University of Pennsylvania Press, 1954.

## PARSONS, LEWIS E. (1817–1895)

A Conservative Democrat, Lewis E. Parsons became Alabama's 19th governor when he was appointed by Andrew Johnson in 1865 to oversee the reestablishment of a loyal government of the state after the Civil War. Previous to this appointment, Parsons served in the presidential Electoral College in 1856 and 1860 and was a member of the Alabama House of Representatives in 1859 and 1865.

Lewis Eliphalet Parsons was born in Boone County, New York, on April 28, 1817. He studied law at an early age, and moved to Talladega, Alabama, in 1840, to practice with Alexander White.

In April 1865, after the Confederate government collapsed, Alabama's civil government was placed under the interim military rule of U.S. Army general George H. Thomas. In June 1865, Johnson called upon Parsons to provisionally reinstate the Alabama government. Parson's first gesture was to urge the people of Alabama to rejoin the Union. Describing the Union as a "life-boat" and mourning the material and personal losses of Alabama's people, he explained that the state itself was in dire need of the justice, domestic tranquility, and protection that the Union could provide. Parsons reinstated officers of the state who were willing to take and subscribe a loyalty oath to the U.S. Constitution and the Union, oversaw the appointment of minor state officials, scheduled and administered county elections, announced that those who did not uphold the new laws of the state would be subject to arrest and punishment, and—with the exception of slavery—reinstated all prewar civil and criminal state laws.

In September 1865, Parsons convened a constitutional convention that ratified the Thirteenth Amendment (which recognized the abolition of slavery nationally) and at the same time passed a Black Code that, while less restrictive than the racial legislations of other states, was still quite onerous. This convention also elected George S. Houston and Parsons to serve in the U.S. Senate. Neither man, however, was able to assume his seat due to the refusal of congressional Republicans to concede representation to states that did not grant full rights to freedmen. Finally, Parsons supervised the final act of the transition: the inauguration of Robert M. Patton as the 20th governor of Alabama.

Parsons was appointed U.S. district attorney for northern Alabama in 1890 by Benjamin Harrison. In 1893, Grover Cleveland attempted to remove Parsons from this office, but Parsons declared that Cleveland had no authority to do so and served what remained of his entire four-year term. Parsons died on June 8, 1895, and is buried in the Oak Hill Cemetery, Talladega, Alabama.

*Michelle LaFrance*

**See also:** Amnesty Proclamations; Black Suffrage; Civil Rights; Congressional Reconstruction; Democratic Party; Lindsay, Robert B. (1824–1902); Presidential Reconstruction; Republicans, Radical.

## Further Reading

Fleming, Walter L. *Civil War and Reconstruction in Alabama*. 1905. Reprint, New York: Peter Smith, 1948.

Sobel, Robert, and John Raimo, eds. *Biographical Directory of the Governors of the United States*. Westport, CT: Meckler, 1978.

## PATTON, ROBERT M. (1809–1885)

Robert M. Patton was elected as Alabama's governor under Andrew Johnson's program of Presidential Reconstruction, serving from December 1865 until superseded by the new Republican governments created through Congressional Reconstruction.

Patton was born in Virginia in 1809, but he spent the bulk of his life outside Florence in Lauderdale County, Alabama. He was a wealthy merchant and a planter, at one time holding some 300 slaves. Patton served in the legislature as a Whig, and he long-opposed secession, backing Northern Democrat Steven Douglas for president in 1860. Upon Alabama's secession, he backed the Southern cause and lost two sons in the Confederate army.

After the Civil War ended, many ex-secessionists were prohibited from assuming leadership roles, but Patton's reputation as a Moderate fit the climate of the immediate postwar situation. Under Johnson's establishment of a provisional government, a new convention rewrote the constitution and began the process of selecting new officials. Patton was elected governor and shared the regional consensus on racial matters, assuring Alabamians that "politically and socially, ours is a white man's government." Patton implemented Johnson's Reconstruction plan, which brought many former confederates into state and local governments. Still, Patton conciliated Northern opinion, vetoing several harsh Black Code provisions. Governor Patton also cooperated with army officials, and worked with of the Bureau of Refugees, Freedmen, and Abandoned Lands, to secure federal food relief for the destitute in devastated Northern Alabama, black and white.

As governor, Patton tried to move Alabama forward economically. He embraced textile mills and railroads, rather than emphasizing sectional controversy and racial extremism. Major public initiatives included restoring the state's credit and pursuing railroad development. With Patton's support, the legislature passed a general transportation aid policy, endorsing $12,000 in bonds for each mile of railroad built in the state.

Patton's political moderation was sorely tested. After the Republicans swept the Northern congressional elections of 1866, all but sweeping aside Johnson's program, Patton encouraged ratification of the pending Fourteenth Amendment. He hoped to stave off congressional intervention—and the superseding of his own government—but the legislature and white public would not endorse so drastic a step. As with nine other former Confederate states, Alabama refused to ratify the amendment, antagonizing Northern Republicans and helping inaugurate an entirely new program of restoration.

The coming of Congressional Reconstruction in 1867 confirmed his fears. Subsequent federal imposition of black suffrage in the Military Reconstruction Acts persuaded him that continued obstruction was dangerous for the state's economic prospects. Patton now endorsed Reconstruction under the terms prescribed by Congress, and he identified himself for months with the Republican Party. His initial hope was that black votes would help bar former secessionist Democrats from power, allowing Moderates to control the state. This position subjected him to criticism from white Alabamians. Yet, the Republican-sponsored newly drafted constitution and its civil rights provisions appalled him, as did the Republican nominees for office. Now a man caught between parties, he opposed ratification of the new constitution in the February 1868 election, but conservative schemes to boycott the vote failed and Congress declared Alabama's Constitution enacted. Patton's nominal authority as governor ceased in July, as he handed the position to the elected Republican successor, William Hugh Smith.

So fluid a political career defies easy categorization. Even after his governorship ended, Patton's flexible public course continued, and after President Ulysses S. Grant's election in 1868, he again found his way into the Republican Party. He also figured prominently in various railroad projects. Patton died in 1885 at his home, Sweetwater.

*Michael W. Fitzgerald*

**See also:** Constitutional Conventions; Elections of 1868; Military Reconstruction Acts (1867–1868).

## Further Reading

Fitzgerald, Michael W. "Wager Swayne, the Freedmen's Bureau, and the Politics of Reconstruction in Alabama." *Alabama Review* (July 1995): 188–218.

Wiggins, Sarah W. *The Scalawag in Alabama Politics, 1865–1881*. Tuscaloosa: University of Alabama Press, 1977.

# PERRY, BENJAMIN F. (1805–1886)

Benjamin Franklin Perry was born November 20, 1805, in the Pendleton District of upcountry South Carolina. He attended public schools and later a preparatory school in Asheville, North Carolina, before studying law. He returned to South Carolina and was admitted to the bar in 1827. Perry never easily fit into a clear political category, as he believed deeply in his state, in state's rights, and in the federal Union. He served in the South Carolina House of Representatives (1836–1842; 1850–1860) and the state Senate (1844–1848).

As the sectional crisis came to a head, Perry remained a Unionist opposed to secession. As with many Southern Unionists, once his state seceded, he supported the Confederate cause. He held several civil offices in the Confederate government, including Confederate states district attorney in 1863 and Confederate states district judge in 1864.

Following the war, Perry, like many former Confederate officials, was unsure of his fate. His luck took a positive turn when President Andrew Johnson initiated his Reconstruction program in May 1865. The president's first move was appointing provisional governors for the former Confederate states, men like Johnson who were Unionists and opponents of the planter elite. Johnson appointed Perry provisional governor of South Carolina in June 1865. Perry tried to restore civil order by reappointing all state officials who had held office at the close of the war. When the South Carolina Constitutional Convention of 1865 met in September, he achieved several reforms, many designed to benefit the underrepresented upcountry portion of the state. These included abolishing the inequitable "parish" system of representation and establishing the popular election of governors, presidential electors, and state judges. He also secured the state's ratification of the Thirteenth Amendment to the federal constitution.

Republicans in Washington approved of these reforms, but were furious when Perry recommended that a committee draw up Black Codes to define the ambiguous position of African Americans in the state. Congressional Republicans and much of the North in general saw these measures as inhumane regressions back to slavery, but Perry believed such laws necessary to fully articulate the extent of blacks' rights, as well as to restore order and efficiency to the state's devastated economy.

Only a provisional appointee, Perry declined to run for governor after the passage of the 1865 Constitution and left office in November. He did not vacate the political scene entirely. As a nationally recognized Southern Unionist, he played a prominent role in Andrew Johnson's National Union Movement and Convention in 1866, and was elected to the U.S. Senate that year. Unfortunately, because of the status of South Carolina and his own Confederate record, the Republican-controlled Congress denied him his seat. When Congress took full control of Reconstruction in 1867, Perry used his prominence and connections to criticize policy; always a Moderate, Perry was an outspoken critic of "Radical" Reconstruction. He served as a delegate to the Democratic National Convention in 1868 and 1876. He ran unsuccessfully for Congress in 1872. For the infamous election of 1876, at the age of 71, Perry campaigned vigorously for Democratic candidate Wade Hampton. He died December 3, 1886, in Greenville, South Carolina.

*John (Rod) Andrew Jr.*

**See also:** Civil Rights Act of 1866; Congressional Reconstruction; Democratic Party; Elections of 1866; Elections of 1876; Orr, James L. (1822–1873); Republicans, Moderate; Republicans, Radical.

## Further Reading

Edgar, Walter B. *South Carolina: A History*. Columbia: University of South Carolina Press, 1998.

Kibler, Lillian Adele. *Benjamin F. Perry: South Carolina Unionist*. Durham, NC: Duke University Press, 1946.

*South Carolina Biographical Dictionary*. St Clair Shores, MI: Somerset Publishers, 2000.

# PIERPONT, FRANCIS H. (1814–1899)

Francis Harrison Pierpont, an antebellum Whig lawyer and businessman in western Virginia, was drawn into politics during the secession crisis of 1861. He took a leading role in opposing secession, was eventually elected governor of the wartime Unionist "Restored government" of the state, helped to create the new state of West Virginia, and served as the postwar Reconstruction governor of Virginia until 1868.

Born on a farm near Morgantown (in what is now West Virginia) on January 25, 1814, Pierpont was educated at Allegheny College in Meadville, Pennsylvania. After graduating in 1839, he taught school and studied law. Admitted to the Virginia bar in 1842, he began a prosperous law practice and became an attorney for the Baltimore & Ohio Railroad in 1848. By 1854, when he married Julia Augustus Robertson, a daughter of Wisconsin abolitionists, he also owned a coal mine, brick factory, and tannery.

A Whig before the Civil War, Pierpont did not become prominent in the political world until the secession controversy of 1861. Like many residents of the western third of the state (typical of many Appalachian areas), he resented the influence and disproportionate power of the eastern slaveholders. When the voters of the Old Dominion voted to secede in May 1861, Pierpont took a leading role in the growing western movement to resist separation from the Union. At a mass meeting of loyalists in Wheeling in June 1861, he provided the legal justification for forming a separate, pro-Union government for the state of Virginia (based on Congress's obligation to guarantee a "republican form of government" in all states). He was elected governor of Virginia by the Wheeling convention on the theory that the state's secessionist officials in Richmond had forfeited their right to hold office. Within a few weeks, both President Abraham Lincoln and the U.S. Congress recognized Pierpont's "Restored" regime in Wheeling as the legitimate state government. Pierpont was an efficient and tireless administrator who raised volunteer regiments for the Union army, created a new bureaucracy to handle state affairs, and provided law and order in western counties. When Congress granted statehood in the summer of 1863, Pierpont declined an invitation to serve as the first governor of West Virginia, arguing he was, technically, still legitimate governor of Virginia. Instead, he moved the Restored government back to old Virginia to continue its administration over the few counties that were firmly in Union hands (mainly near the District of Columbia and Norfolk and on the Eastern Shore).

Under Pierpont's leadership, the Restored government began reconstructing the Old Dominion by holding a constitutional convention in Alexandria (across the river from Washington) in 1864. The new constitution abolished slavery in Virginia and adopted other reforms that other Confederate states would accomplish only after the war. The impact of the "Alexandria constitution" was limited, however, because the Restored government controlled very little area. However, when the war ended in 1865, Pierpont moved his administration down to Richmond, occupied the governor's mansion and called the tiny Restored legislature into session to return the state to normalcy.

But Pierpont's drive was inspired mainly by his devotion to the Union; as the war ended he found that his ideals tended to alienate Virginians on both sides of the political spectrum. He was too conservative for the freedpeople and many white Republicans because he had no real concern for the freedpeople. Yet native white Conservatives and former confederates despised him for his wartime opposition to the Confederacy. When he tried to incorporate former confederates into postwar politics, Unionist allies denounced him as a turncoat. When he urged ratification of the Fourteenth Amendment, former confederates labeled him as a Radical Republican. Caught between these opposing forces, Pierpont became almost an irrelevant figure in Virginia by 1867. Under the Military Reconstruction Acts, Gen. John M. Schofield removed him from office in 1868, and he returned to his old home in Fairmont, part of the new state of West Virginia.

He remained a centrist Republican in his politics after the war and even served one term in the West Virginia legislature, but he gradually faded from public view and spent the last 30 years of his life as a lawyer and businessman. When he died on March 24, 1899, he was known more for his role in the formation of West Virginia than for his courageous and valuable service as the Unionist governor of Virginia.

*Richard Lowe*

**See also:** Amnesty Proclamations; Congressional Reconstruction; Presidential Reconstruction.

## Further Reading

Ambler, Charles H. *Francis H. Pierpont: Union War Governor of Virginia and Father of West Virginia.* Chapel Hill: University of North Carolina Press, 1937.

Curry, Richard O. *A House Divided: A Study of Statehood Politics and the Copperhead Movement in West Virginia.* Pittsburgh: University of Pittsburgh Press, 1969.

Lowe, Richard G. "Francis Harrison Pierpont: Wartime Unionist, Reconstruction Moderate," in Edward Younger et al., eds, *The Governors of Virginia, 1860–1978.* Charlottesville: University Press of Virginia, 1982.

Lowe, Richard G. *Republicans and Reconstruction in Virginia, 1856–70.* Charlottesville: University Press of Virginia, 1991.

## PINCHBACK, PINCKNEY BENTON STEWART (1837–1921)

Pinckney B. S. Pinchback was one of the most important black politicians in Louisiana and a major figure in the state's Republican Party both during and after Congressional Reconstruction. He held various offices, but he is best known as the first black governor in U.S. history and the only black governor during Reconstruction—although his gubernatorial term lasted only 35 days. He was also elected to the U.S. House of Representatives and to the U.S. Senate from Louisiana, but in each instance, his election was successfully

Born a slave in Georgia but raised free in Ohio, Pinckney Benton Stewart Pinchback played a central role in Louisiana politics after the war. Among his achievements was a month-long stint as governor, the first African American governor in U.S. history. (Library of Congress)

contested and he served neither. His career in Louisiana was both testament to the possibilities of the age and an iconic example of the chaos and frustration that accompanied Reconstruction.

Pinchback, the eighth of 10 children, was born near Macon, Georgia, on May 10, 1837, while his father, a white planter, and his mother, a recently manumitted mulatto, were traveling from Virginia to Mississippi. He was sent as a youth to Cincinnati for his education, but upon his father's death and the rest of his family's removal to Ohio to avoid the risk of enslavement, he took a job as a cabin boy on canal boats in the Ohio area. He subsequently worked on riverboats on the Mississippi, Missouri, and Red Rivers and eventually became a steward while also gaining a reputation as a riverboat gambler.

Upon the outbreak of the Civil War and the federal capture of New Orleans, the light-skinned Pinchback made his way to that city in May 1862 and served briefly in a white Unionist regiment from Louisiana. When Gen. Benjamin F. Butler, the federal commander in Louisiana, announced the formation of free black regiments later that year, Pinchback received authorization to recruit volunteers, and in October 1862, he was designated a captain in the Louisiana Native Guards. He held this rank until September 1863, when discriminatory treatment and hostility from white officers prompted him to resign. For the remainder of the war, Pinchback worked with a group of fellow free black men and white radicals who championed civil rights and black suffrage, moving from the arena of military affairs into the sphere of politics.

In 1856, he left New Orleans for Alabama, where he spent the next two years advocating black education, racial equality, and black political rights. With the implementation of Congressional Reconstruction in 1867—which subjected the Southern state governments to military authority—he called for new state constitutions that incorporated black suffrage and mandated that ex-Confederate states ratify the Fourteenth Amendment to the U.S. Constitution for readmission to the Union; Pinchback returned to New Orleans. He joined the Republican Party and served as a delegate to the constitutional convention, where he drafted a key civil rights provision of Louisiana's 1868 Constitution.

At the Louisiana Republican Party's nominating convention in January 1868, in preparation for upcoming state elections, Pinchback was proposed as a possible gubernatorial candidate, but he declined, maintaining that the nomination of a black man was ill-advised at the time. At the April elections, voters approved the new constitution and elected Republican candidates Henry Clay Warmoth, a carpetbagger, as governor and Oscar J. Dunn, Pinchback's rival as the state's leading black Republican, as lieutenant governor. Pinchback was elected to the state senate and he served until December 7, 1871, when he was elected lieutenant governor following Dunn's sudden death.

Pinchback occupied an anomalous position within the Republican Party. As an important power broker who controlled a significant bloc of the state's black votes, he could exercise a certain degree of autonomy. Yet for all his influence, Pinchback was a black man in an organization whose leadership was dominated by whites. Pinchback initially supported Warmoth, and he played an important role in the Republican Party's attempt to secure racial equality, promote economic development, and attract white support. Nonetheless, by 1870, Republican discontent with Warmoth's limited support of black civil rights and differences over state and federal patronage led the party to divide into pro-Warmoth and anti-Warmoth, or "Custom House," factions. The former included mostly state employees while the latter consisted of federal officials headquartered at the U.S. Custom House in New Orleans. In the midst of this strife, Pinchback led his own faction, which maintained an independent position and alternately supported either of the two factions as circumstances dictated. Pinchback's relations with Warmoth, while always personally cordial, were nonetheless driven by political concerns. Although, in 1870, Warmoth vetoed a major civil rights bill that Pinchback had sponsored, Pinchback's reservations about certain Custom House Republicans kept him from splitting with Warmoth. In 1871, moreover, Warmoth supported Pinchback's election as lieutenant governor, if only to secure Pinchback's support in his battle with the Custom House.

By early 1872, Louisiana's Republican Party was hopelessly divided. With both the Warmoth and Custom House factions claiming to be the state's legitimate Republican Party, President Ulysses S. Grant supported the Custom House faction, which gained control of the party and moved to isolate Warmoth.

With the 1872 split in the national Republican Party and the Liberal Republican revolt against Grant, and with Warmoth no longer controlling Louisiana's Republican Party, Warmoth became leader of the state's Liberal Republicans and supported the nomination of Horace Greeley for president. State elections were on the same year, and the gubernatorial nominees included Democrat John D. McEnery and Republican William Pitt Kellogg. Pinchback and his supporters abandoned Warmoth and endorsed Kellogg. The election of 1872 in Louisiana was one of the most controversial in the state's history. Intimidation and violence, especially against blacks, characterized the campaign, and fraud marred the election. In hopes of giving Kellogg an advantage, and to punish Warmoth for having supported the Democrats, the Republican legislature impeached Warmoth in early December, automatically suspending him from office and elevating Pinchback, as lieutenant governor, to the governorship.

Pinchback's term as governor lasted from December 9, 1872 to January 13, 1873, but he was the first black man in U.S. history to hold that office. Once Pinchback's term ended, rival state governments proceeded to hold inaugurations, but Grant eventually recognized the Kellogg government. To complicate matters further, Pinchback had been the

Republican candidate for Louisiana's at-large congressional seat in 1872, and he claimed victory in that race; moreover, the new Republican-majority legislature, upon convening in mid-January 1873, elected Pinchback to the U.S. Senate, making him the only person in U.S. history to simultaneously claim seats in both houses of Congress. Pinchback was eventually denied both seats, owing to allegations of bribery and to the chaos surrounding the 1872 elections, but the senate voted to reimburse him a sum equivalent to the salary he would have received had he served.

Despite these setbacks, Pinchback continued to hold office and to play a prominent role in public life. After the 1877 Redemption of Louisiana, he was appointed to the State Board of Education. He held federal posts in New Orleans from 1879 to 1886 and attended the Republican national conventions of 1880, 1884, and 1892. He served as a delegate at the state constitutional convention in 1879 and was instrumental in establishing historically black Southern University. Pinchback also invested in a number of businesses during and after Reconstruction, including a cotton factorage, a Mississippi River packet company that accommodated black passengers upon the implementation of Jim Crow laws, and a newspaper that addressed the black community's concerns. While Pinchback was a firm supporter of racial equality and black economic advancement, he was also an opportunist tainted by scandal who used public office to enrich himself personally. In 1893, Pinchback moved to Washington, D.C., where he was employed for a time as a federal marshal, established a law practice, and joined the city's black elite. He died in Washington on December 21, 1921, but was buried in New Orleans.

*John C. Rodrigue*

**See also:** Bourbons; Louisiana; Nicholls, Francis Redding Tillou (1834–1912); Packard, Stephen B. (1842–1922); Twitchell, Marshall H. (1840–1905); Wells, James M. (1808–1899)

## Further Reading

Haskins, James. *Pinckney Benton Stewart Pinchback*. New York: Macmillan, 1973.
Lonn, Ella. *Reconstruction in Louisiana after 1868*. New York: G. P. Putnam's Sons, 1918.
Taylor, Joe Gray. *Louisiana Reconstructed: 1863–1877*. Baton Rouge: Louisiana State University Press, 1974.
Warmoth, Henry Clay. *War, Politics and Reconstruction: Stormy Days in Louisiana*. New York: Macmillan, 1930.

## POLL TAX

The poll tax played a critical role in disfranchising African American voters after Reconstruction, in the "redeemed" New South and long thereafter. Following the ratification of the Fifteenth Amendment in 1870, no state could use race, color, or previous condition of servitude as criteria in determining suffrage (the right to vote), but the amendment was "negative" in nature, not directly granting the right to vote but instead prohibiting a few specific provisions. Thus, after Reconstruction collapsed in the face of the Conservative white

Bourbon governments across the South, states began revising their constitutions, using loopholes to circumvent the Fifteenth Amendment. Beginning in 1889, when Florida and Tennessee enacted a poll tax of between $1 and $2 as a prerequisite to vote, many Southern states followed suit and employed the tax as a way to significantly limit black political participation. All prospective voters were asked to show a receipt demonstrating that they had paid their taxes for the year; they were not allowed to vote if they were unable to do so. Black males, most of who did not own land, were rarely required to pay taxes. In some cases, the tax was cumulative for a specific number of years preceding the election, which compounded both its burden on the poor and its anticipated effect of segregating voters according to race and class.

The poll tax, like literacy tests and residence requirements, threatened to undo much of the progress that been gained in black voter participation during Reconstruction, a time in which more than 1,000 African American men were elected to local, state, and national positions. Collectively, these impediments reversed the growing number of African American men able to exercise their right to vote, curbed their political power and presence at all levels of government, and made it so that they would no longer participate fully as members of the nation's democratic system. While poor whites could be targeted by the poll tax (e.g., or literacy laws), provisions like grandfather clauses preserved white voting: a man whose father or grandfather had voted in an election prior to 1867 (or who had previously done so himself) was exempt from the tax. Although nationally guaranteed suffrage rights were not extended to African American women until 1920—when all women citizens gained the right to vote—black women also fell under the tax after being enfranchised.

Eleven states in the American South implemented poll taxes after Reconstruction. In 1964, the Twenty-fourth Amendment to the Constitution prohibited denying or abridging a citizen's right to vote in federal elections on the basis of failing to pay a poll or other tax. It would be more than a year later, however, before the Supreme Court extended prohibition of the poll tax to all elections when it was faced with challenges filed by two African American women from Virginia: Annie Harper and Evelyn Butts. In *Harper v. Virginia State Board of Elections*, the Supreme Court held that a Virginia statute giving voters the choice of either paying a poll tax or filing a residency certificate six months prior to an election violated the equal protection clause of the Fourteenth Amendment. The case was decided together *with Butts v. Harrison* on March 24, 1966, and the nearly 80-year reign of the poll tax finally ended.

*Amanda J. Davis*

**See also:** Black Suffrage; Civil Rights; Congressional Reconstruction; Enforcement Acts (1870, 1871, 1875); Military Reconstruction Acts (1867–1868); New South; Redemption; Republicans, Radical.

## Further Reading

Keyssar, Alexander. *The Right to Vote: The Contested History of Democracy in the United States*. New York: Basic Books, 2000.

Smiley, Tavis and the editors of *Black Issues in Higher Education*. *The Unfinished Agenda of the Selma-Montgomery Voting Rights March*. Indianapolis: Wiley, 2005.

# PORT ROYAL EXPERIMENT

On November 7, 1861, Union military forces under the command of Lt. Gen. William W. Reynolds captured Port Royal, one of the Sea Islands off the coast of South Carolina. Virtually all white inhabitants had fled the island, leaving behind some 10,000 slaves. Northern reformers and investors soon arrived, hoping to help these African Americans make the transition from a slave to a free labor system. This experiment would become the first of many "rehearsals for Reconstruction" in the South during the Civil War.

The most highly publicized reformers to "experiment" with Port Royal slaves were young teachers and missionaries from the North, collectively known as Gideon's Band. These men and women were idealistic abolitionists who believed that slavery had demoralized blacks, making them unable to compete in the competitive world of the marketplace. The Gideonites, assisted by the American Missionary Association, opened schools in Port Royal to educate the former slaves. Some also demanded that the federal government give these freedmen land and not force them to plant cotton.

More influential than the Gideonites were the Northern investors and Union officials. These men, hoping to capitalize on high cotton prices, encouraged Port Royal blacks to plant cotton. Some abolitionists wanted not only to make a profit but also to demonstrate that blacks could work more efficiently as free laborers. Secretary of the Treasury Salmon P. Chase agreed with Northern investors, approving a plan that offered freedmen wages to harvest the valuable cotton.

Nevertheless, Port Royal blacks possessed their own definition of freedom. They did not want to grow cotton, arguing that it was a "slave crop" that had "enriched the masters, but had not fed them." Like most whites, Sea Island blacks desired economic independence. They wanted to own their own land and grow subsistence crops like corn and potatoes. These freedmen resisted Northern reformers' efforts to introduce them to a wage-labor economic system. In the end, however, most blacks were unable to maintain a subsistence lifestyle. Because Union soldiers took most of the foodstuffs on the island, former slaves remained dependent on the federal government for aid. Many had no choice but to sign labor contracts and work for wages. Nor did these freedmen become landowners. Most of the confiscated land that Treasury agents auctioned during the Civil War went to Northern speculators, cotton companies, army officers, and government officials.

The Port Royal experiment foreshadowed many of the problems that African Americans faced in the South after the Civil War. It revealed that former slaves and whites had a different notion of the meaning of freedom. Port Royal blacks, like those elsewhere in the South during Reconstruction, did not want to toil under the supervision of whites. Freedom meant landownership. Although dabbling in the market economy, most desired to grow provision crops, not cotton. Most whites ignored this lesson. Federal officials, wanting former slaves to become wage laborers, were hesitant to redistribute land seized from confederates. The economic independence that blacks desired would remain elusive for the remainder of the 19th century and beyond.

*Bruce E. Stewart*

***See also:*** Amnesty Proclamations; Bureau of Refugees, Freedmen, and Abandoned Lands; Edisto Island, South Carolina; Field Order No. 15; Labor Systems; Pardons; Presidential Reconstruction; Stevens, Thaddeus (1792–1868); U.S. Army and Reconstruction.

## Further Reading

Foner, Eric. *Reconstruction Updated Edition: America's Unfinished Revolution, 1863–1877*. Reprint, New York: HarperCollins, 2014.

Rose, Willie Lee. *Rehearsal for Reconstruction: The Port Royal Experiment*. Athens: University of Georgia Press, 1964.

# PRESIDENTIAL RECONSTRUCTION

Reconstruction, the process of restoring the former states of the Confederacy to the Union during and following the Civil War, proceeded in two distinct phases—Presidential Reconstruction and Congressional Reconstruction. Presidential Reconstruction refers to the stage of that process begun during the war when Presidents Abraham Lincoln and Andrew Johnson took the initiative in determining the restoration policy.

By the spring of 1865, the doctrine of secession had been invalidated by force of arms, and slavery as an institution had been destroyed. Yet, key questions remained unanswered. Who would hold postwar power in the former rebellious states? How would persons formerly in rebellion against the United States be treated? What would be the terms for their readmission to the Union? Who would set these terms and control the process of readmission? What would be the status of the African American freedpeople in American society?

From the beginning of the Civil War to its end, Abraham Lincoln remained convinced that most Southerners were devoted to the Union. He believed, as did others, that Southern Unionists had been either coerced into supporting the Confederacy or hoodwinked by fire-eaters' political rhetoric that conjured up images of slave rebellions and other atrocities. His belief colored and shaped his plans for restoration. Early on, as federal forces began to seize Confederacy territory in 1862, Lincoln hoped that a conciliatory policy would entice the region to lay down its arms. Through an ad hoc process sometimes characterized as "wartime reconstruction," Lincoln encouraged his military commanders to respect the civil and property rights of Southerners. He actively discouraged his officers from interfering with slave property. He appointed military governors in occupied areas and hoped to quickly establish civilian governments in the South and return the nation to its prewar status. However, most Southerners rejected his overtures, and the war only intensified. Lincoln, still reluctant to radically alter Southern society, used emancipation as a last resort to compel the Confederacy to surrender; the Emancipation Proclamation allowed Southerners to keep their slaves if they lay down their arms.

Lincoln genuinely wanted to heal the nation's wounds, but he also hoped that by offering generous peace terms, the Republicans could attract Southern Unionists and former Whigs to the party, thereby broadening its base. In December 1863, Lincoln outlined his program for Reconstruction in a Proclamation of Amnesty and Reconstruction, often called the Ten Percent Plan. In it, he offered pardon to almost all confederates, excluding only high-ranking civilian, military, and diplomatic leaders. These former leaders would take a loyalty oath, swearing allegiance to the U.S. Constitution and pledging to accept all executive orders and congressional resolutions regarding slavery (in anticipation of the passage of the Thirteenth Amendment, which would abolish slavery in the United States). Amnesty carried with it the restoration of all political rights, including suffrage and holding office.

Lincoln's proclamation further stipulated that each of the former Confederate states could organize a new state government once a minimum of 10 percent of the number of white male voters from the 1860 presidential election took the loyalty oath. This new government would create a constitution establishing a republican form of government, abolishing slavery, and providing education for freed blacks; there was no expectation of black political rights. Once these requirements were met, the president would recognize the new governments. Lincoln did not advocate prosecuting prominent ex-confederates, permanently disfranchising rebels, or providing black civil rights.

Congress, reflecting the North itself, was deeply divided over the direction of Presidential Reconstruction. Virtually the entire Northern Democratic Party and most Conservative Republicans supported Lincoln's so-called Ten Percent Plan and did not want to see any sweeping social or economic changes in the South. For them, the war had been about preserving the Union. However, Moderate Republicans, the largest group, believed that the former slaves should receive some basic civil rights, but they stopped short of black suffrage or confiscation of Confederate land. Those in the party who pressed for a far-reaching restructuring of the South came to be known as Radical Republicans. They opposed Lincoln's plan, which they considered too lenient on the ex-rebels. Radicals lobbied for significant civil and political rights for the freedpeople. Many wanted to distribute land confiscated from the planter class, whom the Radicals blamed for the war, to the former slaves. They favored other harsh penalties for former confederates, including disfranchisement and exclusion from holding public office.

Despite differences among them, all these groups shared a frustration that the president had not elicited their advice in devising a Reconstruction policy. With so much at stake, they were determined to play a role in the process. Such an opportunity arose when Lincoln recognized the new governments of Virginia, Tennessee, Louisiana, and Arkansas as being "loyal" and ready for readmission, and Congress refused to admit their representatives to Congress.

Under the direction of Benjamin Wade and Representative Henry Winter Davis of Maryland, Congress formulated its counterproposal for Reconstruction in July 1864, the Wade-Davis bill. Although the bill passed Congress on the final day of the 1864 session, Lincoln killed it with a pocket veto. The president wanted to preserve the Unionist governments he had recognized and move the party toward the political center prior to the elections of 1864. His veto infuriated the Radicals, who countered by issuing the Wade-Davis manifesto in August 1864, accusing Lincoln of usurping Congress's legislative prerogatives.

After the victory of Lincoln and the National Union Party in 1864, the president seemed willing to work with Congress and modify his Reconstruction ideas. For instance, he supported a revised Wade-Davis bill that recognized and preserved his Louisiana and Arkansas governments, but the measure never passed. In January, the president and congressional Republicans did come together to support the Thirteenth Amendment, which would abolish slavery throughout the nation, and in March, Lincoln overcame his reservations and endorsed Congress's establishment of the Bureau of Refugees, Freedmen, and Abandoned Lands, commonly known as the Freedmen's Bureau. In addition, Lincoln allowed to stand, temporarily, Gen. William T. Sherman's Field Order No. 15, which set aside abandoned lands on the Sea Islands and coastal region of South Carolina and Georgia for exclusive use by the region's freed population; for a brief moment, the Radicals were delighted. By the spring, as the war drew to a close, Lincoln even began to consider the idea of limited black suffrage in the South for literate males and Union veterans.

Lincoln's plans ended with John Wilkes Booth's bullet on April 14, 1865. The next day, Andrew Johnson was sworn in as the nation's 17th president. Johnson, a Southern Democrat, faced the enormous task of rebuilding the South and forging a coherent Reconstruction policy. At first, congressional Republicans, even Radicals, were willing to work with the president in shaping policy. Johnson certainly brought great experience to the office. He had built an enviable political career by serving in local, state, and national offices. As the only Southern senator to remain loyal to the Union, Johnson became a leader of the pro-administration War Democrats and Lincoln's choice as the first military governor during wartime Reconstruction. It seemed Johnson had been chosen by Providence to handle Reconstruction. However, Johnson still held to the traditional Democratic doctrines of states' rights, limited federal government activity, a restricted reading of the Constitution, and white supremacy. For him, the Civil War had been about preserving the Union, not remaking Southern society or uplifting African Americans. Johnson quickly disappointed Radicals and their revolutionary expectations. Like Lincoln, the new executive favored a speedy resolution to the problems of Reconstruction. Also like his predecessor, he believed the primary responsibility for Reconstruction rested with the executive branch. On May 29, 1865, with Congress out of session, he issued two proclamations that outlined his restoration policy. The first, similar to Lincoln's 1863 declaration, granted a general pardon to all who would pledge an oath of allegiance and restored complete political rights to former confederates; particular categories of high-ranking individuals needed to petition the president directly for a pardon.

Johnson's second proclamation applied originally to North Carolina but was extended to include all former Confederate states not previously restored to the Union by Lincoln (in Virginia, Tennessee, Arkansas, and Louisiana, Johnson accepted the preexisting Lincoln governments). According to its provisions, Johnson would appoint a provisional governor who would register voters for an election of delegates for a state constitutional convention. The convention would nullify the ordinances of secession, abolish slavery, and repudiate all state debts incurred during the rebellion. Next, elections would be held to select a governor, legislature, and new members of Congress. These new legislatures would then ratify the Thirteenth Amendment. At this stage, Johnson would recognize the new state government, end martial law, and withdraw the army, thereby restoring the state and its citizens to full rights and privileges in the Union. Johnson also reversed Sherman's Special Field Order No. 15 and ordered that abandoned plantations be returned to their former owners.

Johnson's restoration program drew tremendous criticism across the North. A sense of defiance pervaded the new Southern state conventions as they skirted many of the president's requirements. Southern voters elected prominent ex-Confederate officials to the U.S. Congress and to state offices, and new state governments enacted a series of laws, known as Black Codes, that forced former slaves into a caste system, significantly curtailing the rights and liberties that many believed freedpeople deserved. Conservative Southern whites clearly intended to limit black freedom and control black labor, and an equally Conservative president did not believe it constitutional for the federal government to interfere.

Once the Southern states had complied with the structural components of his conditions (such as new constitutions and new representatives, regardless of their quality or composition), Johnson considered Reconstruction complete. In addition to his constitutional conservatism, Johnson's attitude also stemmed from his desire to reshape the national political landscape after the war. He hoped his presidential program would fuse Conservative Republicans, Southern whites, and Northern Democrats into a new national party based on protecting the Constitution and the rights of the states. His National Union Movement would be tested first in the congressional elections of 1866, and then, he reasoned, it would elect him president in 1868.

Johnson's presidential program did not anticipate the cohesion mustered by the Republicans nor did he ever realize how his obstinacy actually forged Republican unity. Republicans were alarmed by Johnson's program, which seemed in so many ways to reward former rebels while it offered nothing to freed slaves, and even threatened the victorious Republican Party.

When the Republican-controlled Congress convened in December 1865, it refused to seat the 80 Southern representatives and senators from Johnson's governments. The Republicans then established the Joint Committee of Fifteen on Reconstruction (usually called the Joint Committee on Reconstruction) to hold hearings on the state of affairs in the South, while they deliberated on their own Reconstruction program. The president's program of Reconstruction had concluded; in his mind the states were ready to rejoin the Union. The Republican Congress disagreed, but without a program of its own it would spend 1866 trying to compromise with Johnson. The president's inability to compromise, and his uncanny tendency to drive rival factions together, would spell the complete undoing of his program and would result in far greater changes that he ever imagined. Congressional—sometimes called Radical—Reconstruction would sweep away his governments, disfranchise his supporters, and establish the foundations of a Southern Republican Party based on black male voting. By the middle of 1867, Presidential Reconstruction had ceased to exist.

*John D. Fowler*

*See also:* Abolition of Slavery; Amnesty Proclamations; Assassination of Abraham Lincoln (1865); Bullock, Rufus B. (1834–1907); Confiscation Acts; Holden, William Woods (1818–1892); Humphreys, Benjamin Grubb (1808–1882); Impeachment of Andrew Johnson (1868); Labor Systems; Military Reconstruction Acts (1867–1868); Parsons, Lewis E. (1817–1895); Sharkey, William L. (1798–1873); U.S. Army and Reconstruction; Wells, James M. (1808–1899).

## Further Reading

Abbott, Richard H. *The Republican Party and the South, 1855–1877*. Chapel Hill: University of North Carolina Press, 1986.

Benedict, Michael Les. *A Compromise of Principle: Congressional Republicans and Reconstruction, 1863–1869*. New York: Norton, 1974.

Carter, Dan T. *When the War Was Over: The Failure of Self-Reconstruction in the South.* Baton Rouge: Louisiana State University Press, 1985.

Donald, David. *The Politics of Reconstruction, 1863–1867*. Baton Rouge: Louisiana State University Press, 1965.

Harris, William C. *With Charity for All: Lincoln and the Restoration of the Union.* Lexington: University Press of Kentucky, 1998.

McKitrick, Eric L. *Andrew Johnson and Reconstruction.* Chicago: University of Chicago Press, 1960. Reprint, New York: Oxford University Press, 1988.

Perman, Michael. *Reunion without Compromise: The South and Reconstruction, 1865–1868*. Cambridge: Cambridge University Press, 1974.

# PROVISIONAL GOVERNORS

As the Civil War ended and Confederate state governments fled, were arrested, or surrendered, President Andrew Johnson appointed provisional governors to organize new civilian governments in their place. These governors would call for and oversee constitutional conventions to write new state constitutions, in preparation for the state resuming its rights under the U.S. Constitution and in the federal Union.

Johnson assumed the presidency after Abraham Lincoln's assassination in April 1865, when Congress was not in session. Instead of recalling Congress, he seized the initiative and presented his vision of Reconstruction in two proclamations issued on May 29, 1865. The first offered amnesty and the restoration of all property, except slaves, to those who had rebelled if they swore future allegiance to the United States. The second proclamation named William W. Holden provisional governor of North Carolina and instructed him to organize an election for delegates to a state constitutional convention. All those who took the oath of allegiance, or received special pardons, and were qualified to vote in 1860 could participate in the election. Lincoln had also appointed governors, but those were civilians who served as military governors in time of war, often overseeing occupied territory.

In June and July 1865, Johnson issued similar proclamations for six other Southern states, appointing provisional governors in Mississippi (William L. Sharkey on June 13), Georgia (James Johnson on June 17), Texas (Andrew Jackson Hamilton on June 17), Alabama (Lewis Parsons on June 21), South Carolina (Benjamin F. Perry on June 30), and Florida (William Marvin on July 13). Because he considered Arkansas, Louisiana, Tennessee, and Virginia restored by Lincoln's Reconstruction policies and wartime governors, Johnson allowed the existing governors to remain in power in those states. The men Johnson appointed were a diverse group. Only two, Marvin and Hamilton, had actively supported the Union. The rest had at least opposed secession early on, although they had remained in the South, either sitting out the war or supporting it to some degree. Johnson believed these men were capable of fulfilling his dream of building a new Union party composed of former Southern Whigs, Democrats, and other Unionists—men like him—who could work with Conservative Northern Republicans and Northern Democrats.

Holden of North Carolina, Johnson's first appointee, was a problematic choice. Because he had changed political positions so many times, many viewed him as an opportunist. Before the war he had been a Whig, switched to the Democracy, signed the state's ordinance of secession, but eventually ran as a peace candidate for governor (1864), urging his state to sue for a separate peace. A prominent Unionist Whig planter, William Sharkey, Johnson's second appointee, had served as chief justice of Mississippi's High Court of Errors since the 1820s. After his state seceded, he refused to support the Southern war effort, retiring from Mississippi politics and, as early as 1863, working for restoration. Indeed, he had been jailed briefly during the war because he refused to sell goods to confederates. But as a respected antebellum politician and planter, Sharkey's appointment encouraged white Mississippians, who knew that Sharkey—at nearly 70—was not interested in reshaping Southern society. Sharkey concentrated on getting the convention to do whatever was necessary so that federal forces would leave, the state could reenter Congress, and white Mississippians could get back to controlling their own state.

In Georgia, Johnson chose a friend who he had shared mess privileges with in Congress in the early 1850s. Provisional governor James Johnson potentially was a good choice for unifying Unionists and Conservative planters, having been a Whig Unionist who never supported secession and who had sat out the war without taking sides. He was a respected Columbus attorney, honest and fair, but as an obscure one-term congressman, Johnson lacked political experience and skill. Andrew Jackson Hamilton of Texas was an Austin attorney who had briefly served in the state legislature. During the 1850s, he joined that faction of the Texas Democratic Party that opposed secession and won election from his western Texas district to Congress in 1858. He served until shortly after Texas seceded. Returning to Austin, he won election to the state senate but had to flee in July 1862, when secessionists plotted against his life. In November 1862, Lincoln appointed him brigadier general of Unionist volunteers and military governor of Texas. As such, he joined the unsuccessful federal expedition into South Texas in late 1863. After that failure, he spent most of the remainder of the war in federally occupied New Orleans.

In Alabama, the president chose Lewis Parsons, a former Whig congressman who had served in the state legislature as a peace advocate. As provisional governor, he sought to build a political base to promote economic development, especially railroad building and industrial development. He believed that to do so he needed to placate the Conservative Whig planter class by promising to seek help in Washington for reduction in the cotton taxes, but he also lobbied for land and tax incentives for railroad construction. In South Carolina, Benjamin Perry symbolized the state's obstinacy toward reconciliation. From the up-country, he was a successful Greenville lawyer long opposed to the planter dominance of his state's politics. Before the war, he fought secession and refused to leave the Democratic Party after the South bolted from the presidential convention in 1860, supporting Northerner Stephen Douglas. Once his state seceded, he served as a judge in the state's Confederate courts. In his first speech to his fellow South Carolinians, he spoke of humiliation and degradation, and applauded Johnson's elevation to the presidency, speculating that Lincoln's death was the South's gain, as Johnson was more able.

William Marvin, Johnson's Florida provisional governor, was a native of New York who moved to Key West, Florida, when President Andrew Jackson appointed him district attorney in 1836. In 1839, he was appointed U.S. district judge for the district of Florida and became a leading expert in admiralty law. As such, he developed close relationships with merchants and insurance executives in New York. During the war, he retained his judgeship until 1863, operating behind Union lines. He had opposed secession and had run as a pro-Union candidate for the state's 1861 secession convention. Support for his appointment as provisional governor came from New York businessmen as well as former slaveholders and Moderate Unionists.

On paper, the provisional governors had tremendous power. They were the president's men. As such, when they spoke, they were seen as speaking for the president. There were, however, limitations to their power. Most white Southerners saw the provisional governors as instruments for relaying the president's requests and reminding them of their humiliating defeat. But to be effective, most provisional governors tried to woo the traditional planter leadership class, rather than create support among the Moderates who would form this new party of Johnson's. When the provisional governors placed men in power who were not part of the traditional ruling groups, organized opposition undermined their positions.

Another hindrance to the provisional governors' powers was the presence of federal troops throughout the South. President Johnson, in his proclamations appointing the provisional governors, had ordered the military to aid but not to interfere with the work of the provisional governors. But Congress had established the Freedmen's Bureau, run by the U.S. Army, to aid African Americans in their transition to freedom. As such, the military and bureau officials supervised labor contracts and refused to allow blacks to be tried in civil courts, because their testimony was not allowed. This often conflicted with the desires and orders of the civil governor.

Sharkey took the lead among the provisional governors, to rid the state of Northern interference as soon as possible. On August 19, only two months after his appointment, he began organizing local militias, essentially arming former confederates, claiming that such action was necessary to maintain law and order; he also told the president this would eliminate the need for federal troops—especially African American soldiers which, he told Johnson, were inflaming tensions. Initially, Johnson ignored Sharkey but then acquiesced, despite the recommendations of Carl Schurz, a Northern politician and general who Johnson had sent to the South to investigate. Schurz was in Mississippi at the time and warned Johnson that Sharkey's militia was persecuting Unionists and former slaves. Johnson ignored Schurz's warnings. After Sharkey's success, all the other governors organized militias and petitioned Johnson for the removal of black troops.

The provisional governors quickly went to work to establish civil governments, but each viewed his task differently. In Georgia, James Johnson restored civil government by simply reinstating all Confederate officials who took the amnesty oath. With the state treasury bankrupt and the statehouse in ruins, he used the state's credit to pay for the delegates to attend the convention and to repair the statehouse and executive mansion. He also authorized contracts to rebuild railroad bridges and purchase rolling stock.

In Florida, Marvin believed that the military was in control, and he worked closely with commanding general J. G. Foster. When he arrived in Florida after his appointment, he told Floridians that he had been appointed to aid loyal citizens in organizing a government. Until then, military authorities would preserve the peace. The military commander would decide which local officials to retain. Marvin campaigned throughout the state, explaining to the citizens that the convention would have to nullify secession, abolish slavery, and repudiate the Confederate war debt. Further, although it was not necessary to give blacks political rights, Florida must guarantee them civil rights and legal rights, including the right to testify in state courts.

By contrast, Holden assumed the Confederacy was dead and that he had full authority to create a new civil government. Declaring all offices vacant, Holden appointed some 4,000 men to offices ranging from state officials to local justices of the peace and town officials. He hoped that his actions would gain him the elective governorship, but in rewarding his political friends and punishing his longtime enemies, he selected many former secessionists. Loyal Unionists, with some justification, began to grumble that Holden was supporting secessionist Democrats over Whigs who had opposed the war before secession. Despite some discontent for his sometimes vindictive use of patronage, Holden did a good job of reestablishing the civil government. He wrote to the president to try to stop the U.S. Treasury from seizing cotton and naval stores and shipping them north. He also received the president's permission to suspend collection of the federal tax on cotton, thereby allowing farmers to market their wartime cotton without paying the tax. Holden also regained control of the state's railroads from federal authorities.

Like Holden, Hamilton in Texas believed that Texas required a new spirit and a new ruling class. His strategy was to delay calling a state convention until early in 1866, when he hoped Texans would be less resentful of the Confederate defeat and more willing to recognize that the freedpeople had rights. He even suggested to President Johnson that he confiscate the property of a few of the leading rebels. As for appointments, he tried to pursue a program of only appointing a small number of officeholders and to limit appointments to former Unionists.

Sharkey, Parsons, and Perry took a completely different path, allowing local Confederate officeholders to remain in their positions. Perry, with his political base in the up-country, believed his actions would bring the low-country planter aristocracy into his camp. This policy proved more popular than that pursued by Marvin, Hamilton, and Holden. Holden and Hamilton were both rejected by their electorates and later joined ultra-Unionists and freedmen to form state Republican parties, while Sharkey, Perry, and Parsons were chosen to serve in the U.S. Senate by the newly elected Conservative state legislatures (although Republicans in Congress refused to seat them).

On August 22, 1865, after receiving numerous complaints that his governors were giving preference to secessionists over ultra-Unionists, Johnson telegraphed his provisional governors. Holden, Johnson, and Hamilton assured him that they were being careful to select original Union men, although their appointees might have supported the Southern war effort for at least some period of time. Sharkey, however, argued that it would be unwise and rash to remove all secessionists from office since they were the experienced, recognized leaders of their communities, but he assured the president that for new appointments, he was selecting only those who had opposed secession. Perry, too, admitted the charges; he replied that there were not more than a dozen Union men in South Carolina and those who were loyalist had not sought office. However, Perry assured Johnson that most South Carolinians—and certainly his appointees—were now loyal.

The second task assigned to the provisional governors was to arrange for the election of delegates to state constitutional conventions. Johnson had authorized his provisional governors to determine who would be pardoned, reasoning that they were more qualified to know the applicants. Perry simply approved all applications. By contrast, in North Carolina, Holden used this power to try to ensure his election as governor, rewarding his friends and punishing his enemies. Governor Johnson in Georgia worked to get officials into the back-country so all had the opportunity to take the oath, and he campaigned vigorously for delegates who supported emancipation and ratification of the Thirteenth Amendment. In Texas, Hamilton viewed pardoning as an important responsibility, diligently trying to recommend only those who he believed to be sincerely repentant. But like many other governors, Hamilton recommended leading confederates for pardons in an effort to either broaden his own political support or neutralize the opposition.

Once delegates were selected and the conventions convened, the issue became fulfilling the requirements set forth by President Johnson. Provisional governors were to see that conventions abolished slavery and declared secession null and void. Because Mississippi was the first to hold a convention, Johnson telegraphed Sharkey with a new suggestion. He urged him to extend the suffrage to literate and property-holding blacks, thereby setting an example he hoped other states would copy and undercutting the efforts of the Radical Republicans. Nonetheless, neither Sharkey nor any of the other provisional governors, except Hamilton of Texas, showed any inclination to do more than grant slaves their freedom. Indeed, most worked to assure their white constituencies that emancipation did not imply any new rights for the freedpeople. Holden expressed his opposition to black suffrage.

Marvin told blacks that emancipation did not imply either political or even civil equality. Sharkey not only ignored Johnson's suggestions for limited black suffrage but insisted that this was a white man's government—and would remain so.

Emboldened by the provisional governors' appointments and lenient pardoning policies, delegates of all the state conventions exhibited reluctance and stubborn pride. Mississippi, Georgia, and Florida refused to nullify their secession ordinances, repealing or rescinding them instead. Alabama only abolished slavery after receiving a strongly worded telegram from President Johnson; before, they simply wanted to pass a resolution acknowledging that slavery had been abolished by the military power of the United States. Georgia's delegates made it clear that in abolishing slavery they were merely acquiescing in an accomplished fact and they passed a resolution urging the government to compensate them for their losses.

After each of the states where Johnson had appointed provisional governors had held their constitutional conventions, rewritten their constitutions, and held elections under those new constitutions for state officers, including governors, the president relieved his provisional governors of their offices, turning the states over to the new elective officials. He relieved all governors between December 4, 1865 (Holden) and August 9, 1866 (Hamilton). For Johnson and his governors, the task seemed complete and readmission—and hence Reconstruction—seemed all but accomplished.

Across the North, Republicans were not convinced, and thus began a struggle over the Reconstruction program, the status of the South, and the future of the nation itself.

*Roberta Sue Alexander*

***See also:*** Abolitionists; Black Codes; Bureau of Refugees, Freedmen, and Abandoned Lands; Congressional Reconstruction; Elections of 1866; Fourteenth Amendment (1868); House Judiciary Committee; Joint Committee on Reconstruction; Labor Systems; National Union Movement (1866); Republicans, Moderate.

## Further Reading

Alexander, Roberta Sue. *North Carolina Faces the Freedmen: Race Relations during Presidential Reconstruction, 1865–67.* Durham, NC: Duke University Press, 1985.

Carter, Dan T. *When the War Was Over: The Failure of Self- Reconstruction in the South, 1865–1867.* Baton Rouge: Louisiana State University Press, 1987.

Foner, Eric. *Reconstruction Updated Edition: America's Unfinished Revolution, 1863–1877.* Reprint, New York: HarperCollins, 2014.

Harris, William C. *Presidential Reconstruction in Mississippi.* Baton Rouge: Louisiana State University Press, 1967.

Harris, William C. *William Woods Holden: Firebrand of North Carolina Politics.* Baton Rouge: Louisiana State University Press, 1987.

McKitrick, Eric L. *Andrew Johnson and Reconstruction.* Chicago: University of Chicago Press, 1960.

Shofner, Jerrell H. *Nor Is It over Yet: Florida in the Era of Reconstruction, 1863–1877.* Gainesville: University Presses of Florida, 1974.

# R

## RACE RIOTS

Race riots provide the most visible and dramatic examples of Southern attempts to deny the Civil War's results, in particular freedmen's rights following abolition. These confrontations stand apart from the rest of the South's Reconstruction-era violence of harassment, intimidation, and even outright terrorism; riots were unique because blacks resisted atrocities forcefully. The best-known street battles occurred in 1866 in Memphis, Tennessee, and New Orleans, Louisiana. Many more, however, took place in Alabama, Georgia, Mississippi, South Carolina, and Virginia.

Reconstruction-era riots built on antebellum and Civil War precedents. They even recalled Atlantic antecedents—especially in the white Southern mind. Every plantation owner knew of the 1794 successful African slave uprising in French Haiti that led to bitter racial warfare. The black victory there terrified Dixie's bravest leaders. During the early 19th century, most American race riots took place in the Northern states. A minority of them were started by free African Americans, including one in 1801 in New York and another in Philadelphia in 1804.

Far more numerous before 1861, however, were white mobs assaulting blacks. During the 1830s, the abolitionist movement gained strength, and growing economic pressures made whites fear workplace competition with former slaves. Large-scale attacks on free African American communities became frequent and persisted through the Civil War, the most infamous (and horrific) being the New York City draft riot in July of 1863. Although triggered by the coming of conscription, rioters—mostly lower-class Irish Americans—targeted African Americans across the city.

Reconstruction-era racial rioting took place in a tense atmosphere. After the war, blacks held great expectations, whereas nightmarish hysteria afflicted Southern whites. At least three types of disturbances can be discerned. First, in a few cases, blacks initiated ill-advised aggression. In South Carolina, newly emancipated African Americans beat whites in Charleston (1866) and at Hunnicut's Crossing (1867). Other raids occurred near Columbia, Tennessee (1868), Shady Grove, Louisiana (1868), and Cross Plains, Alabama (1870). Generally, heavily armed veteran whites responded with enormous overkill.

A second type of Reconstruction-era race riot can be termed "urban popular disorder." Two, in Memphis and New Orleans in 1866, had a major impact on the period's politics. They convinced the Northern public that President Andrew Johnson's overly lenient treatment of defeated confederates was squandering Union army battlefield sacrifices. In both cities, local whites became enraged at African American attempts to exercise social and political equality.

Prominent Memphis natives found the presence of black soldiers an intolerable affront. May 1, 1866, was the day after the area's last African American troops were mustered out of service. Local police attacked them and received fire in return. The military commander, Gen. George Stoneman allowed retreating black veterans to take refuge in nearby Fort Pickering. He then disarmed them and refused to allow them to leave, seeking to placate the city's civilian leaders. Outside, white mobs spent the next 40 hours beating, raping, and murdering all blacks wearing Union blue or those known to have army ties. At least 48 died, including two whites.

In New Orleans, the African Americans' unforgivable sin was trying to secure voting rights. There, at the Mechanics' Institute, Unionists and Republicans reconvened the Louisiana state constitutional convention, seeking to enfranchise blacks and thereby strengthen their political control. Outside, supporters paraded noisily. New Orleans whites, led by the police force, attacked the marchers, who then sought cover inside, among the conventioneers. City lawmen surrounded the building, encouraged surrender, and then slaughtered their disarmed foes. Between 40 and 50 blacks died, as well as three white Unionists. New Orleans experienced subsequent similar riots in 1868, 1873, 1874, and 1877.

Although events in Memphis and New Orleans attracted national attention, many more battles occurred in small Southern towns; these altercations constitute a third type of Reconstruction-era race riot. Outside the large cities, emancipation created divided communities, ready to explode upon some trivial pretext. In virtually every location, elementary black organizations prompted white outrage and massive retaliation.

The rural South's poverty, illiteracy, and absence of cultural institutions left its white residents totally unprepared for revolutionary change. That slavery had been destroyed by outside military force, instead of internal reform, almost certainly stiffened resistance to the new order. Residents had theretofore known only white supremacy, and most country folk sought its return. The full extent of nonurban racial altercations may never be known. The terror was so extreme and so successful that many incidents went unreported.

Experts disagree on the era's total number of race riots. No fewer than 72 took place. Historian Paul A. Gilje has counted 375 between 1865 and 1876 but suspects that still more occurred. The most prominent rural riots occurred in Camilla, Georgia (1868), Opelousas, Louisiana (1868), Meridian, Mississippi (1871), Colfax, Louisiana (1873), and Hamburg and Ellenton, South Carolina, during the 1876 campaign.

The death toll from Reconstruction racial rioting stretched into the thousands, with additional victims raped, beaten, and robbed. Destruction of the property of individual African Americans was often total. For nearly 90 years after 1877, riots—while still occurring—declined in frequency, as the horror of the lynch mob became the most overt public tool of white violence. Many white Southerners justified even the most sadistic atrocities as vital to preserving their civilization.

*James G. Ryan*

**See also:** Black Troops (U.S. Colored Troops) in the Occupied South; Enforcement Acts (1870, 1871, 1875); Fifteenth Amendment (1870); Gun Clubs; Ku Klux Klan (KKK); Lost Cause; Militias; Redemption.

## Further Reading

Formwalt, Lee W. "The Camilla Massacre of 1868: Racial Violence as Political Propaganda." *Georgia Historical Quarterly* 71 (1987): 399–426.

Hardwick, Kevin R. " 'Your Old Father Abe Lincoln Is Dead and Damned': Black Soldiers and the Memphis Race Riot of 1866." *Journal of Social History* 27 (Fall 1993): 109–28.

Keith, Lee Anna. *The Colfax Massacre: The Untold Story of Black Power, White Terror, and the Death of Reconstruction.* New York: Oxford University Press, 2009.

Rable, George C. *But There Was No Peace: The Role of Violence in the Politics of Reconstruction.* Athens: University of Georgia Press, 1984.

Ryan, James G. "The Memphis Riots of 1866: Terror in a Black Community during Reconstruction." *Journal of Negro History* 62 (1977): 243–57.

Shapiro, Herbert. "Afro-American Responses to Race Violence during Reconstruction." *Science and Society* 36 (1972): 158–70.

Vandal, Gilles. *The New Orleans Riot of 1866: Anatomy of a Tragedy.* Lafayette: University of Southwestern Louisiana, 1983.

# RAINEY, JOSEPH HAYNE (1832–1887)

In 1870, Joseph Hayne Rainey became the first African American to serve in the U.S. House of Representatives, an accomplishment not surprising considering his background. Although born a slave in Georgetown, South Carolina, on June 21, 1832, when Rainey was a young child, his father purchased the family's freedom and moved them to Charleston. At some point in the late 1850s, he moved to Philadelphia, where he married a woman named Susan (her last name is unknown) in 1859. The couple moved back to Charleston, risking arrest since free African Americans were not permitted to return to the state having once left.

When the Civil War broke out, Rainey served as a steward on a blockade runner, but in 1862, Rainey and his family escaped to Bermuda. In Hamilton, Bermuda, Rainey began to educate himself and to be active in a fraternal lodge, experiences that prepared him well for political life during Reconstruction. After yellow fever slowed the economy in Bermuda in 1865, Rainey returned to Charleston. In postwar (and post-emancipation) Charleston, Rainey reestablished old ties and by early 1867, moved

Born a slave in South Carolina, Joseph Rainey escaped with his family to Bermuda during the war. He returned to help organize the state's Republican Party, and became the first African American elected to Congress (1870). (National Archives)

back to Georgetown to work as a merchant. He was elected as a delegate to the 1868 Constitutional Convention. In state politics, Rainey was a Conservative Republican, proposing unsuccessfully that the constitution include provisions for a poll tax to support education and for honoring prewar debts from slave purchases. He was not entirely conservative, however, attending the 1869 State Labor Convention and working on the South Carolina Land Commission.

Rainey was elected in 1870 to fill the unexpired term of B. F. Whittemore in the U.S. House of Representatives. He served from December 1870 to March 1879. When the Ku Klux Klan Act (the 1871 Enforcement Act) was debated in Congress, he told stories of atrocities in South Carolina. When Charles Sumner's Civil Rights Act of 1875 was on the floor, Rainey recounted instances when he, a sitting member of Congress, had been refused service. Coming from a district with a heavy African American population, Rainey was able to hold onto his House seat longer than many of his Republican colleagues. Even in the election of 1876, he was voted back in. By 1878, though, Republicans in South Carolina could not muster enough strength to hold even the stronghold of the First District, and Rainey left office in 1879, spending the next two years as an Internal Revenue Service agent in South Carolina. Rainey died on August 2, 1887.

*Bruce E. Baker*

***See also:*** Compromise of 1877; Congressional Reconstruction; Military Reconstruction Acts (1867–1868); Redemption.

## Further Reading

Foner, Eric. *Freedom's Lawmakers: Black Officeholders during Reconstruction*. Rev. ed. Baton Rouge: Louisiana State University Press, 1996.

Packwood, Cyril Outerbridge. *Detour—Bermuda, Destination—U.S. House of Representatives: The Life of Joseph Hayne Rainey*. Hamilton, Bermuda: Baxter's Ltd, 1977.

# RECUSANTS

Following the impeachment of President Andrew Johnson by the U.S. House of Representatives on February 24, 1868, the Senate convened as a high court to decide the president's guilt or innocence. In order to convict—and thereby remove—the executive of the nation, two-thirds of the senators needed to vote guilty. When the votes were taken, first on May 16 and then again on May 30, seven Republicans went against their party and voted with the Democrats to acquit the president. These seven are known as the "recusant senators," or simply the "recusants," a derogatory nickname used against Catholics in England who refused to convert to the Anglican Church.

For nearly three years, the Republican-controlled Congress had struggled with Johnson over Reconstruction policy. After allowing the president some latitude, and seeing that the president's program jeopardized much of what the war might have accomplished, Radical Republicans assumed control of Reconstruction. The elections of 1866 and the passage of the Military Reconstruction Acts in 1867 put the Republicans in a position to reshape the South (and even the nation at large), but the president still retained his position, and with it various methods of obstructing Congressional Reconstruction. The punching and counter-punching finally came to a head in the winter of 1867–1868, when, according to Congress, the president blatantly defied Congress and the law and fired his secretary of war, Edwin M. Stanton. A few weeks later, on February 24, the House voted 128–47 to impeach the president—even though as yet no formal charges existed. The House then drew up 11 formal "articles of impeachment" to serve as the charges and delivered these to seven impeachment managers who would serve as prosecutors, and likewise to the team chosen by Johnson to serve as his defense counsel.

The Senate trial opened on March 30, and the president greeted it with confidence. He believed the central argument of the articles—that he had broken the law by removing Stanton in defiance of the Tenure of Office Act—was weak, and he was right. Many questioned the constitutionality of the law (even Stanton himself) and many believed it did not even apply in this case. Johnson was also confident because the numbers worked in his favor. A two-thirds majority was required for conviction, so the Johnson team needed 19 "not guilty" votes. There were 12 Democrats (or very Conservative Republicans) on whom the president could count for not-guilty votes. Thus, he needed only 7 of the remaining 42 other senators to vote not guilty as well.

After several postponements, the Senate voted for the first time on May 16. The Senate would vote on each article separately, so Republicans opted to open with Article XI, which charged the president with obstructing Congress. Knowing the tenure law was dubious, Radicals believed this to be their strongest charge. Chief Justice Salmon P. Chase proceeded in alphabetical order, and senators and the crowds in the galleries (a limited number of tickets were gifted out) held their breath with each passing name. Especially tense were the senators with Moderate tendencies, who would be the swing voters in the most important trial in American history; of these, Edmund G. Ross weighed the greatest, because he was the last real unknown—the votes of senators after him were obvious. When Justice Chase asked "How say ye?" to Edmund G. Ross of Kansas, there was dead silence. He voted not guilty, after which Chase proceeded to call the rest. The vote was 35 guilty to 19 not guilty; seven Republicans had joined the Democrats to save the president.

Almost immediately, the term "recusant" appeared to label the seven: William Pitt Fessenden of Maine, James W. Grimes of Iowa, Joseph S. Fowler (1820–1902) of Tennessee, Lyman Trumbull of Illinois, Edmund G. Ross of Kansas, John B. Henderson (1826–1913) of Missouri, and Peter Van Winkle (1808–1872) of West Virginia. "Recusant" referred to those Catholics who refused to attend formal Anglican (Church of England) services in England during the 17th and 18th centuries; in the United States of 1868, with its heavily Protestant culture deeply distrustful—even hostile—to Catholics, the epithet stuck.

With the vote failing to convict by the slimmest of margins—one vote—the Senate adjourned to provide time to regroup, and possibly to convince these recusants to vote the proper way. Two weeks later, on May 30, the Senate reconvened as a high court of impeachment, and took up Article II, which charged the president with violating the Tenure of Office Act. The vote was exactly the same, to the person: 35–19. With the most general article having failed, and now the most specific article also being voted down, Republican senators held out little hope for the other articles, which offered vague charges of "conspiracy." The Senate adjourned the court, the trial was over, and the president remained in office.

The controversy did not pass as easily. Impeachment managers immediately charged the recusants—in particular Ross—with receiving bribes for their votes. The Radicals needed a scapegoat, an explanation for the recusants' behavior, who they saw as traitors to their party and to the Republic in general. Investigations into bank accounts and personal finances yielded nothing, although many recusants—including Ross—did benefit significantly from the president's patronage during his remaining months in office. Many different reasons explain why these seven voted as they did. First, one needs to understand that Ross's vote was probably not as critical as history paints it; his later writings played up his vote, and there is evidence that if he had voted guilty, there were Republican senators who might have changed to "not guilty" later on in the count. Readers should remember that there was no vice president at the time; removing Johnson would put in the executive's chair president *pro tem* of the Senate Benjamin Wade, a Radical who was disliked and distrusted on both sides of the aisle. Other theories point to Johnson suddenly being able to compromise. During the trial, he stopped his public ridicule of Congress, supported the readmission of South Carolina and Arkansas under congressional terms, and followed the tenure law to the letter in nominating a new secretary of war, John M. Schofield. Other forces also worked in the president's favor, such as a chief justice who kept the trial from devolving into a Radical kangaroo court, and a superb defense counsel featuring two former attorneys general (Reverdy Johnson and Henry Stanbery) and a former U.S. Supreme Court justice (Benjamin R. Curtis).

Six of the seven recusants actually submitted opinions, as would a judge in a court case. These writings indicate that weak charges worked against conviction. The tenure act was dubious at best, and many of the seven either did not believe a law had been broken or did not believe the charges measured anything really impeachable. For those seeing the trial through a more political lens, there too the president had an advantage. After all, Congress was already veto proof, and Johnson's authority was minimal at best. Several of the seven, William Pitt Fessenden most prominently, openly warned that removing a president was so dangerous, so unprecedented, that it would permanently alter the checks and balances set forth in the U.S. Constitution. With Congress in control of Reconstruction, with the president certainly a lame duck in every way but name, these Moderates saw more harm than good coming from such an unprecedented move. Whereas Radical Republicans saw Johnson as a threat to Reconstruction, some of the seven saw his removal as a threat to the Republic.

Tales abound regarding the fate and later careers of the seven "traitors," some of whom were called "martyrs" because their stand allegedly cost them their careers. Indeed, none of the seven were reelected to the Senate, but many reasons might account for this. For instance, Fessenden, Grimes, and Van Winkle all died before their terms expired; some argue their age and status gave them "nothing to lose," so they voted their conscience willingly. For others, it may be a case of "chicken versus the egg": one can argue that their votes ruined their political careers or one can say that they voted the way they did because they were exasperated with Congress and frustrated with the Republican agenda. If the latter is the case, their leaving politics makes perfect sense. The most famous, Ross, left the Senate in 1871, moved into the Liberal Republican Party, and eventually became a Democrat. He did not return to Washington, but instead went back into the newspaper business, moved to New Mexico, and became territorial governor under President Grover Cleveland. Fowler and Henderson never ran again for the Senate; Fowler moved permanently to Washington, D.C., where he operated a law practice until his death in 1902. Henderson became a U.S. attorney and author. Trumbull served in the Senate until 1873, by which time he also had moved toward the Liberal Republicans and finally retired from politics and returned to law.

*Richard Zuczek*

*See also:* Democratic National Convention (1868); Democratic Party; Presidential Reconstruction; Republicans, Moderate.

## Further Reading

Bergeron, Paul H., Glenna Schroeder-Lein, Marion O. Smith, Lisa Williams, and Richard Zuczek, eds. *The Papers of Andrew Johnson.* Vol. 14. Knoxville: University of Tennessee Press, 1997.

Rehnquist, William H. *Grand Inquests: The Historic Impeachments of Justice Samuel Chase and President Andrew Johnson.* New York: William Morrow, 1992.

Roske, Ralph J. "The Seven Martyrs?" *American Historical Review* 64 (January 1959): 323–30.

Ross, Edmund G. "History of the Impeachment of Andrew Johnson [1868]," taken online from Avalon Project at Yale University, http://www.yale.edu/lawweb/avalon.

Schroeder-Lein, Glenna, and Richard Zuczek. *Andrew Johnson: A Biographical Companion.* Santa Barbara, CA: ABC-CLIO, 2001.

# REDEMPTION

"Redemption" was the name given by Conservative white Southerners for their goal in the South: save white Southern civilization by defeating the Republican Party and its black allies. Those engaged in this struggle were the Redeemers. In selecting the Christian term "Redemption," the Redeemers equated the political restoration of the Southern Democratic Party with the saving of an errant soul headed toward damnation.

The Redeemers' crusade began in response to the enactment of the Reconstruction Acts in 1867. This legislation marked the beginning of Congressional or Radical Reconstruction. It divided the South into military districts and fostered the ascendancy of the Republican Party by dissolving the Conservative state governments that had emerged immediately following the Civil War. Thus, the Southern white Democrats who had been swept from power by the Reconstruction Acts set about formulating a strategy for political restoration or Redemption.

In the Upper South states of Virginia, Tennessee, and North Carolina, Redemption came quite early. The fractiousness of these Republican state governments, a relatively small black voting population, and the application of violent intimidation by organizations such as the Ku Klux Klan, allowed the Redeemers to eke out narrow victories by 1870. A similar set of dynamics led to the Redemption of Georgia in 1871.

In the rest of the South, however, redemption came as a result of several converging forces. Republican infighting often hampered effective governance. These divisions came to a head in 1872, when opponents to the reelection of Ulysses S. Grant formed the splinter Liberal Republican Party. Corruption, both within the Grant administration and Southern Republican state governments, weakened national support for Reconstruction and the regular Republican Party. Racism also worked against the party that had elevated African Americans to full citizenship, especially in the South. Outside factors also favored the Redeemers. The Panic of 1873, a major worldwide financial depression, fueled the perception that garrisoning the South was a waste of taxpayers' money. Meanwhile, the U.S. Supreme Court undermined laws designed to prop up Southern Republican regimes. *United States v. Cruikshank* (1876) effectively gutted the Enforcement Acts that had been passed by Congress to curb violence against Republicans in the South, and the Slaughterhouse Cases (1873) greatly weakened federal authority over the Fourteenth Amendment.

Redeemers, however, were active agents as well. Violence was one tool, although it had limited effectiveness. Ku Klux Klan activity had mostly brought about national support for the Enforcement Acts, and although it played some role in the Redemption of the Upper South, the Klan's activity was poorly coordinated with political objectives. More sophisticated forms of opposition emerged in 1874, with the advent of the White League, Rifle Clubs, and later, the Red Shirts. Unlike the Klan, these paramilitary organizations did not hide behind a mask. They also had strong political underpinnings and orchestrated their activities closely with the Democratic Party. Their martial presence somewhat suppressed black voter turnout. Much of their violence targeted prominent white Republicans, demoralizing black followers and sending an ominous warning to other scalawags and carpetbaggers. Economic intimidation was also a powerful tool available to the Redeemers.

As landlords, they could evict those who worked their land; thus Redeemers could affect Republican voter turnout without resorting to violence and without provoking federal intervention.

Violence and intimidation, combined with a weakened Republican Party, brought about the Redemption of Texas in 1873, Alabama and Arkansas in 1874, and Mississippi in 1875. On the eve of the 1876 presidential contest between Democrat Samuel J. Tilden and Republican Rutherford B. Hayes, only Louisiana, South Carolina, and Florida remained unredeemed. The disputed results from these three states proved pivotal to the outcome of the presidential race, and led to the Compromise of 1877. Among other stipulations, these Southern states gave their electoral votes to Hayes, while the Republican candidate pledged to withdraw federal troops from the South. Left undefended, the remaining Republican governments quickly collapsed. By the spring of 1877, the Democrats had fully redeemed the South.

The Democratic Redeemers who took control of the South were often referred to as "Bourbons," a reference to the Bourbon monarchies that returned to the French throne after the fall of Napoleon. The Redeemer governments quickly instituted a system of fiscal retrenchment, gutting state spending on social services such as education for poor African Americans and whites alike. The Redeemer generation would ultimately usher in the era of the New South by emphasizing sectional reconciliation, encouraging Northern investment in the Southern economy, and eliminating any hint of black political or social equality.

*Justin A. Nystrom*

**See also:** Gun Clubs; Jim Crow Laws; U.S. Army and Reconstruction; *names of individual Southern states.*

## Further Reading

Egerton, Douglas R. *The Wars of Reconstruction: The Brief, Violent History of America's Most Progressive Era.* New York: Bloomsbury Press, 2014.

Fitzgerald, Michael W. *Splendid Failure: Postwar Reconstruction in the American South.* New York: Ivan R. Dee Publishers, 2008

Gillette, William. *Retreat from Reconstruction: 1869–1879.* Baton Rouge: Louisiana State University Press, 1979.

Perman, Michael. *The Road to Redemption: Southern Politics, 1869–1880.* Chapel Hill: University of North Carolina Press, 1984.

Rable, George C. But *There Was No Peace: The Role of Violence in the Politics of Reconstruction.* Athens: University of Georgia Press, 1984.

# RED SHIRTS

The Red Shirts were a paramilitary arm of the Democratic Party in Mississippi and South Carolina that was decisive in the elections of 1875 and 1876, respectively, in those states. Red Shirts were an outgrowth of the politically involved gun clubs that appeared in many Southern states in the mid-1870s.

The Red Shirts first emerged during the Mississippi election of 1875 as part of the Mississippi Plan (also called the Shotgun Plan). When Republicans held political meetings, they were often greeted by mounted white men wielding rifles and shotguns who carefully avoided making direct threats but allowed their intimidating presence to carry a clear message: White Democrats were determined to end Republican rule. Armed Conservative whites, many of whom were Confederate veterans, would gallop about, interrupting and harassing speakers, firing their guns into the air, even demanding "equal time" to address the crowd. The clubs never took open, direct action against Republicans, careful to not draw too much federal attention—and federal intervention. Nonetheless, these groups were involved in several assassinations, attacks on black militia units, and race riots. Their physical presence, plus touches of economic intimidation and outright fraud, doomed the Mississippi Republicans in 1875.

The origin of the red shirt as the uniform of these Democratic paramilitary forces remains unclear. Some argue it was a sarcastic response to the "Bloody Shirt" technique used so successfully by Radical Republicans in Congress. Others contend it had ties to Garibaldi's Red Shirts of the 1860s, who took part in the independence movement that resulted in Italian unification during that decade.

Nonetheless, observing the effectiveness of the Shotgun Plan in Mississippi, South Carolina Democrats decided to emulate it for the election of 1876. Although Wade Hampton III was the Democratic nominee for governor, it was his lieutenant, Martin W. Gary, who took the lead in planning the grassroots mobilization of Democrats across the state. He called for each township in each county to reorganize the party, and out of most of these local Democratic units grew parallel Red Shirt clubs. Historians estimate that at the height of the campaign, there were as many as 290 clubs with 15,000 Red Shirts in South Carolina (in a state with approximately 150,000 men of voting age). One contemporary observer also suggested that earlier Grange organizations formed the nucleus of many Red Shirt clubs, a contention supported by research in Mississippi. Eager to overawe and sway African American voters, the Democrats even encouraged the formation of Red Shirt clubs composed of black members.

Red Shirts in South Carolina carried out several functions, some political and some better described as military. As Wade Hampton toured the state in September and October 1876 campaigning for the governor's office, he was greeted in many towns by tremendous parades of mounted Red Shirts. Red Shirts also crashed Republican meetings, forcing the Republicans to "divide time" with Democratic speakers if they wanted to hold their meeting. This tactic not only deprived potential Republican voters of the information relayed in the speech but also showed that Republican politicians could not defend themselves, much less their constituents. Federal troops were still stationed in the state but had no authority to act against the carefully nuanced intimidation.

There was violence, but considering the demographics and region, soldiers could never track down and locate perpetrators. In violent outbreaks such as the Hamburg Massacre and the Ellenton Riot, Red Shirts played a direct military role, killing dozens of African Americans in these clashes. By election day, the sight of Red Shirts near the polls succeeded in intimidating many would-be Republican voters and nullifying the Republicans' numerical advantage. The Democrats came close enough to contest the election, which remained one of three undecided contests that figured into federal maneuvering during the winters of 1876 and 1877. Again, without the promise of federal support, the situation for the Republican incumbent, Daniel H. Chamberlain, was hopeless. By April 1877, the Red Shirt army had placed Hampton in the governor's chair.

Even after Reconstruction, the Red Shirts remained active in South Carolina politics. In 1878, Red Shirts carried out much the same function as they had in 1876, and in 1880 and 1882, they harassed and attacked candidates and supporters of dissenting political parties such as the Greenback-Labor Party. In the 20th century, many white Southerners approved of their role in "redeeming" the South and lionized the Red Shirts for ending Reconstruction.

*Bruce E. Baker*

*See also:* Bourbons; Compromise of 1877; Hayes, Rutherford Birchard (1822–1893); Redemption; U.S. Army and Reconstruction; White League.

## Further Reading

Fitzgerald, Michael W. *Splendid Failure: Postwar Reconstruction in the American South.* New York: Ivan R. Dee Publishers, 2008

Kantrowitz, Stephen. *Ben Tillman and the Reconstruction of White Supremacy.* Chapel Hill: University of North Carolina Press, 2000.

Williams, Alfred B. *Hampton and His Red Shirts: South Carolina's Deliverance in 1876.* Charleston, SC: Walker, Evans, and Cogswell, 1935.

Zuczek, Richard. *State of Rebellion: Reconstruction in South Carolina.* Columbia: University of South Carolina Press, 1996.

## REED, HARRISON (1813–1899)

Harrison Reed was elected in 1868 as Florida's first governor under Congressional Reconstruction and oversaw the state's readmission into the Union. Although Reed took a very moderate approach in addressing the state's problems during Reconstruction, political infighting, terrorism, and charges of corruption marked his tenure as the state's chief executive. These volatile issues culminated with several attempts on his life and four unsuccessful efforts to impeach and remove him from office.

Reed was born in Littleton, Massachusetts, on August 26, 1813. He moved to Wisconsin in 1837, where he became editor of newspapers in both Milwaukee and Madison. In

1847, he was elected as a delegate to the state constitutional convention and participated in the drafting of the state's first constitution. He joined the Republican Party almost at its inception, in 1854, and his early embracing of the party paid dividends for him with the election of Abraham Lincoln in 1860. Reed received an appointment as a treasury agent in Florida, where he oversaw the sale and distribution of confiscated lands in Florida and Georgia. Removed from office on allegations of distributing land to friends, President Andrew Johnson sent him back to Florida as the state's postmaster, and he was soon one of the most powerful Republicans in the state.

Reed sought to create a coalition between Florida's Moderate Republicans and members of the state's Democratic Party. In 1865, when asked by the Johnson administration for his advice regarding the selection of a provisional governor for the state, he suggested William J. Marvin, a longtime Conservative Florida resident, whom he felt would embrace Presidential Reconstruction and not antagonize local whites. After the disintegration of Johnson's Reconstruction plan, Reed sought to continue the Republican and Democrat coalition by calling for the creation of a new political party. By emphasizing the rebuilding of the state rather than black suffrage, this new alliance of prominent political leaders and businessmen ultimately propelled Reed into the office of governor in 1868 under Congressional Reconstruction.

Reed's election as Florida's governor in 1868 marked the apex of his political career and the end of the fragile coalition of Moderates and Conservatives he had created during Presidential Reconstruction. By early fall 1868, many of his Republican allies had already turned against him, some as a result of his refusal to participate in their plans to develop a railroad in the state, others, including most African Americans living in the state, because of his alliance with Florida's Democrats. Similarly, some Democrats abandoned him once he had subdued the Radical threat in the state. This opposition led to four separate attempts to remove Reed from office. The charges ranged from the theft of government funds to accepting bribes and kickbacks from railroad companies. Reed skillfully fought each impeachment challenge and in each case refused to acknowledge the legitimacy of the indictments.

Reed's relationship with Florida's freedmen was no better than his relationship with his party. Although he appointed an African American, Jonathan C. Gibbs, as his secretary of state in an effort to secure their allegiance, he often fell out of favor with them because of his reluctance to use his executive power to protect them from violence by groups such as the Ku Klux Klan. Under Reed's watch, there were more than 200 reported Klan outrages and vigilante murders in the state, most of which centered in areas where the majority of the population was African American. Reed himself received several death threats from vigilante groups and fled the state capital several times for his own safety.

But the political survivor could not gather enough support to gain his party's nomination in the 1872 gubernatorial election. When Reed's term ended in 1872, he returned to his home near Jacksonville, Florida, and remained there in relative obscurity until his death on May 25, 1899.

*Learotha Williams Jr.*

*See also:* Carpetbaggers; Elections of 1868; Military Reconstruction Acts (1867–1868).

## Further Reading

Current, Richard N. *Three Carpetbag Governors*. Baton Rouge: Louisiana State University Press, 1967.

Shofner, Jerrell H. *Nor Is It over Yet: Florida in the Era of Reconstruction, 1863–1877.* Gainesville: University Presses of Florida, 1974.

## REID, WHITELAW (1837–1912)

Whitelaw Reid was a reporter, editor, publisher, vice presidential candidate, and diplomat.

A clergyman's son, Reid was born near Xenia, Ohio, and given a good classical education. Polished, well read, erudite, reserved, and, when need be, ruthless, he was made for a special correspondent's pen, rather than a day-to-day penny-a-line journalist's. His first serious foray into journalism came as "Agate," the *Cincinnati Gazette*'s lively Washington correspondent during the Civil War. His reports were clear, shrewd, and generally as fair as his Radical Republicanism could make them. There was no love lost for him in the War Department, due to his criticisms of Secretary Edwin M. Stanton, and his confidential relationship with later Supreme Court chief justice Salmon P. Chase which allowed him to accompany the jurist on a postwar tour of the South. Reid's impressions in *After the War* (1866) were chatty, insightful, and deeply skeptical about the way Reconstruction was going. Although he was biased, he clearly sensed the difficulty African Americans were having adjusting to freedom, and the hostility whites had adjusting to defeat.

As a reporter Whitelaw Reid wrote a revealing travel journal of the defeated South called *After the War* (1866). He soon after paired with Horace Greeley to operate the *New York Tribune*, and later managed the latter's 1872 presidential run. (Chaiba Media)

In 1868, Horace Greeley invited him to share the editorial duties on the *New York Tribune*, and Reid made one of America's best newspapers even better, with crackerjack reporting from the South and elsewhere. His articles exposed the rottenness of politics in South Carolina under the so-called negro rule (a series of letters by James S. Pike later turned into a devastating book, *The Prostrate State*) and challenged the credibility of witnesses to racial violence in the Deep South. Perhaps shaken by these developments, Reid moved away from radicalism and became one of the power brokers in the Liberal Republican convention of 1872, a staunch supporter of Greeley's nomination for president.

After Greeley's defeat and untimely death, Reid took over control of the *Tribune*, allegedly with money supplied by railroad speculator Jay Gould. He remained in control for the next 40 years, less and less interested in the day-to-day affairs of the newspaper and sluggish about innovation. It took his son, Ogden Mills Reid, to turn the *Tribune* back into a first-rate paper. Reid himself became minister to France (1889–1892) and vice presidential nominee in 1892. He served ably on the peace commission at the end of the Spanish American War and was all the more ardent an imperialist for his fear that the true white race in the United States, as he saw it, was imperiled by dilution from the scum of the universe—which seemed to include just about everybody everywhere. Theodore Roosevelt made him ambassador to Great Britain in 1905, and he held office until his death in 1912.

*Mark W. Summers*

**See also:** Elections of 1876; Grant, Ulysses S. (1822–1885); Presidential Reconstruction.

## Further Reading

Kluger, Richard. *The Paper: The Life and Death of the New York Herald Tribune.* New York: Alfred A. Knopf, 1986.

# REPUBLICANS, LIBERAL

The Liberal Republicans of the 1870s defined a middle ground in post-Civil War politics that wedded radical demands for human equality with Conservative demands for small government. The Liberal Republican movement came out of Missouri in 1870 and gained enough momentum to field a presidential ticket for the election of 1872. Although it died as a formal organization after flopping in the election, the movement's ideals filtered back into the Republican and Democratic Parties, defining a middle ground in American politics for the rest of the century.

The Liberal Republican movement grew out of the peculiar circumstances of Missouri in the Civil War era. Horrific guerrilla warfare tore the state apart during the conflict, so Republicans rewrote the state's constitution in 1865 in such a way as to disfranchise Democrats. The Republican Party controlled the state, and Senator Charles Drake controlled the party. Prominent politician Carl Schurz of Missouri believed political machines like Drake's threatened American democracy; he opposed Drake's selected nominees, ran for the Senate, and won.

Schurz condemned the spoils system of government administration and also advocated for full restoration of Northern Democrats' political privileges. By 1870, Schurz began a movement to join Democrats and Moderate Republicans to change Missouri's voting restrictions. The regular Republicans drove Schurz and his supporters out of the party, which only emboldened the so-called reformers; in response the coalition nominated B. Gratz Brown for governor and against all odds won the statehouse. Schurz and his allies argued that government dominated by a single powerful party opened the door to tyranny, and the Republican Party's hold on federal and state positions was leading to a corrupt organization designed primarily to keep supporters in office.

Schurz had outlined the principles that would organize opposition to the Republican administration leading up to the election of 1872. In May 1872, reformers seeking an alternative between the national Republican machine and the hostile white Southern Democrats organized the Liberal Republican convention. At the Cincinnati Convention, which opened on May 1, the Liberal Republicans addressed the growing disaffection toward President Ulysses S. Grant's administration. Trying to recapture the liberal dream of individual responsibility and independence within the political strictures of the postwar era, their platform called for the recognition of the Thirteenth Amendment, Fourteenth Amendment, and Fifteenth Amendment to the U.S. Constitution, asserting that all men were equal before the law and that "it is the duty of Government . . . to mete out equal and exact justice to all, of whatever nativity, race, color, or persuasion, religious or political." Insisting on protection for black suffrage, the platform went on to demand "the immediate and absolute removal of all disabilities" imposed on former confederates. Demanding civil service reform, reformers complained that "the civil service of the government has become a mere instrument of partisan tyranny and personal ambition, and an object of selfish greed. It is a scandal and reproach upon free institutions, and breeds a demoralization dangerous to the perpetuity of republican government." Liberal Republicans held a middle course for the nation, refusing to accept the demands of laborers for favorable legislation or the tendency of big businessmen to buy political influence. Unwilling, though, to take a stand on the tariff out of fear of alienating voters on one side or the other, they planted the seeds of their own destruction.

While Schurz was the guiding force of the convention, events quickly ran away from him. Schurz hoped to see B. Gratz Brown as the presidential nominee, but pro-tariff delegations engineered an arrangement to throw the nomination to Horace Greeley, the eccentric editor of the *New York Tribune*, well known as an advocate of protective tariffs. While Greeley answered the needs of the pro-tariff men, his candidacy was deeply problematic. He was a pompous little man, abrasive and dictatorial in print, who supported a wide range of causes—like women's rights—that most Americans regarded with suspicion. Most damaging was that, during the war, he had been vicious towards Southerners and Democrats, an unavoidable fact that struck deep at the heart of the Liberal Republican voting base. Even Schurz washed his hands of Greeley's candidacy.

The campaign itself had troubling implications for American politics. Unwilling to see the writing on the wall, Greeley wore himself out in a frantic campaign that was unable to attract necessary voters. At the same time, the newspapers loyal to Liberal Republicanism hammered home the idea that the Republican administration was catering to lazy African Americans and rich businessmen, tainting American political rhetoric with the idea that black voters were looking only for government handouts, which Republicans were happy to provide in return for the chance to harness the government to the needs of big business. In September, news came of the massive Credit Mobilier scandal, charging prominent congressmen, senators, and even the Grant's vice president with accepting railroad stock in exchange for railroad legislation, but their accusations did little harm. In 1872, African Americans nationwide would vote for the first time in the presidential election, and their political loyalties were with the regular Republican Party and Ulysses S. Grant.

In the fall, most Democrats simply stayed home, refusing to vote for a pro-tariff man who had made a career attacking them, and Grant won handily. Weeks later, exhausted and broken, Greeley died. Angry supporters carried forward the themes of the campaign, blaming African Americans for handing the election to Grant, accusing black men of being interested only in government jobs paid for by tax dollars.

The Liberal Republican movement was more significant than its short history seems to indicate. The ideas that its supporters had articulated became the standard language of late 19th-century America. After 1872, the threat of government corruption at the hands of businessmen or grasping poor became the dominant language of American political rhetoric. While this meant attempts to undercut the political influence of big business and organized labor, it also meant that black voters increasingly bore the blame for an expensive government that seemed not to respond to the average white American. By the turn of the century, Americans would take steps to limit popular suffrage, to reduce the political influence of big business, and, most strikingly, to keep African Americans from the polls.

*Heather Cox Richardson*

**See also:** Abolition of Slavery; Amnesty Proclamations; Congressional Reconstruction; Fifteenth Amendment (1870); Fourteenth Amendment (1868); Labor Systems; New Departure; Presidential Reconstruction; Republicans, Moderate; Republicans, Radical; Thirteenth Amendment (1865).

## Further Reading

Chamberlin, Everett. *The Struggle of '72: The Issues and Candidates of the Present Political Campaign*. Chicago: Union Publishing Co., 1872, http://www.hti.umich.edu/m/moagrp/.

Parrish, William E. *Missouri under Radical Rule, 1865–1870*. Columbia: University of Missouri Press, 1965.

Richardson, Heather Cox. *The Death of Reconstruction: Race, Labor, and Politics in the Post-Civil War North*. Cambridge, MA: Harvard University Press, 2001.

Ross, Earle Dudley. *The Liberal Republican Movement*. New York: Henry Holt and Co., 1919.

Schurz, Carl. *The Reminiscences of Carl Schurz*. Vol. 3. New York: Doubleday, Page and Co., 1909, pp. 292–310.

Sproat, John G. *The Best Men: Liberal Reformers in the Gilded Age*. New York: Oxford University Press, 1968.

## REPUBLICANS, MODERATE

During the Civil War, the separation between Radical and Conservative Republicans was rather clear, turning on whether to take aggressive steps to abolish slavery to prosecute the war. Most Republican congressmen were identified with Radicalism, while many from Border States, some governors, and several of Abraham Lincoln's cabinet members were identified as Conservatives. With the war's end, however, a number of important Republican leaders who had supported Radical measures drew back. Among the most important were William Pitt Fessenden of Maine and Lyman Trumbull of Illinois, who were recognized as senior leaders in the Senate, and Rep. John A. Bingham of Ohio, one of the most influential Republican lawyers in the House. Contemporaries used the term "moderate" to describe these men, practical politicians trying to steer a course between the Radicals and the Conservatives, hoping to hold the support of Northern voters and appeal to Southerners Unionists and former Whigs.

In the first year of Reconstruction, these Moderate Republicans also worked to reconcile the Republican Party and President Andrew Johnson, the former Democrat who became president after Abraham Lincoln's assassination. Interestingly, more historians now recognize that these "Moderate" or "centrist" Republicans played the central role in what once was called "Radical Reconstruction." More and more scholars are simply using the term "Congressional Reconstruction" to identify the Republican program, realizing that Moderates, not Radicals, really shaped the course of Reconstruction and defined the terms of readmission.

At first Moderates' vision of restoration was in step with Johnson's as both sought limited change, no punishment for Southern whites, and a speedy return to the Union. But the total indifference to the plight of newly freed African Americans, or worse, the passing of Black Codes to restrict freedpeople's rights, pushed many Moderates to expand their demands. In 1866, the centrist leadership of Congress passed a Civil Rights Act defining citizenship to include African Americans and guaranteeing them the same basic rights as white citizens. Moderates also proposed a new amendment to the Constitution that would write similar principles into the Constitution itself—civil rights would be guaranteed, but not black suffrage. States would lose representation if they chose not to grant the vote to black males, but Moderates did not impose black suffrage. If the Southern state governments ratified the Fourteenth Amendment and amended their laws and state constitutions to conform to its provisions, Moderate leaders indicated that those states would be restored to normal relations in the Union, and their representatives and senators would be admitted to Congress. When President Johnson vetoed the civil rights bill and publicly opposed ratification of the Fourteenth Amendment, many Moderates began to question if they could work with him at all. When the legislatures of the Johnson-created Southern state governments rejected the Fourteenth Amendment (except Tennessee, which thus escaped most of the Reconstruction process), Republicans joined together to construct a new reconstruction program.

The Military Reconstruction Acts, passed in the spring of 1867, placed Southern states under military supervision until black and white Southerners established new state governments and ratified the Fourteenth Amendment. Again, even the new program represented a compromise between Moderate and more Radical Republicans. Moderates now endorsed some proposals that Radicals had advocated, especially equal suffrage regardless of race, but rejected others, such as land confiscation.

Even with some consensus on Congressional Reconstruction (the so-called Radical Reconstruction), Republicans still remained divided, now over how to deal with President Johnson, who denounced the program as unconstitutional and did everything he could to thwart it. Both on principle and because of its political dangers, Moderates rejected Radical arguments that such presidential obstruction merited impeachment and removal. Losses in local elections in the fall of 1867 reconfirmed their caution. In December 1867, Moderate Republicans joined Democrats to defeat an impeachment resolution by a large margin in the House of Representatives. Perhaps emboldened by this, Johnson became ever more aggressive. In February 1868, he removed Secretary of War Edwin M. Stanton in defiance of the Tenure of Office Act passed a year earlier. Once again, Conservative and Moderate Republicans adopted a Radical policy that they had earlier resisted, and Republicans unified to impeach the president.

However, in the subsequent trial before the Senate, Moderates returned to their reasoned, compromise approach. They sustained rulings by Chief Justice Salmon P. Chase, who presided over the trial and who imposed neutral judicial procedures and decorum. While Radicals argued that impeachment was designed to remedy inherently political abuses of presidential power, most Moderates insisted on a narrower, more legalistic interpretation of the process. In the end, many centrists joined Radicals in voting to convict the president, but the most powerful Republican centrists, including Fessenden and Trumbull, joined Conservative Republicans and Democrats, voting to acquit him.

After Ulysses S. Grant's victory in the presidential election of 1868, Radicals and more Conservative Republicans divided over the last great act of Reconstruction—the framing of the Fifteenth Amendment, which barred racial qualifications for voting. Most Moderates joined Conservatives to reject proposals that would have barred voting tests based not only on race but also on religion, ethnicity, property, and literacy. The Fifteenth Amendment explicitly secured the right to vote only against deprivation on the grounds of race, color, and previous status as a slave.

With the election of a Republican president, the ratification of the Fifteenth Amendment, and the readmission of the last of the former Confederate states to the Union in 1870, contemporaries referred less and less to the divisions among Conservative, Moderate, and Radical Republicans. Although Reconstruction had not fully run its course, and the Republican Party would face decisions on supporting their Southern brethren and enforcing blacks' rights, the questions that delineated Republican wings during the Civil War and Reconstruction had been settled.

*Michael Les Benedict*

**See also:** Elections of 1866; Greeley, Horace (1811–1872); House Judiciary Committee; Joint Committee on Reconstruction; National Union Movement (1866); New Departure; Presidential Reconstruction; Race Riots; Recusants.

## Further Reading

Benedict, Michael Les. *A Compromise of Principle: Congressional Republicans and Reconstruction, 1863–1869*. New York: W. W. Norton, 1974.

Donald, David. *The Politics of Reconstruction, 1863–1867*. Baton Rouge: Louisiana State University Press, 1965. Reprint, Cambridge, MA: Harvard University Press, 1984.

Jellison, Charles A. *Fessenden of Maine, Civil War Senator*. Syracuse, NY: Syracuse University Press, 1962.

Krug, Mark L. *Lyman Trumbull, Conservative Radical*. New York: A. S. Barnes, 1965.

# REPUBLICANS, RADICAL

The Radical Republicans were those members of the Republican Party who before the Civil War opposed any concessions to the South, favored emancipation during the conflict, and afterward insisted on civil rights and suffrage for at least some African Americans. Never an organized group, its membership varied, and its agenda on anything other than race could vary widely.

Often former Free Soilers, or antislavery Whigs or Democrats, during the 1850s, such Radicals as Benjamin F. Wade, Charles Sumner, and Salmon P. Chase in the Senate and George W. Julian and Thaddeus Stevens in the House following the passage of the Kansas-Nebraska Act were instrumental in the creation of the Republican Party. Unable to nominate a candidate in 1860, they supported the Moderate Abraham Lincoln, whose antislavery convictions had been made abundantly clear, so that his end aims were not too different from theirs.

During the secession crisis, the Radicals opposed any concessions to the South, including the surrender of Fort Sumter, an effort that was crowned with success when the president supplied the fort and the Civil War began. During the first months of the war, the Radicals fully supported the administration. In control of many congressional committees after Congress met on July 4, 1861, they freely voted for money, supplies, and arms, and legalized the measures the president had taken to foil the secessionists prior to the meeting of Congress. As time went on, however, they became critical of the administration. In December 1861, they formed the Joint Select Committee on the Conduct of the War, which used its powers to urge more aggressive military action. Beyond preserving the Union, the Radicals' chief aim during the war was to effect total emancipation. Without Radical pressure, it is doubtful that he could have promulgated his Emancipation Proclamation in September 1862, maintained it against Conservative pressure, and carried it into effect on January 1, 1863. Individual abolition measures to end slavery in the Border States followed, as did his pressure to pass the Thirteenth Amendment in the winter of 1864–1865.

One of the Radicals' principal differences with Lincoln involved the problem of Reconstruction. Radicals believed that Congress should control the process, that significant thought be given to complete abolition, and that former confederates be stricken from political power. But Lincoln believed that the states were still in the Union, and that it was up to the president to restore them to their proper relationship with the federal government; when he published his Amnesty Proclamation, Radicals criticized his idea of relying on 10 percent of the voters of 1860 in a state to be restored, as well his failure to fully spell out complete emancipation. Radicals responded with the Wade-Davis Bill, which required 50 percent of the white inhabitants for the initiation of Reconstruction and the swearing of an ironclad loyalty oath for prospective voters. Tension escalated when Lincoln pocket-vetoed the bill, and Radicals in Congress subsequently published a "manifesto" warning that the president was usurping power.

Making relations worse was the open secret that Radicals had tried to drop Lincoln for a more radical candidate in 1864, such as Gen. Benjamin Butler or Treasury secretary Salmon P. Chase. The selection of General George McClellan as the Northern Democrats' candidate forced the Republicans to put aside differences; they united under the Union Party banner and secured Lincoln's reelection. Republican victory, however, did not solve the quarrel about Reconstruction.

The assassination of Abraham Lincoln at first seemed a boon to the Radicals. Although a Southern Democrat, Johnson was the only senator from a seceding state to remain loyal; he had been a member of the Joint Committee on the Conduct of the War and a no-nonsense military governor of Tennessee. Senator Ben Wade said to the new president on Easter Sunday, "Johnson, we have faith in you. By the gods, there will be no trouble now in running the government." "You can judge my policy by the past," replied the new president. "I hold this: Robbery is a crime; rape is a crime; murder is a crime; treason is a crime, and crime must be punished." Yet bluster and background aside, Johnson was more like Lincoln than the Radicals expected: the new president also sought a speedy restoration of Southern states and also believed the executive was the branch to control it.

In accordance with these principles, on May 29, 1865, Johnson issued an Amnesty Proclamation inviting all insurgents except 14 exempted classes to take an oath of allegiance and promising them amnesty. He coupled this with the appointment of a provisional governor for North Carolina who was to call for elections to start reconstituting the government on the basis of white suffrage. Similar proclamations for the other states followed. The result was the election of Conservatives and former confederates who not only attempted to reduce the freedpeople to a condition akin to slavery with the Black Codes, but also elected any number of high ranking ex-confederates, including ex-vice president Alexander H. Stephens, to Congress.

Now the Radicals faced a greater predicament: not only was the president operating on his own, but the former confederates were also in his camp, taking advantage of the lenient program to rebuild their society as they saw fit. Radicals convinced Moderate Republicans to temporarily block the president's program by refusing to admit any Southern representatives, even the most loyal to Congress; Republicans then established a Joint Committee on Reconstruction to investigate the pace and progress of Johnson's program. Radicals constituted a minority of the Republican Party, which consisted of Moderates and Conservatives as well, so they needed help from other factions if they were to redirect Reconstruction efforts.

Help came from the oddest of places: President Johnson. His actions in 1866, particularly his veto of the Freedmen's Bureau and civil rights bills, alienated the Moderates, adding to the Radical's momentum. With the voting support of Moderates, Radicals passed the bills over his veto, then drafted the Fourteenth Amendment, which granted citizenship to blacks, attempted to protect them from discrimination, and provided for the reduction of representation of states that disfranchised (denied the vote to) any males over the age of 21. In addition, it deprived all who had previously held federal office and then joined the Confederacy of the right to hold office. Although these measures all represented compromises between Moderates and Radicals, it was not that Radicals were losing their fire or backing off their goals; rather it was the Moderates who were turning against the president and pushing for greater change in the South.

Johnson continued to defy Congress, and thereby provided more fodder for Radicals. For the congressional elections of 1866, the president embarked on the National Union movement to form a new Conservative party, and he openly advocated rejection of the Fourteenth Amendment. Such obstinacy alienated Northern voters, who delivered a crushing blow to his party's hopes—and delivered the Congress completely to the Republicans. In early 1867, Congressional Reconstruction began, as Republicans placed Southern states under military control and imposed black suffrage on them. Such moves were radical on American soil, but Radicals did not get everything they wanted. Congress stopped short of redrawing state borders, confiscating and redistributing Confederate lands, and pushing black suffrage north.

Congress did restrict the executive's right to dismiss appointees without the consent of the Senate, via the Tenure of Office Act. Once Radicals elected one of their own (Ben Wade) as president *pro tem* of the Senate—and thus next in line for the presidency—they eagerly began impeachment investigations. Again Moderates blocked their initiatives, and again Johnson drove them together; his firing of Secretary of War Edwin M. Stanton convinced Republicans to unite, resulting in Johnson's impeachment. But again Radicals sought too much, and the attempt to remove him from office via Senate trial failed.

In the South, another form of competition played out. The Military Reconstruction Acts ushered in a Southern Republican Party, based on Northern migrants, Southern Unionists, and black males. Certainly the political and social shift was radical, but short-lived. The lack of land severely limited black opportunity, white Southern defiance exceeded everyone's expectations, and Northern dedication faded quickly. During the administration of Ulysses S. Grant, the Radicals succeeded in the adoption of the Fifteenth Amendment, prohibiting the denial of the right to vote on racial grounds, and passed several Enforcement Acts to combat Ku Klux Klan violence; but the specter of corruption and the depth of racism consistently undercut Radical efforts to fundamentally reshape Southern—and American—society.

By the mid-1870s, economic depression and time wore away at the ideals of the Civil War and Reconstruction, and the passing of leading Radicals further eroded the energy required for change. Finally, after the disputed election of 1876, as a result of the Compromise of 1877, President Rutherford B. Hayes withdrew federal troops from the state houses of the remaining Republican states, and Redemption, as the return to conservatism was called, swept away the last of the Republican Southern governments. The Radicals were reformers who had to adapt to circumstances and accept the possible when they could not achieve the ideal. Although many of their tactics and goals harbored vindictiveness and naïveté, many of their ideals possessed great principle and were a century ahead of their time.

*Hans L. Trefousse*

**See also:** Command of the Army Act (1867); Congressional Reconstruction; Recusants; Republicans, Moderate; Tenure of Office Act (1867); Wade-Davis Bill (1864).

## Further Reading

Bogue, Allan G. *The Earnest Men: Republicans of the Civil War Senate*. Ithaca, NY: Cornell University Press, 1981.

Hyman, Harold. *The Radical Republicans and Reconstruction, 1861–1870*. Indianapolis: Bobbs-Merrill, 1967.

Montgomery, David. *Beyond Equality: Labor and the Radical Republicans, 1862–1872*. New York: Alfred A. Knopf, 1967.

Trefousse, Hans L. *The Radical Republicans: Lincoln's Vanguard for Racial Justice*. New York: Alfred A. Knopf, 1969.

## REVELS, HIRAM R. (1827–1901)

Hiram Revels was a prominent African American leader in American politics, religion, and education. Revels's racially mixed family lineage made him one-fourth black. Americans who fell into this racial category were called "quadroons." A free black, he spent his early years in the town of his birth, Fayetteville, North Carolina. Building on the education he had gained at a school for blacks in Fayetteville, Revels left North Carolina and began studying to become a minister, enrolling at two Northern seminaries. After ordination in the African Methodist Episcopal (AME) Church, pastoral work in Baltimore, Maryland, offered him experience in the ministry.

When the Civil War erupted, Revels became a Union army recruiter and an army chaplain. He was especially proud of his record of recruiting African Americans to join the army. After the war, Revels settled in Mississippi, working with the Bureau of Refugees, Freedmen, and Abandoned Lands to aid in its relief efforts in the state. When President Andrew Johnson's government evaporated with the coming of Congressional Reconstruction in 1867, Revels moved into politics. He held several political positions in Mississippi—city alderman, state legislator, and state treasurer—before being elected in 1870 to the U.S. Senate—the first black member of that body. Myth has it he filled Jefferson Davis's abandoned seat, but that honor fell to Adelbert Ames; Revels filled the seat vacated in the war by Albert Brown. Revels was no Radical crusader for black rights and quickly established himself as a Moderate. He pushed for black education, an end to segregation in schools, and

A free black minister, educator, and recruiter for the Union army, Hiram R. Revels was the first African American elected to the U.S. Senate (Mississippi, 1872). (Library of Congress)

even nominated a black man to West Point. Yet he also advocated amnesty for former confederates and a removal of their political disabilities.

In 1871, with the expiration of the Senate term, he returned to Mississippi. Officials of Mississippi's newly chartered black college, Alcorn University, extended an invitation to Revels to become the first president of the institution; Alcorn was the first black land-grant college in the United States. He accepted and held the position until 1882. The state Republican Party lost a great leader, and although many Mississippi whites bristled at the idea of a black college, but were relieved that Revels had left politics. By 1874, Revels had drifted away from the Republicans, horrified by the graft and corruption of the party. He returned to his ministry and the AME Church, in which he remained active until his death in 1901. Holly Springs, Mississippi, became his final resting place.

*James S. Humphreys*

***See also:*** Jim Crow Laws; Military Reconstruction Acts (1867–1868).

## Further Reading

Gravely, William B. "Hiram Revels Protests Racial Separation in the Methodist Episcopal Church." *Methodist History* 8 (April 1970): 13–20.

Gravely, William B. "Hiram Rhodes Revels (1827–1901): Senate, Mississippi," in Stephen Middleton, ed., *Black Congressmen during Reconstruction: A Documentary Sourcebook*. Westport, CT: Greenwood Press, 2002.

Posey, Josephine McCann. *Against Great Odds: The History of Alcorn State University*. Jackson: University Press of Mississippi, 1994.

# S

## SCALAWAGS

"Scalawag" was a derogatory name given to native white Southerners who joined the Republican Party during Congressional Reconstruction. Far more numerous than carpetbaggers, scalawags held a majority of public offices in the Reconstruction states, far outnumbering Northern newcomers and African American politicians. In six states—Texas, Mississippi, Georgia, Alabama, Arkansas, and North Carolina—they comprised a majority of delegates in the constitutional conventions of 1867–1869. Fourteen scalawags were governors during Congressional Reconstruction, totally dominating the executive office in Georgia, North Carolina, Tennessee, Texas, and Alabama. Ten scalawags sat in the U.S. Senate and 52 in the U.S. House of Representatives. Several thousand served as state legislators, judges, sheriffs, mayors, and in diverse other state and local positions; still others held positions in federal post offices, courts, and custom houses. Among the most prominent scalawags were Reconstruction governors William G. Brownlow of Tennessee (also a U.S. senator), Edmund J. Davis of Texas, Rufus Bullock of Georgia, William Woods Holden of North Carolina, and James L. Alcorn of Mississippi (also a U.S. senator). In a few instances, well-known Confederate military heroes became prominent scalawags, notably James L. Longstreet, former corps commander in the Army of Northern Virginia, and Partisan Ranger John S. Mosby.

The word "scalawag" originates from Scalloway, a seaport village in northern Scotland, which in the 17th century was eponymous with low-grade livestock. In English and American slang, vagabonds and other shiftless ne'er-do-wells were sometimes called scalawags. In the context of Reconstruction, by mid-1868 the word was coming into general usage in the Southern states, specifying native (Southern) white Republicans. According to the *Richmond Enquirer* in June of that year, "The term 'scallawag,'[sic] is one that that is derived from the cattle market," where it is "applied to all of the mean, lean, mangy, hidebound, skin[n]y, worthless cattle in every particular drove." White newspapers portrayed scalawags as shiftless poor whites, draft dodgers, and renegades—the scum of Southern society motivated by greed, lust for office and black women, and hatred of their social betters. In Democratic Party newspapers from Virginia to Texas, scalawags joined carpetbaggers and corrupt, ignorant blacks in an unholy trinity of Reconstruction villainy. While some scalawags such as South Carolina governor Franklin J. Moses resembled the press stereotype, most did not, and decades of revisionist scholarship has refuted the scalawag legend. The myth persists in popular culture, however, in part because of Hollywood films such as *Birth of a Nation* (1915) and *Gone with the Wind* (1939).

The great majority of scalawags were drawn from the hardcore Unionists of 1860–1861, the group that presidents Abraham Lincoln and Andrew Johnson believed would serve as the core leadership for a new South. White Southerners, historian David M. Potter has convincingly argued, held dual loyalties simultaneously: They were both Americans and Southerners. Potter's concept of dual loyalties helps explain the choices white Southerners made in the secession crisis. Those whose loyalty, or identity, as Southerners was uppermost supported or accepted secession and joined the Confederacy. On the other hand, those whose loyalty as Americans superseded their regional loyalty opposed secession unconditionally and became wartime Unionists. Such men cooperated with Union occupation regimes, and no small number joined the Union army; others, far from Union lines, supported the Confederacy as little as possible. With the advent of Congressional Reconstruction, most of these wartime Unionists became Republicans. The reality of scalawags' economic status is almost 180 degrees opposite the legend also. Scalawag voters were predominantly small farmers and village tradesmen; the great majority of scalawag leaders were middle-class lawyers, merchants, bankers, planters, engineers, editors, tradesmen, teachers and so on. Though not quite on a par with the so-called redeemers, their education and wealth far exceeded that of most Americans. Moreover, men who bucked the Confederacy as wartime Unionists, then battled Conservative white supremacy as Reconstruction Republicans, were anything but unprincipled. On the whole, it took far more courage and conviction to stand against the white majority than it took to join it.

Like their carpetbagger allies, many scalawags saw the Republican Party as an instrument for overturning the plantation regime and building a progressive New South modeled on the Northern free labor system. Scalawags deserve much of the credit for Reconstruction's liberal reforms: the creation of state-supported free public schools in the South; the elimination of property qualifications on voting, imprisonment for debt, and public whippings; the construction of penitentiaries, orphan and insane asylums, public works, and internal improvements; and black civil rights. Scalawags' overall record on civil rights was weaker than that of carpetbaggers and black leaders. Scalawags were the most conservative component of the Republican coalition, especially concerning black rights. Scalawag leaders such as Mississippi's James L. Alcorn and Georgia's Joseph E. Brown displayed no real commitment to black rights. Indeed, scalawag hostility to black officeholding in Brown's Georgia condemned the state to early redemption in 1871. Scalawags' commitment to black rights in Tennessee, North Carolina, and Virginia was also weak. By 1871, a combination of scalawag defections and ex-confederates regaining their voting rights had ended Reconstruction in all three states. On the other hand, given their starting point in the slave regime, a scalawag minority made progress toward fuller acceptance of blacks' legal and political rights, as well as recognition of their innate dignity as human beings.

When Reconstruction ended, some scalawags left the South. A Texas scalawag named Albert Parsons moved to Chicago where he became an anarchist and champion of labor. In a miscarriage of justice, he was executed for his alleged participation in the 1886 Haymarket Square bombing. The great majority of scalawags, though, remained in the South. White Southern society was largely forgiving of white Republicans who had been labeled tyrants and traitors during Reconstruction. Former Texas governor Edmund J. Davis practiced law in Austin and, as a Republican, ran unsuccessfully for governor in 1880 and Congress in 1882. After fleeing Georgia, ex-governor Rufus Bullock returned to become president of the Atlanta chamber of commerce. James Longstreet returned to Georgia where he had grown up and held a succession of federal offices including U.S. minister to Turkey, U.S. marshal, and U.S. railroad commissioner.

*Ted Tunnell*

***See also:*** Bourbons; Loyalty Oaths; Provisional Governors; Union League of America.

## Further Reading

Baggett, James Alex. *The Scalawags: Southern Dissenters in the Civil War and Reconstruction.* Baton Rouge: Louisiana State University Press, 2003.

Trelease, Allen W. "Who Were the Scalawags?" *Journal of Southern History* 29 (1963): 445–568.

Tunnell, Ted. *Crucible of Reconstruction: War, Radicalism, and Race in Louisiana, 1862–1877.* Baton Rouge: Louisiana State University Press, 1984.

Tunnell, Ted. *Edge of the Sword: The Ordeal of Carpetbagger Marshall H. Twitchell in the Civil War and Reconstruction.* Baton Rouge: Louisiana State University Press, 2001.

Wiggins, Sarah Woolfolk. *The Scalawag in Alabama, 1865–1881.* Tuscaloosa: University of Alabama Press, 1977.

## SCOTT, ROBERT K. (1826–1900)

Carpetbag governor of South Carolina from 1868 to 1872, Scott attended medical school in Columbus, Ohio, where he practiced as a physician before the Civil War.

At the outbreak of hostilities, he entered the army as a major and fought in major engagements including Shiloh, where he had his horse shot from under him. Taken prisoner at Atlanta, he came to Charleston, South Carolina, as a prisoner of war. After the Confederate surrender, he was appointed assistant commissioner for South Carolina of the Bureau of Freedmen, Refugees, and Abandoned Lands (Freedmen's Bureau). In that capacity, he adjudicated thousands of land titles in the Sea Islands, where former white owners and black slaves both claimed property rights.

Scott resigned from the army in July 1868 to accept the nomination of the Republican Party for governor of South Carolina. He won easily—the state had a large black majority, and many white Democrats boycotted the election. As the state's first Republican governor, Scott proved unable to solve the two major problems besetting the state: poverty and violence. His attempts to attract Northern investment in Southern development proved futile, and his management of the state's finances was negligent, perhaps even fraudulent. As governor and as a member of the state's three-person financial board, Scott authorized the overissue of state bonds and the use of them as collateral for high interest loans. When these schemes failed, the state's debt burden, large to begin with, became unbearable; it was left to Scott's successors to oversee the repudiation of much of this debt.

Meanwhile, Scott's government also failed to protect South Carolina Republicans from violence at the hands of Democratic terror groups like the Ku Klux Klan, which hit its climax during his term. Scores of Republicans, including several elected officials, were murdered, hundreds were assaulted, and almost all lived in fear. Scott made several efforts to protect his constituents; he commissioned and armed a state militia, trial justices, and constables, but the Klan's reign of terror did not abate. Scott even tried to cajole and reason with white leaders, warning them that he might need to call for federal help.

Ultimately, this is what happened when in 1871 President Ulysses S. Grant invoked the recently passed Enforcement Acts and suspended the writ of habeas corpus in several up-country counties of South Carolina. Arrests by federal soldiers and Justice Department marshals—and, perhaps equally important, the ensuing calls for restraint by leading white Democrats—eventually ended Klan outrages. Despite Scott's conviction that "the continued presence of the military is a reproach to a Republican State," neither he nor his successors were able to ensure law and order in South Carolina without the use of federal troops.

As governor, Scott was the most powerful Republican in the state, but he had many factional enemies in the party. In 1871, his enemies made an attempt to impeach him on corruption charges stemming from the bond fiasco and other fraudulent official commissions with which he was connected. The move for impeachment came to a vote in the state House of Representatives, but it was foiled amid the bribery of several legislators. It is unclear what role Scott had in the bribery, but the incident did Scott no credit. Nonetheless, Scott was reelected to the governor's chair in 1870. On the larger issue of his commission of frauds, it seems certain that Scott bore a large share of the responsibility for the fiscal disasters that took place during his administration; however, it is less sure that he profited personally from any frauds. He did not, as it was alleged in the *New York Herald*, steal his personal fortune from the state of South Carolina. He was wealthy before the war, and in 1866, even made the preposterous claim that he had $100,000 at his command at any time.

After the expiration of his second term as governor and a failed run for the U.S. Senate, Scott remained in Columbia, South Carolina, but retired from politics and turned to real estate. More successful in business than in public service, Scott continued to lend money to friends and even enemies—in 1871 and 1877, he lent money to R. B. Carpenter, who as a Reform Party candidate for governor in 1870 had accused Scott of fraud. It seemed he no longer cared about politics, or at least had shifted views from his days as an eager Freedmen's Bureau operative. By 1876, Scott had decided that black suffrage had been a mistake and even lent his influence to Wade Hampton's attempt to restore native white rule and white supremacy to South Carolina. Following the victory of Hampton and his Red Shirts and the Redemption of the state, Scott returned to Henry County, Ohio, in 1877. He made headlines once more, in 1880, when he shot and killed a drinking companion of his son, Robert Jr. He was acquitted the following year, as the shooting was ruled an accident. Scott continued in the real estate business until his death in 1900.

*Hyman Rubin III*

**See also:** Congressional Reconstruction; Edisto Island, South Carolina; Field Order No. 15; Forrest, Nathan Bedford (1821–1877); Gordon, John B. (1832–1904); Military Reconstruction Acts (1867–1868); Port Royal Experiment; U.S. Army and Reconstruction.

## Further Reading

Cummings, Charles M. "The Scott Papers: An Inside View of Reconstruction." *Ohio History* 79, no. 2 (1970): 112–18.

Current, Richard N. *Those Terrible Carpetbaggers: A Reinterpretation*. New York: Oxford University Press, 1988.

Simkins, Francis B., and Robert H. Woody. *South Carolina during Reconstruction.* Chapel Hill: University of North Carolina Press, 1932.

Zuczek, Richard. *State of Rebellion: Reconstruction in South Carolina.* Columbia: University of South Carolina Press, 1996.

# SEYMOUR, HORATIO (1810–1886)

Horatio Seymour was born in Pompey Hill, New York. He studied law in Utica, graduated in 1832, and soon after became active in state Democratic Party politics, working under the tutelage of William L. Marcy, a member of the Albany Regency, one of America's first political machines. Seymour's political career skyrocketed in the 1840s, with a seat in the state assembly (New York State Legislature) in 1841, a term as mayor of Utica in 1842, selection as speaker of the state assembly in 1845, and as governor beginning 1852.

During the late 1840s and 1850s, Seymour belonged to Marcy's Hunkers, a Conservative Democratic faction in New York supporting the expansion of slavery into the territories. By 1860, he had shifted over to Illinois senator Stephen A. Douglas and the idea of popular sovereignty in the territories. He campaigned for Douglas in the 1860 presidential election and, after the fall of Fort Sumter in April 1861, tentatively supported the Union war effort.

Seymour became governor of New York again in 1862, as the war waged on. Seymour, who feared the expansion of federal power, gradually drifted further and further from his already-lukewarm support of the war and the Republican administration. He battled often with Republican president Abraham Lincoln, and the hostility intensified in 1863 with the Emancipation Proclamation and the first federal draft. Seymour became an outspoken opponent of emancipation, believing that if the federal government dictated the abolition of slavery, "then the people of the South should be allowed to withdraw themselves from the government which cannot give them the

The powerful Democratic governor of New York during the Civil War, Horatio Seymour opposed the Union draft and the emancipation of slaves. He campaigned for the presidency in 1868, but the Republican Party easily defeated him with their nominee, Ulysses S. Grant. (Library of Congress)

protection guaranteed by its terms." In a speech on July 4, 1863, Seymour compared Lincoln to King Charles I and denounced conscription (the draft) as unconstitutional. This speech added to working-class New Yorkers' resentment of the National Draft Act, and enflamed racial tensions already existing in the city. Only days afterward, New York whites, mostly lower-class Irish immigrants, began to riot in the streets, attacking draft centers, governmental offices, and especially blacks. The New York City draft riots were the most violent and bloody antiwar protests seen during the Civil War. Many Republicans blamed Seymour for the violence.

Not surprisingly, after the Civil War, Seymour emerged as one of the Democratic Party's leading spokesmen. He ceaselessly criticized Radical Republicans while supporting Andrew Johnson, a war Democrat who had become president after Lincoln's assassination in April 1865. Like Johnson, he opposed black suffrage, special "class legislation," and any extreme expression or extension of federal power. By 1868, Seymour was popular enough to earn the Democratic nomination for president, creating a certain awkwardness between the advisor and the executive, since Johnson himself was naively angling for the nomination. Republicans, in turn, rejoiced. Secretary of State William Seward believed that Democrats "could have nominated no candidate who would have taken away fewer Republican votes." Seymour's behavior as governor during the Civil War, combined with his close ties to New York financiers, made it impossible for him to gain the support of veterans and westerners. Republicans shrewdly countered by nominating Union general and war hero Ulysses S. Grant for president. Although Seymour lost the election, he received a surprising 47 percent of the vote, the highest Democratic showing since 1852.

Through the 1870s, Seymour remained an elder statesman in the party and continued to mentor rising Democrats like Samuel J. Tilden. Seymour died in Utica in 1886.

*Bruce E. Stewart*

*See also:* Blair, Francis P. Sr. (1791–1876); Democratic National Convention (1868); Elections of 1868; Elections of 1876; National Union Movement (1866); Presidential Reconstruction; Redemption; U.S. Army and Reconstruction.

## Further Reading

Foner, Eric. *Reconstruction Updated Edition: America's Unfinished Revolution, 1863–1877*. Reprint, New York: HarperCollins, 2014.

Mitchell, Stewart. *Horatio Seymour of New York*. Cambridge, MA: Harvard University Press, 1938.

## SHARKEY, WILLIAM L. (1798–1873)

William Lewis Sharkey was born near Muscle Shoals in Sumner County, Tennessee, on August 12, 1798. Five years later, the family moved to what would become Warren County, Mississippi. An orphan by the age of 15, Sharkey supported his younger brothers and began the study of law. By the early 1820s, he had passed the bar examination in Natchez, returned to Warren County, and begun a successful law practice in Vicksburg.

In 1827, Sharkey was elected to the first of two terms in the lower house of the Mississippi legislature. He positioned himself as a Whig, moved to the state's circuit court, and was later elected a justice of Mississippi's High Court of Errors and Appeals, a position he held for 18 years.

An uncompromising Whig Unionist, Sharkey was one of Mississippi's few leaders who refused to support secession; during the war, he was arrested and imprisoned briefly. Near the end of the war, the state's Confederate governor dispatched Sharkey and William Yerger (another Unionist Whig) to confer with federal officials in Washington. Sharkey and Yerger met with the new president, Andrew Johnson, on June 8, 1865; impressed by Sharkey's Unionism and courage, Johnson appointed Sharkey as Mississippi's provisional governor one week later.

As part of the president's plan for restoring the former Confederate states to the Union, Sharkey called a constitutional convention for the purpose of declaring Mississippi's Ordinance of Secession null and void and abolishing the institution of slavery. He also held a general election to replace state officers. These tasks, of course, were in addition to Sharkey's ordinary duties as provisional governor, such as maintaining public order and attempting to reorganize state affairs. Following the successful completion of these criteria, Sharkey stepped down in December to make way for the newly elected governor, Benjamin Humphreys. The new legislature then selected federal officers—and chose Sharkey as one of its two U.S. senators. It also passed a series of restrictive laws that severely limited the rights of newly freed African Americans, the notorious Black Codes. These codes, which formed part of a greater rift between President Johnson, his Southern governments, and the Republican Congress, were partly responsible for Sharkey being denied his seat by Congress in December 1865. He remained in the nation's capital, however, developing a further political intimacy with President Johnson and advising him to reject any compromise with the Radical Republicans. He was never seated, and did not hold office again.

Instead, he turned back to law as a method of opposing the changes he believed threatened the Union. As a member of the National Union Movement's executive committee in 1866, as a member of the legal teams in *Mississippi v. Johnson*, *Georgia v. Stanton*, and *Ex parte McCardle*, and as a reluctant convert to the Democratic Party in 1868, Sharkey opposed Congressional Reconstruction and its implications with the same single-minded tenacity that he had brought against secession and the Confederacy. Sharkey died in Washington, D.C., on March 30, 1873.

*Martin J. Hardeman*

**See also:** Abolition of Slavery; Amnesty Proclamations; Elections of 1866; Presidential Reconstruction.

## Further Reading

Hall, Marshall. "William L. Sharkey and Reconstruction, 1866–1873." *Journal of Mississippi History* 27 (February 1965): 1–17.

Harris, William C. *The Day of the Carpetbagger: Republican Reconstruction in Mississippi*. Baton Rouge: Louisiana State University Press, 1979.

Harris, William C. *Presidential Reconstruction in Mississippi*. Baton Rouge: Louisiana State University Press, 1967.

# SHERMAN, JOHN (1823–1900)

John Sherman, congressman, U.S. senator, U.S. secretary of the treasury, and secretary of state, was born in Lancaster, Ohio, in 1823, the eighth child of Charles Robert and Mary (Hoyt) Sherman and the younger brother of Gen. William T. Sherman. In the Civil War and Reconstruction, he played a crucial role as a Moderate Republican and financial strategist.

Trained as a lawyer but also successful in lumber and real estate, Sherman entered politics in the 1840s as a Whig. He swiftly moved into the fledgling Republican Party and was elected to the U.S. House of Representatives from Ohio as a Republican in 1854. In 1861, Sherman began the first of two 16-year periods as U.S. senator when he succeeded Salmon P. Chase, who had been appointed Abraham Lincoln's secretary of the treasury. Sherman made his wartime mark helping shape the legislation creating the national banking system and greenback currency. By war's end he had drifted away from Lincoln, supporting Chase's ill-fated push for the 1864 nomination, and endorsing the Wade-Davis Bill that sought to override Lincoln's generous terms of Reconstruction.

As the Civil War came to a close, Sherman's views on the status of the Confederate states were somewhat mixed. Sherman did not concur with Senator Charles Sumner's notion that these states had "committed suicide" in leaving the Union, but neither did he support admitting the Lincoln government's established during the war. Like many in Congress, Sherman initially gave Johnson's Reconstruction policies the benefit of the doubt. In early 1866, after Johnson vetoed the Moderate Freedmen's Bureau Bill and Civil Rights Bill (both of which Sherman had voted for), Sherman still believed reconciliation with the president was possible. Johnson's overt opposition to the Fourteenth Amendment finally convinced Sherman—and many other Republicans—that Johnson should not be allowed to dictate the terms of readmission.

After its success in the congressional elections of 1866, the Republican Party moved ahead with its own Reconstruction bill. On February 16, 1867, as chair of the Senate Republican Party Committee, Sherman wrote a compromise bill to end the deadlock with the House and thereby guaranteed passage of a Reconstruction program before the end of the congressional session. It

A moderate Republican from Ohio (and younger brother of William Tecumseh) John Sherman played pivotal roles not only in designing Reconstruction legislation, but also for structuring Gilded Age finance policy. (Library of Congress)

was Sherman who combined military aspects of congressman Thaddeus Stevens's bill with the readmission requirements created by Senator James G. Blaine, resulting in the Military Reconstruction Act of March 1867. With the passage of the Military Reconstruction Act, Sherman opposed the imposition of any new requirements on the South until the existing legislation was fulfilled. He also expressed reservations over land confiscation and federal interference in Southern public schools.

A year later, the House's impeachment of President Johnson placed Sherman in an awkward position: while serving on the committee that wrote the Tenure of Office Act, Sherman had in fact argued that the law did not apply to cabinet officers. However, Sherman was reluctant to go against the Republican Senate majority, particularly after the president removed—not just suspended—Secretary of War Edwin Stanton. Sherman departed from most Republicans in asserting that the Senate was sitting as a court, while House managers and most Republican senators viewed the Senate's role as a political body, one not bound by evidence that would be only admissible in a court of law. Sherman also favored granting the president's counsel the 40 days requested for trial preparation. Ultimately, Sherman did vote with the Republican majority to convict Johnson on the first article voted upon—Article 11 (concerning the appointment of Thomas).

While the impeachment drama played out, Sherman was just as concerned with the fate of the Fourteenth Amendment, which he viewed as Reconstruction's most critical component. As a result, Sherman worked tirelessly to ensure Northern states ratified the amendment—and that Southern states do so as well. He agreed with many that ratification was requisite for readmission to the Union, and such readmission might be vital for the Republicans to secure victory in the 1868 presidential election. Indeed, Ulysses S. Grant's victory came in part due to black votes from readmitted Southern states.

While Sherman left his mark on the Reconstruction legislation that determined the political status of the South and of African American rights, his greater influence came as Senate Finance Committee chairman. Since Reconstruction encompassed how the government dealt with the many changes brought about by the war, clearly the financial sector had to be considered. Sherman had been a major participant in the creation of the greenback currency and the national banking legislation during the war. In 1868, when Ohio Democrat (and presidential hopeful) George Pendleton proposed the Ohio Plan, which advocated that interest on the national debt would be paid for with greenback currency, expanding the paper money program and inflating the economy. While good for those in debt, this idea was opposed by eastern hard-money interests protected by Johnson's Secretary of the Treasury, Hugh McCulloch. As chairman of the Senate Finance Committee, Sherman labored for years to strike a balance between the two sides; his solution was the Specie Resumption Act of 1875, which stipulated that beginning January 1, 1879, the treasury would redeem all legal tender notes (greenbacks) in specie (gold). By setting the date for resumption four years away, Sherman hoped it might depoliticize the issue and give the treasury time to build up its gold reserves. As fate would have it, Rutherford B. Hayes appointed Sherman secretary of the treasury in 1877, after which Sherman worked tirelessly to increase the nation's gold reserves while convincing the business community of his plan's merits. Sherman's hopes were realized on the first day of resumption in 1879, when the public purchased more greenbacks than redeemed them for gold.

Considered for the Republican nomination for president in 1880, 1884, and 1888, Sherman lost out to more politically skillful and colorful opponents. In 1881, he returned to the U.S. Senate from Ohio, replacing James Garfield, who would have become senator had he not been elected president. Sherman's second 16-year period in the Senate was noted for his role in the passage of the Sherman Anti-Trust Act and the Sherman Silver Purchase Act in 1890. Having served as chairman of the Senate Foreign Relations Committee for nine years, Sherman became President William McKinley's first secretary of state, a post from which he resigned in 1898 because of ill-health and anti-imperialist views that put him at odds with the rest of the cabinet. He died in 1900.

*Robert C. Kenzer*

**See also:** Congressional Reconstruction; Education; Elections of 1864; Elections of 1868; National Union Party (1864); Presidential Reconstruction; U.S. Army and Reconstruction.

## Further Reading

"John Sherman and the Impeachment of Andrew Johnson." *Ohio History* 82 (Summer–Autumn 1973): 176–91.

Kerr, Winfield Scott. *John Sherman, His Life and Public Services.* 2 vols. Boston: Sherman, French and Co., 1907.

Sherman, John. *Recollections of Forty Years in the House, Senate, and Cabinet.* 2 vols. Chicago: The Werner Co., 1895.

Unger, Irwin. *The Greenback Era: A Social and Political History of American Finance, 1865–1879.* Princeton, NJ: Princeton University Press, 1964.

# SHOTGUN PLAN

The Shotgun Plan was one of the names applied to a strategy for securing political control during Reconstruction. It is sometimes called the Mississippi Plan since it was in this state's 1875 election that it was first developed and utilized. Others call it the Edgefield Plan, in honor of Martin W. Gary of Edgefield, South Carolina, who employed it in that state's 1876 campaign. The use of the word "shotgun" highlights the key role that violence played in Reconstruction politics. However, the success of this risky approach depended as much on the indifference in Washington (and the North in general) as it did the audacity in the South.

By the mid-1870s, the Southern Democratic Party began searching for a new way to secure political power. Earlier efforts via "night-riding" and terrorist groups likes the Ku Klux Klan had failed, as had maneuvers in the early 1870s to "fuse" or cooperate with breakaway elements of the Republican Party who had bolted because of scandals, policies, or a desire for moderation. Rather than build alliances or rely on factionalism between Moderate and Radical Republicans, many Democrats decided to support only Democratic candidates to regain control of the state government. This they called the "Straight-Out" or "White Line" strategy. The flaw in this strategy in states like Mississippi and South Carolina was that a substantial portion of the population was African American and committed to supporting the Republican Party. To counter that demographic reality, Democrats had to do three things.

First, they needed to increase the number of Democratic votes by getting all white men on their side. Second, they needed to decrease the number of Republican votes by whatever means necessary. But this approach led to the third element of the Shotgun Plan. It had to be carried out in such a way as to avoid provoking federal action.

Mississippi Democrats in 1875 were confident that they could use considerable force without worrying about federal troops since they had seen the weak support the Grant administration had given to Republican governor William P. Kellogg in Louisiana the year before. The Mississippi Democrats initiated an organized campaign of terror against Republicans at every level during the 1875 campaign. Beginning in Vicksburg, Democrats targeted local Republican leaders for assassination, started riots in which scores of black citizens were killed, broke up campaign meetings with blank-filled cannons and rifle-toting horsemen, and blatantly used violence and fraud at the polls. Their gamble paid off, as Mississippi's state government fell to the Democrats, and as anticipated, the Grant administration had declined to interfere.

Just as Mississippi followed Louisiana's example, so in 1876 South Carolina mimicked Mississippi. There, Wade Hampton III challenged carpetbag governor Daniel H. Chamberlain, and the Democrats' use of harassment and outright terror succeeded again in uniting whites, intimidating Republicans, and still avoid federal interference. South Carolina's version of the Shotgun Plan was not able to entirely dominate the Republican Party, but it was effective enough to throw the election results into dispute and allow Hampton to lay claim to the state house. By the spring of 1877, as a result of violence, intimidation, and the Compromise of 1877, South Carolina had been redeemed as well.

*Bruce E. Baker*

*See also:* Bourbons; Compromise of 1877; Elections of 1876; Gun Clubs; Redemption.

## Further Reading

Fitzgerald, Michael W. *Splendid Failure: Postwar Reconstruction in the American South.* New York: Ivan R. Dee Publishers, 2008

Harris, William C. *The Day of the Carpetbagger: Republican Reconstruction in Mississippi.* Baton Rouge: Louisiana State University Press, 1979.

Rable, George C. *But There Was No Peace: The Role of Violence in the Politics of Reconstruction.* Athens: University of Georgia Press, 1984.

Zuczek, Richard. *State of Rebellion: South Carolina during Reconstruction.* Columbia: University of South Carolina Press, 1996.

# SLAUGHTERHOUSE CASES (1873)

The Slaughterhouse Cases provided an early judicial interpretation of the Fourteenth Amendment, which had been added to the U.S. Constitution only five years earlier. Although the case had little to do with African American rights, representation, or national citizenship—issues shaping the original document—the decision had important implications for how the amendment would be applied.

In 1869, the Republican-controlled Louisiana legislature gave a virtual monopoly over the slaughtering of animals in Orleans, Jefferson, and St Bernard parishes to the Crescent City Live Stock Handling and Slaughterhouse Company. The law was typical for the time; widespread unsanitary conditions existed in the slaughtering business and such a monopoly was a usual exercise of state police power.

A group of complaining butchers made a novel argument, based on Section 1 of the Fourteenth Amendment, that the state's monopoly grant violated their privileges and immunities as citizens. Further they argued that their right to due process had also been violated by the state's restriction on their businesses. In addition, they alleged that the state had created an involuntary servitude in violation of the Thirteenth Amendment. The counterargument was that the Fourteenth Amendment did not provide broad protections but protected only African Americans, the focus of the 39th Congress, which framed the amendment. Also, those supporting Louisiana's action argued that the state's police power gave it the authority to pass the law; it was carrying out its responsibility to protect the public's health. If a state had such power and if the Fourteenth Amendment limited state power, where was the line between constitutional and unconstitutional state action?

In a 5–4 decision, the U.S. Supreme Court emphasized the police-power argument in ruling against the plaintiffs. It also focused on the Fourteenth Amendment's limited purpose: to safeguard the freedom of black Americans. For the majority, Chief Justice Samuel Miller took a narrow view of the amendment, arguing that it had not changed state responsibilities and power in such areas as public health. He also held that the privileges and immunities of national citizens protected by Section 1 were narrow and few and were not likely to be affected by state action. In addition, Miller saw little impact from the Thirteenth Amendment, noting that it was but a broad and inspiring statement about the status of all peoples.

The dissenting judges asserted that the amendment was not designed only to protect the rights of blacks, and that the right to labor was a protected privilege and immunity of American citizens. Significant for future use of the Fourteenth Amendment in economic cases, among the minority were two opinions that would come to affect constitutional thinking in the late 1800s and early 1900s. Justices Stephen J. Field and Joseph P. Bradley gave substantive definitions to due process and liberty as covered by Section 1 of the Fourteenth Amendment. In doing so, they set the stage for judicial voiding of state economic regulations as violations of the amendment's protection of liberty and property.

Their arguments would underpin the concept of "liberty of contract," which state and federal courts used to strike down numerous state regulations between Reconstruction and the last years of the New Deal. Dissents in Slaughterhouse also dealt with the Thirteenth Amendment, with Field arguing that denial of equal rights under law was a badge of slavery; the focus was on the Fourteenth Amendment's implications for the nation.

*Claudine L. Ferrell*

**See also:** Civil Rights; Democratic Party; Republicans, Radical.

## Further Reading

Hyman, Harold M., and William M. Wiecek. *Equal Justice under Law: Constitutional Development, 1835–1875*. New York: Harper and Row, 1982.

Nieman, Donald G. *Promises to Keep: African-Americans and the Constitutional Order, 1776 to the Present*. New York: Oxford University Press, 1991.

# SMALLS, ROBERT (1839–1915)

One of the most influential politicians from South Carolina during Reconstruction, Robert Smalls (sometimes called Robert Small) was born to the slave Lydia Smalls on April 5, 1839, in Beaufort, South Carolina. Smalls spent his early adolescence as a servant in the house of John McKee, who may have been his father. In 1851, Smalls moved with his master, Henry McKee, to a plantation outside of Charleston. Smalls labored as a waiter, lamplighter, stevedore, rigger, and sailor during the 1850s.

At the outbreak of the Civil War, Smalls worked as a sailor on the *Planter*, a private cotton steamer that was incorporated into Confederate service. By late 1861, he had become pilot of the ship, and in the early morning of May 13, 1862, with the Confederate officers ashore, Smalls led a group of slave families aboard. He then sailed out of the harbor and boldly but carefully (it was, after all, a Confederate boat) sailed into the Union Navy's blockade. Smalls turned over ammunition as well as Confederate naval codes and troop locations, winning national fame and a $1,500 reward. He was subsequently commissioned a second lieutenant in Company B, Thirty-third Regiment of the U.S. Colored Troops (he could not officially join the navy because he had not graduated from a naval academy). Smalls piloted various Union ships including the *Planter* and the *Keokuk*; the latter was sunk by confederates during an 1863 Union attack on Charleston.

After the war ended, Smalls served as a civilian pilot and acquired large amounts of property in and around Beaufort. As he grew in wealth and prominence, he provided financial support for the education of former slaves and served as a regent for the State Normal School and the South Carolina Lunatic Asylum. Smalls also held many positions, including brigadier general and major general, in the South Carolina state militia during the 1860s and 1870s.

His greatest postwar impact, however, grew out of his involvement in politics. In the 1860s and 1870s, he built a political machine in Beaufort, helping to organize the Beaufort Republican Club in 1867 and serving as chairman of the Beaufort County Republican Party for most of the 1870s. A delegate to the 1868 Constitutional Convention, he won election to the South Carolina General Assembly later that year, and served as a state senator from 1870 through 1875, when he resigned to accept a seat in the U.S.

A South Carolina slave, Robert Smalls led a party that escaped in 1862—by sailing into the Union blockade. After serving in the U.S. Navy, he returned to his home state to serve in the General Assembly and in the U.S. House of Representatives. (Library of Congress)

House of Representatives. He served one term and then returned during the 1880s for two more terms. Although he failed to gain nomination in the 1890s, his success was still significant when one considers Bourbons had reclaimed the South Carolina government in 1877.

After leaving elected office, Smalls remained actively involved in Republican politics. A delegate to the 1895 state constitutional convention, Smalls vigorously campaigned against disfranchisement clauses. He served as collector of customs in Beaufort from 1890 to 1894 and from 1898 to 1913. Married twice and the father of four children, Smalls died in Beaufort on February 22, 1915.

*Kimberly R. Kellison*

*See also:* New South; Redemption.

## Further Reading

Bailey, N. Louise, Mary L. Morgan, and Carolyn R. Taylor. *Biographical Dictionary of the South Carolina Senate, 1776–1985.* Vol. 3. Columbia: University of South Carolina Press, 1986.

Miller, Edward A. Jr. *Gullah Statesman: Robert Smalls from Slavery to Congress, 1839–1915.* Columbia: University of South Carolina Press, 1995.

Uya, Okon Edet. *From Slavery to Public Service: Robert Smalls, 1839–1915.* New York: Oxford University Press, 1971.

# SMITH, WILLIAM H. (1826–1899)

William Hugh Smith was the first Republican governor of Alabama under Congressional Reconstruction. Not a strong supporter of civil rights, he devoted most of his energies to conciliating Conservative whites and promoting economic development. His administration was memorable for notably irregular practices in state railroad subsidies.

Smith was born in Georgia in 1826 and moved to Alabama in his teens. After becoming a lawyer, he was elected to the legislature for the Democratic Party but emerged as a strong Union man, supporting Steven Douglas for president in 1860. Smith opposed secession, and in 1862, he and several of his brothers fled to federal lines to escape arrest. He then recruited Alabama refugees into the Union army and accompanied Gen. William T. Sherman's forces in the March to the Sea.

Smith returned to Alabama after the war, where the Unionists unsuccessfully promoted him as provisional governor under President Andrew Johnson's restoration program. He briefly served as a judge, but hostility from former confederates forced his resignation. Following the passage of the Military Reconstruction Acts in March 1867, Smith served as head of voter registration and won the election for governor as a Republican later that summer.

As governor, Smith openly reached out to Conservative whites, advocating the elimination of political disabilities, and (even though he was a scalawag) opposing carpetbag influence in the state Republican Party. These efforts won him considerable praise in Democratic circles but hurt his Republicans credentials. He further alienated his party through his inaction against the Ku Klux Klan.

Smith's major public initiative was promotion of railroad development. Under Smith's administration, Alabama's contingent debt escalated several fold. He was particularly supportive of the crucial Alabama & Chattanooga Railroad, running through the mineral district around modern Birmingham. By his own later admission, Smith signed hundreds of thousands of dollars in railroad bonds beyond that authorized by law.

In 1870, Smith's bid for nomination failed; his divided party was defeated in the November canvass, aided by a massive Klan mobilization on behalf of the Democrats and rumored sabotage by Radical Republican rivals. The Democratic candidate, Robert Burns Lindsay, had anti-secessionist credentials also, which enabled him to make inroads into the former Unionist vote. Smith's troubles only worsened. Soon after Smith left office, the state-endorsed Alabama & Chattanooga Railroad suspended its interest payments, and the incoming governor refused to honor Alabama's guarantee of the tainted bonds, ruining the state's credit and resulting in eventual bankruptcy. The subsequent revelation of financial sloppiness damaged Smith's reputation permanently. He returned to Randolph County and resumed the practice of law and, in 1873, was again appointed circuit judge by Republican governor David Lewis. He died in Birmingham in 1899. His Reconstruction career, replete with party infighting and scandals, served as an example of the darker side of Republican Party politics.

*Michael W. Fitzgerald*

**See also:** Presidential Reconstruction; Redemption.

## Further Reading

Summers, Mark W. *Railroads, Reconstruction, and the Gospel of Prosperity: Aid under the Radical Republicans, 1865–1877*. Princeton, NJ: Princeton University Press, 1984.
Wiggins, Sarah Woolfolk. *The Scalawag in Alabama Politics, 1865–1881*. University: University of Alabama Press, 1977.

# SOUTH CAROLINA

It is a mistake to say that South Carolinians lost the Civil War. After all, a majority of South Carolinians were African American, most of whom were enslaved before the conflict. Confederate defeat and African American victory brought tremendous changes to the state. The war and Reconstruction profoundly transformed South Carolina, the most conservative slaveholding state, and home to the South's most intransigent secession movement. Yet by 1880, political power was again concentrated in the hands of a small reactionary class of white landholders who dominated the state's economic fortunes and social life. So in this sense, one could argue that elite white Carolinians may have won the Civil War—in the long run—but they had to accept major changes in race relations, cultural life, and their economy along the way.

South Carolina seceded from the Union on December 20, 1860. It acted independently and without a popular referendum on the issue (a convention decided the vote). Once South Carolina—and 10 other states—formally became the Confederate States of America, internal tensions increased, wartime disruption began, and the reality of living in war atop a slave population became clear. The state's thriving rice and sea-island cotton economy, concentrated in kingly coastal plantations, was quickly disrupted as slaveholders took refuge inland to avoid federal coastal invasions. With community and family members to consider, most slaves stayed on the land, thinking it wiser to value order and routine, however harsh, than to plunge into the unknown.

That decision changed radically with the landing of federal troops at Port Royal on November 7, 1861. By the thousands, slaves simply refused to leave their homes as Beaufort District masters and their families ran off before the Northern host. Within days, local slaves had abandoned field labor for tasks of their own devising: reuniting parted family members, appropriating white property, settling old scores, celebrating—and pondering—their new masterless status. Federal officials and Yankee philanthropists quickly concluded that their foothold on Hilton Head Island offered a splendid opportunity to show how freedmen could be adapted to the steady labor, piety, and thrift of capitalist civilization. The experiment proved confounding for all. Some Northerners found former slaves too immoderate and irrational in religion, too disorderly on domestic matters, too irregular about education, and too shuffling and saucy when it came time to work. Long before the Confederacy's fall, most Northerners had begun to drift away from their partial and ill-defined commitment to social equality, black Carolinians tired of the new shapes racism and exploitation had taken, and elite whites skulked around the edges, waiting for an opening. It was an ominous beginning to the Reconstruction process.

Gen. William T. Sherman's most revolutionary idea did not occur on the battlefield nor was it directed toward an enemy army. Sherman the destroyer evolved into Sherman the creator as the war drew to a close, and took a step that no politician dared take. Sherman's Special Field Order No. 15, issued just before his invasion of South Carolina, set aside the Sea Islands and a 30-mile tract near Charleston for the exclusive settlement of former slaves. Each freed family would receive 40 acres and an army mule to work the land, turning former human property into independent property holders. If successful, the experiment might well have spread to other confiscated and abandoned lands, transforming social relations in the South. Certainly Radical Republicans and even some idealistic officers within the newly formed Bureau of Refugees, Freedmen, and Abandoned Lands (Freedmen's Bureau) looked toward that goal. For President Andrew Johnson, however, the turmoil such redress entailed, plus the overarching threat to private property it posed, was too great. Committed to a policy of speedy reconciliation with defeated Southerners, President Johnson overturned Sherman's offer, returning the land to ex-confederates as he pardoned them. Across South Carolina that autumn, former slaves found themselves neither protected by the paternalism of bondage—such as it was—nor enabled to provide for themselves except by onerous plantation labor, when they could find it, unless fortunate enough to live near the ocean or rivers for harvesting seafood or near the woods for hunting. White fears that freedpeople would rise in revolt, either on July 4, December 25, or January 1, were rampant. That African Americans did not turn to violence is explained by the presence of federal troops, a well-armed veteran white citizenry, and by the New Testament theology of forgiveness and love faith that predominated in the African American community—but one not reciprocated by white South Carolinians. In addition, African Americans had faith that the government capable of emancipation and abolition would, shortly enough, settle the traitors' land upon them as a just reward. Those hopes proved hollow.

For most former confederates, the notion that military defeat should bring social transformation seemed outrageous. Reactions to emancipation were complex—some ex-masters drove their "black families" off the land, some pleaded for them to stay—but almost none envisioned a system promoting racial equality or the enlargement of political rights in any significant way. President Johnson's generous terms for readmission to the Union encouraged that conservative vision. By repealing South Carolina's Ordinance of Secession and ratifying the terms of the Thirteenth Amendment abolishing slavery, the constitutional convention, which met in Columbia in September 1865, seemed to have met his standards for Reconstruction.

Unfortunately, the legislative session of December 1865—dominated by elite ex-confederates—demonstrated how intransigent some white Carolinians still were when they struggled to define their former slaves' new status within the state. "This is a white man's government," explained the new Governor Benjamin Perry, elected under Johnson's plan, "and intended for white men only." South Carolina's Black Code expressly denied freedpeople "social and political equality with white persons" before the law, though they might buy and sell property, make contracts, and seek legal redress through criminal action or civil suits. For the first time, race was defined by statute and interracial marriage was prohibited. Trade, travel, occupation, and judicial redress were all restricted. For Congress and local federal officials, South Carolina's Black Code confirmed their worst fears about former rebels. Although agents of the understaffed Freedmen's Bureau attempted to establish fair terms of contract between white landowners and black labor for the 1866 crop year, collusion, violence, and their own prejudices subverted equity. Before 1870, South Carolina freedmen labored on the same farm units they had worked as slaves or in the near vicinity. Except in a few locales, such as the Promiseland neighborhood of Abbeville County, African Americans found no chance to purchase land of their own, and no opportunity of bettering their lot in a different area. In the low country, the gang-labor requirements of rice cultivation reduced most to grueling wage work.

Congress intended the Civil Rights Act of 1866 and the Fourteenth Amendment to remedy such inequities. South Carolina, however, responded simply by retooling the Black Code in a special session of the legislature early that fall, removing references to race. In December, the General Assembly refused to ratify the Fourteenth Amendment by a vote of 95 to 1. But as the war had shown, state defiance could not match federal power when it decided to operate. In March 1867, Congress passed the Military Reconstruction Acts, which placed the South Carolina government under direct military control and called for yet another constitutional convention, based on universal manhood suffrage. Readmission to the Union required a new constitution rooted in a new legislature, which needed to ratify the Fourteenth Amendment.

For South Carolina blacks and their white allies, the 1868 Constitutional Convention held the promise of a great breakthrough toward political equality and social justice. Scarcely three years after liberating themselves from the slaveholders' Confederacy, South Carolinians—the people, black and white, farmers and townsmen, who comprised the vast majority—sat down to rewrite their state's basic law itself. This step culminated a steady process of organization and institution building by African Americans, establishing churches, schools, and voluntary associations after their own beliefs and ideas, working alongside native whites—derogatorily called scalawags—and Northern immigrants, or carpetbaggers, who shared their values. Politically, they flocked to Union League meetings and the Republican Party, largely confining their advocacy within legal limits, despite the advantage of overwhelming numbers outside the upper piedmont. The constitution they created in 1868 was a model both of racial tolerance and democratic ideals. Based on Ohio's Constitution, delegates—60 percent black—guaranteed voting rights, legal freedoms, and educational opportunity to all Carolinians, and established a new decentralized system of county government that provided a great deal of home rule and local autonomy. The 1868 Constitution won quick ratification, and in elections that fall, Republicans swept to victory across the state at both local and General Assembly levels. A new era, seemingly, was at hand. African Americans controlled a majority of seats in the lower house (and from 1874 to 1876, both the senate and the house), and African Americans won elections as lieutenant governor, secretary of state, and state treasurer, as well as a significant number of local offices, such as sheriff, county commissioner, magistrate, and alderman. Reconstruction in South Carolina lasted longer than in any other state, and South Carolina's black Republicans achieved a tremendous level of importance.

Republican legislators set about trying to reestablish order and promote racial harmony in South Carolina. This was a truly biracial administration, according African Americans more political power than in any other state during Reconstruction—or since. To revitalize the economy and reestablish the state's credit, they floated a massive new bond issue. Universal public education would transform the state, they declared, allowing all with brains and grit a chance to rise. Desegregating public transportation and accommodations would likewise chop down artificial barriers in favor of an unregulated, color-blind marketplace. A new tax code, eliminating the preferential treatment landholders had traditionally enjoyed, would fund initiatives and help redistribute real property, the basis of conservative power. Hundreds of thousands of acres were soon seized by the state for nonpayment of taxes. With the creation of the South Carolina Land Commission (1872), more than 2,000 small farmers, white and black, purchased family-sized tracts. What Sherman's field order failed to achieve, the Land Commission began to redress, albeit on a small scale.

Yet these initiatives failed to gain support from South Carolina whites, even though most stood to benefit from public education, marketplace stability, and government-aided access to land. Higher land taxes hit marginal property holders, and also alienated the largest landowners—while sparing freed slaves who rarely owned land. White Carolinians were susceptible to the propaganda from the Democratic Party of constant charges of corruption in government activities. Many whites grew bitter at what they believed was waste and abuse in government. Spurred on by the hard times caused by low cotton prices, worn lands, soaring interest rates, and the depression that followed the Panic of 1873, many longed to "throw the rascals" out of office. But what brought down the Republican vision in South Carolina was not corruption. It was a bloody, decade-long reign of terror, sponsored and carried out by the very men who claimed to be champions of conservative "order." Whether through secretive activity by the Ku Klux Klan or open mob violence, Democrats resorted to political assassination, murder, physical beatings, arson, and economic intimidation. Klan violence was a direct attack on the Republican vision of political, social, and economic equality itself. By 1871, they had seized effective control of sections of the up-country, forcing President Ulysses S. Grant to suspend habeas corpus in nine counties. Army and justice marshals hunted down and arrested suspected klansmen; mass indictments followed, but prosecutions were slow and convictions few and toothless. The African American community and its white allies waited—with remarkable restraint—for competent federal protection. Instead, Washington's actions showed Conservatives that federals lacked the political will to turn back their assault.

Declining Northern interest, increasing factionalism in the state Republican Party, and growing frustration with taxes and corruption slowly solidified Conservative nerve. Between 1872 and 1876, the Klan evaporated, replaced by gun clubs like the Red Shirts who used intimidation and violence to strengthen the Democratic Party and nibble away at Republican morale. By the election of 1876, terrorism flared again, culminating in the infamous Hamburg and Ellenton Massacres. When no federal action ensued, white Democrats saw the green light for electoral fraud and violence in the gubernatorial and legislative contests that fall. Wade Hampton III, former Confederate general and candidate for governor, tromped the state with vast throngs of armed supporters, while his lieutenant Martin Witherspoon Gary called for all-out guerrilla warfare. When ballots were tallied, Hampton, the Democratic candidate, had been outpolled—though an accurate count is probably beyond meaning or recovery—but was far from outgunned. Refusing to concede defeat to Republican carpetbagger Daniel Chamberlain, Democrats set up a shadow legislature, and anointed Hampton as the state's true leader.

For five months, from late 1876 until April 1877 dual governments existed in Columbia: Daniel Chamberlain's Republicans held the state house, with the aid of federal troops, but Hampton essentially controlled the state; his call to refuse to pay taxes was arguably as powerful as his thousands of armed men. When President Rutherford B. Hayes ordered federal troops out of Columbia in April 1877, Chamberlain was forced to concede, and South Carolina passed to the redeemers.

The Bourbon triumph possessed no real program of its own, except raking up the failures of past administrations and reversing the budding economic and social gains of freedmen and poor whites. In the years after 1877, Conservative regimes tore up the hard-won gains of Reconstruction, and hopes of opportunity, economic advancement, and racial conciliation became little more than wistful alibis. Later as a U.S. senator, the "moderate" Hampton justified fraud, intimidation, and violence to deny South Carolina African Americans the franchise, claiming "the very civilization, the property, the life of the State itself, were involved." Apparently, once again, elite Conservative whites did not see all the people when they spoke of civilization and the state.

*Vernon Burton*

**See also:** Amnesty Proclamations; Black Suffrage; Civil Rights; Confiscation Acts; Delany, Martin R. (1812–1885); Edisto Island, South Carolina; Elliott, Robert B. (1842–1884); Enforcement Acts (1870, 1871, 1875); Moses, Franklin J. Jr. (1838–1906); New South; Orr, James L. (1822–1873); Race Riots; Smalls, Robert (1839–1915).

## Further Reading

Burton, Orville Vernon. *In My Father's House Are Many Mansions: Family and Community in Edgefield, South Carolina.* Chapel Hill: University of North Carolina Press, 1985.

Cooper, William J. Jr. *The Conservative Regime: South Carolina, 1877–1890.* Baltimore: Johns Hopkins University Press, 1968.

Dougherty, Kevin. *The Port Royal Experiment: A Case Study in Development.* Jackson: The University Press of Mississippi, 2014.

Edgar, Walter B. *South Carolina: A History.* Columbia: University of South Carolina Press, 1998.

Holt, Thomas. *Black over White: Negro Political Leadership in South Carolina during Reconstruction.* Urbana: University of Illinois Press, 1977.

Simkins, Francis B., and Robert H. Woody. *South Carolina during Reconstruction.* Chapel Hill: University of North Carolina Press, 1932.

Williamson, Joel. *After Slavery: The Negro in South Carolina during Reconstruction.* Chapel Hill: University of North Carolina Press, 1965.

Zuczek, Richard. *State of Rebellion: Reconstruction in South Carolina.* Columbia: University of South Carolina Press, 1996.

## SOUTHERN CLAIMS COMMISSION (SCC)

Created by Congress in 1871, the Southern Claims Commission (SCC) evaluated the claims made by Southern Unionists for goods and supplies taken by Union forces during the Civil War. Dedicated to reimbursing only those claimants who had been loyal throughout the conflict, the three-member commission amassed detailed testimonies and other records that are an invaluable source for the history of Unionism in the South, the transition from slavery to freedom, and the significance of community during and after the war.

Southern Unionists had lost goods and property to the Union military through official confiscation, unsanctioned confiscation, and simple destructiveness. Troops often did not know or care about the allegiance of the property owners they encountered. Occasionally, Southerners received payment from officers for what was taken; more often they received written or oral assurances that the government would make good on the transactions after the war. Such redress did not come immediately. Congress did not establish the SCC until March 3, 1871, after two years of debate within the 41st Congress.

Appointed by President Ulysses S. Grant and approved by the Senate, the commissioners were Asa Owen Aldis of Vermont, who served as president of the commission; Orange Ferriss of New York; and James B. Howell of Iowa. All three were former Whigs who had become Radical Republicans. They developed a strict loyalty test, with the burden on claimants to prove that they had been loyal—despite their wartime residence within the Confederacy. The commissioners forwarded their recommendations on each claim to the U.S. House of Representatives, which almost always approved the commissioners' recommendations.

Individuals and organizations ultimately filed 22,298 claims for more than $60 million in lost goods. Congress approved 7,092 of the claims at a cost of $4.6 million. Claimants included whites, free blacks (African Americans who had been free before the war), and even former slaves. Although slaves in particular had difficulty proving to the commissioners that they had truly owned the goods declared, SCC records clearly reflect property holding, particularly communal ownership, among slaves. While skeptical of slave property ownership, the commissioners placed great faith in the detailed testimonies of former slaves regarding the losses experienced by Unionist planters during the war.

Claimants who sought reimbursement for losses of more than $10,000 had to appear with their witnesses before the three commissioners in Washington, D.C. The considerable cost of such a trip deterred some applicants altogether and encouraged others to keep their claims below the $10,000 threshold and thus only incur the moderate fees for filing a claim.

Approximately 220,000 witnesses testified on behalf of SCC claimants. The testimonies of witnesses regarding claimants' loyalty illustrate the intimidation and harassment that Unionists had faced within the Confederacy, reveal the deep interest that blacks took in the war's outcome, and expose the lingering bitterness of political divisions that carried over into Reconstruction. The language used by witnesses conveys at once the acrimony, weariness, and hope of the period.

Many Northern Republican congressmen and newspapers, particularly the *New York Tribune*, voiced opposition to Southern claims. Claims became part of the Bloody Shirt politics of the period, as Northerners accused Southerners of greed and expressed fear over a drain on the treasury. The commission itself, however, received praise in the North for its thrift and discretion. Many residents of the South, on the other hand, criticized the commission for the strictness of its loyalty test. The commission concluded its work on March 10, 1880. The Bowman Act (1883) and the Tucker Act (1887) gave unsuccessful SCC claimants the opportunity to present their claims to the U.S. Court of Claims, which usually upheld the SCC's decisions.

*Antoinette G. van Zelm*

***See also:*** Civil Rights; Congressional Reconstruction; Fourteenth Amendment (1868); Loyalty Oaths.

## Further Reading

Klingberg, Frank W. *The Southern Claims Commission*. Berkeley: University of California Press, 1955.

Mills, Gary B. *Southern Loyalists in the Civil War: The Southern Claims Commission*. Baltimore: Genealogical Publishing Co., 1994.

Storey, Margaret M. "Civil War Unionists and the Political Culture of Loyalty in Alabama, 1860–1861." *Journal of Southern History* 69 (2003): 71–106.

Washington, Reginald. "The Southern Claims Commission: A Source for African-American Roots." *Prologue* 27 (1995): 374–82.

# SOUTHERN HOMESTEAD ACT (1866)

In the wake of the Civil War, more than 46 million acres of public land remained unsold in the states of Arkansas, Alabama, Florida, Louisiana, and Mississippi. To facilitate its distribution and respond to pressure to assist former slaves seeking land, Congress passed the Southern Homestead Act. Although he opposed what he called "class legislation"—the offering of assistance to former slaves—President Andrew Johnson signed it into law on June 21, 1866, believing it would help poor whites. Under its terms, individuals could claim up to 80 acres for homesteading (40 acres for land originally priced at $2.50 per acre), although prior to January 1, 1870, only blacks and loyal white Southerners could file for land.

The law prohibited the acquisition of government land by cash sale or preemption in order to ensure the land was acquired by homesteaders and not timber companies or other business interests. It also allowed former slaves five years to pay their registration fee to facilitate settlement by the cash-poor freedpeople, and included unprecedented language stating, "No distinction or discrimination shall be made in the construction or execution of this act on account of race or color."

Despite these favorable provisions and attempts by the Bureau of Refugees, Freedmen, and Abandoned Lands to assist former slaves wishing to take advantage of the law, the Southern Homestead Act actually proved of little help to blacks trying to acquire land during Reconstruction. First, many well-to-do white Southerners objected to the law, both to the principle of black landownership and because it threatened to drain the plantations of laborers. Southern whites opposed any legislation that bolstered the independence of African Americans. Fraud also was rampant, with timber companies in particular skirting the law's intent by filing false claims through front men. Third, much of the best land was off-limits, as it was already reserved for grants to railroads or military reservations. The parcels left often proved too poor for farming.

In short, numerous obstacles existed to keep former slaves and poor whites from acquiring land under the Southern Homestead Act. In the 10 years the law existed, about 67,600 claims were made for land, with about a quarter of those made by black people. Around 28,000 claims were successfully patented, meaning the applicant eventually acquired title to the land. While some of these patents went to former slaves, the Southern Homestead Act did not become a vehicle to mass black landownership during Reconstruction.

*Donald R. Shaffer*

*See also:* Edisto Island, South Carolina; Field Order No. 15; Port Royal Experiment.

## Further Reading

Hoffnagle, Warren. "The Southern Homestead Act: Its Origins and Operation." *Historian* 32 (August 1970): 612–29.

Lanza, Michael L. *Agrarianism and Reconstruction Politics: The Southern Homestead Act.* Baton Rouge: Louisiana State University Press, 1990.

Pope, Christie Farnham. "Southern Homesteads for Negroes." *Agricultural History* 44 (April 1970): 201–12.

## STANTON, EDWIN M. (1814–1869)

Aside from perhaps only Abraham Lincoln and Ulysses S. Grant, Edwin McMasters Stanton was the indispensable man during the Civil War. Vain and dedicated, Stanton brought a Victorian intensity and work ethic to his position as secretary of war. He was universally unpopular, but his commitment to the Union cause remained constant as the American world changed. As a Radical Republican during and after the war, he played a large role in the direction of the new America. Ultimately, his clash with President Andrew Johnson was the last battle in Congress's ongoing conflict with the executive.

Born in Steubenville, Ohio, to David Stanton, a physician, and Lucy Norman, Edwin was a bright but sickly child, a victim of an asthmatic condition that shaped his behavior and his personality. He was active member of the Episcopal Church, and religious sentiments and values shaped his intellectual world. He attended local schools until his father's death, briefly attended Kenyon College, and eventually turned to law. Stanton supported the Democracy, served as the county attorney, and generally, kept his antislavery sentiments to himself.

After moving his practice several times, he settled in Pittsburgh where his partnership with Charles Shalter led to more financial rewards and opportunities to network in the party. He moved to Washington, D.C., and joined the James Buchanan

Edwin M. Stanton, a Democrat-turned-Radical Republican, brilliantly served as President Lincoln's secretary of war. He clashed constantly with President Johnson, and his removal led to the president's impeachment. (Library of Congress)

administration. As a government lawyer, Stanton earned a reputation for honesty and diligence, and many of his cases revolved around rooting out corruption and fraud. In the final year of Buchanan's term, Stanton served as U.S. attorney general.

As part of the president's inner circle during the secession crisis of 1860, Stanton was shocked by Buchanan's reasoning that secession was illegal but that the government was powerless to prevent it. It was during this tenuous period that Stanton, railroad mogul and future general George McClellan, and others formed the nucleus of the "War Democrats," Democratic leaders in the North who put Union above party.

Early on, this Democrat displayed Radical Republican characteristics, such as his support for the use of African Americans in the Union army. Even the new Republican president, Abraham Lincoln, feared this would alienate Northern soldiers and the Border States. Early in 1862, when Secretary of War Simon Cameron resigned under a cloud of corruption, Lincoln, knowing Stanton's reputation as a hardworking, honest Democrat, saw the opportunity to clean up the department and create cross-party alliances. It was a brilliant choice. He brought order to the growing department, worked (i.e., lobbied) Congress successfully, and developed an early form of a "war council" that discussed the military events, policies, and programs to formulate advice for Lincoln. Lincoln and Stanton worked together on a "hands-on" policy in directing the Union's military efforts. Slowly, Stanton left his Democratic fold and evolved into a Radical Republican, arguing for a "hard war" policy with confiscation of slaves and other property of rebel leaders. Stanton enthusiastically supported the Emancipation Proclamation and was thrilled with its provisions for admitting African Americans into the Union army. Stanton supported Grant's strategy, and when assassins killed Lincoln, he was personally responsible for bringing the conspirators to justice.

The new president, Democrat Andrew Johnson, knew his legitimacy was thin and so deliberately retained the cabinet of his successor. Johnson was not unlike Stanton, or so it seemed. Johnson was a War Democrat, thoroughly committed to preserving the Union and crushing the rebellion, but whereas Stanton developed during the war and moved to embrace the active federal government and the possibilities awakened by abolition, Johnson remained rooted in the antebellum period. The new president sought a quick and painless reconciliation, with little punishment for former rebels and little offerings to former slaves. As a result, Stanton and Johnson soon clashed, with a great deal at stake: The secretary of war had charge of the army, a central player in all Reconstruction agendas. During Presidential Reconstruction, the South was an occupied territory, and beginning in 1867 and continuing through Congressional Reconstruction, the U.S. Army actually helped govern the region. So, the man in charge of the War Department had considerable influence over the restoration programs in the former Confederate states. He issued orders, countermanded orders, delivered interpretations favorable to Radical needs, and generally interfered with the president's use of the military.

By 1867, the president believed Stanton a traitor who was undermining executive power to advance a Radical Republican agenda. For just this reason, congressional Republicans had passed the Tenure of Office Act in March 1867, which prohibited the president from removing, without Senate consent, anyone appointed via Senate consent. In August, Johnson, believing the Act unconstitutional (he had vetoed it) and inapplicable in Stanton's case (since he was appointed under another administration), took advantage of a loophole in the Tenure of Office Act, and suspended the secretary while the Senate was in recess. The president appointed Gen. Ulysses S. Grant as secretary *ad interim* and believed that he and Grant had an agreement: If the Senate did not consent in the suspension, the office would revert back to the president (not to Stanton). The Senate did not consent, but Grant shocked Johnson by returning the office to Stanton, who gladly reoccupied his old position. Johnson reacted swiftly and possibly irrationally by then removing Stanton altogether. Radicals in Congress charged the president with violating the Tenure of Office Act, and the first successful impeachment of a president followed.

Andrew Johnson escaped conviction in the Senate and continued as president for the remainder of the term. Not so for Stanton, who did not actually stay in office; in an odd sort of compromise, Johnson held firm in his removal of Stanton but appointed Moderate John M. Schofield as the new secretary of war. Congressional Republicans concurred in the nomination since the issue had already been decided, and Johnson was eliminated as an obstacle. In a way, Stanton was no longer necessary, for the entire crisis had revealed a new ally and by this time Republican presidential nominee, Gen. Ulysses S. Grant.

After leaving office, Stanton's health declined; asthma, stress, and long hours took their toll. Grant appointed him to the U.S. Supreme Court in December 1869, but he died before taking office. A man some referred to as "Lincoln's Mars" was a lightning rod for controversy and criticism, but he faced incredible challenges with professional aplomb and grim determination. Perhaps the fact that, in his last months, he was financially supported by his friends gives a sense of what others thought of him. He had contributed all his health and wealth for his nation, and its continued existence was due in some part, to him.

*Donald K. Pickens*

***See also:*** Command of the Army Act (1867); Impeachment Managers; Military Reconstruction Acts (1867–1868).

## Further Reading

Hendrick, Burton J. *Lincoln's War Cabinet*. Boston: Little, Brown, 1946.

Hyman, Harold M. "Johnson, Stanton, and Grant: A Reconsideration of the Army's Role in the Events Leading to Impeachment." *American Historical Review* 66 (October 1960): 85–96.

Pratt, Fletcher. *Stanton, Lincoln's Secretary of War*. New York: Norton, 1953.

Thomas, Benjamin P., and Harold M. Hyman. *Stanton: The Life and Times of Lincoln's Secretary of War*. New York: Knopf, 1962.

## STEVENS, THADDEUS (1792–1868)

The leading Radical Republican in the U.S. House of Representatives during the Civil War and early Reconstruction, Thaddeus Stevens's motives, policies, and ideology have fascinated both contemporaries and historians. Born in Danville, Vermont, of a poor family—a situation made worse when his father abandoned it—Stevens benefitted from a zealously religious mother who pushed his education. Stevens developed into an unusual man: handicapped (he had a clubfoot), not handsome, with a caustic, argumentative style. He gambled, did not attend church, never married, and yet raised two nephews.

Stevens graduated from Dartmouth College in 1814. By 1815, Stevens moved to York, Pennsylvania, where he taught and studied law. Passing the bar, he moved to Gettysburg, Pennsylvania. He soon emerged as a leader in the county, taking a Whig stance on internal improvements, banking, and public education. Elected to the Pennsylvania House of Representatives in 1833, he led the fight to strengthen the state educational system, which he saw as a means of social mobility.

In 1842, Stevens moved to Lancaster, Pennsylvania, where his reputation grew due to his aggressive advocacy of controversial subjects. For instance, he defended the suffrage rights of the state's free black population, and pushed for stronger laws against Southern slave catchers operating in the state. In 1848, Stevens won election to the U.S. House of Representatives.

In Congress, Stevens quickly became an articulate foe of the "Slave Power," arguing that free land (i.e., non-slave) makes free men. Wearing a red wig (his baldness the result of a fever as a young man) that often slipped in the heat of debate, Stevens took no verbal prisoners. By the 1850s, the central issue facing the nation was the spread of slavery into the West. The Whig Party disintegrated over the debate, with the Democratic Party staking its future on slavery, while a new Northern party, the Republicans, opposed the expansion of the slave system. Stevens was almost too radical for the Republicans, but he recognized that only the Republican Party could preserve the West as free soil.

Some historians believe that Stevens even welcomed the coming of the Civil War. As a promoter of capitalism, free enterprise, public education, and national banking, Stevens could see the American South as a disease, a rejection of everything he believed in. The war was a way of cleansing America; of moving forward in a moral and practical way; reshaping Southern society along just, fair, and "modern" lines. Stevens early on pushed for sterner war measures and a harsher prosecution of the war, including proposing national conscription (a draft) and the suspension of the writ of habeas corpus to allow the government to squash unpatriotic activity. Stevens was frustrated with President Abraham Lincoln's failure to see how the future of the Union and the abolition of slavery were innately connected (the same argument made to Lincoln by abolitionist Frederick Douglass). Stevens urged that African Americans be enrolled in the Union army and that civil rights be extended to all blacks—and even suffrage to males.

Union victory was to Stevens a godsend, a preordained, destined event by which the South—and its former slaves and former confederates—were to be delivered over to the North, and the Radical Republicans, for judgment and reforming. Stevens's concept of Reconstruction established him as the radical vanguard: the rebel states were conquered territories. They had waged war, been beaten, and now awaited whatever course of action the victors intended. The most important action to Stevens was entirely consistent with his career and ideology: a plan of land distribution to the freedpeople. Stability and justice in an agricultural region could only occur through land ownership. Stevens argued confiscation and redistribution fulfilled many goals: it punished traitors, rewarded blacks, and equalized an economically regressive society.

But Stevens's plan was too extreme in a country obsessed with private property and white supremacy. His initiative was dead by February 1866, as he met with no support from the new president, Andrew Johnson, and little from his Republican colleagues in Congress. Undaunted, Stevens continued his agitation for social justice while providing leadership in the House of Representatives. In 1866 and 1867, he defended the Bureau of Refugees,

Freedmen, and Abandoned Lands, the Civil Rights Act, and the Fourteenth Amendment. As the founder of and ranking member on the Joint Committee on Reconstruction, Stevens urged a total reshaping of Southern institutions, particularly landownership. He introduced the Tenure of Office Act, and a series of bills that became the 1867 Military Reconstruction Act. Stevens envisioned these as the vehicle for advanced economic change, but it fell short of his ideal; many in Congress, including his peer in the Senate, Charles Sumner, saw political rights as more important than economic ones. Stevens was never swayed, arguing that a more equitable distribution of land superseded political roles.

Obviously, Stevens was a bitter opponent of President Johnson. Considering Johnson's lenient treatment of former confederates, eagerness to extend amnesty, total rejection of land confiscation (even overturning Sherman's meager Field Order No. 15), and open disdain for what he called "class legislation" to help African Americans, reconciliation between the men was impossible. Seeing the congressman as a dangerous fanatic, Johnson lashed out at Stevens publicly in public addresses and during the 1866 National Union Party campaign. Not surprisingly, Stevens was among the first to openly call for the impeachment and removal of President Andrew Johnson. Following Johnson's removal of Secretary of War Edwin Stanton, the House voted to impeach the president and created a committee of impeachment managers to serve as the prosecution in his Senate trial. Stevens was, of course, named to the body, but his health had declined rapidly, so he was unable to play an active role; during the trial, proxies had to read his speeches and comments, as Stevens was unable to rise and sometimes even attend.

As with his dreams of creating a new economic and social order, Stevens's mission to remove the president failed as well. Johnson survived the trial, was acquitted in May, and continued as president. Stevens never recovered his health and died in Washington in August, feeling bitter and betrayed. Stevens had chosen for his burial an interracial cemetery in Lancaster, Pennsylvania. His tombstone's epitaph, written by Stevens himself, is a fitting summary of his life as a critical contributor to the America that emerged from the ashes of the Civil War: "I repose in this quiet and secluded spot, not from any natural preference for solitude But, finding other Cemeteries limited as to Race, by Charter Rules, I have chosen this that I might illustrate in my death, the Principles which I advocated Through a long life: EQUALITY OF MAN BEFORE HIS CREATOR."

*Donald K. Pickens*

**See also:** Amnesty Proclamations; Ashley, James M. (1824–1896); Black Suffrage; Butler, Benjamin Franklin (1818–1893); Civil Rights Act of 1875; Confiscation Acts; Congressional Reconstruction; Edisto Island, South Carolina; Freedmen's Relief Societies; Labor Systems; Loyalty Oaths; National Union Party (1864); Port Royal Experiment; Presidential Reconstruction; Republicans, Moderate.

## Further Reading

Brodie, Fawn N. *Thaddeus Stevens, Scourge of the* South. New York: Norton Library, 1966.

Current, Richard N. *Old Thad Stevens, A Story of Ambition.* Madison: University of Wisconsin Press, 1942.

Palmer, Beverly Wilson, ed. *The Selected Papers of Thaddeus Stevens.* Pittsburgh: University of Pittsburgh Press, 1997.

# SUFFRAGE

Nineteenth-century thought was divided over whether suffrage was a right of citizenship or a privilege based on education and responsibility. In colonial America, suffrage was curbed everywhere by religious affiliation, gender, property holding, and—in most instances—race. Since, as men believed, government was established to defend liberty and property, voters and government officials needed to possess a modicum of each. Between 50 and 80 percent of adult white males were eligible to cast ballots, depending on local restrictions; this represented between 10 and 16 percent of the total adult population. In practice, however, average voter turnout ranged from 40 percent in Virginia down to 10 percent in Massachusetts and Connecticut.

After 1776, everything changed. With the political and legal upheaval of the American Revolution and the economic changes of the market revolution, a veritable "age of democracy" sprang up after 1815. Property and religious qualifications for suffrage were swept away everywhere by 1840, while race became even more entrenched as an obstacle. By the late antebellum period, between 70 and 80 percent of white male citizens turned out to vote. Extending the franchise had played an important role in defusing class antagonism. The expansion of white suffrage went hand in hand with the elimination of black voting rights across the antebellum North. Abraham Lincoln himself publicly opposed equal suffrage for free blacks as late as 1858. Midwestern states such as Ohio, Illinois, Indiana, and Wisconsin worked hard to bar black immigration altogether (the latter three wrote racial bans into their constitutions), and emigrants carried exclusionary ideas westward to Oregon and California. New Yorkers never denied blacks the right to vote, but held them to discriminatory property qualification rules after 1821.

At the outset of the Civil War, only five states in the nation, all in New England, permitted blacks to vote on the same basis as whites. All states denied women, and many states from each section of the country had additional suffrage restrictions, denying Chinese, illiterates, or those too poor to pay taxes. Between 1863 and 1870, proposals to enfranchise African Americans were overwhelmingly defeated in more than 15 Northern states and territories.

After Appomattox, Radical Republicans took up the cause of black suffrage in spite of the considerable political risk it entailed. Although radicals like Charles Sumner and Salmon Chase had goaded him to act, Abraham Lincoln considered the franchise a state matter on which he doubted his authority to intervene, even as commander in chief charged with subduing a rebellion. Privately, he urged Louisiana's governor to consider limited African American suffrage in writing a new state constitution, and he lent support to congressmen who proposed extending the franchise to black troops, but both efforts failed. Following his reelection in 1864, Lincoln called for allowing "the very intelligent, and those who served our cause as soldiers" to vote. The suggestion had no effect. Lincoln's successor, Andrew Johnson, made no move toward black suffrage, eager to reestablish prewar voting arrangements as quickly as possible. Although African American enfranchisement was a cherished goal for Radical Republicans, many insisted on a go-slow approach during 1865–1866. It was mostly social reformers, North and South, who championed immediate voting rights for freedmen during this period.

Southern intransigence gave congressional Radicals the opportunity they sought. In the winter of 1865–1866, Johnson-backed legislatures packed with elite ex-confederates passed a series of Black Codes, expressly denying African Americans social and political equality with whites. The Black Codes brought people to conclusion that the ballot was necessary if African Americans were to protect their own civil rights. The African American church, voluntary organizations, and individuals knew that the right to vote was essential to securing liberty.

African Americans in the South (not the nation as a whole) gained access to suffrage when Congress passed the 1867 Military Reconstruction Act. The act divided the South into five military districts for law enforcement and set up the protocol for states to gain readmission to the Union. State governments existed at the mercy of army officials, former confederates were broadly disfranchised, and new constitutional conventions set in motion. Specifically, states had to ratify the Fourteenth Amendment and write new state constitutions. For the purpose of choosing electors to these meetings, universal manhood suffrage was established, regardless of race.

Across the South, black and white convention delegates advocated universal male suffrage, and wrote new constitutions protecting that right. Unsurprisingly, across the South in 1867 and 1868, Republican-dominated conventions and legislatures ratified the Fourteenth Amendment and codified the right of African Americans to vote in state elections and to hold public office. Congress itself had already pointed the way in January 1866, affirming African Americans' suffrage rights in the District of Columbia. By contrast, diehards in Kentucky (which had never seceded, and so was exempt from these measures) did not ratify the amendment until 1976. By June 1868, seven states had passed new constitutions granting citizenship and the right to vote to previously enslaved men.

African American men responded in a big way. Louisiana was typical; approximately 90 percent of black males of voting age in the state registered to vote in 1867. Suffrage meant that, where a coalition of African Americans and white Republicans were in the majority, African American leaders won elections. In the presidential election of 1868, Republican Ulysses S. Grant won by 300,000 votes in an election in which 700,000 African Americans voted.

The right to vote meant political power, and political power directly and personally influenced economic opportunity by prohibiting job discrimination. Moreover, in areas where Republicans controlled the political process, African Americans brought about reform in women's rights and divorce laws. They ended some of the exploitation of children in apprenticeship. They reformed orphanages and asylums. A lasting legacy of Reconstruction was the support of public education for all children in the South. They also reformed the penal system, ending inhumane punishments such as disfigurement, and ending imprisonment for debt. They outlawed discrimination on any public transportation, and most Jim Crow legislation (social segregation) in the South did not come about until Reconstruction was actively overturned.

Imposed by Congressional act and enforced by the U.S. Army, by 1870, Southern state constitutions allowed universal male suffrage—but most Northern and Western states did not. Between 1865 and 1869, 8 Northern states held 11 referendums on equal manhood suffrage. All but two went down to defeat. In solidly Republican states like Minnesota, Kansas, and Ohio, voters refused to extend franchise rights and punished politicians who promoted them. In Illinois, Indiana, Pennsylvania, and New Jersey, such measures were considered too risky to even bring before the electorate.

To secure the right to vote nationwide, congressional leadership mobilized Northern members of Congress to propose on February 26, 1869, an amendment to the Constitution,

"The right of citizens of the United States to vote shall not be denied or abridged by the United States or by any State on account of race, color, or previous condition of servitude." When Republican legislators in New York ratified the Fifteenth Amendment in 1869, voters turned them out in favor of gloating Democrats, who promptly rescinded the measure. Illinois, Pennsylvania, and Ohio—crucial Electoral College states—all refused to affirm equal suffrage.

Women interested in suffrage for themselves expected to be included in the Fifteenth Amendment. African American suffragist Sojourner Truth pointed out that everyone, "whatever their sex or color," had a "common cause" in needing the right to vote. As the Civil War ended and Reconstruction began, women like Truth, Lucy Stone, Elizabeth Cady Stanton, and Susan B. Anthony were optimistic about the future. These women anticipated that democracy outlined in the proposed Fifteenth Amendment would also apply to women.

Anthony and Stanton were among the women suffragists who thought voting was a privilege better left to the educated and well-off; these women thought they were better qualified than poor, "ignorant" former slaves, or for that matter, than Northern immigrants who might be dependent upon machine politics for jobs.

Their optimism was unfounded. Men were not willing to give women the right to vote. Frederick Douglass openly put aside women in the quest for black suffrage: "I must say that I do not see how any one [*sic*] can pretend that there is the same urgency in giving the ballot to woman as to the negro. With us, the matter is a question of life and death, at least, in fifteen States of the Union." Even the now-famous Julia Ward Howe concurred with Douglass; at a political rights convention she stated, "I am willing that the negro shall get the ballot before me."

Women continued to take collective, direct action by attempting to register and cast ballots wherever they could. In a few cases, such bids succeeded; other challenges were turned away or channeled into the court system. A case brought by suffragist Virginia Minor claimed that the Fourteenth Amendment defining citizenship automatically granted the right to vote. In 1875, the case (*Minor v. Happersett*, 88 U.S. 162) reached the U.S. Supreme Court and met crushing defeat. The court ruled unanimously that the Constitution did not "confer the right of suffrage upon any one." Voting was not a right of citizenship, but a privilege granted by government, which was charged with maintaining social order. Not only did this decision give American women the back of high court's hand, but it also laid the legal groundwork for African American disfranchisement in the years ahead. Nationwide, women were not granted the right to vote until 1920, with the passage of the Nineteenth Amendment.

The Fifteenth Amendment was ratified on February 3, 1870, carried by eight of the former Confederate states as well as states in the North and West. The amendment declared that a citizen's right to vote could not be abridged on the grounds of race or previous condition of servitude. It upheld *impartial*, but not *universal* suffrage. Within months, bitter racist reaction set in. In the South, paramilitary violence spiked and continued at high levels through 1876. Before 1868, Ku Klux Klan terror had focused on racial control of land and labor; after the achievement of African American suffrage, political assassination, voter intimidation, and election fraud ruled the agenda. In the North, whites simply turned their backs on the Republican cause in the 1870 elections. Even in counties where African Americans had a higher-than-average presence among the electorate, in many—perhaps most—cases, they were unable to counteract the effects of the majority of local whites who switched sides or stayed home. The high price Republicans paid for backing the suffrage amendment may partially explain why Congress failed to enact legislation addressing violence at Southern polling places. A large majority of Northern white voters had never been assembled to fight for African American rights in their own region.

After 1876, voting rights for African Americans and other racial minorities, as well as immigrants and poor whites—were rapidly rolled back, often in the name of positive reform and the usually half-baked desire to eliminate "corrupt" elements from the ranks of potential voters. By the 1890s, disfranchisement was the norm. (Native Americans were not declared citizens until 1924, but voting rights were determined on the state level. Americans of Asian descent became eligible for citizenship in the 1940s and 1950s.) In the South, the Fifteenth Amendment's support of the right to vote was diluted after Redemption and the overthrow of Reconstruction. Poll taxes, multiple ballot boxes, and the use of literacy tests, while outwardly race-neutral and so in keeping with the requirements of the Fifteenth Amendment, were actually ruthlessly biased in conception and administration. In response to public outcry that poor and illiterate whites would be turned away from the polls, Southern legislatures adopted the "grandfather clause," allowing males the right to vote if one of their grandparents had voted. The color line had come down on political life across the South and beyond. It would take a second Reconstruction, three generations hence, to restore what had been snatched away.

*Vernon Burton*

**See also:** Bourbons; Bureau of Refugees, Freedmen, and Abandoned Lands; Carpetbaggers; Compromise of 1877; Congressional Reconstruction; Democratic Party; Elections of 1864; Enforcement Acts (1870, 1871, 1875); Freedmen's Relief Societies; Pardons; Presidential Reconstruction; Republicans, Moderate; Union League of America.

## Further Reading

Goldman, Robert M. *Reconstruction and Black Suffrage: Losing the Vote in Reese & Cruikshank*. Lawrence: University Press of Kansas, 2001.

Keyssar, Alexander. *The Right to Vote: The Contested History of Democracy in the United States*. New York: Basic Books, 2000.

Perman, Michael. *Struggle for Mastery: Disfranchisement in the South, 1888–1908*. Chapel Hill: University of North Carolina Press, 2001.

Valelly, Richard M. *The Two Reconstructions: The Struggle for Black Enfranchisement*. Chicago: University of Chicago Press, 2004.

Wang, Xi. *The Trial of Democracy: Black Suffrage and Northern Republicans, 1860–1910*. Athens: University of Georgia Press, 1997.

## SUMNER, CHARLES (1811–1874)

Pompous, vain, and brilliant, Charles Sumner was the voice of moral certainty during the Civil War and Reconstruction. One of most educated and talented senators in American history, Sumner's policy voice carried a moral imperative.

Born in Boston to Relief Jacob and Charles Pinckney Sumner, a lawyer and sheriff, the family was committed to humanitarian reform and middle-class uplift. He married late in life and divorced after one year; although he remained close to his immediate family, his crusades in reform and justice dominated his life. Sumner entered Harvard when he was 15, graduated, and moved into Harvard Law School. Sumner enjoyed legal scholarship, writing, and rhetoric, yet found himself very unhappy practicing law. So, by the 1840s, he moved his legal focus in the direction of reform, including antislavery, public education, and prison reform. A Conscience Whig, Sumner condemned American aggression in the Mexican War as an immoral plot to expand the slave system. By the war's end, Sumner and many other Northern Whigs had joined the Free Soil Party, which proposed halting the spread of slavery into the West and granting homesteads to white farmers moving westward. He also fought (unsuccessfully) for school integration in Boston in 1849, which gained him such a following that Free Soilers and antislavery Massachusetts Democrats elected him to the U.S. Senate.

Sumner was a Republican from the birth of the party, a virulent anti-South, antislavery New Eng-

Longtime Massachusetts senator Charles Sumner (served 1851–1875) was the most powerful, uncompromising, and consistent proponent of abolition and equal rights. He saw the war as an opportunity to perfect the nation; by the 1870s he believed squabbling politicians and vile racism undercut real chances for real change. (Library of Congress)

lander who saw American progress itself hanging in the balance. His caustic speeches on the floor of the Senate were famous, and led to one of the most infamous events in the history of Capitol Hill. In May 1856, Sumner insulted South Carolina senator Andrew Butler in a speech condemning violence in Kansas, which led to an attack by Butler's cousin Preston Brooks. Brooks beat Sumner into a coma as the statesman read his mail at his desk; Sumner was absent from the Senate for three years. He did not return to the Senate until 1859, weaker, slightly hobbled, but as aggressive and forceful as ever. When the Civil War came, Sumner saw an opportunity, not a catastrophe. He believed the North would triumph, and anticipated great changes stemming from Union victory—including abolition, equal rights, and even black suffrage. He constantly appealed to President Abraham Lincoln to take action against slavery, and pushed the commander in chief to recruit African Americans for the Union army. Like many, he came to appreciate Lincoln's genius and was shocked and horrified by his assassination. Of his successor, Andrew Johnson, little was known: Sumner had been in the Senate with the Southern Democrat and was encouraged by his Unionism and strong performance as military governor of Tennessee. But it soon became apparent that Johnson was no friend of former slaves or champion of reform.

Disappointed, the brilliant Sumner believed (correctly) that Johnson's obstinate behavior would alienate potential Moderates and unify Republicans against him. While events bore this out, he was not to see party acceptance of his "state suicide" theory, Sumner's contention that rebel states lost all rights and privileges when they attempted to leave the Union; states no longer existed, as they had reverted to territorial status, under the control of Congress. Like his Radical counterpart in the House of Representatives Thaddeus Stevens, Sumner watched as his initiatives were watered down and frittered away to make Moderate legislation possible, as Moderate Republicans really controlled the tempo of Congress. He enjoyed a few real successes—including the act to enfranchise black males in the District of Columbia—but most of Congressional Reconstruction was too conservative for his goals.

Reconstruction never approached the possibilities Sumner saw in it. For him, it seemed as though the cost of the war, the expenditure in blood and treasure, was wasted, as golden opportunities for real reform and progress evaporated. President Johnson was part of the problem, and Sumner was an early advocate of impeaching and removing him. Sumner was frustrated with the Senate's failure to remove the president and angry with his fellow Republicans (some say it was Sumner who first charged Edmund Ross with receiving a bribe to vote "not guilty").

Even the advent of a Republican president left Sumner hollow. He had low expectations for Ulysses S. Grant, not really seeing him as a proponent of African American rights or human equality in general. Sumner was unfortunately accurate, and the senator found himself drifting from Grant and the Republicans. Alarmed by the rise in violence in the South, Sumner criticized the half-hearted enforcement policy, and admonished Congress for turning its back on Southern Republican governments. To show his exasperation, Sumner even voted against the Fifteenth Amendment, because of its "negative" phrasing; again Sumner was prophetic, predicting blacks would be disfranchised as a result. By the early 1870s, Sumner clashed with Grant head-on: as chair of the Senate Foreign Relations Committee he derailed negotiations over Civil War claims with Great Britain (Sumner demanded Canada as compensation for British aid to the Confederacy) and neutralized several of Grant's annexation schemes, including taking the Dutch West Indies and the Dominican Republic.

The disagreements over Grant's aggressive foreign policy and the administration's growing problems with scandal drove Sumner from the party fold; by 1872, he was part of the Liberal Republican bolt. But Sumner never wavered from his goal of African Americans' full citizenship and their right to a decent living. To the end of his career, he fought for civil liberties and against discrimination in all its various forms. Legend has it that his dying words were a plea to save his civil rights bill, awaiting vote in Congress; the senator died March 11, 1874, in Washington. In a bittersweet final act, perhaps in honor of the great senator, Congress did pass the Civil Rights Act of 1875—but, as usual, without the key components and most important provisions that Sumner had proposed. Despite his vanity and failings, Sumner saw clearly the necessity for a significant and lasting reformation of American life and politics. Unfortunately, it took more than a century for the nation to realize the validity of his vision.

*Donald K. Pickens*

**See also:** Amnesty Proclamations; Ashley, James M. (1824–1896); Black Suffrage; Butler, Benjamin Franklin (1818–1893); Civil Rights Act of 1875; Confiscation Acts; Congressional Reconstruction; Edisto Island, South Carolina; Freedmen's Relief Societies;

Impeachment of Andrew Johnson (1868); Loyalty Oaths; National Union Party (1864); Port Royal Experiment; Presidential Reconstruction; Republicans, Moderate.

## Further Reading

Blue, Frederick. *Charles Sumner and the Conscience of the North.* Arlington Heights, IL: Harlan Davidson, 1994.

Donald, David. *Charles Sumner and the Coming of the Civil War.* New York: Knopf, 1967.

Donald, David. *Charles Sumner and the Rights of Man.* New York: Knopf, 1970.

# SUPREME COURT

Before the Civil War, the Supreme Court had accommodated and even promoted slavery. Republicans had condemned its ruling in the Dred Scott case, *Dred Scott v. Sandford* (1857), that African Americans were not citizens of the United States and that Congress lacked the authority to ban slavery from the territories. Although the Court had generally sustained the government's wartime policies, the fear that it would undermine measures to abolish slavery was a powerful motive for securing emancipation with the Thirteenth Amendment to the U.S. Constitution. President Abraham Lincoln hoped to create a more sympathetic Court by naming Salmon P. Chase chief justice upon the death of Roger B. Taney. Chase had been the Republican Party's leading constitutional expert, the foremost proponent of the Republican argument that the federal government was constitutionally obligated to promote freedom rather than accommodate slavery. Lincoln hoped Chase would not only influence the Court but also help restore its prestige.

Despite Chase's presence as chief justice, working with four other justices appointed by Lincoln, several decisions suggested that the Court was not in full sympathy with the Republican program of Reconstruction. Moreover, Chase, who was required by the Constitution to preside over the impeachment trial of President Andrew Johnson, played a key role in securing his acquittal. Although Republican president Ulysses S. Grant named several more Republican justices, the Court's restrictive interpretation of federal power under the Fourteenth Amendment and Fifteenth Amendment undermined the government's ability to protect the rights of its citizens after the war.

Those restrictions came early in the Republicans' Reconstruction efforts. Most Republicans insisted that the federal government retain military control over the Southern states after the war, exercising martial law where necessary and using the army and military courts to maintain order. However, in April 1866, the Court in *Ex parte Milligan* freed an Indiana Copperhead who had been sentenced to death by a presidentially authorized military commission. Its opinion held that civilians could not be tried by military commissions where the civil courts were open. The opinion questioned Congress's authority to maintain military government in the South, just as most Republicans were concluding that it was necessary.

Other justices joined Chase's concurring opinion that Milligan's trial was illicit because it was authorized only by the president and not by Congress. In similar 5–4 decisions, the justices continued to throw doubt on the constitutionality of Congressional Reconstruction policy; early in 1867, the Court ruled unconstitutional the state and federal laws that required people to take "test oaths." These loyalty oaths were oaths that one had never supported the rebellion, required in order to practice various influential professions. The U.S. Constitution explicitly banned such "bills of attainder" and "ex post facto laws," the majority of the justices held in the Test Oath cases, *Cummings v. Missouri* and *Ex parte Garland*. The decisions undermined the ability of reconstructed Southern governments to limit the influence of former confederates and drew into question disfranchisement provisions of the Military Reconstruction Acts of 1867.

Overall, however, the Court did not challenge Reconstruction directly. For instance, encouraged by the court's restrictions, state governments established under President Johnson's Reconstruction program asked the Court to prohibit the enforcement of the Reconstruction Act (which would ultimately eliminate Johnson's governments). In *Mississippi v. Johnson* and *Georgia v. Stanton*, the justices unanimously agreed that Reconstruction policy was within the discretion of the political branches of government and that the cases therefore presented political questions beyond the competence of judges. Although the impact of these decisions may be exaggerated, they led to the claim that the Reconstruction Court refused to rule on so-called political matters. However, Republican leaders in Congress were very concerned that the Milligan precedent might lead the Court to overturn key provisions of the Reconstruction act that supported military control of the South.

While that did not occur, Republicans took no chances: in *Ex parte McCardle* (1868) Congress actually repealed the provision from the Habeas Corpus Act that allowed the plaintiff to seek court intervention (he had been convicted in Mississippi by military commission). In the 1869 case *Texas v. White*, the court sustained Congressional Reconstruction albeit after most of the Southern states had been restored to normal relations in the Union under its provisions. At the same time, Chief Justice Chase's majority opinion reconfirmed the importance of state rights in the federal system, challenging the growing nation-centeredness of the dominant Republican Party. "The preservation of the States, and the maintenance of their governments, are as much within the design and care of the Constitution as the preservation of the Union and the maintenance of the National government," he wrote.

Although he largely sustained congressional authority over Reconstruction, Chief Justice Chase made clear his distaste for military government in the South. He had instead urged Republicans to turn power over to Southern Unionists and African Americans. Until 1890, Supreme Court justices were supposed to join district judges to hear cases in their circuits, made up of several states. The chief justice refused to hear circuit court cases in the former Confederate states in his circuit until they were freed from military authority. He believed it unseemly for the chief justice to preside over a court whose authority could be superseded by martial law. Required by the Constitution to preside over the trial of Andrew Johnson in the Senate after the House impeached him for high crimes and misdemeanors in 1868, Chase used his influence as chief justice to slow the process down and to bring a court-like atmosphere to the Senate. He worked to influence senators' views of the law of the case through his rulings on the admissibility of evidence, which generally supported the president's position. All recognized that the chief justice played the crucial role in converting a political procedure into a judicial one, culminating in Johnson's acquittal. In fact, despite his reputation as a Radical Republican, Chase became a contender for the Democratic Party's presidential nomination.

In spite of the tension between the Supreme Court and Republicans, Congress gave the federal courts the key role in administering the transformation in American civil liberty and civil rights that they attempted in Reconstruction. While the army could provide temporary protection for citizens' rights in the South, Republicans knew that the region could not be subjected permanently to military control. Instead, they framed the language of the Fourteenth Amendment and Fifteenth Amendment to give courts major responsibility for the protection of rights. Rather than simply authorizing Congress to define and protect civil and political rights, the Reconstruction-era amendments specified that "no state shall" abridge the privileges of U.S. citizens, deny any person due process or the equal protection of the laws, or interfere with suffrage by imposing racial tests. If state laws or actions violated these provisions, it would be the responsibility of the courts, state and federal, to rule them unconstitutional, even in the absence of the congressional legislation that the amendments also authorized. Expecting state courts to be less enthusiastic than federal courts about enforcing these provisions, Congress broadened the right of people to transfer cases from state to federal courts, a process that culminated in the Judiciary Act of 1875, which allowed plaintiffs or defendants to remove cases from state to federal courts whenever they involved rights claimed under federal law.

However, the Supreme Court proved reluctant to expand federal power to protect civil and political rights as far as the Reconstruction amendments might have made possible. If interpreted broadly, the vague language of the Fourteenth Amendment would precipitate a revolution in the federal system, enabling Congress and the courts to intervene whenever they thought ordinary state legislation violated basic rights. Republicans had wanted the government to have broad power to protect the rights of the freed slaves, but it is doubtful that they had intended that Congress and the courts second-guess ordinary state legislation. The Slaughterhouse Cases, decided in 1873, brought the revolutionary potential of the Fourteenth Amendment clearly into focus. In it, New Orleans butchers argued that a health law requiring them to slaughter animals in a single, state-sanctioned slaughterhouse deprived them of the right of American citizens freely to follow their professions and deprived them of liberty and property without due process of law. By a 5–4 margin, the justices ruled that ordinary rights belonged to Americans as citizens of their states rather than as national citizens; the Fourteenth Amendment prohibited states only from infringing the latter. The same majority denied that a health regulation could amount to a deprivation of liberty or property without due process. The Court also interpreted restrictively Congress's power to enforce the Fourteenth Amendment. In the Civil Rights Cases of 1883, the justices established the "state action doctrine." The amendment explicitly forbade states from infringing rights; it said nothing about private individuals. Thus, Congress had no authority to punish ordinary people from violating their neighbors' rights. To rule otherwise would transfer ordinary law enforcement away from the states and to the federal government, the justices explained. The Fourteenth Amendment left that responsibility to the states, where it had always resided.

The Court took similar steps to reduce the revolutionary potential for federalism of the Fifteenth Amendment. It worked to make sure that the federal government would not take over a general responsibility for policing all elections. The Fifteenth Amendment authorized the federal government to protect African Americans' right to vote, even from private action, the Court ruled, but any indictment must allege the racial motivation of the offense. It ruled unconstitutional federal laws that did not require this motivation as far as they applied to voting in state elections, although the justices conceded broad federal power to protect the integrity of federal elections. By the turn of the 20th century, the Court decided that the Fifteenth Amendment, too, only applied to state action.

Finally, in 1896, the Court ruled in *Plessy v. Ferguson* that state-mandated separation of the races did not deprive African Americans of the equal protection of the laws. As long as both races were treated reasonably equally, mere separation could not be interpreted to violate the Fourteenth Amendment. Advocates of equal civil and political rights for women were likewise disappointed by the Supreme Court's interpretation of the Fourteenth Amendment. Since citizenship had long been identified with the fulfillment of such public responsibilities as voting and jury service, a number of woman suffragists argued that the Fourteenth Amendment's ban on state abridgement of the rights of U.S. citizens meant that they could not deny any American citizen's right to vote. However, in the 1875 case of *Minor v. Happersett*, the Supreme Court rejected that argument as well.

Although the Supreme Court had weakened its position by accommodating slavery so fully before the Civil War, and although it alienated many Republicans by apparently threatening their program after it, the Court exerted a profound influence upon the course of Reconstruction and the enforcement of the Reconstruction-era constitutional amendments. The court proved more committed to preserving the basics of the federal system than to protecting the rights of American citizens. By undermining Republicans' ability to maintain their Reconstruction policy, the Supreme Court demonstrated its continued power in American government.

*Michael Les Benedict*

**See also:** Amnesty Proclamations; Civil Rights; Civil Rights Act of 1866; Civil Rights Act of 1875; Compromise of 1877; Democratic National Convention (1868); Enforcement Acts (1870, 1871, 1875); Hayes, Rutherford Birchard (1822–1893); Jim Crow Laws; Presidential Reconstruction; Redemption; Tilden, Samuel J. (1814–1886).

## Further Reading

Fairman, Charles. *Five Justices and the Electoral Commission of 1877*. New York: Macmillan, 1988.

Fairman, Charles. *Reconstruction and Reunion, 1864–1868*. New York: Macmillan, 1971–1987.

Kaczorowski, Robert J. *The Politics of Judicial Interpretation: The Federal Courts, Department of Justice and Civil Rights, 1866–1876*. Dobbs Ferry, NY: Oceana Publications, 1985.

Kutler, Stanley. *Judicial Power and Reconstruction Politics*. Chicago: University of Chicago Press, 1968.

Labbe, Ronald, and Jonathan Lurie. *The Slaughterhouse Cases: Regulation, Reconstruction and the Fourteenth Amendment*. Lawrence: University Press of Kansas, 2003.

# T

## TENNESSEE

Reconstruction in Tennessee was relatively short (1862–1870) but always turbulent. The period can best be described as a vicious political power struggle between the state's Radical Republican Party and its ex-Confederate majority. While in power, the Radicals proved among the South's most zealous advocates of Reconstruction, often governing Tennessee through authoritarian force. In the process, Tennessee became the first former Confederate state that Congress readmitted to the Union, largely because it was the only Southern state to voluntarily ratify the Fourteenth Amendment—and thus the only Southern state not subjected to military rule under the Reconstruction Acts. It was also the first state in the entire nation to bestow universal suffrage on its adult black male population. These noteworthy accomplishments notwithstanding, Tennessee, the birthplace of the Ku Klux Klan, experienced a violent Reconstruction and consistently teetered on the edge of a second civil war.

As Northern armies overran Tennessee, the federal government initiated Reconstruction in the state. In March 1862, President Abraham Lincoln appointed Tennessee senator Andrew Johnson as military governor. A Tennessee Unionist who strongly opposed secession, Johnson was determined to restore civil government under reliable Unionist leadership. To this end, he imposed stringent loyalty oaths on the occupied populace and ostracized Confederate politicians. Despite these measures, Johnson experienced repeated frustration. Secessionists often interfered with elections, and the tidal nature of military operations left much of the state in chaos. Further complicating Johnson's Reconstruction plan was a growing rift within the ranks of Tennessee's Unionists. Two competing factions emerged: Radical Unionists, who embraced the unconditional war aims of the Republican Party and displayed a vindictive attitude toward former rebels, and Conservative Unionists, who rejected the policy of emancipation and promoted lenient treatment of ex-confederates. In January 1865, the Radicals, most of whom came from the Unionist stronghold of East Tennessee, asserted themselves by taking control of a Unionist convention in Nashville, where they issued resolutions repudiating Tennessee's allegiance to the Confederacy, drafted a new state amendment abolishing slavery, and nominated Radical candidates for a new state government. In a referendum held in February, Tennessee voters approved the Radical agenda, which fulfilled the stipulations of Lincoln's Amnesty Proclamation, also called the Ten Percent Plan. The following month, most of the Radical candidates won their elections by similar returns. Prominent among the Radical leadership was the new governor, William G. Brownlow, an acerbic newspaper editor who soon implemented a stern Reconstruction program.

Like Andrew Johnson before him, Brownlow's principal concern was establishing an electorate that was thoroughly loyal to the Union. Radicals in the legislature agreed, and on June 5, 1865, they passed the first of a series of controversial franchise laws. The first act disfranchised—temporarily forbade from voting—some 80,000 ex-confederates. As a political minority of perhaps 40,000 voters, Radicals understandably believed this law was imperative lest the "traitors" who ruptured the Union in 1861 regained power. When former confederates continued to push into politics, Radicals enacted a second, more repressive franchise law (May 3, 1866) that permanently barred all former confederates from voting.

With the ballot box seemingly under control, Brownlow called for a special legislative session to consider ratification of the Fourteenth Amendment. Having cast aside President Andrew Johnson's plan for Reconstruction, congressional Republicans made readmission to the Union contingent on ratifying this amendment. Tennessee Radicals eagerly complied but encountered strong opposition from legislative Conservatives—21 of whom withdrew from the general assembly in an attempt to thwart ratification by preventing a quorum—and from President Johnson who urged states to reject the amendment. But the Volunteer State ratified the amendment and Tennessee rejoined the Union on July 24, 1866.

Political Reconstruction in Tennessee reached its climax with yet another franchise law, one that bestowed the suffrage on some 40,000 freedmen. Concerned about numerical weaknesses in Middle and West Tennessee, many Radicals sought to bolster the strength of their fledgling party by enrolling African Americans into its ranks. Thus, on February 25, 1867, the state legislature granted all adult black males the right to vote. Through political organizations known as Union Leagues, Radical leaders effectively mobilized and indoctrinated the new black electorate into the Radical Republican Party. Although Tennessee was ostensibly in the vanguard of racial equality, black suffrage was in some respects a political expedient. Blacks in Tennessee never held any important political offices during Reconstruction and white Radicals rarely encouraged them to run. Nevertheless, blacks eagerly embraced their new political rights. Even before gaining access to the polls, blacks peacefully agitated for civil and political reforms. In August 1865 and 1866, blacks had held conventions in Nashville for the "Colored Citizens of Tennessee."

Passing laws was one thing; enforcing them was quite another. Opponents of Reconstruction branded the Brownlow administration a tyranny and lambasted black citizenship as a perversion of race order. Ex-confederates in particular vowed to resist, and violence soon became common. The most infamous example occurred with the Memphis Riot in May 1866, a terrible event where a white mob murdered 46 blacks. More ominous than any race riot, however, was the growing paramilitary challenge to Reconstruction. No sooner had the Civil War ended than Rebels in many parts of Middle and West Tennessee reorganized themselves into vigilante bands. In Sumner County, for instance, the wartime guerrilla leader "King" Ellis Harper commanded a force of some 150 horsemen and ruled the county like a warlord. Harper and numerous other Rebel outfits fearlessly attacked the Reconstruction process by persecuting blacks, disrupting elections, and assassinating local Radical leaders.

The magnitude of the paramilitary threat justified a forceful response, but the Brownlow administration adopted an erratic approach to law enforcement. For reasons of cost and convenience, Tennessee Radicals preferred calling on the federal garrison for assistance, but the army was hesitant to involve itself in state matters. Gen. George H. Thomas, the army's commander in Tennessee, was sympathetic to the Radical cause, and on several occasions dispatched U.S. Army units to trouble spots, but he rightly believed that law enforcement was the governor's responsibility, especially after Tennessee's readmission to the Union. Accordingly, Brownlow searched for an effective and inexpensive way to combat Rebel lawlessness. The Metropolitan Police Act (May 14, 1866) seemed promising. This law created urban police forces in the state's three largest cities—Memphis, Nashville, and Chattanooga—all under the governor's control. Although innovative for its time, the metropolitan police force was no use against a largely rural insurgency. Instead, in February 1867, with black suffrage imminent, Radicals created a new weapon: the Tennessee State Guard. Consisting of nearly 1,900 men, including about 500 blacks, the Guard was partisan (virtually all were Radicals) but well trained and disciplined, with many veterans of the Union army. Under the command of militia general Joseph A. Cooper, the Guard occupied 33 counties in the weeks prior to the August election. In the process, it provided security for Radical party rallies and ensured the safe registration of thousands of black voters. The election passed off quietly and Brownlow and the Radicals won in a landslide.

In addition to political power, Radicals pursued economic prosperity as well. They enthusiastically heeded the call for a "New South," one where Southerners emulated the wealthy North by diversifying their economies through industrial development. To this end, on December 7, 1867, Tennessee Radicals enacted the so-called Omnibus Bill, which allocated large sums for various railroad projects. Similarly, Brownlow urged his followers to develop the coal and iron resources in the mountains of East Tennessee. Hoping to attract white labor to the state, Brownlow also created a bureau of immigration to advertise Tennessee's employment opportunities. As with other Southern states, Tennessee fell short. The railroad venture suffered from corruption and mismanagement, and although productivity grew during Reconstruction, it was due to cottage manufacturing and not industrial development. Also as with other states, farming remained the principal livelihood in Tennessee, and for many poor whites and a majority of freedmen, the most significant agricultural development of the Reconstruction period was sharecropping. Sharecropping denied blacks their dream of owning land but it did afford the freedmen some privacy and some control over the pace of their work.

Although Reconstruction failed to fulfill the political and economic aspirations of many blacks, African Americans were testing the boundaries of their new freedom. Black Tennesseans enjoyed moving about freely. Many searched for family members taken away by the prewar slave trade, while others migrated to the towns and cities looking for jobs. Blacks voluntarily segregated themselves from the white control: all-black churches, mostly Methodist and Baptist in denomination, emerged throughout the state, and all-black communities arose, be it the rural "Mount Africa" in Maury County or the urban neighborhood of "Hell's Half Acre" in Nashville. If owning land was beyond the reach of most blacks, acquiring an education was not. Education was arguably Reconstruction's most important gift to the freedmen, and blacks of all ages avidly attended school. While blacks themselves often took the lead in establishing rudimentary public school facilities, they were greatly aided by Northern missionaries. The federal Bureau of Refugees, Freedmen, and Abandoned Lands also sponsored the construction of schools. In March 1867, the Radical state government assumed control over all public schools in Tennessee and, by 1870, Tennessee's public education system blossomed to 500 schools with more than 25,000 students.

For most Tennessee whites, the experiment in racial equality, as well as the alleged political despotism of the Brownlow administration, was more than they could tolerate. In

1868, paramilitary bands resumed their activities with violent intensity. The most notorious organization was the hooded Ku Klux Klan. Founded in Pulaski, Tennessee, in 1866, the Klan laid low during the militia deployment of 1867. In early 1868, however, after Brownlow imprudently disbanded the State Guard, the Klan rapidly expanded its influence until dens existed in dozens of counties throughout Middle and West Tennessee. Under the titular leadership of the fearsome Confederate cavalry commander Nathan B. Forrest, the Klan instigated a deadly campaign of terror. The Radicals' response to the Klan menace was firm but belated, and Klan depredations reduced the Radical voting significantly. Brownlow finally mobilized the militia and on February 20, 1869, he declared martial law in nine selected counties. Unlike its first deployment, the State Guard in 1869 was all white in order to avoid a race war. In the field from February to June, the Guard (1,600 strong) neutralized the Klan, which basically went underground, but irreparable damage had already been done.

Toward the end of February 1869, Brownlow departed Tennessee to take a seat in the U.S. Senate. His departure deprived the Radical party of its most dynamic leader, and competing Radical factions soon battled for control of the Reconstruction process. DeWitt C. Senter, the new governor and a Moderate Radical, substantially modified the harsh policies of his predecessor. Hoping to garner Conservative support for the upcoming gubernatorial election in August, Senter disbanded the State Guard and announced his intention to seek the repeal of all franchise restrictions. Radical hardliners and most freedmen rallied around William B. Stokes, a Radical from Middle Tennessee who warned that ex-confederates could never be trusted. Delighted by the Radical rift, Conservatives did indeed back the Senter candidacy while running a full slate of their own under the banner of the Democratic Party. As the overseer of registration, Senter ensured his victory by replacing most of Brownlow's commissioners with handpicked men; in the ensuing election, Senter crushed Stokes, and Democrats won a majority in the legislature.

The Democrats moved quickly to dismantle the work of Reconstruction. They immediately repealed the militia act and the anti-Klan law. More important, in December 1869, they issued a call for a constitutional convention. The following March, Tennesseans approved a new constitution, which limited gubernatorial power and undermined black suffrage. Although blacks retained the right to vote, a new poll tax effectively disfranchised them. These changes allowed John C. Brown, a former Confederate general and Klan leader, to become governor in 1871; Democrats completely controlled the state government. Reconstruction in Tennessee was clearly over.

*Ben H. Severance*

**See also:** Congressional Reconstruction; Democratic Party; Redemption; Republicans, Radical.

## Further Reading

Alexander, Thomas B. *Political Reconstruction in Tennessee.* Nashville, TN: Vanderbilt University Press, 1950.

Coulter, E. Merton. *William G. Brownlow: Fighting Parson of the Southern Highlands.* Chapel Hill: University of North Carolina Press, 1937.

Egerton, Douglas R. *The Wars of Reconstruction: The Brief, Violent History of America's Most Progressive Era.* New York: Bloomsbury Press, 2014.

Fitzgerald, Michael W. *Splendid Failure: Postwar Reconstruction in the American South.* New York: Ivan R. Dee Publishers, 2008.

Patton, James W. *Unionism and Reconstruction in Tennessee, 1860–1869.* Chapel Hill: University of North Carolina Press, 1934.

Severance, Ben H. *Tennessee's Radical Army: The State Guard and Its Role in Reconstruction, 1867–1869.* Knoxville: University of Tennessee Press, 2005.

# TENURE OF OFFICE ACT (1867)

On February 19, 1867, Congress passed the Tenure of Office Act. It forbade the removal, without further senatorial approval, of any federal official who had been appointed with the advice and consent of the Senate. This included presidential cabinet members who were to retain their offices "for and during the term of the President by whom they may have been appointed, and for one month thereafter, subject to the advice and consent of the Senate." The act also stipulated that anyone accepting an appointment in violation of the act or anyone attempting to appoint or remove an official without the consent of the Senate would be guilty of a "high misdemeanor." If Congress was not in session, the president could remove and appoint officials until the Senate reconvened and voted on the matter.

The impetus for the act began in 1866 with the struggle between President Andrew Johnson and Republicans in Congress for control of the Reconstruction process. Following the midterm elections that year, the combination of Radical and Moderate Republicans held a large majority in Congress and could easily override a presidential veto. However, as the chief executive and commander in chief, Johnson still had means to interfere with Reconstruction legislation. So the Republicans passed a series of acts, including the Tenure of Office Act, designed to limit Johnson's authority.

The law was designed to protect patronage appointments, since such favors were crucial to the continued success of any political party. In 1866, Johnson had removed hundreds of Republicans to make room for his supporters—and curry their favor and votes. Republicans sought to do the same, of course. Congressional Republicans also intended for the measure to prevent the president from removing Secretary of War Edwin Stanton, the only cabinet member who supported the Republican Reconstruction program. (Johnson had retained Lincoln's entire cabinet intact.) Johnson kept hoping Stanton would resign, but the secretary of war knew his position was vital to protecting the Republican's Reconstruction agenda.

Johnson considered the act to be unconstitutional. His cabinet, including Stanton, concurred. In fact, Stanton helped Secretary of State William Seward draft the president's veto message. However, Congress passed the act over Johnson's veto on March 2, 1867 as part of a flurry of Congressional Reconstruction activity, which included the Army Appropriations Act and most important, the Military Reconstruction Acts. Waiting until Congress adjourned Johnson suspended Stanton on August 12, 1867, and appointed Ulysses S. Grant as the interim secretary of war. If the Senate refused to concur with Stanton's suspension, Johnson asked that Grant return the office to the executive, and Johnson planned to challenge the constitutionality of the act in the courts. On January 13, 1868, the Senate rejected Stanton's suspension, but Grant returned the office to Stanton. Confused and stymied, Johnson made a fateful decision. On February 21, 1868, with the Senate in session, Johnson removed Stanton and nominated Adjutant General Lorenzo Thomas the new interim secretary.

A call for a vote on impeachment went up again (an earlier attempt had been voted down), charging the president with violating the Tenure of Office Act. The House voted along straight party lines to impeach Johnson, and then, after the vote, drew up a formal list of charges, called articles of impeachment. Most of the articles were based in the alleged violation of the Tenure Act, which most agreed was confusing and ambiguous. In the Senate, as court of impeachment, Johnson's salvation came from senatorial Democrats and several Republicans—the so-called recusants—who doubted both Johnson's guilt and the constitutionality of the law. As Johnson's legal team pointed out, even if the tenure law were valid, Abraham Lincoln, not Johnson, had appointed Stanton. Moreover, Johnson's supporters doubted the wisdom of curtailing the presidential power of appointment, and even his opponents, pushed to the brink, had second thoughts about Congress removing an executive.

In 1869, almost immediately after Republican president Ulysses S. Grant assumed office, Congress modified the Tenure of Office Act to allow the president to remove officials as long as new nominations were submitted within 30 days of the beginning of a new congressional session. Historical myths notwithstanding, the Court has never ruled the act unconstitutional. It was repealed in 1887, when President Grover Cleveland challenged its constitutionality. The U.S. Supreme Court concurred with Cleveland's position in *Myers v. United States* (1926), declaring presidential removal powers to be unlimited, a finding restricted by the latter case *Rathbun v. United States*, in which the Court stated those unlimited powers only related to cabinet appointments.

*John D. Fowler*

**See also:** Chase, Salmon Portland (1808–1873); Command of the Army Act (1867); Impeachment Managers; Presidential Reconstruction; Stevens, Thaddeus (1792–1868); Sumner, Charles (1811–1874).

## Further Reading

Benedict, Michael Les. *The Impeachment and Trial of Andrew Johnson.* New York: Norton, 1973.

Trefousse, Hans L. *Impeachment of a President: Andrew Johnson, the Blacks, and Reconstruction.* Knoxville: University of Tennessee Press, 1975. Reprint, New York: Fordham University Press, 1999.

## TEXAS

Confederate forces in Texas surrendered on June 12, 1865. Large numbers of federal troops began arriving in the state almost immediately as a show of force in an area left largely untouched by the war and as a demonstration of force against the French incursion into Mexico. The army found little interest in continued fighting among Texans, and the majority of soldiers moved to the Rio Grande border. The smaller number that occupied the state's coastal and interior points found the task of Reconstruction left to them for nearly two months because of the delayed arrival of President Andrew Johnson's provisional governor, Andrew J. Hamilton, and similar problems in setting up the administration of the Bureau of Refugees, Freedmen, and Abandoned Lands (the Freedmen's Bureau). Gen. Gordon Granger announced the Emancipation Proclamation at Galveston on June 19, and commanders in the field began supervising freedmen's affairs, including overseeing labor contracts.

Governor Hamilton finally arrived in Texas on July 22, but did not reach the state capital until the end of the month. Hamilton, a Unionist who had fled the state to avoid arrest during the war, had the advantage of hearing news of other states' progress; he concluded that Johnson's policy did not produce governments that reflected the truly loyal people of the state, and in fact actually encouraged resistance. By the fall of 1865, Texas saw growing violence between freedmen and whites, and also witnessed conflict between former confederates and Unionists as each settled old scores. Hamilton believed that Unionists had little chance in an election and he successfully put off the state's constitutional convention until February 1866. Even then, he did not believe a loyal government could be created.

Results of the convention supported his conclusions. The old secessionists of the Democratic Party allied with some prewar Unionists who had supported the Confederacy and gained control. This Conservative Party elected James W. Throckmorton president of the convention, a Unionist who had served as a colonel in the Confederate army. The majority accepted the abolition of slavery, and fulfilled other requirements set by President Johnson, while excluding blacks from suffrage and officeholding, serving on juries, testifying in most court cases, and marrying whites. The Conservative coalition asserted itself again in the general election of 1866, running Throckmorton for governor at the head of a Conservative Union Party. He faced prewar governor Elisha M. Pease, who ran on a Union Party ticket. Throckmorton's supporters painted Pease as a radical on race issues and an ally of the Radical Republicans, even though at this time Pease was not. Throckmorton received 49,277 votes as opposed to Pease's 12,168 and Conservatives seized the new Eleventh Legislature.

The legislature pursued an agenda that sparked concern in Washington and suggested that Texas leaders had learned nothing from the Civil War. It refused to vote on the proposed Thirteenth Amendment and rejected the Fourteenth. It elected Oran M. Roberts, president of the state's secession convention, to Washington as one of the state's two senators. The legislature enacted Black Codes similar to those produced in other Southern states, designed to control the lives and labor of the freedmen.

Because of both Southern and presidential stubbornness, Congress passed the Military Reconstruction Act on March 2, 1867; Texas became a part of the Fifth Military District under Gen. Philip H. Sheridan, and Gen. Charles Griffin assumed command of local affairs. Griffin and Sheridan, tired of Throckmorton's repeated challenges to federal authority, removed him on July 30, 1867, replacing Throckmorton with Elisha Pease. Congressional Reconstruction required that states hold new constitutional conventions chosen by an electorate that allowed black suffrage (for males). Most Unionists moved into the state's Republican Party, and the Union League appeared to organize black voters. Unlike states like South Carolina, however, Texas lacked the large black population that could form a substantial core of the state's Republican Party. Republican success depended on keeping white Conservatives away from the polls or converting them to their cause.

The constitutional convention of 1868–1869 met at Austin on June 1, 1868. Unfortunately for the Republicans, the convention exposed serious internal differences within the party. Republican delegates quickly divided into groups referred to as "Radicals" and "Conservatives." The president of the convention, Edmund J. Davis, became the principal leader of the Radicals, while former governor Hamilton headed the Conservatives. Radical delegates came primarily from southern Texas and supported the extension of greater rights to blacks, continued disfranchisement of former Confederate leaders, and a cautious program of economic development. Moderates generally supported less civil rights for blacks, greater state support for railroad construction, and the removal of restrictions on former confederates. Eventually—waiting until after Ulysses S. Grant had been elected president—the constitutional convention removed constraints upon political participation other than those imposed by the federal constitution. Radicals tried to dissolve the convention, but received no help from Washington so could do little in the convention itself. Questions over the rights of freedmen and economic issues continued to divide members, however, and the party entered the election divided.

The Radicals nominated Edmund J. Davis, while Conservative Republicans put forward Andrew J. Hamilton. The Radicals managed to draw some Conservative Republicans from eastern Texas to their support, but won with only a narrow majority, 39,838 votes to Hamilton's 39,055. The Twelfth Legislature met in a special session on February 8, 1870, and adopted the Fourteenth Amendment and Fifteenth Amendment. They also elected U.S. senators Morgan C. Hamilton and James W. Flanagan. These steps finished the Reconstruction process established by Congress and resulted in Congress's acceptance of the delegation from the state. On March 30, 1870, President Grant signed the legislation acknowledging Texas's formal readmission to the Union.

The Twelfth Legislature assembled on April 26, 1870. The legislature created a state police force, gave the governor increased power over the state militia, and expanded the state's judiciary. In addition, legislators created the state's first public school system, a highly centralized graded school system with a standard curriculum directed by a state board of education that included the governor and his superintendent of public instruction. On railroad issues, Davis found himself fighting a combination of Democratic Conservatives, Conservative Republicans, and members of his own wing who generously offered state bonds to help support railroad construction. He failed in his efforts to block such legislation when this combination ultimately proved strong enough to override the governor's vetoes.

Conservative Republicans and Conservatives arrayed themselves against the administration from the beginning. They attacked the Radicals on the grounds that the police measures and even the public schools represented a suppression of freedom and reflected Gov. Davis's tyrannical designs on the state. They pointed to Davis's declarations of martial law in several election conflicts and his use of the state police and militia as proof. Taking their cue from Conservative campaigns elsewhere in the South, they also charged the Davis government with corruption and fraud, even though the Texas Radicals never had the problems of other Southern Republican governments. In the fall of 1871, when Conservatives encouraged people to withhold their taxes and to file lawsuits to prevent the collection of school taxes, the Democratic Conservatives precipitated a financial crisis that forced the governor to seek operating funds through the issue of bonds, an action that only worsened the state's fiscal situation.

It was clear Radicals would have difficulty maintaining hold of state government. The removal of all disabilities from former confederates swelled opposition numbers. Attacks upon the Davis administration for its taxes, its authoritarianism, and its support of African Americans alienated many whites. A flood of white immigrants from other former Confederate states counterbalanced Republican votes from the black community. Again, as in other Southern states, Conservatives, originally willing to cooperate with the Conservative Republicans, began to reassert themselves as the white-line Democratic Party. In 1871, Democrats ran for all congressional seats and carried them. In the presidential contest of the following year, Democrats carried the state for Horace Greeley and his anti-Grant Liberal Republicans. The general election also gave them control of the state House of Representatives for the next session. When the Thirteenth Legislature met in 1873, it moved quickly to dismantle the school system, putting schools into the hands of local rather than state officials. It repealed the state police law and limited the power of the governor to use the state militia. Few Republicans showed themselves willing to stand in the way of what most considered their inevitable fall from power.

Texas held another general election in the fall of 1873. Davis campaigned against Democrat Richard Coke, in an election marked by what had become the usual intimidation and violence. Coke soundly defeated the incumbent Davis, and Democrats retained the house and finally gained control of the state senate.

In December, the state Supreme Court heard the case of *Ex parte Rodriguez* from Houston, challenging the election. The justices ruled that the election was unconstitutional, because of controversy surrounding the number of days for balloting. The decision depended on a semicolon dividing two phrases in the constitution, giving the Court thereafter the nickname the "the semicolon court." The Court had no power to enforce its decision, but Governor Davis believed he had the responsibility of upholding the judiciary. His stand led to a confrontation between himself and the new legislature and governor-elect Coke, called the Coke-Davis Imbroglio. But the Grant administration refused to intervene, leading Davis to step down in favor of the Coke government. So ended Reconstruction in Texas, paving the way for Democratic Conservative domination into the next century.

*Carl H. Moneyhon*

**See also:** Elections of 1868; Labor Systems; Redemption.

## Further Reading

Baum, Dale. *The Shattering of Texas Unionism: Politics in the Lone Star State during the Civil War Era*. Baton Rouge: Louisiana State University Press, 1998.

Campbell, Randolph B. *Grass-Roots Reconstruction in Texas, 1865–1880*. Baton Rouge: Louisiana State University Press, 1997.

Crouch, Barry. *The Freedmen's Bureau and Black Texans*. Austin: University of Texas Press, 1992.

Moneyhon, Carl H. *Republicanism in Reconstruction Texas*. Austin: University of Texas Press, 1980.

Moneyhon, Carl H. *Texas after the Civil War: The Struggle of Reconstruction*. College Station: Texas A&M University Press, 2004.

# THIRTEENTH AMENDMENT (1865)

Although some Americans sought a constitutional amendment to protect state-based slavery before the Civil War, few looked to the amendment process as the best way to end slavery in the United States. Then came the Civil War, limited emancipation, and finally, in 1864, the National Union Party of President Abraham Lincoln which called for a constitutional amendment abolishing slavery. In February 1865, in the last days of the Civil War, the Republican-dominated 38th Congress sent a proposed Thirteenth Amendment to the states for their approval. Ratified that December, the Thirteenth Amendment was the first addition to the U.S. Constitution in more than 60 years and the first of three Reconstruction-era amendments.

In words largely taken from the Northwest Ordinance of 1787, the Thirteenth Amendment provides that "neither slavery nor involuntary servitude, except as punishment for crime whereof the party shall have been duly convicted, shall exist in the United States, or any place subject to their jurisdiction." It includes no provision for the compensation of slave owners. Its words do not limit the actions of any particular group or limit its prohibition to slavery based on race. Section 2 authorizes Congress to enforce the abolition of slavery with "appropriate legislation."

Considering that as late as 1861, the nation sought to save the Union by providing slavery with permanent protection, the path to the amendment during the Civil War was surprisingly easy. In 1862, Congress provided for compensated emancipation in the District of Columbia and ended slavery in federal territories. Then followed Lincoln's Emancipation Proclamation of January 1, 1863, which formally ended slavery in Confederate-held areas of the 11 seceded states. It did not affect slavery in the four non-seceded slaveholding states; the western counties of Virginia; by 1863, the state of West Virginia; or in federally held areas of Louisiana. In addition, its authority as a war measure did not bar the future re-creation of slavery of some type; the proclamation and the war ended slavery militarily, but the institution's legal existence was unclear, and many believed that Congress did not have the power to end slavery in the nation by statute. This was emancipation—the freeing of slaves—not abolition, the destruction of the institution itself.

In December 1863, Congressman James M. Ashley of Ohio proposed a constitutional amendment; the following month, John B. Henderson of Missouri did so in the Senate. These men sought the broad and permanent abolition of slavery in the United States through amending the Constitution, but in April 1864, the proposed amendment failed in the House of Representatives. After Lincoln's victory in the election of 1864 and Maryland's voluntary abolition of slavery, the president helped push the amendment through the House on January 31, 1865, by a vote of 119 to 56.

Since Secretary of State William H. Seward did not consider the Southern states out of the Union, 27 of the 36 states had to ratify the amendment. The death of Lincoln on April 15, 1865, did not stall the process, and the new president, Andrew Johnson, supported abolition. Encouraged by Johnson to approve the amendment, all former Confederate states did so except slow-moving Florida and Texas. On December 15, 1865, the Thirteenth Amendment went into effect. Kentucky and Delaware, the so-called Border States that had slavery but stayed in the Union, rejected the amendment.

While the amendment clearly prohibited slavery, its real impact was uncertain. Radical Republicans clearly intended the amendment to do more than permanently end the enslavement of African Americans. At least some of its framers believed it suggested equality before the law for everyone, and they believed that Section 2 gave the national government the responsibility to prevent denial of rights, the so-called badge of slavery.

An example of the amendment's broad definition was its use as the constitutional foundation of the Civil Rights Act of 1866. The statute was prompted by the Southern states' passage in 1865 and 1866 of Black Codes, laws that did not formally reinstitute slavery but which limited the freedom of freedpeople. As enacted by the 39th Congress in early 1866, the statute covered various civil and economic rights, such as making contracts, owning and selling property, and bringing lawsuits. Supporters of the measure argued that without these rights, freedom had no meaning; denial of these rights—whether by government or private individual—was a badge of slavery, thus violating the Thirteenth Amendment.

Despite these early victories, opponents of the amendment had little to fear about its broad reach. The framers' goal was undermined by the country's state-based federal system and by its entrenched racism. Ironically, the ratification of the Fourteenth Amendment (1868) and the Fifteenth Amendment (1870) diluted the amendment as lawmakers and courts now gave the Fourteenth and Fifteenth amendments priority. As the century waned, the Supreme Court also reduced the reach of the amendment.

In the Civil Rights Cases (1883), the Court argued that while the amendment abolished slavery and its badges, the denial of admission to a theater or an inn was not a badge of slavery. Fundamental civil or economic rights were protected, not social ones. The tug of war continues, however, as the broader interpretation of the amendment was confirmed a century after Reconstruction when the Supreme Court in *Jones v. Alfred H. Mayer Co.* (1968) ruled that a homeowner's refusal to sell property to a black buyer was a badge of slavery, as intended by the Thirteenth Amendment.

*Claudine L. Ferrell*

*See also:* Civil Rights; Congressional Reconstruction; Contraband, Slaves as; Enforcement Acts (1870, 1871, 1875); Jim Crow Laws; New South; Presidential Reconstruction; Trumbull, Lyman (1813–1896); U.S. Army and Reconstruction.

## Further Reading

Buchanan, G. Sidney. *The Quest for Freedom: A Legal History of the Thirteenth Amendment*. Houston: Houston Law Review, 1976.

Hyman, Harold M., and William M. Wiecek. *Equal Justice under Law: Constitutional Development, 1835–1875*. New York: Harper and Row, 1982.

Maltz, Earl M. *Civil Rights, the Constitution, and Congress, 1863–1869*. Lawrence: University Press of Kansas, 1990.

McPherson, James M. *The Struggle for Equality: Abolitionists and the Negro in the Civil War and Reconstruction*. Reprint, Princeton, NJ: Princeton University Press, 2014.

## THROCKMORTON, JAMES W. (1825–1894)

James Webb Throckmorton, Conservative Reconstruction governor of Texas, was born in Sparta, Tennessee, on February 1, 1825, but moved with his family to Collin County, Texas, in 1841. After initially studying medicine, Throckmorton decided to begin a law practice instead. He also developed an interest in politics and served as a Whig in the Texas House of Representatives from 1851 to 1857. As the Whigs disintegrated, Throckmorton moved into the Democratic Party. During the sectional crisis of the 1850s, he urged moderation, ran for the state secession

A tepid Texas Unionist before the war, James W. Throckmorton was elected governor in 1866 under presidential Reconstruction. As he was hostile to freedpeople and Republicans, General Philip Sheridan removed him from office in 1867. (Library of Congress)

convention on a pro-Union platform, and was one of seven delegates who refused to vote for secession.

Like many Texas Unionists, Throckmorton supported his state once the war began. He organized a company of cavalry, fought at Pea Ridge, and negotiated treaties with American Indian tribes in the Indian Territory. Following Confederate defeat, Throckmorton at first found Reconstruction bewildering. Despite his role during the war, he sought a role in the restoration process. The state's provisional governor, Andrew J. Hamilton, and other unionists did not consider his course truly loyal, since he supported the Confederacy once war began. Throckmorton, whose racism found even white foreigners inferior, was also disturbed by returning Unionists supporting abolition, promoting African Americans rights, and even discussing the possibility of suffrage. Throckmorton realized he had no place among these Unionists and began working in opposition to them.

In 1866, Throckmorton ran for the state constitutional convention and was elected by an overwhelming margin. At the state capital, he became the central figure among Unionists similar to him. These became known as the Conservative Unionists, as opposed to the Radicals of Hamilton's party. Old leaders of the Democratic Party, calling themselves Conservatives, allied with Throckmorton, giving the appearance of loyalty and control of the convention. For the governor's race in June, this coalition allowed Throckmorton to decisively defeat the Radical Unionist candidate, former governor Elisha M. Pease.

By the time Throckmorton took office, Texans sensed the growing opposition in the North to President Andrew Johnson's Southern governments, and the governor urged the new legislature to avoid antagonizing the North or the Radical Republicans in Congress. Yet, his actions contradicted this. He supported the legislature's refusal to act on the Thirteenth Amendment and its outright rejection of the Fourteenth Amendment. Subsequently, he did little to stand in the way as that body passed Black Codes designed to regulate the lives of freedpeople, gerrymander legislative districts to limit the power of Radical Unionists, and protect the interest of former Confederate officeholders.

With the onset of Congressional Reconstruction in the spring of 1867, Throckmorton's position became precarious, as the Military Reconstruction Acts allowed district commanders (army generals) to remove officials they perceived as obstructionist. Uncertain at first about their power, military officials delayed, but on July 30, 1867, Maj. Gen. Philip H. Sheridan, commander of the military district, removed Throckmorton from office.

Throckmorton returned to McKinney following his removal. He resumed the practice of law but openly criticized the opposition Republicans and the administration of Edmund J. Davis. Throckmorton played a major role in developing the charges that the Davis administration was extravagant and abused power, while at the same time, he served as a lobbyist for various railroad interests. Political opponents even charged Throckmorton with bribing members of the legislature to secure benefits for the railroads from the state, although the accusations were never proven.

Following the end of Reconstruction, Throckmorton remained popular in his local district. He was elected to Congress in 1874, 1876, 1882, 1884, and 1886. In Washington, he continued to push for the development of his community, particularly supporting federal aid to railroads.

Throckmorton grew weak due to kidney disease and never recovered from a serious fall in March 1894. He died on April 21, 1894, and was buried at McKinney.

*Carl H. Moneyhon*

**See also:** Amnesty Proclamations; Bureau of Refugees, Freedmen, and Abandoned Lands; Civil Rights; Civil Rights Act of 1866; Elections of 1866; Loyalty Oaths; National Union Movement (1866); Presidential Reconstruction.

## Further Reading

Elliott, Claude. *Leathercoat: The Life History of a Texas Patriot.* San Antonio, TX: Standard Printing Co., 1938.

Moneyhon, Carl H. *Texas after the Civil War: The Struggle of Reconstruction.* College Station: Texas A&M University Press, 2004.

## TILDEN, SAMUEL J. (1814–1886)

Samuel Jones Tilden was born in New Lebanon, New York, the son of a successful farmer. Tilden began his political career in 1832 by writing political manifestos for William Marcy, a Democrat senator and member of the Albany Regency, one of America's first political machines. While enrolled at New York University in 1840, he abandoned his legal studies to work for the reelection of President Martin Van Buren. After Van Buren's defeat, Tilden became a corporate lawyer in New York City, where he made a fortune representing railroad companies in court.

Although not holding office during the late 1840s and 1850s, Tilden continued as a voice in Democratic Party affairs, despite his opposition to the expansion of slavery into the territories. In 1860, he was a delegate to the National Democratic Convention and supported Illinois senator Stephen A. Douglas for president. Like many other Northern Democrats, Tilden supported the Union cause during the Civil War, but remained hostile to Republican attempts to expand federal power and impose harsh measures on the South. In 1862, he was instrumental in recruiting Horatio Seymour as governor of New York.

After the Civil War, Tilden supported the policies of Andrew Johnson, the Unionist War Democrat who became president after Abraham Lincoln's assassination in April 1865. Like Johnson, Tilden opposed military rule, feared an overly expansive federal program, and had significant reservations about advocating black rights. Although never really close to Johnson, the relationship grew more distant because of the election of 1868. The president openly—and naively—sought the Democratic presidential nomination, but it went to Horatio Seymour of New York. By this time, Tilden had become chair of the New York State Democratic Party, and he agreed to manage Seymour's campaign for president.

After Seymour's loss to Ulysses S. Grant, Tilden turned his attention to corruption in New York. In the fall of 1871, he launched a campaign against the infamous Tweed Ring of New York City's Tammany Hall. In 1874, he ran for governor, defeating his Republican opponent that November.

Tilden's place in Reconstruction history is usually remembered because of his role in the 1876–1877 election dilemma. Possessing impeccable reform credentials, he easily won the Democratic nomination for president in 1876. Like Democrats before him, Tilden opposed African American equality, favored a weak central government, and advocated for states' rights. His opponent, Republican Rutherford B. Hayes from Ohio, chastised Tilden's record during the Civil War and attacked the Democratic nominee for having filed fraudulent income tax returns. In the actual election, Tilden won a majority of the national popular vote, but because of the problems in the South, it was unclear how the electoral votes would be apportioned. Months of debates, discussions, and dealings passed, and America was without a president-elect just weeks before the inauguration. Finally, a special electoral commission was created, which awarded 20 disputed electoral votes to Hayes, giving him the election. This so-called Compromise of 1877 resulted in the last Republican governments collapsing in the South, but that was little consolation to the man who believed he should be president. Following this controversial election, Tilden retired to his estate in suburban Yonkers, where he died in 1886.

*Bruce E. Stewart*

**See also:** Black Suffrage; Civil Rights; Democratic National Convention (1868); Elections of 1876; Florida; Louisiana; Presidential Reconstruction; Redemption; South Carolina; U.S. Army and Reconstruction.

## Further Reading

Flick, Alexander C. *Samuel Jones Tilden: A Study in Political Sagacity.* New York: Dodd, Mead and Co., 1939.

Rehnquist, William. *Centennial Crisis: The Disputed Election of 1876.* New York: Alfred A. Knopf, 2004.

## TOURGÉE, ALBION WINEGAR (1838–1905)

Albion Winegar Tourgée, author and advocate for freedmen's rights, was born in Williamsfield, Ohio, to parents of French Huguenot and Swiss ancestry. When Tourgée was nine years old, his family moved to nearby Kingsville, Ohio.

As the Civil War loomed near, Tourgée joined the Wide-Awakes, an organization devoted to spreading the values of the Republican Party. In April 1861, he and several other classmates joined what ultimately became the 27th New York Volunteer Infantry. At the

Battle of First Bull Run, Tourgée suffered a severe back injury when hit by the wheel of a gun carriage. Shot in the hip at Perryville, Kentucky, in 1862, he continued to fight with his men in Kentucky and Tennessee until captured in 1863 at Stone's River. Tourgée spent four months in various prison camps before receiving his freedom as part of a prisoner exchange. Tourgée rejoined his regiment in Tennessee where he saw action at the Battle of Chickamauga. In Chattanooga, a fall renewed his back injury; he resigned his army post in late 1863 and returned to civilian life in Ohio where he practiced law, taught school, and worked as a reporter for the Erie, Pennsylvania, *Dispatch*.

Intrigued by the opportunities the South offered for business investment and seeking a warmer climate for his health, Tourgée took a trip to North Carolina in summer 1865. Soon after, he and his wife Emma left Ohio and established residence on the outskirts of Greensboro, North Carolina. With several partners, he rented a nursery and 750 acres of farmland, speculated in railroad construction, and established a law firm. Life in postwar North Carolina shaped his views about African American rights, and Tourgée publicly promoted land reform, manhood suffrage, and equal rights for all citizens. The Tourgées leased land to freedmen and, through his law firm, Tourgée helped Southern Unionists establish legal claim to property destroyed by Union armies. He also played a formative role in the creation of the Loyal Reconstruction League, an organization similar to the Union Leagues, mainly comprised of supporters of former Unionist governor William W. Holden.

Tourgée's political activism led to his election as delegate to the first state Republican convention, in March 1867. As delegate to the 1868 constitutional convention, he helped secure a number of constitutional measures including black suffrage, abolition of the poll tax, and debt reform. The convention appointed Tourgée one of three commissioners to reform the state's law codes, a position he held until Democrats dissolved the commission in 1873.

In 1868, Tourgée won election as Superior Court Judge of the Seventh Judicial District, a circuit position covering eight counties in the piedmont of North Carolina. During Tourgée's tenure as judge, he tried various civil and criminal cases, including prosecutions of members of the Ku Klux Klan. After being ousted from his judgeship in 1874, Tourgée continued to champion political and educational rights for freedmen. As a Republican delegate to the Democratic-controlled constitutional convention of 1875, he helped prevent a complete overhaul of the constitution of 1868.

Although he continued to promote freedmen's rights through legal and economic channels, the Conservative political climate of post-Reconstruction North Carolina proved frustrating to Tourgée, who, in the fall of 1879, moved with his family to Denver, Colorado. Tourgée worked on the editorial staff of the *Denver Evening Times* and speculated in real estate and mining ventures; he also witnessed the publication that same fall of two novels, *Figs and Thistles* and *A Fool's Errand by One of the Fools*. Largely based on Tourgée's experience in Reconstruction North Carolina, *A Fool's Errand* depicted the racial injustice of the postwar South and emphasized the need for federal programs, particularly regarding education, to transform racial inequities. The novel became a best seller in the early 1880s prompting a move to New York, where Tourgée continued a prolific writing career. He published a number of subsequent novels, including *Bricks without Straw* (1880) and *An Appeal to Caesar* (1884), both of which stressed the need for federal education programs. He also regularly published articles in periodicals including *Inter Ocean*, *The Basis*, and *War of the Standards*. His writings consistently emphasized the need for federal support for social, economic, and educational reform. Although no longer living in the South, for the remainder of his life, Tourgée remained firmly committed to racial and economic justice for African Americans. He joined other white activists at the Lake Mahonk Conference on the Negro in the summer of 1890, and in 1891, helped launch the National Citizens Rights Association, an interracial organization that promoted equal rights.

In 1896, Tourgée received an appointment as U.S. consul to Bordeaux, France. The family moved to Bordeaux in 1897, where, apart from his consular duties, Tourgée continued to write and to champion racial justice. He died in Bordeaux on May 21, 1905, at the age of 68. Only months later, in November 1905, the newly formed Niagara Movement offered a testimony to Tourgée's lifelong efforts to promote racial equality. The organization held national memorial services for three "Friends of Freedom"—William Lloyd Garrison, Frederick Douglass, and Albion Tourgée.

*Kimberly R. Kellison*

*See also:* Abolition of Slavery; Bourbons; Bureau of Refugees, Freedmen, and Abandoned Lands; Carpetbaggers; Congressional Reconstruction; Democratic Party; Enforcement Acts (1870, 1871, 1875); Jim Crow Laws; New South; Redemption; Southern Claims Commission (SCC); U.S. Army and Reconstruction; Worth, Jonathan (1802–1869).

## Further Reading

Fredrickson, George. "Introduction," in Albion W. Tourgée, *A Fool's Errand: A Novel of the South during Reconstruction*. Prospect Heights, IL: Waveland Press, 1991, pp. vii–xxv.

Olsen, Otto H. *Carpetbagger's Crusade: The Life of Albion Winegar Tourgée*. Baltimore: Johns Hopkins Press, 1965.

# TRUMBULL, LYMAN (1813–1896)

Judge, senator, and candidate for governor, Lyman Trumbull embodied the rise of the Republican Party, the critical role of Moderate Republicans during Reconstruction, and the conflicts that wracked the party in the 1870s.

The seventh son of Benjamin Trumbull and Elizabeth Mather, Trumbull was born in Colchester, Connecticut, but moved to St Clair County, Illinois, in 1837 to pursue a career in law. Trumbull's career throve and he gained attention as an up-and-coming member for the Democratic Party. He was elected assemblyman in 1840, secretary of state the following year, and by 1848 sat on the state supreme court. By the 1850s, as sectional issues came to the fore, he fit less well with the Democrats. Indeed, he had made something of a name for himself as a defender of blacks, including *Jarrot v. Jarrot* (1845), in which he put the courts on record that no slavery could exist on Illinois soil. Like many Northern Democrats, Trumbull saw Stephen Douglas's Kansas-Nebraska bill of 1854 as a betrayal of Northern interests in favor of the expansion of slavery. Trumbull took a leading role among the anti-Nebraska Democrats, but by 1855 found himself drifting into the Republican Party—and earning a seat in the U.S. Senate.

During the Civil War, many classified Trumbull as one of the early Radical Republicans because of his support for an aggressive war. The author of the first and second Confiscation

Acts, Trumbull saw emancipation as a means of defeating the Confederacy. Concerned that the Emancipation Proclamation might not survive court challenges, he helped design the Thirteenth Amendment to make sure that freedom could not be reversed.

Once peace came, however, Trumbull fell instead into the Moderate Republican camp. When it came to the freedpeople, he favored neither confiscation to provide land nor suffrage to promote political roles. He hoped that Congress and President Andrew Johnson could compromise on African American rights and bring a speedy readmission for the Southern states. One sees this in his legislation, most notably the 1866 Freedmen's Bureau bill and Civil Rights Act. Johnson's antagonism toward these Moderate measures convinced Trumbull—and many like him—that more forceful methods were needed, resulting in the Military Reconstruction Acts and the Fourteenth and Fifteenth Amendments.

A Moderate Republican, Illinois senator Lyman Trumbull drafted the Civil Rights Act, opposed President Johnson's impeachment, and supported the Liberal Republican Party in 1872. (Library of Congress)

As Reconstruction progressed, he became more jaded and less enthusiastic about the extraordinary use of national power to protect civil equality. His moderation was clearly evident in Johnson's impeachment trial, when he joined six other "recusant" Republicans in voting for the president's acquittal. Over the next four years, Trumbull separated further from the rest of his party, and openly opposed the federal government's efforts to prop up the Southern Republican governments. He called the so-called Ku Klux bill of 1871 a usurpation of states' rights, insisting that the Fourteenth Amendment had not expanded national authority, and joined the Liberal Republican revolt of 1872 supporting Horace Greeley for president instead of Ulysses S. Grant. Greeley's defeat drove Trumbull out of political life, too. His term ended in 1873, and while he ran unsuccessfully for governor as a Democrat later, he never held office again.

*Mark W. Summers*

**See also:** Congressional Reconstruction; Enforcement Acts (1870, 1871, 1875); Fessenden, William Pitt (1806–1869); Presidential Reconstruction.

## Further Reading

Krug, Mark M. *Lyman Trumbull, Conservative Radical.* New York: A. S. Barnes and Co., 1965.

# TWITCHELL, MARSHALL H. (1840–1905)

Marshall H. Twitchell was a prominent carpetbagger in Louisiana who, along with most of his family, became a Republican martyr during the "redemption" of the state. Graphic and tragic, the story of the Twitchell clan mirrors the rise and destruction of Republican hopes in the state—and perhaps the South in general.

Twitchell was born on February 29, 1840, on a small farm in Townshend, Vermont, to Harvey Daniel and Elizabeth Scott Twitchell. He graduated from Townshend's Leland Seminary in 1860 and entered the Fourth Vermont Infantry the first summer of the Civil War. He served three years in the Fourth Vermont, suffered a near-fatal head wound at the Battle of the Wilderness, and in 1864, became captain in the 109th U.S. Colored Troops. In September 1865, he accepted an assignment as the agent for the Bureau of Refugees, Freedmen, and Abandoned Lands in Bienville Parish, Louisiana. He left the Freedmen's Bureau in 1866, married Adele Coleman, the daughter of a prominent Bienville Parish planter, and purchased a plantation overlooking Lake Bistineau. Aided by his Louisiana in-laws, he prospered as a planter. During 1867–1868, he was a delegate to Louisiana's constitutional convention under Congressional Reconstruction. In 1869, he purchased a new plantation on the upper Red River in De Soto Parish, just before winning election to the state senate as a Republican. In 1871–1872, with his friend and ally, Edward W. Dewees, a member of the lower house, Twitchell guided legislation through the General Assembly creating Red River Parish, with the town of Coushatta the parish seat. Although both Twitchell and Dewees were carpetbaggers, the creation of Red River Parish had broad backing from Coushatta's business elite, most of whom were members of the Democratic Party. Twitchell constructed a disciplined political organization in which his relatives, in concert with African American Republicans, held the key offices in the parish and town government.

Twitchell's rise to power coincided with the first upswing of the Southern economy after the war. Unfortunately, the recovery was all too brief; Coushatta's and Louisiana's prosperity was on the decline even before the Panic of 1873, which devastated the Red River Valley. As the economy turned sour, white toleration of the so-called carpetbag rule plummeted. In the summer of 1874, the white-line movement swept Louisiana and the Deep South. Coushatta's business elite formed a branch of the "White Man's Party," or White League, whose avowed purpose was the overthrow of the Twitchell organization. In July and August, the Red River White League orchestrated the "Coushatta massacre." In the space of a few days in late July and early August 1874, the White League in and about Coushatta, Red River Parish, murdered 10 Republicans, 6 whites and 4 blacks. Three of the murdered whites included Twitchell's brother, Homer, and two of his brothers-in-law; all of the white victims were officeholders and members of the Twitchell organization. Two years later on May 2, 1876, in a deadly ambush, a disguised assassin killed the surviving brother-in-law, George King, and shot Twitchell six times. He survived the attack, but both of his arms were amputated. The devastation led to more suffering, as Twitchell's three younger sisters died of disease, with stress and heartbreak contributing to their untimely deaths.

The reign of terror neutralized Republican rule in Red River Parish and precipitated the fall of the Republican Party across northwest Louisiana. The murder of so many officeholders and the virtual destruction of the entire Twitchell family is one of the most brutal chapters in the story of Southern redemption.

A convalescing Twitchell returned North in 1876. Of the nine members of his family who had settled in Louisiana, only the carpetbagger and his mother survived. In 1878,

President Rutherford B. Hayes appointed him the American consul in Kingston, Canada, where he remained until his death in 1905.

*Ted Tunnell*

**See also:** Ku Klux Klan (KKK); Military Reconstruction Acts (1867–1868); Race Riots; Union League of America; U.S. Army and Reconstruction.

## Further Reading

Tunnell, Ted, ed. *Carpetbagger from Vermont: The Autobiography of Marshall Harvey Twitchell.* Baton Rouge: Louisiana State University Press, 1989.

Tunnell, Ted. *Edge of the Sword: The Ordeal of Carpetbagger Marshall H. Twitchell in the Civil War and Reconstruction.* Baton Rouge: Louisiana State University Press, 2001.

# U

## UNION LEAGUE OF AMERICA

The Union League, also called Loyal League, was the Republican Party's mechanism for mobilizing African American voters during the early phases of Reconstruction.

The League originated during the Civil War as a Northern patriotic organization backing the Lincoln administration. After Appomattox, the Union League turned its attention to the former Confederate states. It initially secured a following among white Unionists and absorbed local networks of draft resisters and anti-Confederate groups like North Carolina's "Red Strings." Concentrated in the up-country, the league became the political expression of the most intransigent white opponents of Presidential Reconstruction. With the Military Reconstruction Acts in March 1867, congressional Republicans utilized this existing organization to appeal to the newly enfranchised freedmen.

Agents from the Bureau of Refugees, Freedmen, and Abandoned Lands, Northern missionaries, native Unionists, and other activists swore in vast numbers of black males. Although whites were the prominent organizers—either carpetbaggers from the North or Unionist scalawags—local leadership was often African American. League speakers offered basic instruction on politics and voting and taught locals how to hold clandestine meetings at secluded locations to avoid detection. An explosive politicization of the freedpeople resulted in the summer and fall of 1867, as hundreds of thousands reportedly flocked to league councils and similar local groups. Although the formal organization had political goals, leagues also formed the backbone of many of the so-called black militia units that Republican governors created later on to combat white violence.

The league also had economic effects. Following abolition, many plantation owners sought to reinstate mass labor gangs on their lands; freedpeople needed employment and landowners needed labor, and for whites a system as near as possible to slavery made the most sense. But the League saw this as an attempt to rebuild the economic and power relationships present before the war, and quickly stepped in to readjust the economic picture. Working with the Freedmen's Bureau and local courts, the Union League proved vital in moving many African Americans to tenant labor on rented land.

The league mobilized virtually the entire male black population, and thus it contributed to the speedy approval of Reconstruction constitutions in most of the Southern states operating under the Military Reconstruction Acts. Readmission soon followed, as did state governments dominated by white and black Republicans. This success brought backlash, and the organization suffered terribly with the appearance of the terrorist Ku Klux Klan and its offshoots in early 1868. With white violence on the rise and the promise of federal assistance in the offing, the league's Republican sponsors concluded that the secret organization had served its purpose. Vestiges of the organization survived locally and as a paper organization at the national level through the 1880s. While transient, the Union League had tremendous political and economic effects: it created a tradition of Republican voting, and it also encouraged lasting changes in the plantation system.

*Michael W. Fitzgerald*

**See also:** Abolition of Slavery; Black Suffrage; Congressional Reconstruction; Constitutional Conventions; Democratic Party; Enforcement Acts (1870, 1871, 1875); Fifteenth Amendment (1870); Freedmen's Relief Societies; Labor Systems; Suffrage; U.S. Army and Reconstruction.

## Further Reading

Fitzgerald, Michael W. *The Union League Movement in the Deep South*. Baton Rouge: Louisiana State University Press, 1989.

Foner, Eric. *Reconstruction Updated Edition: America's Unfinished Revolution, 1863–1877*. Reprint, New York: HarperCollins, 2014.

## *UNITED STATES v. CRUIKSHANK* (1876)

*United States v. Cruikshank* (1876) was one of the first Reconstruction-era judicial decisions to limit the reach of the three amendments added to the U.S. Constitution after the Civil War. It reflected the Supreme Court's respect for state-based federalism and its growing concern with expanded federal powers under the amendments.

To combat intimidation and violence in the postwar South, Congress passed four Enforcement Acts in 1870 and 1871 to protect black civil rights, in particular suffrage. The statutes were based on the Fourteenth Amendment and Fifteenth Amendment and prohibited certain types of private as well as state action. Under the new laws, federal marshals and troops arrested hundreds, but the violence against blacks and their white Republican supporters continued in many areas of the South. The single bloodiest day of Reconstruction occurred in Louisiana, on Easter Sunday in 1873, providing the situation that led to *United States v. Cruikshank*.

In Colfax, located in Grant Parish, whites attacked and killed more than 100 blacks who were guarding a courthouse; the attackers fired into the courthouse where they had taken refuge, set the building on fire, and shot blacks who fled or surrendered. Federal troops arrested scores, and dozens were indicted under the Enforcement Act of May 31, 1870. After a mistrial, three attackers were convicted in federal circuit court of violating Section 6, the provision that prohibited conspiracies to deny the constitutional rights of citizens. Among the three was William Cruikshank, who appealed his conviction.

In the circuit court case *United States v. Cruikshank* (1874), Justice Joseph P. Bradley broadly read the power given to Congress in Section 2 of the Thirteenth Amendment to enforce the amendment's prohibition of slavery, but he held that Congress could act against private individuals only if they were motivated by race. Because his ruling differed from that of the other circuit court member, the trial judge from the case, the dispute went to the Supreme Court.

Two years later, the opinion issued by Chief Justice Morrison R. Waite for the unanimous Supreme Court (including Bradley) focused on the indictments, declaring them to be defective, and announced that the defendants should not have been tried under the Enforcement Act. The court ruled that the Fourteenth Amendment had "add[ed] nothing to the rights of one citizen as against another." The rights that Cruikshank was accused of violating were protected from limitation by the national government; they were not restrictions on private citizens or on states. Specifically, the Fourteenth Amendment limited the actions of states, not of private individuals. Murder by a mob or private army was not state action. Despite the amendment, racially motivated murder by an individual was still murder, a state crime, and still punishable only by the state. Thus, such crimes could not be covered by an Enforcement Act growing out of the Fourteenth Amendment.

In the companion case of *United States v. Reese*, the court emphasized the general impact of its interpretation of the Reconstruction amendments. As in *Cruikshank*, the court limited the scope of federal power. Under the Fifteenth Amendment's enforcement section, the national government could not act to stop state-imposed restrictions on suffrage if these restrictions were not based on race. The court, therefore, held that sections of the Enforcement Act of 1870 were too broad and vague.

*Claudine L. Ferrell*

**See also:** Ku Klux Klan (KKK); Race Riots; Supreme Court.

### Further Reading

Nieman, Donald G. *Promises to Keep: African-Americans and the Constitutional Order, 1776 to the Present*. New York: Oxford University Press, 1991.

Rable, George C. *But There Was No Peace: The Role of Violence in the Politics of Reconstruction*. Athens: University of Georgia Press, 1984.

# U.S. ARMY AND RECONSTRUCTION

The army's roles and involvement in Reconstruction produced successes and controversy throughout the 1860s and 1870s.

As the Civil War ended, the Union army's soldiers and officers found themselves scattered throughout the former Confederate states. More than 1 million men had served in the Union's volunteer army, greatly outnumbering approximately 16,000 members of the regular army on duty in 1860. Naturally, in the summer of 1865, most Northern volunteers wanted to return home as soon as possible, and their representatives in the U.S. Congress obliged them. Between June and December 1865, in a remarkable and swift mustering out, most of the federal volunteers were dismissed from service, leaving less than 200,000 soldiers in the army. Demobilization continued, but one of the points of controversy was the size of the army. By 1867, only about 60,000 men, all regulars, were in the army, and by 1870, the number was reduced to 37,000. Of course, the size of the army related directly to the number of posts the army would maintain and the kinds of influence the army might exercise near those posts, especially in the South.

A controversial element of this shrinking army was the Republicans' decision to enlist African American soldiers. In July 1866, Congress authorized for the first time in American history that black men could serve in segregated army units in peacetime. The black regiments would be led by white officers but have black sergeants and enlisted men. At first, Congress appropriated funds for six black regiments, four of infantry and two cavalry, later reduced to two each of infantry and cavalry. Recruiting and posting those black units in the South made most white Southerners uncomfortable, and African Americans in army uniforms were a reminder of social changes—soon including admitting a few black cadets to the U.S. Military Academy at West Point. By the 1870s, the black regiments had been shifted to the Trans-Mississippi region, where they served with distinction. No matter if the soldiers were black or white, during the 1860s and 1870s, Americans debated if the army had enough soldiers to fulfill its multiple duties of defending the seacoasts, patrolling the western states and territories, fighting Native Americans, and conducting Reconstruction in the South.

In 1865, U.S. government leaders had to decide which federal agencies might carry out the administrative duties of Reconstruction in the former Confederacy. Primary possibilities included agents of the U.S. Treasury Department, employees of the U.S. Justice Department (including a handful of federal marshals), and the army. Adding to the list, Republicans in Congress passed a bill in March to create an experimental organization for one year, the Bureau of Refugees, Freedmen, and Abandoned Lands, to assist the former slaves. Many of the bureau's agents were Union volunteer army officers waiting to be mustered out. Other bureau agents, still wearing their army uniforms, were former Union officers who elected to stay in the South to assist in Reconstruction. Therefore, the process of Reconstruction took on a military flavor, naturally aggravating some white Southerners, who were aware of the important American tradition that expected the military to remain out of politics. For the next seven years, the entire time the Freedmen's Bureau existed, Gen. Oliver O. Howard served as its commissioner and regular army officers held the subordinate assignments as assistant commissioners, administering the bureau's activities in the Southern states.

In 1865 and 1866, soldiers still on active duty also became caught up in practical matters of reunion and physical rebuilding in the South. After the collapse of the Confederacy, many state and local offices were vacant, government services were not operating, roads and bridges had been damaged or fallen into disrepair, and railroads were not running, leaving state economies in a shambles. Army officers made ad hoc decisions to rebuild roads and bridges, reopen or establish public schools—including ones for freedmen—and authorize the operation of major businesses, such as banks and railroads. In some cases, army officers operated banks and railroads until their owners could be found or new owners acquired them. Where local and state officeholders remained in place, the army dealt with them, but elsewhere army officers performed the functions of vacant offices until elections could be held or new appointments were made.

From the summer of 1865 to the end of 1866, President Andrew Johnson created new state governments to supplement Lincoln's wartime governments, but he and Republican leaders in Congress disagreed on matters related to Reconstruction. Disagreements included rechartering the Freedmen's Bureau, passing the Civil Rights Act, and approving the proposed Fourteenth Amendment to the U.S. Constitution. In addition, a number of violent incidents took place in the South, especially riots in Memphis and New Orleans, leading most Republicans to conclude that Johnson's plan of Reconstruction was ineffective. Therefore, in March 1867, congressional Republicans passed the Military Reconstruction Acts.

The Military Reconstruction Acts placed much of the responsibility for carrying out Reconstruction on the army in the former Confederate states that were divided into five military districts. President Johnson appointed five senior generals as district commanders, but how he later removed or reassigned them raised new controversy. Furthermore, those military districts were unique in American history; in them, the generals supervised the steps that states were required to take leading toward regaining their representation in Congress. The army's instrumental role drew criticism, and many complained about the army's intrusion into politics—especially the capability under the Reconstruction Acts of army generals to remove civilians from office and appoint their replacements. It was ironic that Congress called on the army to carry out much of the process of Reconstruction because most of the senior officers could be classified as politically Moderate or Conservative. Of the leading generals, some, including Philip Sheridan, Joseph Reynolds, John Pope, and Daniel Sickles, were considered or accused by Democrats of being "radicals." By contrast, other generals, including Winfield Hancock, John Schofield, Edward Canby, E.O.C. Ord, George G. Meade, Irvin McDowell, and William T. Sherman were either Moderate or Conservative. Notably, when serving as the army's general in chief, Sherman criticized or opposed most of the Republicans' goals and objectives. On the other hand, while he was in uniform, Gen. Ulysses S. Grant adhered closely to the spirit of the Reconstruction Acts before he was elected president in 1868. From the passage of the Military Reconstruction Acts to the readmission of the former Confederate states, the army carried the burden of Reconstruction. The generals, their subordinate officers, and soldiers, registered voters (including freedmen), supervised elections, and organized and guarded constitutional conventions. The district commanders removed numerous public officials, including state governors and other politicians, and appointed new men in their place, and even decided the validity of elections.

By 1870, most of the former Confederate states had completed the terms of the Military Reconstruction Acts and gained the admission of their senators and representatives in the U.S. Congress. Readmission brought a total return to civil law and civil government, thus the role of the army in political affairs diminished significantly.

But after readmission, the army remained attentive to matters related to protecting the rights of freedmen and Southern Republicans. U.S. marshals arrested and then federal attorneys charged and prosecuted persons accused of violating federal laws, usually involving crimes violating the civil or political rights of freedmen and Republicans in the South. Soldiers acted as a *posse comitatus* for marshals who needed the army's help to serve arrest warrants. The army appeared to be especially active in assisting marshals and prosecutors in South Carolina in suppressing the Ku Klux Klan. In other former Confederate states, army units tried to counteract persons opposed to Reconstruction, such as gun clubs, White Leagues, and Knights of the White Camellia, groups that employed a low level of guerrilla warfare against Republicans in the South. During elections, the army patrolled to discourage intimidation of voters and guarded ballot boxes to prevent vote fraud. Although Democrats and former confederates contended that "bayonet rule" dominated the South, the army was spread too thin across the South to stop Reconstruction's opponents everywhere. Nevertheless, the army made the effort to protect citizens' rights under federal laws, especially when state authorities or state militias were unreliable or unavailable.

The presidential election of 1876 produced a contested result between the supporters of Democratic candidate Samuel J. Tilden and Republican candidate Rutherford B. Hayes. By 1876, only three former Confederate states still had Republican governments—South Carolina, Louisiana, and Florida—and the army in the South was limited to a few posts, mostly on the coasts or near state capitals. Democrats, North and South, contended that the army unfairly intruded in politics by propping up the last Southern Republican governments in opposition to the will of "the people," though in two of the states, Louisiana and South Carolina, African Americans formed 50 percent or more of the population. To resolve the contested election, Congress established an extraordinary Electoral Commission. It ruled in favor of Hayes. As part of the so-called Compromise of 1877, Hayes and his advisors agreed to withdraw army support from Southern Republicans contesting elections, but Hayes did not withdraw all soldiers from Louisiana, South Carolina, or Florida, or the rest of the South.

As Reconstruction drew to a close, the army's status and roles remained contentious. The Democrats passed the Posse Comitatus Act, prohibiting the army's direct involvement in "executing the laws" without the express authorization of Congress. In effect since 1878, this long-standing federal law reflected the residue of the Democrats' bitterness against the variety of actions that the army had taken in the South during the previous 17 years.

*Joseph G. Dawson III*

**See also:** Command of the Army Act (1867); Memphis Riot (1866); New Orleans Riot (1866).

## Further Reading

Dawson, Joseph G. III. *Army Generals and Reconstruction: Louisiana, 1862–1877*. Baton Rouge: Louisiana State University Press, 1982.

Rable, George C. *But There Was No Peace: The Role of Violence in the Politics of Reconstruction*. Athens: University of Georgia Press, 1984.

Richter, William L. *The Army in Texas during Reconstruction, 1865–1870*. College Station: Texas A&M University Press, 1987.

Sefton, James E. *The United States Army and Reconstruction, 1865–1877*. Baton Rouge: Louisiana State University Press, 1967.

# V

## VIRGINIA

Reconstruction in Virginia was a quiet affair compared to the upheaval in some other former Confederate states. Unlike elsewhere, Conservative former confederates controlled the state government without serious challenge as early as the presidency of Andrew Johnson. Congressional Reconstruction lasted only three years, and Conservative whites regained control of the state in early 1870, with less violence and intimidation than in states of the lower South. Likewise, the newly enfranchised African Americans rarely resorted to violent means, preferring to exercise their new rights and enjoy their freedom by staying within traditional bounds of political behavior. In reality, the Virginia Republican Party wielded significant power only during military rule. Nevertheless, the Reconstruction era did bring about some significant, long-term changes in the life of the Old Dominion.

The process to restore Virginia to its normal place in the Union—the original meaning of the word "reconstruction"—began only weeks after the firing on Fort Sumter in April 1861. When the Virginia secession convention voted to secede on April 17, white Unionists in the northwestern third of the state immediately began organizing to resist the move toward the Southern Confederacy. When the voters of the Old Dominion nevertheless approved the secession ordinance by a margin of four to one, Northwestern Unionists— including Whigs, Democrats, and Republicans—stormed into Wheeling (in the panhandle between Pennsylvania and Ohio) on June 11 to construct a common response. The convention, acting for the loyal citizens of Virginia, declared vacant all state offices held by secessionists, appointed Francis H. Pierpont (a Whig lawyer and small manufacturer) governor, and accepted those Unionist members of the state general assembly who could meet in Wheeling as the only legitimate legislature of the Old Dominion. President Abraham Lincoln and Congress officially recognized this "Restored" government by July, thereby readmitting Virginia—officially, at least—to its position in the Union. Immediately after establishing their loyalist government, western Virginians began organizing for separate statehood, with the consent of the Restored government. Lincoln and Congress approved a statehood bill in December 1862, but demanded that the new state add a gradual emancipation clause to its constitution. This was quickly done (there were not many slaves in Appalachian Virginia, anyway) and West Virginia entered the Union officially on June 20, 1863. Pierpont and his staff moved the records and offices of the Restored regime (technically the Unionist government of old Virginia) to Alexandria, across the Potomac River from Washington, in August. This group now represented, in effect, a "third" Virginia, speaking for the occupied areas of the state near Washington and in southeastern Virginia. Pierpont authorized a constitutional convention in 1864 to rewrite the antebellum constitution; this "Alexandria constitution" abolished slavery, disfranchised nearly all Confederate soldiers and officials, civilians, authorized the state's first public education system, switched from the voice vote to the ballot, and reformed the tax system.

When President Andrew Johnson assumed control of Reconstruction policy after Lincoln's assassination, he appointed provisional governors for the former Confederate states and ordered those states to write new constitutions reflecting postwar realities (i.e., outlawing slavery, renouncing the Confederate debt, and repudiating secession). Thanks to the Restored government, Virginia already had a Unionist governor (Pierpont) and a new constitution that included the required reforms, so Johnson allowed the Old Dominion to proceed directly to the election of state and federal officers. Now relocated to Richmond, Pierpont, much to the surprise and disappointment of Virginia Unionists and freedmen, administered Johnson's plan in a manner that reinvigorated the antebellum ruling class of Conservative white men, many of them former slaveholders. Under his leadership, the Restored legislature removed most of the Alexandria Constitution's disabling clauses that barred former confederates from political participation; white Unionists and former slaves could hardly believe their ears and eyes.

Pierpont—the man who had stood bravely against secession in 1861, the governor who had raised troops for the Union, the chief executive who had urged the Restored government to draw up an antislavery constitution in 1864—was now restoring to power the old secessionists. Some white Unionists for the first time publicly called for black suffrage in the summer of 1865. Meanwhile, black Virginians held numerous meetings of their own to protest Pierpont's policies, form Union Leagues, and demand the vote. In the state's first postwar elections, held in October 1865, Conservative whites easily brushed aside these Republican stirrings. Conservatives won almost every contest for the General Assembly and national House of Representatives and quickly removed all restrictions on voting and officeholding by former confederates. Over the next year, the new legislature then removed from office key Unionist allies of Pierpont and replaced them with former confederates, and adopted restrictive codes hat limited African Americans' legal and economic rights.

Republican hopes soared in November 1866, when the first postwar national elections sent an overwhelmingly Republican Congress to Washington. Virginia Republicans counted on their federal colleagues to act and act fast, a desire only reinforced when the Virginia legislature refused to ratify the Fourteenth Amendment in January 1867.

Congressional Republicans, tired of failed attempts to compromise with President Johnson, assumed control of Reconstruction in March 1867, when they passed the first of four Military Reconstruction Acts. This law divided the South into five military districts, placed each under supervision of an army general, required new constitutional conventions to guarantee black voting and officeholding (and disfranchise some former confederates), and demanded ratification of the Fourteenth Amendment.

Virginia Republicans now looked forward to real change in the Old Dominion. Indeed, with tens of thousands of new black voters, the party might control the governorship, the General Assembly, and the state's congressional delegation.

To prepare for the constitutional convention, the state Republicans held two conventions to mobilize leading blacks, test the waters of black suffrage and tax reform, and try to diffuse controversial issues like land confiscation. These meetings, one in April and one in

August, also demonstrated the meager power Republicans had: even with the onset of black activity, without attracting substantial white support, the Republicans were in trouble. Such notable Northern leaders as Senator Henry Wilson of Massachusetts and newspaper editor Horace Greeley tried to lure more whites to the party, but hostile responses by Virginia blacks drove many whites away.

Nonetheless, state Republicans won their first significant political victory ever in the elections of delegates to the constitutional convention required by the March 1867 Reconstruction law. On October 22, voters sent 72 Republicans and only 33 Conservatives to the convention, scheduled to begin in December. The Republican delegates included 24 black men, the first ever elected to public office in the Old Dominion. Intense interest in the election by black Virginians (88% of registered blacks actually voted, despite intimidation by white employers), sullen apathy on the part of white Conservatives (only 63% of those registered actually voted), and the geographical concentration of black voters in eastern counties (which magnified the importance of their numbers) led to the stunning result.

A side effect of this Republican victory was the political reawakening of white Conservatives. Jolted by their crushing defeat, thousands of white Virginians who had turned away from politics in disgust now lined up for voter registration. In December 1867, former Whigs and members of the Democratic Party joined to create a new organization, the Conservative Party, in December 1867.

The constitutional convention (sometimes called the "Underwood convention" for its presiding officer, the Radical federal judge, John C. Underwood) met in Richmond from December to April. Republicans revised the tax system to place more of the burden on property holders, established Virginia's first public education system, made more state offices elective, provided homestead protection for delinquent debtors, opened voter rolls to men of both races (except for ex-confederates disqualified for office by the Fourteenth Amendment), and disqualified for public office every man who had supported the Confederacy in any way—even down to privates in the ranks and farmers who had sold food to the Confederate government. This "test-oath" clause was the most controversial in the entire document; even the military commander of Virginia, the Moderate John Schofield, waited to schedule a referendum on the proposed constitution until he received approval from Washington to submit the officeholding clause for a separate vote.

Conservatives and Republicans spent the next 12 months lobbying in Washington, mainly to control the referendum on the constitution. Virginia Republicans, including the new governor, Henry H. Wells (a former U.S. Army officer appointed by Schofield to replace Pierpont, whose term had expired), lobbied for a quick referendum on the entire Underwood Constitution without any separate votes. Conservatives and less-radical Republicans demanded separate votes on both disabling clauses (voting and office-holding) and won the support of important Northern newspapers as well as Gen. Schofield. In April 1869, President Ulysses S. Grant and Congress provided funds for a referendum on the Underwood Constitution, with separate votes on the two disabling clauses.

The alliance of these Moderate Republicans and the Conservatives continued to cooperate in preparations for the crucial July vote. The Moderate Republicans nominated Gilbert C. Walker—a former New York Democrat, strong Unionist, and banker in Norfolk—to run against the regular Republican candidate, provisional governor Henry H. Wells. The leading centrists among the Conservatives convinced their own party to withdraw from the gubernatorial competition and join with the Moderates Republicans—now calling themselves "True Republicans"—against Wells. Although both parties appealed for black votes, invited black voters to barbecues, and promised a new and better Virginia for the former slaves, the great majority of the freedmen would turn out for the regular Republican Wells.

In an orderly election on July 6, voters approved the proposed constitution overwhelmingly (96% in favor) and rejected the two disabling clauses by wide margins (about 60% to 40% in both cases). Walker, with 54 percent of the vote, defeated Wells, and coalition candidates won 30 of 43 seats in the state senate, 97 of 140 seats in the state house, and 5 of 8 positions in the Congressional delegation. Although Walker was a native New Yorker and strong Unionist during the war, and although he ran on the "True Republican" ticket, the election was a victory for the Conservative Party, which had provided most of the votes.

Provisional governor Wells resigned in September and was replaced by Walker. A new legislature approved the Fourteenth and Fifteenth Amendments in October, and President Grant recommended readmission of Virginia into Congress in December. Congress agreed in January 1870, bringing Congressional Reconstruction to an end in the Old Dominion. Nevertheless, Reconstruction had brought black Virginians into the political process for the first time, democratized the state government in a variety of ways, established the state's first public education system, and created a more modern constitution that would serve as the state's basic law until 1902.

*Richard Lowe*

**See also:** Amnesty Proclamations; Black Codes; Carpetbaggers; Elections of 1866; Labor Systems; Loyalty Oaths; Redemption.

## Further Reading

Chesson, Michael B. *Richmond after the War, 1865–1890*. Richmond: Virginia State Library, 1981.

Lowe, Richard. "Another Look at Reconstruction in Virginia." *Civil War History* 32 (March 1986): 56–76.

Lowe, Richard. *Republicans and Reconstruction in Virginia, 1856–70*. Charlottesville: University Press of Virginia, 1991.

Maddex, Jack P. Jr. *The Virginia Conservatives, 1867–1879: A Study in Reconstruction Politics*. Chapel Hill: University of North Carolina Press, 1970.

W

# WADE, BENJAMIN FRANKLIN (1800–1878)

Benjamin Franklin Wade, Radical Republican senator from Ohio, was born in Feeding Hills, Massachusetts, the son of James and May Woodham Wade, descendants of famous Puritans. Educated by his mother, the daughter of a minister, and in the local schools, at 21 he moved to Andover, Ohio, where he taught school and labored on the Erie Canal. He also read law and, by 1831, had established himself as an attorney in partnership with Joshua Giddings, later a famous antislavery leader in Congress. Wade supported the Whigs, and in 1837 and again in 1841 was elected to the state senate. He built a reputation—and many enemies—defending and supporting women, laborers, and African Americans.

When Congress passed the Fugitive Slave Bill 1850, Wade, now a state judge, announced that he would not enforce it. Consequently, a combination of Whigs and Free Soiler selected him to the U.S. Senate, where he stood out as one of a small band of antislavery radicals. He opposed the Kansas-Nebraska Act, and consequently helped found the Republican Party, under whose banner he won election to the Senate in 1856.

During the secession crisis, he opposed any compromise with the South. During the war, Wade favored vigorous prosecution of the war and the abolition of slavery, goals he urged from his position as chair of the Joint Select Committee on the Conduct of the War, a Radical body that sought to influence Lincoln to move against slavery and to rely on Radical generals.

Wade disapproved of Lincoln's Amnesty Proclamation and coauthored the Wade-Davis Bill as an alternative. Wade, Henry Davis, and other Radicals wanted a greater congressional role and a smaller Confederate one; their bill required that 50 percent, not Lincoln's 10 percent, of voters needed to take a loyalty oath before Reconstruction could begin. Furious when the president pocket-vetoed this measure, he and Davis posted the Wade-Davis Manifesto accusing Lincoln of seeking to win reelection by means of rotten boroughs. But when the Democratic Party nominated George B. McClellan on a peace platform in 1864, he rallied behind his party and its candidate, Lincoln.

The assassination of the president and the accession of Andrew Johnson at first pleased Wade. "Johnson, we have faith in you," he reportedly told the new executive. "By the gods, there will be no trouble now in running the government." However, he was soon disappointed and became one of the president's most determined opponents. Wade's strong advocacy for black rights and belief in congressional (not executive) power put them on a collision

Ardent antislavery senator from Ohio, Radical Republican Benjamin F. Wade clashed with both presidents Lincoln and Johnson; Wade sought rights for the freedpeople and severe punishment for Confederates. (Library of Congress)

course. Wade pushed for civil rights, supported the Military Reconstruction Acts, backed the Fourteenth Amendment, and was an early voice calling for the impeachment of Johnson. Here he needed to tread carefully, because in March 1867 he was elected president *pro tem* of the Senate, an office that put him next in line for the presidency (no vice president existed when Johnson became president).

As such, he was in a difficult position during the impeachment trial. Following Johnson's impeachment in 1868, the Senate faced the unprecedented issue of placing the executive on trial, with a guilty verdict bringing his removal. Although his opponents demanded that Wade refrain from voting, he held that Ohio was entitled to two senators—and two votes—and thus he cast his ballot for conviction (although, because of his place in the alphabet, it had no effect on the outcome). Ironically, to some extent, Wade was responsible for saving the man he sought to oust: some senators' voted not-guilty out of fear of Wade's radicalism. That radicalism also cost him his seat; his strenuous campaign for black suffrage in Ohio, in 1867, proved too much for voters and they returned the Ohio legislature to the Democrats.

After leaving the Senate, he served on the board of the Union Pacific Railroad and as a commissioner to Santo Domingo. In 1876, he served as a presidential elector and was horrified that Republican Rutherford B. Hayes removed federal troops from Southern capitals as part of the Compromise of 1877. Although too radical for many and personally dislikeable to most, Wade nonetheless believed in human progress and human rights, often in advance of the rest of society. Whatever personal flaws he possessed, time would bear out that his social views were humane and noble. He died at Jefferson, Ohio, in 1878.

*Hans L. Trefousse*

***See also:*** Compromise of 1877; Congressional Reconstruction; Presidential Reconstruction; Recusants; Redemption; Republicans, Radical.

## Further Reading

Trefousse, Hans L. *Benjamin Franklin Wade, Radical Republican from Ohio*. New York: Twayne Publishers, 1963.

# WADE-DAVIS BILL (1864)

The Wade-Davis Bill represented congressional Republicans' first plan to reestablish loyal governments in the Confederate states during the Civil War. Introduced by Maryland congressman Henry Winter Davis and supported by Ohio senator Benjamin F. Wade, the bill attempted to weaken the Confederacy by ending military resistance, abolishing slavery, and building loyal, Unionist states. It also represented another example of growing tension between the executive and legislative departments over control of the war and the readmission process.

By 1863, the federal government had conquered enough territory to begin considering how to readmit areas to the Union. Central to Abraham Lincoln's plan were the abolition of slavery and the establishment of state governments loyal to the Union. To facilitate this transition, Lincoln developed the Proclamation of Amnesty and Reconstruction, which offered amnesty to citizens willing to take a loyalty oath to the U.S. Constitution and pledge obedience to all laws of the United States. This included the Emancipation Proclamation, so these states needed to formally emancipate their slaves. In order for the readmission process to begin, at least 10 percent of citizens who voted in the 1860 elections were required to take a loyalty oath. After these citizens established a republican form of government, representatives would be readmitted to Congress.

But many more radical members of Congress thought the plan to be far too lenient. Lincoln's so-called Ten Percent Plan needed only minimal population loyalty for proceeding, guaranteed property rights (except slaves), disfranchised few former confederates, and made no provision for African Americans. The growing number of Radical Republicans in Congress wanted stricter controls over who would come to power in the new South. Congress's counterproposal was the Wade-Davis Bill, which placed tougher restrictions on former Confederate states. First, after all military resistance ceased, the president would appoint a provisional governor in the state. The governor would require white male citizens to take a loyalty oath supporting the Constitution of the United States. Only when 50 percent of eligible white male voters declared loyalty could a state convention be held. To attend the convention, eligible citizens swore to an ironclad oath, a declaration that they never aided or served in the Confederacy; this was much more binding than Lincoln's oath, as Lincoln required participants to swear future loyalty, whereas this required past loyalty as well. Those declaring the oath were allowed to vote for and serve as convention delegates. Under the Wade-Davis Bill's loyalty requirements, no persons holding office during the Confederacy could participate at the convention. At the convention, eligible voters would draft and adopt a new state constitution. In addition, the bill prohibited involuntary servitude and guaranteed freedom to all persons.

Despite similarities, the Wade-Davis Bill imposed stricter loyalty requirements than Lincoln's plan, with voter eligibility resting on past loyalty to the Union. Also, Lincoln's plan did not clearly address the status of freedmen. The Wade-Davis Bill allowed blacks habeas corpus protection, equal rights to trial, and extended liberties to all freedmen. Neither bill clearly defined the status of freed slaves, nor did it promote black suffrage. Congress hastily passed the Wade-Davis Bill in July 1864. Concerned that the rapid passing of the bill could jeopardize reconstruction progress in Louisiana, Lincoln pocket-vetoed it. Furious, Radical Republicans charged Lincoln with failure to acknowledge congressional legislative powers. In retaliation, Congress refused to recognize the new Southern governments constructed under Lincoln's plan.

Congressional Republicans also adopted the Wade-Davis Manifesto in August 1864 in response to Lincoln's veto. This complained of the executive's abuse of authority and failure to recognize the jurisdiction of the legislature. But Lincoln never accepted the congressional plan, and the status of the Lincoln governments remained cloudy. The war wound down with no clear understanding of what would follow.

*Janice E. Fowler*

***See also:*** Confiscation Acts; Congressional Reconstruction; Constitutional Conventions; Joint Select Committee on the Conduct of the War; Pardons; Presidential Reconstruction.

## Further Reading

Abbott, Richard H. *The Republican Party and the South, 1855–77*. Chapel Hill: University of North Carolina Press, 1986.

Barney, William L. *The Civil War and Reconstruction: A Student Companion*. New York: Oxford University Press, 2001.

Neely, Mark E. Jr. *The Abraham Lincoln Encyclopedia*. New York: Da Capo Press, 1982.

## WARMOTH, HENRY CLAY (1842–1931)

Henry Clay Warmoth was a carpetbagger who helped found the Republican Party in Louisiana and served as governor of the state from its readmission to the Union in 1868 until his impeachment in December 1872. He remains one of the most controversial figures of the Reconstruction era and in all of Louisiana history.

Warmoth was born in McLeansboro, Illinois, on May 9, 1842. He developed an interest in law from his father, a justice of the peace, and in 1860, at the age of 18, he relocated to Missouri to practice law. Despite his youth and lack of military training, Warmoth was made a colonel of Missouri militia at the outbreak of the Civil War. He was seriously wounded at Vicksburg, inadvertently discharged, then reinstated and sent to Louisiana. Warmoth arrived in New Orleans in February 1864, as the Unionist state government was forming under Lincoln's Ten Percent Plan. He became judge on the provost court for the military Department of the Gulf, and when war ended, he decided to remain in New Orleans and open a law practice.

In the spring of 1865, Warmoth played a central role in organizing the Republican Party in Louisiana, despite the fact that Lincoln's assassination placed a more Conservative Andrew Johnson in control. Johnson's restoration process excluded African Americans, so Louisiana Republicans operated in parallel, somewhat illegally. Befitting Louisiana in general and New Orleans in particular, the party had a diverse nature, built of native white Moderates, white and black Radicals, influential free blacks from before the war, and carpetbaggers like Warmoth. Their first party convention in September 1865 horrified the new president: it embraced the idea that the ex-Confederate states had reverted to "territorial" status, and it advocated black suffrage and racial equality. When elections for state officials and members of Congress were held in Louisiana in November under the president's restoration policy, state Republicans held their own extralegal election that included blacks and that chose Warmoth as a "territorial delegate." Although Warmoth was not formally seated in Congress, he spent early 1866 conferring with important Republican leaders in Washington, D.C. Warmoth returned to Louisiana and witnessed the New Orleans riot of July 30, 1866, in which a white mob massacred dozens of black and white Republicans. He spent that fall in the North campaigning for Republican congressional candidates and for the defeat of Johnson's policy in the elections of 1866.

Warmoth and others like him rejoiced when the fall elections handed control of Congress over to the Republicans; the Military Reconstruction Acts of spring 1867 swept the Johnson governments from power, and allowed former Confederate states to "start from scratch." New conventions needed to write new constitutions, and this time black suffrage and the Fourteenth Amendment would be included—and many ex-confederates would not. Although Warmoth did not participate in the Louisiana constitutional convention of late 1867 and early 1868, he gained the Republican nomination for governor in January 1868. Warmoth and a Republican-majority legislature were elected in April 1868; Louisiana ratified the Fourteenth Amendment and was readmitted in June.

Warmoth had just turned 26 years old when he became governor of Louisiana. Handsome, personable, and self-confident, he exuded a charm that enchanted even his political opponents. He was also a formidable political figure who, despite his Northern background, mastered the ways of Louisiana politics. As part of the Republican Party's attempt to remake Southern society in the image of the free-labor North, Warmoth promoted state spending on internal improvements, attempting to rebuild Louisiana's devastated infrastructure and transportation system, and he tried to foster economic development by attracting Northern investment and industry. He oversaw creation of Louisiana's first statewide system of public education, and, in hopes of drawing white support to the Republican Party and of building a biracial political coalition, Warmoth appointed a number of white Conservatives to office.

Despite Warmoth's talents, these initiatives met with little success. Instead, the Warmoth administration was mired in controversy. Warmoth's opponents relentlessly accused him of corruption, and although there is no evidence that Warmoth took bribes, he undoubtedly used the powers of his office to make himself wealthy. The large majority of white Louisianans, moreover, saw neither Warmoth's administration nor the entire process of Congressional Reconstruction as legitimate, and they opposed them every way they could. When the Ku Klux Klan and other terrorist groups disrupted the presidential election of 1868 in Louisiana, Warmoth and the legislature created a body known as the Returning Board, which was authorized to exclude any election results that it believed had been tainted by illegal methods. Although intended to preserve electoral integrity, the Returning Board itself sparked much controversy.

Making matters worse, Warmoth's party was plagued by bitter factional infighting. Warmoth's appointment policy and his limited support of black civil rights alienated many Republicans, especially influential blacks. Squabbles also arose over state and federal patronage, state contracts, and other spoils of office. By 1870, the party had split into pro-Warmoth and anti-Warmoth (called the "Custom House") factions. The former included mostly state employees, while the latter consisted of federal officials headquartered at the U.S. Custom House in New Orleans. Both factions claimed to be the legitimate Republican Party of Louisiana, but President Ulysses S. Grant, with whom Warmoth had quarreled during the war (Grant had discharged him for erroneous reasons) supported the Custom House faction.

When Warmoth blocked the election of James F. Casey, a member of the Custom House faction and Grant's brother-in-law, to the U.S. Senate, relations decayed further. Louisiana's Democratic Party encouraged and capitalized upon Republican infighting. When the

Liberal Republican schism in 1872 led to a party revolt against Grant's reelection, Warmoth became the leader of the Liberal Republicans in Louisiana. State elections were also scheduled for 1872, and the gubernatorial nominees included Democrat John D. McEnery and Republican William Pitt Kellogg. During the summer, there remained the possibility that Louisiana Republicans and Liberal Republicans might reunite, but Warmoth could not bring himself to support Grant's reelection. Instead, Democrats and Liberal Republicans in Louisiana formed a "Fusion" ticket headed by McEnery, with Warmoth pulling the strings. Warmoth used his power as governor to aid the Fusion ticket, firing Republican state election officials and replacing them with Democrats.

The election of 1872 in Louisiana was marred by fraud, violence, and controversy. Both Kellogg and McEnery claimed victory, as did rival Republican and Democratic legislatures. Opposing Returning Boards, of which there were eventually four, likewise declared conflicting results. In hopes of giving Kellogg an advantage, the Republican legislature impeached Warmoth in early December, thereby suspending him from office with only one month left in his term. Although he never faced trial before the state senate, Warmoth's impeachment effectively ended his governorship. The black lieutenant governor, Pinckney B. S. Pinchback, completed Warmoth's term and thus became the first black governor in U.S. history. Rival state governments held inaugurations in January 1873, but Grant, not surprisingly, recognized the Kellogg government.

Unlike many other carpetbaggers, Warmoth remained in the South for the rest of his life. After leaving office, he purchased a sugar plantation and became a leading modernizer of the Louisiana sugar industry. Returning to the Republican fold, he served in the state legislature at the end of Congressional Reconstruction, ran as Republican candidate for governor in 1888, and in the early 1890s, served as collector of customs in New Orleans.

In 1930, he published his memoirs, *War, Politics and Reconstruction*, a defense of his administration and record. He died in New Orleans on September 30, 1931, and is buried in Metairie, Louisiana.

*John C. Rodrigue*

**See also:** Amnesty Proclamations; Packard, Stephen B. (1842–1922); Presidential Reconstruction; Twitchell, Marshall H. (1840–1905); Wells, James M. (1808–1899).

## Further Reading

Current, Richard Nelson. *Those Terrible Carpetbaggers: A Reinterpretation*. New York: Oxford University Press, 1988.

Taylor, Joe Gray. *Louisiana Reconstructed: 1863–1877*. Baton Rouge: Louisiana State University Press, 1974.

Warmoth, Henry Clay. *War, Politics and Reconstruction: Stormy Days in Louisiana*. New York: The Macmillan Co., 1930.

## WELLS, JAMES M. (1808–1899)

A planter and politician, James Madison Wells served as governor of Louisiana during Reconstruction. A native of Alexandria, Louisiana, Wells received a good education by attending schools in Kentucky, Connecticut, and Ohio. He became one of the largest slave owners in Louisiana, but in politics, he was inherently Conservative: a Whig devoted to the Union, he opposed both abolition and secession before the Civil War. As federal troops occupied portions of the state, wartime Reconstruction began in 1864, with Unionist Michael Hahn elected governor and Wells lieutenant governor. When the legislature selected Hahn as U.S. senator, Wells succeeded to the governorship in March 1865.

Wells, like former president Abraham Lincoln and the new president, Andrew Johnson, sought a speedy return to normal operations—minus slavery, of course. But while Wells favored abolition, other policies were less clear. He vacillated between Conservative former confederates and the Democratic Party on the one hand and, on the other hand, more liberal men belonging to Louisiana's new Republican Party—including Union army veterans, freedmen, and prewar Unionists. He sided with Johnson's forgiving plan of Reconstruction, finding himself at odds with some U.S. Army officers who supervised the state's economy and politics. Running as a Democrat, Wells won the governorship in the special election of November 1865. Sliding away from conservatism, Wells remarkably appeared to entertain the possibility of suffrage for African American men, a point to be considered when the wartime constitutional convention of 1864 planned to reconvene in July 1866. However, his actions seemed to betray Radical Republicans and freedpeople: Wells took no steps to stop a bloody race riot in New Orleans that disrupted the convention, left dozens dead and wounded, and severely affected the state's—and the president's—political fortunes. Despite announcing his support for ratifying the Fourteenth Amendment to the U.S. Constitution and calling for the legislature to appropriate money for black schools, Wells failed to convince Gen. Philip Sheridan that he genuinely supported Congress's plan for Reconstruction. When the Military Reconstruction Acts of 1867 gave Sheridan authority over all civil officeholders in the Fifth Military District (Louisiana and Texas), Sheridan removed the governor as an "impediment to Reconstruction."

Out of office a few years, Wells returned to politics as a Republican in 1872, when Louisiana's Republican leaders made him chairman of the State Returning Board, an organization that determined the validity of ballots cast in the state's elections. His board helped count votes favoring his new party in the elections of 1874, and that led to Wells being appointed to the lucrative post of surveyor of customs for the port of New Orleans. In 1876, Wells and the Republican majority on the Returning Board determined that Republican presidential candidate Rutherford B. Hayes had carried Louisiana, contributing to a dispute at the national level over the winner of the presidency between Hayes and Democrat Samuel Tilden. As a part of the subsequent Compromise of 1877, Francis R. T. Nicholls was counted in as Louisiana's Democratic governor after Hayes gained the presidency. Yet despite the Democratic redemption, Wells continued to serve as surveyor of customs until 1880.

*Joseph G. Dawson III*

**See also:** Congressional Reconstruction; Elections of 1866; Presidential Reconstruction; Redemption; Republicans, Moderate; Scalawags.

## Further Reading

Dawson, Joseph G., III. *Army Generals and Reconstruction, 1862–1877*. Baton Rouge: Louisiana State University Press, 1982.

Taylor, Joe Gray. *Louisiana Reconstructed, 1863–1877*. Baton Rouge: Louisiana State University Press, 1974.

# WEST VIRGINIA

The majority of citizens living in the far western counties of Virginia opposed the decision of the state's political leaders to secede in 1861. Residing hundreds of miles from Virginia's capital, Richmond, and relying less heavily on slavery than whites living in the eastern section of the state, they saw little to gain from secession. Nevertheless, Virginia became a Confederate state. Strong Unionist sentiment in the West provided the impetus for a statehood movement for the far western counties during the Civil War. President Abraham Lincoln, striving to undermine the Confederacy in any way possible, also favored statehood. The movement culminated in 1863, when U.S. Congress recognized the state of West Virginia.

West Virginia's infant status did not protect it from the difficulties of Reconstruction. Three issues affecting the state after the Civil War stand out as especially significant. The first issue dealt with the debate over whether to grant political and civil rights to former confederates in West Virginia. A second issue dealt with the power of the Republican government, which controlled West Virginia at the outset of Reconstruction, to implement its policies in the face of Democratic and Conservative Unionist opposition. A third issue concerned the site of a permanent capital for the state. The manner in which state and federal leaders addressed these issues determined the course of Reconstruction in West Virginia and affected the state long after the Reconstruction era. Former confederates in West Virginia found themselves bound by laws that severely limited their political rights. These laws won the staunch support of leaders of the state's Republican Party, which struggled to maintain political control by disfranchising (denying voting rights) many "rebel" whites while supporting black suffrage. Comprising a miniscule percentage of the population of the state, and residing mainly in the northern and eastern corners of West Virginia, blacks exerted only a limited influence over state politics.

Reconstruction presented West Virginia blacks with innumerable challenges in adjusting to freedom. Not least among these was the necessity of overcoming white racism. Local white leaders were sometimes slow to build new schools for blacks, even though a state law mandated that such schools be constructed and despite the offer of Freedmen's Bureau officials to assist. Other whites resorted to more dangerous forms of opposition: harassment, intimidation, and violence. High prices for basic goods such as shoes, exorbitant rent prices, and diseases such as cholera also bedeviled the freedmen. These dismal conditions slowly improved during the Reconstruction period. Federal officers working for the Freedmen's Bureau sometimes noted in their reports examples of black advancement, praising many of the freedmen as hardworking and responsible. Blacks benefited from the fact that no Black Codes, such as the ones passed by legislatures in many of the former Confederate states, existed in West Virginia.

The federally operated Freedmen's Bureau was especially strong in the eastern corner of the state, a region dubbed the "eastern panhandle." Blacks and poor whites both received aid from bureau officials. The rations and medical aid dispensed by bureau officials rescued many recipients from privation, and the education they provided helped to unlock the shackles of ignorance that had bound blacks as slaves. Only three years after the Civil War, however, the federal government ended Freedmen's Bureau operations, and states were left to their own resources.

In 1868, after being impeached by the U.S. House of Representative, President Andrew Johnson was tried in the Senate and acquitted by a single vote. Had he failed to garner the support of a small number of Republicans, he probably would have been convicted. One of the so-called recusant Republicans who voted for President Johnson's acquittal was West Virginia senator Peter G. Van Winkle. Like Kansas senator Edmund G. Ross, today the most famous of the band of Republicans who supported President Johnson, Van Winkle believed that the president was a victim of a cynical Radical Republican ploy to oust him from office. In voting to acquit the president of the charges against him, Senator Van Winkle not only challenged his own party but also violated the wishes of a large majority of West Virginia's legislature, which supported the president's conviction. In 1869, his Senate term ended, and with it, his career as an elected official.

The influence of the Republican Party in West Virginia slowly ebbed as Reconstruction progressed. Elections in1869 and 1870 produced favorable results for the Democrats, and, as a consequence, Republican political control of state government dissolved. After West Virginia's "redemption," former confederates no longer faced discriminatory laws, and they became a significant political force. "Redemption" is a term historians employ to describe the collapse of the Republican Party's power in a Southern state during Reconstruction, and the subsequent takeover by Democratic or Conservative forces. With the rise of Democrats to power in the early 1870s, African Americans were forced to attend schools separate from whites, and only whites were allowed to serve on juries. The Fifteenth Amendment to the U.S. Constitution, ratified in 1870, prevented voting discrimination based on race but left open many other methods of denying suffrage.

The last major issue during Reconstruction was the debate whether to place the state capital in Wheeling, Charleston, or some other town. Dominated by Radical Republicans, Wheeling was unacceptable to the large Democratic contingent in the state. Resting in the "northern panhandle," the state's far northwestern corner, its remote location also made Wheeling unattractive as a state capital. Although Charleston, which could not be reached by train, had its weaknesses as well, it became West Virginia's permanent capital in 1885, the state's voters approving the move in a referendum.

The impact of the events of the Reconstruction period in West Virginia held long-term consequences for the state. Charleston, of course, remained the capital. More significant, redemption brought the rise of retrenchment through a Bourbon government, and the treatment of blacks during Reconstruction would pave the way for the later development of Jim Crow laws. In West Virginia, as well as throughout the United States, developing a just society would prove a far more arduous task than simply forming a new state.

*James S. Humphreys*

**See also:** Abolition of Slavery; Bureau of Refugees, Freedmen, and Abandoned Lands; New South; Pierpont, Francis H. (1814–1899).

## Further Reading

Engle, Stephen D. "Mountaineer Reconstruction: Blacks in the Political Reconstruction of West Virginia." *Journal of Negro History* 78 (Summer 1993): 137–65.

Rice, Otis K. *West Virginia: A History*. 2nd ed. Lexington: University Press of Kentucky, 1993.

Stealey, John Edmund III, ed. "Reports of Freedmen's Bureau Operations in West Virginia: Agents in the Eastern Panhandle." *West Virginia History*4 2 (Fall 1980–Winter 1981): 94–129.

## WHITE LEAGUE

The White League was a paramilitary-style organization of white Southern men that had emerged in Louisiana in 1874 to support the political objectives of the state's Democratic Party. By both intimidating its opponents and rallying potential supporters, the White League played a central role in the Redemption of the Pelican State.

The White League differed considerably from its predecessor in Louisiana, the Klan-like Knights of the White Camellia. Although the Knights sometimes attacked freedmen's agents or other representatives of Republican authority, they lacked political focus, directing most of their activities against the freedmen. Ultimately, the Enforcement Acts put an end to the Knights' activities in Louisiana. In contrast, the White League eschewed night-riding for targeted military-style campaigns against prominent Republicans and timed their activities for maximum political effect.

The White League emerged from Louisiana's contested gubernatorial election of 1872 between Republican William Pitt Kellogg and Fusion candidate John McEnery. The defeated Fusionists, dominated by members of the Democratic Party, refused to recognize the legitimacy of Kellogg's government. Kellogg, however, enjoyed the support of President Ulysses S. Grant as well as the protection of the Metropolitan Police—essentially a private army of Louisiana's Republican Party. When the White League appeared in 1874, its objective was to reverse the results of the election of 1872 and bring about Redemption.

The Redeemers used the White League to overcome two main obstacles. They needed to rally the support of disaffected white men around the Redemption crusade, and at the same time, form them into an army capable of challenging Kellogg's Metropolitan Police. To accomplish this, the league staged rallies where they promoted the idea of white supremacy, declaring the Democratic Party the "white man's party." At the same time, the White League took on a military character, purchased weapons, and organized itself into companies.

Because the White League lacked a statewide organizational structure, its character varied considerably from parish to parish. In some locations, the league relied mostly upon both physical and economic intimidation to accomplish its

Thomas Nast drawing depicting the evolution of white intimidation. By the early 1870s in Louisiana, the Klan had morphed into a larger, more open, and more successful organization, called the White League. This armed paramilitary body supported the state's Democratic Party, and helped secure white conservative control by early 1877. (Library of Congress)

goals. In Red River Parish, however, a rural chapter of the White League assassinated several members of the local Republican government and severely wounded the parish's state senator, Marshall H. Twitchell. In September 1874, a full-scale battle took place between more than 1,000 members of the Crescent City White League and several hundred of the Republican's Metropolitan Police on Canal Street in New Orleans. The clash produced more than 30 fatalities and led to the temporary overthrow of Kellogg. Although Grant sent federal troops to Louisiana to restore Kellogg's Republican regime, he left the White League unmolested. Grant's failure to punish the White League's leaders strengthened the organization.

The White League played its final role during the contested national election of 1876. As had been the case in 1872, both the Republicans and Democrats claimed victory in Louisiana's gubernatorial election in 1876. Nationally, the electoral contest hinged on the outcome in Louisiana and two other unredeemed Southern states. The Compromise of 1877 resolved this conflict by giving the presidency to Republican Rutherford B. Hayes of Ohio. In return, Hayes ordered federal troops to abandon the remaining Southern Republican regimes. With this turn of events, the White League forcibly ejected the Republican Party's claimant to the governorship of Louisiana, and seated in his stead the Redeemer governor, Francis Redding Tillou Nicholls. After Redemption, the White League formed the core of the official Louisiana National Guard.

*Justin A. Nystrom*

**See also:** Gun Clubs; Redemption; Shotgun Plan.

## Further Reading

Keith, Lee Anna. *The Colfax Massacre: The Untold Story of Black Power, White Terror, and the Death of Reconstruction.* New York: Oxford University Press, 2009.

Perman, Michael. *The Road to Redemption: Southern Politics, 1869–1880.* Chapel Hill: University of North Carolina Press, 1984.

Rable, George C. *But There Was No Peace: The Role of Violence in the Politics of Reconstruction.* Athens: University of Georgia Press, 1984.

Trelease, Allen. *White Terror: The Ku Klux Klan Conspiracy and Southern Reconstruction.* Baton Rouge: Louisiana State University Press, 1971.

## WORTH, JONATHAN (1802–1869)

Jonathan Worth, lawyer, businessman, Whig politician, state treasurer, peace advocate, and Presidential Reconstruction governor, was born on November 18, 1802, in Randolph County, North Carolina. As the son of a county doctor, Worth enjoyed a variety of educational opportunities. The most significant such opportunity came on 1823, when he relocated to Hillsborough to study law. After completing his legal training, Worth established his own law practice and entered public service as a member of the Whig Party. Between 1830 and 1860, he held a variety of state offices. Worth demonstrated a strong devotion to the Union, fought for economic development and public education, and attained both status and wealth before the war.

The secession crisis weighed heavily on Southern Whigs like Worth who resisted disunion, but as the crisis deepened, he had to take a stand. State senator Worth confronted secession head-on as the legislature debated a bill calling for a statewide secession convention. When the bill finally faced a vote, only Worth and two other legislators rejected it.

The attack on Fort Sumter in Charleston Harbor forced North Carolinians to choose between joining the Confederacy and suppressing the rebellion. When his state chose the Confederacy in late May 1861, Worth, like many Southern Unionists, reconciled himself to secession. Ironically, secession proved favorable to Worth's political career. Like many former Whigs, Worth found himself in a new political party soon after the war began. As North Carolinians realized that the war required greater sacrifice than the Democratic secessionists led them to believe, they found a new alternative, called the Conservative Party, founded by William W. Holden. Although little more than the Whigs under a new guise, the Conservatives placed former Whigs in the ascendance, and Worth became the state's treasurer under Conservative governor Zebulon B. Vance in 1862.

Worth grew increasingly disenchanted with the Confederacy. Frequent squabbles with national officials over financial matters and the relationship between the state and federal governments reaffirmed the treasurer's belief that secession had been an error. He became involved in a statewide peace movement in 1863, also led by Holden. North Carolina's peace movement, however, did little to hasten the Confederacy's demise and even as late as 1864, Vance won reelection as governor in a landslide over Holden.

On May 29, 1865, President Andrew Johnson initiated his Reconstruction policy with a series of proclamations, using North Carolina as a model. Johnson appointed the former peace leader Holden provisional governor and ordered him to reorganize the state government and convene a state constitutional convention. Now in the office that had been denied him only a few months earlier by North Carolina's voters, the Unionist newspaper editor undertook the tasks before him. He appointed new local officials, advised President Johnson on pardoning former confederates, and called a constitutional convention into session.

Despite their working relationship during the war, Holden's actions as governor strained his relationship with Worth. The provisional governor hoped to create a political base that would keep him in office, so he attempted to appoint men to local office that favored his policies and used his influence over men's pardons to gain their support. Worth resented Holden's actions because he felt that the governor endorsed the pardons of former confederates while blocking the amnesty petitions of former Whigs who might stunt Holden's political ambitions.

The growing differences between Holden and Worth proved beneficial to the former confederates searching for a candidate to oppose Holden in the gubernatorial election scheduled for November 9, 1865, Conservatives needed to be careful. A candidate too closely associated with secession and the war might upset the president and Congress, but they also desired a man of Conservative political principles who would preserve as much of the antebellum status quo as possible. Worth's record as a pro-Union Whig before the war and as Confederate state treasurer suited the Conservatives' needs perfectly. During the abbreviated campaign, Holden's supporters boldly claimed that a vote for Worth would continue Reconstruction, while a ballot cast for Holden would restore the Union. Such tactics failed. Worth carried most of the eastern and central parts of the state en route to an impressive victory, while Holden carried many of the mountain counties and their higher number of white Unionists.

Once in office, Worth demonstrated a strong ideological commitment to the president's Reconstruction policy. The new governor felt that the former Confederate states should be returned to the Union once they repudiated secession and abolished slavery. A quick restoration complemented Worth's political ideology, which limited public power to white male property holders.

Politics as usual did not come as easily as Worth hoped. Blacks asserted their rights and struggled to gain control over their families. Lower-class whites, many of whom resented shouldering what they felt was an unfair share of wartime sacrifices, also challenged the political hierarchy that the governor sought to preserve. Such subversive behavior by social lessers confused Worth. He blamed federal officials, especially the army and Bureau of Refugees, Freedmen, and Abandoned Lands, for upsetting the status quo. Worth believed that these organizations undermined the restoration of North Carolina's civil government, and he devoted himself to resisting them. In particular, the Freedmen's Bureau galled Worth. Designed to oversee the South's transition from a slave to free labor society, the Freedmen's Bureau was empowered to supervise labor contracts between the former slaves and their former masters and to hold military courts to try cases involving blacks. As executive of state laws, Worth believed he must uphold the state's judges and lawyers. Reports that Freedmen's Bureau agents intervened in state courts and, at times, overturned their decisions infuriated the governor. Worth became so frustrated with the federal presence by July 1866 that he became blind to several other problems. Violence raged across the state as Unionists and secessionists settled old scores, embittered whites lashed out at former slaves, and poorer whites resisted tax collectors. The governor dismissed many accounts as false reports by bad men, even attempts by Holden and other enemies to restore military government in the state to further their own political careers.

The challenges and tribulations of Reconstruction politics taxed Worth's health. Near the end of his term, he battled a variety of ailments that limited his ability to perform his duties as governor. For that reason, his removal from office for a newly elected governor in 1868 granted him a grim sense of relief. Once out of office, however, Worth's condition failed to improve. He passed away in September 1869.

*Steven E. Nash*

**See also:** Abolition of Slavery; Black Codes; Civil Rights; Civil Rights Act of 1866; Congressional Reconstruction; Labor Systems; Loyalty Oaths; Military Reconstruction Acts (1867–1868); Presidential Reconstruction; Thirteenth Amendment (1865).

## Further Reading

Escott, Paul D. *Many Excellent People: Power and Privilege in North Carolina, 1850–1900.* Chapel Hill: University of North Carolina Press, 1985.

Hamilton, J. G. de Roulhac, ed. *The Correspondence of Jonathan Worth.* 2 vols. Raleigh, NC: Edwards & Broughton Printing Co., 1909.

Zuber, Richard L. *Jonathan Worth: A Biography of a Southern Unionist.* Chapel Hill: University of North Carolina Press, 1965.

Zuber, Richard. *North Carolina during Reconstruction.* Raleigh, NC: The State Department of Archives and History, 1969.

# Primary Documents

## PRESIDENT ABRAHAM LINCOLN'S EMANCIPATION PROCLAMATION (JANUARY 1, 1863)

*By the summer of 1862, Radical Republicans in Congress, military leaders, and the Northern public were pushing for a more aggressive approach to crushing the Confederacy. At the same time, abolitionists reiterated that slavery and its immorality lay at the center of the sectional crisis. These two forces merged with President Abraham Lincoln's decision, shared with his cabinet in the summer of 1862, that he was ready for limited emancipation. On September 22, 1862, five days after Union forces repulsed General Robert E. Lee's invasion at the battle of Antietam, Lincoln announced the preliminary Emancipation Proclamation, to go into effect on January 1, 1863. Historians still debate the impact and meaning of the proclamation. Issued as a war measure, it was limited in scope; it did not promote abolition, but merely emancipation, and did not even apply to the entire South, but its significance was still profound. The proclamation represents a complete reversal of the War Aims Resolution of 1861, as victory was now linked to emancipation. Also, the first inklings of equality can be seen, as the proclamation admits African Americans to military service.*

By the President of the United States of America: A Proclamation.

Whereas, on the twenty-second day of September, in the year of our Lord one thousand eight hundred and sixty-two, a proclamation was issued by the President of the United States, containing, among other things, the following, to wit:

That on the first day of January, in the year of our Lord one thousand eight hundred and sixty-three, all persons held as slaves within any State or designated part of a State, the people whereof shall then be in rebellion against the United States, shall be then, thenceforward, and forever free; and the Executive Government of the United States, including the military and naval authority thereof, will recognize and maintain the freedom of such persons, and will do no act or acts to repress such persons, or any of them, in any efforts they may make for their actual freedom.

That the Executive will, on the first day of January aforesaid, by proclamation, designate the States and parts of States, if any, in which the people thereof, respectively, shall then be in rebellion against the United States; and the fact that any State, or the people thereof, shall on that day be, in good faith, represented in the Congress of the United States by members chosen thereto at elections wherein a majority of the qualified voters of such State shall have participated, shall, in the absence of strong countervailing testimony, be deemed conclusive evidence that such State, and the people thereof, are not then in rebellion against the United States.

Now, therefore I, Abraham Lincoln, President of the United States, by virtue of the power in me vested as Commander-in-Chief, of the Army and Navy of the United States in time of actual armed rebellion against the authority and government of the United States, and as a fit and necessary war measure for suppressing said rebellion, do, on this first day of January, in the year of our Lord one thousand eight hundred and sixty-three, and in accordance with my purpose so to do publicly proclaimed for the full period of one hundred days, from the day first above mentioned, order and designate as the States and parts of States wherein the people thereof respectively, are this day in rebellion against the United States, the following, to wit:

Arkansas, Texas, Louisiana (except the Parishes of St. Bernard, Plaquemines, Jefferson, St. John, St. Charles, St. James Ascension, Assumption, Terrebonne, Lafourche, St. Mary, St. Martin, and Orleans, including the City of New Orleans), Mississippi, Alabama, Florida, Georgia, South Carolina, North Carolina, and Virginia (except the forty-eight counties designated as West Virginia, and also the counties of Berkley, Accomac, Northampton, Elizabeth City, York, Princess Ann, and Norfolk, including the cities of Norfolk and Portsmouth[)], and which excepted parts, are for the present, left precisely as if this proclamation were not issued.

And by virtue of the power, and for the purpose aforesaid, I do order and declare that all persons held as slaves within said designated States, and parts of States, are, and henceforward shall be free; and that the Executive government of the United States, including the military and naval authorities thereof, will recognize and maintain the freedom of said persons.

And I hereby enjoin upon the people so declared to be free to abstain from all violence, unless in necessary self-defence; and I recommend to them that, in all cases when allowed, they labor faithfully for reasonable wages.

And I further declare and make known, that such persons of suitable condition, will be received into the armed service of the United States to garrison forts, positions, stations, and other places, and to man vessels of all sorts in said service.

And upon this act, sincerely believed to be an act of justice, warranted by the Constitution, upon military necessity, I invoke the considerate judgment of mankind, and the gracious favor of Almighty God.

In witness whereof, I have hereunto set my hand and caused the seal of the United States to be affixed.

Done at the City of Washington, this first day of January, in the year of our Lord one thousand eight hundred and sixty three, and of the Independence of the United States of America the eighty-seventh.

By the President: ABRAHAM LINCOLN

WILLIAM H. SEWARD, Secretary of State.

*Source:* Emancipation Proclamation, January 1, 1863. Presidential Proclamations, 1791–1991. Record Group 11, General Records of the United States Government, National Archives.

## THIRTEENTH AMENDMENT TO THE U.S. CONSTITUTION (RATIFIED DECEMBER 18, 1865)

*The two most important results of the Civil War were the preservation of the federal Union and the destruction of slavery. Slavery had begun to crumble during the war, through the actions of military officers, congressional acts, Lincoln's Emancipation Proclamation, and even the efforts of slaves themselves. But emancipation—gaining freedom—did not end slavery as an institution. By war's end, congressional Republicans, Lincoln, and even Johnson expected Southern states to abolish slavery within their borders; but what of new states, or the North? Sadly, the United States was well behind most other Western powers in abandoning the system on a national level (even eastern European empires had moved away from serfdom before the United States eradicated slavery). Not until the passage and ratification of the Thirteenth Amendment was slavery formally abolished as a legal institution in the United States. The amendment said nothing of the freed people's rights or other privileges, and introduced a new component to amending the Constitution—the enforcement clause—which left the door open for congressional action in the future.*

## Article XIII

Section 1. Neither slavery nor involuntary servitude, except as punishment for crime whereof the party shall have been duly convicted, shall exist in the United States, or any place subject to their jurisdiction.

Section 2. Congress shall have power to enforce this article by appropriate legislation.

*Source:* The House Joint Resolution proposing the 13th amendment to the Constitution, Ratified on December 18, 1965. Enrolled Acts and Resolutions of Congress, 1789–1999. General Records of the United States Government, Record Group 11, National Archives.

# MISSISSIPPI BLACK CODES (1865)

*While the Civil War and the Thirteenth Amendment proved that African Americans were slaves no more, neither did anything to indicate what they were. What was the status of the freed people? What rights, opportunities, and privileges would they have? Under Andrew Johnson's program of restoration, these questions were left to the judgment of the individual southern states. State after state of the former Confederacy passed Black Codes, rules, and restrictions that enforced a plantation-based, white supremacist system. The discrimination, inhumanity, and outright arrogance displayed in the codes helped convince many Republicans that the president's program was a betrayal of Union victory.*

## An Act to Confer Civil Rights on Freedmen, and for Other Purposes

Section 1. All freedmen, free negroes and mulattoes may sue and be sued, implead and be impleaded, in all the courts of law and equity of this State, and may acquire personal property, and chooses [sic] in action, by descent or purchase, and may dispose of the same in the same manner and to the same extent that white persons may: Provided, That the provisions of this section shall not be so construed as to allow any freedman, free negro or mulatto to rent or lease any lands or tenements except in incorporated cities or towns, in which places the corporate authorities shall control the same.

Section 2. All freedmen, free negroes and mulattoes may intermarry with each other, in the same manner and under the same regulations that are provided by law for white persons: Provided, that the clerk of probate shall keep separate records of the same.

Section 3. All freedmen, free negroes or mullatoes [*sic*] who do now and have here before lived and cohabited together as husband and wife shall be taken and held in law as legally married, and the issue shall be taken and held as legitimate for all purposes; and it shall not be lawful for any freedman, free negro or mulatto to intermarry with any white person; nor for any person to intermarry with any freedman, free negro or mulatto; and any person who shall so intermarry shall be deemed guilty of felony, and on conviction thereof shall be confined in the State penitentiary for life; and those shall be deemed freedmen, free negroes and mulattoes who are of pure negro blood, and those descended from a negro to the third generation, inclusive, though one ancestor in each generation may have been a white person.

Section 4. In addition to cases in which freedmen, free negroes and mulattoes are now by law competent witnesses, freedmen, free negroes or mulattoes shall be competent in civil cases, when a party or parties to the suit, either plaintiff or plaintiffs, defendant or defendants; also in cases where freedmen, free negroes and mulattoes is or are either plaintiff or plaintiffs, defendant or defendants. They shall also be competent witnesses in all criminal prosecutions where the crime charged is alleged to have been committed by a white person upon or against the person or property of a freedman, free negro or mulatto: Provided, that in all cases said witnesses shall be examined in open court, on the stand; except, however, they may be examined before the grand jury, and shall in all cases be subject to the rules and tests of the common law as to competency and credibility.

Section 5. Every freedman, free negro and mulatto shall, on the second Monday of January, one thousand eight hundred and sixty-six, and annually thereafter, have a lawful home or employment, and shall have written evidence thereof as follows, to wit: if living in any incorporated city, town, or village, a license from that mayor thereof; and if living outside of an incorporated city, town, or village, from the member of the board of police of his beat, authorizing him or her to do irregular and job work; or a written contract, as provided in Section 6 in this act; which license may be revoked for cause at any time by the authority granting the same.

Section 6. All contracts for labor made with freedmen, free negroes and mulattoes for a longer period than one month shall be in writing, and a duplicate, attested and read to said freedman, free negro or mulatto by a beat, city or county officer, or two disinterested white persons of the county in which the labor is to [be] performed, of which each party shall have one: and said contracts shall be taken and held as entire contracts, and if the laborer shall quit the service of the employer before the expiration of his term of service, without good cause, he shall forfeit his wages for that year up to the time of quitting.

Section 7. Every civil officer shall, and every person may, arrest and carry back to his or her legal employer any freedman, free negro, or mulatto who shall have quit the service of his or her employer before the expiration of his or her term of service without good cause; and said officer and person shall be entitled to receive for arresting and carrying back every deserting employee aforesaid the sum of five dollars, and ten cents per mile from the place of arrest to the place of delivery; and the same shall be paid by the employer, and held as a set off for so much against the wages of said deserting employee: Provided, that said arrested party, after being so returned, may appeal to the justice of the peace or member of the board of police of the county, who, on notice to the alleged employer, shall try summarily whether said appellant is legally employed by the alleged employer, and has good cause to quit said employer. Either party shall have the right of appeal to the county court, pending which the alleged deserter shall be remanded to the alleged employer or otherwise disposed of, as shall be right and just; and the decision of the county court shall be final.

Section 8. Upon affidavit made by the employer of any freedman, free negro or mulatto, or other credible person, before any justice of the peace or member of the board of police, that any freedman, free negro or mulatto legally employed by said employer has illegally deserted said employment, such justice of the peace or member of the board of police issue his warrant or warrants, returnable before himself or other such officer, to any sheriff, constable or special deputy, commanding him to arrest said deserter, and return him or her to said employer, and the like proceedings shall be had as provided in the preceding section; and it shall be lawful for any officer to whom such warrant shall be directed to execute said warrant in any county in this State; and that said warrant may be transmitted without endorsement to any like officer of another county, to be executed and returned as aforesaid; and the said employer shall pay the costs of said warrants and arrest and return, which shall be set off for so much against the wages of said deserter.

Section 9. If any person shall persuade or attempt to persuade, entice, or cause any freedman, free negro or mulatto to desert from the legal employment of any person before the expiration of his or her term of service, or shall knowingly employ any such deserting freedman, free negro or mullato, or shall knowingly give or sell to any such deserting freedman, free negro or mulatto, any food, raiment, or other thing, he or she shall be guilty of a misdemeanor, and, upon conviction, shall be fined not less than twenty-five dollars and not more than two hundred dollars and costs; and if the said fine and costs shall not be immediately paid, the court shall sentence said convict to not exceeding two months imprisonment in the county jail, and he or she shall moreover be liable to the party injured in damages: Provided, if any person shall, or shall attempt to, persuade, entice, or cause any freedman, free negro or mullatto to desert from any legal employment of any person, with the view to employ said freedman, free negro or mullato without the limits of this State, such costs; and if said fine and costs shall not be immediately paid, the court shall sentence said convict to not exceeding six months imprisonment in the county jail.

Section 10. It shall be lawful for any freedman, free negro, or mulatto, to charge any white person, freedman, free negro or mulatto by affidavit, with any criminal offense against his or her person or property, and upon such affidavit the proper process shall be issued and executed as if said affidavit was made by a white person, and it shall be lawful for any freedman, free negro, or mulatto, in any action, suit or controversy pending, or about to be instituted in any court of law equity in this State, to make all needful and lawful affidavits as shall be necessary for the institution, prosecution or defense of such suit or controversy.

Section 11. The penal laws of this state, in all cases not otherwise specially provided for, shall apply and extend to all freedman, free negroes and mulattoes . . .

## An Act to Regulate the Relation of Master and Apprentice, as Relates to Freedmen, Free Negroes, and Mulattoes

Section 1. It shall be the duty of all sheriffs, justices of the peace, and other civil officers of the several counties in this State, to report to the probate courts of their respective counties semiannually, at the January and July terms of said courts, all freedmen, free negroes, and mulattoes, under the age of eighteen, in their respective counties, beats, or districts, who are orphans, or whose parent or parents have not the means or who refuse to provide for and support said minors; and thereupon it shall be the duty of said probate court to order the clerk of said court to apprentice said minors to some competent and suitable person on such terms as the court may direct, having a particular care to the interest of said minor: Provided, that the former owner of said minors shall have the preference when, in the opinion of the court, he or she shall be a suitable person for that purpose.

Section 2. The said court shall be fully satisfied that the person or persons to whom said minor shall be apprenticed shall be a suitable person to have the charge and care of said minor, and fully to protect the interest of said minor. The said court shall require the said master or mistress to execute bond and security, payable to the State of Mississippi, conditioned that he or she shall furnish said minor with sufficient food and clothing; to treat said minor humanely; furnish medical attention in case of sickness; teach, or cause to be taught, him or her to read and write, if under fifteen years old, and will conform to any law that may be hereafter passed for the regulation of the duties and relation of master and apprentice: Provided, that said apprentice shall be bound by indenture, in case of males, until they are twenty-one years old, and in case of females until they are eighteen years old.

Section 3. In the management and control of said apprentices, said master or mistress shall have the power to inflict such moderate corporeal chastisement as a father or guardian is allowed to infliction on his or her child or ward at common law: Provided, that in no case shall cruel or inhuman punishment be inflicted.

Section 4. If any apprentice shall leave the employment of his or her master or mistress, without his or her consent, said master or mistress may pursue and recapture said apprentice, and bring him or her before any justice of the peace of the county, whose duty it shall be to remand said apprentice to the service of his or her master or mistress; and in the event of a refusal on the part of said apprentice so to return, then said justice shall commit said apprentice to the jail of said county, on failure to give bond, to the next term of the county court; and it shall be the duty of said court at the first term thereafter to investigate said case, and if the court shall be of opinion that said apprentice left the employment of his or her master or mistress without good cause, to order him or her to be punished, as provided for the punishment of hired freedmen, as may be from time to time provided for by law for desertion, until he or she shall agree to return to the service of his or her master or mistress: Provided, that the court may grant continuances as in other cases:

And provided further, that if the court shall believe that said apprentice had good cause to quit his said master or mistress, the court shall discharge said apprentice from said indenture, and also enter a judgment against the master or mistress for not more than one hundred dollars, from the use and benefit of said apprentice, to be collected on execution as in other cases.

Section 5. If any person entice away any apprentice from his or her master or mistress, or shall knowingly employ an apprentice, or furnish him or her food or clothing without the written consent of his or her master or mistress, or shall sell or give said apprentice spirits without such consent, said person so offending shall be guilty of a misdemeanor, and shall, upon conviction there of before the county court, be punished as provided for the punishment of person enticing from their employer hired freedmen, free negroes or mulattoes.

Section 6. It shall be the duty of all civil officers of their respective counties to report any minors within their respective counties to said probate court who are subject to be apprenticed under the provisions of this act, from time to time as the facts may come to their knowledge, and it shall be the duty of said court from time to time as said minors shall be reported to them, or otherwise come to their knowledge, to apprentice said minors as hereinbefore provided.

Section 9. It shall be lawful for any freedman, free negro, or mulatto, having a minor child or children, as provided for by this act.

Section 10. In all cases where the age of the freedman, free negro, or mulatto cannot be ascertained by record testimony, the judge of the county court shall fix the age. . . .

## An Act to Amend the Vagrant Laws of the State

Section 1. All rogues and vagabonds, idle and dissipated persons, beggars, jugglers, or persons practicing unlawful games or plays, runaways, common drunkards, common night-walkers, pilferers, lewd, wanton, or lascivious persons, in speech or behavior, common railers and brawlers, persons who neglect their calling or employment, misspend what they earn, or do not provide for the support of themselves or their families, or dependents, and all other idle and disorderly persons, including all who neglect all lawful business, habitually misspend their time by frequenting houses of ill-fame, gaming-houses, or tippling shops, shall be deemed and considered vagrants, under the provisions of this act, and upon conviction thereof shall be fined not exceeding one hundred dollars, with all accruing costs, and be imprisoned, at the discretion of the court, not exceeding ten days.

Section 2. All freedmen, free negroes and mulattoes in this State, over the age of eighteen years, found on the second Monday in January, 1866, or thereafter, with no lawful employment or business, or found unlawful assembling themselves together, either in the day or night time, and all white persons assembling themselves with freedmen, Free negroes or mulattoes, or usually associating with freedmen, free negroes or mulattoes, on terms of equality, or living in adultery or fornication with a freed woman, freed negro or mulatto, shall be deemed vagrants, and on conviction thereof shall be fined in a sum not exceeding, in the case of a freedman, free negro or mulatto, fifty dollars, and a white man two hundred dollars, and imprisonment at the discretion of the court, the free negro not exceeding ten days, and the white man not exceeding six months.

Section 3. All justices of the peace, mayors, and aldermen of incorporated towns, counties, and cities of the several counties in this State shall have jurisdiction to try all questions of vagrancy in their respective towns, counties, and cities, and it is hereby made their duty, whenever they shall ascertain that any person or persons in their respective towns, and counties and cities are violating any of the provisions of this act, to have said party or parties arrested, and brought before them, and immediately investigate said charge, and, on conviction, punish said party or parties, as provided for herein. And it is hereby made the duty of all sheriffs, constables, town constables, and all such like officers, and city marshals, to report to some officer having jurisdiction all violations of any of the provisions of this act, and in case any officer shall fail or neglect any duty herein it shall be the duty of the county court to fine said officer, upon conviction, not exceeding one hundred dollars, to be paid into the county treasury for county purposes.

Section 4. Keepers of gaming houses, houses of prostitution, prostitutes, public or private, and all persons who derive their chief support in the employment's that militate against good morals, or against law, shall be deemed and held to be vagrants.

Section 5. All fines and forfeitures collected by the provisions of this act shall be paid into the county treasury of general county purposes, and in case of any freedman, free negro or mulatto shall fail for five days after the imposition of any or forfeiture upon him or her for violation of any of the provisions of this act to pay the same, that it shall be, and is hereby, made the duty of the sheriff of the proper county to hire out said freedman, free negro or mulatto, to any person who will, for the shortest period of service, pay said fine and forfeiture and all costs: Provided, a preference shall be given to the employer, if there be one, in which case the employer shall be entitled to deduct and retain the amount so paid from the wages of such freedman, free negro or mulatto, then due or to become due; and in case freedman, free negro or mulatto cannot hire out, he or she may be dealt with as a pauper.

Section 6. The same duties and liabilities existing among white persons of this State shall attach to freedmen, free negroes or mulattoes, to support their indigent families and all colored paupers; and that in order to secure a support for such indigent freedmen, free negroes, or mulattoes, it shall be lawful, and is hereby made the duty of the county police of each county in this State, to levy a poll or capitation tax on each and every freedman, free negro, or mulatto, between the ages of eighteen and sixty years, not to exceed the sum of one dollar annually to each person so taxed, which tax, when collected, shall be paid into the county treasurer's hands, and constitute a fund to be called the Freedman's Pauper Fund, which shall be applied by the commissioners of the poor for the maintenance of the poor of the freedmen, free negroes and mulattoes of this State, under such regulations as may be established by the boards of county police in the respective counties of this State.

Section 7. If any freedman, free negro, or mulatto shall fail or refuse to pay any tax levied according to the provisions of the sixth section of this act, it shall be prima facie evidence of vagrancy, and it shall be the duty of the sheriff to arrest such freedman, free negro, or mulatto, or such person refusing or neglecting to pay such tax, and proceed at once to hire for the shortest time such delinquent taxpayer to any one who will pay the said tax, with accruing costs, giving preference to the employer, if there be one.

Section 8. Any person feeling himself or herself aggrieved by judgment of any justice of the peace, mayor, or alderman in cases arising under this act, may within five days appeal to the next term of the county court of the proper county, upon giving bond and security in a sum not less than twenty-five dollars nor more than one hundred and fifty dollars, conditioned to appear and prosecute said appeal, and abide by the judgment of the county court; and said appeal shall be tried de novo in the county court, and the decision of the said court shall be final.

*Source: An Act to Confer Civil Rights on Freedmen, and for Other Purposes, November 25, 1865. Laws of the State of Mississippi, Passed at a Regular Session of the Mississippi Legislature, Held in the City of Jackson, October, November and December, 1865. Jackson, MS, 1866, 82–86.*

# CIVIL RIGHTS ACT (APRIL 1866)

*Seeking a compromise between the desires of some Radical Republicans and the conservative approach of President Johnson, Moderate Republicans succeeded in maneuvering a new Civil Rights Bill through Congress. This bill overturned the obnoxious Black Codes in the South by guaranteeing under federal law certain civil, judicial, and economic rights of the freed people. This action was radical in terms of its expansion of federal jurisdiction and its promise of federal enforcement, but still kept clear of the extreme issues, such as black suffrage and officeholding. As with the previous version, Johnson vetoed the bill. Congress passed the bill into law over the president's veto, the first time in U.S. history Congress overturned a presidential veto of a significant piece of legislation.*

## An Act to Protect all Persons in the United States in their Civil Rights, and Furnish the Means of their Vindication

Be it enacted by the Senate and House of Representatives of the United States of America in Congress assembled, That all persons born in the United States and not subject to any foreign power, excluding Indians not taxed, are hereby declared to be citizens of the United States; and such citizens, of every race and color, without regard to any previous condition of slavery or involuntary servitude, except as a punishment for crime whereof the party shall have been duly convicted, shall have the same right, in every State and Territory in the United States, to make and enforce contracts, to sue, be parties, and give evidence, to inherit, purchase, lease, sell, hold, and convey real and personal property, and to full and equal benefit of all laws and proceedings for the security of person and property, as is enjoyed by white citizens, and shall be subject to like punishment, pains, and penalties, and to none other, any law, statute, ordinance, regulation, or custom, to the contrary notwithstanding.

Sec. 2. And be it further enacted, That any person who, under color of any law, statute, ordinance, regulation, or custom, shall subject, or cause to be subjected, any inhabitant of any State or Territory to the deprivation of any right secured or protected by this act, or to different punishment, pains, or penalties on account of such person having at any time been held in a condition of slavery or involuntary servitude, except as a punishment for crime whereof the party shall have been duly convicted, or by reason of his color or race, than is prescribed for the punishment of white persons, shall be deemed guilty of a misdemeanor, and, on conviction, shall be punished by fine not exceeding one thousand dollars, or imprisonment not exceeding one year, or both, in the discretion of the court.

Sec. 3. And be it further enacted, That the district courts of the United States, within their respective districts, shall have, exclusively of the courts of the several States, cognizance of all crimes and offences committed against the provisions of this act, and also, concurrently with the circuit courts of the United States, of all causes, civil and criminal, affecting persons who are denied or cannot enforce in the courts or judicial tribunals of the State or locality where they may be any of the rights secured to them by the first section of this act; and if any suit or prosecution, civil or criminal, has been or shall be commenced in any State court, against any such person, for any cause whatsoever, or against any officer, civil or military, or other person, for any arrest or imprisonment, trespasses, or wrongs done or committed by virtue or under color of authority derived from this act or the act establishing a Bureau for the relief of Freedmen and Refugees, and all acts amendatory thereof, or for refusing to do any act upon the ground that it would be inconsistent with this act, such defendant shall have the right to remove such cause for trial to the proper district or circuit court in the manner prescribed by the "Act relating to habeas corpus and regulating judicial proceedings in certain cases," approved March three, eighteen hundred and sixty-three, and all acts amendatory thereof. The jurisdiction in civil and criminal matters hereby conferred on the district and circuit courts of the United States shall be exercised and enforced in conformity with the laws of the United States, so far as such laws are suitable to carry the same into effect; but in all cases where such laws are not adapted to the object, or are deficient in the provisions necessary to furnish suitable remedies and punish offences against law, the common law, as modified and changed by the constitution and statutes of the State wherein the court having jurisdiction of the cause, civil or criminal, is held, so far as the same is not inconsistent with the Constitution and laws of the United States, shall be extended to and govern said courts in the trial and disposition of such cause, and, if of a criminal nature, in the infliction of punishment on the party found guilty.

Sec. 4. And be it further enacted, That the district attorneys, marshals, and deputy marshals of the United States, the commissioners appointed by the circuit and territorial courts of the United States, with powers of arresting, imprisoning, or bailing offenders against the laws of the United States, the officers and agents of the Freedmen's Bureau, and every other officer who may be especially empowered by the President of the United States, shall be, and they are hereby, specially authorized and required, at the expense of the United States, to institute proceedings against all and every person who shall violate the provisions of this act, and cause him or them to be arrested and imprisoned, or bailed, as the case may be, for trial before such court of the United States or territorial court as by this act has cognizance of the offence. And with a view to affording reasonable protection to all persons in their constitutional rights of equality before the law, without distinction of race or color, or previous condition of slavery or involuntary servitude, except as a punishment for crime, whereof the party shall have been duly convicted, and to the prompt discharge of the duties of this act, it shall be the duty of the circuit courts of the United States and the superior courts of the Territories of the United States, from time to time, to increase the number of commissioners, so as to afford a speedy and convenient means for the arrest and examination of persons charged with a violation of this act; and such commissioners are hereby authorized and required to exercise and discharge all the powers and duties conferred on them by this act, and the same duties with regard to offences created by this act, as they are authorized by law to exercise with regard to other offences against the laws of the United States.

Sec. 5. And be it further enacted, That it shall be the duty of all marshals and deputy marshals to obey and execute all warrants and precepts issued under the provisions of this act, when to them directed; and should any marshal or deputy marshal refuse to receive such warrant or other process when tendered, or to sue all proper means diligently to execute the same, he shall, on conviction thereof, be fined in the sum of one thousand dollars, to the use of the person upon whom the accused is alleged to have committed the offence. And the better to enable the said commissioners to execute their duties faithfully and efficiently, in conformity with the Constitution of the United States and the requirements of this act, they are hereby authorized and empowered, within their counties respectively, to appoint, in writing, under their hands, any one or more suitable persons, from time to time, to execute all such warrants and other process as may be issued by them in the lawful performance of their respective duties; and the persons so appointed to execute any warrant or process as aforesaid shall have authority to summon and call to their aid the bystanders or posse comitatus of the proper county, or such portion of the land or naval forces of the United States, or of the militia, as may be necessary to the performance of the duty with which they are charged, and to insure a faithful observance of the clause of the Constitution which prohibits slavery, in conformity with the provisions of this act; and said warrants shall run and be executed by said officers anywhere in the State or Territory within which they are issued.

Sec. 6. And be it further enacted, That any person who shall knowingly and willfully obstruct, hinder, or prevent any officer, or other person charged with the execution of any warrant or process issued under the provisions of this act, or any person or persons lawfully assisting him or them, from arresting any person for whose apprehension such warrant or process may have been issued, or shall rescue or attempt to rescue such person from the custody of the officer, other person or persons, or those lawfully assisting as aforesaid, when so arrested pursuant to the authority herein given and declared, or shall aid, abet, or assist any person so arrested as aforesaid, directly or indirectly, to escape from the custody of the officer or other person legally authorized as aforesaid, or shall harbor or conceal any person for whose arrest a warrant or process shall have been issued as aforesaid, so as to prevent his discovery and arrest after notice or knowledge of the fact that a warrant has been issued for the apprehension of such person, shall, for either of said offences, be subject to a fine not exceeding one thousand dollars, and imprisonment not exceeding six months, by indictment and conviction before the district court of the United States for the district in which said offence may have been committed, or before the proper court of criminal jurisdiction, if committed within any one of the organized Territories of the United States.

Sec. 7. And be it further enacted, That the district attorneys, the marshals, their deputies, and the clerks of the said district and territorial courts shall be paid for their services the like fees as may be allowed to them for similar services in other cases; and in all cases where the proceedings are before a commissioner, he shall be entitled to a fee of ten dollars in full for his services in each case, inclusive of all services incident to such arrest and examination. The person or persons authorized to execute the process to be issued by such commissioners for the arrest of offenders against the provisions of this act shall be entitled to a fee of five dollars for each person he or they may arrest and take before any such commissioner as aforesaid, with such other fees as may be deemed reasonable by such commissioner for such other additional services as may be necessarily performed by him or them, such as attending at the examination, keeping the prisoner in custody, and providing him with food and lodging during his detention, and until the final determination of such commissioner, and in general for performing such other duties as may be required in the premises; such fees to be made up in conformity with the fees usually charged by the officers of the courts of justice within the proper district or county, as near as may be practicable, and paid out of the Treasury of the United States on the certificate of the judge of the district within which the arrest is made, and to be recoverable from the defendant as part of the judgment in case of conviction.

Sec. 8. And be it further enacted, That whenever the President of the United States shall have reason to believe that offences have been or are likely to be committed against the provisions of this act within any judicial district, it shall be lawful for him, in his discretion, to direct the judge, marshal, and district attorney of such district to attend at such place within the district, and for such time as he may designate, for the purpose of the more speedy arrest and trial of persons charged with a violation of this act; and it shall be the duty of every judge or other officer, when any such requisition shall be received by him, to attend at the place and for the time therein designated.

Sec. 9. And be it further enacted, That it shall be lawful for the President of the United States, or such person as he may empower for that purpose, to employ such part of the land or naval forces of the United States, or of the militia, as shall be necessary to prevent the violation and enforce the due execution of this act.

Sec. 10. And be it further enacted, That upon all questions of law arising in any cause under the provisions of this act a final appeal may be taken to the Supreme Court of the United States.

SCHUYLER COLFAX, Speaker of the House of Representatives.

LA FAYETTE S. FOSTER, President of the Senate, pro tempore.

In the Senate of the United States, April 6, 1866

*Source:* Civil Rights Act of 1866, 14 Stat. 27–30 (1866).

# MILITARY RECONSTRUCTION ACTS (1867–1868)

*Congressional Reconstruction (or "Radical Reconstruction") began on March 2, 1867, when Congress overrode President Andrew Johnson's same-day veto of the First Military Reconstruction Act. Supplemental acts passed by the following Congress attempted to plug loopholes in the initial measure. From this point on, the Republican Party and Congress directed Reconstruction. The acts began a total political restructuring of 10 of the 11 former Confederate states (Tennessee had already been readmitted to the Union). The acts imposed radical elements, including stringent measures for readmission, broad disfranchisement of former confederates, new state constitutions, military supervision of all civil officials, and African American male voting, but certain moderate characteristics existed. For instance, the acts did not displace Johnson's governments outright nor did they call for land confiscation or territorial and geographic adjustments. Nevertheless, these measures resulted in actions and reactions that defined Reconstruction for the next decade.*

## Act of March 2, 1867

Reconstruction Act of the Thirty-Ninth Congress

An Act to provide for the more efficient government of the rebel states. Whereas no legal State governments or adequate protection for life or property now exist in the rebel States of Virginia, North Carolina, South Carolina, Georgia, Mississippi, Alabama, Louisiana, Florida, Texas, and Arkansas; and whereas it is necessary that peace and good order should be enforced in said States until loyal and republican State governments can be legally established: Therefore

Be it enacted, &c., That said rebel States shall be divided into military districts and made subject to the military authority of the United States, as hereinafter prescribed, and for that purpose Virginia shall constitute the first district; North Carolina and South Carolina the second district; Georgia, Alabama, and Florida the third district; Mississippi and Arkansas the fourth district; and Louisiana and Texas the fifth district.

Sec. 2. That it shall be the duty of the President to assign to the command of each of said districts an officer of the army, not below the rank of brigadier general, and to detail a sufficient military force to enable such officer to perform his duties and enforce his authority within the district to which he is assigned.

Sec. 3. That it shall be the duty of each officer assigned as aforesaid to protect all persons in their rights of person and property, to suppress insurrection, disorder, and violence, and to punish, or cause to be punished, all disturbers of the public peace and criminals, and to this end he may allow local civil tribunals to take jurisdiction of and to try offenders, or, when in his judgment it may be necessary for the trial of offenders, he shall have power to organize military commissions or tribunals for that purpose; and all interference under color of State authority with the exercise of military authority under this act shall be null and void.

Sec. 4. That all persons put under military arrest by virtue of this act shall be tried without unnecessary delay, and no cruel or unusual punishment shall be inflicted; and no sentence of any military commission or tribunal hereby authorized, affecting the life or liberty of any person, shall be executed until it is approved by the officer in command of the district, and the laws and regulations for the government of the army shall not be affected by this act, except in so far as they conflict with its provisions: Provided, That no sentence of death under the provisions of this act shall be carried into effect without the approval of the President.

Sec. 5. That when the people of any one of said rebel States shall have formed a constitution of government in conformity with the Constitution of the United States in all respects, framed by a convention of delegates elected by the male citizens of said State twenty-one years old and upward, of whatever race, color, or previous condition, who have been resident in said State for one year previous to the day of such election, except such as may be disfranchised for participation in the rebellion, or for felony at common law, and when such constitution shall provide that the elective franchise shall be enjoyed by all such persons as have the qualifications herein stated for electors of delegates, and when such constitution shall be ratified by a majority of the persons voting on the question of ratification who are qualified as electors for delegates, and when such constitution shall have been submitted to Congress for examination and approval, and Congress shall have approved the same, and when said State, by a vote of its legislature elected under said constitution, shall have adopted the amendment to the Constitution of the United States, proposed by the Thirty-Ninth Congress, and known as article fourteen, and when said article shall have become a part of the Constitution of the United States, said State shall be declared entitled to representation in Congress, and Senators and Representatives shall be admitted therefrom on their taking the oaths prescribed by law, and then and thereafter the preceding sections of this act shall be inoperative in said State: Provided, That no person excluded from the privilege of holding office by said proposed amendment to the Constitution of the United States shall be eligible to election as a member of the convention to frame a constitution for any of said rebel States, nor shall any such person vote for members of such convention.

Sec. 6. That until the people of said rebel states shall be by law admitted to representation in the Congress of the United States, any civil governments which may exist therein shall be deemed provisional only, and in all respects subject to the paramount authority of the United States at any time to abolish, modify, control, or supersede the same; and in all elections to any office under such provisional governments all persons shall be entitled to vote, and none others, who are entitled to vote under the provisions of the fifth section of this act; and no person shall be eligible to any office under any such provisional governments who would be disqualified from holding office under the provisions of the third article of said constitutional amendment.

## Act of March 23, 1867

Supplementary Reconstruction Act of Fortieth Congress, An Act supplementary to an act entitled "An act to provide for the more efficient government of the rebel states," passed March second, eighteen hundred and sixty-seven, and to facilitate restoration.

Be it enacted, &c., That before the first day of September, eighteen hundred and sixty-seven, the commanding general in each district defined by an act entitled "An Act to provide for the more efficient government of the rebel States," passed March second, eighteen hundred and sixty-seven, shall cause a registration to be made of the male citizens of the United States, twenty-one years of age and upwards, resident in each county or parish in the State or States included in his district, which registration shall include only those persons who are qualified to vote for delegates by the act aforesaid, and who shall have taken and subscribed the following oath or affirmation: "I, do solemnly swear, (or affirm,) in the presence of Almighty God, that I am a citizen of the State of ; that I have resided in said State for months next preceding this day, and now reside in the county of, or the parish of, in said State, (as the case may be) that I am twenty-one years old; that I have not been disfranchised for participation in any rebellion or civil war against the United States, nor for felony committed against the laws of any State or of the United States; that I have never been a member of any State legislature, nor held any executive or judicial office in any State and afterwards engaged in insurrection or rebellion against the United States, or given aid or comfort to the enemies thereof; that I have never taken an oath as a member of Congress of the United States, or as an officer of the United States, or as a member of any State legislature, or as an executive or judicial officer of any State, to support the Constitution of the United States, and afterwards engaged in insurrection or rebellion against the United States or given aid or comfort to the enemies thereof; that I will faithfully support the Constitution and obey the laws of the United States, and will, to the best of my ability, encourage others so to do, so help me God;" which oath or affirmation may be administered by any registering officer.

Sec. 2. That after the completion of the registration hereby provided for in any State, at such time and places therein as the commanding general shall appoint and direct, of which at least thirty days' public notice shall be given, an election shall be held of delegates to a convention for the purpose of establishing a constitution and civil government for such state loyal to the Union, said convention in each State, except Virginia, to consist of the same number of members as the most numerous branch of the State legislature of such State in the year eighteen hundred and sixty, to be apportioned among the several districts, counties, or parishes of such State by the commanding general, giving to each representation in the ratio of voters registered as aforesaid, as nearly as may be. The convention in Virginia shall consist of the same number of members as represented the territory now constituting Virginia in the most numerous branch of the legislature of said State in the year eighteen hundred and sixty, to be apportioned as aforesaid.

Sec. 3. That at said election the registered voters of each State shall vote for or against a convention to form a constitution therefor under this act. Those voting in favor of such a convention shall have written or printed on the ballots by which they vote for delegates, as aforesaid, the words "For a convention," and those voting against such a convention shall have written or printed on such ballots the words "Against a convention." The person appointed to superintend said election, and to make return of the votes given thereat, as herein provided, shall count and make return of the votes given for and against a convention; and the commanding general to whom the same shall have been returned shall ascertain and declare the total vote in each State for and against a convention. If a majority of the votes given on that question shall be for a convention, then such convention shall be held as hereinafter provided; but if a majority of said votes shall be against a convention, then no such convention shall be held under this act: Provided, That such convention shall not be held unless a majority of all such registered voters shall have voted on the question of holding such convention.

Sec. 4. That the commanding general of each district shall appoint as many boards of registration as may be necessary, consisting of three loyal officers or persons, to make and complete the registration, superintend the election, and make return to him of the votes, lists of voters, and of the persons elected as delegates by a plurality of the votes cast at said election; and upon receiving said returns he shall open the same, ascertain the persons elected as delegates according to the returns of the officers who conducted said election, and make proclamation thereof; and if a majority of the votes given on that question shall be for a convention, the commanding general, within sixty days from the date of election, shall notify the delegates to assemble in convention, at a time and place to be mentioned in the notification, and said convention, when organized, shall proceed to frame a constitution and civil government according to the provisions of this act and the act to which is it [sic] supplementary; and when the same shall have been so framed, said constitution shall be submitted by the convention for ratification to the persons registered under the provisions of this act at an election to be conducted by the officers or persons appointed or to be appointed by the commanding general, as hereinbefore provided, and to be held after the expiration of thirty days from the date of notice thereof, to be given by said convention; and the returns thereof shall be made to the commanding general of the district.

Sec. 5. That if, according to said returns, the constitution shall be ratified by a majority of the votes of the registered electors qualified as herein specified, cast at said election, (at least one half of all the registered voters voting upon the question of such ratification,) the president of the convention shall transmit a copy of the same, duly certified, to the President of the United States, who shall forthwith transmit the same to Congress, if then in session, and if not in session, then immediately upon its next assembling; and if it shall, moreover, appear to Congress that the election was one at which all the registered and qualified electors in the State had an opportunity to vote freely and without restraint, fear, or the influence of fraud, and if the Congress shall be satisfied that such constitution meets the approval of a majority of all the qualified electors in the State, and if the said constitution shall be declared by Congress to be in conformity with the provisions of the act to which this is supplementary, and the other provisions of said act shall have been complied with, and the said constitution shall be approved by Congress, the State shall be declared entitled to representation, and Senators and Representatives shall be admitted there from as therein provided.

Sec. 6. That all elections in the States mentioned in the said "Act to provide for the more efficient government of the rebel States," shall, during the operation of said act, be by ballot; and all officers making the said registration of voters and conducting said elections shall, before entering upon the discharge of their duties, take and subscribe the oath prescribed by the act approved July second, eighteen hundred and sixty-two, entitled "An act to prescribe an oath of office:" Provided, That if any person shall knowingly and falsely take and subscribe any oath in this act prescribed, such person so offending and being thereof duly convicted, shall be subject to the pains, penalties, and disabilities which by law are provided for the punishment of the crime of willful and corrupt perjury.

Sec. 7. That all expenses incurred by the several commanding generals, or by virtue of any orders issued, or appointments made, by them, under or by virtue of this act, shall be paid out of any moneys in the treasury not otherwise appropriated.

Sec. 8. That the convention for each State shall prescribe the fees, salary, and compensation to be paid to all delegates and other officers and agents herein authorized or necessary to carry into effect the purposes of this act not herein otherwise provided for, and shall provide for the levy and collection of such taxes on the property in such State as may be necessary to pay the same.

Sec. 9. That the word article, in the sixth section of the act to which this is supplementary, shall be construed to mean section.

## Act of July 19, 1867

Supplementary Reconstruction Act of July 19, 1867

An Act supplementary to an act entitled "An Act to provide for the more efficient government of the rebel states," passed on the second day of March, 1867, and the act supplementary thereto, passed on the 23d day of March, 1867.

Be it enacted, &c., That it is hereby declared to have been the true intent and meaning of the act of the 2d day of March, 1867, entitled "An act to provide for the more efficient government of the rebel States," and of the act supplementary thereto, passed on the 23d day of March, 1867, that the governments then existing in the rebel States of Virginia, North Carolina, South Carolina, Georgia, Mississippi, Alabama, Louisiana, Florida, Texas, and Arkansas, were not legal State governments; and that thereafter said governments, if continued, were to be continued subject in all respects to the military commanders of the respective districts, and to the paramount authority of Congress.

Sec. 2. That the commander of any district named in said act shall have power, subject to the disapproval of the General of the army of the United States, and to have effect till disapproved, whenever in the opinion of such commander the proper administration of said act shall require it, to suspend or remove from office, or from the performance of official duties and the exercise of official powers, any officer or person holding or exercising, or professing to hold or exercise, any civil or military office or duty in such district under any power, election, appointment, or authority derived from, or granted by, or claimed under, any so-called State or the government thereof, or any municipal or other division thereof; and upon such suspension or removal such commander, subject to the disapproval of the General as aforesaid, shall have power to provide from time to time for the performance of the said duties of such officer or person so suspended or removed, by the detail of some competent officer or soldier of the army, or by the appointment of some other person to perform the same, and to fill vacancies occasioned by death, resignation, or otherwise.

Sec. 3. That the General of the army of the United States shall be invested with all the powers of suspension, removal, appointment, and detail granted in the preceding section to district commanders.

Sec. 4. That the acts of the officers of the army already done in removing in said districts persons exercising the functions of civil officers, and appointing others in their stead, are hereby confirmed: Provided, That any person heretofore or hereafter appointed by any district commander to exercise the functions of any civil office, may be removed either by the military officer in command of the district, or by the General of the army. And it shall be the duty of such commander to remove from office, as aforesaid, all persons who are disloyal to the Government of the United States, or who use their official influence in any manner to hinder, delay, prevent, or obstruct the due and proper administration of this act and the acts to which it is supplementary.

Sec. 5. That the boards of registration provided for in the act entitled "An act supplementary to an act entitled 'An act to provide for the more efficient government of the rebel States,' passed March 2, 1867, and to facilitate restoration," passed March 23, 1867, shall have power, and it shall be their duty, before allowing the registration of any person, to ascertain, upon such facts or information as they can obtain, whether such person is entitled to be registered under said act, and the oath required by said act shall not be conclusive on such question, and no person shall be registered unless such board shall decide that he is entitled thereto; and such board shall also have power to examine, under oath, (to be administered by any member of such board,) any one touching the qualification of any person claiming registration; but in every case of refusal by the board to register an applicant, and in every case of striking his name from the list as hereinafter provided, the board shall make a note or memorandum, which shall be returned with the registration list to the commanding general of the district, setting forth the grounds of such refusal or such striking from the list: Provided, That no person shall be disqualified as member of any board of registration by reason of race or color.

Sec. 6. That the true intent and meaning of the oath prescribed in said supplementary act is, (among other things,) that no person who has been a member of the Legislature of any State, or who has held any executive or judicial office in any State, whether he has taken an oath to support the Constitution of the United States or not, and whether he was holding such office at the commencement of the rebellion, or had held it before, and who has afterwards engaged in insurrection or rebellion against the United States, or given aid or comfort to the enemies thereof, is entitled to be registered or to vote; and the words "executive or judicial office in any State" in said oath mentioned shall be construed to include all civil offices created by law for the administration of any general law of a State, or for the administration of justice.

Sec. 7. That the time for completing the original registration provided for in said act may, in the discretion of the commander of any district, be extended to the 1st day of October, 1867; and the boards of registration shall have power, and it shall be their duty, commencing fourteen days prior to any election under said act, and upon reasonable public notice of the time and place thereof, to revise, for a period of five days, the registration lists, and, upon being satisfied that any person not entitled thereto has been registered, to strike the name of such person from the list, and such person shall not be allowed to vote. And such board shall also, during the same period, add to such registry the names of all persons who at that time possess the qualifications required by said act who have not been already registered; and no person shall, at any time, be entitled to be registered or to vote, by reason of any executive pardon or amnesty, for any act or thing which, without such pardon or amnesty, would disqualify him from registration or voting.

Sec. 8. That section four of said last-named act shall be construed to authorize the commanding general named therein, whenever he shall deem it needful, to remove any member of a board of registration and to appoint another in his stead, and to fill any vacancy in such board.

Sec. 9. That all members of said boards of registration, and all persons hereafter elected or appointed to office in said military districts, under any so-called State or municipal authority, or by detail or appointment of the district commanders, shall be required to take and to subscribe the oath of office prescribed by law for officers of the United States.

Sec. 10. That no district commander or member of the board of registration, or any of the officers or appointees acting under them, shall be bound in his action by any opinion of any civil officer of the United States.

Sec. 11. That all the provisions of this act and of the acts to which this is supplementary shall be construed liberally, to the end that all the intents thereof may be fully and perfectly carried out.

*Source:* Military Reconstruction Acts of 1867. March 2, 1867, 14 Stat. 428–430, c.153; March 23, 1867, 15 Stat. 2–5, c.6; July 19, 1867.

# FOURTEENTH AMENDMENT TO THE U.S. CONSTITUTION (RATIFIED JULY 28, 1868)

*One of the most complex and controversial amendments, the Fourteenth Amendment was Congress's attempt to protect civil rights legislation from presidential vetoes or future congressional revocations. As passed in 1866, the Fourteenth Amendment represented another compromise for Republicans, as it completely redefined citizenship in the United States, yet stopped well short of defining exactly what that citizenship entailed. Similarly, the amendment was the first national projection of black suffrage, but did not actively confer it; instead, it linked black voting to congressional representation in an effort to encourage state action. Congressional Republicans hoped it could be the "peace treaty" ending the rebellion and Reconstruction, for ratification by the Johnson governments in the former Confederate states brought readmission to the Union. In the end, only Tennessee ratified the amendment—and became the first state readmitted. The rejection of the amendment by the other southern states marked the final break between Congress and the president, and those 10 states faced an entirely new program for readmission. Only under the Southern Republican governments created by the Military Reconstruction Acts did the amendment finally gain enough state support to become part of the Constitution.*

## Article XIV

Section 1: All persons born or naturalized in the United States, and subject to the jurisdiction thereof, are citizens of the United States and of the State wherein they reside. No State shall make or enforce any law which shall abridge the privileges or immunities of citizens of the United States; nor shall any State deprive any person of life, liberty, or property, without due process of law; nor deny to any person within its jurisdiction the equal protection of the laws.

Section 2: Representatives shall be apportioned among the several States according to their respective numbers, counting the whole number of persons in each State, excluding Indians not taxed. But when the right to vote at any election for the choice of electors for President and Vice President of the United States, Representatives in Congress, the Executive and Judicial officers of a State, or the members of the Legislature thereof, is denied to any of the male inhabitants of such States, being twenty-one years of age, and citizens of the United States, or in any way abridged, except for participation in rebellion, or other crime, the basis of representation therein shall be reduced in the proportion which the number of such male citizens shall bear to the whole number of male citizens twenty-one years of age in such State.

Section 3: No person shall be a Senator or Representative in Congress, or elector of President or Vice President, or hold any office, civil or military, under the United States, or under any State, who, having previously taken an oath, as a member of Congress, or as an officer of the United States, or as a member of any State legislature, or as an executive or judicial officer of any State, to support the Constitution of the United States, shall have engaged in insurrection or rebellion against the same, or given aid or comfort to the enemies thereof. But Congress may by a vote of two-thirds of each House, remove such disability.

Section 4: The validity of the public debt of the United States, authorized by law, including debts incurred for payment of pensions and bounties for services in suppressing insurrection or rebellion, shall not be questioned. But neither the United States nor any State shall assume or pay any debt or obligation incurred in aid of insurrection or rebellion against the United States, or any claim for the loss or emancipation of any slave; but all such debts, obligations and claims shall be held illegal and void.

Section 5: The Congress shall have power to enforce, by appropriate legislation, the provisions of this article.

*Source:* The House Joint Resolution proposing the 14th amendment to the Constitution, June 16, 1866. Enrolled Acts and Resolutions of Congress, 1789–1999. General Records of the United States Government, Record Group 11, National Archives.

# ARTICLES OF IMPEACHMENT AGAINST PRESIDENT ANDREW JOHNSON (FEBRUARY 21, 1868)

*On February 24, 1868, the House of Representatives voted 128–47 to impeach President Johnson for "high crimes and misdemeanors." No formal charges actually existed, so Speaker Schuyler Colfax requested that a committee draw some up. Called the "articles of impeachment," they were formally adopted on March 3, and then backdated to the 21st, the day the Committee on Reconstruction introduced the impeachment resolution. These 11 articles served as the House's accusations against Johnson, and formed the case taken by the impeachment managers into the Senate trial. The first eight revolved around Johnson's alleged violation of the Tenure of Office Act. Article IX involved the Army Appropriations Act, Article X (written by Benjamin Butler) charged Johnson with publicly ridiculing Congress, and Article XI (written by Thaddeus Stevens) accused him of failing to execute the law—and thus his duties—by interfering with the Reconstruction Acts. After the prosecution and defense rested, the Senate voted on Article XI first, believing it the most likely to bring conviction. When that failed, the Senate took up Article II, hoping it best summarized the Tenure Act crisis; this too failed, and with it, the case against Johnson.*

Articles were exhibited by the House of Representatives of the United States in their name and all the people of the United States, against Andrew Johnson, president of the United States, in maintenance and support of their impeachment against him for high crimes and misdemeanors in office.

## Article I

That said Andrew Johnson, President of the United States, on the 21st day of February, in the year of our Lord eighteen hundred and sixty-eight, at Washington, in the District of Columbia, unmindful of the high duties of his office, of his oath of office, and of the requirement of the Constitution that he should take care that the laws be faithfully executed, did unlawfully, and in violation of the Constitution and laws of the United States issue an order in writing for the removal of Edwin M. Stanton from the office of Secretary for the Department of War, said Edwin M. Stanton having been theretofore duly appointed and commissioned by and with the advice and consent of the Senate of the United States, as such secretary, and said Andrew Johnson, President of the United States, on the twelfth day of August in the year of our Lord eighteen hundred and sixty-seven, and during the recess of said Senate, having suspended by his order Edwin M. Stanton from said office, and within twenty days after the first day of the next meeting of said Senate, that is to say, on the twelfth day of December in the year last aforesaid having reported to said Senate such suspension with the evidence and reasons for his action in the case and the name of the person designated to perform the duties of such office temporarily until the next meeting of the Senate, and said Senate there afterwards, on the thirteenth day of January, in the year of our Lord eighteen hundred and sixty-eight, having duly considered the evidence and reasons reported by said Andrew Johnson for said suspension, and having refused to concur in said suspension, whereby and by force of the provisions of an act entitled "An Act regulating the tenure of certain civil offices," passed March second, eighteen hundred and sixty-seven, said Edwin M. Stanton did forthwith resume the functions of his office, whereof the said Andrew Johnson had then and there due notice, and said Edwin M. Stanton, by reason of the premises, on said 21st day of February, being lawfully entitled to hold said office of Secretary for the Department of War, which said order for the removal of said Edwin M. Stanton is in substance as follows, that is to say:

EXECUTIVE MANSION, WASHINGTON, D.C., FEB. 21, 1868.

Sir:—By virtue of the power and authority vested in me as President by the Constitution and laws of the United States you are hereby removed from office as Secretary for the Department of War, and your functions as such will terminate upon the receipt of this communication. You will transfer to Brevet Major General Lorenzo Thomas, Adjutant General of the army, who has this day been authorized and empowered to act as Secretary of War ad interim, all records. books, papers, and other public property now in your custody and charge.

*Respectfully yours, Andrew Johnson.*
*To the Hon. Edwin M. Stanton, Washington, D.C.*

Which order was unlawfully issued with intent then and there to violate the act entitled "An Act regulating the tenure of certain civil offices," passed March 2d, 1867, and with the further intent contrary to the provisions of said act, in violation thereof, and contrary to the provisions of the Constitution of the United States, and without the advice and consent of the Senate of the

United States, the said Senate then and there being in session, to remove said Edwin M. Stanton from the office of Secretary for the Department of War, the said Edwin M. Stanton being then and there Secretary for the Department of War, and being then and there in the due and lawful execution and discharge of the duties of said office, whereby said Andrew Johnson, President of the United States, did then and there commit and was guilty of a high misdemeanor in office.

## Article II

That on the said twenty-first of February, in the year of our Lord one thousand eight hundred and sixty-eight, at Washington, in the District of Columbia, said Andrew Johnson, President of the United States, unmindful of the high duties of his office, of his oath of office, and in violation of the Constitution of the United States, and contrary to the provisions of an act entitled "An act regulating the tenure of certain civil offices," passed March second, eighteen hundred and sixty-seven, without the advice and consent of the Senate of the United States, said Senate then and there being in session, and without authority of law, did, with intent to violate the Constitution of the United States, and the act aforesaid, issue and deliver to one Lorenzo Thomas a letter of authority in substance as follows, that is to say:

EXECUTIVE MANSION. WASHINGTON, D.C., FEBRUARY 21, 1868.

Sir:—The Hon. Edwin M. Stanton having been this day removed from office as Secretary for the Department of War, you are hereby authorized and empowered to act as Secretary of War ad interim, and will immediately enter upon the discharge of the duties pertaining to that office. Mr. Stanton has been instructed to transfer to you all the records, books, papers, and other public property now in his custody and charge.

*Respectfully yours, Andrew Johnson. To Brevet Major General Lorenzo Thomas. Adjutant General U.S. Army, Washington, D.C.*

Then and there being no vacancy in said office of Secretary for the Department of War, whereby said Andrew Johnson, President of the United States, did then and there commit and was guilty of a high misdemeanor in office.

## Article III

That said Andrew Johnson, President of the United States, on the twenty-first day of February, in the year of our Lord one thousand eight hundred and sixty-eight, at Washington, in the District of Columbia, did commit and was guilty of a high misdemeanor in office in this, that, without authority of law, while the Senate of the United States was then and there in session, he did appoint one Lorenzo Thomas to be Secretary for the Department of War ad interim, without the advice and consent of the Senate, and with intent to violate the Constitution of the United States, and no vacancy having happened in said office of Secretary for the Department of War during the recess of the Senate, and no vacancy existing in said office at the time, and which said appointment, so made by said Andrew Johnson, of said Lorenzo Thomas, is in substance as follows, that is to say:

EXECUTIVE MANSION, WASHINGTON, D.C., FEB. 21, 1868.

Sir:—The Hon. Edwin M. Stanton having been this day removed from office as Secretary for the Department of War, you are hereby authorized and empowered to act as Secretary of War ad interim, and will immediately enter upon the discharge of the duties pertaining to that office. Mr. Stanton has been instructed to transfer to you all the records, books, papers, and other public property now in his custody and charge.

*Respectfully yours, Andrew Johnson. To Brevet Major General Lorenzo Thomas, Adjutant General, U.S. Army, Washington, D.C.*

## Article IV

That said Andrew Johnson, President of the United States, unmindful of the high duties of his office and of his oath of office, in violation of the Constitution and laws of the United States, on the twenty-first day of February, in the year of our Lord one thousand eight hundred and sixty-eight, at Washington, in the District of Columbia, did unlawfully conspire with one Lorenzo Thomas, and with other persons to the House of Representatives unknown, with intent, by intimidation and threats, unlawfully to hinder and prevent Edwin M. Stanton, then and there the Secretary for the Department of War, duly appointed under the laws of the United States, from holding said office of Secretary for the Department of War, contrary to and in violation of the

Constitution of the United States, and of the provisions of an act entitled "An act to define and punish certain conspiracies," approved July thirty-first, eighteen hundred and sixty-one, whereby said Andrew Johnson, President of the United States, did then and there commit and was guilty of a high crime in office.

## Article V

That said Andrew Johnson, President of the United States, unmindful of the high duties of his office and of his oath of office, on the twenty-first day of February, in the year of our Lord one thousand eight hundred and sixty-eight, and on divers other days and times in said year, before the second day of March, in the year, of our Lord one thousand eight hundred and sixty-eight, at Washington, in the District of Columbia, did unlawfully conspire with one Lorenzo Thomas, and with other persons to the House of Representatives unknown, to prevent and hinder the execution of an act entitled "An act regulating the tenure of certain civil offices," passed March second, eighteen hundred and sixty-seven, and in pursuance of said conspiracy, did unlawfully attempt to prevent Edwin M. Stanton, then and there being Secretary for the Department of War, duly appointed and commissioned under the laws of the United States, from holding said office, whereby the said Andrew Johnson, President of the United States, did then and there commit and was guilty of a high misdemeanor in office.

## Article VI

That said Andrew Johnson, President of the United States, unmindful of the high duties of his office and of his oath of office, on the twenty-first day of February, in the year of our Lord one thousand eight hundred and sixty-eight, at Washington, in the District of Columbia, did unlawfully conspire with one Lorenzo Thomas by force to seize, take and possess the property of the United States in the Department of War, and then and there in the custody and charge of Edwin M. Stanton, Secretary for said Department, contrary to the provisions of an act entitled "An act to define and punish certain conspiracies," approved July thirty-one, eighteen hundred and sixty one, and with intent to violate and disregard an act entitled "An act regulating the tenure of certain civil offices," passed March second, eighteen hundred and sixty-seven, whereby said Andrew Johnson, President of the United States, did then and there commit a high crime in office.

## Article VII

That said Andrew Johnson, President of the United States, unmindful of the high duties of his office and of his oath of office, on the twenty-first day of February, in the year of our Lord one thousand eight hundred and sixty-eight, at Washington. in the District of Columbia, did unlawfully conspire with one Lorenzo Thomas with intent unlawfully to seize, take, and possess the property of the United States in the Department of War, in the custody and charge of Edwin M. Stanton Secretary for said Department, with intent to violate and disregard the act entitled "An act regulating the tenure of certain civil offices" passed March second, eighteen hundred and sixty-seven, whereby said Andrew Johnson, President of the United States, did then and there commit a high misdemeanor in office.

## Article VIII

That said Andrew Johnson, President of the United States, unmindful of the high duties of his office and of his oath of office, with intent unlawfully to control the disbursements of the moneys appropriated for the military service and for the Department of War, on the twenty-first day of February, in the year of our Lord one thousand eight hundred and sixty-eight, at Washington, in the District of Columbia, did unlawfully and contrary to the provisions of an act entitled "An act regulating the tenure of certain civil offices," passed March second, eighteen hundred and sixty-seven, and in violation of the Constitution of the United States, and without the advice and consent of the Senate of the United States, and while the Senate was then and there in session, there being no vacancy in the office of Secretary for the Department of War, and with intent to violate and disregard the act aforesaid, [did] then and there issue and deliver to one Lorenzo Thomas a letter of authority in writing, in substance as follows, that is to say:

EXECUTIVE MANSION, WASHINGTON, D.C., FEB. 21, 1868.
Sir:—The Hon. Edwin M. Stanton having been this day removed from office as Secretary for the Department of War, you are hereby authorized and empowered to act as Secretary of War ad interim, and will immediately enter upon the discharge of the duties pertaining to that office. Mr. Stanton has been instructed to transfer to you all the records, books, papers, and other public property now in his custody and charge. Respectfully yours, Andrew Johnson. To Brevet Major General Lorenzo Thomas, Adjutant General, United States Army, Washington, D.C. Whereby said Andrew Johnson, President of the United States, did then and there commit and was guilty of a high misdemeanor in office.

## Article IX

That said Andrew Johnson, President of the United States, on the twenty second day of February, in the year of our Lord one thousand eight hundred and sixty-eight, at Washington, in the District of Columbia, in disregard of the Constitution, and the laws of the United States duly enacted, as commander-in-chief of the army of the United States, did bring before himself then and there William H. Emory, a major-general by brevet in the army of the United States, actually in command of the department of Washington and the military forces thereof, and did then and there, as such commander-in-chief, declare to and instruct said Emory that part of a law of the United States, passed March second, eighteen hundred and sixty-seven entitled "An act making appropriations for the support of the army for the year ending June thirtieth, eighteen hundred and sixty-eight and for other purposes," especially the second section thereof, which provides, among other things, that "all orders and instructions relating to military operations issued by the President or Secretary of War, shall be issued through the General of the army, and, in case of his inability, through the next in rank," was unconstitutional, and in contravention of the commission of said Emory, and which said provision of law had been theretofore duly and legally promulgated by General Orders for the government and direction of the army of the United States, as the said Andrew Johnson then and there well knew, with intent thereby to induce said Emory, in his official capacity as commander of the department of Washington, to violate the provisions of said act, and to take and receive, act upon, and obey such orders as he, the said Andrew Johnson, might make and give, and which should not be issued through the General of the army of the United States, according to the provisions of said act, and with the further intent thereby to enable him, the said Andrew Johnson, to prevent the execution of the act entitled "An act regulating the tenure of certain civil offices," passed March second eighteen hundred and sixty-seven and to unlawfully prevent Edwin M. Stanton then being Secretary for the Department of War, from holding said office and discharging the duties thereof, whereby said Andrew Johnson, President of the United States, did then and there commit and was guilty of a high misdemeanor in office.

And the House of Representatives by protestation saving to themselves the liberty of exhibiting at any time hereafter any further articles, or other accusation or impeachment against the said Andrew Johnson, President or the United States, and also of replying to his answers which he shall make unto the articles herein preferred against him, and of offering proof to the same, and every part thereof, and to all and every other article, accusation, or impeachment which shall be exhibited by them, as the case shall require, do demand that the said Andrew Johnson may be put to answer the high crimes and misdemeanors in office herein charged against him, and that such proceedings, examinations, trials, and judgments may be thereupon had and given as may be agreeable to law and justice.

## Article X

That said Andrew Johnson, President of the United States, unmindful of the high duties of his office, and the dignity and proprieties thereof, and of the harmony and courtesies which ought to exist and be maintained between the executive and legislative branches of the government of the United States, designing and intending to set aside the rightful authority and powers of Congress, did attempt to bring into disgrace, ridicule, hatred, contempt and reproach, the Congress of the United States, and the several branches thereof, to impair and destroy the regard and respect of all the good people of the United States for the Congress and legislative powers thereof, (which all officers of the government ought inviolably to preserve and maintain,) and to excite the odium and resentment of all the good people of the United States against Congress and the laws by it duly and constitutionally enacted; and in pursuance of his said design and intent, openly and publicly, and before divers assemblages of the citizens of the United States, convened in divers parts thereof to meet and receive said Andrew Johnson as the Chief Magistrate of the United States, did, on the eighteenth day of August, in the year of our Lord one thousand eight hundred and sixty-six, and on divers other days and times, as well before as afterward, make and deliver, with a loud voice, certain intemperate, inflammatory, and scandalous harangues, and did therein utter loud threats and bitter menaces. as well against Congress as the laws of the United States duly enacted thereby, amid the cries, jeers, and laughter of the multitudes then assembled and in hearing.

## Article XI

That said Andrew Johnson, President of the United States, unmindful of the high duties of his office, and of his oath of office, and in disregard of the Constitution and laws of the United States, did, heretofore, to wit, on the eighteenth day of August, A.D. eighteen hundred and sixty-six, at the City of Washington, and the District of Columbia, by public speech, declare and affirm, in substance, that the thirty-ninth Congress of the United States was not a Congress of the United States authorized by the Constitution to exercise legislative power under the same, but, on the contrary, was a Congress of only part of the States, thereby denying, and intending to deny, that the legislation of said Congress was valid or obligatory upon him, the said Andrew Johnson, except in so far as he saw fit to approve the same, and also thereby denying, and intending to deny, the power of the said thirty-ninth Congress to propose amendments to the Constitution of the United States; and, in pursuance of said declaration, the said Andrew Johnson, President of the United States, afterwards, to-wit, on the twenty first day of February, A.D. eighteen hundred and sixty-eight, at the city of Washington, in the District of Columbia, did, unlawfully, and in disregard of the requirements of the Constitution that he should take care that the laws be faithfully executed, attempt to prevent the execution of an act entitled "An act regulating the tenure of certain civil offices," passed March second, eighteen hundred and sixty-seven, by unlawfull devising and contriving, and attempting to devise and contrive means by which he should prevent Edwin M. Stanton from forthwith resuming the functions of the office of Secretary for the Department of War, notwithstanding the refusal of the Senate to concur in the suspension theretofore made by said Andrew Johnson of said Edwin M. Stanton from said office of Secretary for the Department of War; and, also, by further unlawfully devising and contriving, and attempting to devise and contrive means, then and there, to prevent the execution of an act entitled "An act making appropriations for the support of the army for the fiscal year ending June thirtieth, eighteen hundred and sixty-eight, and for other purposes," approved March second, eighteen hundred and sixty-seven; and also, to prevent the execution of an act entitled "An act to provide for the more efficient government of the rebel States," passed March second, eighteen hundred and sixty-seven, whereby the said Andrew Johnson, President of the United States, did then, to wit, on the twenty-first day of February, A.D. eighteen hundred and sixty-eight, at the city of Washington, commit, and was guilty of, a high misdemeanor in office.

Schuyler Colfax,

Speaker of the House of Representatives.

Attest: Edward McPherson,

Clerk of the House of Representatives.

*Source:* Ross, Edmund G. *History of the Impeachment of Andrew Johnson.* New York: Burt Franklin, 1868, 79–84.

## SAMPLE CONSTITUTION UNDER CONGRESSIONAL RECONSTRUCTION, TEXAS (1869)

*As mentioned above, Texas had its "Congressional Reconstruction" constitution submitted for a statewide referendum. With only minor edits, that new constitution is published below. Note its "radical" and progressive aspects, including equality before the law, universal male suffrage, free public education, government homesteads, and the nullification of all acts while Texas was in the Confederacy, but the constitution is moderate as well. For instance, this version eliminated the controversial proposal to disfranchise former confederates. With a small black population, Republicans recognized that the state party needed white allies to survive.*

The constitution of the State of Texas, adopted by the convention, and to be submitted to a vote of the people at a time to be indicated by the President, contains in the preamble an acknowledgment, with gratitude, of the grace of God in permitting them to make a choice of our form of government.

In the bill of rights are these declarations:

That the heresies of nullification and secession, which brought the country to grief, may be eliminated from political discussion, that public order may be restored, private property and human life protected, and the great principles of liberty and equality secured to us and our posterity, we declare that—

The Constitution of the United States, and the laws and treaties made and to be made in pursuance thereof, are acknowledged to be the supreme law; that this constitution is framed in harmony with and in subordination thereto; and that the fundamental principles embodied herein can only be changed subject to the national authority.

All freemen, when they form a social compact, have equal rights, and no man or set of men is entitled to exclusive separate public emoluments or privileges.

No law shall be passed depriving a party of any remedy of the enforcement of a contract which existed when the contract was made.

No person shall ever be imprisoned for debt.

No citizen of this State shall be deprived of life, liberty, property, or privileges, outlawed, exiled, or in any manner disfranchised, except by due course of the law of the land.

Perpetuities and monopolies are contrary to the genius of a free government, and shall never be allowed; nor shall the law of primogeniture or entailment ever be in force in this State.

The equality of all persons before the law is herein recognized, and shall ever remain inviolate; nor shall any citizen ever be deprived of any right, privilege, or immunity, nor be exempted from any burdens or duty, on account of race, color, or previous condition.

Importation of persons under the name of "coolies," or any other designation, or the adoption of any system of peonage, whereby the helpless and unfortunate may be reduced to partial bondage, shall never be authorized or tolerated by the laws of the State; and neither slavery nor involuntary servitude, except as a punishment for crime, whereof the party shall have been duly convicted, shall ever exist in the State.

Every male person who shall have attained the age of twenty-one years, and who shall be (or who shall have declared his intention to become) a citizen of the United States, or who is at the time of the acceptance of this constitution by the Congress of the United States a citizen of Texas, and shall have resided in the State one year next preceding an election, and the last six months within the district or county in which he offers to vote and is duly registered, (Indians not taxed excepted,) shall be deemed a qualified elector; and should such qualified elector happen to be in any other county, situated in the district in which he resides, at the time of an election, he shall be permitted to vote for any district officer; provided that the qualified elector shall be permitted to vote anywhere in the State for State officers; and provided further, that no soldier, seaman, or marine in the army or navy of the United States shall be entitled to vote at any election created by this constitution.

Senators shall be chosen for six years, and representatives for two. The governor for four.

The legislature shall not authorize any lottery, and shall prohibit the sale of lottery tickets.

It shall be the duty of the legislature to immediately expel from the body any member who shall receive or offer a bribe, or suffer his vote influenced by promise of preferment or reward; and every person so offending and so expelled shall thereafter be disabled from holding any office of honor, trust, or profit in this State.

The legislature shall proceed, as early as practicable, to elect senators to represent this State in the Senate of the United States; and also provide for future elections of representatives to the Congress of the United States; and on the second Tuesday after the first assembling of the legislature after the ratification of this constitution the legislature shall proceed to ratify the XIIIth and XIVth articles of amendment to the Constitution of the United States of America.

The governor may at all times require information in writing from all the officers of the executive department on any subject relating to the duties of their offices, and he shall have a general supervision and control over them. He shall have the power of removal of each of said officers, except the lieutenant governor, for misfeasance, malfeasance, or nonfeasance; but the reasons and causes of such removal shall be communicated in writing by him to the senate at the first meeting of the legislature which occurs after such removal, for its approval or disapproval; if disapproved by the senate, it may restore the displaced incumbent by a vote of that body.

The governor has the veto power, subject to an overriding vote of two-thirds of each House.

The supreme judges to be appointed by the governor, with the approval of the senate, to serve for nine years.

Every male citizen of the United States, of the age of twenty-one years and upwards, not laboring under the disabilities named in this constitution, without distinction of race, color, or former condition, who shall be a resident of this State at the time of the adoption of this constitution, or who shall hereafter reside in this State one year, and in the county in which he offers to vote sixty days next preceding any election, shall be entitled to vote for all officers that are now or hereafter may be elected by the people, and upon all questions submitted to the electors at any election; provided, that no person shall be allowed to vote or hold office who is now or hereafter may be disqualified thereby by the Constitution of the United States, until such disqualification shall be removed by the Congress of the United States; provided, further, that no person while kept in any asylum, or confined in prison, or who has been convicted of felony, or who is of unsound mind, shall be allowed to vote or hold office.

It shall be the duty of the legislature of the State to make suitable provisions for the support and maintenance of a system of public free schools, for the gratuitous instruction of all the inhabitants of this State between the ages of six and eighteen years.

The legislature shall establish a uniform system of public free schools throughout the State.

The legislature at its first session (or as soon thereafter as may be possible) shall pass such laws as will require the attendance on the public free schools of the State of all the scholastic population thereof for the period of at least four months of each and every year; provided, that whenever any of the scholastic inhabitants may be shown to have received regular instruction for said period of time in each and every year from any private teacher having a proper certificate of competency, this shall exempt them for the operation of the laws contemplated by this section.

As a basis for the establishment and endowment of said public free schools, all the funds, lands, and other property heretofore set apart and appropriated for the support and maintenance of public schools shall constitute the public school fund; and all sums of money that may come to this State hereafter from the sale of any portion of the public domain of the State of Texas shall also constitute a part of the public school fund. And the legislature shall appropriate all the proceeds resulting from sales of public lands of this State to such public school fund. And the legislature shall set apart, for the benefit of public schools, one-fourth of the annual revenue derivable from general taxation, and shall also cause to be levied and collected an annual poll-tax of one dollar on all male persons in this State between the ages of twenty-one and sixty years for the benefit of public schools. And said fund and the income derived therefrom, and the taxes herein provided for school purposes, shall be a perpetual fund, to be applied, as needed, exclusively for the education of all the scholastic inhabitants of this State, and no law shall ever be made appropriating such fund for any other use or purpose whatever.

The legislature shall, if necessary, in addition to the income derived from the public school fund and from the taxes for school purposes provided for in the foregoing section, provide for the raising of such amount, by taxation, in the several school districts in the State, as will be necessary to provide the necessary school-houses in each district and insure the education of all the scholastic inhabitants of the several districts.

The public lands heretofore given to counties shall be under the control of the legislature, and may be sold under such regulations as the legislature may prescribe, and in such case the proceeds of the same shall be added to the public school fund.

The legislature shall, at its first session, (and from time to time thereafter, as may be found necessary,) provide all needful rules and regulations for the purpose of carrying into effect the provisions of this article. It is made the imperative duty of the legislature to see to it that all the children in the State, within the scholastic age, are without delay provided with ample means of education. The legislature shall annually appropriate for school purposes, and to be equally distributed among all the scholastic population of the State, the interest accruing on the school fund and the income derived from taxation for school purposes, and shall, from time to time, as may be necessary, invest the principal of the school fund in the bonds of the United States Government, and in no other security.

To every head of a family, who has not a homestead, there shall be donated one hundred sixty acres of land out of the public domain, upon the condition that he will select, locate, and occupy the same for three years, and pay the office fees on the same. To all single men twenty-one years of age there shall be donated eighty acres of land out of the public domain, upon the same terms and conditions as are imposed upon the head of a family.

Members of the legislature, and all officers, before they enter upon the duties of their offices, shall take the following oath . . .

Laws shall be made to exclude from office, serving on juries, and from the right of suffrage, those who shall hereafter be convicted of bribery, perjury, forgery, or other high crimes. The privilege of free suffrage shall be supported by laws regulating elections, and prohibiting under adequate penalties all undue influence thereon from power, bribery, tumult, or other improper practice.

The legislature shall provide by law for the compensation of all officers, servants, agents, and public contractors . . .

General laws, regulating the adoption of children, emancipation of minors, and the granting of divorces, shall be made; but no special law shall be enacted relating to particular or individual cases.

The rights of married women to their separate property, real and personal, and the increase of the same, shall be protected by law; and married women, infants, and insane persons shall not be barred of their rights of property by adverse possession or law of limitation of less than seven years from and after the removal of each and all of their respective legal disabilities.

The legislature shall have power, and it shall be their duty, to protect by law from forced sale a certain portion of the property of all heads of families . . . All persons who at any time heretofore lived together as husband and wife, and both of whom, by the law of bondage, were precluded from the rites of matrimony, and continued to live together until the death of one of the parties, shall be considered as having been legally married, and the issue of such cohabitation shall be deemed legitimate, and all such persons as may be now living together in such relation shall be considered as having been legally married, and the children heretofore or hereafter born of such cohabitations shall be deemed legitimate.

No minister of the Gospel, or priest of any denomination whatever, who accepts a seat in the legislature as representative, shall, after such acceptance, be allowed to claim exemption from military service, road duty, or serving on juries, by reason of his said profession.

The ordinance of the convention passed on the first day of February, A.D. 1861, commonly known as the ordinance of secession, was in contravention of the Constitution and laws of the United States, and therefore null and void from the beginning; and all laws and parts of laws founded upon said ordinance were also null and void from the date of their passage. The legislatures which sat in the State of Texas from the 18th day of March, A.D. 1861, until the 6th day of August, A.D. 1866, had no constitutional authority to make laws binding upon the people of the State of Texas: Provided, That this section shall not be construed to inhibit the authorities of this State from respecting and enforcing such rules and regulations as were prescribed by the said legislatures which were not in violation of the Constitution and laws of the

United States, or in aid of the rebellion against the United States, or prejudicial to citizens of this State who were loyal to the United States, and which have been actually in force or observed in Texas during the above period of time, nor to affect prejudicially private rights which may have grown up under such rules and regulations, not to invalidate official acts not in aid of the rebellion against the United States during said period of time. The legislature which assembled in the city of Austin on the 6th day of August, A.D. 1866, was provisional only, and its acts are to be respected only so far as they were not in violation of the Constitution and laws of the United States, or were not intended to reward those who participated in the rebellion or discriminate between citizens on account of race or color, or to operate prejudicially to any class of citizens.

All debts created by the so-called State of Texas from and after the 28th day of January, A.D. 1861, and prior to the 5th day of August, 1865, were and are null and void . . .

All the qualified voters of each county shall also be qualified jurors of such county.

Four congressional districts are established, to continue until otherwise provided by law.

The election on the adoption of the constitution to be held on the first Monday in July, 1869, at the places and under the regulations to be prescribed by the commanding general of the military district.

*Source:* McPherson, Edward. *The Political History of the United States of America during the Period of Reconstruction.* Washington: Philp & Solomons, 1871, 430–432.

# FIFTEENTH AMENDMENT TO THE U.S. CONSTITUTION (RATIFIED MARCH 30, 1870)

*Taken by many as the "capstone" of Republican Reconstruction, the Fifteenth Amendment was really the usual blend of radical possibilities tempered by moderate practicalities.*

*True, it was the first federal imposition of suffrage regulation at the national level; the Military Reconstruction Acts only applied to 10 states, and the Fourteenth Amendment offered a reward versus penalty motivation for states to expand suffrage. However, the Fifteenth Amendment was phrased in a "negative" fashion—it stated on what basis states could not restrict suffrage, rather than specifically guaranteeing who could vote. This was done deliberately to avoid alienating whites opposed to universal suffrage. As a result, states North and South found many ingenious methods to exclude women, blacks, immigrants, and others from the ballot.*

## Article XV

Section 1: The right of citizens of the United States to vote shall not be denied or abridged by the United States or by any State on account of race, color, or previous condition of servitude.

Section 2: The Congress shall have power to enforce this article by appropriate legislation.

*Source:* The House Joint Resolution proposing the 15th amendment to the Constitution, December 7, 1868. Enrolled Acts and Resolutions of Congress, 1789–1999. General Records of the United States Government, Record Group 11, National Archives.

# ENFORCEMENT ACT OF APRIL 1871 (KU KLUX KLAN ACT)

*Unlike many of the general, sweeping measures passed by Congress during Reconstruction, the Klan Act was designed for a narrow, specific purpose: to allow the federal government to break up paramilitary white terrorist organizations preying on Republicans in the South. Violence against black and white Republicans was rampant and well organized, well beyond the ability of the state governments to confront. Basing its authority in earlier measures, the Klan Act placed voting harassment under federal jurisdiction and provided both enforcement and punishment mechanisms for perpetrators, but these definitions were open to interpretation, and the latitude given to the president and federal forces made the law an easy target for conservative opponents. All these facets came into play in 1871, when President Ulysses Grant invoked military provisions to combat Klan activity in South Carolina (in other states, officials relied on the 1870 Enforcement Act).*

## Chap. XXII.—An Act to Enforce the Provisions of the Fourteenth Amendment to the Constitution of the United States, and for Other Purposes.

Be it enacted by the Senate and House of Representatives of the United States of America in Congress assembled, That any person who, under color of any law, statute, ordinance, regulation, custom, or usage of any State, shall subject, or cause to be subjected, any person within the jurisdiction of the United States to the deprivation of any rights, privileges, or immunities secured by the Constitution of the United States, shall, any such law, statute, ordinance, regulation, custom, or usage of the State to the contrary notwithstanding, be liable to the party injured in any action at law, suit in equity, or other proper proceeding for redress; such proceeding to be prosecuted in the several district or circuit courts of the United States, with and subject to the same rights of appeal, review upon error, and other remedies provided in like cases in such courts, under the provisions of the act of the ninth of April, eighteen hundred and sixty-six, entitled "An act to protect all persons in the United States in their civil rights, and to furnish the means of their vindication"; and other remedial laws of the United States which are in their nature applicable in such cases.

Sec. 2. That if two or more persons within any State or Territory of the United States shall conspire together to overthrow, or to put down, or to destroy by force the government of the United States, or to levy war against the United States, or to oppose by force the authority of the government of the United States, or by force, intimidation, or threat to prevent, hinder, or delay the execution of any law of the United States, or by force to seize, take, or possess any property of the United States contrary to the authority thereof, or by force, intimidation, or threat to prevent any person from accepting or holding any office or trust or place of confidence under the United States, or from discharging the duties thereof, or by force, intimidation, or threat to induce any officer of the United States to leave any State, district, or place where his duties as such officer might lawfully be performed, or to injure him in his person or property on account of his lawful discharge of the duties of his office, or to injure his person while engaged in the lawful discharge of the duties of his office, or to injure his property so as to molest, interrupt, hinder, or impede him in the discharge of his official duty, or by force, intimidation, or threat to deter any party or witness in any court of the United States from attending such court, or from testifying in any matter pending in such court fully, freely, and truthfully, or to injure any such party or witness in his person or property on account of his having so attended or testified, or by force, intimidation, or threat to influence the verdict, presentment, or indictment, of any juror or grand juror in any court of the United States, or to injure such juror in his person or property on account of any verdict, presentment or indictment lawfully assented to by him, or on account of his being or having been such juror, or shall conspire together, or go in disguise upon the public highway or upon the premises of another for the purpose, either directly or indirectly, of depriving any person or any class of persons of the equal protection of the laws, or of equal privileges or immunities under the laws, or for the purpose of preventing or hindering the constituted authorities of any States from giving or securing to all persons within such States the equal protection of the laws, or shall conspire together for the purpose of in any manner impeding, hindering, obstructing, or defeating the due course of justice in any State or Territory, with intent to deny any citizen of the United States the due and equal protection of the laws, or to injure any person in his person or his property for lawfully enforcing the right of any person or class of persons to the equal protection of the laws, or by force, intimidation, or threat to prevent any citizen of the United States lawfully entitled to vote from giving his support or advocacy in a lawful manner towards or in favor of the election of any lawfully qualified person as an elector of President or Vice-President of the United States, or as a member of the Congress of the

United States, or to injure any such citizen in his person or property on account of such support or advocacy, each and every person so offending shall be deemed guilty of a high crime, and, upon conviction thereof in any district court or circuit court of the United States or district or supreme court of any Territory of the United States having jurisdiction of similar offences, shall be punished by a fine not less that five hundred nor more than five thousand dollars, or by imprisonment, with or without hard labor, as the court may determine, for a period of not less than six months nor more than six years, as the court may determine, or by both such fine and imprisonment as the court shall determine. And if any one or more persons engaged in any such conspiracy shall do, or cause to be done, any act in furtherance of the object of such conspiracy, whereby any person shall be injured in his person or property, or deprived of having and exercising any right or privilege of a citizen of the United States, the person so injured or deprived of such rights and privileges may have and maintain an action for recovery of damages occasioned by such injury or deprivation of rights and privileges against any one or more of the persons engaged in such conspiracy, such action to be prosecuted in the proper district or circuit court of the United States, with and subject to the same rights or appeal, review under error, and other remedies provided in like cases in such courts under the provisions of the act of April ninth, eighteen hundred and sixty-six, entitled "An act to protect all persons in the United States in their civil rights, and to furnish the means of their vindication."

Sec. 3. That in all cases where insurrection, domestic violence, unlawful combinations, or conspiracies in any State shall so obstruct or hinder the execution of the laws thereof, and of the United States, as to deprive any portion or class of the people of such State of any of the rights, privileges, or immunities, or protection, named in the Constitution and secured by this act, and the constituted authorities of such State shall either be unable to protect, or shall, from any cause, fail in or refuse protection of the people in such rights, such facts shall be deemed a denial by such State of the equal protection of the laws to which they are entitled under the Constitution of the United States; and in all such cases, or whenever any such insurrection, violence, unlawful combination, or conspiracy shall oppose or obstruct the laws of the United States of the due execution thereof, or impede or obstruct the due course of justice under the same, it shall be lawful for the President, and it shall be his duty to take such measures, by the employment of the militia or the land and naval forces of the United States, or of either, or by other means, as he may deem necessary for the suppression of such insurrection, domestic violence, or combinations; and any person who shall be arrested under the provisions of this and the proceeding section shall be delivered to the marshal of the proper district, to be dealt with according to law.

Sec. 4. That whenever in any State or part of a State the unlawful combinations named in the preceding section of this act shall be organized and armed, and so numerous and powerful as to be able, by violence, to either overthrow or set at defiance the constituted authorities of such State, and of the United States within such State, or when the constituted authorities are in complicity with, or shall connive at the unlawful purposes of, such powerful and armed combinations; and whenever, by reason of either or all of the causes aforesaid, the conviction of such offenders and the preservation of the public safety shall become in such district impracticable, in every such case such combinations shall be deemed a rebellion against the government of the United States, and during the continuance of such rebellion, and within the limits of the district which shall be so under the sway thereof, such limits to be prescribed by proclamation, it shall be lawful for the President of the United States, when in his judgment the public safety shall require it, to suspend the privileges of the writ of habeas corpus, to the end that such rebellion may be overthrown: Provided, That all the provisions of the second section of an act entitled "An act relating to habeas corpus, and regulating judicial proceedings in certain cases," approved March third, eighteen hundred and sixty-three, which relate to the discharge of prisoners other than prisoners of war, and to the penalty for refusing to obey the order of the court, shall be in full force so far as the same are applicable to the provisions of this section: Provided further, That the President shall first have made proclamation, as now provided by law, commanding such insurgents to disperse: And provided also, That the provisions of this section shall not be in force after the end of the next regular session of Congress.

Sec. 5. That no person shall be a grand or petit juror in any court of the United States upon any inquiry, hearing, or trial of any suit, proceeding or prosecution based upon or arising under the provisions of this act who shall, in the judgment of the court, be in complicity with such combination or conspiracy; and every such juror shall, before entering upon any such inquiry, hearing, or trial, take and subscribe an oath in open court that he has never, directly or indirectly, counseled, advised, or voluntarily aided any such combination or conspiracy; and each and every person who shall take this oath, and shall therein swear falsely, shall be guilty of perjury, and shall be subject to the pains and penalties declared against that crime, and the first section of the act entitled "An act defining additional causes of challenge and prescribing an additional oath for grand and petit jurors in the United States courts," approved June seventeenth, eighteen hundred and sixty-two, be, and the same is hereby repealed.

Sec. 6. That any person or persons, having knowledge that any of the wrongs conspired to be done and mentioned in the second section of this act are about to be committed, and having power to prevent or aid in preventing the same, shall neglect or refuse so to do, and such wrongful act shall be committed, such person or persons shall be liable to the person injured, or his legal representatives, for all damages caused by any such wrongful act which such first-named person or persons by reasonable diligence could have prevented; and such damages may be recovered in any action on the case in the proper circuit court of the United States, and any number of persons guilty of such wrongful neglect or refusal may be joined as defendants in such action:

Provided, That such action shall be commenced within one year after such cause of action shall have accrued; and if the death of any person shall be caused by any such wrongful act and neglect, the legal representatives of such deceased person shall have such action therefore, and may recover not exceeding five thousand dollars damages therein, for the benefit of the widow of such deceased person, if any there be, or if there be no widow, for the benefit of the next kin of such deceased person.

Sec. 7. That nothing herein contained shall be construed to supersede or repeal any former act or law except so far as the same may be repugnant thereto; and any offences heretofore committed against the tenor of any former act shall be prosecuted, and any proceeding already commenced for the prosecution thereof shall be continued and completed, the same as if this act had not been passed, except so far as the provisions of this act may go to sustain and validate such proceedings.

Approved, April 20, 1871.

*Source:* The Civil Rights/Enforcement Act of 1871. 17 Stat. 13 (1871).

# Appendix 1

## Reconstruction Governors for Former Confederate States

Listed below are the governors who served in the former Confederate states under the various phases of Reconstruction.

| State | Provisional Governor under Andrew Johnson | Elected Governor under Johnson's Plan | First Elected Governor under Congressional Reconstruction |
|---|---|---|---|
| Alabama | Lewis E. Parsons | Robert M. Patton | William H. Smith |
| Arkansas | Isaac Murphy[1] | Isaac Murphy[2] | Powell Clayton |
| Florida | William Marvin | David S. Walker | Harrison Reed |
| Georgia | James Johnson | Charles J. Jenkins/ Rufus B. Bullock[3] | Rufus B. Bullock |
| Louisiana | Michael Hahn[1] | James Madison Wells | Henry C. Warmoth |
| Mississippi | William L. Sharkey | Benjamin G. Humphreys | James L. Alcorn[4] |
| North Carolina | William W. Holden | Jonathan Worth | William W. Holden |
| South Carolina | Benjamin F. Perry | James L. Orr | Robert K. Scott |
| Tennessee | William G. Brownlow[1] | William G. Brownlow[2] | None[5] |
| Texas | Andrew J. Hamilton | James W. Throckmorton | Edmund J. Davis |
| Virginia | Francis H. Pierpont[1] | Francis H. Pierpont/ Henry H. Wells[2] | Gilbert C. Walker |

[1] Murphy, Hahn, Brownlow, and Pierpont took office during Lincoln's administration, and Johnson accepted them as legitimate.

[2] Johnson allowed Murphy, Brownlow, and Pierpont to serve out their terms as governor rather than require new gubernatorial elections. In Virginia, General John A. Schofield appointed Wells to succeed Pierpont when the latter's term expired in 1868.

[3] General George G. Meade removed Jenkins from office in January 1868. Rufus Bullock was appointed new provisional governor and was elected later that summer.

[4] From 1868 to 1870, General Adelbert Ames served as military provisional governor (he was elected governor in1873). Alcorn was the first legitimately elected governor under the Military Reconstruction Acts.

[5] Tennessee had ratified the Fourteenth Amendment in 1866 so was not subject to the Military Reconstruction Acts.

# Appendix 2

## Dates of Readmission, Redemption, and Ratification of Thirteenth and Fourteenth Amendments for Former Confederate States

| State | State Readmission | Ratification of Thirteenth Amendment | Ratification of Fourteenth Amendment | Redemption |
|---|---|---|---|---|
| Alabama | June 25, 1868 | December 2, 1865 | July 13, 1868 | November 14, 1874 |
| Arkansas | June 22, 1868 | April 14, 1865 | April 6, 1868 | November 10, 1874 |
| Florida | June 25, 1868 | December 28, 1865 | June 9, 1868 | January 2, 1877 |
| Georgia | July 15, 1870 | December 6, 1865[1] | July 21, 1868 | November 1, 1871 |
| Louisiana | June 25, 1868 | February 17, 1865 | July 9, 1868 | January 2, 1877 (April 24)[3] |
| Mississippi | February 23, 1870 | March 16, 1995 | January 17, 1870 | November 3, 1875 |
| North Carolina | June 25, 1868 | December 4, 1865 | July 4, 1868 | November 3, 1870 |
| South Carolina | June 25, 1868 | November 13, 1865 | July 9, 1868[2] | November 12, 1876 (April 11, 1877)[3] |
| Tennessee | July 24, 1866 | April 7, 1865 | July 19, 1866 | October 4, 1869 |
| Texas | March 30, 1870 | February 18, 1870 | February 18, 1870 | January 14, 1873 |
| Virginia | January 26, 1870 | February 9, 1865 | October 8, 1869 | October 5, 1869[4] |

[1] Georgia provided the required three-quarters vote for ratification of the Thirteenth Amendment.

[2] South Carolina provided the required three-quarters vote for ratification of the Fourteenth Amendment.

[3] In Louisiana and South Carolina, the contested election led to rival governments and nearly civil war. The date in parentheses represents the actual date that Conservatives resumed power, following President Rutherford Hayes's withdrawal of federal troops.

[4] Conservatives returned to power in Virginia before the state was readmitted to the Union.

# Selected Bibliography

Benedict, Michael Les. *A Compromise of Principle: Congressional Republicans and Reconstruction.* New York: W. W. Norton, 1974.

Berlin, Ira et al., eds. *Freedom: A Documentary History of Emancipation, 1861–1867.* New York: Cambridge University Press, 1986–ongoing.

Blight, David W. *Race and Reunion: The Civil War in American Memory.* New York: Belknap Press, 2000.

Bynam, Victoria. *Unruly Women.* Chapel Hill: University of North Carolina Press, 1992.

Carter, Dan T. *When the War Was over: The Failure of Self-Reconstruction in the South, 1865–1867.* Baton Rouge: Louisiana State University Press, 1985.

Clinton, Catherine. *Tara Revisited: Women, War, and the Plantation Legend.* New York: The Abbeville Press, 1995.

Clinton, Catherine, and Nina Silber, eds. *Divided Houses.* New York: Oxford University Press, 1992.

Curry, Richard O. "The Civil War and Reconstruction, 1861–1877: A Critical Overview of Recent Trends and Interpretations." *Civil War History* 20 (September 1974): 215–38.

Donald, David H. *The Politics of Reconstruction, 1863–1867.* Baton Rouge: Louisiana State University Press, 1965.

Dougherty, Kevin. *The Port Royal Experiment: A Case Study in Development.* Jackson: The University Press of Mississippi, 2014.

Du Bois, W.E.B. Black *Reconstruction in America.* New York: Harcourt, Brace, 1935.

Edwards, Laura F. *Gendered Strife and Confusion: The Political Culture of Reconstruction.* Urbana: University of Illinois Press, 1997.

Egerton, Douglas R. *The Wars of Reconstruction: The Brief, Violent History of America's Most Progressive Era.* New York: Bloomsbury Press, 2014.

Fitzgerald, Michael W. *Splendid Failure: Postwar Reconstruction in the American South.* New York: Ivan R. Dee Publishers, 2008.

Foner, Eric. *Reconstruction Updated Edition: America's Unfinished Revolution, 1863–1877.* Reprint, New York: HarperCollins, 2014.

Foster, Gaines M. *Ghosts of the Confederacy: Defeat, the Lost Cause, and the Emergence of the New South, 1865–1913.* New York: Oxford University Press, 1985.

Franklin, John Hope. *Reconstruction after the Civil War.* Chicago: University of Chicago Press, 1961.

Gillette, William. *Retreat from Reconstruction, 1869–1879.* Baton Rouge: Louisiana State University Press, 1979.

Guelzo, Allen C. *Fateful Lightning: A New History of the Civil War and Reconstruction*. New York: Oxford University Press, 2012.

Harris, William C. *With Charity for All: Lincoln and the Restoration of the Union*. Lexington: University of Kentucky Press, 1997.

Hogue, James K. *Uncivil War: Five New Orleans Street Battles and the Rise and Fall of Radical Reconstruction*. Baton Rouge: Louisiana State University Press, 2006.

Hyman, Harold. *A More Perfect Union: The Impact of the Civil War and Reconstruction on the Constitution*. New York: Knopf, 1973.

Jones, Jacqueline. *Labor of Love, Labor of Sorrow*. New York: Basic Books, 1985.

Keith, Lee Anna. *The Colfax Massacre: The Untold Story of Black Power, White Terror, and the Death of Reconstruction*. New York: Oxford University Press, 2009.

Kolchin, Peter. *American Slavery, 1619–1877*. New York: Hill and Wang, 1993.

Lane, Charles. *The Day Freedom Died: The Colfax Massacre, the Supreme Court, and the Betrayal of Reconstruction*. New York: Paperbacks, 2009.

McFeely, William. *Yankee Stepfather: General O.O. Howard and the Freedmen*. New Haven, CT: Yale University Press, 1968.

McKitrick, Erik L. *Andrew Johnson and Reconstruction*. Chicago: University of Chicago Press, 1960.

McPherson, James M. *The Struggle for Equality: Abolitionists and the Negro in the Civil War and Reconstruction*. Reprint, Princeton, NJ: Princeton University Press, 2014.

Noe, Kenneth W., ed. The *Yellowhammer War: The Civil War and Reconstruction in Alabama*. Tuscaloosa: University of Alabama Press, 2014.

Rable, George C. *Civil Wars: Women and the Crisis of Southern Nationalism*. Urbana: University of Illinois Press, 1989.

Richardson, Heather Cox. *The Death of Reconstruction: Race, Labor, and Politics in the Post–Civil War North, 1865–1901*. Cambridge, MA: Harvard University Press, 2004.

Richardson, Heather Cox. *West from Appomattox: The Reconstruction of America after the Civil War*. New Haven: Yale University Press, 2008.

Saville, Julie. The *Work of Reconstruction: From Slave to Wage Laborer in South Carolina, 1860–1870*. New York: Cambridge University Press, 1994.

Silber, Nina. *The Romance of Reunion: Northerners and the South, 1865–1900*. Chapel Hill: University of North Carolina Press, 1993.

Stampp, Kenneth. *The Era of Reconstruction, 1865–1877*. New York: Vintage Books, 1967.

Stampp, Kenneth, and Leon Litwack, eds. *Reconstruction: An Anthology of Revisionist Writings*. Baton Rouge: Louisiana State University Press, 1969.

Summers, Mark Wahlgren. *A Dangerous Stir: Fear, Paranoia, and the Making of Reconstruction*. Chapel Hill: University of North Carolina Press, 2009.

Summers, Mark Wahlgren. *The Ordeal of the Reunion: A New History of Reconstruction*. Chapel Hill: University of North Carolina Press, 2014.

Trefousse, Hans L. *The Radical Republicans: Lincoln's Vanguard for Racial Justice*. New York: Knopf, 1969.

Weisberger, Bernard A. "The Dark and Bloody Ground of Reconstruction Historiography." *Journal of Southern History* 25 (November 1959): 427–47.

Wharton, Vernon Lane. *The Negro in Mississippi, 1865–1890*. New York: Harper and Row, 1965.

Whites, Lee Ann. *The Civil War as a Crisis in Gender: Augusta, Georgia, 1860–1890*. Athens: University of Georgia Press, 1995.

Williamson, Joel. *After Slavery: The Negro in South Carolina during Reconstruction, 1861–1877.* Chapel Hill: University of North Carolina Press, 1965.

Woodward, C. Vann. *The Future of the Past.* New York: Oxford University Press, 1989.

Woodward, C. Vann. *The Origins of the New South, 1877–1913.* Baton Rouge: Louisiana State University Press, 1971.

Woodward, C. Vann. *Reunion and Reaction: The Compromise of 1877 and the End of Reconstruction.* Boston: Little Brown and Co., 1951.

Wright, Gavin. *Old South, New South: Revolutions in the Southern Economy since the Civil War.* New York: Basic Books, 1986.

# Index

Note: Page numbers in **boldface** reflect main entries in the book.

# About the Editor

**RICHARD ZUCZEK,** professor of history at the U.S. Coast Guard Academy (USCGA), served as editor-in-chief of the two-volume *Greenwood Encyclopedia of the Reconstruction Era* (2006). Before joining the USCGA in 1999, Zuczek taught at the University of Tennessee, where he was both an assistant professor and an assistant editor of *The Papers of Andrew Johnson*. His publications include *State of Rebellion: South Carolina during Reconstruction* (University of South Carolina Press, 1996), *Andrew Johnson: A Biographical Companion* (with Glenna Schroeder-Lein; ABC-CLIO, 2000), and most recently "The Foreign Policy of Andrew Johnson" in *A Companion to the Reconstruction Presidents* (Wiley-Blackwell, 2014). Professor Zuczek lives with his wife, Etsuko, and their two boys in Westerly, Rhode Island.